"As a study in the sociology of religion this book will be of lasting interest and importance, and it will be indispensable for understanding the century from the Reformation to the Civil War"
Gerald Aylmer in *The Guardian*

"The masterly application of the author's enormous reading gives vitality to every page of this book, while a nice sense of humour and of style make it a delight to read"
C. V. Wedgwood in *The Daily Telegraph*

"Christopher Hill's consistent attitude is a simple and rare one – a belief that it is the underdog who matters, and a refusal to accept uncritically the plausible justifications of the successful. 'The light which burned in a Milton, a Lilburne, a Winstanley' lights all Mr. Hill's work, and with it an analytical study of society cannot be arid or impersonal"
History Today

Christopher Hill, one of the most eminent historians of our day, is Master of Balliol College, Oxford. His previous authoritative study, *Puritanism and Revolution*, is already available in this series

Christopher Hill

Society and Puritanism in Pre-Revolutionary England

Panther History

Society and Puritanism in
Pre-Revolutionary England

A Panther Book

First published in Great Britain by
Martin Secker & Warburg Limited 1964
Mercury Books edition published 1966
Panther edition published 1969

Copyright © Christopher Hill 1964

Printed in England by
C. Nicholls & Company Ltd.,
The Philips Park Press, Manchester,
and published by Panther Books,
3 Upper James Street, London, W.1.

for Bridget, but for whom . . .

Contents

Preface

In 1956 I published a book entitled *Economic Problems of the Church, from Archbishop Whitgift to the Long Parliament*. In it I tried to suggest some of the non-theological reasons which might lead men to oppose the Laudian régime in the English church. The present book deals with the same period and approaches the same problem from another angle. It tries to suggest that there might be non-theological reasons for supporting the Puritans, or for being a Puritan. The two books were conceived, and in part drafted, together, which explains why there are so many cross-references from the present volume to *Economic Problems*. It must also serve to explain some of the limitations of the present book. For instance, I have not examined the extent to which the ideas of Puritans were shared with or derived from continental protestantism. These connections are important, but a proper study of them would demand far more knowledge than I possess, and in any case my theme was the roots of Puritanism in English society. Men took arguments from the common protestant heritage, and developed them to meet English circumstances. Nor have I discussed at all the economic changes of the sixteenth and seventeenth centuries. I have taken them for granted, since my book was too long anyway. I hope to return to this subject later.

I am grateful to the Master and Fellows of Balliol College for making it possible for me to have sabbatical terms in 1951 and 1958, during which much of this book was written; and to the Leverhulme Trustees for a grant towards my expenses in 1951. I also thank the University of Oxford for appointing me, through the Modern History Board, to a Special Lectureship which had the effect of reducing my teaching hours over the past three years. For advice and help of various kinds my thanks are due to Professor G. E. Aylmer, Mr. J. Bebbington, Sheffield City Librarian, Mrs. D. M. Garman, Mrs. Hilliard, Mr. A. Jenkin, Mr. M. H. Keen, Dr. Valerie Pearl, Mrs. Joan Simon, Mr. R. L. Taverner, Miss M. Weinstock, and Professor C. M. Williams. I am grateful to Dr. D. M. Barratt,

Miss I. Cassidy, Miss D. Slatter, Mr. D. W. Boorman, Dr. H. G. Owen, Professor J. M. Patrick and Dr. T. O. Ranger for permission to quote from their unpublished theses. A certain Buckinghamshire emphasis in the examples given in this book derives from a course of W.E.A. lectures delivered at Great Missenden in 1956: I thank the members of this class for their help. A shortened version of Chapter 5 was read as a paper to the Anglo-Dutch Historical Conference at Utrecht in September 1962: thanks are due to all those who made helpful criticisms and suggestions during and after the discussion. This paper will be published in *Britain and the Netherlands*, II (ed. J. S. Bromley and E. H. Kossmann, Groningen). My greatest debts are to the late Miss Dona Torr, with whom I discussed much of this book; to my pupils, who treated its ideas with useful scepticism; to Mr. Keith Thomas, who added to many kindnesses by vigilantly reading the proofs; and to my wife, who ruthlessly kept me at it.

Spelling, punctuation and capitalization have been modernized in all quotations, but not in the titles of books.

OXFORD, November 1962.

Preface to the Panther Edition

FOR this edition I have made a number of corrections. I am very grateful to the Rev. W. K. Lowther Clarke, Mr. F. G. Emmison, Professor G. R. Potter, Professor I. A. Roots and especially the Rev. G. F. Nuttall for pointing out errors and misprints.

Puritanism is a subject into which research is at the moment being pursued with great vigour. Since this book was first published, a number of studies have further explored its subject matter. First and foremost is Dr. Patrick Collinson's *The Elizabethan Movement* (1967). This magisterial book sheds new light on puritanism in Elizabeth's reign and relates it to social and political history with a thoroughness and insight that make it the necessary starting point for all future discussions of the subject. Dr. Collinson also contributed "The Beginnings of English Sabbatarianism" to *Studies in Church History*, I; "Episcopacy and Reform in England in the Later Sixteenth Century" to *ibid.*, III; and another paper on "The Godly: Aspects of Popular Protestantism in Elizabethan England" to a *Past and Present* Conference on Popular Religion, held in July 1966. Professor A. G. Dickens' excellent *The English Reformation* (1964) is essential reading, as is Michael Walzer's stimulating *The Revolution of the Saints* (Harvard University Press, 1965), though the discerning reader will note differences of emphasis between Professor Walzer and myself. C. H. George has an interesting article on "Puritanism as History and Historiography" in *Past and Present*, No. 41, 1968.

Professor George Yule's "Developments in English Puritanism in the Context of the Reformation" (*Studies in the Puritan Tradition*, a joint supplement of the Congregational Historical Society's *Transactions* and the Presbyterian Historical Society's *Journal*) and his "Some Problems in the History of the English Presbyterians in the Seventeenth Century" (Presbyterian Historical Society's *Journal*, May 1965) also deals with matters treated in this book. So does Mr. John Addy's pamphlet, *The Archdeacon and Ecclesiastical Discipline in Yorkshire, 1598–1714* (St. Antony's Hall Publications, No. 24, York, 1963), Professor I. Breward's article, "The Significance of William Perkins", *Journal of Religious History*, 1966, Mr. A. L. Beier's "Poor Relief in Warwickshire, 1630–1660", *Past and Present*, No. 35, 1966, and Mr. P. Tyler's "The Significance of the Ecclesiastical Commission at York", *Northern History*, II, 1967. Mr. Keith Thomas' "Work and Leisure in Pre-Industrial Society", *Past and Present*, No. 29, 1964, must be read. So must Mr. E. P. Thompson's "Time, Work Discipline and Industrial Capitalism", *Past and Present*, No. 38, 1967. Dr. Claire Cross's excellent life of the third Earl of Huntingdon (The Puritan Earl, 1966) contains a case study of the political and social uses to which Puritan preachers could be put. Kenneth Charlton's *Education in Renaissance England* (1965) and Mrs. Joan Simon's important *Education and Society in Tudor England* (1966) will lead to serious revision of traditional attitudes to Puritanism and education in England.

I have pursued one subject of this book further in "The Many-Headed Monster in Late Tudor and Early Stuart Political Thinking", a contribution to *From the Renaissance to the Counter-Reformation: Essays in Honor of Garrett Mattingly* (ed. C. H. Carter, New York, 1965). *Society and Puritanism* was demolished by B. S. Manning in *English Historical Review*, LXXXI (1965–66). It was subjeced to less wholesale but very perceptive criticism by R. B. Grassby in the *Oxford Magazine* of 6 May 1965. I commend these reviews, each by a former pupil of mine, to any reader who is in danger of thinking I have said the last word on the wide open subject of society and Puritanism.

Christopher Hill, March 1969

Abbreviations

The following abbreviations have been used:

C.J.	*Commons' Journals*
C.S.P.D.	*Calendar of State Papers, Domestic*
C.S.P., *Venetian* (or *Irish*, or *Scottish*)	*Calendar of State Papers, Venetian* (or *Irish*, or *Scottish*)
E.H.R.	*English Historical Review*
Econ. H.R.	*Economic History Review*
E.P.C.	C. Hill, *Economic Problems of the Church, from Archbishop Whitgift to the Long Parliament* (1956)
H.M.C.	Historical Manuscripts Commission
L.J.	*Lords' Journals*
N.R.S.	Ed. W. Notestein, F. H. Relf and H. Simpson, *Commons Debates, 1621* (Yale University Press, 1935)
P. and P.	*Past and Present*
S.P.	State Papers
T.R.H.S.	*Transactions of the Royal Historical Society*
V.C.H.	*Victoria County History*

Chapter One

The Definition of a Puritan

Thus far it appears what a vast circumference this word "Puritan" has, and how by its large acception it is used to cast dust in the face of all goodness, theological, civil or moral: so that scarce any moderate man can avoid its imputation.

> [Henry Parker], *A Discourse concerning Puritans*
> (2nd ed., 1641), p. 60.[1]

I

SOME of the difficulties in making precise statements about the relation of religion and politics in the seventeenth century are linguistic. The words "Presbyterian" and "Independent" are productive of a great deal of confusion, as Professor Hexter demonstrated in 1938:[2] many historians have illustrated the confusion since. The word "Puritan" too is an admirable refuge from clarity of thought. Mr. Allen expressed this with pleasing trenchancy when he declared that "Puritanism seems to be a discovery of later thought and research"; "there were, in my view, very few in the Long Parliament who ought to be called Puritans".[3] Professor and Mrs. George deny the existence of a separable puritan trend, even among ministers.[4]

1. This tract is sometimes attributed to John Ley, for whom see p. 155 below.
2. J. H. Hexter, *Reappraisals in History* (1961), pp. 163–84.
3. J. W. Allen, *English Political Thought, 1603–1644* (1938), pp. 255–62, 302.
4. C. H. and K. George, *The Protestant Mind of the English Reformation, 1570–1640* (Princeton, 1961), esp. pp. 6–8, 399–407. Although I cannot accept their main conclusion, that there was nothing in Puritanism

These heroic remedies are salutary; but contemporaries did use the word, and we have to decide what, if anything, they meant by it.

Like most political nicknames it was "a reproachful name", given, the fifth Earl of Huntingdon told his son, "either by Papists that do hate all ministers except those of their own sect, or atheists or men extremely vicious".[1] "The adversary", said a petition to the Privy Council about 1580, "very cunningly hath new-christened us with an odious name . . . of Puritanism; we detest both the name and the heresy".[2] The word was often used as a very general term of abuse. "I find many that are called Puritans", wrote Feltham in 1628; "yet few or none that will own the name".[3] "That odious and factious name of Puritans", Pym called it.[4] Some such words – "Anabaptist", e.g. or "Communist" – are similarly used by extension to describe persons whom one dislikes; but in these cases there is a definable restricted meaning to which precision can be given, so that we can say that some sectaries denounced as "bloody Anabaptists" by their opponents were improperly so described. But is there any inner core of precise meaning to which the word "Puritan" can be related? Or was it always a vague mist through which hostile or ludicrous figures were seen threatening and posturing?

Many to whom the name was applied agreed with the Earl of Huntingdon in thinking it had been invented by papists and atheists. "I know no Puritans", wrote Udall in 1588; "but Satan taught the papists so to name the ministers of the gospel".[5] Marprelate made his Papist say, "It was never merry world since there was so many Puritans and such running to

---

significantly different from the position of the hierarchy before the Laudian innovations, there is much excellent material in this book.

1. *Hastings MSS.* (H.M.C.), IV, p. 330.

2. [Anon.], *A parte of a Register* (Middelburg, 1593), p. 129. Cf. the minister accused of Puritanism in 1574 who said that the Archdeacon of Nottingham "knoweth no more what a Puritan is than his old horse" (R. Marchant, *The Puritans and the Church Courts in the Diocese of York, 1560–1642*, 1960, p. 135).

3. Owen Feltham, *Resolves, Divine, Morall and Politicall* (Temple Classics), p. 9. First published 1628.

4. N.R.S., IV, p. 63.

5. J. Udall, *Diotrephes* (ed. E. Arber, 1879), p. 9.

sermons as there is now".[1] Bacon, in urging the Duke of
Buckingham to patronize the Puritan party, insisted that he
must not let "the name of Puritans in a papist's mouth . . .
make you withdraw your favour from such as are honest and
religious men".[2] The Spanish Ambassador Gondomar was
said in 1620 to aim "to breed distaste and jealousies in the
King towards his best subjects under the false and adulterate
nickname of Puritans, and so to prevent all future Parliaments".[3] The Jesuits and the Jesuited faction, said Calybute
Downing in a sermon of 1640, "revile the wisdom, conscience
and representation of a state in Parliament as a faction, a
combination, a pack of Puritans".[4] George Wither held
Puritans in high esteem

> *". . . If by that name you understand*
> *Those whom the vulgar atheists of this land*
> *Do daily term so".*[5]

Those who denounce Puritans, said Henry Parker sweepingly
in 1641, are "papists, hierarchists, ambidexters and neuters
in religion"; also "court-flatterers, time-serving projectors and
the rancorous caterpillars of the realm . . . and the scum of the
vulgar. . . . In the mouth of a rude soldier, he which wisheth
the Scotch war at an end without blood" is a Puritan.[6] "I love
and reverence only bear to such" as some men call Puritans

1. M. Marprelate, *A Dialogue wherein is plainly layd open the Tyran-
nicall Dealing of the Lord Bishops over Gods Church* (1640 reprint), Sig.
C 4. This reprint includes the poem, *The Interpreter*, quoted on page 23
below.

2. Ed. J. Spedding, R. L. Ellis and D. D. Heath, *Works of Francis
Bacon* (1872-74), XIV, pp. 448-9; cf. an anonymous pamphlet, *Of the
Name of Puritans* (c. 1620-40), printed in *Trans. Congregational Hist.
Soc.*, VI (1913), pp. 76-88.

3. Ed. J. O. Halliwell, *The Autobiography and Correspondence of Sir
Simonds D'Ewes* (1845), I, pp. 158-9. D'Ewes was summarizing Thomas
Scott's *Vox Populi* (1620).

4. C. Downing, *A Sermon preached to the Renowned Company of
Artillery*, September 1, 1640, p. 29. (Published by order of the House of
Commons.) The last phrase was in constant use: cf. the pamphlet, *A
Pack of Puritans*, referred to on p. 314 below.

5. G. Wither, *Juvenilia* (Spenser Soc. reprint, n.d.), I, p. 299. First
published 1622.

6. H. Parker, *A Discourse concerning Puritans* (2nd ed., 1641), pp.
58-60.

"in scorn and spite": so John Taylor, who is not usually classified with the radicals.[1]

The suggestion that the wide meaning of the word was deliberately exploited to create confusion was also a commonplace. On Whitgift's definition, Cartwright observed, Puritans made the Book of Common Prayer.[2] Bacon said that those whom he called "honest religious men . . . traduced by that name" of Puritan were "the greatest part of the body of the subjects".[3] "The name, I know, is sometimes fastened upon those that deserve it not", observed a future bishop; "rascal people will call any man that beareth but the face of honesty a Puritan".[4] Sanderson was right: he was called a Puritan himself.[5] So, at one time or another, even more surprisingly, were Archbishop Whitgift, Elizabeth's Earl of Essex, Sir Walter Raleigh, James Hay, Earl of Carlisle, King James, Prince Charles (by Venetian and French diplomats, in 1624), Inigo Jones, the Earl of Strafford (by the Papal Agent, in 1640!). Digby told the Spanish Ambassador in 1620 that the Court swarmed with Puritans. Fifteen years later the Venetian Ambassador spoke of Henrietta Maria's party as Puritan.[6] In most of these cases "Puritan" seems to be used to denote an advocate of an anti-Spanish foreign policy. But the Hostmen of Newcastle used to refer to those London and Ipswich merchants who opposed their monopoly as Puritans.[7]

One is inclined to agree with a pamphleteer of 1631

1. J. Taylor, *The Water-Cormorant His Complaint* (1622), p. 4; cf. his *Mad Fashions, odd Fashions* (1642), pp. 4–5.

2. Ed. J. Ayre, *The Works of John Whitgift* (Parker Soc., 1851–3), I, p. 172.

3. Bacon, *Works, XIV*, p. 449.

4. R. Sanderson, *XXXV Sermons* (1681), p. 16.

5. Sanderson, *Pax Ecclesiae*, in appendix to J. Hough, *Sermons and Charges* (1821), p p. 331–4.

6. W. M. Lamont, *Marginal Prynne* (1963), p. 44; Sir J. E. Neale, *Elizabeth I and her Parliament 1584–1601* (1957), p. 151; Sir Walter Ralegh, *History of the World* (1820), VI, p. 97; S. R. Gardiner, *History of England* (1883–4), III, pp. 241–2, 337; V, p. 251; VIII, p. 85; IX, p. 88; C. H. and K. George, *The Protestant Mind of the English Reformation*, pp. 401, 404.

7. J. U. Nef, *The Rise of the British Coal Industry* (1932), II, pp. 280, 282; cf. Miss E. Rosenberg, "Leicester can be seen as a genuine 'Puritan' if we abandon the nonconformist overtones of that word" (*Leicester Patron of Letters*, Columbia University Press, 1955, pp. 196–7).

who said "the name [Puritan] . . . is ambiguous, and so it is fallacious".[1] So ambiguous was it that James I, who had made some ill-advised generalizations about Puritans in the *Basilikon Doron*, had to explain in his 1603 Preface to the Reader that the word Puritan properly belonged only to the vile sect known as the Family of Love, and that he used it principally of them, the Brownists and their sympathizers. This was presumably not the sense he attached to the word in 1619 when he urged the University of Cambridge to check and reform "any fanciful conceit savouring of . . . Puritanism, disagreeing from the laudable and approved customs of our Church of England".[2]

Originally, as James's apology indicates, separatists were called Puritans rather than those who wished to reform the Church from within. Udall's anti-Puritan, Diotrephes, said that by Puritan he meant those "that are not contented with the state, but mislike the government of the church, and would have a new form of government".[3] But Marprelate accounted "no Brownist to be a Puritan",[4] and in the seventeenth century the word was normally used, in its religious sense, to indicate those who wanted reform from within the Church, as contrasted with separatists on the one hand, and those who were satisfied with the established discipline on the other.[5] Many who were called Puritans were conformists with no objection to set forms of worship, like Richard Baxter's father,[6] or like Richard Capel, John Dod, Arthur Hildersam, John Downame, Richard Sibbes, Richard Stock, Nicholas Byfield.[7] But it was used generically as "the common term of

1. Giles Widdowes, *The Schismatical Puritan* (1631), Sig. A 3, quoted by Perry Miller, *Orthodoxy in Massachusetts, 1630–50* (Harvard University Press, 1933), p. 21.

2. M. H. Curtis, *Oxford and Cambridge in Transition, 1558–1642* (1959), p. 172. Cf. pp. 23–4 below.

3. J. Udall, *Diotrephes* (1879), p. 9.

4. M. Marprelate, *Hay any Work for Cooper?* (1589), p. 25.

5. e.g. W. Bradshaw, *English Puritanisme* (1605); J. Wilkinson, *An Exposition of the 13 Chapter of the Revelation* (1619), pp. 34–5.

6. Ed. M. Sylvester, *Reliquiae Baxterianae* (1696), I, p. 3; John Geree *The Character of an old English Puritane* (1646), *passim*.

7. The list is from *Capel's Remains* (1658), with Life by Valentine Marshall, Sig. A 8. First published 1633.

derision of the professors in England from about . . . 1600 to the year 1640 and after".[1]

When contemporaries came to define Puritanism in religious terms, Sabbatarianism, opposition to popery and hostility to oaths were often mentioned.[2] "Men and brethren, I am a Puritan", cried Donne, if Puritanism means opposing oaths and profanation of the Sabbath.[3] Many found the name a stumbling-block. Zeal in religion is called Puritanism, complained Bishop Bayly.[4] Dod and Cleaver, two ministers deprived early in James I's reign, rebuked "their dastardliness, that are afraid to keep the Sabbath, or to do any other religious duty, because they should be counted and called Puritans".[5] Wither made the same point:

> "And do we not perceive that many a man,
> Fearing to be entitled Puritan
> Simply neglects the means of his salvation?"[6]

Sir Robert Cotton noted that fear of being called "a bloodsucker, a busybody, or a Puritan" restrained many from enforcing the laws against recusants.[7] "If I reproved the vanity of the time", said Francis Quarles's Persecuted Man, "it derided me with the style of Puritan".[8] Attorney-General Noy accused Prynne of implying, more simply, that Jesus Christ was a Puritan.[9] Henry Parker almost echoed Donne when he said to his reader "If thou art not an anti-Puritan of the worst kind, I am not a Puritan. . . . If thou thinkest some men religious which affect not the name of Puritan, I think so too; if thou thinkest most men irreligious which hate the name of

1. Ed. E. B. Underhill, *The Records of a Church of Christs meeting in Broadmead Bristol, 1640–97* (Hanserd Knollys Soc., 1847), p. 6.

2. For the social significance of swearing, see pp. 405–6 below.

3. J. Donne, *LXXX Sermons* (1640), p. 493.

4. L. Bayly, *The Practice of Piety* (55th ed., 1723), p. 115.

5. J. Dod and R. Cleaver, *A plain and familiar Exposition of the Ten Commandements* (19th ed., 1662), p. 7. Dod, a protégé of the Knightleys, had been a member of a classis in the fifteen-eighties. Cf. also H. Smith, *Sermons* (1675), p. 31. First published 1592.

6. Wither, *Juvenilia*, I, p. 264.

7. *Cottoni Posthuma* (1679), II, pp. 61–3.

8. F. Quarles, *Judgment and Mercy* (1807), p. 302. First published 1644.

9. J. Rushworth, *Historical Collections* (1680), II, p. 224.

Puritan, I think so too".[1] "All conscientious men in the nation shared the contempt", said Francis Osborn, hardly a Puritan himself; "the breadth and newness of the name . . . stifled the seeds of goodness".[2]

Fuller thought that the word Puritan changed its meaning in the sixteen-twenties. Before then it signified "such as dissented from the hierarchy in discipline and church government". Henceforth it was extended to brand anti-Arminians.[3] Since the Arminian party was also a political party, this helped to confuse the religious and political senses of the word Puritan. "Absolutely to define him", Feltham thought, "is a work . . . of difficulty. . . . As he is more generally in these times taken, I suppose we may call him a church-rebel, or one that would exclude order, that his brain might rule".[4]

So contentious did the issues around the word Puritan become that a serious attempt seems to have been made to obtain an official definition of it. Emmanuel Downing wrote to Ussher in October 1620 that the priests "have now stirred up some crafty papists, who very boldly rail both at ministers and people, saying they seek to sow this damnable heresy of Puritanism among them: which word, though not understood, but only known to be most odious to his Majesty, makes many afraid of joining themselves to the Gospel. . . . So to prevent a greater mischief that may follow, it were good to petition his Majesty to define a Puritan, whereby the mouths of those scoffing enemies would be stopped".[5] An undated paper in the *Rutland MSS.*, probably from the same period, also asked for definition of a Puritan, "so that those who deserve the name may be punished, and others not calumniated".[6] In February 1621 a letter attributed to Sir Robert Harley said: "I think the Parliament will not proceed to define a Puritan".[7] Francis Osborn may have been referring to this episode when he

1. H. Parker, *A Discourse concerning Puritans*, To the Reader.
2. F. Osborn, *Traditionall Memoyres on the Raigne of King James the First*, in *Secret History of the Court of James I* (ed. Sir W. Scott, 1811), I, pp. 188–9.
3. Fuller, *Church History* (1842), III, p. 307. Contrast P. Heylyn, *Cyprianus Anglicus* (1671), p. 119.
4. Feltham, *Resolves*, p. 9.
5. R. Parr, *Life of . . . James Usher* (1686), p. 16.
6. *Rutland MSS. Belvoir* (H.M.C.), IV pp. 212–13.
7. *Portland MSS.* (H.M.C.), III, p. 13.

wrote of "a people styled Puritans", who met "no nearer a
definition than the name. . . . Court sermons were fraught with
bitter invectives against these people . . . ; yet the wisest durst
not define them".[1] For contemporaries the word thus had
wide and ill-defined meanings, which were at least as much
political as religious.

II

The shrewd Henry Parker insisted that it was necessary to
distinguish at least four types of Puritans – Puritans in Church
policy, Puritans in religion, Puritans in State and Puritans in
morality.[2] Puritans in Church policy and religion I shall take,
as contemporaries did, to be those who remained within the
state Church but wanted a cleaner break with popery. I shall
not normally, in the period before 1640, use it to include
separatists, except in so far as their views seem to me a logical
extension of those of the non-separating Puritans.

But always we must remember the broader, looser sense in
which the word was used to describe any opponents of the
policies pursued by hierarchy and Court. Let us consider
"Puritans in State" first, difficult though it is to distinguish
them from "Puritans in Church policy". "If they could . . . they
would change her [the Queen's] government", wrote Archbishop Parker to Burghley in 1575. "Does your lordship think
that I care either for cap, tippet or surplice, or wafer-bread, or
any such ? But the laws so established, I esteem them".[3] Parker
referred here to the government of the Church. But slowly the
word Puritan began to be used in a purely political context.
Three out of every four members of the House of Commons at
the beginning of James I's reign were said to be Puritans.[4] In
1641 Henry Parker wrote: "All the Commons in Parliament,
and almost all the ancient impartial temporal nobility, and all
such as favour or relish the late proceedings of both the houses,
which is the main body of the realm, papists, prelates and
courtiers excepted, . . . all these are Puritans".[5] Many other
examples could be given in the four decades between.

1. Osborn, *Traditionall Memoyres*, pp. 187–8.
2. Parker, *A Discourse concerning Puritans*, p. 13.
3. Ed. J. Bruce and T. T. Perowne, *Correspondence of Matthew
Parker* (Parker Soc., 1853), p. 478.
4. Gardiner, *History of England*, I, p. 178.
5. Parker, *op. cit.*, p. 11.

> "*A Puritan is he that speaks his mind*
> *In Parliament: not looking once behind*
> *To others' danger; nor just sideways leaning*
> *To promised honour his direct true meaning*
> *But for the laws and truth doth fairly stand . . .*
> *His character abridged if you would have,*
> *He's one that would a subject be, no slave*".[1]

"Turbulent and factious spirits, . . . adverse to the government of the church" were possible meanings which Bacon thought might be given to the word.[2] In 1624 John Davenport denied being a Puritan "if by a Puritan is meant one opposite to the present government" [of the church], or "one that secretly encourageth men in opposition to the present government".[3] The label was often applied to one who advocated a forward foreign policy: "It was made an infallible note of a Puritan, and consequently of an ill subject", wrote Thomas Scott, "to speak on behalf of the King's children, and a certain proof of a good Protestant, or a discreet and moderate man, to plead against them for the Emperor and the King of Spain".[4]

> "*A Puritan is he that rather had*
> *Spend all to help the States (he is so mad!)*
> *Than spend £100,000 a year*
> *To guard the Spanish coasts from pirates' fear:*
> *The whilst the Catholic King might force combine*
> *Both Holland, Beame and Palz to undermine*".[5]

When a newsletter writer in 1619 said "Buckingham . . . is held to be no inward friend to Spain, whatsoever demonstration he maketh outwardly", he thought it necessary to add, "Yet he is no Puritan".[6]

But most often the word was applied to home politics. James I described Puritans to his first Parliament as "a sect rather

1. *The Interpreter*, attributed to Thomas Scott, in E. Arber, *An English Garner* (1895), VI, pp. 235–6. Originally published, abroad, in 1622.
2. Bacon, *Works*, XIV, p. 449.
3. Ed. I. M. Calder, *Letters of John Davenport* (Yale, 1937), p. 13.
4. T. Scott, *Vox Regis* (1624), p. 21.
5. *The Interpreter, loc. cit.*, p. 233. "Beame and Palz" are Bohemia and the Palatinate. For Puritanism defined in terms of foreign policy, see J. Rous, *Diary* (Camden Soc., 1856), p. 44.
6. T. Birch, *The Court and Times of James I* (1848), II, p. 134.

than a religion – ever discontented with the present government
and impatient to suffer any superiority, which maketh their
sect unable to be suffered in any well-governed commonwealth".[1] In 1616 he told the judges of J.P.s who opposed the
prerogative and monarchy "through their puritanical itching
after popularity".[2] The Elector Palatine was no doubt
echoing his father-in-law's views (and repudiating those of
Thomas Scott) when he told his son's tutor to "take heed he
prove not a Puritan, which is incompatible with princes who
live by order, but they by confusion".[3]

"Some few that labour to bring in a new faction of their
own", said Christopher Sherland in the House of Commons of
1628, "drop into the ears of his Majesty that those that oppose
them oppose his Majesty (putting him upon designs that stand
not with the public liberty), and tell him that he may command
what he listeth, and do as he pleaseth with our goods, lives and
religion, whereby they have involved all good true-hearted
Englishmen and Christians under the name of Puritans".
"I am persuaded that the greater part of the nobility, clergy
and gentry are firm", Sherland added.[4] Arthur Wilson, "being
bred with a master who ever affected . . . natural and just
freedom for the subject, could not relish this growing way the
clergy had gotten, to make themselves great by undoing
the King". So at Chillingworth's college of Trinity, Oxford, in
the sixteen-thirties he "was accounted a kind of Puritan among
them".[5] The word had acquired sufficient precision in this
popular usage for it to be reported in 1634 that "in most
parishes in Wiltshire, Dorsetshire and the West parts, there is
still a Puritan and an honest man chosen churchwardens
together".[6] So local disputes were compromised with a

1. C. J., I, p. 144 (March 19, 1604).
2. King James I, Workes (1616), p. 564.
3. Quoted by E. Godfrey, A Sister of Prince Rupert (1919), p. 44.
4. Sir Thomas Crewe, The Proceedings and Debates of the House of
Commons in . . . 1628 (1707), pp. 13–14. Sherland was one of the Feoffees
for Impropriations, and an original member of the Providence Island
Company (E.P.C., p. 255; E. W. Kirby, "The Lay Feoffees: A Study in
Militant Puritanism", Journal of Modern History, XIV, p. 6, and references there cited).
5. Arthur Wilson, Life, in F. Peck, Desiderata Curiosa (1779), p. 470.
The "master" was the Earl of Essex, whose secretary Wilson had been.
6. "Archbishop Laud's Visitation of Salisbury in 1634", Wiltshire
Notes and Queries, I (1893), p. 75.

common sense that was not shown higher up the political ladder.

"All those that desire to preserve the laws and liberties of the kingdom, and to maintain religion in the power of it" are included under the name of Puritan by the Jesuited papists, said the Grand Remonstrance.[1] "If they ascribe anything to the laws and liberties of this realm, or hold the prerogative royal to be limitable by any law whatsoever", men are called Puritans, said Henry Parker. "If they hold not against Parliaments and with Ship Money, they are injurious to kings; and to be injurious to kings is *proprium quarto modo* to a Puritan. . . . If all reformers are Puritan, then Parliament is Puritan".[2] To show how far from religious the use of the word could be, we may quote a gamekeeper writing to the Earl of Suffolk in 1629 about a "mechanic" who poached the royal game as if he had no king to command him or had obtained exemption from the obedience of a subject, "which is a damnable opinion of a Puritan".[3]

Finally, Puritans were also defined in social terms. Mary Proude was told that "no gentleman, none but mean persons" were Puritans.[4] The Puritan is "naturally covetous of his purse and liberal of his tongue"; the epigram was attributed to King James.[5] Bishop Curle defined a Puritan as "such an one as loves God with all his soul but hates his neighbour with all his heart".[6] Another bishop said that Puritanism allowed "usury, sacrilege, disobedience, rebellion, etc.".[7] John Marston in 1598 described how an advocate of the "new discipline" "bit me

1. Gardiner, *Constitutional Documents of the Puritan Revolution* (3rd ed., 1906), p. 216.

2. Parker, *op. cit.*, p. 45; cf. pp. 11, 52, 59. Cf. also [Anon.], *Twenty Lookes Over all the Round-heads that ever lived in the world* (1643).

3. Quoted by F. Rose-Troup, *John White, the Patriarch of Dorchester* (New York, 1930), pp. 40–1. The men of Dorchester acquired the reputation of being Puritans because they "factiously contemn all law and justice that is without their own precincts".

4. Maria Webb, *The Penns and Penningtons of the Seventeenth Century* (1867), p. 18. She married one nevertheless.

5. *Crumms fal'n from King James's Table* in *The Miscellaneous Works . . . of Sir Thomas Overbury* (ed. E. F. Rimbault, 1890), p. 262.

6. Ed. J. Bruce, *Diary of John Manningham* (Camden Soc., 1868), p. 156.

7. Parker, *A Discourse concerning Puritans*, p. 57. The bishop was Henry Leslie of Down.

sore in deepest usury".[1] Thomas Heywood's definition of a
Puritan ran

> "*And when the poor his charity entreat* –
> '*You labour not, and therefore must not eat*'".[2]

An unsigned letter of about 1626–8, drawing up a comprehensive list of enemies of the Duke of Buckingham, included
covetous landlords, papists, needy and indebted persons,
Puritans and sectaries, malcontents, lawyers, City merchants
and republicans. Puritans and sectaries, "though scarce two
of them agree in what they would have, yet they all in general
are haters of government". They are strong amongst "the
lawyers, citizens and western men" – i.e. clothiers.[3] Wentworth
described John Hampden to Laud as "a great brother": "the
very genius of that nation of people leads them always to
oppose, as well civilly as ecclesiastically, all that ever authority
ordains for them".[4]

III

So it is important, in discussing Puritanism, to remember
that for contemporaries the word had no narrowly religious
connotation. Above all we must clear our minds of the post-
1660 stereotype. Our leading authority on Puritan London
writes "Ardent propagandist and pleasure-seeking citizen
alike – few had the kill-joy qualities given to all Puritans by
later legend".[5] It was the "Puritan" Nicholas Fuller who in
Darcy v. Allen defended the right to play cards as a lawful use
of leisure.[6] In so far as there were killjoys of the type caricatured

1. *The Metamorphosis of Pygmalion's Image*. quoted in G. B. Harrison,
A Second Elizabethan Journal (1931), p. 280.

2. T. Heywood, *Troia Britanica* (1608), quoted in Harrison, *A Second
Jacobean Journal* (1958), p. 166.

3. *Cabala* (1654), pp. 225–7.

4. Ed. W. Knowler, *The Earl of Strafforde's Letters and Dispatches*
(1739), II, p. 138. Such people, the Archbishop agreed, should ideally be
"whipped into their right wits".

5. Valerie Pearl, *London and the Outbreak of the Puritan Revolution*
(1961), p. 279. This consideration will become especially important to
bear in mind when we come to discuss Sabbatarianism (see Chapter 5
below, esp. pp. 160–1). See also P. Miller and T. H. Johnson, *The Puritans*
(New York, 1938), pp. 115–16, 124, 226.

6. F. Thompson, *Magna Carta: its role in the making of the English
Constitution. 1300–1629* (University of Minnesota Press, 1948), p. 230.

by Zeal-of-the-Land Busy, they are to be found among the separatists. On the other hand, we can find plenty of "Puritanism" in the poems of George Herbert and Henry Vaughan; and it was the future bishop, Jeremy Taylor, who insisted that Jesus Christ never laughed.[1] There were on the royalist side in the civil war many "Puritans" like the Sabbatarian Sir Ralph Hopton, Sir Bevil Grenville with his dislike of oaths, or Samuel Ward, expelled from Sidney Sussex College by the Parliamentarians. But among those whom I define as Puritans there were many Malvolios. Contemporary references to puritan hypocrisy are frequent, and they usually refer to the combination of godly phrases with economic or other less noble motives. It was an accusation to which a puritan leader like John Preston was especially sensitive.[2]

Thus Marston's Quicksilver in *Eastward Hoe* (1605), who was an apprentice, has a curious remark to the effect that "your only smooth skin to make fine vellum is your Puritan's skin; they be the smoothest and slickest knaves in a country".[3] George Wither, whilst praising some Puritans, recognized that there was also "the hollow crew, the counterfeit elect".[4] And Osborn noted how the elasticity of the name "did not only delight and cover all those that cheated under a pretence of sanctity, but stifled the seeds of goodness: so as probity was obstructed by deceit in the general commerce, and religion, the guard of property, rendered useless, if not destructive, to human society".[5] Clarendon wrote caustically of that distinguished pirate and empire-builder the Earl of Warwick that "a man of less virtue could not be found out", but that by his patronage and generosity towards the silenced ministers "he became the head of that party and got the style of *a godly man*."[6]

1. Jeremy Taylor, *The Whole Works* (1836), III, p. 747.
2. J. Preston, *The Breastplate of Faith and Love* (5th ed., 1634), Sermon IV, pp. 99–101; *A Patterne of Wholesome Words*, in *Riches of Mercy to Men in Misery* (1658), pp. 280–2. Mr. P. N. Siegel has collected many examples in his "Shylock and the Puritan Usurers", *Studies in Shakespeare* (Miami, 1952), pp. 129–38. Cf. Richard Carew's sneers at usurers in the tin industry "who make greatest pretence of zeal in religion" (*Survey of Cornwall*, 1811, p. 49. First published 1602).
3. John Marston, *Plays* (1934–9), III, p. 110.
4. Wither, *Juvenilia*, p. 299.
5. Osborn, *Traditionall Memoyres*, p. 189.
6. Clarendon, *History of the Rebellion*, (ed. W. D. Macray, 1888), II,

Contemporaries were thus aware of the social and political overtones of the word Puritan, and Osborn's phrase, "religion, the guard of property", shows that social functions were not attributed to one brand of belief only. Let us look again at some of the famous definitions in this light. "To bewail the distresses of God's children, it is Puritanism", said Job Throckmorton in 1587. "I fear me we shall shortly come to this, that to do God and her Majesty good service shall be counted Puritanism".[1] Sir Benjamin Rudyerd said in the Long Parliament: "Whosoever squares his action by any rule, either divine or human, he is a Puritan. Whosoever would be governed by the King's laws, he is a Puritan.[2] He that will not do whatsoever other men would have him do, he is a Puritan. Their great work, their masterpiece now is to make all those of the religion to be the suspected party in the kingdom".[3] Mrs. Hutchinson was probably drawing on recollections of this speech in the more famous passage in her *Life of Colonel Hutchinson*:

"If any were grieved at the dishonour of the kingdom, or the griping of the poor, or the unjust oppressions of the subject by a thousand ways invented to maintain the riots of the courtiers and the swarms of needy Scots the King had brought in to devour like locusts the plenty of this land, he was a Puritan; if any, out of mere morality and civil honesty, discountenanced the abominations of those days, he was a Puritan, however he conformed to their superstitious worship; if any showed favour to any godly, honest person, kept them company, relieved them in want, or protected them against violent and unjust oppression, he was a Puritan; if any gentleman in his county maintained the good laws of the land, or stood up for any public interest, for good order or government, he was a Puritan. In short, all that crossed the views of the needy courtiers, the

---

p. 544. Such figures are familiar in the history of Puritanism, from the Duke of Northumberland and his son onwards. In the fifteen-nineties John Penry cast the Earl of Essex for the role of godly land-grabber, and in the sixteen-twenties John Preston had similar hopes of the Duke of Buckingham.

1. Neale, *Elizabeth I and her Parliaments, 1584–1601*, p. 151.
2. The reference is presumably to the recusancy laws.
3. T. May, *The History of the Parliament of England* (1647), I, p. 74. "Those of the religion" is the technical term usually employed to describe the French Huguenots.

proud encroaching priests, the thievish projectors, the lewd nobility and gentry, . . . all these were Puritans; and if Puritans, then enemies to the King and his government, seditious, factious hypocrites, ambitious disturbers of the public peace, and finally the pest of the kingdom".[1]

"Puritan" came to be used to describe almost any opponent of the Court. A pamphlet published in 1643, allegedly by the Venetian Ambassador, described three factions in England – Protestant, Catholic and Puritan. The last-named "is the most potent, consisting of some bishops, all the gentry and commonalty".[2] "Those whom we ordinarily call Puritans", said Henry Parker, "are men of strict life and precise opinions, which cannot be hated for anything but their singularity in zeal and piety. . . . The number of such men is . . . small, and their condition . . . low and dejected. But they which are the Devil's chief artificers in abusing this word . . . can so stretch and extend the same, that scarce any civil honest Protestant . . . can avoid the aspersion of it".[3] "Laud's faction", Roger Coke agreed, "stigmatized all others (except papists) which were not of their faction with the name of Puritans". As the popish and prerogative parties grew more insolent, so "the Puritan party gained strength and reputation among the vulgar and became more than all the other three".[4]

The Puritans, wrote Vicars in 1644, included "all that were zealous for the laws and liberties of the kingdom, and for the maintenance of religion".[5] Or as Sir Arthur Haslerig summed it up, "I was bred a Puritan, and am for public liberty". Sir Arthur, who was speaking in 1659, went on to say that he was no Leveller, and to distinguish between men of property (Puritans) and lovers of anarchy (Levellers).[6] But the Levellers agreed with him on the significance and usage of the word "Puritan". Their *Large Petition* of 1647 reminded the House of

1. Lucy Hutchinson, *Memoirs of the Life of Colonel Hutchinson* (1846), pp. 80–1. The omitted passage refers to disapproval of oaths and Sabbath-breaking, and support for preaching.
2. *The Popes Nuntioes*, in *Somers Tracts* (1748–51), IX, p. 386. Cf. Bacon, quoted on p. 18 above.
3. Parker, *op. cit.*, p. 11.
4. R. Coke, *A Detection of the Court and State of England* (1694), II, pp. 317–18; I, pp. 206–7. The third party was the "country or legal party".
5. J. Vicars, *Jehovah-Jireh* (1644), p. 12.
6. Ed. J. T. Rutt, *Diary of Thomas Burton* (1828), IV, p. 77.

Commons that "those who found themselves aggrieved formerly at the burdens and oppressions of those times, that did not conform to the church government then established, refused to pay Ship Money or yield obedience to unjust patents, were reviled and reproached with nicknames of Puritans, heretics, schismatics, sectaries . . .", just as, the Petition continued, the Levellers were now.[1]

So I agree with contemporaries in thinking that there was in England in the two or three generations before the civil war a body of opinion which can usefully be labelled Puritan. There was a core of doctrine about religion and Church government, aiming at purifying the Church from inside. This doctrine for various reasons won the support of a substantial and growing group of laymen. It is not to be identified with either Presbyterianism or Independency. The former was always primarily a clerical theory, and the English Presbyterian movement was effectively persecuted out of existence in the fifteen-nineties by Whitgift and Bancroft. There was no real continuity between it and the Presbyterianism imposed on England in the sixteen-forties as the price of the Scottish alliance, which in any case was a very watered down erastian affair compared with what prevailed in Scotland or with what the Westminster Assembly of Divines would have liked to see.[2] Independency as a significant body of opinion in England post-dates the civil war. The main stream of puritan thought, as I define it, is associated with men like Perkins, Bownde, Preston, Sibbes, Thomas Taylor, William Gouge, Thomas Goodwin, Richard Baxter. Their thought was not monolithic, but they adopted comparable attitudes to most of the problems examined in this book; and these attitudes seem to have appealed to the larger circle of lay opinion which we can conveniently describe as Puritan, the body of opinion without which the civil war could never have been fought.[3] What I have tried to do in this book is to examine some of the themes to which doctrinal Puritans attached importance, and to account for their appeal to laymen.

1. *The Large Petition* (1647), Sig. A 3–3v, in *Tracts on Liberty in the Puritan Revolution* (ed. W. Haller, Columbia University Press, 1934), III, pp. 401–2.
2. H. R. Trevor-Roper, "Scotland and the Puritan Revolution", in *Historical Essays, 1600–1750, presented to David Ogg* (1963), p. 93; cf. pp. 247–8, 473–5, 487–8 below.
3. See Chapter 4 below.

Chapter Two

The Preaching of the Word

There will be a perpetual defection, except you keep men in by preaching, as well as law doth by punishing.

> Francis Bacon, Speech to the judges, 1617
> (*Works*, XIII, p. 213).

Traveller. – You divines have the sway of men's minds, you may as easily persuade them to good as to bad, to truth as to falsehood.

> Samuel Hartlib, *A Description of the famous Kingdom of Macaria*. (1641), in *Harleian Miscellany* (1744–56), I, p. 567.

Military preparations had effected little, had not the fire been given from the pulpit.

> [Anon.], *A Letter from Mercurius Civicus to Mercurius Rusticus* (1643), in *Somers Tracts* (1748–51), V, p. 400.

I

PREACHING is necessary to salvation, said Hus in 1412. Two hundred and twenty-eight years later Stephen Marshall told the House of Commons that preaching of the Word was the chariot on which salvation came riding into the hearts of men.[1] Between the two dates the sentiment was often repeated, by heretics under Henry VIII, by Elizabethan bishops, and by Puritans and radicals like Thomas Sampson, John Penry, Martin Marprelate.[2] Preaching was "the only mean and instrument

1. S. Marshall, *A Sermon Preached before the Honourable House of Commons . . . November 17, 1640*, p. 33.
2. Ed. D. Williams, John Penry's *Three Treatises Concerning Wales* (1960), pp. 3, 67, 119, and *passim*; Martin Marprelate, *The Epistle* (ed. E. Arber, 1895), p. 27. Published 1588.

of the salvation of mankind", Archbishop Grindal told
Elizabeth in 1576.[1] But he was in trouble with the Queen at the
time, precisely for, in her view, over-valuing preaching. Whitgift's formulation was more cautious: preaching was "the most
ordinary and usual means that God useth to work by in the
hearts of the hearers".[2] The difference between these two
emphases played a large part in Penry's examination before the
High Commission in 1587. Bishop Cooper of Winchester
accused him of "an execrable heresy" for saying that preaching
was "the only ordinary means" of salvation, and Whitgift
concurred.[3]

Henceforth Grindal's view became a puritan shibboleth,
echoed by Robert Browne, by Richard Greenham, William
Perkins, William Gouge, Thomas Taylor, the Westminster
Assembly and its two catechisms, by Thomas Hooker and the
1650 Code of Connecticut, and by Baxter and Bunyan.[4]
Evangelist is in a sense the most important character in
Pilgrim's Progress. But the hierarchy and its spokesmen, from
Whitgift onwards, sheered away from Grindal's position. The
judicious Richard Hooker noted that "it hath grown to be a
question, whether the Word of God be any ordinary mean to
save the souls of men, . . . or else only as the same is preached".
Hooker thought catechizing and reading Homilies were also
forms of preaching, and attacked Cartwright's view that the
sacraments were "not effectual to salvation, without men be

1. Ed. W. Nicholson, *The Remains of Edmund Grindal* (Parker Soc.,
1843), p. 379.

2. Whitgift, *Works* (Parker Soc., 1851–3), III, p. 32.

3. Martin Marprelate, *The Epistle*, p. 28. Cooper denied the words, but
not the doctrine (T. Cooper, *An Admonition to the People of England*,
ed. Arber, 1895, pp. 58–9. First published 1589).

4. Ed. A. Peel and L. H. Carlson, *Writings of Robert Harrison and
Robert Browne* (1953), pp. 408–10; R. Greenham, *Workes* (1612), pp.
173, 341; W. Perkins, *Workes* (1612), I, p. 71; W. Gouge, *A Commentary
on the whole Epistle to the Hebrews* (1866), I, p. 101; T. Taylor, *A
Commentary Upon the Epistle of St. Paul written to Titus* (1658), pp.
34–5; ed. A. F. Mitchell and J. Struthers, *Minutes of the Sessions of
the Westminster Assembly of Divines* (1874), p. 276; *The Shorter Catechism* of 1647 (1897), p. 14; *The Larger Catechism* of 1648 (1865), pp.
115, 194–5; Perry Miller, *Errand into the Wilderness* (Harvard University Press, 1956), p. 35; T. Hooker, *The Saints Dignitie* (1651), p. 234;
Reliquiae Baxterianae, I, p. 8; W. Dell, *Several Sermons and Discourses*
(1709), p. 143: published 1652; J. Bunyan, *Works* (1860), III, p. 685; cf.
D. Featley, *Ancilla Pietatis* (5th ed., 1639), p. 74. See also p. 65 below.

instructed by preaching before they be partakers of them". Sacraments, Hooker thought, do far more than "teach the mind", since they are holy mysteries, not mere signs.[1]

Hooker thus justified theoretically a retreat to Sacramentalism which was to be carried further by Laud. But the emphasis on preaching had been one of the essentials of Protestantism, and was strongly reinforced by the marginal notes to the Geneva Bible, the most widely read version until well into the seventeenth century.[2] The proposition that preaching was one of the marks of the true church had been laid down by Luther and the Augsburg Confession, by Calvin and Bullinger, by the Thirty-nine Articles and the Homilies. It was accepted by Whitgift no less than by Richard Fitz's "Privy Church" in 1571, or by John Penry. The retreat therefore could not go too far.

II

We may consider the importance of preaching from another angle. In the sixteenth and seventeenth centuries the Church had a monopoly of thought-control and opinion-forming. It controlled education; it censored books. Until 1641 the publication of home news was prohibited; privately circulated newsletters were available to the rich, but were beyond the means of the poor.[3] So in the absence of other media of communication, sermons were for the majority of Englishmen their main source of political information and political ideas. Men come to church for news, said Silver-Tongued Smith: "if the preacher say anything of our armies beyond the sea, or council at home, or matters at court", they are happy.[4] This was as true of the North as of London. A King's Preacher in Lan-

1. R. Hooker, *Of the Laws of Ecclesiastical Polity* (Everyman ed.), II, pp. 55–76, 98–9, 234. Cf Bacon on the Puritans: "they have made it almost of the essence of the sacrament of the supper to have a sermon precedent" (*Works*, I, p. 93, *On the Controversies of the Church*; cf. E. Troeltsch, *Social Teaching of the Christian Churches*, transl. O. Wyon, 1931, II, pp. 479–80).
2. See H. Schultz, *Milton and Forbidden Knowledge* (New York, 1955), pp. 229, 233.
3. Godfrey Davies, "English Political Sermons, 1603–40", *Huntington Library Quarterly*, III, p. 4.
4. Quoted by J. L. Lievsay, "Silver-Tongued Smith", *Huntington Library Quarterly*, XI, pp. 34–5.

cashire said in 1614 "Report to them [some] human history; tell them some strange news or a tale for their worldly profit or corporal health, they will keep it well enough".[1] "The first publication of extraordinary news was from the pulpit", said Clarendon of the civil war period.[2] The pulpit fulfilled indeed quite different functions from those which are expected of it to-day. In addition to disseminating news, sermons had replaced the confessional as a source of guidance on moral and economic conduct. Even an orthodox clergyman like Robert Sanderson used the pulpit to denounce monopolies and the corruptions and excessive fees of the law courts.[3] Nor should we forget the illiteracy of a large proportion of the population. For all except a favoured few the words of the parson, even when they were not accepted as gospel, necessarily formed the starting-point for discussion.[4]

This being so, control of the Church was of vital political importance. Thanks to the Reformation the nomination of ministers had come increasingly into the hands of well-to-do laymen.[5] But nearly all clergymen, once presented, were subject to the authority of bishops; and bishops appointed by the Crown very rarely forgot their maker. By precept and punishment, through bishops or immediately, governments went far to determine what was said in most pulpits.

Direct governmental control of preachers goes back to long before the Reformation, though this gave it a new urgency. Cromwell's Injunctions of 1536 instructed the clergy to preach down papal claims, and preach up the royal supremacy, twice in each year. The Visitation Articles of 1559 included an inquiry whether ministers "have exhorted the people to obedience to the Queen's majesty and ministers".[6] The mediaeval custom of licensing preachers and schoolmasters, revived under Edward VI, was continued by Elizabeth: only those officially licensed were allowed to preach. In March 1565 licences to preachers were called in, and reissued only to min-

1. W. Harrison, *The Difference of Hearers* (1614), p. 39.

2. Clarendon, *History of the Rebellion*, IV, p. 194.

3. R. Sanderson, *XXXV Sermons* (1681), pp. 130, 203.

4. I have discussed this at greater length in my *Century of Revolution* (1961), pp. 75–7.

5. *E.P.C.*, Chapter 4.

6. Ed. E. Cardwell, *Documentary Annals of the Reformed Church of England* (1839), I, p. 211.

isters who had been "diligently examined for their conformity in unity of doctrine established by public authority". They were to be "admonished to use sobriety and discretion in teaching he people", especially in "matters of controversy". Many earned men were lost to the ministry; but those who remained were, from the Government's point of view, more discreet and amenable. Henceforth every minister on admission to a living had to make a protestation, "I shall not preach, or publicly interpret, but only read that which is appointed by public authority, without special licence of the bishop under his seal".[1] The savage persecution of the fifteen-nineties aimed to prevent preaching by deprived ministers or by persons whose ordination lacked the approval of "public authority".

Nor were the laity forgotten. The Injunctions of 1559 dealt with "rash talkers of Scripture". "No man shall talk or reason of the holy Scriptures rashly or contentiously, nor maintain any false doctrine or error, but shall commune of the same, when occasion is given, reverently, humbly and in the fear of God". The 1562 Introduction to the Thirty-nine Articles ordered "all further curious research" into theological matters to be laid aside; no man should in a sermon or in print draw aside the meaning of any article.[2]

Under the 46th Canon of 1604 any minister who was not himself licensed to preach must procure the services of a licensed preacher once a month, and pay for it himself if his benefice could stand the charge. On other Sundays, or if he occupied a poor living, as most vicars in market towns did, he had to fall back upon the Book of Homilies. In 1606 there was another relicensing of preachers. "No minister whatsoever", Yonge noted, "may preach before he get a new licence from the ordinary of the diocese wherein he is, albeit he hath been a preacher these twenty years".[3]

Control also took more positive forms. "Queen Elizabeth used to tune her pulpits, as her saying was".[4] In 1579 the Council, alarmed by John Stubbes's criticism of the Queen's proposed marriage to the Duke of Anjou in *The Gaping Gulph*, instructed the Archbishop of Canterbury to admonish

1. Ed. A. Sparrow, *A Collection of Articles* (1684), pp. 123, 128.
2. *Ibid.*, pp. 78, 90; cf. pp. 80–1.
3. Ed. G. Roberts, *Diary of Walter Yonge* (Camden Soc., 1848), p. 9.
4. P. Heylyn, *Cyprianus Anglicus* (1671), p. 153.

preachers in his diocese "that in their sermons and preachings
they do not intermeddle with any such matters of state, being
in very deed not incident nor appertaining to their profession,
. . . but rather teach the people to be thankful towards Almighty God for the great benefits both of liberty of conscience,
peace and wealth which they have hitherto enjoyed by her
Majesty's good means".[1] The anniversary of Queen Elizabeth's
accession was an unfailing occasion for sermons which were
pure Government propaganda.[2] In the famine year of 1596
Whitgift, through the bishops, issued instructions to preachers
"to exhort the wealthier sort . . . to contribute more liberally
towards the relief of the poor", and to denounce hoarders.
Next year farmers and engrossers of corn were to be attacked,
and prayers were asked for the success of the Cadiz expedition.[3]
Burghley seems to have derived especial pleasure from drafting
prayers in connection with military and naval enterprises.[4]

Sermons at Paul's Cross were almost official Government
pronouncements. As early as Edward VI's reign we find Cecil
briefing Gardiner for a sermon to be delivered there.[5] On the
day of Mary's death he noted that he must look into "the
condition of the preacher of Paul's Cross, that no occasion be
given by him to stir any dispute touching the governance of the
realm". A month later Elizabeth forbade all preaching,
particularly in London.[6] The preacher at Paul's Cross each
Sunday morning was appointed by the Bishop of London or
some other Government official. Towards the end of her reign
Elizabeth several times vetoed a preacher when his name was
submitted to her.[7] The bishop was normally held responsible to
the Privy Council for the soundness of the doctrine preached.
("The preacher standeth up as the wolf doth in a vizard",
sneered Browne; "he hath the Bishop's name in a parchment,

1. Cardwell, *Documentary Annals*, I, p. 383.

2. For an example by Whitgift himself in 1583, see Strype, *Life of
Whitgift* (1822), III, pp. 70–81.

3. *Ibid.*, III, p. 350; Peck, *Desiderata Curiosa* (1779), pp. 168–72.

4. C. Read, *Lord Burghley and Queen Elizabeth* (1960), p. 521.

5. M. A. S. Hume, *The Great Lord Burghley* (1898), pp. 459–60.

6. Strype, *Annals of the Reformation . . . during Queen Elizabeth's
happy reign* (1824), I, part i, pp. 7, 59.

7. M. Maclure, *The Paul's Cross Sermons, 1534–1642* (Toronto,
1958), pp. 13–14; J. O. W. Haweis, *Sketches of the Reformation and
Elizabethan Age* (1844), pp. 51–2.

for that is his licence, it is a thieves' quittance".[1]) On important occasions the preacher was given detailed instructions, not only as to his theme but as to the manner of its presentation. Thus Bancroft dictated the Paul's Cross sermon after Essex's rising in 1601, and there was considerable interference at the time of the Spanish marriage negotiations in the early sixteen-twenties.[2] Such sermons reached a wider audience than that at the Cross: they were often repeated elsewhere. In James's reign Cromwell's teacher Dr. Beard refused to obey his bishop's orders to "rehearse" at Huntingdon a sermon preached at Paul's Cross by Dr. Alabaster, which Beard (and his pupil) thought contained flat popery.[3] Beard was soundly rated, and Cromwell raised the matter in Parliament, many years later. It marked a minor revolution when in 1642 Isaac Penington persuaded the House of Commons that henceforth the Lord Mayor and aldermen of London should appoint the preachers at Paul's Cross; and it was startling evidence of the City's new importance in national politics.[4] In 1581 Bishop Aylmer's chaplain, preaching at Paul's Cross, had said that if the appointing of preachers were committed to the City authorities, "they would appoint such as would defend usury, the Family of Love and Puritanism".[5]

In a letter which he wrote to the Archbishop of Canterbury in 1622, James I started from the historically accurate assumption that "the abuses and extravagances of preachers in the pulpit have been in all times suppressed in this realm by some act of council or state, with the advice and resolution of grave and learned prelates"; and went on to lay down detailed regulations. Afternoon sermons were to be confined to some part of the catechism, or to a text from the Creed, the Ten Commandments or the Lord's Prayer. (This restriction on afternoon sermons, Fuller said, lost the Puritans half the preaching in England.) No preacher was to stray outside the

1. R. Browne, *Treatise upon the 23 ... of Matthew* (1582), in *Writings of Harrison and Browne*, pp. 199–204.
2. F. O. White, *Lives of the Elizabethan Bishops* (1898), p. 379; Maclure, *op. cit.*, pp. 241–4; ed. T. Birch, *The Court and Times of James I* (1848), II, pp. 334–5.
3. Ed. W. C. Abbott, *Writings and Speeches of Oliver Cromwell* (Harvard University Press, 1937–47) I, p. 62.
4. Pearl, *London and the Outbreak of the Puritan Revolution*, p. 262.
5. Maclure, *op. cit.*, p. 212.

theological fold of the Thirty-nine Articles and the Homilies; no one below the rank of dean was to touch thorny problems such as predestination, or to meddle with matters of state; or to attack papists. In particular they were not to advocate restrictions on "the power, prerogative, jurisdiction, authority or duty of sovereign princes". As the Arminians came to hold all the best bishoprics and deaneries in England, the restriction by rank was in effect a party restriction. It silenced, to quote Fuller again, "mean ministers in popular congregations".[1]

James criticized the bishops "for their former remissness" in licensing preachers, and ordered them to withdraw any permission given to their deputies to grant licences. They were to be more careful in future.[2] Henceforth all lecturers were to be licensed. The King was worried lest "every young man should take unto himself an exhorbitant liberty to teach what he listeth, to the offence of his Majesty and to the disturbance and disquiet of the church and commonwealth". It is hardly surprising that these instructions gave rise to rumours among "some few churchmen and many of the people" that the King's orders tended "to the restraint of the exercise of preaching".[3] But the mesh seemed to have been drawn tightly enough, and the point had been underlined in 1614 by the trial, torture and death sentence imposed on Edmund Peacham for having in his possession a sermon (which he said he had never preached, but which was written out fair) which the Government thought seditious. Peacham died in prison.[4]

In 1620 James I instructed preachers in London "to inveigh ... against the insolency of our women, and their wearing of broad-brimmed hats" and other undesirable garments. Less than three weeks later "our pulpits ring continually of the insolence and impudence of women", and the King had to intervene to stop enthusiasts carrying the attack beyond its intended object, the wives of London citizens, so far as to check "ladies and gentlewomen" for wearing yellow

1. Clarendon, *Life* (1759), I, p. 50; Fuller *Church History*, III, p. 321.
2. Rushworth, *Historical Collections*, I, p. 65.
3. Ed. H. R. Wilton Hall, *Records of the Old Archdeaconry of St. Albans* (St. Albans and Herts. Architectural and Archaeological Soc. 1908), pp. 147–8, 150. In the previous year "divers preachers" had "cast out words in the pulpit as if there were some danger that religion should be changed amongst us" (*ibid.*, p. 147).
4. Gardiner, *History of England*, III, pp. 272–83.

ruffs.[1] Mr. Godfrey Davies collected much evidence of "definite attempts to dictate the contents of sermons" under the first two Stuarts. "What might almost be called the censorship of sermons runs parallel to the censorship of the press", each becoming more stringent after Charles I's accession. He gives many examples,[2] and there was no doubt more Government interference than the surviving evidence reveals. The Canons of 1640 insisted that the doctrine of the Divine Right of Kings should be preached in all pulpits on one Sunday in each quarter: in some parishes this might amount to a high proportion of all the sermons preached.[3]

Control of the pulpit was a question of political power. "People are governed by the pulpit more than the sword in times of peace", Charles I told his son.[4] John Wilkins often said to Oliver Cromwell that "no temporal government could have a sure support without a national church that adhered to it".[5] Marchamont Nedham, a pamphleteer who wrote for either side, expressed the point with more cynical candour: "No state can permit ministers to pretend scruples".[6] It was on the basis of English experience that Fuller concluded both that "in all state alterations, be they never so bad, the pulpit will be of the same wood with the Council Board", and that "those who hold the helm of the pulpit always steer the people's hearts as they please".[7]

iii

It was not only the government which used the pulpit for political purposes. Puritans were presented to livings by lay

1. Ed. N. E. McClure, *The Letters of John Chamberlain* (American Philosophical Soc., 1939), II, pp. 286–94.

2. G. Davies, "English Political Sermons", *Huntington Library Quarterly*, III, esp. pp. 7–8.

3. Cf. F. H. West, *Sparrows of the Spirit* (n.d.), p. 23 – a pamphlet, *God and the King*, bought in the sixteen-thirties for the vicar of Upton to read in church, commending Divine Right monarchy in obsequious language.

4. Ed. Sir C. Petrie, *Letters, Speeches and Proclamations of King Charles I* (1935), p. 200.

5. G. Burnet, *History of My Own Time* (ed. O. Airy, 1897), I, p. 114.

6. *Mercurius Politicus*, quoted by Margaret James, *Social Problems and Policy during the Puritan Revolution* (1930), p. 32.

7. Fuller, *Church History* (1842), III, p. 102; G. P. Gooch, *The History of English Democratic Ideas in the Seventeenth Century* (1898), p. 62.

patrons, lecturers were appointed by town corporations and City Companies.[1] The judges, through the J.P.s, instructed ministers to read their orders from the pulpit, though in 1632 Chief Justice Richardson was rapped over the knuckles by Laud for issuing Sabbatarian orders which conflicted with the archbishop's policy.[2] Rival viewpoints might thus be expressed within the Church. But the Government used all the advantages of its position, with increasing effectiveness, to suppress views which it did not like.

Whitgift in 1574 used language which suggests the existence of a powerful *political* opposition inside the Church: "If a man in some congregations commend the magistrates and such as be in authority, if he exhort to obedience, if he move unto peace, if he confirm the rites and orders by public authority established . . . , he shall scarcely be heard with patience; nay, he shall be sent away with all kind of opprobries and reproaches. But if he nip at superiors and reprove those that be in authority, . . . if he shall inveigh against laws and orders established, and talk of matters that tend to contention rather than edification (though it be done never so untruly, never so unlearnedly, as commonly it is), they flock to him like bees . . .".[3] An example of what Whitgift was attacking may be given from 1564. Melchior Smyth, vicar of Hessle and Hull, was accused, among many other things, "that in his sermons he hath divers times to the estimation of his hearers inveighed against the rulers and nobility and difference of blood, and persuaded all men to be equal and like". This was reported to the Ecclesiastical Commissioners at York, with a view to disciplinary action against Smyth.[4] A sermon preached in 1600 assumed as a matter of course that a sensational preacher would be silenced.[5]

Down to 1589 the Earl of Leicester saw to it that learned

1. See pp. 91–109 below.
2. See p. 184 below.
3. Whitgift, *Works*, III, p. 572.
4. Ed. J. S. Purvis, *Tudor Parish Documents of the Diocese of York* (1948), pp. 212, 217. This aspect of the case against Smyth is not mentioned in Marchant, *The Puritans and the Church Courts in the Diocese of York*.
5. Haweis, *Sketches of the Reformation and Elizabethan Age*, pp. 99–100. Examples from James's reign are given by Mr. Davies, "Engl sh Political Sermons", pp. 8–9.

puritan preachers were promoted in the Church, or gave them large stipends out of his own purse.[1] But after Leicester's death, and with the simplification of foreign policy issues after 1588, the influence of Puritanism declined. It grew again as a new threat to Protestantism appeared in the Thirty Years War. Foreign policy, so closely bound up with religion, was a subject which many preachers found difficult to resist. Mr. Davies holds that there is "good evidence" of an intensified interest in politics after the exposure of James I's pro-Spanish policy.[2] This was wholly to the advantage of the Puritans. The negotiations for the marriage of Prince Charles gave rise to much pulpit controversy. As early as 1617 Dr. Samuel Page, preaching the annual Easter Monday "Spittal sermon" before the Council, spoke "too broadly against the Spanish match" and was committed.[3] In December 1620 the Bishop of London received instructions to call all his clergy before him and order them, from the King, "not to meddle in their sermons with the Spanish match nor any other matter of state".[4] But evasion was possible. One preacher spoke of the great sheep murrain of Edward VI's reign, caused, it was said, by the importation of scabbed sheep from Spain; another, after denouncing those who should break their faith, concluded by saying he would make no application as he did not want to go to jail.[5]

In 1622, shortly before Charles's visit to Spain, the Venetian Ambassador noted that recently preachers had been expressing "seditious and most dangerous opinions, offering the strongest opposition to the Spanish marriage". A directive, however, had clearly gone round, for he reported that now preachers "daily exhort the people to obedience".[6] In March of the next year, when Charles was actually in Spain with Buckingham," many of our churchmen are hardly held in, and their tongues itch to be talking".[7] The Bishop of London, on James's orders, again

1. Ed. P. Collinson, *Letters of Thomas Wood, Puritan, 1566–77* (Bulletin of the Institute of Historical Research, Special Supplement No. 5), p. 13.

2. Davies, "English Political Sermons", p. 4.

3. *Letters of John Chamberlain*, II, p. 74.

4. *Ibid.*, II, p. 331.

5. Davies, "English Political Sermons", pp. 12–13; cf. Birch, *Court and Times of James I*, II, pp. 265–6.

6. *C.S.P., Venetian*, 1621–3, p. 445.

7. *Letters of John Chamberlain*, II, p. 486.

instructed his clergy not to "prejudicate the prince's journey by
their prayers", but only to pray God to bring him safely home
and no more. One parson reconciled his instructions with his
conscience by praying publicly "that God would return our
noble prince home again and no more".[1] Mr. Davies spoke of
the protests in this period as "perhaps . . . the first definite
example of an attempt to marshal public opinion in opposition
to the foreign policy of a government in England". John
Everard, preacher of St. Martin's in the Fields, was reputed to
have been "six or seven times in prison" for his obstinate
preaching against the Spanish match.[2] Many who were not
Puritans must have sympathized with him.

The powers of the Crown were always a risky subject for
preachers, yet one to which they continually adverted because
of their crucial importance in all disputes, religious or political.
Thus in the ticklish year 1617 the Rev. John Drope of Mag-
dalen College, Oxford, preached a sermon at Paul's Cross
"wherein out of Proverbs among other things he would prove
that kings might steal as well as meaner men, both by borrow-
ing and not paying, and by laying unreasonable and undue
impositions upon their subjects".[3] That was getting very near
the knuckle indeed, and Mr. Drope can hardly have been
surprised to find himself in trouble. Five years later John
Knight, in a sermon preached at Oxford, was alleged to have
proved from "Paraeus upon Romans" that tyrannical kings
might be brought into order by the inferior magistrate. This
doctrine seemed to James so extravagant that he threatened
to have the sermon publicly burnt as *heretical*. Knight was
only spared because he made due submission. All copies of
Paraeus's offending work were hunted out from libraries,
private studies and bookshops in Oxford, and publicly burnt;
and all Oxford graduates were compelled to sign a declaration
of passive obedience and non-resistance.[4] In July of the same

1. Birch, *Court and Times of James I*, II, p. 381. A newsletter noted
that the clergy "do not obey" the Bishop's command (Davies, *op. cit.*,
p. 9).
2. Davies, *op. cit.*, pp. 9–10.
3. *Letters of John Chamberlain*, II, p. 71.
4. *Ibid.*, II, p. 434; Roberts, *Diary of Walter Yonge*, p. 62. Piquancy
was added to the situation by the fact that Paraeus was a Calvinist divine
of Heidelberg, long a centre of influence on English Puritans, more
recently now the capital of James's son-in-law, the Elector Palatine,

year the Bishop of London was put up at Paul's Cross to urge
contributions to the benevolence: his argument was that
"what we have is not our own, and what we gave was but
rendering and restoring"[1] – unpopular doctrine with the
citizens of London.

In June 1626 Charles I issued a proclamation again threatening severe penalties against those who preached views not
warranted by the doctrine and discipline of the Church of
England – a proclamation which, Heylyn says, was largely
ignored by Puritan ministers outside London.[2] It was followed
by a letter from the Privy Council to the archbishops, telling
them to mobilize preachers to explain the miseries of disunity,
to urge supply for the Spanish war, begun on Parliament's
advice, and to explain that it was sinful to refuse aid.[3] A spate
of loyal sermons ensued, of which the most notorious are
those of Manwaring, Sibthorpe and Montague. They drove
an M.P. to cry out in the Parliament of 1628 "It hath been
preached, or rather prated in pulpits, that all is the King's".[4]
Here we see one of the most obvious points at which control
of the pulpit was an essential political weapon. The government was able to get sermons preached in favour of Ship
Money, and to suppress the few preached against it.

When the Scottish war came, the government's monopoly
control over pulpit and press was used to the fullest extent. All
Scottish manifestoes were suppressed, but the royal proclamation against the Scots was ordered to be read in all the churches
of England.[5] It was therefore a political demonstration when

---

whom James regarded as a rebel against his sovereign and many Englishmen regarded as the defender of Protestantism against papist aggression.

1. *Letters of John Chamberlain*, II, p. 443.

2. Davies, "The Character of James VI and I", *Huntington Library
Quarterly*, V, p. 59.

3. Davies, "English Political Sermons", pp. 14–17; M. A. Judson,
The Crisis of the Constitution (Rutgers University Press, 1949), p. 175.

4. Quoted in *Crises in English History* (ed. B. D. Henning, A. S.
Foord and B. L. Mathias, New York, 1949), p. 237. Mr. Davies notes
that infinitely greater attention was paid to the pulpit in this Parliament
than in earlier ones ("English Political Sermons", p. 17).

5. T. May, *History of the Parliament*, I, p. 45. John Aston's Diary for
1639 shows that preaching against the Scottish war was not the way to
become popular – in Berwick at least (ed. J. C. Hodgson, *Six North
Country Diaries*, Surtees Soc., 1910, p. 21). Cf. Gardiner, *History of
England*, VIII, pp. 389–91; Davies, "English Political Sermons", p. 20.

at the end of 1640 large crowds flocked to hear the sermons preached by the chaplains of the Scottish Commissioners in London.[1] At the same time Pym was denouncing in the House "preaching for absolute monarchy, that the King may do what he list".[2] Ministers electioneered vigorously in 1640, as they had sometimes done earlier; and when civil war came, "Some of them cried to the rude, wicked people, in their idol-temples, 'Fight, lads, for the Gospel' ".[3] Clergymen acted as recruiting agents for both sides, and both King and Parliament expected their declarations to be read from the pulpit.[4]

IV

Enough has perhaps been said to illustrate the *political* importance of the pulpit and of the struggle to control it. When Bishop Aylmer spoke of the surplice as "the Queen's livery", apparently with nothing but pride in the fact that he was the Queen's servant, and when Joseph Hall defended the wearing of "the bishops' liveries" by ministers, men with a less feudal outlook did not need profound puritan convictions to be shocked.[5] This aspect of the controversy over ceremonies has perhaps been insufficiently emphasized. In 1565 English Protestants criticized Papists for justifying the honouring of the sacrament by the ceremonial respect shown to princes:[6] but forty-five years later Joseph Hall drew the identical parallel between kneeling to God and kneeling to the King.[7] Laud was merely a trifle tactless when he compared the ecclesiastical

1. Clarendon, *History of the Rebellion*, I, p. 251. Clarendon, with his unfailing class instinct, records that the citizens attended "out of humour and faction", whilst the motives of others were mixed.

2. Davies, "English Political Sermons", pp. 21–2.

3. E. Burroughs, *The Memorable Works of a Son of Thunder and Consolation* (1672), p. 191.

4. *Portland MSS.* (H.M.C.), I, pp. 212, 297, 704–5; Sanderson, *XXXV Sermons* (1681), p. 29; *Somers Tracts* (1748–51), VI, p. 48; ed. D. H. Pennington and I. A. Roots, *The Committee at Stafford, 1643–45* (1957), pp. xxxiii, 27, 95, 168. See pp. 75–7 below.

5. W. Pierce, *An Historical Introduction to the Marprelate Tracts* (1908), p. 78; J. Hall, *Works* (1837–9), X, pp. 89–90.

6. J. Jewel, *Works* (Parker Soc., 1845–50), II, pp. 557–8; J. Calfhill, *An Answer to John Martiall's Treatise of the Cross* (Parker Soc., 1846), p. 340.

7. J. Hall, *Works*, X, p. 69.

ceremonies which he imposed with those of the Order of the Garter. Miss Wedgwood quotes a similar defence made by a London minister in 1640: "A hat, a knee, a reverent posture of the body, are no such tyrannies as some please to fancy them. You would do more in a great man's presence, more for a small temporal encouragement. . . . You have more ceremonies in your companies and corporations, and you observe them strictly".[1] Such defences must have inclined many others to the view attributed to a Fifth Monarchy man, who "so hates a gentleman as he cannot endure that God should be served like one".[2] Part of the trouble was that by the seventeenth century some men were coming to question the desirability of exaggerated deference even to their fellow men.

A proud spirit like Milton refused to "subscribe slave" by donning the bishops' livery. He later ascribed the "low dejection and debasement of mind" of the English people first of all to "the prelates and their fellow-teachers, . . . whose pulpit-stuff . . . hath been the doctrine and perpetual infusion of servility and wretchedness to all their hearers".[3] For the Earl of Clarendon, on the other hand, no sin might more reasonably be thought the sin against the Holy Ghost than a minister turning rebel against his prince and preaching rebellion to the people as the doctrine of Christ.[4] Bishop Bramhall could not understand how a fellow bishop could even hold a discussion with a nonconformist who criticized the orders of the Church. It was more, he thought, than could be justified *to the state*. For such fellows whipping was more fit than reasoning.[5] Monck was perhaps being a little naïve, but there was sound military sense in his retrospective observation that, if you want to prevent civil wars, "the second thing is (if it be possible to be done without the endangering of a kingdom or state)

1. C. V. Wedgwood, *Seventeenth Century English Literature* (1950), p. 92.

2. R. F., *Fifty-Five Enigmatical Characters* (1665), quoted in J. M. Patrick's unpublished thesis, "A History of Utopianism in the 17th century".

3. J. Milton, *Prose Works* (Bohn ed.), I, p. 313; cf. p. 217. Milton made this point several times. Cf. the reference in his Commonplace Book to the clergy as "commonly the corrupters of kingly authority, turning it to tyranny by their wicked flatteries even in the pulpit" (*Complete Prose Works*, Yale ed., I, p. 439).

4. Clarendon, *History of the Rebellion*, II, p. 322.

5. W. J. Sparrow Simpson, *Archbishop Bramhall* (1927), p. 29.

that there be but one religion".[1] Life would have been much
simpler if it had been possible.

As opinions diverged, the bishops came increasingly to use
suppression to maintain their control. The savage sentences
imposed on Leighton, Prynne, Burton, Bastwick and Lilburne
sprang in part from a realization that they – like Marprelate
before them – had broken through to spread popular opinions
in opposition to those officially promulgated. Puritans like
Thomas Taylor concluded that if men studied their Bibles
more "there would be fewer spiritual monopolists or in-
grossers of these spiritual commodities, who having gathered
great store will not utter them but at excessive rates. Oh how
the church laboureth under this burden, never was any
monopoly so mischievous, never any called louder for
reformation".[2] Lay opinion was hostile to monopolies of any
description, and more secular spirits would soon carry the
argument further. Thus Lilburne wrote that "of all monopolies or patents . . . the monopolizing or ingrossing the
preaching of God's Word into the tithing and griping claws of
the clergy" was the worst.[3] When Parliament forbade lay
preaching by its ordinance of 1645, some men thought this
was to perpetuate "a monopoly of the spirit worse than the
monopoly of soap".[4]

The issues in Church and state were thus closely parallel.
The bishops had tried to maintain a perfect monopoly in the
production of opinion, driving their unlicensed competitors
out of business by the power of the state; whilst Milton and
others ultimately evolved a theoretical justification of free
trade in ideas (among Protestants).

V

There was thus rivalry for control of the pulpit, as men came
increasingly to want different doctrines preached. But attitudes

1. George, Duke of Albemarle, *Observations upon Military and
Political Affairs* (1671), p. 145; cf. *Economic Writings of Sir William
Petty* (ed. C. H. Hull, 1899), II, pp. 472–3.

2. T. Taylor, *Works* (1653), p. 238; cf. J. Hall, *Works* (1837–9), VII,
pp. 381–3.

3. J. Lilburne, *Englands Birth-right Justified* (1645), p. 42. Printed in
W. Haller, *Tracts on Liberty in the Puritan Revolution*, III, p. 300.

4. R. Barclay, *Inner Life of the Religious Societies of the Commonwealth* (1876), p. 159.

towards preaching as such also came to diverge. The approach of the Puritans was simple. They wanted more preaching, as much more as possible, so as to carry the Gospel into all corners of the land, even the darkest, and to raise the educational and disciplinary level of all members of all congregations. Since salvation came through the Word, it could not be preached too much. "There is not a sermon which is heard, but it sets us nearer heaven or hell", said Preston confidently.[1] Government and hierarchy saw things differently. They appreciated very clearly the explosive, anarchic possibilities of unlimited preaching: their emphasis was on control from above. Elizabeth disapproved on principle of too much preaching, and ridiculed the idea of putting a preaching minister into every pulpit. Three or four to a county was quite enough. Much safer, she thought, to have "honest, sober and wise men, and such as can read the Scriptures and Homilies well unto the people".[2]

Hence Elizabeth's resolute hostility to "prophesyings" — discussion classes among ministers which offered some chance of raising the level of information and eloquence among the less gifted clergy. The prophesyings were encouraged by many bishops, and by Archbishop Grindal himself. They appeared to be countenanced by 1 Corinthians xiv. 1–3. Bacon thought prophesyings "the best way to frame and train up preachers".[3] But they were held in public; laymen sometimes attended, nay, even participated. In consequence, Elizabeth informed her bishops in May 1577, "great numbers of our people, especially the vulgar sort, meet to be otherwise occupied with honest labour for their living, are brought to idleness and seduced: and in manner schismatically divided among themselves into variety of dangerous opinions".[4] "Especially the vulgar sort": there lay the danger. Despite the opposition of her Council and her archbishop, Elizabeth sent orders over Grindal's head to

1. J. Preston, *A Patterne of Wholesome Words*, in *Riches of Mercy to Men in Misery* (1658) p 288.

2. Sir J. E. Neale, *Elizabeth I and her Parliaments, 1584–1601*, p. 71. Professor Knappen speaks of Elizabeth's "implacable opposition to the programme of instructing the clergy and the laity . . . Ignorance was a small price to pay for docility" (M. M. Knappen, *Tudor Puritanism*, Chicago, 1939, pp. 251–7).

3. Bacon, *Works*, X, pp. 119–20.

4. Strype, *Life of Grindal* (1821), p. 574. For "prophesying" as discussion, see W. Dell, *Several Sermons and Discourses* (1709), pp. 273–5.

the bishops to suppress prophesyings. Dr. Collinson describes the prophesyings as "probably the most effective means that had been found for propagating the reformed religion in the rural areas of England". But he also sees them as "a first step in the partial delegation of the bishop's pastoral functions to permanent moderators of local synods", a step which was warmly supported by "the country gentry and Leicester".[1]

James VI came from Scotland with a prejudice in favour of preaching.[2] Bacon recommended to him that the Lancashire system of itinerant preachers should be extended to other areas: liberal stipends might be provided at the expense of non-preaching clergymen in rich benefices.[3] This line of approach would hardly have commended itself to the bishops, and they seem to have persuaded the King, early in his reign, to change his mind. At the Hampton Court Conference James agreed that, whilst preaching might be all very well in country villages, there could be too much of it in towns; more emphasis should be laid on the Homilies there.[4] James's attitude hardened as the reign progressed. "I had rather have a comfortable man with but ordinary parts", the King used to reply to those who pleaded for favour to able Puritan ministers, "than the rarest man in the world, that will not be obedient".[5] His son's reign shows how right these pronouncements were.

Yet because of the fundamental protestant emphasis on preaching, the authorities found themselves in difficulties. When they ejected Puritan preachers, and were complacent about a ministry largely composed of dumb dogs, it was natural for the average educated layman to sympathize with those who protested. It seemed ridiculous for many parishes to lack preachers whilst talented men were deprived of the opportunity to preach. Lay patrons, town corporations and

1. Collinson, *Letters of Wood*, pp. xvii, xxxvii. "There is no evidence" Dr. Collinson adds, "that the doctrinal attack by the Presbyterians on the principle of imparity in the ministry made the same appeal". The distinction is important for the later history of Puritanism. See pp. 30 above.

2. M. H. Curtis, "Hampton Court Conference and its Aftermath", *History*, No. 156, pp. 6, 9, 11.

3. Bacon, *Works*, X, p. 124, XI, p. 154; cf. my "Puritans and 'the Dark Corners of the Land' ", *T.R.H.S.*, 1963, pp. 90–1.

4. Cardwell, *A History of Conferences* (1840), p. 192.

5. G. Davies, "The Character of James VI and I", *Huntington Library Quarterly*, V, p. 59.

gentlemen with private chaplains did something to absorb the unemployed and to further preaching; but they did it in face of opposition from the hierarchy, supported increasingly in the seventeenth century by the Government. The way of thought which Protestantism had inculcated, and which had been thoroughly absorbed by at least the educated middle-class laity, put the hierarchy at a tactical disadvantage. It was only very late that Hooker, Andrewes and Laud evolved a theology which restored some of the traditional emphasis on the sacraments, elevated prayer as against preaching; and then it was easy for Puritans to say that this was a reversion to popery, and for ordinary lay Protestants to believe them. This is the background against which we should see the demand for a preaching minister in every parish.

The study and exposition of the Bible in English both contributed to the stability of Protestantism and ultimately tended to produce a more rational and critical attitude. Study *and* exposition: it was only the educated minority which fully profited by the translation of the Bible to study it carefully for themselves, though this minority was steadily growing. (Hobbes, looking back, could suppose that by the sixteen-forties many boys and wenches had "read the Scriptures once or twice over".)[1] But the mass of the population still perforce approached the Bible through the preachers. English Bibles had been installed in every church throughout the country, but that was not enough unless they were used to full advantage by an educated preaching clergy. Before 1575 no even relatively cheap Bibles were printed in England - and then it was the Puritan Geneva Bible which filled the gap.[2]

For the convinced Protestant and English patriot, preaching and the instruction of laymen were not merely desirable religious activities: they were vital political necessities. Knox told Cecil in 1559 that perpetual concord between England and Scotland might be effected by the preaching of Jesus Christ crucified.[3] Right down to 1640 men could not be sure that Protestantism had come to stay in England. All the weight of

1. T. Hobbes, *English Works* (ed. Sir W. Molesworth, 1839-45), VI, pp. 190-1.

2. W. M. Southgate, *John Jewel and the Problem of Doctrinal Authority* (Harvard University Press, 1962), pp. 157-8.

3. *C.S.P., Scotland, 1547-1563*, p. 218.

tradition, custom, inertia, laziness, communal village life, the influence of many powerful landlords, helped to prolong the old ways of thought and behaviour. From Elizabeth's reign onwards they were abetted by courageous and skilful Jesuit propaganda, with powerful lay backing. On a world scale two ideologies were in conflict, and it was by no means clear that Protestantism was not going to be driven under, as so many heresies had been before. In the sixteen-twenties and -thirties the outlook was perhaps even blacker than one or two generations earlier. So there was a sense of bitter urgency about the demand for a preaching clergy. Victory, as Miss White puts it, was still to be won in the parishes.[1] The Convocation of 1562 feared that the people would revert to paganism unless every living were raised to £20 in order to supply preachers.[2] Sixty-six years later Sir Benjamin Rudyerd declared that "in the uttermost skirts of the North", and "in divers parts of Wales", "God was little better known than amongst the Indians".[3]

The demand then was for organized effort in the ideological war being waged all over Europe. If the mass of Englishmen could not be roused to active defence of the new religion, then it and all that it stood for might go under. Faced with the threat from the European Counter-Reformation, with the ignorance and indifference of so many Englishmen, not only convinced Protestants but all patriots must have felt that not to be in favour of such education and propaganda was to be disloyal to the country. In 1626 Daniel Featley drew a harrowing picture of "atheists, papists, bankrupts and all kinds of malcontents" who had been lying in wait to make "havoc of all things" on 5 November 1605.[4]

Yet it was not as simple as that, and many outside Government circles knew it. Luther's preaching in Germany had been followed by the Peasant's Revolt of 1525, and by the Münster Anabaptists. The godly reformation under Edward VI had been followed by Ket's rebellion: the demands of the Norfolk

1. H. C. White, *Social Criticism in 16th century English Literature* (New York, 1944), pp. 102–3.
2. Strype, *Annals of the Reformation . . . during Queen Elizabeth's happy reign* (1824), I, part i, p. 513.
3. J. A. Manning, *Memoirs of Sir Benjamin Rudyerd* (1841), pp. 135–8. See pp. 58–60 below.
4. D. Featley, *Ancilla Pietatis: Or, The Hand Maid to Private Devotion* (5th ed., 1639), pp. 499–500.

rebels had included a resident and preaching clergy.[1] So suppress preaching, said the conservatives. No, said the men of the centre. Popular revolts, Lever asserted after 1549, were not due to the translation of the Bible into English "but because the rude people, lacking the counsel of learned men to teach them the true meaning when they read it or hear it, must needs follow their own imagination in taking of it". Since the imagination of most "rude people" was by definition corrupt, men like Crowley, Latimer and Lever were able to argue with some force that expenditure on a preaching clergy would be a sound social investment. Some "unworthy curates", it was admitted, "have been the stirrers up of the simple people in the late tumults"; but this would not have happened if their rectors had not been absentee pluralists. "The reformed clergy", Miss White sums up, "can be counted on to teach a social doctrine that will restrain even a suffering and indignant people from resorting to rebellion".[2] The preachers hoped to build up a central alliance with the Crown against Catholics on the one hand and social revolutionaries on the other.

This remained the hope of the main body of Puritans right down to 1640. Marprelate argued that it was to the interest of the bishops themselves to set at liberty those preachers who had been restrained from preaching. For "the people are altogether discontented for want of teachers. Some of them already run into corners and more are like, because you keep the means of knowledge from them. Running into corners will breed Anabaptists. Anabaptists will alienate the hearts of the subjects from their lawful governors. And you are the cause hereof".[3] The bishops were indeed on the horns of a dilemma: they refused to face the necessity of reform, and so in the long run they got the revolution with which Marprelate threatened them. But the short-run difficulties were all too clear. Would they and the government be able to control the consciences of educated, well-paid and therefore independent clergy? On balance dumb dogs seemed safer: they could not go far wrong if they stuck to the Prayer Book and the Homilies. Spenser's "formal priest" presents the type:

1. Ed. A. E. Bland, P. A. Brown and R. H. Tawney, *English Economic History: Select Documents* (1914), pp. 248–9.
2. White, *op. cit.*, pp. 130–1.
3. M. Marprelate, *The Epistle*, p. 47.

> *"All his care, was his service well to say,*
> *And to read Homilies upon holy days;*
> *When that was done, he might attend his plays:*
> *An easy life, and fit high God to please".*[1]

Of the "great and alarming scarcity" of preaching ministers[2] in the sixteenth century there can be no doubt at all. It is stated clearly in the *Homily against Peril of Idolatry*, which connects it directly with the danger of popery.[3] John Stockewood, preaching at Paul's Cross in 1579, feared that scarce one parish in twenty was provided with an able teacher. "No marvel therefore if there dwell in the people such horrible and wonderful ignorance".[4] "Scarce one in a hundred", Dering had said, more rashly, a few years earlier.[5] Such men were allowed for "pastors of men's souls", a puritan pamphlet alleged in 1584, "whom no careful owner of cattle would make overseer of his sheep's bodies".[6] The evidence for the ignorance of the clergy revealed by Hooper's Visitation of Gloucester in 1551–2 is familiar.[7] In Devon in 1561 only 1 in 12 of the beneficed clergy was licensed to preach, and most of these in their own benefices only: 58 out of 288 had degrees. In Cornwall there were not half a dozen preachers.[8] In Wiltshire in the same year only 20 out of 220 parochial clergy were able to preach, and not all of these were licensed.[9] In the diocese of

1. E. Spenser, *Mother Hubberds Tale* (c. 1579), in *Works* (Globe ed., 1924), p. 516. Cf. Jeremiah Dyke, *A Caveat for Archippus* (ed. B. Winstone, 1898), p. 69. First published 1619.

2. Jewel, *Works* (Parker Soc., 1845–50), IV, p. 1241.

3. *Sermons or Homilies appointed to be read in Churches* (1802), pp. 199–200.

4. J. Stockewood, *A Very Fruiteful Sermon preached at Paules Crosse* (1579), Sig. A 3.

5. E. Dering, *Works* (1614), Sig. A 2v–A 6v. One in three qualified men, said John Dillingham in 1645 (J. Frank, *The Beginnings of the English Newspaper, 1620–1660*, Harvard University Press, 1961, p. 326).

6. [Anon.], *A Briefe and plaine declaration concerning the desires of all those faithful Ministers that . . . seeke for the Discipline and reform of the Church of Englande* (1584), p. 44, quoted in Pierce, *Historical Introduction to the Marprelate Tracts*, p. 137.

7. F. D. Price, "Gloucester Diocese under Bishop Hooper, 1551–3", *Trans. Bristol and Gloucestershire Archaeological Soc.*, LX, passim.

8. A. L. Rowse, *Tudor Cornwall* (1941), p. 324.

9. *V.C.H. Wiltshire*, III, p. 33. In 1649, by striking contrast, 88 out of 91 Wiltshire churches had regular sermons, 49 of them twice a Sunday (*ibid.*, p. 42).

Worcester more than 3 out of 4 were non-preachers; in Gloucester in 1562 there were 54 preachers among 247 ministers.[1] One in five could preach in the diocese of Rochester; less than 1 in 8 in the archdeaconry of Leicester, one in twenty-two in the archdeaconry of Coventry.[2] In the archdeaconry of Canterbury itself, in 1569 there was one preacher for every thousand communicants.[3]

Things improved slightly towards the end of the reign: the number of preachers in the large diocese of Lincoln trebled between 1585 and 1603.[4] In the archdeaconry of St. Albans there were 11 non-preachers in 1586, only 7 in 1603.[5] In 1586 the Puritan *Supplication to Parliament* listed 472 preachers as against 1,773 non-preachers for ten counties or portions of counties.[6] Puritan standards of what constituted a preacher would no doubt be high; but the bishops' own figures do not differ widely. In 1592-3 they gave 106 preachers out of 484 ministers in Norfolk; 84 out of 253 in Gloucester; 172 out of 385 in Chester; 207 out of 579 in York; and 79 out of 117 in the favoured diocese of Ely.[7] In 1597 8 churches in Norfolk had no quarterly sermon, 88 no monthly sermon, 17 no homilies read either. In Suffolk 42 churches had no monthly or quarterly sermon, some not even homilies.[8] In the sixteen-thirties Bishop Wren confirmed that in the 34 churches of puritan Norwich itself there were only 4 Sunday morning sermons.[9] A relatively

1. I owe this to Miss D. M. Barratt's unpublished Oxford D.Phil thesis, "The condition of the Parochial Clergy from the Reformation to 1660, with special reference to the Dioceses of Oxford, Worcester and Gloucester" (1949).

2. W. H. Frere, *The English Church in the Reigns of Elizabeth and James I* (1904), p. 107.

3. Strype, *Life of . . . Matthew Parker* (1821), I, p. 564.

4. C. W. Foster, *The State of the Church in the Reigns of Elizabeth and James I* (Lincolnshire Record Soc., XXIII), p. lvii.

5. Wilton Hall, *Records of the Old Archdeaconry of St. Albans*, pp. 2, 4.

6. Ed. A. Peel, *The Seconde Parte of a Register* (1915), II, p. 88.

7. A. Tindal Hart, *The Country Clergy in Elizabethan and Stuart Times* (1958), p. 30.

8. Ed. J. F. Williams, *Bishop Redman's Visitation*, 1597 (Norfolk Record Soc., 1946), p. 17. There were 542 churches in Norfolk, 260 in Suffolk.

9. M. Wren, *Parentalia* (1750), p. 47. In the other churches sermons were "all put off to the afternoon" – i.e. presumably preached by lecturers provided by lay initiative rather than by regular incumbents. See p. 66 below.

virtuous clergyman like John Prideaux, Rector of Exeter College, Oxford, could preach in person only once a quarter at one of the four livings he held in plurality. He provided sermons by a curate "for the most part every third week", but none at all during harvest.[1]

It was this universally admitted lack of competent protestant preachers that made the invasion of England by learned, well-trained and wholly devoted Jesuits so dangerous to the precariously balanced Elizabethan settlement. The Jesuit martyrs formed a marked contrast to the average rude and uneducated English parish priest. But just as the Puritans in Parliament showed themselves most keenly aware of the foreign menace, so it was largely thanks to puritan efforts that the position with regard to preaching improved by the early seventeenth century.[2] "The zealous preachers of the gospel" were "the most diligent barkers against the popish wolf", and should not be silenced for Puritanism, Knollys insisted to Burghley in 1584.[3]

Fundamentally the problem was economic. Scandalous livings, said Sir Benjamin Rudyerd, created scandalous ministers. "To plant good ministers in good livings was the strongest and surest means to establish true religion"; and he quoted with approval James's establishment of churches in Scotland with £30 a year.[4] But how were good livings to be endowed? The main defence of pluralism was that it enabled at least some able men to be attracted to the ministry. Bacon mocked those who wanted to abolish pluralism and supply a preaching minister in every parish: it was "to desire things contrary".[5] His logic was not impeccable, for the shortage of preachers was due to the hierarchy's campaign to turn Puritans out of their livings. Yet many of those who wanted a preaching ministry also wanted to abolish bishops, deans and chapters, and to use their wealth to finance preaching. This would have been a minor social revolution: it was in fact carried out after 1641. But so long as the hierarchy retained its power, bishops supported dumb dogs and pluralists, both because they suspected that preaching ministers might be financed at their

1. Quoted in S. Marshall, *Oxford* (Diocesan Histories, 1882), p. 142.
2. See below, pp. 60–1, 115–17.
3. Quoted by M. M. Knappen, *Tudor Puritanism* (Chicago, 1939), p. 275.
4. Manning, *Memoirs of Sir Benjamin Rudyerd*, pp. 135–8.
5. Bacon, *Works*, X, p. 124.

expense and because they feared the probable theological sentiments of a vastly expanded preaching ministry. This gives its point to Milton's bitterness:

"While none think the people so void of knowledge as the prelates think them, none are so backward and malignant as they to bestow knowledge upon them; both by suppressing the frequency of sermons and the printed explanations of the English [i.e. Geneva] Bible. No marvel if the people turn beasts, when their teachers themselves, as Isaiah calls them, 'are dumb and greedy dogs'.... Had they but taught the land, or suffered it to be taught ... then the poor mechanic might have so accustomed his ear to good teaching as to have discerned between faithful teachers and false. But now, with a most inhuman cruelty, they who have put out the people's eyes reproach them of their blindness".[1]

These were the last words of those who – from Lever and Marprelate onwards – believed that Protestantism could be prevented from disintegrating into sectarian anarchy only by a preaching ministry and discipline.

VI

There were thus many reasons for the demand for preaching which the Puritans voiced. It was part of the protestant theological emphasis, which we can if we wish trace back to Wyclif, to elevate teaching, discussion, the rational element in religion generally, against the sacramental and ceremonial aspects. The Reformation was due to preaching, especially in cities and princes' palaces, Sir Edwin Sandys declared in 1599.[2] The object of worship was to edify. Hence the congregation must understand all that was done in the service.[3] Hence the

1. Milton, *Prose Works* (Bohn ed.), III, pp. 153–4. Cf. Macaulay: "The heads of the church and state reaped only that which they had sown. The government had prohibited free discussion: it had done its best to keep the people unacquainted with their duties and their rights. The retribution was just and natural. If our rulers suffered from popular ignorance, it was because they themselves had taken away the key of knowledge. If they were assailed with blind fury, it was because they had exacted an equally blind submission". This was written in 1825 (T. B. Macaulay, *Critical and Historical Essays*, 1854, I, pp. 38–9). Macaulay might have expressed himself differently after 1848.
2. [Sir E. Sandys], *Europae Speculum* (The Hague, 1629), pp. 77–8. First published 1599.
3. Cf. M. Bucer, *Scripta Anglicana* (1577), quoted by G. W. O.

vernacular rather than Latin, congregational rather than choir singing, communion rather than the mass;[1] hence preaching was more important than ceremonial. Churches became little more than auditoria for the pulpit.[2] Hence too the puritan insistence on a plain style in preaching, as against the florid extravagances of the university and Court divines. "So then preach as that we may rather make our people scholars than show ourselves scholars to our people", advised Jeremiah Dyke at a visitation sermon.[3]

Pious Protestants were horrified at that popular ignorance of the elementary facts of Christianity which centuries of popery had left behind. The ignorance of the priesthood was a pale reflection of the ignorance of the lower orders of the laity. Josias Nichols, puritan rector of Eastwell, Kent, worried because so little attention was paid to his preaching, found on investigation that in a parish of 400 communicants scarcely 40 had any knowledge "of Christ, what he was in his person: what in his office: how sin came into the world: what punishment for sin: what becomes of our bodies being rotten in the graves". Hardly one got the right answer to the question "whether it were possible for a man to live so uprightly that by well-doing he might win heaven".[4] This last was a question to which Calvinists expected one specific answer, and would not accept replies which would have satisfied other theologians;[5] stories of this sort should be discounted to the extent of reading "non-Calvinist" where the author says "non-Christian". But Whitgift had admitted the "dissoluteness" and "ignorance" of

Addleshaw and F. Etchells, *The Architectural Setting of Anglican Worship* (1948), pp. 245–6.

1. Cf. Jewel's opposition to private masses in the name of "a communion in very deed, common and indifferent to a great number" (*Apology of the Church of England*, Parker Soc., 1848, p. 92).

2. See pp. 478–9 below.

3. J. Dyke, *A Caveat to Archippus*, p. 76.

4. J. Nichols, *The Plea of the Innocent* (1602), pp. 212–13. Nichols attributed this ignorance to his predecessors' non-residence and the consequent lack of preaching in the parish. He was deprived himself in 1603. Cf. also Strype, *Life of Whitgift* (1822), II, p. 479. Nichols's account was inevitably used by separatists to demonstrate the necessity of leaving the corrupt national Church (Henry Ainsworth, *Counterpoyson*, 1608, pp. 183–5).

5. Cf. Perkins, *Workes*, I, pp. 537, 631; II, pp. 290, 300; III, pp. 493–500 583 595.

"the common sort" in 1591, though his remedy was catechizing.[1] Nichols's account, and others like it, is evidence that the attitudes which the Puritans wished to inculcate were conspicuously absent in early seventeenth-century England.[2] "The meaner or ordinary sort of people", wrote Thomas Hooker as late as 1632, "it is incredible and unconceivable, what ignorance is among them".[3] Herbert Palmer suggested some of the political anxieties when in the dangerous year 1646 he declared: "There are many places of this kingdom where men have been rebellious against God, even for many generations . . .; and of late they have proved rebellious against you" (the House of Commons). He was referring to "the remote parts of the kingdom, specially northward": the royalist areas. When preaching was established there, Palmer thought, "what a blessing and a happiness will that be to their people, and even to you. . . . Churches will be your strongest castles, if you furnish them well with ministers. . . . Send spiritual commanders among them, to subdue them to God".[4] Hugh Peter, more brutally, said "the common people will worship any dunghill-god if preaching be neglected". He was advocating the establishment of itinerant ministers.[5] Many laymen shared his fears and aspirations.

Bullinger had thought that the common people were like sheep, "that being carefully fed and discreetly ordered, they prove gentle and loving towards their shepherds; . . . but, being neglected and left to themselves, they degenerate into bloody wolves, watching every opportunity when they may rent in pieces their shepherds and all other sheep which are not degenerated into their wolfish nature".[6] For such men preaching was the necessary positive accompaniment of negative

1. Strype, *Life of Whitgift*, III, p. 288.

2. Cf. T. Taylor, *A Commentary on the Epistle of St. Paul to Titus* (1658), p. 438; T. Goodwin, *Works* (1861–3), I, pp. 557–8. See pp. 242–3 below.

3. T. Hooker, *The Souls Preparation for Christ* (1632), p. 70, quoted in P. Miller and T. H. Johnson, *The Puritans*, p. 12.

4. H. Palmer, *The Duty and Honour of Church-Restorers*, pp. 42–4 (a sermon preached to the House of Commons, 30 September 1646).

5. *Mr. Peters Last Report of the English Wars* (1646), pp. 12–13.

6. Ed. T. Harding, *The Decades of Henry Bullinger* (Parker Soc. 1849–52), I, p. 4. Thomas Goodwin thought it was the duty of preachers "to discover the wickedness and vanity of the heart by nature" (*Works* 1861–3, III, p. 510).

restraint by discipline.[1] At a time when lay educational standards were rising fast in the populous centres of the South and
East of the country, the ignorance of many rural areas and of
the "dark corners" of Wales and the North seemed an insult to
God, a menace to the salvation of many thousands of Englishmen, and a political danger in that survivals of popery and
superstition in these regions offered a basis for revolt or support
for foreign invasion.

I have tried to document elsewhere the especial shortage of
protestant preaching in Wales and the North. John Penry,
himself a Welshman, said in 1587 that for one Welsh parish
that had a quarterly sermon, 20 had none.[2] Wales and parts of
the North, Rudyerd told Parliament in 1628, are "scarce in
Christendom. . . . The prayers of the common people are more
like spells and charms than devotions".[3] The Welsh bishops
themselves confirmed the absence of learned or preaching
ministers.[4] In the diocese of Carlisle at the end of the sixteenth
century most of the clergy could not read English truly and
distinctly.[5] In the South-west the position was the same. In
1586 a "Supplication of the people of Cornwall" to Parliament
alleged that "the greatest part" of the country's 160 churches
were served by men guilty of "gross sins". Ninety thousand
souls "for want of the word are in extreme misery".[6] In Devon
there were the Gubbings, outlaws "exempt from bishop,
archdeacon and all authority either ecclesiastical or civil".
They lived like swine and "multiplied without marriage".[7] At
least four ministers in the diocese of Exeter who were described by Puritans as "mass-men" or papists held on to their
livings until well into the seventeenth century.[8]

1. See Chapter 6 below; cf. pp. 169–70, 461.
2. J. Penry, *Three Treatises on Wales* (ed. D. Williams, 1960), p. 36.
3. Manning, *Memoirs of Sir Benjamin Rudyerd*, pp. 135–6.
4. See my article "Puritans and 'the Dark Corners of the Land' "
T.R.H.S., 1963; cf. Strype, *Annals of the Reformation . . . during . . .
Queen Elizabeth's happy reign* (1824), III, part ii, pp. 471–5.
5. *V.C.H. Cumberland*, II, pp. 75–6; cf. *V.C.H. Durham*, II, p. 39;
V.C.H. Lancashire, II, p. 59.
6. Ed. A. Peel, *The Seconde Parte of a Register* (1915), II, pp. 174–6.
7. T. Fuller, *The History of the Worthies of England* (1840), I, p. 398.
8. I owe this information to the Oxford B.Litt. thesis of Miss Irene
Cassidy, "The Episcopate of William Cotton, Bishop of Exeter (1598–
1621), . . ." (1963). Cf. *Master Peters Message from Sir Thomas Fairfax*
(1645), p. 11.

Concern for the provision of preaching in dark corners was shown by the Commons, the Feoffees for Impropriations, and countless men up and down the country – from the merchants whose endowment of preaching Professor Jordan has catalogued down to George Campion who in 1615 left a close in Theydon Bois towards the maintenance of a preacher in Epping.[1] The will of Peter Blundell, clothier (1599), created scholarships at Balliol for the increase of "good and godly preachers of the gospel". At Halifax the inhabitants subscribed to maintain 10 preachers, "and by the special grace of God there is [c. 1612] not one popish recusant" in the parish.[2] Above all those who endowed preaching wanted to safeguard it against the hierarchy. Nathan Walworth, ex-steward to the Earl of Pembroke and merchant of London, built a chapel for his birthplace in 1635. He endowed the minister's stipend with lands, and left it in the care of a lay trust. Three years later, also in Lancashire, Dorothy Legh placed £400 in the hands of lay trustees on a private understanding that the money was to be used to pay a minister at the chapel of Ellenbrook, of whom "the bishop should have no hand in the putting in, placing or displacing".[3]

Preaching, Archbishop Grindal told Elizabeth, had kept London loyal in 1569 when the ignorant North revolted.[4] Yet there was still not enough preaching or education. Popish seminaries abroad sent forth more priests than our two universities at home do ministers, Sir Edwin Sandys declared at the end of Elizabeth's reign.[5] Output from Oxford and Cambridge increased in the seventeenth century, and the standard of clerical education certainly rose significantly between 1558 and

1. W. K. Jordan, *Philanthropy in England, 1480–1660* (1959), *The Charities of London* (1960), *The Forming of the Charitable Institutions of the West of England* (Trans. American Philosophical Soc., New Series L, 1960), *The Charities of Rural England* (1961), *The Social Institutions of Lancashire* (Chetham Soc., 3rd Series, XI, 1962), *Social Institutions in Kent* (Archaeologia Cantiana, LXXV, 1961), *passim. E.P.C.*, pp. 267–71; T. W. Davids, *Annals of Evangelical Nonconformity in . . . Essex* (1863), p. 388. Cf. pp. 91–5 below.

2. H. W. C. Davis, *History of Balliol College* (revised ed., 1963), p. 108; H. Heaton, *The Yorkshire Woollen and Worsted Industries* (1920) p. 183.

3. Jordan, *Lancashire*, pp. 20, 64–5; *V.C.H. Lancashire*, IV, p. 391.

4. E. Grindal, *Remains* (Parker Soc., 1843), p. 379.

5. Sandys, *Europae Speculum*, pp. 81–2.

1640. The number of graduates among London incumbents rose from 41% in 1560 to 72% 35 years later; the number of preachers rose from 27% to 88% between 1561 and 1601.[1] But in the archdeaconry of Nottingham in 1603 the graduates among the clergy were still less than half.[2]

Lay educational standards rose simultaneously, and so long as any dumb dogs remained they had to endure the contempt of serious-minded artisans and yeomen in their congregations. Those who took preaching to popular audiences most seriously were the puritan ministers, with their simpler style. As late as 1622 Archbishop Abbot was complaining of the "defections . . . to popery and anabaptism", for which he blamed the "lightness, affectedness and unprofitableness of that kind of preaching which hath been of late years too much taken up in court, university, city and country".[3] Despite occasional drives against them by Whitgift and Bancroft, Puritans in some remoter dioceses continued to enjoy a certain *de facto* tolera-tion right down to the Laudian decade, simply because they filled a need.[4] Conversely, their sense of the desperate need for preaching persuaded many ministers to conform in 1604, and no doubt on other occasions when their consciences were under strain.[5]

If we allow for his bias, the younger Matthew Wren helps to explain the reasons for the Puritans' success, in an essay "Of the Origin and Progress of the Revolutions in England". The Puritans, he says, "screwed themselves into all good and opulent towns and rich families (especially such as were governed by women), . . . erected schools in every corner, and procured a college or two to be founded in a manner solely for themselves. But above all things they laboured to gain the

1. H. G. Owen, "Lecturers and Lectureships in Tudor London", *Church Quarterly Review* (Jan.–March, 1961), p. 73; cf. H. R. Wilton Hall. *Records of the Old Archdeaconry of St. Albans* (St. Albans and Hertfordshire Architectural and Archaeological Soc., 1908), pp. 53–5, 96–8.
2. A. C. Wood, "An Archiepiscopal Visitation of 1603", *Trans. Thoroton Soc.* (1949), p. 3.
3. Quoted in P. A. Welsby, *George Abbot* (1962), p. 107.
4. R. A. Marchant, *The Puritans and the Church Courts in the Diocese of York, 1560–1642* (1960), pp. 87, 140–4. Miss Barratt arrived at the same conclusion in her unpublished Oxford D.Phil. thesis (see p. 53, note 1, above).
5. S. B. Babbage, *Puritanism and Richard Bancroft* (1962), pp. 224–5.

possession of the pulpits. . . . Hence the so many lectures, afternoon sermons, repetitions, buying in of impropriations, and other arts of the same stamp. . . . So that, within a while, preaching had almost justled out of the church all other parts of public divine worship; the people relishing nothing besides a sermon, as being withal the cheapest way of serving God".[1]

The sneers are ungenerous; but the passage throws light on the reasons for the support given to Puritans by so many M.P.s and town corporations. There can be no doubt about the astonishing popularity of preaching, so much so that authority began to attack "the superstitious opinion of sermons". It seems to have prevailed especially among merchants and business men, from the early days of the Reformation when Otwell Johnson ended a letter "in much haste, going to a good sermon".[2] Chamberlain noted it in 1621, as "an idle custom ... lately brought up" that when men from Cheshire, Staffordshire, Northamptonshire, Sussex and Suffolk (and other counties) met in London for an annual feast at some hall, "it must not be done without a sermon". Merchants of the Virginia Company had a sermon at their feast at Grocers' Hall; and there had been three or four other instances, Chamberlain observed, within ten days.[3] Sermons were preached – and printed – as propaganda for (for instance) the Virginia Company.[4] At a lower level, to have a good preacher was an economic asset to a market town, since it drew crowds in to listen to his market day lecture.[5]

VII

In Edward VI's reign Laurence Saunders, defending his "much preaching", admitted that "there be . . . of them that think it an high point of divinity to use seldom preaching, thinking to make it as a dainty dish; . . . but I take God's Word to be that necessary quotidian, ghostly food to feed the soul

1. Ed. J. Gutch, *Collectanea Curiosa* (1781), I, pp. 230–1. See p. 83 below.

2. B. Winchester, *Tudor Family Portrait* (1955), p. 43.

3. *Letters of John Chamberlain*, II, p. 408; *Relequiae Baxterianae*, I, pp. 95–6.

4. L. B. Wright, *Religion and Empire* (University of North Carolina Press, 1943), pp. 76, 87–117, 138.

5. See pp. 96–7 below.

withal".[1] The hierarchy and its spokesmen grew less and less enthusiastic about preaching: some Puritans attached so great importance to it that they thought only a preacher could be a true minister. Article xxii of the Scottish Confession of Faith (1560) declared that sacraments were not rightfully administered except by ministers "appointed to the preaching of the Word". Cartwright maintained this position against Whitgift, and so did the 1572 *Admonition to Parliament*.[2] Penry added that it was a sin to receive the sacrament from a dumb dog, and suggested that tithes should be withheld from a non-preaching minister.[3] Whitgift denounced this view as heretical, and defended reading ministers.[4]

The matter was of more than academic concern. In 1600 a burgess of Salisbury refused to come to church "without there be a sermon annexed to the praise there". At Box, Wiltshire, three years later, a weaver and a rough mason alleged that a non-preaching minister could not properly administer the sacraments.[5] That preaching was not necessary to the efficacy of the sacrament became official doctrine in Canon 57 of 1604; but these Canons were never confirmed by Parliament. In 1614 a minister in Nottinghamshire said that "a child baptized with an unpreaching minister is damned, and the minister too".[6] John Cotton in the same year declared it a flat error to think any man a lawful minister who did not preach.[7] The same

1. Winchester, *Tudor Family Portrait*, pp. 48–9.

2. Whitgift, *Works*, II, pp. 454–5; cf. III, pp. 30–42; T. Rogers, *The Faith, Doctrine and Religion professed and protected in the Realm of England* (1681), p. 209. First published 1607. Cf. also pp. 31–3 above.

3. Penry, *Three Treatises*, pp. 55, 69, 36. The last agreeable suggestion was often made by lay anti-clericals; cf. Sir David Lindsay, *Poetical Works* (1871), II, pp. 51–2, 241–4.

4. Strype, *Annals*, III, pp. 573–4; Whitgift, *Works*, III, p. 52. Cf. *ibid.* III, p. 1: "It may be that he that preacheth but once in the month taketh more pains, . . . edifieth more . . . than you [the authors of *The Admonition to Parliament*] do. . . . For what is it to preach every day and to spend the time with words only?"

5. *V.C.H. Wiltshire*, III, p. 37.

6. Marchant, *The Puritans and the Church Courts in the Diocese of York*, p. 174. The minister, James Collie, had been in trouble 13 years earlier for making treasonable remarks about the execution of the Earl of Essex (*ibid.*, p. 299).

7. Precentor Venables, "Primary Visitation of the Diocese of Lincoln", *Associated Architectural Societies' Reports and Papers*, XVI, 1881, p. 51. Cf. p. 169 below.

doctrine was advanced three years later by John Crosse, a grocer's apprentice of London who became a curate in Huddersfield. He believed that "all unpreaching ministers . . . are damned persons, and whosoever goeth to them cannot be saved".[1] In the sixteen thirties Gerrard Dobson, who had been presented to the vicarage of High Wycombe by the Feoffees for Impropriations, expressed similar if less violent sentiments.[2]

"A greater part of the people", said a preacher at Paul's Cross in 1598, hold it "the only exercise of the service of God to hear a sermon".[3] At the Hampton Court Conference, according to one account, King James himself taxed "the hypocrisy of our times, which placeth all religion in the ear, through which there is an easy passage".[4] "As the extolling of the sacrament bred the superstition of the mass", declared Bacon, "the extolling of liturgies and prayers bred the superstition of the monastic orders and oraisons, and so no doubt preaching likewise may be magnified and extolled superstitiously, as if all the whole body of God's worship should be turned into an ear".[5] "All our holiday holiness, yea and our working day too", complained Lancelot Andrewes, "both are come to this, to hear (nay, I dare not say that, I cannot prove it) but to be at a sermon".[6] There are "few true hearers; the rest are but a sort of sermon-hypocrites".[7] "I will not speak against preaching", Andrewes said, "nor against those that preach twice every Sunday; . . . but I would he [John Vicars, who had invited persons from other parishes to attend his sermons], would preach less and consider what he saith". Andrewes roused the ire of Puritans by excusing an alderman who slept in sermon-time. The Puritans, not illogically,

1. Marchant, *op. cit.*, p. 35.
2. W. H. Summers, "State Papers relating to Beaconsfield", *Records of Bucks.*, VII, pp. 107, 111.
3. John Howson, *A Second Sermon preached at Paules Crosse* (1598), quoted in Maclure, *Paul's Cross Sermons*, pp. 77, 220. Howson was later Bishop of Oxford and Durham.
4. Cardwell, *A History of Conferences*, p. 191. But James thought that ministers must preach in order to teach people how to pray (Curtis, "Hampton Court Conference", p. 9).
5. Bacon, *Works*, X, p. 115.
6. L. Andrewes, *XCVI Sermons* (1629), p. 992.
7. *Ibid.*, p. 232. Cf. C. H. and K. George, *The Protestant Mind*, pp. 335–41.

thought sleeping during the sermon evidence of reprobation.[1]

The near-papist Bishop Goodman thought it "a lamentable thing . . . to consider how all the exercises of religion are laid aside, as if preaching alone would suffice".[2] The Laudian Gilbert Ironside found that it was taken for "a maxim in religion, that unless there be preaching in a parish, the Lord's Day cannot be sanctified by the parishioners". In view of the shortage of preachers, this was likely to lead to conventicles. Worse still, "*many of our common people . . . think it an obliga-*tion to have an afternoon sermon too".[3] "The beauty of preaching (which is a beauty too) hath preached away the beauty of holiness", said Shelford.[4] "Such rotten stuff", Archbishop Ussher called Shelford's book, which "the Jesuits of England sent over . . . hither [to Ireland] to confirm our Papists in their obstinacy".[5] But from the Interregnum the Laudian view became a commonplace with anti-Puritans. "Hearing", said the author of *The Whole Duty of Man*, "is the most lazy of all religious offices", and "this insatiate appetite of it is originally founded either in the not having business or not attending to it". That, the author thought, was why sermons were especially popular with servants, mechanics and shopmen, and why towns and cities had been "the great nurseries of faction".[6]

The sectaries later freed themselves from this accusation of mere passive listening, by encouraging discussion after the sermon: though this would hardly have pleased the hierarchy. Some sectaries, like William Dell, distinguished sharply between mere "legal preaching" and "the ministration of the

1. Ed. S. R. Gardiner, *Reports of Cases in the courts of Star Chamber and High Commission* (Camden Soc., 1886), p. 234; J. Aubrey, *Brief Lives* (1898), I, p. 30.

2. G. Goodman, *Trinity and Incarnation* (1653), pp. 107–8.

3. G. Ironside, *Seven Questions of the Sabbath Briefly disputed after the Manner of the Schooles* (1637), pp. 265–6. My italics.

4. R. Shelford, *Five Pious and Learned Discourses* (1635), quoted in T. T. Carter, *Nicholas Ferrar* (1892), p. 111.

5. R. Parr, *The Life of . . . James Usher* (1686), II, p. 477.

6. [Anon.], *The Works of the . . . Author of the Whole Duty of Man* (1704), I, pp. 359–60; II, pp. 49–51 (*The Ladies Calling*). Cf. Jeremy Taylor, *Whole Works* (1836), III, p. 716; I. Walton, "Life of Sanderson", in *Lives* (World's Classics), p. 395; W. Nicholson, *A plain and full Exposition of the Catechism of the Church of England* (1655), Epistle Dedicatory; G. Davies, "Arminians versus Puritans in England, ca. 1620–40", *Huntington Library Bulletin*, V, p. 173.

spirit", the contributions to discussion made by any godly member of the congregation, clerical or lay.[1]

VIII

The Laudians thus came to see a great many objections to the enthusiasm for sermons which was so strong among the "middling men" in town and country. Gilbert Ironside was more explicit than most about the reasons for distrusting preaching. Adulation of sermons made every youth straight down from the university insist on becoming a preacher as soon as he was ordained. So, "partly through ignorance, partly through impudence, faction is fomented, the people humoured and misled".[2] Puritans welcomed the habit of taking notes at sermons which so impressed foreigners, and which led to the popularity of shorthand.[3] For the object was to be able to repeat and discuss the sermon afterwards in the household circle – an exercise recommended by Puritans but unwelcome to the hierarchy. "The good hearer will confer and talk of that which he hath heard, to help others – children, servants, and neighbours of less understanding".[4] Men left their own parish churches to seek out preaching, when their own minister was a dumb dog. No less personages than Dod and Cleaver, like John Penry, advised their readers to break the law in this way:

> "But if in place thou have abode where ignorance dark
>   doth reign,
> I wish thee further seek forth truth, or there do not
>   remain".[5]

A Northamptonshire mercer felt it obligatory for a Christian to go from his own church when it did not provide two sermons a Sunday, "preaching being the ordinary means ordained by

1. W. Dell, *Several Sermons and Discourses* (1709), pp. 148, 297–300. Dell gives rules for the conduct of such discussions.
2. Ironside, *Seven Questions of the Sabbath*, p. 266.
3. R. F. Young, *Comenius in England* (1932), p. 65; cf. R. Baillie, *Letters and Journals* (1775), I, p. 414 – all the people write at sermons.
4. John Mayne, *The English Catechism Explained* (3rd ed., 1623), p. 561. See Chapter 13 below.
5. Dod and Cleaver, *Ten Commandments* (1662), Sig. A 3v. For Penry, see p. 58 above.

God for salvation".[1] It was of course easier to escape detection in London, where one had a large choice of churches.[2] Alderman Atkins in 1637 gave as one reason for leaving Norwich (of which he had been elected mayor) and moving up to London (where he had been elected sheriff) his wish for more preaching, week-day lectures and afternoon sermons having been put down in Norwich.[3] In the 1621 Parliament complaints had been made that men and women in the diocese of Peterborough were cited to church courts for going to another parish when they had no sermon in their own. Lambe assured James I in reply that "the Puritans go by troops from their own church (though there be a sermon) to hear another whom their humour better affecteth". This exercise of consumers' choice – by John Hampden, among others – rendered men liable to heavy fines.[4] It was one of the "common grievances groaning for reformation" of which John Winthrop complained.[5] When the assembly of the Long Parliament enabled the victims of the courts to give their version, we learn from John James of Olney, who no doubt exaggerated, that he had "to sell his inheritance, and to spend above £100" including £4 for a beaver for this same Sir John Lambe, in consequence of a suit arising from his going to hear a sermon outside his parish church. None were preached there because the vicar had been suspended for not reading the Book of Sports.[6]

This passion among the laity for hearing sermons, and the conviction of the importance of the Word of God spoken

1. *C.S.P.D.*, *1634–5*, pp. 22–3. In addition he had repetitions of sermons and other religious exercises in his family on Sunday afternoons.

2. H. G. Owen, "The Episcopal Visitation: Its Limits and Limitations in Elizabethan London", *Journal of Ecclesiastical History*, XI, p. 181; contrast J. F. Williams, *Bishop Redman's Visitation, 1597* (Norfolk Record Soc., 1946), p. 24.

3. Ed. J. Bruce and S. R. Gardiner, *Documents relating to the Proceedings against William Prynne* (Camden Soc., 1877), p. 73; cf. *C.S.P.D.*, *1637*, p. 219. Wren had recently suppressed sermons in Norwich: see p. 104 below.

4. N.R.S., II, p. 368; VI, pp. 471–6, VII, p. 606. One man was alleged to have been fined 33s. for leaving his own parish where there was no sermon, in order to hear preaching elsewhere. For Hampden (in 1634) see *V.C.H. Bucks*, II, p. 288. Cf Marchant, *Church Courts in the Diocese of York, passim*. See also p. 304 below.

5. S. E. Morison, *Builders of the Bay Colony* (n.d., ?1930), p. 59.

6. *H.M.C., Fourth Report, Appendix*, p. 49; J. Brown, *John Bunyan* (1928), p. 11.

through a true believer, made it inevitable that lay Puritans should wish to preach. From Sir Francis Bigod in the fifteen-thirties[1] to the mechanic tub-thumpers of the Interregnum the pressure for lay preaching came both from without (the great shortage of gifted preachers) and from within (all believers are priests). "The preaching of the Word being a gift", said Penry, "and not depending upon the very ordination, is not so tied to the person of a minister but that he which hath not the outward calling may offer the trial of his gifts unto the church".[2] This of course was just what Government and hierarchy feared. They found ordained and licensed ministers difficult enough to control. Yet lay preaching could be justified by the logic of Protestantism itself, and it found a ready welcome outside official circles.

In 1660 Pepys thought Lord Sandwich "a perfect sceptic" because he said "all things would not be well while there was so much preaching, and that it would be better if nothing but homilies were to be read in churches".[3] Sandwich had had the benefit of the experience of the Interregnum; but many ruling persons had arrived at the same conclusion before him. The judicious Hooker explained that catechizing and reading were forms of preaching and James I commended exposition of the catechism as most profitable.[4] On the other side, Bullinger, Greenham and Penry argued that reading was not preaching;[5] and the Warwickshire Classis in 1588 declared that it was not lawful for the Homilies to be read in church – or so Bancroft would have us believe.[6] It was with grim satisfaction that Richard Baxter recorded that a reading minister in Suffolk had been exposed as a witch.[7]

1. A. G. Dickens, *Lollards and Protestants in the Diocese of York, 1509–58* (1959), pp. 59, 71–4, 77.

2. Penry, *Three Treatises*, p. 83; cf. p. 38.

3. S. Pepys, *Diary* (ed. H. B. Wheatley, 1946), I, p. 246. Cf. Monck's similar opinion, quoted on p. 45 above. The coincidence of view in the two chief makers of the restoration is interesting.

4. Hooker, *Of the Laws of Ecclesiastical Polity* (Everyman ed.) II, pp. 55–7; Cardwell, *Documentary Annals*, II, pp. 153–4.

5. Bullinger, *Decades*, I, pp. 70–80; Greenham, *Workes*, p. 72; Penry, *Three Treatises*, pp. 7, 53, 59, 69.

6. R. Bancroft, *Dangerous Positions* (1640), p. 86. First published 1593.

7. Quoted in I. G. Smith and P. Onslow, *Worcester* (Diocesan Histories, 1883), p. 224.

Puritans who referred to the necessity of *both* preaching *and* prayer usually made it clear that they thought preaching the more important of the two.[1] So authority came to emphasize the virtues of prayer as against preaching. In 1587 Sir Christopher Hatton in the House of Commons attacked a proposed Puritan prayer book for its emphasis on the sermon – "which is, indeed, the whole service" – and contrasted the set prayers of the Book of Common Prayer, which illiterate common people could learn by heart.[2] (John Field had professed to find "a deep silence throughout the whole book" of Common Prayer on the subject of preaching.)[3] A praying ministry is as needful as a preaching ministry, said Bancroft – formerly Hatton's chaplain – at the Hampton Court Conference.[4] Great play was made with the distinction by Attorney-General Noy in the Exchequer case against the Feoffees for Impropriations in 1632-3. He called for their suppression "to the end that ministers that pray as well as preach may have some part of the charity of well-disposed givers".[5] At Little Gidding the pulpit and the reading desk were of equal height to show that prayer was of equal value with preaching: George Herbert had intended to make the same symbolic arrangements at Leighton Bromswold.[6]

"There should be more praying and less preaching", the Duke of Newcastle summed up after the civil wars; "for much preaching breeds faction, but much praying causes devotion".[7] This doctrine had been popular with the denser type of old-fashioned cleric under Laud. "It was never a merry world since there was so much preaching", one of them was reported

1. e.g. Greenham, *Workes*, p. 776; G. Wither, *Brittans Remembrancer* (Spenser Soc. reprint, 1880), pp. 231, 496. First published 1628.

2. Neale, *Elizabeth I and her Parliaments, 1584-1601*, p. 159.

3. Quoted by P. Collinson, "John Field and Elizabethan Puritanism" in *Elizabethan Government and Society* (ed. S. T. Bindoff, J. Hurstfield and C. H. Williams, 1961), p. 151.

4. R. G. Usher, *The Reconstruction of the English Church* (New York, 1910), I, p. 325.

5. Ed. I. M. Calder, *Activities of the Puritan Faction of the Church of England, 1625-33* (1957), p. 61; cf. pp. 50, 102.

6. F. Higham, *Catholic and Reformed* (1962), p. 149.

7. Ed. C. H. Firth, *The Life of the Duke of Newcastle, by the Duchess* (London Library, n.d.), p. 124. The Duchess echoed her husband: see her *Philosophical and Physical Opinions* (1655), quoted by D. Grant, *Margaret the First* (1957), p. 198.

to have said; "for now all hospitality and good fellowship was laid abed". An absentee clergyman was alleged to have affirmed preaching to be properly no service of God, adding that "it was never a merry world since there was so much of it, and that if he could preach twice a day he would not, and that once hearing of common prayer is better than ten sermons". He was, naturally, an enthusiast for the Book of Sports.[1] A subtler and more sophisticated argument was put forward by Bishop White of Ely. He pointed out that prayer was not for the individual only, but for the King, lords, bishops, magistrates, the sick and all estates of people: and so was as important as preaching.[2] The same point was made by Hacket in his defence of deans and chapters in 1641; not only did cathedrals provide week-day lectures, but they also performed the public duty of praying for society as a whole. So service to the community was contrasted with the individualist emphasis on preaching.[3]

The authorities came similarly to elevate catechizing against preaching. In the early days of the Reformation catechizing had been an essential means of instilling the rudiments of Protestantism into the mass of the population.[4] It was "the easiest and best way to train up young ones and the ruder sort", said a member of the Dedham Classis in 1584.[5] Innumerable catechisms were published, and used, in our period. But learning answers by rote was, in a fully reformed country, an unsatisfactory manner of stimulating that intelligent comprehension of faith which Protestantism demanded. It was far inferior to preaching. Dering, who wrote *A Briefe and necessarie Catechism or Instruction, very needfull to be knowne of all Householders*, regarded it as a second best which would not be required if "every congregation had a sufficient pastor to

1. Davids, *Annals of . . . Nonconformity in . . . Essex*, pp. 240, 439. Cf. T. Taylor: "Whilst they are siding and contending against the Word, they lay all the blame upon the Word. 'We were quiet, we never had such contention in the parish before this preacher and preaching came in among us, and we were better before'" (*Works*, 1653, p. 200). Cf. F. Osborn, *Miscellaneous Works*, II, p. 215.

2. Francis White. *A Treatise of the Sabbath-day* (1635), Sig. A 3v; cf. *C.S.P.D., 1635*, p. xliii.

3. Fuller, *Church History* (1842), III, p. 420. Cf. p. 478 below.

4. Gouge, *Commentary on . . . Hebrews*, I, p. 374.

5. Ed. R. G. Usher, *The Presbyterian Movement in the Reign of Queen Elizabeth* (Camden Soc., 1905), p. 90. Cf. pp. 440–1 below.

instruct those that were ignorant".[1] But in 1622, as part of the campaign against lecturers and controversial preaching, James I ordered that exposition of the catechism should replace Sunday afternoon sermons; and in 1633 Charles I ordered even exposition to cease.[2] Many ministers continued to preach in spite of these orders.[3] In some churches a sermon followed the catechism;[4] in others the minister evaded the prohibition by expounding the catechism in what was in effect a sermon.[5] The Bishop of Bath and Wells, Prynne tells us, reproved this "catechizing sermon-wise", by saying it was "AS BAD AS PREACHING".[6] Where the order was obeyed, and there was no afternoon sermon, some parishioners refused to come to church.[7] Others, like Alderman Penington at Chalfont St. Peter, cajoled or coerced their minister into defying the order.[8] Others again followed Perkins' *Six Principles* when they catechized, and not the Common Prayer catechism.[9]

In November 1641 the House of Commons ordered sermons to be preached on Sunday afternoons in all parishes of England. "Ever since sermonizing hath justled out this necessary instruction enjoined on the Lord's Day", said William Nicholson of catechizing, "our people have been possessed with strange errors in religion, and hurried on by the spirit of giddiness, of faction, of rebellion".[10]

1. E. Dering, *Works* (1614), Sig. A 2v.
2. Cardwell, *Documentary Annals*, II, pp. 149, 178.
3. e.g. Marchant, *op. cit.*, pp. 75, 77.
4. Ed. F. R Goodman, *The Diary of John Young* (1928), p. 88.
5. Marchant, *op. cit.*, p. 83.
6. W. Prynne, *Canterburies Doome* (1646), p. 378.
7. Marchant, *op. cit.*, p. 109.
8. See p. 114 below.
9. *V.C.H. Bucks.*, I. p. 321. But catechizing was recommended by the Provincial Assembly of London in November 1648, chiefly for children and servants not yet admitted to communion (ed. C. E. Surman, *The Register-Book of the 4th Classis in the Province of London, 1646–59*, Harleian Soc. Pubs., Vols. 82–3, 1952–3, p. 67).
10. Nicholson, *A plain and full Exposition of the Catechism* (1655), Epistle Dedicatory. The complaint was echoed by many high-flying Anglicans during and after the Interregnum (H.R. McAdoo, *The Structure of Caroline Moral Theology*, 1949, pp. 168–71; J. W. F. Hill *Tudor and Stuart Lincoln*, 1956, p. 180).

IX

Ever since the bishops had taken fright at Lollard preaching, and the Lollards had attacked non-preaching bishops, the problem had existed. Bishop Rowland Lee, who had "the eye of an inspecting general for soldiers and military equipment", said in 1535 when asked to preach against the pope, "I was never heretofore in the pulpit", though he was a bishop of twelve months standing.[1] But the Reformation committed the bishops to a theology which made it difficult for them to ignore the importance of preaching. Penry described the Welsh bishops as "the butchers and stranglers of the souls of my dear countrymen".[2] And Whitgift – unfairly – accused Marprelate of saying that the archbishop mortally abhorred and prosecuted "the heresy of preaching".[3] But Bishop Cooper came very near to justifying these criticisms of the hierarchy when he wrote nostalgically in 1589: "When there were fewer preachers and less teaching by great odds than of late years hath been, the people did not revolt as now they do. . . . In the first ten years of her Majesty's most gracious reign, there was little or no backsliding from the Gospel, in comparison of that now is; yet was there not then so much preaching by half, nor so many preachers in the Church of England by a thousand, as now there are. And since that time . . . in divers places where there hath been often preaching, and that by learned and grave men, there have been many that have revolted, and little good affection declared among the residue".[4] At Hampton Court Bancroft, whilst admitting that preaching was necessary in a church newly planted, thought that a praying ministry was now equally necessary. He wished to prevent every humorous or discontented fellow using the pulpit to traduce his superiors.[5]

It became a stock and not entirely unfair jibe, to say with George Wither "As mute as some rich clergyman".[6] When the Earl of Leicester boasted to Thomas Wood of the number of

1. P. Williams, *The Council in the Marches of Wales under Elizabeth I* (1958), p. 16.
2. Penry, *Three Treatises*, p. 62; cf. pp. 27, 59.
3. Strype, *Life of Whitgift*, III, p. 219.
4. T. Cooper, *An Admonition to the People of England* (1895), p. 91.
5. Cardwell, *A History of Conferences* (1840), pp. 191–2.
6. Wither, *Juvenilia* (Spenser Soc. reprint), II, p. 49; cf. *Brittans Remembrancer*, p. 384, for Wither against dumb dogs.

preachers he had caused to be elevated to the episcopal bench, the Puritan replied sourly "As for the bishops whom your Lordship hath commended, I know not. But there was one Young, preferred in the beginning to be one of the chiefest, and of many thought to be your Lordship's doing, who was no divine but a simple civilian, and never preached at York but one sermon (as the report was) which he conned so ill by heart that he was forced to cut it off in the midst".[1] One of William Prynne's rare jokes was made in reply to Laud's taunt that he could not have written *Histriomastix* single-handed. "It may be their [the bishops'] laborious preaching once or twice a year permits them not to read or study half so much as meaner men".[2] Lord Brooke in 1641, after accusing some of the bishops of Arminianism and Socinianism, could rely on raising an easy laugh by saying that this was evidenced by their writings, "yea and sermons, though these be very rare".[3] It was a common jest in Dublin in the sixteen-thirties that the archbishop had only one sermon, on the text "Touch not mine Anointed" – "which once a year he commonly read" on the King's birthday. His congregation knew it by heart.[4]

The wily John Williams thought that the Puritans "had nothing but much preaching to make them plausible and popular". Fuller agreed that what won the Puritans most respect "was their ministers' painful preaching in populous places". Williams drew the conclusion that "the way to get credit from the nonconformists was to out-preach them".[5] But this was not the Laudian view. The archbishop discouraged afternoon sermons, and encouraged his bishops to harry lecturers. In his Metropolitan Visitation churchwardens were asked "Doth your minister, curate or lecturer in his or their sermons deliver such doctrine as tends to obedience and the edifying of their auditory in faith and religion, without

1. Collinson, *Letters of Thomas Wood*, pp. 13, 19. Thomas Young was Archbishop of York from 1561 to 1568.

2. Ed. Bruce and Gardiner, *Documents relating to the Proceedings against William Prynne*, p. 36.

3. Brooke, *A Discourse opening the Nature of that Episcopacie which is exercised in England*, (1642) in Haller, *Tracts on Liberty*, II, p. 135.

4. Ed. E. S. Shuckburgh, *Two Biographies of William Bedell* (1902), p. 146.

5. Fuller, *Church History*, III, p. 102; Hacket, *Scrinia Reserata* (1693), I, p. 34.

intermeddling with matters of state, not fit to be handled in the pulpit, but to be discussed by the King and his Council?"[1] (It was unfit, however, only for the humbler clergy. Laud thought that a bishop "may preach the Gospel more publicly, and to far greater edification, in a court of judicature or at a council table, where great men are met together to draw things to an issue, than many preachers in their several charges can do".)[2]

When Bishop Wren was impeached in 1641, he was accused not only of discouraging sermons, but even of preventing the ringing of a different peal on church bells when there was no sermon. "That he ever preached himself in his diocese saving once, I never heard affirmed by any", declared one of the managers of the impeachment.[3] Bishop Pierce of Bath and Wells became notorious for putting down sermons when they interfered with Church ales. He was alleged to have said that preaching might have been all very well in apostolic times, but was unnecessary now.[4] Only 13 licences to preach were granted during the 8 years of Neile's tenure of the archbishopric of York. "At that rate of issue enough preachers would never have been found to preach the monthly sermons in each parish required by the Canons", let alone provide a preaching minister in every church.[5] Men saw it as all part of a considered policy when in 1636 a book of prayers was reprinted, omitting a collect which "magnifies continual often preaching of God's Word". This seemed to Robert Reyce a sign that the bishops have "conspired together to extirpate our frequent powerful preachers and continual preaching of God's Word".[6] "What edification", asked a pamphlet of 1641, "have we by our bishops, unless edification of altars, images and popery? But for edification of souls by the Word, who are greater enemies thereunto than bishops? Preaching twice a day is sufficient to put a comformable minister into their black bill. . . . There are

1. Laud, *Works*, V, p. 427.

2. *Ibid.*, VI, p. 191.

3. J. Nalson, *An Impartial Collection of the Great Affairs of State* (1683), II, p. 397; N. Wallington, *Historical Notices of events occurring chiefly in the Reign of Charles I* (1869), I, pp. 153–5.

4. Nalson, *op. cit.*, II, p. 413; Prynne, *Canterburies Doome*, pp. 377–8. See pp. 182, 189 below for Pierce.

5. Marchant, *op. cit.*, p. 87; cf. pp. 129, 186.

6. *Massachusetts Historical Soc. Collections*, 4th series, VI, pp. 426–7.

divers thousands of congregations without a preaching ministry".[1] It was a hostile and unfair statement; but it expressed a conviction on which many men, and many M.P.s, were prepared to act.[2] Herbert Palmer in 1643 urged the Commons to "make a law for preaching".[3]

X

Preaching was thus a sword to divide. When in January 1619 the Common Council of Gloucester voted that preaching was "the only ordinary means of salvation", it was inaugurating a great conflict with the hierarchy over the lecturer it had appointed.[4] Even a relatively inoffensive book of characters published in 1631 described "a double-beneficed parson" who "hath two pulpits and one sermon". The author did not fail to note that "he's very fearful of another Parliament, lest one of his livings should fall short of his reckoning".[5] Richard Sibbes spoke in similar vein in the same year of clergymen who "raise temporal advantage to themselves out of the spiritual misery of others, such as raise estates by betraying the church, and are unfaithful in the trust committed unto them; when the children shall cry for the bread of life and there is none to give them, bringing thus upon the people of God that heavy judgment of a spiritual famine".[6] A man like Sir Simonds D'Ewes saw preaching as the crucial issue of his time. "I could be willing to redeem the reunion of his Majesty and the two Houses with my dearest blood, that so religion might be established in that power and purity amongst us, and preaching so settled in those places where atheism, profaneness and ignorance now reigns,

1. [Anon.], *The Petition for the Prelates Examined* (1641), p. 19.
2. See pp. 115–18 below. Cf. G. Davies, "English Political Sermons", p. 21: "Within a month of the meeting of the Long Parliament members were denouncing royal advisers, ecclesiastical and lay, because they 'have a mind to quell preaching and to draw the religion to old ceremonies' ".
3. H. Palmer, *The Necessity and Encouragement of Utmost Venturing for the Churches Help*, pp. 52–3 (a sermon preached before the House of Commons, 28 June 1643).
4. J. N. Langston, "John Workman, Puritan Lecturer in Gloucester", *Trans. Bristol and Gloucestershire Archaeological Soc.*, LXVI (1945), p. 220. See pp. 31–3 above for preaching as the only ordinary means of salvation, and pp. 89, 102–3 below for Workman.
5. F. Lenton, *Characterismi* (1631), No. 15.
6. R. Sibbes, *The Bruised Reed and Smoking Flax* (1838), p. 89. First printed 1631.

as that all men might know their duty to God and the King".[1]

A City corporation, a Puritan minister, and the Long Parliament's leading antiquarian, were perhaps committed; but the inhabitants of the remote Oxfordshire village of Toot Baldon agreed with them. In 1638 they represented to their bishop that "some of the parishioners, for want of an able minister, have of late fallen into popery: and some others being dangerously sick have wanted spiritual instruction". All this because the minister was a pluralist, holding his other benefice $1\frac{1}{2}$ miles away, well within the permitted 30 miles.[2] Arise Evans too was a church-and-king man; but he went rather further than Sibbes when he looked back in 1653. "In the late King's days all the ministers sought after great church livings, to the end that they might follow the gentry rather than the ministry, so that they forgot to preach. . . . Thus the people were starved for want of knowledge, and adversaries, finding this opportunity, steal in . . . and carry the people away with them. The bishops and protestant [i.e. non-Puritan] ministers thought to do all with the club, and that preaching was but a vain thing to establish them. . . . Many of our ministers", he concluded, "make but a jest of Master Hugh Peter's preaching; but I tell ye, ye may all go learn to preach of him".[3] A few years previously this same Hugh Peter looked back too to the times when bishops "thought to do all with the club": "those ill times, when a base messenger from a proud prelate could shut up the doors, stop the mouths of the most godly ministers, that the best noble-man here" – Peter was preaching before the House of Lords – "could not enjoy the worship of God freely".[4] Allowing for the difference of idiom, Evans paints the same picture as Sibbes and Peter.

XI

Royalists were agreed on the importance of preaching in stimulating support for Parliament. "This strange wildfire among the people", said Clarendon, "was not so much and so

1. Ed. J. O. Halliwell, *The Autobiography and Correspondence of Sir Simonds D'Ewes* (1845), II, p. 292.

2. Quoted in D. McClatchey, *Oxfordshire Clergy, 1777–1869* (1960), p. 30.

3. Arise Evans, *An Eccho to the Voice from Heaven* (1653), pp. 100–1.

4. H. Peter, *Gods Doings and Mans Duty* (1646), p. 15. Cf. pp. 341–2 below.

furiously kindled by the breath of the Parliament as of the clergy, who both administered fuel and blowed the coals in the Houses too". They "infused seditious inclinations into the hearts of men against the present government of the church, with many libellous invectives against the state too". They "inveighed in the presence of the King . . . to incense and stir up the people".[1] Colonel Axtell, we are assured, was literally preached into taking up arms for Parliament, since he and others like him "verily believed they should have been accursed of God for ever if they had not acted their part".[2] London ministers used the pulpit to recommend contributions to the Parliamentary cause; the Presbyterian Christopher Love claimed that "the clergy had done as much service . . . in their pulpits as your regiments in the field".[3] Stephen Marshall urged his congregation to invest in "the insurance office of Heaven" – i.e. the Parliamentary cause – and get all back a hundredfold even in this life.[4] The influence of Marshall (and Cornelius Burges) on Parliament in 1641, Clarendon tells us, was greater than that of Laud had ever been on the Court.[5] In 1643, at the order of the Common Council, pulpits rang with the call to defend the City. Ministers were ordered to "stir up the prentices" to complete the fortifications, with the aid of children and servants.[6] In August of the same year the Commons demonstrated the function of preachers as propa-

1. Clarendon, *History of the Rebellion*, II, pp. 319–21.
2. R. South, *Sermons*, I, p. 513, quoted in the Bohn edition of Milton's *Prose Works*, II, p. 3n. I have not been able to identify the edition. South added: "it was the pulpit that supplied the field with swordsmen, and the Parliament house with incendiaries". As a former panegyrist of Oliver Cromwell, South was well qualified to assess the influence of the clergy on Parliament's side.
3. Pearl, *London and the Outbreak of the Puritan Revolution*, pp. 230–2; W. Dell, *Right Reformation*, a sermon preached in 1646, printed in *Several Sermons and Discourses* (1709), p. 120.
4. S. Marshall, *Meroz Cursed*, quoted by E. Vaughan, *Stephen Marshall* (1907), p. 49.
5. Clarendon, *History of the Rebellion*, I, p. 401.
6. Pearl, *London and the Outbreak of the Puritan Revolution*, p. 264. Of course the pulpit was not used on one side only. The chief inhabitants of one Suffolk hundred declared in December 1643 that they had "observed by several long experience what prevailing influences their ["the ill-affected clergy's"] bold advices and conversations" had upon "unstable and weak people" (A. Everitt, *Suffolk and the Great Rebellion*, Suffolk Records Soc., 1960, p. 46; cf. pp. 62–3).

gandists by issuing an order "for sending divers godly ministers into divers counties . . . to possess the people with the truth and justice of the Parliament's cause in taking up of defensive arms".[1]

So it was only natural that when in April 1642 the House of Commons issued its Declaration on Church Reform, the one positive proposal should be the establishment of "learned and preaching ministers, with a good and sufficient maintenance, throughout the whole kingdom, wherein many dark corners are miserable destitute of the means of salvation".[2] One of the demands put forward by Parliament in the Isle of Wight Treaty of November 1648 was an act for the advancement of preaching.[3] Three generations of puritan endeavour lay behind it, and it would have the sympathy of many laymen who were in no doctrinal sense Puritans.

1. *C.J.*, III, p. 202; cf. Clarendon, *History of the Rebellion*, I, p. 387, II, pp. 319–22; Osborn, *Miscellaneous Works*, I, p. 193. Cf. also Lt.-Col. Jackson, who in 1647 was alleged to be so overawed by Thomas Edwards, his "ghostly father", that he dared not comply with the Army against Parliament (ed. C. H. Firth, *Clarke Papers*, Camden Soc., 1891, I, p. 113).

2. Gardiner, *Constitutional Documents of the Puritan Revolution*, pp. 247–8.

3. F. Peck, *Desiderata Curiosa* (1779), p. 407.

It is interesting that a modern work on "the thought and practice of the Church of England, illustrated from the religious literature of the 17th century", contains nothing about preaching in 783 pages (ed. P. E. More and F. L. Cross, *Anglicanism*, 1935).

Chapter Three

The Ratsbane of Lecturing

Stipendiaries or lecturers, that signify little less than an anti-clergy.

Francis Osborn, *Advice to a Son* (1656), in
Miscellaneous Works (11th ed., 1722), I, p. 106.

The breach of that unity and uniformity in the church hath principally been caused . . . by lecturers . . . I dare promise myself nothing when the preacher shall be forced to suit his business to the fancy of his auditors, and to say nothing but what pleases them, at leastwise nothing that may displease them; and this needs he must do if his means have not some competency in it, and if a competency then so much the worse if no certainty, but wholly depending on the will and pleasure of his hearers.

Matthew Wren, Bishop of Norwich, Tanner MS. 68,
f. 92, quoted in Gardiner, *History of England*, VIII, p. 225.

I

WHEN John Penry was in prison in 1593, awaiting trial and execution as a seditious sectary, questions which troubled him were whether papists preached in the time of popery; and "whether there be any lecturers in popery?"[1] Preaching had come to be thought of as a specifically *protestant* activity; and lecturers were the most advanced and independent of the protestant preachers. They had been imitated from the French Huguenots, Heylyn thought.[2] It was only in the seventeenth

1. Ed. A. Peel, *The Notebook of John Penry, 1593* (Camden Soc., 1944), p. 21.
2. P. Heylyn, *Historical and Miscellaneous Tracts* (1681), I, p. 171.

century that men began to draw parallels between lecturers and preaching friars, not least in their destructive effects upon the Church to which they ostensibly belonged.[1]

Heylyn was wrong, of course. Lecturers existed in England before French influence was likely to have been felt, and arose naturally from what were felt as English needs. The appetite for sermons, at least in towns, seems to have been insatiable. It was stimulated by, as well as stimulating, the protestant emphasis on "the priesthood of all believers", on the importance of each individual striving to understand the Bible for himself. Preaching should have aided the flock in this all-important task. But whilst the sheep looked up to the parochial clergy with considerable interest, they were inadequately fed. Lecturers were appointed to give what they wanted to congregations whose educational standards and demands were rising.

Lecturers were free-lance clergy. "A new body", James I called them in 1622, "severed from the ancient clergy, as being neither parsons, vicars nor curates".[2] They were usually men who had been ordained, who were qualified to preach (though they might not be licensed), but who had been appointed to no benefice. They were thus far less subject to episcopal control than parochial ministers.[3] In 1582 Robert Browne denounced lecturers as hirelings no less than parish priests. But that was because they had the bishop's licence to preach and observed some at least of the Church's ceremonies.[4] As the conflicts of the century developed, an increasing number of lecturers were unlicensed and managed to evade compliance with many of the ceremonies. This lack of control by the hierarchy was part of the attraction of lectureships for men of independent views. Thus Henry Smith, "the silver-tongued preacher", refused to take a parish because he had conscientious scruples about the subscription required. Instead he became lecturer at St. Clement Dane's in 1587, "at the desire of many of the parish-

1. J. Selden, *Table Talk* (1847), p. 75; J. Cleveland, *Works* (1687), p. 483; T. Hobbes, *Behemoth* (1679), in *English Works* (1839–45), VI, p. 193; J. Nalson, *An Impartial Collection* (1683), II, p. 478.

2. J. Rushworth, *Historical Collections*, I, pp. 64–5.

3. H. G. Owen, "Lecturers and Lectureships in Tudor London" *Church Quarterly Review*, Jan.–March, 1961, p. 66.

4. Ed. A. Peel and L. H. Carlson, *The Writings of Robert Harrison and Robert Browne* (1953), p. 209.

ioners, and by the favour of the Lord Treasurer [Burghley], who dwelt in the same parish and yielded contribution to him".[1] John Boyes became lecturer at Halifax after he had been "banished out of Kent for his nonconformity".[2] As lecturer at Bridgnorth in the sixteen-thirties Richard Baxter enjoyed a welcome immunity from episcopal jurisdiction. If a lecturer had scruples about using the Prayer Book, he could get a curate to read the service for him, and concentrate solely on preaching.[3]

There were various types of lecturers. A lectureship might be a means of augmenting the stipend of an underpaid minister of whom his congregation approved. Thus at Castle Hedingham in 1632 the minister was given £20 a year by the parish on condition that he preached three lectures each week. Such additions to income were immune from taxation.[4] The withdrawal of such an increment might be financially disastrous. In 1636 Farrar of Burstall had been inhibited from preaching; but the bishop was prepared to consider leniency "because his whole means will be withdrawn if they have not some sermons".[5] By such payments congregations gained effective economic control. A lecturer might be "superinducted . . . in another man's cure and pastoral charge". Such individuals, Bishop Montagu admitted, were "the first, most hugged, followed, admired and maintained". Or there might be a "combination" by a group of ministers, who would agree to take turns in preaching at a neighbouring town on market days. Montagu was worried about the conformity of ministers in such combinations in his diocese of Norwich in 1638.[6] A fourth type was the "running lecturer", an itinerant preacher going from village to village. In 1638 the Bishop of Coventry and Lichfield suppressed a running lecturer who had been

1. Ed. J. Brown, *The Sermons of Henry Smith* (1908), p. vii; W. Haller, *The Rise of Puritanism* (Columbia University Press, 1938), p. 29.
2. Ed. J. H. Turner, *Autobiography, Diaries . . . and Event Books of Oliver Heywood* (1882–5), IV, p. 16.
3. S. B. Babbage, *Puritanism and Richard Bancroft* (1962), pp. 229–30.
4. Davids, *Nonconformity in Essex*, p. 171. For examples in London see Owen, *op. cit.*, pp. 71, 73. See also *E.P.C.*, pp. 194, 219, 290, 294–5.
5. Tanner MS. 68, f. 182. I owe this reference to Mr. D. W. Boorman's unpublished Oxford B.Litt. thesis, "The Dioceses of Norwich and Ely under Wren . . ." (1959).
6. R. Montagu, *Articles of Enquiry and Direction for the Diocese of Norwich* (1638), Tit. 4.

"ordained to illuminate the dark corners of that diocese".[1]

Lectureships might be endowed in many ways – by an individual, by a group of merchants, by contributions from some or all the members of a congregation (as in the case of Henry Smith, or of the lecturer of St. Margaret's, Lothbury, to whom 34 parishioners made a "free offer" in 1584 of sums ranging from 2*d*. to 6*s*. 8*d*. a year),[2] or by town corporations.

II

A favourite accusation made by the defenders of the hierarchy was that through lecturers the puritan opposition was threatening the established order in the Church. Sir John Harington thought that "the true theorique and practique of Puritanism" was to impugn the bishops secretly by lecturers and at the same time to impoverish their livings by long leases. There was a very real sense in which through lectureships a rival and independent organization was being built up.[3] The maintenance of ministers, especially in the towns, was inadequate; the hierarchy and Government failed to take action to remedy this, and consequently the thirst for preaching remained unsatisfied. In towns the establishment of lecturers was also a part of the struggle for patronage. When the rich few who "rule the roost" could not get their nominee appointed to a rectory or vicarage, "ten to one but they will strain themselves to bring him in as a lecturer, which is a thing they reverence beyond the parson of the parish by many degrees".[4]

At Banbury William Whately, son of a former mayor of the town, was appointed lecturer in 1604, and succeeded to the vicarage six years later.[5] On the other hand, when in the

1. Laud, *Works*, V, p. 320.
2. S. L. Ware, *The Elizabethan Parish in its Ecclesiastical and Financial Aspects* (Baltimore, 1908), p. 89; cf. J. Stoughton, *History of Religion in England* (1881), I, p. 46 (St. Michael Royal).
3. Sir John Harington, *A Briefe View of the State of the Church of England* (1653), pp. 149–50; cf. *E.P.C.*, Chapter 2, and the passage from Osborn quoted as epigraph to this chapter.
4. T. Powell, *The Art of Thriving* (1635), in *Somers Tracts* (1809–15), VII, p. 196. See pp. 101–6 below for examples. On conflicts between lecturers and beneficed ministers, see *A Seasonable Discourse Written by Mr. John Dury* (1649), p. 5.
5. Jordan, *Philanthropy in England*, p. 184. Cf. Robert Todd, lecturer at Leeds parish church in 1630, made incumbent of St. John's church in

sixteen-twenties Francis Higginson had been ejected from his
living at Leicester for nonconformity, he was maintained by
popular support as a lecturer for ten years until driven into
emigration.[1] A "combination lecturer", a "running lecturer"
or a lecturer who drew people from other parishes to listen to
him – each of these to a greater or less extent helped to
disrupt the old community of the parish and to create new
voluntary communities in which men were uniting to pay for
services which they wanted and which the traditional parochial
system failed to supply.[2]

It was natural that subscribers should want their money to
be spent on preachers of a type of whom they would approve.
They were unenthusiastic about paying more to existing incumbents of livings, except in the rare cases where these were
able and willing to preach, and to preach an acceptable
theology. Since nearly all those who both desired and had the
means to establish lectureships were the richer classes in the
towns, lecturers tended to reflect their general outlook, to be
puritan and parliamentarian. Henry Smith, for instance, was
elected by his congregation, and a petition to Burghley asking
for his support was signed by "the two churchwardens, one a
grocer, the other a locksmith, and a good number besides of
ordinary tradesmen, as smiths, tailors, saddlers, hosiers,
haberdashers, glaziers, cutters and such-like", most of whom
could not write their names.[3]

The lectureship at Trinity Church, Cambridge, which
Richard Sibbes the Feoffee held from 1610 onwards, was
maintained by subscriptions, some of the subscribers signing
by making a mark.[4] It was so popular that it became the

1634 (B. Dale, *Yorkshire Puritanism and Early Nonconformity*, n.d.,
?1910, p. 155).

1. Cotton Mather, *Ecclesiastical History of New England* (1702), III,
p. 71, quoted by J. Simon, "The Two John Angels", *Trans. Leicestershire
Archaeological and Historical Soc.*, XXXI, pp. 37, 47.

2. See Chapter 14 below.

3. Strype, *Life of Aylmer* (1821), pp. 101–2. Cf. E. Grindal, *Remains*
(Parker Soc., 1843), pp. 288–9 – petition of women on behalf of a suspended lecturer in 1566 (St. Giles's parish without Cripplegate).

4. T. Ball, *Life of the renowned Dr. Preston* (1885), pp. 98–101
(probably written in the late sixteen-thirties); Haller, *Rise of Puritanism*,
pp. 56, 66, 73. Stock was another of the Feoffees who as a lecturer had
been in trouble – in his case in 1603 for attacking the over-assessment
of the poor to taxation by the Lord Mayor and aldermen of London.

public town lecture of Cambridge, and the mayor, aldermen and burgesses obtained a say in the choice of the lecturer. In 1615 Sibbes's tenure of it was terminated by a royal prohibition of the "new erected lectures that might draw scholars away from catechizing".[1] The lectureship was subsequently held by John Preston, at a stipend raised from £50 to £80 a year. Preston is said to have refused an offer of the bishopric of Gloucester in order to retain this lectureship: so influential was it. Preston also opposed the King's express instructions that the university should have the final say in appointing lecturers to Cambridge churches.[2]

Since lectureships were not normally given to incumbents, we can understand the accusation that subscribers tended to appoint "factious" and "popular" lecturers; that lecturers, so appointed, were dependent on the good will of their congregations, and so had to preach doctrines which would please them; and (often in the same breath) that lecturers preached sedition. Lecturers, said Laud in 1629, "by reason of their pay are the people's creatures".[3]

Lecturers have been described as an intellectual proletariat, the result of over-production of graduates in the early seventeenth century.[4] The universities, which had lagged behind demand in the sixteenth century, were in the early seventeenth century turning out a vastly increased supply of graduates. Emmanuel and Sidney Sussex colleges were founded in 1584 and 1596 respectively for the express purpose of supplying preachers.[5] The number of undergraduates admitted to Oxford and Cambridge reached a peak in the fifteen-eighties, and between 1620 and 1640 was *absolutely* greater than ever again until the eighteen-sixties, when of course the national population had increased many times over.[6] Mulcaster and Bacon were worried by graduate unemployment, and the question was raised in the House of Commons in 1606 by Nicholas

---

1. *V.C.H. Cambridge*, III, p. 16.
2. Ball, *The Life of the renowned Dr. Preston*, pp. 41–4. After Preston the lectureship was held by Thomas Goodwin (1628–33).
3. Rushworth, *Historical Collections*, II, p. 7.
4. M. H. Curtis, 'The Alienated Intellectuals of Early Stuart England' *P. and P.*, No. 23, *passim*.
5. Haller, *Rise of Puritanism*, p. 20.
6. J. A. Venn, *Matriculations at Oxford and Cambridge, 1544–1906* (1908).

Fuller.[1] The fact that "unhappy scholars" are prized "at a hireling rate", and are driven to "seeking maintenance by base vassalage" is the theme of the three Parnassus Plays performed at Cambridge in 1598–1601. Unemployment, the authors suggest, might lead either to melancholy or to popery: they do not suggest Puritanism as a possible alternative.[2]

Mr. Curtis has shown that the vast majority of lecturers in the diocese of Lincoln in 1614 were university graduates. Seventy per cent had M.A.s or higher degrees: only two out of 70 had no degree at all.[3] Some bishops, Heylyn said, admitted many men promiscuously to holy orders, for the sake of the fees: such men either became gentlemen's chaplains or stipendiary lecturers.[4] Petty suggested in 1662 that unemployed clerics "will seek ways how to get themselves a livelihood; which they cannot do more easily than by persuading the people that the 12,000 incumbents do poison or starve their souls". Recent experience, he suggested, had shown that lecturers succumbed to this temptation. So he argued against training too many parsons.[5]

But this is altogether too facile. The over-population which was believed to exist in the country as a whole at the beginning of the seventeenth century was in fact not absolute: it was relative to the capacity of the economy to absorb labour. So in the Church, the surplus of clerics which concerned many men in the early seventeenth century was related to the lack of adequate rewards offered to educated ministers.[6] The puritan programme of abolishing pluralism and non-residence, and of endowing a preaching minister in every parish, could easily have absorbed all the graduates Oxford and Cambridge turned out: though the higher incomes to which the fortunate few

1. *C.J.*, I, pp. 333 sq.
2. Ed. J. B. Leishman, *The Three Parnassus Plays* (1949), pp. 350, 356, 308–9, 213, 251. Robert Burton agreed about melancholy. Cf. T .Dekker, *Works*, Cambridge, (1953–61), II, pp. 528–36.
3. Curtis, "The Alienated Intellectuals", p. 36.
4. Heylyn, *Cyprianus Anglicus* (1671), p. 239. The instruction given in 1633 that no minister was to be ordained without a cure was an attempt to prevent this practice (*ibid.*, p. 241). See pp. 112–12 below.
5. Ed. C. H. Hull, *Economic Writings of Sir William Petty* (1899), I, pp. 79–80.
6. It was also related to the snobbism of graduates. The heroes of the Parnassus Plays regarded the profession of Shakespeare as beneath them (*Three Parnassus Plays*, pp. 336–49).

attained would have been reduced. As the Parnassus Plays suggest, men did not become Puritans because they were an unemployed intellectual proletariat; there was an unemployed intellectual proletariat, among other reasons, because there were Puritans. The fact that Puritans *were* employed as lecturers shows, indeed, that the demand for preaching existed: it was the hierarchy's refusal to satisfy it that created the problem. In August 1644 Baillie wrote gleefully "Presently all the youths of England, who for many years have waited for a pure ordination, shall be admitted to churches". Yet even when all these mute church-outed Miltons, "and what more Scotland can afford of good youths for the ministry here, are provided, it is thought some thousands of churches must vaick for want of men".[1] By this date there had been some ejections, but not "some thousands"; the abolition of pluralism would create far more vacancies. The reformer, John Hall, in fact thought that the over-endowment of the universities had created a super-fluity of jobs, which turned many a potential good craftsman into an ecclesiastical or literary drone.[2]

The sermons delivered by a lecturer have been described as the seventeenth-century equivalent of an adult education course. The lecture was "specifically and avowedly a teaching medium: closer attention was expected for a longer time. The audience would be the puritan elect who came on week-days to supplement the simpler Sunday fare". The congregation assembled voluntarily, and subscribed to pay for the lecturer. "Those who attended were inspired by a firm belief in the value of an instructed membership, and the people's eagerness to learn usually matched the minister's desire to teach".[3] It has rather the flavour of the early days of the W.E.A., when its classes provided something not otherwise obtainable and anxiously sought after: something perhaps a little daring and unorthodox.

In 1614 a sour report from the diocese of Lincoln tells us that lecturers showed little respect for higher academic degrees. It spoke in particular of David Allen, who was lecturer in three places and often lectured three times a week. "By which his

1. R. Baillie, *Letters and Journals* (1775), II, pp. 54–5.

2. J. Hall, *The Advancement of Learning* (*1649*) (ed. A. K. Croston, 1953), pp. 16–17.

3. G. R. Cragg, *Puritanism in the Period of the Great Persecution* (1957), pp. 210, 165.

unnecessary pains above his fellows he hath won to himself the name of an apostolic man". "This lecturing hath brought many of God's holy and good ordinances into contempt", the report continued. "For the multitude is drawn to this conceit, that the preaching of the Word is not only a principal but even the sole and only means of men's salvation, and that all religious worship consists only in speaking and in hearing".[1] So lecturers came to figure prominently in the theological controversies over preaching.[2] "Busy, idle lecturers", thought even a moderate like Fulke Greville, moulded "petty dividing schisms . . . sprung from . . . misty opinion".[3]

A lectureship which began by voluntary contributions might evolve in either of two directions. First, such lectureships were often officially taken over, in whole or in part, by town corporations. This happened, for instance, at Barnstaple, Gloucester and Newcastle-on-Tyne. At Newcastle lecturers were nominated by the mayor, aldermen and common council, with the approval of the Bishop of Durham. Their salary was not fixed, but rose or fell as the town authorities thought fit.[4] Under such circumstances men were hardly likely to preach doctrine too displeasing to their makers. Corporation lecturers, therefore, both because of the way they were chosen and of the way they were paid, were particularly likely to reflect the views of the richer citizens. Bishop Neile of Lincoln was insisting in 1614 that "the preachers shall not be beholden . . . to the mayor or bailiff of the town where the sermon is held, but that every minister pay for his own lecture".[5] When Laud (Neile's protégé) tried to suppress lecturers, in many towns the municipal authorities themselves necessarily became involved in struggles with the bishops.[6]

Secondly, where lectureships continued to be maintained by

1. Precentor Venables, "The Primary Visitation of the Diocese of Lincoln by Bishop Neile, A.D. 1614", *Associated Architectural Societies, Reports and Papers*, XVI (1881), pp. 46–7.
2. See pp. 61–74 above.
3. F. Greville, *Life of Sir Philip Sidney* (1907), p. 45. Written *c.* 1610–12?
4. J. F. Chanter, *The Life and Times of Martin Blake* (1910), pp. 33–5, 49–51, 62–4; W. B. Willcox, *Gloucestershire, 1590–1640* (Yale, 1940), pp. 216–17; ed. W. H. D. Longstaffe, *Memoirs of Mr. Ambrose Barnes* (Surtees Soc., 1867), p. 300.
5. Venables. "Primary Visitation of the Diocese of Lincoln", p. 47.
6. See pp. 95–109 below.

voluntary subscriptions, they naturally evolved in the direction of congregational independency. In 1571 the lecturer of Christ Church, Newgate, was dismissed for lack of attendance and because his teaching "doth not edify the people".[1] Nineteen years later, when there was a dispute between vicar and vestry of St. Lawrence Jewry over the right to appoint a parish clerk, parochial contributions to the vicar's lecture were suspended. This would have cost him £13 6s. 8d. a year: he surrendered within two months.[2] The lectureship at Wetherfield, Essex, was endowed by a yeoman on condition that the lecturer "be chosen by twenty of the chief inhabitants of the parish, or the greater part of them". When Stephen Marshall held this lectureship he was presented with "a library at the cost of £50" in return for a promise not to leave.[3] A lectureship given to an incumbent as a means of augmenting his stipend might be withdrawn from his successor if the congregation, or its richer members, did not like his theology. Where the lectureship was financially more valuable than the living itself, as was often the case, this gave the congregation the whip hand, as even a bishop like Wren had to recognize.[4] Wren's Norwich Visitation Articles of 1636 asked if there was a regular stipend settled on the lectureship, or merely an *ad hoc* contribution for a particular lecturer. Herbert Palmer's lectureship at St. Alphage's, Canterbury, was put down by the dean in 1630 because he drew "factious persons" out of other parishes.[5] Such lectures thus cut across parochial boundaries.

The subscribers might well expect to choose their own minister; we are on the way to a gathered church. John Smyth, later the Se-Baptist, was a lecturer at Lincoln for 2 years before

1. H. G. Owen, "Lectures and Lectureships in Tudor London", *Church Quarterly Review*, Jan.–March, 1961, p. 68. Cf. Pearl, *London and the Outbreak of the Puritan Revolution*, pp. 163–4 – canvassing and house-to-house collections for the lecturers of St. Antholin's.

2. H. G. Owen, "Lectures and Lectureships in Tudor London", p. 68; Owen, "The London Parish Clergy in the Reign of Elizabeth I" London Ph.D. Thesis, 1957.

3. E. Vaughan, *Stephen Marshall* (1907), pp. 13, 114. See also *E.P.C.*, pp. 295–7, for examples of effective election of lecturers by congregations.

4. See pp. 80–82 above. Cf. Owen, "Lecturers and Lectureships", pp. 68, 74.

5. The lectureship was revived as a result of influential pressure on the not unsympathetic Archbishop Abbot (*Dictionary of National Biography*). For Palmer, see pp. 176–7 below.

his dismissal in 1602 for having preached "untimely against divers men of good place". He then went off to found a separatist church.[1] As late as 1644 Baillie noted that some of the Independent divines in London were lecturers, but none held a settled parochial cure.[2] Many ministers who had conscientious scruples about accepting tithes had none about voluntary contributions, just as later they were to have none about a State maintenance.[3]

London citizens, we are told, "would rather . . . give a lecturer of their own choice twice as much as their full tithe came to than pay their dues to the parson".[4] For so they retained control, both of their own money and of its recipient. We may note as a parallel Clarendon's observation that many men would have paid Ship Money voluntarily who objected to it as a legal tax.[5] And Professor Jordan has shown how generous was the endowment of poor relief by private charity, whatever objections might be raised to compulsory rating for poor relief at Government instance.[6] In all these ways society was being remoulded by the voluntary actions of men with money: in comparison with what they were doing, Government activity would have been almost irrelevant if it had not been such an irritant. When most effective, it took the form of merely negative repression.

By stimulating the idea that the minister should be elected by the congregation, the existence of lecturers helped to undermine the hierarchical principle and the patronage system, and to prepare men's minds for democratic ideas.[7] Daniel Elliott, merchant tailor of London, in 1629 bequeathed £20 per annum for a Thursday afternoon lecture at All Hallows', Bread St. (Milton's parish), the lecturer to be chosen by the parish.[8] Some at least of the lecturers subsidized by the Feoffees for Impropriations seem to have been elected by the con-

1. C. Burrage, *The Early English Dissenters* (1912), I, pp. xi, 227–8.
2. Baillie, *Letters and Journals*, II, p. 24.
3. G. Nuttall, *Visible Saints* (1957), pp. 139–40.
4. [Anon.], *Persecutio Undecima* (1648), pp. 10–11. For the tithe controversy in London, see *E.P.C.*, Chapter 12, and pp. 297, 300.
5. Clarendon, *History of the Rebellion*, I, p. 86.
6. See p. 266 below.
7. Haller, *Liberty and Reformation in the Puritan Revolution* (Columbia University Press, 1955), p. 115.
8. Calder, *Activities of the Puritan Faction*, p. xiv. Richard Stock, one of the Feoffees, was rector of All Hallows'.

gregations concerned, though no doubt the Feoffees retained a right of veto.[1] John Workman, the contentious lecturer of Gloucester in Laud's time, thought that the choice of a minister properly belonged to the people.[2] Once the hierarchy had gone, lecturers of this type owed allegiance only to their congregations.

The fundamental cause, then, of this drift towards a "non-doctrinal" independency was economic. It sprang from the failure of the parochial system to provide adequate remuneration for ministers, at a time when the wealth of merchants and of other professional groups like lawyers and stewards was rising; and from the not unnatural desire of subscribers to get value for their money. Nor is there anything surprising in the lecturers' acceptance of the opposition point of view. Professor Haller has shown how Cambridge became a seminary for "a kind of puritan order of preaching brothers. The members sprang as a rule from the gentry or merchant class, or had immediate connections with that class". Such men, with their own preaching programme for the Church, might accept a living from a sympathetic patron, but tended increasingly to prefer the position of lecturer, at once freer and more re-munerative.[3] To get a nobleman's chaplaincy or a lectureship, we are told, was in the sixteen twenties a principal ambition of the Fellows of Preston's Emmanuel. It was a comprehensible ambition, whether the stimulus came from a desire "to exercise their ministry" or "to make themselves known unto such as had it in their power to prefer them."[4] It was often no doubt difficult to differentiate between these two motives. A lecture-ship offered possibilities of advancement, through winning a reputation as a preacher, or through making valuable contacts.[5]

A nominal chaplaincy or curacy might be a disguised lecture-ship, a way in which a peer or a gentleman gave protection and financial support to a minister who had difficulties with the bishop. Bancroft described how Puritan ministers "creep into noblemen's bosoms in the country (a matter of no great

1. Calder, "A 17th century attempt to purify the Anglican Church" *American Historical Review*, LII, p. 768.
2. *C.S.P.D., 1635*, p. 195. See pp. 102–3 below.
3. Haller, *Rise of Puritanism*, pp. 52–4, and *passim*.
4. Ball, *Life of . . . Preston*, pp. 81–4.
5. Owen, "Lecturers and Lectureships" p. 71.

difficulty, considering what necessary instruments they are to some purposes)".[1] Before the Canons of 1604 stopped it, bishops often ordained a minister on the strength of a guaranteed stipend from an aristocratic family in their diocese: this was especially frequent in areas like Wales, where such chaplains helped the parish incumbent, normally a non-preacher.[2] In 1605 Bancroft recognized that despite the Canons, private lectureships or gentlemen's chaplaincies were protecting Puritans whom he was trying to root out of the Church.[3] When one of the lecturers appointed by the Feoffees for Impropriations was silenced by Laud, he fled to Warwick to become chaplain to Lord Brooke.[4] In 1632 a lecturer at Saffron Walden was "disguised as a curate".[5] Two years later Mr. Eden of Peterborough kept a schoolmaster in his house who preached an afternoon lecture in the church at Warrington.[6] Thomas Shepard served as chaplain in the family of Sir Richard Darley between the suppression of his Essex lecture-ship and his emigration to New England.[7] Lectures abounded in Suffolk, Wren reported to Laud in 1636, many of them maintained by private gentlemen without reference to the bishop.[8] He fined the churchwardens of Dullam 40s. apiece for permitting Lord Brooke's chaplain to preach a Sunday afternoon sermon in their church.[9] Even where chaplains were genuinely retained to perform family duties they could be something very like lecturers, since the private chapel would be thrown open when sermons were preached.

1. Ed. A. Peel, *Tracts ascribed to Richard Bancroft* (1953), p. 57. The ascription to Bancroft is not absolutely certain, though probable.
2. Ed. A. I. Pryce, *The Diocese of Bangor in the Sixteenth Century* (1923), pp. xxx–xxxi. Lady Hoby had a chaplain who was also a lecturer (ed. D. M. Meads, *Diary of Lady Margaret Hoby, 1599–1605*, 1930, pp. 63–5, 243–4).
3. D. Wilkins, *Concilia* (1737), IV, pp. 409–10.
4. Pearl, *London and the Outbreak of the Puritan Revolution*, p. 165. Cf. p. 101 below.
5. Davids, *Nonconformity in Essex*, pp. 170–3.
6. Hart, *The Country Clergy in Elizabethan and Stuart Times*, p. 91.
7. J. A. Albro, *The Life of Thomas Shepard* (Boston, 1870), p. 135.
8. Laud, *Works*, V, p. 340.
9. Prynne, *A Looking-Glasse for all Lordly Prelates* (1636), pp. 71–5.

III

Those who invested their money in the endowment of lectureships might have more than one reason for doing so. On the one hand, they themselves no doubt wished to listen to sound theology, of a type which beneficed ministers of the Church of England were less and less likely to preach in the two or three decades before 1640. But a second reason was a genuine anxiety to preserve the mass of the population from popery and superstition, to indoctrinate them. This seems to have been a particular concern of merchants. Partly, no doubt, they are conspicuous in the financing of lecturers because their wealth took the form of cash and was not tied up in land. But even when allowances have been made, their prominence (as against the peerage and gentry) is remarkable. Those annual feasts at which London merchants who hailed from the same county used to meet were not only themselves introduced by a sermon: they also often led to consultations "what good they might do to their native county by settling some ministers (or some other good work)" for the benefit of their less fortunate countrymen who had stayed at home. London merchants of Lancashire origin contributed an annual sum sufficient to maintain five or six ministers in their native county in places "where there was neither preaching nor means to maintain it".[1] About 1633 John Shaw, previously lecturer at Brampton, Derbyshire, preached at a meeting of Devon merchants in London: next year they sought him out and appointed him lecturer at Chulmleigh in their county. Their custom was to maintain a lecturer for three years at their expense, after which they hoped his congregation would continue his maintenance; if it did not, the merchants would support him elsewhere. But before Shaw's three years were up the Laudian campaign had got rid of him.[2] In the sixteen-fifties Worcestershire Londoners

1. *Life of Master John Shaw*, in *Yorkshire Diaries and Autobiographies in the 17th and 18th centuries* (Surtees Soc., LXV, 1875), pp. 126–9; W. Walker, *A Sermon Preached in St. Pauls Church in London*, 28 November 1628, *Epistle Dedicatory*.
2. *Life of Shaw, loc. cit.*; A. G. Matthews, *Calamy Revised* (1934), pp. 434–5; cf. *E.P.C.*, p. 268. Shaw then went to York, in his native county, as lecturer (see pp. 105–6 below). He was later chaplain to the Yorkshire Parliamentary Committee (J. G. Miall, *Congregationalism in Yorkshire*, 1868, p. 93).

collected £30 and sent it to Richard Baxter to set up a lecture
called "the Londoners' lecture". This was for one year only,
but now the times were happier, and the local inhabitants
were able to continue the lecture from their own contributions
until the Restoration.[1]

London-endowed lectureships often gave rise to controversies. From St. Ives Oliver Cromwell wrote in January 1636
about such a lectureship to Mr. Storie, "at the sign of the Dog
in the Royal Exchange", urging the wealthy founders to continue their subscriptions: "it were a piteous thing to see a
lecture fall . . . in these times wherein we see they are suppressed
with too much haste and violence by the enemies of God his
truth".[2] At Huntingdon Cromwell's beloved schoolmaster,
Dr. Beard, held a lectureship until his death in 1633, when
Laud managed to suppress it. But then the Mercers' Company
of London, with Richard Fishbourne's money, set up a
lecturer to preach on Sundays and market days, reserving to
themselves, Laud said indignantly, the right to dismiss him
"upon any dislike they may have of him", at a month's or a
fortnight's notice, "without any relation to bishop or archbishop". "My humble suit to your Majesty", the archbishop
added, "is that no layman whatsoever, and least of all companies or corporations, may . . . have power to put in or put
out any lecturer or other minister". Charles replied to this
demand for a new directive on policy: "Certainly I cannot
hold fit that any lay person or corporation should have the
power these men would take to themselves. For I will have
no priest have any necessity of a lay dependency. Wherefore
I command you to show me the way to overthrow this, and
to hinder the performance in time to all such intentions".
Those were brave words. But 1633 was rather late in the day
to utter them. Laud got the Huntingdon lecturer dismissed,
but a few months later the Mercers appointed him to a vacant
vicarage in the same town.[3]

1. *Reliquiae Baxterianae*, I, pp. 95–6. Cf. p. 94 below.
2. W. C. Abbott, *The Writings and Speeches of Oliver Cromwell*
(1937–47), I, pp. 80–1. This lecturer appears subsequently to have been
a chaplain in the Parliamentary army.
3. Repositories of the Acts of the Court of the Mercers' Company,
1637–41, ff. 57v–58 (I owe this reference to the kindness of Dr. Valerie
Pearl); Laud, *Works*, V, p. 321, VI, pp. 349–51. See also *E.P.C.*, pp.
270–1. For the Mercers' activities see also p. 106 below.

The religious zeal of the merchants was manifested in many places. Hugh Peter's lectureship at St. Sepulchre's, London, was financed by a chandler.[1] The Clothworkers' Company gave a lecturer at Burton-on-Trent £30 a year, and also nominated the reader at Whittington College, London.[2] William Jones in 1615 left funds to the Haberdashers to endow lectureships in London and at Monmouth and Newland, Gloucestershire. Puritans were appointed to them all.[3] The Haberdashers nominated other lecturers, and, like the Mercers, the other big livery company which consistently used its patronage to promote Puritans, on occasion received a royal command to dismiss their nominees.[4] It was no doubt to such activities of puritan merchants that a royalist pamphleteer referred when he said that the same men who incorporated themselves into a distinct Church and "set up an upstart ministry of lecturers" also "had their mutual intelligence throughout the kingdom and engrossed almost all the inland trade to men of their faction".[5]

Merchants were aware of the hierarchy's opposition to what they were doing. In 1626 John Juxon, a relative of the later Bishop of London and a merchant tailor, left money by will for the establishment of lectures in the City. Foreseeing trouble ahead, he stipulated that if the lectures were discontinued, the money should go to the Company for the foundation of scholarships. His forebodings were justified: by July 1634 the

1. R. P. Stearns, *The Strenuous Puritan* (University of Illinois Press, 1954), pp. 35–6.

2. Strype, Life of Parker (1821), II, p. 377; ed. W. N. Landon, *Staffordshire Incumbents and Parochial Records (1530–1680)* (William Salt Archaeological Soc., 1915), p. 44. The Whittington lectureship was held by the Puritan Thomas Sampson until 1574. Archbishop Parker then prevented Edward Dering succeeding him.

3. W. M. Warlow, *A History of the Charities of William Jones ... of Monmouth and Newland* (1899), *passim*; Jordan, *Charities of London*, pp. 108, 153 4, 236, 285 6, 338; *E.P.C.*, pp. 61, 268 9.

4. *E.P.C.*, p. 268; Pearl, *London and the Outbreak of the Puritan Revolution*, p. 242. For other endowment of lecturers through City Companies, see Owen, "Lecturers and Lectureships", p. 69.

5. [Anon.], *Persecutio Undecima* (1648), p. 55. This pamphlet is attributed to Robert Chestlin, a minister who had been deprived in 1642 and replaced by a former lecturer; so he is hardly an impartial witness (see p. 118 below). But cf. William Strode's reference to "a faction/Brought in with merchandize from foreign ports" (*Poetical Works*, 1907, p. 189).

lectures had been put down.[1] In 1633 a London citizen left
money to pay a lecturer, who was to be appointed by the
Drapers' Company, but with a proviso that if there should be
any alteration in religion the bequest was to lapse to the
Company.[2]

The Feoffees for Impropriations, who had four merchants
among their number as well as four lawyers and four ministers,
had as one of their main aims the endowment of lecturers,
especially in market towns. Conversely, lecturers were
accused of stirring up the rich to contribute to the Feoffees'
funds.[3] One of the Feoffees, Alderman Rowland Heylyn,
had bought an impropriation in Shropshire in 1613 (before the
Feoffees existed as a body) and used it to set up a lecturer at
St. Alkmund's, Shrewsbury. Julius Hering, a protégé of the
Feoffees, was lecturer there.[4] The Feoffees were accused of
bringing in lecturers over an incumbent's head, to preach
against him and "triumph over him". They made bigger
grants to lecturers than to perpetual vicars, because the former
were "removable men".[5] As an example of their method of
proceeding, we may take the Essex lectureship endowed
through the Feoffees by John Preston's friend Dr. Thomas
Wilson. This lectureship was to rotate among various towns
in the county, staying at none of them for more than three
years: since if any good at all was to come of it, it would have
been achieved in that period. The placing of the lecturer was
left to the discretion of a conference of ministers which met
regularly at different towns in Essex. The lectureship was
originally intended for Coggeshall, but in fact the first holder
was Thomas Shepard at Earls Colne. At the end of the initial
period, the parishioners of Earls Colne decided to take over
and increase Shepard's maintenance themselves, which they

1. W. H. Marah, *Memoirs of Archbishop Juxon and his times* (1869)
p. 13.

2. Gardiner, *History of England*, VII, p. 305.

3. *A Letter from Mercurius Civicus to Mercurius Rusticus, Somers
Tracts* (1748–51), V, p. 400.

4. Samuel Clarke, *A General Martyrologie* (1677), Life of Hering;
E.P.C., p. 260; A. C. Carter, *The English Reformed Church in Amsterdam
in the Seventeenth Century* (Amsterdam, 1964), pp. 64, 96.

5. Calder, *Activities of the Puritan Faction*, pp. 51–2, 110, 119–20;
Somers Tracts, V, pp. 400–2. Nominating lecturers had been no part of
the intention of those who subscribed money to the Feoffees, it was
alleged against them (Rushworth, *Historical Collections*, II, p. 152).

did until the lecture was suspended in 1630.[1]

Professor Jordan's researches give us some idea of the scale of endowment of lecturers. In the 9 counties and 2 cities which he investigated, £46,250 was left for lecturers between 1601 and 1640, over and above £37,500 to augment the maintenance of the clergy. These two sums together amount to about one-third of the money given to religious purposes in these decades, and between 6 per cent and 7 per cent of what was given for all purposes. The four decades are quite exceptional in the amounts devoted to preaching (82.37 of the capital endowment of lectureships between 1480 and 1660 was made between 1610 and 1650). Half of the money with which lectureships were endowed in the first four decades of the seventeenth century came from London merchants.[2] At Bristol, too, many merchants made provision for lectureships in the early seventeenth century. Appointment to one of these endowed in 1630, was to be "at the discretion of the mayor and his brethren": the lecturer was to preach every Sunday.[3]

IV

But it was the appointment of lecturers by town corporations that gave rise to the greatest controversies. The urban middle and lower classes were those most inclined to religious radicalism. But there were other especial reasons for the establishment of lectureships in towns. Owing to the "decay" of personal tithes, ministers there were often very badly paid. "Vicars in great market towns", Laud told Charles I in 1633, "where the people are very many, are for the most part worst provided for".[4] In most urban livings, where the educational

1. Davids, *Nonconformity in Essex*, p. 164; Albro, *Life of Thomas Shepard*, p. 119. Lady Wooley also acted through the Feoffees when she established a lectureship at Wonersh, in Surrey (E. W. Kirby, "The Lay Feoffees: A Study in Militant Puritanism", *Journal of Modern History* XIV, p. 12).

2. Jordan, *Philanthropy in England*, pp. 249, 300–1, 312–14, 350, 374 5; *The Charities of London*, p. 72. For details of merchant endowment of lectureships see these and Professor Jordon's related works, *passim*.

3. Ed. P. McGrath, *Merchants and Merchandise in 17th century Bristol* (Bristol Record Soc., 1955), pp. xix, 55–6. Cf. Jordan, *The Forming of the Charitable Institutions of the West of England* (American Philosophical Soc., 1960), pp. 10, 17, 42, 72.

4. Laud, *Works*, V, p. 327. Cf. *E.P.C.*, Chapter 5.

level of congregations was highest, the endowment was least likely to attract able preachers. So there was a case for supplementing them by lecturers. Alternatively, if the minister found favour in the eyes of his flock, a lectureship might be given to him to augment his salary and encourage him in preaching. A lecturer once brought in might succeed to the cure if the congregation could prevail upon the patron to make the nomination, which of course was easiest when the town corporation itself owned the advowson. Where the town authorities did not possess the patronage, they might welcome the introduction of lecturers. Thus at Exeter the city oligarchy would have liked to bring the parishes directly under the control of the chamber; failing that they sponsored lecturers, over whom there were naturally quarrels with the bishop. Since lecturers received from £40 to £60 a year, and no benefice in the city was worth more than £20, this was a powerful lever in the city fathers' hands.[1]

Contemporaries saw the establishment of lectures in towns as a deliberate policy of the Puritans, which aimed at influencing the main centres of population, and in particular those boroughs which returned members to the House of Commons. There seem to be no grounds for doubting the truth of this accusation, which is to be found as early as 1585: "They bend not themselves to preach abroad in the country, and where there is greatest need, but in the most populous places, as in the market towns, shire towns and cities, where they know that, strange devices and novelties finding always most friends and best entertainment, they might with less labour sow their contentions".[2] In 1584 the puritan Earl of Huntingdon had said "I do all that I can to get good preachers planted in the market towns of this county" (Lincolnshire).[3] In the same year a bill for the provision of maintenance for ministers and preachers in towns corporate was "dashed" in the House of Commons after "much dispute".[4] The Feoffees for Impropriations were accused of concentrating their efforts on boroughs which returned M.P.s to the House of Commons,

1. W. T. MacCaffrey, *Exeter, 1540–1640* (Harvard University Press, 1958), pp. 201–2, 266. See pp. 101–2 below.
2. Peel, *Tracts Ascribed to Richard Bancroft*, p. 57.
3. Quoted by C. J. Billson, *Leicester Memoirs* (1924), p. 42.
4. Sir Simonds D'Ewes, *The Journals of all the Parliaments during the Reign of Queen Elizabeth* (1682), p. 339.

a charge which their defenders did not trouble to deny.[1]

There were also no doubt economic reasons for the success of unorthodox lecturers in towns. The vicar of Braintree, writing to the Chancellor of the Diocese of London in 1629, reported that the town of Chelmsford would insist on having a lecturer "who may draw tumults and troops of the country to their inns and shops, which a regular man cannot do, let his sufficiency and honesty be what it will".[2] Regularity, sufficiency and honesty no doubt lacked box-office appeal. "Not a bowling green or an ordinary could stand without" a lecturer, commented Bishop Wren of Norwich sourly in 1636.[3] He had just received a petition from Norwich citizens complaining that trade was likely to decay if he suspended their preachers: for gentlemen normally came to the city not only to trade but also to hear sermons.[4]

> "It was the market and the lecture day.
> Lecturers sell sermons, as the lay
> Do sheep and oxen; have their reasons just
> For both their markets."

So sang Bishop Corbett of the market-day lecturer at Daventry, maintained by the voluntary contributions of the inhabitants.[5]

Towns then provided the most favourable congregations for puritan preachers; they were badly supplied with beneficed preaching ministers, for economic reasons; and the Puritans set themselves deliberately to influence the main centres of population. Contemporaries had no doubt of their success. "The first great hazard [of schism]", wrote a royalist sadly wise after the event, "is when popular persons are put in popular employments and in populous places. A cunning and a factious minister is a dangerous instrument in a city;

1. Nalson, *An Impartial Collection*, I, p. 279; Heylyn, *Cyprianus Anglicus* (1671), pp. 198 9.

2. H. Smith, *Ecclesiastical History of Essex* (Colchester, n.d.), pp. 33–4.

3. *C.S.P.D., 1636–7*, p. 223.

4. Tanner MS. 68, ff. 151–2, 115. I owe this reference to Mr. Boorman's B.Litt. thesis.

5. Ed. J. A. W. Bennett and H. R. Trevor-Roper, *The Poems of Richard Corbett* (1955), p. 32; Laud, *Works*, V, p. 349. Laud thought in 1637 that the Bishop of Peterborough should keep an eye on this lecture.

and the more dangerous if tolerated, for then he stirs up tumults by authority, and who shall blame the flock for following the shepherd ?"[1]

The fight, therefore, which was waged over lecturers was recognized as being a fight for key positions of political influence. Dugdale tells us how "under a seeming devout and holy pretence, to advance and promote the preaching of the Gospel, they got in a number of lecturers into most of the corporate towns and populous places of this realm (according to the pattern of Geneva), especially into the City of London; whom they maintained by voluntary contributions, to the end they might be engaged to preach such doctrine as should (upon occasion) prepare the people for any disloyal attempt, and dispose them to rebellion when opportunity served".[2]

A royalist pamphleteer of 1643 spoke of lecturers, "whose maintenance being dependent, . . . must preach such doctrine as may foment disloyalty, and instil such principles into their auditors as may first dispose them to, and after engage them in, rebellion when things were ripe; or else they shall want bread to put into their heads".[3] Selden agreed that lecturers won for themselves "not only the affections but the bounty that should be bestowed upon the minister". They "get a great deal of money because they preach the people tame . . . and then they do what they list with them". "If there had been no lecturers", he thought, "the Church of England might have stood and flourished at this day".[4] In these widely accepted accusations against lecturers we have one of our most impressive pieces of evidence for the growing alienation of the solid, God-fearing urban middle classes from the government and the hierarchy of the established Church. Just because lecturers were independent of the establishment, and dependent on those who maintained them, they give us some understanding of the mode of thought and the aspirations of the opposition. "Not a soul", a royalist observed after the Restoration, "that by the instigation

1. [Anon.], *A Memento* (n.d., *c*. 1660–5), p. 168.

2. Sir W. Dugdale, *A Short View of the Late Troubles in England* (1681), p. 36; cf. Sig. A 2–3.

3. *A Letter from Mercurius Civicus to Mercurius Rusticus* (1643), in *Somers Tracts* (1748–51), V, p. 400; cf. Heylyn, *Cyprianus Anglicus* (1671), p. 9.

4. Selden, *Table Talk*, pp. 113, 75; cf. Burnet, *History of the Reformation* (1825), III, p. 2 10.

of schismatical lecturers deserted the church, but become an enemy to the state".[1] "Every corporation is a petty free state against monarchy", the Duke of Newcastle told Charles II, "and they have done your Majesty more mischief in these late disorders with their lecturers than anything else". The latter "have preached your Majesty out of your kingdoms". "Therefore no lecturers at all, in no place", the Duke recommended.[2]

Bishop Burnet, in a passage which illuminates the political background of the Clarendon Code, tells us how after the Restoration Archbishop Sheldon persuaded Charles II that "nothing had spoiled the late King's affairs so much as the credit that the factious lectures had in all corporations, for this had so great an influence on their elections that he ascribed all the war to that half-conformity, and therefore he said it was necessary in order to the having a good Parliament that all the clergy should be hearty conformists; and no wonder if this satisfied the King, for it was very plausible".[3] Bunyan's Mansoul, it will be recalled, was a corporation and a market town. There Diabolus first set up and maintained "a sufficient ministry, besides lecturers"; but after Emmanuel's victory the corporation was purged by a commission, and new lecturers established.[4] Sheldon's explanation of the civil war was possibly a little over-simplified, though (as Burnet said) it had plausibility. It had been put with even greater brevity by a royalist pamphleteer of 1649: "Three things have been the bane of monarchy:

(1) First, weekly lectures;
(2) Corporations;
(3) Trained bands".[5]

V

Few were the towns in which, during the decades before the Revolution, there were no disputes over the appointment of lecturers. A few examples may be given of the sorts of conflict

1. *A Memento*, p. 166.
2. S. A. Strong, *A Catalogue of Letters . . . at Welbeck* (1903), pp. 185–9, 206.
3. Ed. H. C. Foxcroft, *A Supplement to Burnet's History of My Own Time* (1902), p. 71; cf. p. 69. Cf. also pp. 119–20 below.
4. Bunyan, *Works* (1860), III, pp. 255, 293, 322, 356.
5. [Anon.], *Lex Talionis* (1649), p. 9; cf. J. Walker, *The Sufferings of the Clergy* (1714), I, pp. 18–22.

that arose. At Leicester the Earl of Huntingdon succeeded in establishing a town preacher in 1576, paying him an annuity of £30 per annum over and above his salary of £13 11s. 8d. In 1590, "by the earnest suit and labour of the Earl of Huntingdon", the town preacher was given an official salary of another £30. In consequence of this the town claimed the right to nominate the preacher. They tended by preference to select marked Puritans. In 1586 the town asked Huntingdon to try to persuade Walter Travers to accept the post. This was just after Travers had been silenced by Whitgift, following his preaching contest with Hooker at the Temple. But Travers went elsewhere.[1] In the sixteen-twenties, when Francis Higginson was deprived of his living in Leicester for nonconformity, the town is said to have obtained the permission of the complaisant Bishop Williams to retain him as their lecturer. Here he remained until Laud got on to his track and proceedings were started against him in the High Commission. He then fled to New England. In 1634 John Angel, the town preacher, was suspended by the Dean of the Arches for preaching without a licence. He continued to be honoured at Leicester, and as soon as political circumstances permitted he was restored to his office at an increased salary. Angel was a staunch Parliamentarian during the civil war.[2] Arthur Hildersam, another protégé of the Earl of Huntingdon, was vicar of Ashby-de-la-Zouch from 1593 onwards. He was frequently in trouble with the ecclesiastical authorities, and in 1605 was deprived. He then established himself as lecturer at Burton-on-Trent and Repton, where he survived until Neile, newly appointed Bishop of Coventry and Lichfield, suppressed the lectures in 1611. Declining an invitation to the pastorate of the English church at Leiden, Hildersam somehow managed to return to Ashby-de-la-Zouch as a lecturer, where he continued a running battle with his ecclesiastical superiors until his death in 1632.[3]

At Colchester a lecture was established about 1564, at first

1. S. J. Knox, *Walter Travers: Paragon of Elizabethan Puritanism* (1962), p. 82.

2. C. J. Billson, *Leicester Memoirs* (1924), pp. 43–51; J. Simon, "The two John Angels", *Trans. Leicestershire Archaeological and Historical Soc.*, XXXI (1955), pp. 35–40. The story about Higginson has been queried: see Billson, *op. cit.*, p. 52.

3. S. B. Babbage, *Puritanism and Richard Bancroft* (1962), pp. 183–6, 229.

endowed by subscription; but in 1576 this was converted into a salary of £40 a year paid by the town. This rose gradually, until in 1620 it stood at £100 plus £10 for a house. The holders of this lectureship, nominated by the mayor and corporation, included the famous William Ames (1609–10), William Bridge (1631–2) and John Knowles (1635–7), all three of whom ultimately emigrated. There were at least 23 other lectures in Essex, among the holders of which we find the names of such well-known puritan preachers as Samuel Ward (Havershill), John Rogers and Matthew Newcomen (Dedham), Samuel Fairclough (Clare), Thomas Shepard (Earls Colne), Stephen Marshall (Wethersfield). It was Thomas Hooker, lecturer at Chelmsford, of whom a correspondent wrote to Laud's Chancellor in 1629: "I . . . have seen the people idolizing many new ministers and lecturers, but Hooker surpasses them all". Hooker was expelled the next year, and soon afterwards emigrated to New England.[1]

At Coventry a weekly lecture was founded in 1608 "during the pleasure of Mr. Mayor and his brethren, the preacher to be at their discretion". To this Samuel Clarke, later the martyrologist, was appointed about 1630. He was fiercely attacked by Dr. Buggs, who held two livings in the town. Bishop Morton of Coventry and Lichfield supported Buggs, and forbade Clarke to preach in the diocese. Clarke disregarded this order, having a licence from the archbishop and the support of some aldermen who were prepared to spend money in his defence; but he was finally dismissed when a new mayor took Buggs's side. Clarke was then invited to a lectureship at Warwick, but the vicar there frustrated this offer. The Earl of Warwick came to Clarke's rescue by making him his chaplain, and virtually ordering the vicar to accept him as his assistant.[2]

At Exeter the Merchant Adventurers took the lead in introducing a lecturer. In 1599 they agreed to contribute £10 a year for a preacher nominated by the chamber. The city contributed

1. Davids, *Nonconformity in Essex*, pp. 151, 547–8 and *passim*; Smith, *Ecclesiastical History of Essex*, pp. 21–41 and *passim*; *V.C.H. Essex*, II, pp. 51–3; *C.S.P.D.*, *1629–31*, p. 186; Laud, *Works*, V, p. 348. For Shepard, see pp. 90, 95 above. For Newcomen, see p. 116 below.

2. J. Sibree and M. Carton, *Independency in Warwickshire* (1855), pp. 19–21; *C.S.P.D.*, *1631–3*, pp. 358–62, 492; S. Clarke, *The Lives of Sundry Eminent Divines of this later Age* (1683), I, pp. 5–6; S. Palmer, *The Nonconformists' Memorial* (1775), I, p. 90.

a further £20 per annum. But contributions were difficult to collect, and the lectureship lapsed between 1607 and 1610. In 1613 two lecturers were appointed at £50 each a year. Three years later a third was added, thanks to a legacy from Laurence Bodley and £200 from a merchant, which made possible the purchase of an impropriation yielding £40 a year. For this lectureship the name of John Hazard was put forward to Bishop Cotton by the Chamber. Hazard was willing to undertake the lecture for £20 per annum, "having other livings among us in the right of his wife". But the bishop refused to accept him. Hazard gives a vivid account of their interview in April 1616. Cotton accused him of pushing into two other churches where there already were preachers. Hazard replied that these churches had been chosen as the largest and so the fittest to contain a large congregation. Laurence Bodley's object in leaving the money was that "not only the people of the same parish, but also such poor people of the city as could not come to hear at St. Peter's might be present at this, it being a public lecture and not to be appropriated to the inhabitants of any one particular parish". The bishop asked whether Hazard would take upon him "that none of the higher sort come, but only the poor?" The mingling of congregations, Cotton added, might lead to the spreading of infection. He regretted that he had ever ordained Hazard, since he had preached false doctrine, "but would not show me wherein, because I know he could not". Cotton threatened to suspend Hazard if he preached again before producing his letters dimissory from his last place, and warned him not to rely on the Archbishop of Canterbury's licence to preach. This quarrel ended with the death of Hazard in 1617. Nine years later Laurence Bodley's nephew was complaining that his uncle's preacher was negligent and debauched. It would appear that the Bishop of Exeter had succeeded in preventing the appointment of another Puritan.[1] At Plymouth the King intervened personally in 1631 to forbid the corporation to appoint the lecturer of their choice – Edmund Ford, who had just been sent down from Oxford for preaching seditious sermons.[2]

In 1619 John Workman was unanimously elected lecturer by

1. *City of Exeter MSS.* (H.M.C.), pp. 92–8; MacCaffrey, *Exeter 1540–1640*, pp. 157, 197–202.

2. *E.P.C.*, pp. 59–60.

the Common Council of Gloucester. He held this appointment unquestioned until 1633, the year of Laud's accession to the primacy. Then the new archbishop wrote to say that Workman "had done so much harm, and made such a faction in Gloucester, as that the High Commission thought it not fit to continue him there". Ostensibly for preaching against sports and images, Workman was suspended, excommunicated and imprisoned. He was also alleged to have prayed for the States of Holland and the King of Sweden before he prayed for Charles I, and to hold that the election of ministers belonged to the people. The city fought back, confirming their lecturer's stipend of £20 "so long as he shall be pleased to inhabit and live in this city, whether he preach or not". For this gesture the mayor, town clerk and three aldermen were fined £10 apiece by the Privy Council. One of those fined was Alderman Pury, a vigorous opponent of episcopacy, and a witness against Laud at his trial. Laud's actions in this case indeed formed the basis of an article in his impeachment. Workman, after his release from prison, was successively inhibited from working as a tutor and practising as a physician. In 1638 the Bishop of Hereford tracked him down to the house of Mr. Kyrle, subsequently a supporter of the Parliamentary cause in Herefordshire; the good bishop drove him out, "God knows whither". Workman in fact appears to have returned to Gloucester, where the city voted him £20 during his sickness in 1640, and an annuity to his widow in the following year.[1]

In Norfolk and Suffolk there were many disputes. A lectureship at Lynn was held from 1619 by Samuel Fairclough, who received £50 from the town authorities, and a similar sum in voluntary contributions. But he soon got into trouble with the bishop and had to move.[2] At Yarmouth the mayor and corporation appointed not only the incumbent but also three town preachers; and there were lecturers maintained by congrega-

1. J. N. Langton "John Workman, Puritan lecturer in Gloucester", *Trans. Bristol and Gloucestershire Archaeological Soc.*, LXVI (1945), pp. 219–32; Willcox, *Gloucestershire, 1590–1640* (Yale University Press, 1940), pp. 216–17; J. and T. W. Webb, *Memorials of the Civil War in Herefordshire* (1879), I, p. 23; Laud, *Works*, IV, pp. 234–5, V, p. 357; G. Soden, *Godfrey Goodman* (1953), pp. 170–1; Prynne, *Canterburies Doome*, pp. 104–8. For other lecturers in Gloucestershire, see *V.C.H. Gloucestershire*, II, pp. 32, 34.

2. Palmer, *Nonconformists' Memorial*, II, p. 430.

tions as well.[1] One of the lectureships was established in 1632
against the opposition of four prebendaries, who described
the move as being due to "the restless importunity of some few
of the faction without the general allowance". "Great divisions" followed in the town, the lecturer was hauled before the
High Commission and driven into emigration.[2] George
Burdett, who was "merely a lecturer" and lived "upon the
benevolence of the people" was deprived in 1635 for opposing
the incumbent, preaching against ceremonies, and saying that
ministers should be elected.[3] At Norwich John Robinson, later
the separatist, was a lecturer until he was ejected in 1604. There
were lectures at St. Andrew's on Monday, Thursday and
Friday, the first two at the corporation's expense, the latter
financed by the parish. In 1634 the Bishop of Norwich tried to
suppress the Friday lecture, delivered by William Bridge. The
city fathers protested, but Bridge was suspended and emigrated.[4] There were many other lecturers in Norfolk, three of
whom Wren inhibited in 1636.[5]

At Ipswich the practice of levying a rate on houses for the
maintenance of ministers (authorized by 13 Eliz. cap. 24) had
developed into something very like a system of maintenance by
voluntary contributions. In consequence, as his Chancellor
told Wren, ministers "dance after their pipe from whom they
receive the livelihood, which is stopped or runs as the Levites
popularize".[6] In 1624 there were two lecturers here, John
Yates and Samuel Ward, who were responsible for gathering
the Arminian points out of Montagu's *New Gag for an Old
Goose* for presentation to Parliament. Ten years later Ward
was up before the High Commission on a variety of charges,
and he was sent to prison for contumacy. Despite his dismissal,

1. Nuttall, *Visible Saints*, pp. 24–5. At least one of these lecturers
emigrated to New England in 1635 (Marchant, *The Puritans and the
Church Courts in the Diocese of York*, p. 236).
2. *Cowper MSS.* (H.M.C.), I, pp. 465, 480; Laud, *Works*, V, p. 340;
C.S.P.D., *1635*, p. xxxii.
3. *C.S.P.D.*, *1634–5*, pp. 537–9.
4. W. L. Sachse, *Minutes of the Norwich Court of Mayoralty, 1630–1*
(Norfolk Record Soc., XV, 1942), pp. 49-50; *V.C.H. Norfolk*, II,
pp. 281–2, 286, 289; Laud, *Works*, V, pp. 328, 340; cf. Wren, *Parentalia*,
pp. 47, 98–9; *E.P.C.*, p. 261.
5. *C.S.P.D.*, *1636–7*, p. 223.
6. Tanner MS. 68, f. 3. I owe this reference to Mr. Boorman's B.Litt.
thesis.

Ipswich continued to be "very factious", refused to appoint anyone in Ward's place, and went on paying his stipend to his widow and eldest son after his death in 1640.[1] There was also a lectureship at Bury St. Edmunds. The holder of this, "one Mr. Peartree", was deprived of his licence to preach during Brent's visitation of 1635 for "great ignorance", since he was unable to say what "*ecclesia*" signified. But this may be a little official joke: Peartree no doubt said it meant "congregation". For he also "opposed the ceremonies of our church" and "drew many after him from neighbouring parishes".[2]

At Barnstaple in the early years of the seventeenth century there were disagreements between the vicars and the lecturers, the latter being appointed and paid by the corporation. In order to outflank one lecturer the vicar in 1606 persuaded the bishop to make his parish clerk a deacon. Two successive parish clerks in this town were deacons, covering the period from 1606 to the abolition of episcopacy.[3] In 1630 the then vicar, Martin Blake, presented some of the lecturers for non-compliance with the instructions of 1629. One of them, Mr. Crompton, began a preaching feud with the vicar, whose sermons he attacked in his afternoon lecture. When in 1636 Crompton publicly accused Blake of heresy, the latter tried to get his appointment terminated. At once the corporation was up in arms in defence of its lecturer. The vicar argued that Crompton's appointment was invalid, since he lacked the bishop's licence and consent. The bishop, the moderate Joseph Hall, prudently referred the matter to the arbitration of the deputy recorder of Barnstaple, on the plea that legal points were involved. Crompton's lectureship was terminated.[4]

At York there was a city preacher, normally a Puritan, appointed by the corporation.[5] After John Shaw was ejected from his lectureship in Devon, he moved to York, in his native county, where he became lecturer at All Saints'. His first

1. Heylyn, *Cyprianus Anglicus* (1671), p. 120; Laud, *Works*, V, pp. 328, 334; N. Bacon, *Annals of Ipswich* (1880), pp. 419, 424, 433, 518, 523–4 (first published in 1654); *C.S.P.D.*, *1635–6*, pp. xxxii–lx.

2. *C.S.P.D.*, *1635*, p. xxxiii.

3. J. F. Chanter, "The Parish Clerks of Barnstaple, 1500–1900", in *Report and Transactions of the Devonshire Association for the Advancement of Science, Literature and Art*, XXXVI, pp. 401–3.

4. J. F. Chanter, *The Life and Times of Martin Blake* (1910), pp. 33–5, 49–51, 62–4.

5. *V.C.H.*, *York*, pp. 152, 201.

sermon caused him to be summoned by Archbishop Neile, who told him he had heard that Shaw was "brought in by the Lord Mayor of York to head the Puritan faction against me". Only the fact that Neile knew Shaw was chaplain to the Earl of Pembroke saved him.[1]

At Berwick too there were squabbles throughout the early decades of the seventeenth century, between the vicar and his lecturer. The vicar received a bare 20 marks from the Dean and Chapter of Durham, the impropriators, plus a pension of £40 from the King, which was paid irregularly and with large defalcations. The lecturer was originally maintained by voluntary subscriptions, but from about 1630 the Mercers' Company of London gave him £50 per annum. In 1637, in conjunction with Robert Fenwick (the "prime man" of the puritan faction in Berwick) the Mercers appointed John Jennett to this lectureship. He proved so unsatisfactory to authority, in this key military post, that in November 1639 Charles I wrote to the Company asking them to suspend him. The King tactfully took it for granted that the Mercers had not been aware of Jennett's factious disposition when they appointed him, and asked for him to be replaced by George Sydserf, an episcopalian refugee from Scotland.[2] In Newcastle-on-Tyne the lecturer was appointed by the mayor, aldermen and common council, and his salary was increased or diminished as they thought fit. In 1639 a Puritan lecturer was deprived. The vicar complained to Laud of "those mischiefs and inconveniences which had heretofore happened and may again arise in this corporation through the multiplicity of lecturers".[3]

There were many more quarrels and disagreements – e.g. between rival parties at Lincoln for many years after 1602,

1. *The Life of Master John Shaw*, in *Yorkshire Diaries and Autobiographies in the 17th and 18th centuries* (Surtees Soc., 1875), p. 129; Marchant, *The Puritans and the Church Courts in the Diocese of York*, p. 277. See p. 91 above.

2. *C.S.P.D.*, *1636–7*, pp. 549–50; *1637–8*, pp. 60–1; *1638–9*, pp. 217–18; *1639*, pp. 104, 393. The Mercers had also established a lectureship at Hexham under Fishbourne's will (*City of Exeter MSS.*, H.M.C., pp. 195–6).

3. R. Welford, *A History of Newcastle and Gateshead in the 15th–17th centuries* (1887), III, pp. 164–5, 368–81; cf. *C.S.P.D.*, *1639–40*, pp. 384–5. The burgesses of Newcastle were Puritans, the gentry in the surrounding countryside papists almost to a man (Welford, *op cit.*, III, p. 209).

when John Smyth was city preacher;[1] between the vicar and the mayor and jurats of Rye in 1623–5;[2] between vicar and lecturer at Grantham in 1627;[3] at Leeds, Bradford and Beverley in the 'thirties;[4] between corporation and dean and chapter at Worcester.[5] There were long disputes at Shrewsbury in the 'thirties, in which the Privy Council ultimately intervened.[6] Hull, the first city to oppose Charles I in the civil war had, Hacket thought, been corrupted by its lecturers, one of whom was Andrew Marvell, father of the poet.[7] It is interesting to reflect that the other two towns which held up Charles's advance on London in 1643, Plymouth and Gloucester, may have been similarly influenced by their lecturers.[8] In civil wars the factor of morale is apt to be more decisive than generalship or military experience.

London, Heylyn tells us, set the example to other towns in establishing lectureships as well as in other "innovations". For in London the beneficed clergy were so meanly provided for that they had to augment their livings. One way of doing this was to undertake lectures, "in the hope that gaining the good will thereby of the chief in their parish they might be gratified by them with entertainments, presents and some other helps to mend their maintenance. Lecturers", Heylyn added, "as being creatures of the people, and depending wholly on the purse of the wealthier citizens, . . . overtopped them [the beneficed clergy] in power, reputation, and generally profit and revenue too".[9] That is an interesting piece of evidence for

1. Hill, *Tudor and Stuart Lincoln*, pp. 101–16, 166, 227–32.

2. *Rye Corporation MSS.* (H.M.C.), pp. 162, 174.

3. Gardiner, *History of England*, VII, p. 16.

4. Marchant, *The Puritans and the Church Courts in the Diocese of York*, pp. 116–17, 239, 271–2.

5. I. G. Smith and P. Onslow, *Worcester* (Diocesan Histories, 1883), pp. 231–2; W. Urwick, *Nonconformity in Worcestershire* (1897), pp. 28–34; *C.S.P.D., 1629–31*, pp. 266–7, 287; *V.C.H. Worcestershire*, II, pp. 63–6.

6. *C.S.P.D., 1637–8*, pp. 58–9; and see pp. 94–5 above. See also J. H. Thomas, *Town Government in the 16th century* (1933), p. 27, for an ingenious device by which the Shrewsbury corporation endowed their lecturer in 1582.

7. J. Hacket, *Scrinia Reserata* (1693), II, p. 186; cf. Marchant, *The Puritans and the Church Courts in the Diocese of York*, pp. 118, 121. The father of another poet, William Crashawe, had been lecturer of Beverley only a few miles away.

8. See pp. 74, 102–3 above.

9. Heylyn, *Cyprianus Anglicus*, p. 282. Cf. H. Burton, *A Censure of Simonie* (1624), p. 105, for profitability of lectureships.

the popularity and profitability of lectureships, at least in the capital.

By 1583 nearly 1 in 3 of London's parishes had lectureships. Some lecturers were elected by congregations. Most were paid by voluntary contributions, and could be dismissed at will.[1] A few were endowed, including St. Antholin's.[2] As more and more wealthy citizens left money to endow lectureships in the seventeenth century, so the position of lecturers became more secure. Among the puritan lecturers in London we may mention Thomas Sampson, Henry Smith, Thomas Gataker and Richard Greenham; John Field, until his suspension in 1585; and among the pre-revolutionary generation John Downame, Thomas Taylor, John Stoughton, Thomas Edwards, Henry Burton, Thomas Foxley, John Archer, Hugh Peter, Edmund Calamy.[3] When John Brinsley was dismissed from being minister and schoolmaster at Ashby-de-la-Zouch he came to London as a lecturer.[4]

There were quarrels in London as in other towns. At St. Botolph's some unknown "well-disposed persons" bestowed a lecture upon the parish, to which Thomas Edwards was appointed, with the approval of Thomas Swadlin, the minister. It was alleged that Swadlin had received a promise of £30 a year for his good will. Despite this, and despite Edwards' declaration of conformity to the Church of England, he was dismissed by Laud in 1629 "for causes unknown".[5] At East Ham it was alleged that the pluralist William Fairfax refused to let the parish have a lecturer on Sunday afternoons unless he was paid £50; and that for eight years he blocked a weekday lecture which had been endowed by testament and a lecturer appointed. Fairfax was naturally included in the *First Century of Scandalous Ministers*.[6] Edward Finch, vicar of

1. Owen, "Lectures and Lectureships", pp. 65, 67–8, 74.

2. See next page.

3. Owen, *op. cit.*, p. 69; "Tradition and Reform: Ecclesiastical Controversy in an Elizabethan London Parish", *The Guildhall Miscellany*, II, 2 (1961), pp. 3, 7; Collinson, "John Field and Elizabethan Puritanism", in *Elizabethan Government and Society* (ed. Bindoff, Hurstfield and Williams, 1961), pp. 143, 150; Pearl, *London and the Outbreak of the Puritan Revolution*, pp. 165–6. Samuel Purchas maintained himself by lecturing.

4. William Lilly, *History of His Life and Times* (1826), pp. 12–13.

5. *C.S.P.D.*, *1628–9*, pp. 543, 593; *1629–31*, p. 1.

6. Davids, *Nonconformity in Essex*, pp. 233–4.

Christ Church, and William Grant, vicar of Isleworth, were likewise accused by their parishioners in 1641 of accepting payments to permit a lecturer to preach in their churches, and then withdrawing from the bargain without returning the money. Finch admitted the accusation.[1] The parishioners of St. Martin Orgar said that Brian Walton neither preached himself on Sunday afternoons nor would allow them to hire anyone else to do so, though he demanded £20 a year "for afternoon sermons" for himself.[2]

In the very puritan parish of St. Antholin's, money subscribed and invested for the maintenance of six lecturers brought in about £70 a year. To this sum the Chamber of London added £40 between 1622 and 1630. In consideration of this the Court of Aldermen demanded the right to nominate when a vacancy occurred. But a rival with even greater available financial resources appeared on the scene. Some time between 1625 and 1628 the Feoffees for Impropriations began to augment the stipend of each of the lecturers to £30 per annum, and therefore also insisted on the right to nominate. After a brief skirmish the City fathers recognized defeat, and discontinued their contribution in 1630.[3] In 1635 the lecturers of Aldermanbury, St. Margaret's, New Fish St., St. Swithin's and St. Lawrence, Old Jewry, were all in trouble with the Bishop of London.[4]

VI

The bishops had less control over lecturers than over parochial clergy, especially when a preacher enjoyed the support of a corporation or an influential gentleman. But in theory at least lecturers were not completely independent. The Canons of 1604 provided that they were to be licensed by an archbishop, a bishop or one of the two universities, after sub-

1. *E.P.C.*, p. 301, and references there cited.
2. *The Articles aud Charge proved in Parliament against Dr. Walton, Minister of St. Martins Orgars* (1641), p. 4. There was also trouble over a lecturer at St. Giles-in-the-Fields (*C.S.P.D.*, *1628–9*, pp. 416–17).
3. *Ibid.*, p. 495; D. A. Williams, "Puritanism in the City Government, 1610–40", *Guildhall Miscellany*, No. 4, 1955, pp. 4–8; see *E.P.C.*, pp. 259–60.
4. Laud, *Works*, V, p. 333; I. M. Calder, "The St. Antholin's Lectures" *Church Quarterly Review*, CLX, p. 52.

scribing to the royal supremacy, the Prayer Book and the Thirty-nine Articles. In 1606, under Bancroft, all preachers were re-licensed. In 1622 James ordered that lecturers were to be licensed by the Court of Faculties only, on presentation of a written recommendation from the bishop of their diocese, the fiat of the Archbishop of Canterbury and confirmation under the Great Seal.[1]

But in the relatively lenient interlude between the death of Bancroft and Laud's rise to political dominance, no steady pressure came from Lambeth to carry out these instructions. Abbot seems to have disliked the campaign against lecturers.[2] Lionel Cranfield, Bishop Goodman's merchant friend who rose to be Lord Treasurer, even proposed that clerical poverty should be ended by using impropriations to finance conformable lecturers.[3] But conformable lecturers were rare. Much seems to have been left to the discretion of each bishop in his diocese. Miles Smith, Bishop of Gloucester from 1612 to 1624, was even reputed to countenance lecturers against the lawful minister of the parish.[4] The high-flying Neile of Lincoln, on the other hand, inquired searchingly after lecturers in nine towns of his great diocese in his visitation of 1614. Lectureships, his registrar thought, encourage "factious spirits", who are "so desirous to preach in other men's parishes upon working days" that they "very seldom or never preached upon the saints' days in their own".[5] In the Addled Parliament Nicholas Fuller accused Neile, *inter alia*, of suppressing lecturers in his diocese.[6] Another high-flyer, John Cosin, in his 1627 visitation of the archdeaconry of the East Riding could ask whether lecturers travelled about the country from one church to another; who paid them; whether they meddled with civil matters "in rude and undecent reviling of persons"; or whether they chiefly laboured "to exhort the people unto

1. Rushworth, *Historical Collections*, I, p. 65.
2. P. A. Welsby, *George Abbot* (1962), p. 137.
3. R. H. Tawney, *Business and Politics under James I* (1958), p. 282.
4. Heylyn, *Cyprianus Anglicus*, p. 64.
5. Venables, "The Primary Visitation of the Diocese of Lincoln by Bishop Neile, A.D. 1614", *Associated Architectural Socs.' Reports*, XVI (1881), p. 47.
6. T. L. Moir, *The Addled Parliament of 1614* (1958), p. 126. Neile was also said to demonstrate his lack of enthusiasm for preaching by sleeping during sermons.

obedience, peace and justice".[1] But the harrying of lecturers only became official policy again under Laud.

In March 1629 Laud submitted a series of suggestions to the King, including a number of proposals about lecturers, of whom he thought "a special care" should be taken. For lecturers, by their economic dependence, were "the people's creatures, and blow the bellows of their sedition". Laud made four suggestions for abating the lecturers' power:

"(1) That the afternoon sermons in all parishes may be turned into catechizing by questions and answers, according to an order set out by King James of blessed memory. If this cannot be, then

"(2) That every bishop ordain in his diocese that every lecturer do read divine service in his surplice before the lecture.

"(3) That when a lecture is set up in a market town, it is read by a combination of grave and orthodox divines near adjoining.

"(4) That if an incorporation do maintain a lecturer, he be not suffered to preach till he take upon him cure of souls within that incorporation".[2]

These suggestions were issued in the same year, with only trifling alterations, as Instructions from the King to Archbishop Abbot.[3] The object of this part of the Instructions, Heylyn makes it clear, was to keep "the greatest part of the rigid Calvinists" out of lectureships.[4] Bishops were to arrange to have spies to report on lecturers' sermons, and were to suffer none below the rank of peer, or men otherwise legally qualified, to keep private chaplains in their houses. Laud himself summoned all the ministers and lecturers in his diocese of London

---

1. Ed. G. Ornsby, *The Correspondence of John Cosin* (Surtees Soc., 1868), I, pp. 122–3.

2. Rushworth, *Historical Collections, II*, pp. 7–8.

3. In the Instructions, clauses (1) and (2) of Laud's suggestions became supplementary, not alternatives, to clause (3); since combination lecturers were not always reliable (see p. 80 above), a provision was added that the grave and orthodox divines should all be of the same diocese, and should preach in gowns, not cloaks "as too many do use"; in clause (4), profession of willingness to take a living with cure of souls was sufficient, provided the lecturer "actually take such benefice or cure so soon as it shall be fairly procured for him" (Rushworth, *op. cit.*, II, 30–2). See *C.S.P.D., 1629–31*, for enquiries by Bishop Wright of Bristol whether a lecturer paid by the Chamber of the City was to be regarded as a lecturer maintained by a corporation.

4. Heylyn, *Cyprianus Anglicus*, pp. 189–91.

and insisted on their obedience to these Instructions.[1]

After the suppression of the Feoffees for Impropriations in 1633 Laud, now archbishop, made a serious attempt to put an end to lectureships altogether. In September a royal letter forbade bishops to ordain ministers unless to undertake a cure of souls.[2] In January 1634 the Instructions of 1629 were reissued, this time with Laud in a position to make sure that all the bishops took them seriously. The archbishop's annual accounts of his Province drawn up for the King are full of the battle of the lecturers. Thus in 1633 the Bishop of Coventry and Lichfield had suppressed several lecturers; the Bishop of Llandaff proudly reported that he had only two lecturers in his diocese. Bishop Pierce of Bath and Wells had put down several lecturers in market towns because, being beneficed outside his diocese, the lecturers were apt to retire from his jurisdiction when he wished to proceed against them. At Bridgwater Robert Blake was one of those who protested when Pierce suspended the minister for preaching a lecture in his own church on a market day.[3] But notwithstanding protests, Pierce was soon able to boast that "thank God, he had not one lecturer left in his diocese". Suppression of lecturers was one of the articles charged against this bishop in his impeachment of 1641.[4]

In the diocese of Norwich a determined attempt was made to abolish "that ratsbane of lecturing, . . . the virulence whereof hath intoxicated many thousands". All weekly lectures were put down.[5] Neile in 1635 reported a welcome decrease in the number of market-day lecturers in the diocese of York.[6] The

1. For the rigour with which they were enforced, see Wilton Hall, *Records of the Old Archdeaconry of St. Albans*, p. 155.

2. Cardwell, *Documentary Annals*, II, pp. 182–3.

3. H. Dixon, *Robert Blake* (1852), p. 27.

4. Laud, *Works*, V, pp. 319–21, 334, 339, 349; Heylyn, *Cyprianus Anglicus*, p. 294; Prynne, *The Second Part of the Antipathie of the English Lordly Prelacie both to regall Monarchy, and Civill Unitie* (1641), unnumbered pages between pp. 304 and 305.

5. Charles Corbett, Chancellor of the Diocese, to Matthew Wren, 3 June 1636, Tanner MS. 68, f. 2 (I owe this reference to Mr. Boorman's unpublished Oxford B.Litt. thesis). See also letters from Robert Reyce to John Winthrop, in *Massachusetts Historical Soc. Collections*, 4th Series, VI, pp. 409–13. The resultant "famine", Reyce thought, was a punishment for "our high contempt of the Word when we had it abundantly".

6. Marchant, *The Puritans and the Church Courts in the Diocese of York*, p. 129.

visitation articles of Laud himself, and of Bishops Wren and Montagu, show how narrowly lecturers might be inquired into, and how political was the bishops' interest. "Doth he intermeddle with matters of state, government, foreign from his profession, above his understanding? Doth he gird at the discipline of the church?"[1] If lecturers set up a lecture of their own authority on working days, Wren later admitted in reply to the articles of impeachment "and so to draw a conflux of the country people . . . from their houses and from their labours", it might well be that he advised a chancellor or commissary to inhibit them.[2] When Laud forbade any afternoon sermons at all, this instruction was carried out at least by Neile and Wren.[3]

Any bishop who showed lack of enthusiasm for the good work was himself closely watched. Joseph Hall learnt that he was complained of at Court because he willingly gave way "to orthodox and peaceable lecturers in several parts of my diocese" of Exeter.[4] Bishop Dove of Peterborough also claimed to have taken no action against peaceable and conformable lecturers.[5] Goodman of Gloucester put down some lectures and set up others, "which he conceives he did without offence", Laud reported drily in 1634, "being done upon different occasions". Charles I underlined the word "occasions", and commented "I must be satisfied that the occasions were very necessary, otherwise he shall answer it".[6] Goodman was no favourer of Puritans, but he might well have been lazy; or he might have been recompensing himself for the poverty of his see, to which he had often drawn the government's attention. Heylyn suggested that some bishops in the poorer sees had been making money by admitting all and sundry to holy orders.[7] In the diocese of Lincoln, of which the recalcitrant John Williams was Bishop, Laud was informed that the vicar of Chalfont St. Peter, who wanted to catechize in the after-

1. *H.M.C., Second Report, Appendix*, p. 108; Prynne, *Canterburies Doome*, pp. 375–8; Cardwell, *Documentary Annals*, II, p. 206; Montagu, *Articles of Enquiry and Direction for the Diocese of Norwich* (1638).

2. Wren, *Parentalia*, p. 88.

3. Cardwell, *Documentary Annals*, II, p. 178; Marchant, *op. cit.*, pp. 55, 65.

4. J. Hall, *Works*, I, p. xxxv.

5. *Buccleugh MSS., Montague House* (H.M.C.), I, p. 275.

6. Laud, *Works*, V, p. 330.

7. See p. 84 above.

noon, was "violently importuned" to lecture "by some new-comers to the parish, namely by one Mr. Penington, a citizen". The vicar yielded, since he was "wonderful timorous . . . as all the rest of the clergy in these parts are, because they are overawed by the justices and lay gentry". The parts were Puritan, and Penington was to be a supporter of Pym in the Long Parliament, and Lord Mayor of London after the revolution of 1641–2. "In this county", Laud's informant continued, "where government, both ecclesiastical and civil, is so slackly looked unto, men of some little pretty worldly fortunes are persuaded that they may say or do anything both against government and governors (both ecclesiastical or laic) without check or controlment".[1]

By 1638, Heylyn thought, most lecturers had been outed. They survived only "where they had a constant or certain maintenance, or where they had become more pliant or conformable".[2] In London, Prynne agrees, they had been virtually suppressed. Even in the cathedrals they were some-times put down,[3] though in 1641 Hacket was to plead their provision of week-day lectures in defence of deans and chap-ters.[4] And in 1640 when Mr. Rudge of Evesham left money to the churchwardens for a lecturer, to be appointed by four London Puritan ministers, he provided that if the lecture were "prohibited by authority", the money should go to the poor of the parish.[5]

Many lecturers emigrated, some persuading their congrega-tions to accompany them.[6] The few conforming lecturers who survived could not meet the demands of their congregations for preaching. "If they did not fancy the man, the church was half empty", Wren tells us. "Mr. Cock, an honest, conform-able man", who lectured in Norwich, had little support from

1. W. H. Summers, "State Papers relating to Beaconsfield", *Records of Bucks*, VII, p. 110.

2. Heylyn, *Cyprianus Anglicus*, pp. 342–3.

3. Prynne, *Canterburies Doome*, p. 373; cf. Laud, *Works*, V, pp. 343, 348, 492.

4. Fuller, *Church History* (1842), III, p. 420.

5. Smith and Onslow, *Worcester* (Diocesan Histories), pp. 234–6.

6. Heylyn, *Cyprianus Anglicus*, p. 344; cf. Miller and Johnson. *The Puritans*, pp. 117–18, 490; and *E.P.C.*, pp. 260, 266; B. M. Levy "Preaching in the first half century of New England History", *American Soc. of Church History, Studies in Church History*, VI (1945), p. 11.

the citizens.[1] Congregations would conclude that, so long as the Laudian régime survived, they could not have the preaching they wanted even by paying for it. "The word preaching is obsolete", Robert Reyce wrote to Winthrop in September 1636.[2] But it was shortly to be resurrected; and with it many of the *émigré* lecturers returned.

VII

In 1614 the "graver and learneder sort of men" in Neile's diocese of Lincoln had advised that high-flyer not utterly to extinguish lecturing, "since that would make a clamour in the country as though your lordship was the enemy to the preaching of the Gospel".[3] The Laudians took no heed of this sensible advice, and so there was some ground for the charges brought against the bishops in 1641–2, that they had tried to suppress certain types of preaching altogether. Falkland, who was to die defending the royal cause in the civil war, declared in a speech of 8 February 1641 that the bishops "have brought in catechizing only to thrust out preaching, cried down lecturers by the name of factions, either because other men's industry in that duty appeared a reproof of their neglect of it . . . or with intention to have brought in darkness that they may the easier sow their tares while it was night; and by that introduction of ignorance, introduce the better that religion which accounts it the mother of devotion".[4] George Wither, even more confidently, saw Jesus Christ as a persecuted lecturer:

> "*Possession of his house he got,*
> *The merchants thence expelled;*
> *And though the priests were mad thereat*
> *His lectures there he held*".[5]

Archbishop Laud argued that he suppressed afternoon sermons to preserve peace between ministers and people, the lecturers being for the most part factious, and the occasion of great contentions in the parishes where they preached.[6] But the

1. Prynne, *Canterburies Doome*, p. 375.
2. *Massachusetts Historical Soc. Collections*, 4th series, VI, p. 408.
3. Venables, "Primary Visitation of the Diocese of Lincoln", p. 47.
4. J. A. R. Marriott, *The Life and Times of Lucius Cary, Viscount Falkland* (1907), pp. 182–3.
5. G. Wither, *Hymns and Songs of the Church* (1856), p. 194. First published 1623.
6. Prynne, *Canterburies Doome*, p. 537.

House of Commons would be more impressed by the analysis made by Matthew Newcomen, the Smectymnuan, in a sermon preached before them on 5 November 1642. Newcomen described what he believed to have been a subtle plot for the destruction of true religion and the advancing of popery. "To suspend all the orthodox preachers in the land at once would have made too great a noise; therefore proceed by degrees. And first suspend all lecturers which will not constantly practice the ceremonies. Then, after a little pause, clap down all lecturers as an order of vagrants not to be tolerated in the Church. When that is done, forbid all pastors and incumbents preaching in their own parish churches upon week days. Next inhibit preaching upon the Lord's Day in the afternoon, under pretence of advancing catechizing by that means: and yet within a little while after forbidding all catechistical exposition, tying men to the bare words of the primer catechism; as soon after they forbade all praying but in the words of the Canon. Now what can any ingenious man think the design of all this was, but to rob us of preaching and praying?"[1]

Newcomen's audience would not find it difficult to accept his argument. Laud may not have wanted to put down preaching as such. But he certainly wanted to stop the sort of preaching which the influential members of many congregations wished to hear. It is this wider divergence of interest which we must have in mind if we are to appreciate the reasons which led respectable conservatives like Falkland and Newcomen to make the accusations they did.

The friars had been silenced; but in the generations between Reformation and Revolution little had been done to provide protestant preachers in their place. Ultimately it was the Baptists, the Seekers and especially the Quakers who were to fill – with very new wine – the bottles emptied a century earlier. This fact suggests reflections about the decades before 1640. The conservative Puritans hoped then, through parish ministers and lecturers, to be able to supply the preaching which public opinion demanded, without disrupting the national Church. Their approach was reformist where that of the sectaries was to be revolutionary. The preachers had a double

1. M. Newcomen, *The Craft and Cruelty of the Churches Adversaries* (1642), pp. 25–6. The sermon was printed by order of the House of Commons.

battle to fight – against the hierarchy which wished to prevent them instructing and arousing their congregations, and against the sectarian separatism into which the mere repression of the hierarchy threatened to drive the sober and conscientious section of the middle and lower classes.[1] This perhaps helps us to understand in retrospect not only why a preaching ministry and a godly discipline were so closely associated in the minds of conservative Puritans, but also why uncontrolled separatism and mechanic preaching at once appeared when the hierarchy was overthrown.

VIII

In 1641 the House of Commons reversed what had seemed to be Laud's victory over the lecturers. On September 7th Stephen Marshall, preaching before the House, had reminded members that there was much still to be done. "The ministry is not purged. . . . Great cities and towns, and many thousand other places in the kingdom, want bread for their souls".[2] Next day, on petition from the parishioners of Stepney for permission to set up a Sunday lecture, and on the motion of Oliver Cromwell, who no doubt remembered St. Ives and Huntingdon, the House ordered "It shall be lawful for the parishioners of any parish . . . to set up a lecture, and to maintain an orthodox minister at their own charge to preach every Lord's Day where there is no preaching, and to preach one day in every week where there is no weekly lecture".[3]

The House of Lords, always more conservative on such issues than the House of Commons, got this order shelved two months later. But it had started activities from below which could not so easily be checked. Petitions flowed in from parishes anxious to set up lectures and elect lecturers. Ministers in their turn complained that to have lecturers forced upon them was an invasion of their freehold rights in their livings.[4] Many were the battles waged in the parishes for the control of this key position, with the House of Commons frequently

1. See pp. 50–5 above and Chapter IV below.
2. S. Marshall, *A Peace-Offering to God* (1641), quoted by Haller, *Liberty and Reformation in the Puritan Revolution*, p. 28.
3. Nalson, *An Impartial Collection*, II, p. 477; see pp. 91–2 above.
4. W. A. Shaw, *History of the English Church . . . 1640–1660* (1900), II, pp. 184, 300–6.

intervening to insist, under threat of penalty, that ministers must allow the lecturers chosen by the parish free use of their pulpits.[1] We get a vivid picture of the struggle between the old order and the new spirit in a letter from the vicar of Cranbrook to his M.P., asking for support against his parishioners who wanted "to force a lecturer upon me" of their own choice and paid by them. The vicar declared that he was "resolute yet, that no man shall possess my pulpit against my will, who am settled in it by law". He wanted only to enjoy his £100 a year in peace, with a "humble and quiet-spirited man" as lecturer "who would not cross shins with me to the fomenting of popular spirits against laws. . . . To have my conscience, credit and pains trampled upon by my people after 24 years is an hard task, to say no more".[2] In St. Matthew's parish, London, the parishioners tried to reinstate Henry Burton in the cure from which he had been dispossessed. The incumbent resisted, whereupon "some of the factious of the parish combined to make him [Burton] their lecturer", and by 1642 he was back in the parsonage, the intruding Mr. Chestlin having been deprived as a seditious preacher.[3]

Under the circumstances it is hardly surprising that many lecturers became ardent propagandists for the Parliamentary cause. "Furious promoters of the most dangerous innovations", Charles I called them in August 1642; in October 1643 he referred to the agitation, "under the pretence of religion, in pulpits and prayers and sermons of many seditious lecturers, to stir up and continue the rebellion raised against us".[4] "To blow up the people into a perfect rebellion", wrote Dugdale, "they appointed weekly lectures to be generally set up; which was accordingly performed by the most seditious and turbulent spirits that could be found".[5] Nalson wrote in the same vein of the "spiritual militia of these lecturers". "These were the men that debauched the people with principles of disloyalty, and

1. See, e.g. *C. J.*, II, pp. 673, 735, 864, 909; cf. R. Culmer, *Cathedrall Newes from Canterbury* (1644), p. 3.

2. Quoted in *The Journal of Sir Simonds D'Ewes* (ed. W. H. Coates, Yale University Press, 1942), p. 20.

3. [B. Ryves], *Angliae Ruina* (1647), pp. 147–51. For Chestlin see p. 93 above.

4. Charles I's *Declaration* of 12 August 1642; Rushworth, *Historical Collections*, V, p. 364.

5. Dugdale, *The Late Troubles in England*, pp. 87–8.

taught them to worship . . . the pretended liberty of the subject, and the glorious reformation that was coming; which the common people adored. . . . These hirelings . . . preached many deluded souls out of their lives by a flagrant rebellion; and were so far from advancing the gospel of peace that they sounded the trumpet for war; and always their pulpit harangues to the people were the repeated echoes of the votes, orders, remonstrances and declarations of Westminster".[1]

Such statements no doubt exaggerate: yet the political importance of lecturers was sufficient for them to be specifically included in one draft of the Newcastle Propositions of 1646: "that liberty be given to all ministers though they cannot conform to the present government in all things, being not sequestered or sequestrable, to preach any lecture or lectures in any church or chapel where they shall be desired by the inhabitants thereof", provided that it be not at such hours as the minister preaches.[2]

This was a logical consequence of the position into which most lecturers had been forced in the decades before 1640. They arose in order to preach a theology, usually puritan, which seems to have been more acceptable, at least to urban congregations, than that which was preached by most of the parochial clergy. The opposition of the hierarchy to their views, and to their economic dependence on their congregations, which was both cause and effect of those views, drove them to associate their liberty to preach with the assertion of Parliament's dominance in the state. So when civil war broke out the majority of them naturally felt that God's cause was at stake. The only danger was that some of them might go too far. Lecturers, said a conservative pamphleteer in 1641, should be chosen only by scot and lot householders, not by the poor.[3] So the lower orders were driven into the arms of the sectaries, many of whom in any case preached a scheme of universal salvation much more acceptable for mass consumption (given free consumers' choice) than the narrow predestinarianism of the orthodox ministers and lecturers.

After the Restoration, naturally, lecturers lost their privileged position. But since ministers also lost the augmentations

1. Nalson, *An Impartial Collection*, II, p. 478.
2. Ed. T. Birch, *Thurloe State Papers* (1742), I, p. 83.
3. [Anon.], *Good Workes* (1641), pp. 8–9.

which they had enjoyed during the revolutionary period, the economic need for lectureships still remained. And during the revolution the Anglicans had found that they too could make use of lectures.[1] The restored bishops were mainly concerned to see that lecturers were subordinated to the parish clergy and the hierarchy.[2] Some post-Restoration bishops actually took the initiative in instituting lectureships.[3] Funds originally intended to support Puritans were absorbed by the hierarchy to maintain its nominees, contrary to the intentions of the donors.[4] The Act of Uniformity stipulated that lecturers should be licensed by the archbishop or a bishop, should assent to the Thirty-nine Articles, and should always read the Book of Common Prayer.[5] This was a return to the Canons of 1604, an abandonment of the attempt to get rid of lecturers altogether. Burnet called it "maintaining conformity to the height",[6] but it was not being maintained in the way that Laud, Neile and Wren had wished. The restoration atmosphere was very different from that of the Laudian decade. With the subsequent rise of licensed non-conformity the whole position was transformed.

1. G. B. Tatham, *The Puritans in Power* (1908), pp. 229–32; R. S. Bosher, *The Making of the Restoration Settlement* (1951), p. 12.
2. *Reliquiae Baxterianae*, I, p. 175.
3. Bosher, *op. cit.*, pp. 235–6.
4. Jordan, *Philanthropy in England*, p. 52.
5. 14 Car. II cap. xxiv; cf. Cardwell, *Documentary Annals*, II, p. 273.
6. G. Burnet, *The History of My Own Time* (1897), I, p. 322.

Chapter Four

The Industrious Sort of People

Whereas all other creatures live unto themselves, man was appointed to live as well to others as to himself: the church, the country, the family, the poor, every man challengeth a part in every man. . . . Ask thyself then, "What good doth my life to church, to commonwealth, to family, to men?" and if thy conscience answer "Truly, little or none" then must thou conclude "Surely I am rather a belly than a man." But many such bellies want ears.

> T. Taylor, *A Commentary upon the Epistle of St. Paul written unto Titus* (1658), p. 183.

Be ashamed of idleness as thou art a man, but tremble at it as thou art a Christian. . . . What more wretched estate can there be in the world? First to be hated of God as an idle drone, not fit for His service; then through extreme poverty to be contemned of all the world.

> Elizabeth Jocelinc, *The Mothers Legacie to her unborne Childe* (1632), pp. 27–9.

I

MR COLEMAN has expressed in usefully modern terms the besetting problem of seventeenth-century society. It was the problem of any backward economy – failure to use the full human resources of the country. Mr. Coleman gives many examples of voluntary underemployment arising from the social habits of the community – idleness on saints' days,[1] the instability of labour and its lack of regularity to which the Statute of Artificers bears witness, the habit of working short

1. See pp. 142–5 below.

time when wages were high. So long as there are few consumer goods within the purchasing power of the mass of the population, there is little incentive to earn more than the subsistence minimum wage.[1] Petty recorded how far England was from the classical model of a supply-and-demand economy. "It is observed by clothiers and others who employ great numbers of poor people, that when corn is extremely plentiful . . . the labour of the poor is proportionably dear, and scarce to be had at all (so licentious are they who labour only to eat, or rather to drink)". Prices must be kept up if men are to be made to labour.[2] Until men work harder there will be no cheap consumer goods. An ideology advocating regular systematic work was required if the country was to break through this vicious circle to economic advance. "Hunger and poverty make men industrious", observed Sir Walter Ralegh;[3] but the ministers could help too.

The Statute of Artificers and the Act of 1597–8 for the maintenance of husbandry and tillage included idleness, drunkenness and unlawful games among the "lewd practices and conditions of life" which interfered with agricultural or industrial production.[4] Thomas Mun referred in the early sixteen-twenties to "the general leprosy of our piping, potting, feasting, factions and mis-spending of our time in idleness and pleasure", which placed England at such a disadvantage in commercial competition with the industrious Dutch.[5] George Herbert's Parson thought that idleness was "the great and national sin of this land";[6] its "*malus genius*", Robert Burton

1. D. C. Coleman, "Labour in the English Economy of the 17th century", *Econ. H.R.*, Second Series, VIII, pp. 290–2; cf. R. H. Hilton, "Y eut-il une crise générale de la féodalité?", *Annales*, Jan.–March, 1951, p. 29.

2. Ed. C. H. Hull, *Economic Writings of Sir William Petty* (1899), I, pp. 274–5.

3. Sir Walter Ralegh, *Works* (1751), I, p. 107.

4. Ed. Tawney and Power, *Tudor Economic Documents*, I, pp. 360, 384.

5. T. Mun, *England's Treasure by Forraign Trade*, reprinted in J. R. McCulloch, *Early Tracts on Commerce* (1856), p. 193; cf. L. Roberts, *The Treasure of Traffike, ibid.*, p. 34.

6. G. Herbert, *A Priest to the Temple*, Chapter xxxii; cf. R. Carew, *A Survey of Cornwall* (1811), pp. 185–6; Ralph Venning, *Orthodox Paradoxes* (Howe's Reprints, n.d.), p. 54. This last named work was first published in 1657.

agreed.[1] Robert Sanderson in 1625 denounced "riot and excess" as "the noted proper sin of this nation".[2] This view was held not only by Englishmen, like Fynes Moryson in 1617; even a French visitor like Sorbière in 1663 thought the English were "naturally lazy and spend half their time taking tobacco".[3] The country's shortage of skilled labour even in the early seventeenth century was shown by the Virginia Company's importation of Dutchmen, Swedes, Poles and Frenchmen to supervise every industry which it attempted to establish in America.[4] The object of this chapter is to survey some of the ways in which Puritanism helped in the task of imposing labour discipline.[5]

II

Professor Haller has some shrewd words on the economic application of Puritanism which are of relevance for our present purposes:

"The unloveliness of [the puritan] code in some of its later manifestations should not blind us to its positive and bracing effect upon common life in Stuart times. The merry England doomed by puritan asceticism was not all cakes and ale, may-pole dancing and frolics on the village green". In face of the "social chaos and moral corruption of many a swollen town and decaying country neighbourhood", the Anglican Church seemed to be "being used simply as a bulwark to protect privilege against reform": it gave little spiritual guidance. The puritan preachers were trying "to adapt Christian morality to the needs of a population which was being steadily driven from its old feudal status into the untried conditions of competition between man and man in an increasingly commercial and industrial society under a money economy".[6] It is the limitation

1. R. Burton, *The Anatomy of Melancholy* (Everyman ed.), I, p. 88; cf. II, pp. 139–40.

2. R. Sanderson, *XXXV Sermons* (1681), p. 129; cf. pp. 87 97, 197–9, and Jeremy Taylor, *The Whole Works* (1836), III, p. 727.

3. F. Moryson, *An Itinerary* (1617), Part III, p. 147; S. Sorbière, *A Voyage to England* (1709), p. 54.

4. S. M. Kingsbury, *An Introduction to the Records of the Virginia Company of London* (1905), p. 105.

5. Cf. Archdeacon W. Cunningham, *The Moral Witness of the Church on the Investment of Money and the Use of Wealth* (1909), p. 25.

6. Haller, *The Rise of Puritanism*, pp. 116–17; cf. V. G. Kiernan, "Puritanism and the Poor", *P. and P.*, No. 3, pp. 45–51.

of national resources, and the backwardness of the country's economic organization, especially its organization of labour, that accounts for the severity towards idleness shown not only by the poor law but also by charitable Puritans.[1]

Problems of labour discipline were of general concern to statesmen and divines during our period. As early as 1536 Richard Morison stressed the importance of hard work in a pamphlet entitled *A Remedy for Sedition*, written as propaganda to convince the northern rebels.[2] Edward VI in his *Discourse about the Reformation of Many Abuses* also dealt with the training of youths in agriculture and the crafts, and with the punishment of vagabonds.[3] Industrial slavery was introduced into England for a short time during his reign, and the forced labour provided by the English Statute of Artificers of 1563 and the Scottish Act of 1663 was little better.[4] An anonymous commentator on the English Act in 1573, and Burghley in 1581, had the same concern for the prevention of idleness, whether stimulated by unlawful games or by multiplicity of taverns.[5] Sir Edward Coke thought that education of the youth in industry, and the execution of good laws to set the idle on work, would prevent the "lamentable case" of seeing so many men and women hanged for theft.[6] Richelieu in France no less than Ralegh in England believed that the mass of men would never work unless driven by hunger.[7] Colbert thought of religion as a useful reinforcement of labour discipline. In addition to reducing the number of holidays, he criticized indiscriminate alms-giving, and gave his support to schemes for using religious foundations to

1. This has been cogently argued by Professor Jordan in his *Philanthropy In England, 1480–1660*, esp. pp. 99–101. See also my *Puritanism and Revolution*, pp. 215–38.

2. I owe this reference to the late Dr. Felix Raab's *The English Face of Machiavelli* (1964).

3. Burnet, *History of the Reformation*, IV, pp. 83–9.

4. William Perkins thought slavery lawful, under certain carefully defined conditions (*Workes*, III, pp. 697–8). See pp. 274–7 below.

5. Tawney and Power, *Tudor Economic Documents*, I, pp. 360, 363; II, p. 125.

6. Sir E. Coke, *III Institutes* (1648), Epilogue. Hobbes made similar demands (*Leviathan*, Everyman ed., p. 185).

7. "Tous les politiques sont d'accord que si les peuples étaient trop à leur aise il serait impossible de les contenir dans les règles de leur devoir" (H. Hauser, *La Pensée et l'action économiques de Richelieu* Paris, 1944, p. 145); for Ralegh see p. 122 above.

employ the poor profitably.[1] The great Earl of Cork expected the introduction of preaching, common law, industry and the poor law to civilize Ireland, to get rid of idleness and popery.[2] Although no longer phrased in religious terms, the cry for labour discipline still went up in restoration England. "'Tis for want of discipline that any poverty appears in England", cried Petty.[3] Unemployment, Locke believed in 1697, was caused by "nothing else but the relaxation of discipline and corruption of manners".[4]

It is difficult, indeed, for us to-day imaginatively to recapture the modes of thought of a pre-industrial society so as to understand the urgent necessity of imposing a new ethic. A few analogies may help. *The Times* on 17 December 1948, discussing labour problems in Africa, observed that "most Europeans have for centuries embraced a religious code which condemned idleness as wicked; his cults and taboos have more frequently taught the African that work is degrading or evil". Mediaeval society and religion had perhaps advanced too far to encourage the serf to think that his labour was degrading and evil: but it was not honourable in itself, since it was the consequence of sin. (In *Paradise Lost* Milton twice went out of his way to emphasize that Adam and Eve worked *before* the Fall.[5]) In an agricultural society labour was very intense for short periods, in seasonal fits and starts, dominated by natural forces: it provided no stimulus to prolonged and consistent effort. From nineteenth-century literature we are familiar with the passive, fatalistic attitude of the pre-revolutionary Russian peasant: and the Soviet Government, in an entirely different social environment, has had its own problems of labour discipline, especially in ensuring *continuity* of labour. Part of the answer in the U.S.S.R. has been the education of the population in a new body of ideas which, like Puritanism, stresses the dignity and social value of labour.

1. P. Boissonade, *Colbert* (Paris, 1932), pp. 274–5; C. W. Cole, *Colbert and a Century of French Mercantilism* (Columbia University Press, 1939), II, pp. 499–501.
2. I owe this point to Dr. T. O. Ranger's Oxford D.Phil. thesis, "The Career of Richard Boyle, first Earl of Cork, in Ireland, 1588–1643" (1959) which is shortly to be published. Cf. *C.S.P., Ireland, 1625–32*, p. 611.
3. Petty, *Economic Writings*, I, p. 118.
4. H. R. Fox-Bourne, *The Life of John Locke* (1876), II, p. 378.
5. Milton, *Paradise Lost*, Books IV and IX.

III

Labour then was a social duty: this point was emphasized again and again by the protestant divines. The classic statement comes in the *Homily Against Idleness*:

"A great part of the begging that is among the poor can be imputed to nothing so much as idleness" and bad upbringing. Children must be trained to work so as to be able "not only to sustain themselves competently, but also to relieve and supply the necessity and want of others". "The labouring man and his family, whilst they are busily occupied in their labour, be free from many occasions of sin, which they that live in idleness are subject unto. . . . The serving-men of this realm, who spend their time in much idleness of life, nothing regarding the opportunity of their time", would be wiser to "expend their idle time in some good business, whereby they might increase in knowledge, and so be the more worthy to be ready for every man's service".[1]

The doctrine that labour was a duty to one's neighbour, to society, to the commonwealth, to mankind, came to be especially emphasized by the puritan preachers. Dod and Cleaver,[2] Gouge,[3] Preston,[4] may be cited to represent the orthodox wing. Thomas Taylor thought that production for society is the distinguishing *human* quality.[5] Among the more radical Puritans, Robert Browne in 1588–9 thought that an

1. *Sermons or Homilies appointed to be read in Churches* (1802), pp. 330, 443–4. Observe the tell-tale confusion in that last "every man": it means, of course, "every employer".

2. J. Dod and R. Cleaver, *A Plain and Familiar Exposition of the Ninth and Tenth Chapters of Proverbs* (1612), pp. 65–6; XI and XII, pp. 92, 139–40; XIII and XIV, pp. 11, 73, 123; XVIII–XX, pp. 10-11; *Ten Commandments* (19th ed., 1662), pp. 93–4, 274–6, 294. Cf. Robert Hill, *The Pathway to Prayer and Pietie* (1610), pp. 82–3, quoted by L. B. Wright, *Middle-Class Culture in Elizabethan England* (Chapel Hill, 1935), pp. 256–7.

3. W. Gouge, *Of Domesticall Duties* (1626), p. 2.

4. For Preston see my *Puritanism and Revolution* (1958), pp. 272–3, and the passages there quoted. Labour as a duty to one's neighbour is discussed at greater length in my contribution to *Essays . . . in honour of R. H. Tawney* (1961), pp. 31–3.

5. See epigraph to this chapter. Cf. T. Taylor, *Works*, "Christian Practice", pp. 256–7; Peel, *Tracts attributed to Richard Bancroft*, p. 72; G. Webb, *A Garden of Spirituall Flowers* (1643), Part I, p. 134; Part II, p. 278.

idle person ceased to be a member of the church of God;[1] the Fenstanton Baptists in 1657 resolved that it was unlawful to maintain at home in idleness a daughter who was capable of earning her own living. The parents concerned were sharply reproved and exhorted to put her to service.[2] Such passages bring home to us the extent to which at least radical Puritanism appealed to the small men in town and country. The point is illustrated in the Cambridge play *The Return from Parnassus*, which throughout shows great hostility to a society in which

> "*The partial heavens do favour each rude boor*
> *Makes droviers rich, and makes each scholar poor.*"

"A solemn senseless oration against idleness" is given to "an old churl" who employed Studioso as chaplain.[3]

The peasant regulates his life by the sun and the seasons; but when Melanchthon made an appointment he fixed not only the hour but the minute as well.[4] The Puritan horror of waste of time helped not only to concentrate effort, to focus attention on detail, but also to prepare for the rhythms of an industrial society, our society of the alarm clock and the factory whistle. Thoughts, said Thomas Goodwin in an illuminating metaphor, are vagrants, which must be diligently watched for, caught, examined, whipped and sent on their way.[5] John Wilkins saw frugality as a law of the universe, a principle at work in nature.[6] There was a great increase in the literature advocating thrift in the years 1600–40.[7]

It was a seventeenth-century commonplace that Protestant-

1. *Writings of Robert Harrison and Robert Browne*, p. 528; cf. pp. 362–3.

2. Ed. E. B. Underhill, *Records of the Churches of Christ gathered at Fenstanton, Warboys and Hexham* (Hanserd Knollys Soc., 1854), p. 290; cf. pp. 228–37.

3. Ed. J. B. Leishman, *The Three Parnassus Plays* (1949), pp. 141, 166; cf. pp. 97, 110, 267–8.

4. S. Johnson, *The Rambler*, No. 60. A Soviet cartoon of the nineteen-thirties showed a man running to catch a train, who breathlessly asked a peasant by the side of the road what the time was. "In the tenth hour", was the reply. The cartoon was labouring the same point as many a seventeenth-century sermon.

5. T. Goodwin, *Works* (1861–3), III, pp. 527–8.

6. S. F. Mason, "The Scientific Revolution and the Protestant Reformation, I", *Annals of Science*, IX, pp. 83–4.

7. L. B. Wright, *op. cit.*, pp. 185–200.

ism was peculiarly suited to a commercial and industrial community, and that popish religion created an unaptness for trade, hard work and accumulation.[1] Popery, Richard Sibbes believed, was "set up by the wit of man to maintain stately idleness".[2] An anonymous Elizabethan poet thought that foreign foes conspired England's distress "for reforming the abuse Of such as lived in sloth".[3] The worst that could be said of Little Gidding in 1641 was that "men and women in health, of able and active bodies and parts", had "no particular callings", or else abandoned them for a "contemplative and idle life, as if diligence in our particular lawful callings were no part of our service to God". This was "nearly complying with Popery".[4] In Slingsby Bethel's account of the weakness of popery, published in 1668, he listed five main heads, all economic. First, monks, nuns and friars live in idleness, making no contribution to national production.[5] England, Bethel added, "was richer and fuller of trade" during the revolutionary decades, when the bishops could neither hoard up "money which before went in trade" nor drive "into corners the industrious sort of people, by imposing upon their consciences". Secondly, an unmarried clergy causes a declining population. Thirdly, superstition leads to extravagance in adorning

1. The *locus classicus* is De Souligné's *Political Mischiefs of Popery* (English translation, 1698). De Souligné was a Huguenot who fled to England after the revocation of the Edict of Nantes. See also a curious work, *The Social Effects of the Reformation* by a Fellow of the Statistical Society (privately printed, 1852), a reprint of articles replying to William Cobbett's *History of the Reformation*. As against Cobbett's argument that the Reformation had had a deleterious effect on the economic position of the working class, the Fellow of the Statistical Society had no difficulty in showing that the abolition of popery enormously added to the actual and potential wealth of the nation. But he did not follow Cobbett in asking which classes were the main beneficiaries. See also *The Memoirs of the Life of Mr. Ambrose Barnes* (Surtees Soc., 1867), p. 47.

2. R. Sibbes, *The Bruised Reed* (1838), p. 119; cf. p. 113. First published in 1631.

3. Ed. E. Farr, *Select Poetry, Chiefly Devotional, of the Reign of Elizabeth* (Parker Soc., 1845), II, p. 329.

4. *The Arminian Nunnery* (1641), quoted by H. R. Trevor-Roper, *Archbishop Laud* (1940), p. 138.

5. Cf. Petty's estimate that England had fewer than 20,000 clerics, whereas France was burdened with some 270,000 (*Economic Writings*, I, pp. 291–2). This made the advantages of protestantism self-evident to economists who were acutely aware of a shortage of "hands".

churches, wasteful expenditure on pilgrimages and similar useless functions: this checks accumulation and investment. Fourthly, there are too many holidays, again to the detriment of production. Finally, friars and other mendicants live especially on the alms of the poor, and so the latter can never rise above a mean condition.[1]

It is a comprehensive indictment, and it is the indictment of one system of ideas and social relationships in terms of the values of another. Popery is suited to a static agricultural society, which offers the mass of the population no possibility of becoming richer than their fellows, and in which poverty is a holy state. Protestantism is suited to a competitive society in which God helps those who help themselves, in which thrift, accumulation and industry are the cardinal virtues, and poverty very nearly a crime. The Laudian ceremonies were believed to be leading the country back to popery – social and economic popery as well as doctrinal. The Rev. John Tombes, in a sermon preached in 1641, used milder language than Milton was employing that year on the same subject: but the economic implications of his indictment are clear, as is his emphasis on the unity of interest between propertied laymen and the lower clergy: –

"This evil ['will-worship' – i.e. Laudianism] tends to the detriment of men's goods, the pillaging of men's purses, for no benefit to the owners, much hindrance to the poor, labouring ministers and commonwealth on which it should be bestowed. Many a pound is given in legacies and contributions, is extorted by courts for maintaining vestments, organs, processions, windows, buildings and other things unnecessary, when the poor want, painful preachers live on a small stipend, and the commonwealth is brought to straits. For superstition is costly, and superstitious persons are either lavishly profuse or slavishly ready to bestow their goods for very vanities which do them no good, when by a right bestowing of their goods they might make themselves friends of the unrighteous Mammon and be received into everlasting habitations".[2]

1. S. Bethel, *The World's Mistake in Oliver Cromwell*, in *Harliean Miscellany* (1809–15), VII, pp. 358–9.

2. J. Tombes, *The Leaven of Pharisaicall Wil-Worship* (1643), p. 11. There had been similar, though longer, denunciations of the costliness of popery in William Tyndale's *Obedience of a Christian Man* (1527–8), in *Doctrinal Treatises* (Parker Soc., 1848), pp. 237–40. Cf. also Bishop

Bethel's phrase "the industrious sort of people" accurately describes those yeomen, artisans and small and middling merchants who supported lecturers and Puritanism generally.[1] ("Such as were dubbed with the title of yeomanry" was Bishop Aylmer's contemptuous description of men who petitioned for the restoration of a puritan minister to his living.)[2] I shall use the phrase henceforth to describe the economically indepen-dent men, householders, to the exclusion both of the property-less and of the privileged classes.[3] The latter might be landed aristocrats or members of the ruling oligarchies of the big cities, great financial magnates, monopolists, customs farmers, who would expect to be called "gentlemen" and who might aspire to knighthood. They took no direct part in productive activity, were not "industrious" in Bethel's sense of the word, and their interests lay with the rentier class into which they were rising, rather than with "the industrious sort of people" from whom they sometimes originated.[4]

Bale's attack on non-labouring Church officials (*Select Works*, Parker Soc., 1849, pp. 518–19). Even a conservative like Sir Henry Spelman stressed the Reformation's contribution to the accumulation of capital (*A Dialogue concerning the Coin of the Kingdom*, in *English Works*, 1727, II, p. 209; cf. Sir E. Sandys, *Europae Speculum*, pp. 50–1). Sir Thomas Overbury's "devilish usurer" "likes our religion best because 'tis best cheap" (ed. E. F. Rimbault, *Miscellaneous Works . . . of Sir Thomas Overbury*, 1890, p. 134). Cf. the sneers of William Chillingworth (*Works*, 1838, III, p. 171), of Matthew Wren the younger (*Of the Origin and Progress of the Revolutions in England*, in *Collectanea Curiosa*, ed. Gutch, I, p. 231) and of John Dryden (*Religio Laici*, 1682, in *Poetical Works*, Globe ed., p. 200); and the uneasiness shown on this question by Thomas Adams (*The Soules Sickness*, in *Works*, 1861–2, I, p. 495) and Sir Benjamin Rudyerd (Manning, *Memoirs of . . . Rudyerd* p. 137).

1. Peel, *Tracts Ascribed to Richard Bancroft*, p. 57.

2. Dyke, *A Caveat for Archippus*, p. 40. Cf. a Puritan petition of 1604 from 200 yeomen of Essex, quoted in Babbage, *Puritanism and Richard Bancroft*, p. 124. For much evidence of lay Puritanism below the rank of gentleman, see *ibid*., pp. 360–6, 374–5.

3. See Chapter 13 below. Cf. M. H. Dobb, *Studies in the Development of Capitalism* (1946), Chapter IV; H. K. Takahashi, "The Transition from Feudalism to Capitalism", *Science and Society*, XVI, pp. 313–65.

4. It is necessary to emphasize this distinction, often ignored by historians anxious to argue that there were "capitalists" on both sides in the civil war. There were: but since Dr. V. L. Pearl's *London and the Outbreak of the Puritan Revolution* (1961), it is inexcusable to ignore the real economic differences and difference of interest which separated the two groups of "capitalists". The distinction was made in my *The English Revolution, 1640* (1940), pp. 35–7.

The economic appeal of puritan asceticism to industrious artisans and aspiring peasants, in an age of nascent industrialization, can be paralleled from China in the present century. There revolutionary feeling among the peasantry in the nineteen-twenties manifested itself in opposition to any form of conspicuous waste, whether it arose from ostentatious extravagance by the rich, from the sycophantic idleness of strolling players, or from religious ritual. The peasants, a shrewd observer noted, "have to cultivate frugality as a means of self-protection".[1]

Protestantism, then, and more specifically Puritanism, appealed especially to those smaller employers and self-employed men, whether in town or country, for whom frugality and hard work might make all the difference between prosperity and failure to survive in the world of growing competition. "They are very hot for the Gospel", said Thomas Adams of such laymen; "they love the Gospel: who but they? Not because they believe it, but because they feel it: the wealth, peace, liberty that ariseth by it".[2]

Puritanism also of course appealed to a section of the gentry, who as patrons and M.P.s were important in furthering the cause out of all relation to their numbers; it had staunch supporters among the common lawyers, usually of gentry families;[3] and there was always the hope that, not necessarily for primarily religious reasons, some great Court aristocrat might lead an attack on the Church – the Earl of Leicester, the Earl of Essex, the Duke of Buckingham. But though such men were potentially very important, and the puritan gentry in the House of Commons were indispensable, still without the backing of large numbers of humbler men puritanism could never have challenged the Crown and the bishops: the civil war could never have been fought and won. I shall concentrate on the industrious sort because my subject is the formation of this wider climate of opinion; but my failure to emphasize the role of the puritan gentry, except incidentally, should not be taken to imply any disparagement of its importance. If there had been no lay patrons there could have been no puritan ministers to preach to a wider public.

1. Mao Tse-Tung, *Report of an investigation into the peasant movement in Hunan*, in *Selected Works*, I (1954), pp. 52–4.
2. T. Adams, *The Wolf Worrying the Lamb*, in *Workes* (1629), p. 389.
3. See pp. 329–30 below.

A late seventeenth-century pamphlet, *St. Paul the Tent-Maker*, attempted to show "how religion has in all ages been promoted by the Industrious Mechanick". Starting with the 12 Apostles, the author jumped with significant haste to the Reformation, which began in "those parts of Germany . . . wherein trades, arts and sciences flourish most". The majority of English protestant martyrs were laymen, generally tradesmen and their wives. Popery drew men and women to idleness and poverty. It caused them "to part with the necessary support of themselves and their families, to purchase the prayers and benedictions of the church. The Protestants proceeded in a way diametrically opposite to this, and instructed their converts as well in the method of an industrious course of life, as in the principles of religion and virtue: and at the same time that they educated them in the service of God . . . they likewise proved that one part of their duty consisted in making a necessary provision for their families". Hence Protestantism and a multitude of beggars are mutually exclusive. Unlike the Spaniards, Protestants in America make the Indians *work*.[1]

"Our reformation sprang up among the same people of industry and labour" as the Apostles: like the Apostles the early Protestants encouraged a "delight in secular employments". The author believed that men's public and private devotions should "be so proportioned as not to hinder" those other duties which "they owe to themselves and families, which both God and nature require from them". "The more diligently we pursue our several callings, the more we are capacitated" (after looking after ourselves, our friends and our relations) "to extend our charity to such as are in poverty and distress".[2] It is therefore an erroneous opinion, although maintained by the practice of too many gentlemen, "that a competent estate disobliges them from business, and by consequence gives them an unlimited freedom of pursuing their pleasures at random".[3] "Only industrious and laborious

---

1. *St. Paul the Tent-Maker* (1689), pp. 18–21, 24.
2. *Ibid.*, pp. 16, 19, 25. Cf. Henry Newcome's *cri de coeur* in 1661: "This is now my constant fear, lest I die and shall leave nothing for my wife and children; and so men will say, 'This was his strictness, and this is Puritanism! See what it gets them! What it leaves to wife and children!'" (*Autobiography*, ed. R. Parkinson, Chetham Soc., 1852, pp. 135–6). The implied standards are interesting.
3. *St. Paul the Tent-Maker*, pp. 10–12. See pp. 135–8 below.

people are the riches of any nation", said a pamphlet of 1690; "not such as are wholly unemployed, as gentry, clergy, lawyers, serving-men and beggars".[1]

The statement of his thesis by the author of *St. Paul the Tent-Maker* is late and highly sophisticated: and yet there are few elements in the author's case which cannot be found in very early protestant writings, or which cannot be deduced from the logic of those writings. The protestant religion was in fact promoted most of all by the Industrious Mechanick in the sixteenth and seventeenth centuries: many contemporary papists testify to this.[2] The point was put with especial naïveté in a pamphlet of 1674: "the reformed part of the world, being manumitted from such slavery and incumbrances [as ceremonies and observances] beat out the Popish everywhere in trading, and generally excel them in all arts and sciences. . . . Presently after the Reformation, the English grew potent at sea, sent forth great colonies and plantations, maintained traffic and commerce over the world, and brought home honour, plenty and riches to the nation".[3] In the light of such later passages, it is easy to mock the preachers' glorification of hard work, thrift, economy of time, accumulation;[4] their emphasis on the advantages of a cheap Church.[5] We smile when we hear Roger Williams begging Parliament to give the people absolute freedom "so that no person be forced to pay nor pray otherwise than as his soul believeth and consenteth".[6] But if we merely mock we miss the essential social truth underlying the naïvetés. England's retention of

1. Dalby Thomas, *An Historical Account of the Rise and Growth of the West India Colonies* (1690), in *Harleian Miscellany* (1744–56), II, p. 343.

2. Cf. a report by Nicholas Sanders written at the beginning of Elizabeth's reign, in *C.S.P., Rome, 1558–71*, p. 61; F. de Rémond, *Histoire de la naissance, progrés et décadence de l'Hérésie de ce siècle* (1605–17), book VII, p. 931.

3. W. Staveley, *The Romish Horsleech* (1674), Sig. A 8.

4. Cf. a funeral sermon on an alderman of London: "Shall any be reputed covetous or an oppressor for looking to have his own goods restored according to law, that he may husband them himself, *for the glory of God and the good of others*?" (Edward Browne, *A rare Paterne of Justice and Mercy*, 1642, pp. 43–4 – my italics). For Alderman Cambel see pp. 259, 313 below.

5. Cf. H. T. Buckle, *History of Civilization in England* (World's Classics), II, p. 277.

6. Roger Williams, *The Fourth Petition, Presented by Major Butler to the Honourable Committee of Parliament* (1652), quoted by Perry Miller, *Roger Williams* (New York, 1953), p. 194.

her independence in the sixteenth century owed much to men like Drake, who "hated idleness like the devil".[1] The British Empire did not expand any more slowly because men like Richard Hakluyt advised "That there be appointed one or two preachers for the voyage, that God may be honoured, the people instructed, mutinies the better avoided and obedience the better used, that the voyage may have the better success".[2] And it *was* by hard work and labour discipline that England won its industrial lead over the rest of the world.

In 1580 Robert Hitchcock thought that the endowment of itinerant preachers would help "to root out idleness, the mother and breeder of vagabonds".[3] At Halifax the great Calvinist preacher John Favour ruled from 1593 to 1623. "He encouraged the development of the cloth industry; . . . he subdued the roistering and the criminal with the breath of fire in his sermons"; and he collected more than 60 bequests, from far and near, for the improvement and education of his community.[4] John White the Patriarch of Dorchester encouraged men to work, "piety breeding industry, and industry procuring plenty unto it. A beggar was not then to be seen in the town".[5] Baxter had a similar success later at Kidderminster in fitting the poor for employment in the clothing industry. Even an old reprobate like Sir Arthur Ingram hoped to supply the workers in his Yorkshire alum mines with "comfort both by food and raiment for their bodies, and instruction for their souls by sufficient and good preachers, and education for their children by schoolmasters there kept and maintained".[6] Like Hitchcock 35 years earlier, he undoubtedly regarded money spent on such social services as prudently invested. In 1646, to round off the story, Hugh

1. Quoted by R. A. J. Walling, *The Story of Plymouth* (1950), p. 38.
2. R. Hakluyt, *A Discourse of Westerne Planting*, in *The Original Writings and Correspondence of the two Richard Hakluyts* (ed. E. G. R. Taylor, Hakluyt Soc., 1935), II, p. 324.
3. R. Hitchcock, *A Politic Plat*, in E. Arber, *An English Garner* (1897), II, p. 141. See p. 268 below.
4. W. K. Jordan, *The Rural Charities of England, 1480–1660*, pp. 323–6.
5. Fuller, *Worthies*, III, p. 25. I owe this reference to Mr. Brown Patterson.
6. A. F. Upton, *Sir Arthur Ingram* (1961), p. 108. On the need for labour discipline among Ingram's workers, see *ibid.*, pp. 117, 132. For Ingram's general interest in preaching, see *ibid.*, pp. 241, 251, 263.

Peter thought that a preaching ministry was the way to establish "justice, charity and industry" in England, and so to catch up economically with the Netherlands.[1]

IV

So there were social reasons for the puritan ministers' special emphasis on the duty of working hard, for extolling the dignity of labour. But a theory that dignifies labour is as double-edged as the labour theory of value which is its secularized counterpart, already to be found in the writings of Hobbes and Locke. The Hussites had held that every Christian should earn his living through work: "They are unworthy of bread that in their deeds have no care for the commonweal".[2] This was the lower-class heresy throughout the centuries. The propertied class had always been able to suppress it until the sixteenth century; but then it won its way to respectability, thanks in part at least to the growing social importance of the industrious sort of people.

In England the *Homily Against Idleness* taught that "by corruption of nature through sin" man "taketh idleness to be no evil at all, but rather a commendable thing, seemly for those that be wealthy". But God commanded that every man should work. If we live "like drone bees by the labours of other men, then do we break the Lord's commandment". This was sailing pretty near the wind. The Homily hedged by declaring "whosoever doth good to the commonweal and society of men with his industry and labour . . . is not to be accounted idle, though he work no bodily labour".[3] Yet this still left the mere rentier open to criticism. As early as the fifteen-sixties Bishop Jewel had to counter the view that the protestant doctrine of labour was socially subversive. He argued, developing the hints dropped by the Homily, that "the nobleman and magistrate, if he regard his country, be careful for the laws, aid the poor, repress tyranny, comfort the weak, punish the wicked, is not

1. *Mr. Peters Last Report of the English Wars* (1646), pp. 12–13; cf. S. Hartlib, *Considerations Tending to the Happy Accomplishment of Englands Reformation in Church and State* (1647), pp. 22–3.

2. See two sermons preached by Jan Želivsky in 1419, quoted by J. Macek, *The Hussite Movement in Bohemia* (Prague, 1958), p. 117. Želivsky, like Winstanley and Lenin after him, quoted II Thessalonians iii, 10: "If any would not work, neither should he eat".

3. *Sermons or Homilies* (1802), pp. 438–40.

idle".[1] But when Arthur Dent reproduced the argument, it
followed a flat statement "God doth allow none to live idly".[2]
The common man would not necessarily always be convinced
that his betters' activities – as magistrates, for instance – were
socially useful.

It was easy to express the doctrine in ways that could give
offence to the landed class. In a sermon preached at Paul's
Cross in 1581 James Bisse attacked all who lived in no
vocation, no craft, no trade, no profession.[3] The high priest of
the Puritans, William Perkins, declared that "such as live *in
no calling*, but spend their time in eating, drinking, sleeping
and sporting" were guilty of disobedience and rebellion
against God. It was no defence that you had inherited a
private income.[4] A marginal note to Genesis xiii, I, in the
Geneva Bible pointed out that Abraham's "great riches gotten
in Egypt hindred him not to follow his vocation".

Emphasis on the dignity of labour becomes almost a democratic doctrine in the mouths of Dod and Cleaver. "They that
apply themselves to labour for their livings do eat their own
bread, and are profitable to others; whereas those stately idle
persons are driven to put their feet under other men's tables,
and their hands into other men's dishes". Since God "doth
prefer the poor, despised, industrious, laborious, and giveth
His voice for their precedency, why should we give titles to
ruffians and roisters . . . that have nothing in them of grace and
goodness, . . . of art or skilfulness?"[5] It was a difficult question
to answer on puritan assumptions: but the social implications
were very dangerous. "Turning of recreation into a vocation
. . . is not allowable by God's word", the authors added.[6]
"Every man, of every degree, as well rich as poor, as well

1. J. Jewel, *An Exposition upon the Two Epistles . . . to the Thessalonians*, in *Works* (Parker Soc., 1845–50), II, p. 864. First published
1583.
2. A. Dent, *The Plaine Mans Path-way to Heaven* (1601), pp. 191–2.
Richard Baxter was still making the same exceptions in 1683, but again
he started by saying "It is swinish and sinful not to labour" (*The Catechizing of Families*, 1683, p. 278).
3. J. Bisse, *Two Sermons Preached* (1581), Sig. B 5.
4. Perkins, *Workes*, III, pp. 63–4; I, p. 756. See also my *Puritanism
and Revolution*, pp. 235–7.
5. Dod and Cleaver, *Proverbs*, XI–XII, pp. 139–40; cf. XVIII–XX,
pp. 10–11.
6. Dod and Cleaver, *Ten Commandements*, pp. 93–4.

mighty as mean, as well noble as base, must know that he is born for some employment to the good of his brethren, if he will acknowledge himself to be a member, and not an ulcer, in the body of mankind".[1]

John Preston warned young gentlemen against the dangers of idleness.[2] Richard Bernard criticized "those hangers-on who brag of their gentry and will not work", but sponged on their rich relations: "Work they cannot, they will not; but it is no shame for them to live dishonestly and idly, contrary to nature, contrary to God's injunction that men should labour, contrary to the practice of all the godly. . . . Let him or they whosoever, which think themselves religious indeed, make conscience to take pains in some calling and beware of living idly". No one should live merely in "the calling of a gentle-man". This was a profession "so abused to advance sin and Satan's kingdom as nothing more".[3] Those were harsh words, and they came from a minister who trembled on the verge of separatism. But even a future bishop, Robert Sanderson, pointed out, very circumspectly, that idleness was no more justifiable in the nobility and gentry than in monks and beggars.[4] A good deal depended on one's definition of idleness.

In the model puritan community, New England, labour was not only desirable but essential to survival. The signatories to the first church covenant of Salem promised to "shun idleness as the bane of every state". In 1648 idleness was made a punish-able offence in Massachusetts.[5] So in New England, as so often, the full theoretical consequences latent in puritan teach-ing were drawn out. In his famous Discourse of 1622 Robert Cushman declared that "idle drones are intolerable in a settled commonwealth, much more in a commonwealth which is but as it were in the bud. Of what earth, I pray thee, art thou

1. Dod and Cleaver, *Proverbs*, XVII–XX, p. 11. The authors also make the more familiar point about self-help: "He that is painful and prudent in his business (notwithstanding his wealth be small) is rising from the bottom towards the top, and he that is remiss and careless (though his substance be great) is falling from the top towards the bottom" (*ibid.*, XIII–XIV, p. 71).
2. J. Preston, *The Saints Qualification* (2nd ed., 1634), p. 75; cf. *Four Godly and Learned Treatises* (3rd ed., 1633), p. 346.
3. R. Bernard, *Ruth's Recompence* (1628), printed with R. Stock and S. Torshell's *Commentaries upon Malachi* (1865), pp. 37, 57–8.
4. Sanderson, *XXXV Sermons*, pp. 196–7, 251.
5. S. E. Morison, *Builders of the Bay Colony* (n.d., ?1930), pp. 166–7.

made? Of any better than the other of the sons of Adam? And thou sit idle at home, or takest thy pleasure abroad?" To make this assertion of human equality more precise, Cushman applied it to "men that have taken in hand either to come, out of discontentment in regard to their estates in England, . . . affecting it to be gentlemen, landed men". And he made the link, always implicit but rarely explicit in puritan teaching, between "gentry and beggary": both forms of idleness were intolerable in a well-ordered commonwealth.[1]

From the doctrine of the dignity of labour, and the argument that property was justified by labour, it was possible to conclude that idleness should lead to expropriation: no labour, no property. Attributing the doctrine to Calvin, Heylyn pointed out its consequences: "No man is sure of his estate, but may be stripped of it as an idle boy, or an unprofitable servant, when the brethren please".[2] Such conclusions were not in fact drawn by Calvin but they were by some of the radical English revolutionaries. In Chelmsford in 1643, we are told by a royalist, the principle was preached that there were no grounds "neither in nature nor in Scripture . . . that one man should have £1,000 a year, another not £1; . . . therefore it is now fit that the nobility and gentry should . . . work for their own maintenance; and if they will not work, they ought not to eat".[3] In the same year Robert Kyrle, giving his reasons for deserting Parliament for the King, said that his eyes had been opened to the true nature of the Parliamentarian cause by the preaching of John Sedgwick: "if they cannot prove any of quality to be a Papist, yet as he is a gentleman he shall want grace; and that is title enough to possess the estates of all that are more richer than themselves".[4]

1. *Cushman's Discourse*, in *Chronicles of the Pilgrim Fathers* (Everyman ed.) pp. 235–6, 239. There was to be no hereditary aristocracy in Massachusetts, as even godly peers like Saye and Sele and Brooke were firmly told in 1635.
2. P. Heylyn, *History of the Presbyterians* (1670), p. 35. Cf. C. H. George's interesting "Social Interpretation of Puritanism", *Journal of Modern History*, XXV, pp. 339–41.
3. [Bruno Ryves], *Angliae Ruina* (1643), pp. 26–7.
4. J. and T. W. Webb, *Memorials of the Civil War in Herefordshire* (1879), II, pp. 349–51. We should not take Sergeant-Major Kyrle too seriously. A more potent reason may have been that his family estates were under the control of the royal forces. He changed back again as soon as Parliament was clearly winning. Nevertheless, if he was inventing

These were the propagandist accounts of enemies of Parliament. Yet all the elements in the arguments are by now familiar to us in the ideas of respectable puritan preachers who would themselves have shrunk from a doctrine of dominion by grace. Even in the following rough plebeian declaration of the class war we can hear unmistakable echoes of William Perkins. Gentlemen and priests, said a pamphlet of 1649, "do live altogether out of God's way, and in rebellion to His laws: first because they live without a calling, and so are idle, being vagabonds, . . . and by their own law ought to be put into a house of correction and to be made work".[1] Gerrard Winstanley carried the doctrine to its logical conclusion when he wrote: "No man can be rich but he must be rich either by his own labours or by the labours of other men helping him. If a man have no help from his neighbour he shall never gather an estate of hundreds and thousands a year. If other men help him to work, then are those riches his neighbours' as well as his; for they be the fruit of other men's labours as well as his own. . . . Rich men receive all they have from the labourer's hand".[2] In 1655 Major-General Boteler was "taking note of all profane and idle gentry . . . and all inferior persons that are dangerous and live without callings".[3] We can understand why there was less support from the gentry for nonconformity after 1660 than there had been for Puritanism before 1640.

In 1660 the industrious sort of people were put back into their place. Indeed the backwardness of this class was cited by Moses Wall to Milton in 1659 as an explanation of the failure of the Revolution: "Whilst people are not free but straitened in accommodations for life, their spirits will be dejected and servile. . . . There should be an improving of our native commodities, as our manufactures, our fishery, our fens, forests and commons and our trade at sea, etc., which would give the body of the nation a comfortable subsistence".[4]

arguments, that was all the more reason, in a propagandist pamphlet, for making them plausible.
1. [Anon.], *More Light Shining in Buckinghamshire* (1649), in G. H. Sabine's edition of *The Works of Gerrard Winstanley* (Cornell University Press, 1941), p. 633. For Perkins see p. 136 above.
2. Winstanley, *The Law of Freedom* (1652), *ibid.*, p. 511. Cf. P. Chamberlen, *The Poore Mans Advocate* (1649), pp. 12, 20, 30.
3. Ed. T. Birch, *Thurloe State Papers* (1742), IV, p. 218.
4. D. Masson, *Life of Milton* (1875–94), V, pp. 602–3.

Yet something of the doctrine survived. As the nonconformists sloughed off their political ideals, so their emphasis on the
duty of labour outweighed their emphasis on the rights of
those who work. This shift was encouraged by the ruling class.
Reviving the doctrine of the Homily, they hoped that hard
work would distract the poor from sedition and crime.[1] If men
could only be brought to be industrious, Lord Clarendon
thought, there would be no stealing.[2] And industry of a kind
became fashionable even in the highest circles. The self-made
Duke of Albemarle "very well knew . . . how unable the
nobility are to support their own esteem and order, or to assist
the crown, whilst they make themselves contemptible and
weak by the number and weight of their debts and the continual
decay of their estates. And if the wealth of the nation come to
centre most among the lower and trading part of the people, at
one time or other it will certainly be in their power, and
probably in their desires, to invade the government". These
and the like considerations had moved the Duke of Albemarle
to become as great an example to the nobility of honourable
good husbandry "as he had been before of loyalty and allegiance".[3] The argument owes more to Harrington than to
Puritanism: but it illustrates how some at least of the aristocracy tried to live up to their social responsibilities, and to
accept some form of economic activity as a duty. By 1690
Locke could assert the origins of property in labour with no
more danger than when he asserted the origins of government
in the people: it was as though such things as Levellers and
Diggers had never existed.[4]

1. For examples, see R. B. Schlatter, *The Social Ideas of Religious
Leaders, 1660–88* (1940), pp. 161–9.

2. Clarendon, *A Compleat Collection of Tracts* (1747), p. 139.

3. T. Skinner, *The Life of General Monck, Duke of Albemarle* (2nd
ed., 1724), p. 384.

4. See pp. 490–4 below.

Chapter Five

The Uses of Sabbatarianism

As frequenting of markets maketh a rich man, so keeping of Sabbaths maketh a rich Christian. And as we count him a bad husband that followeth games on the market day, so may we as well count him a spiritual unthrift that spendeth the Sabbath in that sort.
Thomas Gataker, "The Gaine of Godlinesse", in *Sermons* (1637), p. 145.

Member of the Massachusetts General Court. – "You are not to do unnecessary work on the Sabbath".
Indian chiefs. – "That will be easy: we haven't much to do any day, and can well take our ease on the Sabbath".
Discussion *c.* 1643, quoted in S. E. Morison, *Builders of the Bay Colony*, p.290.

It is the Sabbath, the most useful day in seven, that is set apart for divine service and religious exercise as well as resting from bodily labour; and it is a duty incumbent on all magistrates to take a particular care of that day. The poor more especially and their children should be made to go to church on it both in the fore- and afternoon, because they have no time on any other. By precept and example they ought to be encouraged and used to it from their very infancy; the wilful neglect of it ought to be counted scandalous, and if downright compulsion to what I urge might seem too harsh, and perhaps impracticable, all diversions at least ought strictly to be prohibited, and the poor hindered from every amusement abroad that might allure or draw them from it.
Bernard Mandeville, *An Essay on Charity and Charity Schools* in *The Fable of the Bees* (1724), I, p. 352.

I

AT first sight the seventeenth-century controversies over the
Sabbath seem mere irrational Bibliolatry: and this element
certainly enters into the fierce discussions as to whether God
intended Saturday or Sunday to be observed as the day of rest.
But many historians have observed that there is far more to it
than that. The Bible had been read for centuries without
sabbatarian inferences being drawn by significant sections of
the population. Part of the explanation lies in the availability
of the Bible in English; not only clerics and scholars but the
industrious sort of people could now read it for themselves.
The ministers especially directed their preaching to the latter –
as in the passage from Gataker quoted at the head of this
chapter – and Sabbatarianism seems especially to have
appealed to them. The Bible is a large book, in which men
find different things in different ages and different circumstances. In the sixteenth century newly-literate people were
reading it for the first time, with no historical sense and
believing all its texts to be divinely inspired. So in explaining
sixteenth- and seventeenth-century use of the Bible it is as
important to take into consideration the pressures and demands of society as the text itself.

Protestants and especially Puritans elevated the Sabbath, the
regular day of rest and meditation suited to the regular and
continuous rhythms of modern industrial society: they attacked the very numerous and irregular festivals which had
hitherto marked out the seasons. To celebrate a hundred or
more saints' days in a year was all very well in an agricultural
society like that of mediaeval England, or the more primitive
pre-Christian societies whose festivals the saints' days so often
preserve. Agricultural labour is spasmodic, very intense for
brief periods. But an industrialized society, such as England
was becoming in the sixteenth century, needs regular, disciplined labour. Machinery that is not regularly used is
wasted: mines that are not regularly worked may deteriorate.
Holy-days, said the Order of 1536 abrogating them, are the
occasion of much sloth and idleness, riot and superfluity, and
lead to the decay of industrial crafts.[1] Artificers and labourers,
the Bishop of Exeter observed in 1539, still needed "spiritual

1. Sparrow, *A Collection of Articles*, p. 167.

instruction", backed up by punishment, to persuade them to work on saints' days.[1]

In 1579 Sheffield miners observed 13 saints' days each year, in addition to taking a week off at Christmas, 4–5 days at Easter, and 3 days at Whitsuntide.[2] It was no doubt the nature of their toil that made them cling to the old holidays. South Wales miners also kept "all abolished holy days, and cannot be weaned from that folly".[3] The tinners of Cornwall, Richard Carew observed in 1602, work to a calendar which "alloweth them more holidays than are warranted by the church, our laws or their own profit". Carew attributed this to the arduous nature of their toil.[4] Even at Ipswich, even in the sixteen-thirties, Samuel Ward still had to "cross that vulgar super-stitious conceit that whosoever works on any of the twelve days [after Christmas] shall be lousy".[5]

Buckle indeed suggested that the abolition of saints' days at the Reformation did more to harm the poor than the dissolu-tion of the monasteries, by effectively lowering wages: "and this gave rise to the poor laws".[6] Erasmus used exactly the opposite argument, that the festivals of the Church robbed labourers of regular earnings that would otherwise have been theirs.[7] The flat contradiction between Erasmus's analysis (which was to become a protestant commonplace) and Buckle's is resolvable only when we realize that the former adopts the standpoint of the independent small producer or

1. A. L. Rowse, *Tudor Cornwall* (1941), pp. 232–3.

2. L. Stone, "An Elizabethan coalmine", *Econ. H.R.*, Second Series, III, pp. 101–2.

3. J. U. Nef, *The Rise of the British Coal Industry* (1932), II, p. 175.

4. R. Carew, *A Survey of Cornwall* (1811), p. 5. The severe nature of the tinners' labour, which made it impossible for them to work more than 4 hours a day, was emphasized by J. Childrey in 1661 (*Britannia Baconica*, p. 8). It is interesting evidence of changing standards that Carew's nineteenth-century editor denied that tinners worked hard. They took nearly half each month off; none in fact worked so little. But by then regular industrial labour had become the national rule, not the exception; and men's ideas had changed with this economic transforma-tion. For the sixteenth century, cf. Rowse, *Tudor Cornwall*, pp. 230–3.

5. *C.S.P.D.*, *1635–6*, p. xlii.

6. H. T. Buckle, *Miscellaneous and Posthumous Works* (1872), I, p. 539. Buckle refers to Blanqui's *Histoire de l'Economie Politique*.

7. Ed. P. S. Allen, *Erasmi Epistolae* (1906), IV, p. 117 (letter to John Slechta, 1 November 1519); F. Seebohm, *The Oxford Reformers* (Everyman ed.), p. 306.

labourer on short wage contract, whilst the latter is thinking
of a peasant doing week-work or a household servant hired by
the year, or at least for long periods. For peasants and independent artisans, or for day labourers, the abolition of
holidays must have increased their potential earnings, at least
as expressed in money. We are dealing with a period of transition between two different economic systems. But it is the
former group, more typical of modern economy, that was
increasing in numbers, not peasants doing week-work, or
household servants hired by the year.

The attack on saints' days became common form for Protestants. In Geneva in 1561 it was decided that the traditional
Wednesday holiday which the apprentices enjoyed was
"against God"; and it was suppressed, with Beza's approval,
and probably on his initiative. Some of the smaller employers
said that the holiday improved the morale of their workers,
and so increased production; but this did not prevent Wednesday labour being violently enforced.[1] In England in 1608
Nicholas Bownde said that there should not be so many holy
days "lest thereby men should be hindered from the necessary
works of their callings; which hath moved the reformed
churches . . . to cut off many that were used in time of popery".[2]
It was even necessary in the last years of Elizabeth's reign to
defend the celebration of her accession day (November 17) as a
national holiday.[3]

In 1624 James Howell contrasted protestant England with
catholic Spain: in the latter, he calculated, days amounting to
more than five months in the year were dedicated to some saint
or other and kept festival: "a religion that the London apprentices would like well".[4] In France Colbert succeeded in
reducing saints' days to 92 per annum in 1666:[5] so Howell's

1. Paul Chaix, *Recherches sur l'imprimerie à Genève de 1550 à 1564*
(Geneva, 1954), pp. 27–9, quoted in R. M. Kingdon, *Geneva and the
Coming of the Wars of Religion in France*, 1555–63 (Geneva, 1956), p. 97.

2. N. Bownde, *The Unbelief of St. Thomas* (1817), pp. 8–9.

3. T. Holland πανηγύρις *D. Elizabeth . . . A Sermon preached at Pauls
Cross in London* (1601), quoted in M. Maclure, *The Paul's Cross Sermons*
(Toronto, 1958), pp. 116–17, 220; J. Howson, *A sermon preached at St.
Maries in Oxford, in defence of the festivities of the Church of England,
and namely that of her majesties coronation* (1602).

4. J. Howell, *Familiar Letters or Epistolae Ho-Elianae* (Temple
Classics), I, p. 217.

5. P. Boissonade, *Colbert*, p. 274.

calculation was not so wildly out. Roman Catholics have so many saints' days, the Duke of Newcastle thought, "as poor tradesmen and labouring men cannot live of their several callings for them".[1] A late seventeenth-century economist estimated that every holiday lost £50,000 to the nation.[2] That was the new attitude with a vengeance.

We have seen the campaign against saints' days repeated in our own time in the U.S.S.R., with equal moral fervour though with a different ideology. "What tremendous material loss", a recent pamphlet observed, "is caused by these religious holidays, of which there are hundreds in the year". The connection between saints' days and drunkenness was emphasized in true seventeenth-century manner.[3]

As with so many of the doctrines we discuss, the view that no day should be kept holy except Sunday goes back to the Lollards, whose main strength also came from the industrious sort of people. Luther recommended the conversion of most or all saints' days into working days. "We increase the wrath of God more on holy days than on others". The point was taken up with alacrity by the German princes in 1522.[4] Edwardian Parliaments, and some Edwardian reformers, including Protector Somerset, had been prepared to allow work on Sundays, whilst prohibiting amusements. The Injunctions of 1547 and 1559 instructed the clergy to teach the people that to be idle on holy and festival days in time of harvest was a grievous offence to God.[5] Ridley as Bishop of London in 1550 ordered his clergy to prevent the celebration of any of the suppressed holy

1. S. A. Strong, *A Catalogue of Letters . . . at Welbeck*, p. 188. On the other hand, Newcastle added, the Presbyterians have so many week-day exercises that they too interrupt the industry of the poor. The Church of England has found the *via media*! It would be interesting to know if "poor tradesmen and labouring men" agreed with the Duke. Cf. Hobbes, *English Works*, VI, pp. 193–4. See pp. 47–8, 64–5, 110, 113 above, and 146–7, 162–3, 458 below.

2. H. Pollexfen, *A Discourse of Trade and Coin* (1697), p. 50.

3. Khudryakov, *Overcoming Religious Survivals in the U.S.S.R.*, cited by E. Crankshaw in *The Observer*, 7 December 1958.

4. Ed. B. L. Woolf, *The Reformation Writings of Martin Luther* (1952–6), I, p. 166, II, p. 314. Luther's phrase was echoed by Philip Stubbes in 1583; and cf. p. 166 below.

5. Cardwell, *Documentary Annals*, I, pp. 16, 46, 188. Cf. Khudryakov's pamphlet, as quoted in *The Observer* of 7 December 1958: "Religious holidays do particularly great harm to agriculture. . . . The harvest is not gathered in because of absenteeism on account of these holidays".

days, and to stop men absenting themselves from their lawful callings on these days – even for the purpose of attending sermons.[1] 5 and 6 Ed. VI cap. 3, repealed under Mary but re-enacted in 1604, authorized labour in harvest on Sundays (and on the few saints' days still observed) "or at any other times in the year when necessity shall require to labour, ride, fish or work any kind of work, at their free wills and pleasure".[2]

In the early days of the Reformation, indeed, enthusiasm for preaching was carried to what many employers thought excessive lengths. "If there be a sermon *any time* of the day", said Richard Whytford,[*] masters should let their households "be there present all that be not occupied in needful and lawful business".[3] In Edward VI's reign the liberated preachers began to deliver long sermons on all days of the week. Masters complained that servants were drawn away from work, and in 1552 the Council wrote to the Bishop of London criticizing the habit of preaching on working as well as holy days. This "may increase the people's idleness, who of themselves are so much disposed to it, as all the ways that may be devised are little enough to draw them to work".[4] Ridley accordingly instructed his clergy that sermons were not to be preached at times when they would distract labourers and artisans from their lawful trades:[5] this is no doubt why market-day lectures became popular in the towns. In the Convocation of 1563 a demand for the abrogation of all holy days except Sunday and "prin-

1. J. G. Ridley, *Nicholas Ridley* (1957), pp. 215, 235.
2. Thomas Shepard, in seventeenth-century New England, was even prepared to allow the fires in iron furnaces to be kept going on Sundays (Morison, *Builders of the Bay Colony*, p. 278). But in Ireland, where the problem of labour discipline was at its most acute, the hierarchy was even in the seventeenth century much more inclined to Sabbatarianism than in England. (Cf. the 56th Article of the Irish Convocation in 1615.) Petty early in the reign of Charles II thought that priests opposed the introduction of trade and manufactures; it was essential for the improvement of Irish trade "that the people be dissuaded from the observation of superstitious holy-days" (*Economic Writings*, I, pp. 199, 223). Cf. the views of the great Earl of Cork, quoted on p. 125 above. 7 William III cap. 17 limited Irish holy days to 33.
3. R. Whytford, *A Work for Householders* (?1530), Sig. D iv (my italics). Men should "keep the preachings rather than the mass, if by case they may not hear both". Whytford was an Erasmian, not a Protestant.
4. Cardwell, *Documentary Annals*, I, pp. 84–5; cf. Burnet, *History of the Reformation*, III, p. 210.
5. Ridley, *op. cit.*, p. 235.

cipal feasts of Christ" was defeated by only one vote.[1] "Super-stitious holidays" were "the breakneck of the Lord's Sab-baths", and propaganda was concentrated against them: sometimes, Greenham thought, to the detriment of Sunday itself, "men now not sparing to work on the Lord's day also, because they have not been taught to sanctify it". Anabaptists and members of the Family of Love "so far reject holy days that they take away the Lord's day also".[2]

The early reformers, determined to finish with idleness, had thus been prepared to tolerate Sunday work in an emergency. But their successors adopted a simpler either-or attitude, and emphasized more insistently the necessity of the regular weekly rest. "There is more cause why men should rest upon the Sabbath in harvest", declared Bownde, "than at any other time of the year".[3] Given the rapid economic development of the period, emergencies were there all the time, especially for the industrious sort of people in industry and agriculture, upon whom the preachers increasingly fixed their eyes. Gild regula-tions were breaking down, and in many of the new industries in which capitalist relations were developing most rapidly there were no gilds at all. There was a tendency towards cut-throat competition. It was an age in which the margin between suc-cess and failure was very narrow: and hard work seemed to be the key to success. There was thus every inducement for the small producer to work long hours, and 7 days a week: not only to work himself, but also to make his apprentices and journeymen work. It is the small family shopkeepers to-day who have the maximum of temptation and the maximum of opportunity to stay open on Sundays and early-closing days.

In the seventeenth century there was only one way in which the industrious sort could be protected from themselves: by the total prohibition of Sunday work, and of travel to and from markets; and by the strict enforcement of this prohibition, in the interests of the class as a whole, against the many in-dividual members of the class who would try to evade

1. Cardwell, *A History of Conferences*, pp. 39–41.

2. Greenham, *Workes*, pp. 359, 374; cf. Whitgift, *Works*, II, pp. 565–6, 577–9. For an assumption that there is all the difference in the world between Sundays and saints' days, made by someone who did not take the contrast seriously, see two poems attributed to Sir Philip Sidney in his *Poems* (ed. W. A. Ringler, 1962), pp. 356–8.

3. N. Bownde, *The True Doctrine of the Sabbath* (1606), p. 142.

it.[1] This could not be left to private decision or to gild regulation. It must be done either by the ecclesiastical disciplinary apparatus, or by national legislation enforced by J.P.s. In 1583 the Dedham Classis was concerned about clothiers "setting their woad vats on the Sabbath", and decided to talk to "the godliest of that trade" about it.[2] In the Buckinghamshire lace-making industry, a new industry in the sixteenth century, men "who continually travailed to sell bone lace on the Sabbath day" were presented to the Church court at Newport Pagnell in 1611. In an even newer industry, paper-making, the owner of a mill at Milton's village of Horton was presented to the ecclesiastical court in 1635 for working his mill on the Sabbath throughout the year. The wages he paid were so bad that they had to be supplemented by poor relief. This desperate infringer of the law was a high constable.[3]

We may recall Dryden's sneer at Slingsby Bethel, who

> "*Did wisely from expensive sins refrain,*
> *And never broke the Sabbath but for gain*".[4]

All employers would tend towards Sunday work unless prevented; so its prohibition was very important not only for the craftsmen but still more for their employees. The Sabbath "was without doubt instituted to give a comfortable relaxation to beasts and men", wrote Francis Osborn.[5] Once saints' days were abolished, it was essential for prentices and journeymen that the Sunday rest should be rigidly enforced. On some of the old saints' days work had been permitted after service.[6] "Surely meet it were", said Nowell's *Catechism*, "that servants should, *together with us*, sometimes serve Him that is the common master of them and us. . . . It is also profitable for the masters themselves that servants should sometimes rest between their workings, that after respiting their work awhile

1. We may perhaps compare the attitude of some trade unions to-day towards overtime: there must either be a universally enforceable prohibition or no restriction at all.
2. Ed. R. G. Usher, *The Presbyterian Movement in the Reign of Queen Elizabeth* (Camden Soc., 1903), p. 53.
3. *V.C.H. Bucks.*, II, pp. 106, 111. See pp. 416–20 below.
4. Dryden, *Absalom and Achitophel*, in *Poetical Works* (Globe ed. 1886), p. 108. For Bethel, see p. 128 above.
5. Osborn, *Miscellaneous Works* (1722), II, p. 212.
6. W. B. Whitaker, *Sunday in Tudor and Stuart Times* (1933), pp. 141–3, 157–8. I have found this book very useful.

they may return more fresh and lusty to it again".[1] Nicholas
Bownde too pointed out that a regular Sabbath rest would be
to the advantage of all employers if it were generally enforced.[2]
It was much better for worldly business, two members of the
Assembly of Divines added, to have one day in seven set apart
for God, than parts of each of the seven days: the latter would
hinder "day-labourers and all men of much business exceedingly".[3]

II

There are two points, then. First, "the liberty of working six
days in the week", disregarding the interruptions of the old
saints' days. This was argued out when "certain Londoners"
were examined before the Ecclesiastical Commission in June
1567. God's law says six days shalt thou labour, pleaded White,
one of the accused; "but the prince's law saith 'Thou shalt not
labour seven [i.e. six] days, but shall keep the popish holy
days' ". He had no objection to hearing sermons on holy days.
"But what shall we do when the sermon be done?" he asked.
"If we do any work, we are commanded to your courts". The
bishop (Grindal) replied: "You may well be occupied in serving
God". "So we are all occupied when we are at our work that
God commandeth", White retorted. "The Sabbath is appointed to rest in, and to serve God. . . . I think him to be no
Christian, that doth not pray and serve God every day, before
he begins his work".[4] Here we see how the Sabbath family
prayers and the protestant emphasis on serving God by industry in one's calling, all combined against the wasteful observance of the traditional holy days. They are all aids to
productive labour.

"This permission to work on the six days cannot be restrained for any religious use", Greenham added.[5] The point
was made in the Millenary Petition, and was repeated by a man

1. A. Nowell, *A Catechism* (Parker Soc., 1853), p. 129. This catechism
was approved by Convocation in 1562, but published in 1570 by Nowell
on his own authority. I have italicized a passage which conveys the social
assumptions of men like Nowell.
2. See pp. 163–9 below.
3. Daniel Cawdrey and Herbert Palmer, *Sabbatum Redivivum: or The
Christian Sabbath Vindicated* (1645), p. 132. See also Cartwright, quoted
on pp. 150–1 below.
4. Grindal, *Remains*, pp. 215–16.
5. Greenham, *Workes*, p. 810.

presented in 1607 for working on a holy day.[1] Joseph Hall attributed to the Brownists an unkind emphasis on the profits which Church courts made out of those who used "the least and the most lawful labour" on saints' days, "notwithstanding the liberty of the six days' labour which the Lord hath given",[2] but one may suspect that men far more orthodox harboured similar thoughts when they observed that some Church courts themselves sat upon holy days.[3] When the Prayer Book of 1637, with its full calendar of saints' days, was being imposed on Scotland, George Gillespie declared that "the law of God hath allowed us to labour six days of every week, which liberty no human power can ever take from us".[4]

Secondly, there was the prohibition of Sunday labour, and also of certain forms of Sunday recreation. This point was fairly generally accepted. Churchwardens presented men for selling, loading or transporting goods on Sundays, or keeping markets, or for certain kinds of sports; bishops sometimes excommunicated such offenders.[5] Lancelot Andrewes himself in his young days spoke strongly in favour of strict Sabbath observance.[6] Even Whitgift admitted that "all the punishments appointed cannot keep a number of [men] from their worldly affairs" on saints' days. Yet he wished to enforce their observance.[7] Cartwright said that "the church nor no man" can

1. W. H. Hale, *A Series of Precedents and Proceedings . . . in the Diocese of London* (1847), pp. 233–4.

2. J. Hall, *Works* (1837–9), X, p. 78; cf. p. 129.

3. R. Peters, *Oculus Episcopi; Administration in the Archdeaconry of St. Albans, 1580–1625* (1962), p. 52.

4. G. Gillespie, *A Dispute against the English popish ceremonies* (1637), quoted by G. Donaldson, *The Making of the Scottish Prayer Book of 1637* (1954), p. 74. The liberty of working six days a week ultimately became a duty, which even the rich could not escape (R. Baxter, *The Catechizing of Families*, 1683, p. 278).

5. W. P. M. Kennedy, *Elizabethan Episcopal Administration* (Alcuin Club Collections, XXV), pp. cxx, cxxiv; Usher, *Reconstruction of the English Church*, II, p. 39; J. Brown, *John Bunyan* (1928), p. 6; ed. W. M. Palmer, *Episcopal Returns for Cambridgeshire, . . . 1638–65* (1930), pp. 51–3, 59–61, 68–9; D. Wilkins, *Concilia* (1737), IV, p. 269. But Mr. E. R. Brinkworth found that very few presentments for working on Sunday led to convictions at this period; and there were no convictions for Sunday sports ("The Study and Use of Archdeacon's Court Records: illustrated from the Oxford Records (1566–1759)", *T.R.H.S.*, 1943, p. 105).

6. See p. 164 below.

7. Whitgift, *Works*, II, pp. 578–9.

take away men's liberty of working 6 days a week; nor can it "drive them to a necessary rest of the body".[1] Whitgift replied: "If you have such a regard to their worldly affairs, is it not more commodious for them to abstain wholly from work upon these holy days, when they fall, than twice or thrice every week half the day ?"[2]

The campaign against the Puritans in the fifteen-nineties seems to have marked a turning-point. In the Archdeacon of Huntingdon's Court, between 1590 and 1596 there were 19 cases where the charge was working on holy days, and only one concerning work on Sunday.[3] Bancroft, even more than Whitgift, seems to have been the influential figure. Where his predecessors had endeavoured to put down both work and games on Sundays,[4] Bancroft inquired in his diocese of London whether anyone had worked or kept shops open on Sundays or holy days.[5] His chaplain in 1607 went out of his way to attack Cartwright's contention that "the church cannot take away this liberty of working six days in the week".[6]

Battle was joined. The hierarchy committed itself to the attempt to stop gainful labour on saints' days: the puritan opposition insisted on the right to work every day except Sunday. On this issue the Puritans would have the support of many of the industrious sort. In the same year 1607 Crashawe, preaching at Paul's Cross, called not on the bishops but on heads of households, magistrates and especially the Lord

1. Cartwright, *A Replye to an answere made of M. Doctor Whitgifte Aguynste the Admonition to the Parliament* (n.d.   c. 1574), p. 129.

2. Whitgift, *Works*, II, pp. 578–9. See pp. 148–9 above for the Puritan answer to this question.

3. F. G. Emmison, "Abstract of the Act Book of the Archdeacon of Huntingdon's Court", *Trans. of the East Herts. Archaeological Soc.*, VIII, pp. 28–9. For other examples of church courts penalizing work on saints' days in Elizabeth's reign, see J. Raine, *The Injunctions and other Ecclesiastical Proceedings of Richard Barnes, Bishop of Durham* (Surtees Soc., 1850), p. 126; W. J. Pressey, "Some Essex Dialect Entries", *Essex Review*, XLV, pp. 134–5; A. C. Yorke, "John Morden, Rector of Fowlness", *History Teachers' Miscellany*, III, p. 105; ed. J. S. Purvis, *Tudor Parish Documents in the Diocese of York* (1948), p. 52 and *passim*.

4. For an example, see J. Tait, "The Declaration of Sports for Lancashire" *E.H.R.*, XXXII, pp. 566–7.

5. Kennedy, *Elizabethan Episcopal Administration* (Alcuin Club Collections, XXVII), pp. 179–83, 345–7.

6. T. Rogers, *The Faith, Doctrine and Religion professed and protected in . . . England*, pp. 105, 206. Cf. also S. Patrick *A Treatise of Repentance* (1841) p. 129; published 1686.

Mayor of London to stop the horrible abuse of the Sabbath by fairs, markets, buying, selling and bargaining – and by May games and morris dances, wakes and feasts.[1] "We present a good reformation for the Sabbath day", said the churchwardens of King's Sutton, Oxfordshire, in 1619; but "for festival days, it is a thing never observed so strictly with us from buying and selling: nor in the time of harvest to abstain from labouring about corn; for very few of the parish", they continued ominously, "but we think are faulty herein".[2] Few came to church on holy days except churchwardens, we learn from Bucks, in 1634; yet few are presented, and none of the gentry or the rich.[3] One of the charges made against Dr. Lambe in the 1621 Parliament was that he tried to stop men opening their shops on holy days.[4]

There is any amount of evidence that throughout the reigns of the first two Stuarts churchwardens were expected to present men who worked on saints' days, and that Church courts imposed penalties on such men. Examples come from counties as widely scattered as Hampshire, Kent, Essex, Norfolk, Huntingdonshire, Lincolnshire, Bedfordshire, Oxfordshire, Hertfordshire, Buckinghamshire, Somerset, Dorset, Sussex, Yorkshire, the Isle of Man. The offences vary too: ploughing, getting in harvest, threshing, grinding corn, shearing sheep, making bricks, making a pig-sty, opening shops, lace-making, "horsing barges", shoeing or treating a horse, barbering, carrying out a constable's duty and arresting, "charming teeth", setting servants to work.[5] In 1627 the very poor rector

1. W. Crashawe, *The Sermon Preached at the Crosse* (1607), pp. 173–4; cf. John Sprint, *Propositions, tending to proove the necessarie use of the Christian Sabbaoth* (1607), pp. 37, 55.

2. S. A. Peyton, *The Churchwardens' Presentments in the Oxfordshire Peculiars of Dorchester, Thame and Banbury* (Oxfordshire Record Soc., 1928), p. 298. There were several sermons against profanation of the Sabbath at Paul's Cross in 1611, 1615, 1616: see Maclure, *The Paul's Cross Sermons*, pp. 233, 237–8. "Few or none cometh to the church upon such light holidays", said the curate of Wragby in 1627, of Easter Tuesday and St. Mark's Day (Marchant, *The Puritans and the Church Courts in the Diocese of York*, p. 239).

3. W. H. Summers "State Papers relating to Beaconsfield", *Records of Bucks.*, VII, pp. 99, 104.

4. N.R.S., II, p. 368, III, p. 260, IV, pp. 346–7, V, p. 607.

5. A. J. Willis, *A Hampshire Miscellany, I* (1963), pp. 20, 36; A. Hussey, "Visitations of the Archdeacon of Canterbury", *Archaeologia Cantiana*, XXV, pp. 17–18, XXVII, p. 215; E. G. Breton, "17th century

of Shenley, Hertfordshire, was himself presented for ploughing on a saint's day.[1]

As the ministers and their lay supporters tried to elevate the especial sanctity of the Sabbath, so the hierarchy and the government played it down. In 1629 Laud had a quarrel with the Lord Mayor of London, because the latter, after issuing a drastic order against working on the Sabbath, arrested an old apple woman and forbade her to sell her goods in St. Paul's churchyard on a Sunday.[2] Yet Laud tried hard to compel abstention from labour on saints' days.[3] In the puritan archdeaconry of Bucks, presentments for working on Sundays and holy days increased ominously under Laud. There were 19 in 1633, 32 in 1634, 72 in 1635; but they dropped to 23 in 1636.[4] Evidence from elsewhere makes it difficult not to suppose that

Church Discipline", *History Teachers' Miscellany*, IV, p. 28; W. J. Pressey, "Some Essex Dialect Entries", *Essex Review*, XLV, pp. 134–5; ed. J. F. Williams, *Bishop Redman's Visitation, 1597* (Norfolk Record Soc., 1946), pp. 30–2, 35–6, 157–8; F. G. Emmison, "Abstract of the Act Book of the Archdeacon of Huntingdon's Court", *Trans. East Hertfordshire Archaeological Soc.*, VIII, pp. 28–9; Babbage, *Puritanism and Richard Bancroft*, pp. 344–6; *V.C.H. Bedfordshire*, I, p. 336; *V.C.H. Oxfordshire*, II, p. 41; Peyton, *Churchwardens' Presentments in the Oxfordshire Peculiars of Dorchester, Thame and Banbury*, pp. lxx, 27–30, 205–9, 288; W. Urwick, *Nonconformity in Hertfordshire* (1884), p. 458; Brinkworth, "The Laudian Church in Duckinghamshire" pp. 34, 50; Summers, "State Papers relating to Beaconsfield", p. 99; C. Jenkins, "Act Book of the Archdeacon of Taunton", *Collectanea*, II (Somerset Record Soc., XLIII), *passim*; J. M. J. Fletcher, "A Century of Dorset Documents", *Proceedings of the Dorset Natural History and Antiquarian Field Club*, XLVII, pp. 40–6; H. Johnstone, *Churchwardens' Presentments (17th century), Part I, Archdeaconry of Chichester* (Sussex Record Soc., XLIX), *passim;* Marchant, *The Puritans and the Church Courts in the Diocese of York*, pp. 77–8, 171; R. H. Skaife, "Extracts from Visitation Books at York", *Yorkshire Archaeological Journal*, XV, pp. 237, 241; ed. J. Raine, *The Injunctions and other Ecclesiastical Proceedings of Richard Barnes, Bishop of Durham* (Surtees Soc., 1850), p. 126; ed. F. R. Raines, *Private Devotions and Miscellanies of James, Seventh Earl of Derby* (Chetham Soc., 1867), I, p. xliii.

1. Urwick, *Nonconformity in Hertfordshire*, p. 460.
2. D. A. Williams, "Puritanism in the City Government, 1610–40", *Guildhall Miscellany*, I, No. 4, p. 9. The City authorities seem henceforth to have abandoned their attempt to stop Sabbath-breaking, presumably under government pressure. Cf. Rushworth, *Historical Collections*, II, pp. 22–3; Levy, *Der Sabbath in England*, p. 141; Pearl, *London and the Outbreak of The Puritan Revolution*. p. 79.
3. Laud, *Works*, V, pp. 391, 430–1, 445; VII, p. 299.
4. Brinkworth, "The Laudian Church in Buckinghamshire", p. 50.

the majority of these cases were for profaning saints' days.[1] In 1639 a stationer in London declared that he dared not sell parchment on Ascension Day, though he might without risk on a Sunday.[2] "The practice of the ecclesiastical courts" in trying "to charge upon men's consciences all the church holy days", was indeed "too injurious to men's worldly occasions", and it proved impossible to get local co-operation. "The people everywhere (specially in the country) do without any scruple reject them [saints' days] for the most part".[3]

In December 1640 the Commons' Committee for Religion reported, among many other "impossibilities" in the visitation articles for the diocese of London: "To present every householder not at church on holy days, Wednesdays and Fridays. What shops are open, etc."[4] At the same time signatures were being gathered all over London to a petition against the bishops, one clause of which complained against "the pressing of the strict observation of the saints' days, whereby great sums of money are drawn out of men's purses for working on them; a very high burthen on most people who, getting their living on their daily employments, must either omit them and be idle, or part with their money, whereby many poor families are undone, or brought behindhand: yet many church-wardens are sued, or threatened to be sued, for not presenting their parishioners who failed in observing holy days". For such "vain, idle and trivial matters as working or opening a shop on a holy-day", men were liable to excommunication.[5]

When the opposition – puritan and parliamentary – tried to find justifications for its different attitude, it looked for them in the Bible, the traditional protestant counter-authority to the authority of the hierarchy. Some of the extremes to which later Sabbatarianism resorted arose from belief in the literal inspiration of the Bible and equation of Sunday with the Jewish

1. Cf. pp. 150–1 above.
2. *H.M.C., Ninth Report, Appendix*, II, p. 498; cf. G. Ironside, *Seven Questions of the Sabbath*, pp. 228, 234, for examples of labour which a spokesman of the hierarchy would have permitted on Sundays. See also pp. 162–3 below.
3. Cawdrey and Palmer, *Sabbatum Redivivum*, p. 199.
4. Ed. W. Notestein, *The Journal of Sir Simonds D'Ewes* (Yale University Press, 1923), pp. 111–12.
5. Gardiner, *Constitutional Documents of the Puritan Revolution*, pp. 141–2.

Sabbath. But these extreme views came later, *after* the hierarchy had broken the virtual unanimity of early Elizabethan times on the subject of Sunday observance, which is summed up in that very "Puritan" document, the Homily *Of the Place and Time of Prayer*. Striking evidence of this sense that it was the Laudians who were the innovators, as well as of the passion which the subject aroused, is to be found in a private letter of Robert Reyce, written to John Winthrop in September 1636.[1]

III

If we want evidence that far profounder causes were at work than fanaticism or Bibliolatry, Mr. Whitaker has provided it. Thus in the two generations after 1572, the J.P.s of Lancashire, Cheshire, Devon, Cornwall, Yorkshire, Norfolk, Somerset, Middlesex, Worcestershire, Warwickshire, were all taking action to enforce Sunday observance: so were the municipal authorities of Ipswich, Rochester, Manchester, Rochdale, Liverpool, Lincoln, London, Southwark, Preston, Canterbury, Shrewsbury, Salisbury, Cambridge, Norwich, Maldon, Okehampton, Exeter and York.[2] There is no reason to suppose these are anything like complete lists: but they represent a fair cross-section of those areas of industrial England from which evidence happens to survive. In all these areas, local authori-

1. *Massachusetts Historical Soc. Collections*, 4th Series, VI, pp. 396–409; cf. *ibid.*, pp. 422–4, where Reyce copied out Prynne's *Newes from Ipswich*, which contains passages on the subject of the Sabbath. Cf. also J. Ley, *Sunday a Sabbath* (1641), pp. 101–15. Ley was anxious to show the Laudians that "Sabbath" was a respectable word, used by James I and many bishops.

2. *Whitaker, op. cit.*, pp. 37–9, 74–8, 81–4, 101–2, 117–19, 124; S. Clarke, *A Collection of the Lives of Ten Eminent Divines* (1662), p. 482; N. Bacon, *Annals of Ipswich* (1880), p. 427 (published 1654); R. L. Taverner, *The History of All Saints Church, Okehampton* (1961), p. 14; G. Chandler, *Liverpool Under James I* (1960), p. 260; Hill, *Lincoln*, pp. 99–100, 104; *V.C.H. Cambridgeshire*, III, p. 16; W. L. Sachse, "Minutes of the Norwich Court of Mayoralty, 1630–1", *Norfolk Record Soc.*, XV, p. 51; MacCaffrey, *Exeter*, pp. 97, 198; *V.C.H. Lancashire*, II, pp. 61–2; Halley, *Lancashire: its Puritanism and Nonconformity*, I, p. 147; *Kenyon MSS.* (H.M.C.), pp. 16–17; W. P. Baker, "The Observance of Sunday", in *Englishmen at Rest and Play* (ed. R. Lennard, 1931), p. 107; Tait, "The Declaration of Sports for Lancashire", *E.H.R.*, XXXII, p. 566; ed. A. Clark, *The Shirburn Ballads (1585–1616)* (1907), pp. 48–9; Frere, *The English Church in the Reigns of Elizabeth and James I*, p. 381; *V.C.H. York*, p. 202.

ties were far keener to prevent work on Sundays than government or hierarchy.

For further confirmation, consider the attitude of Parliament. As early as 1585 Elizabeth vetoed a bill for "the better and more reverent observing of the Sabbath", even though Burghley had been on the committee which steered it through the House of Lords. It was not a puritan bill. In 1601 there was another bill prohibiting the holding of fairs and markets on Sunday, and handing the enforcement of compulsory church attendance over to J.P.s. This also failed to get on to the statute book.[1] In 1606 a bill for the Sabbath passed the Commons, failed in the Lords: in the next Parliament the first bill that passed the Lower House was for the keeping of the Sabbath. It was accepted after amendment in the Lords, but Parliament was dissolved before it became law. In 1621 a bill was introduced which seems to have been aimed directly against James I's 1618 Declaration of Sports, since it forbade dancing and May games on the Sabbath.[2] It was passed *nem. con.* by the Commons, accepted by the Lords, but rather naturally did not receive the royal assent. In 1624 the same thing happened. Such a bill, an M.P. declared, "hath ever, since 27 Elizabeth, passed this House".[3] Next year a similar bill was the first item minuted in the *Commons' Journals*, and it passed both Houses, to receive the royal assent at last. This Act, unlike most earlier bills, was directed exclusively against unlawful sports, especially in towns: it said nothing about labour on the Sabbath. That subject was tackled again in 3 Car I. cap. 2, which forbade various kinds of work and travel on Sunday, and meetings of people outside their own parishes for common plays or unlawful sports. Carriers were forbidden to travel, butchers to kill or sell on Sundays. All that the House of Commons had to do in April 1641 was to order that "the statutes for the due observing of the Sabbath be put in execution".[4]

In 1621 an M.P. had by unanimous consent been deprived of

1. Neale, *Elizabeth I and her Parliaments, 1584–1601*, pp. 58–60, 394–5, 402–5.

2. N.R.S., II, p. 164, VII, p. 300; cf. T. L. Moir, *The Addled Parliament of 1614* (1958), p. 203.

3. *C.J.*, I, p. 671.

4. Whitaker, *Sunday in Tudor and Stuart Times*, pp. 104–15, 144–61, 188–92; N.R.S., VII, pp. 643–4; *Portland MSS.* (H.M.C.), III, p. 13; *C.J.*, II, p. 118.

his seat for a violent speech attacking a bill against profanation of the Sabbath, and for inveighing not only against Puritans but also against J.P.s. This last point aroused the fiercest indignation, and called forth Pym's first recorded speech in the House. For Shepherd had been guilty of "slander upon the Justices, as if they were ever ready to protect such as were refractory to his Majesty's laws".[1]

Responsible men outside Parliament were coming to take a similar view of the Sabbath. The mediaeval custom of electing churchwardens on a Sunday was abandoned.[2] In 1562 the Ironmongers' Company ordered that the day on which they yearly gave a great dinner should be altered from Sunday to Monday.[3] In 1613 the parishioners of Buxted, Sussex, agreed that their parish feast should not be held on St. James's day when that day happened to be a Sunday.[4] The previous year the municipal authorities of Cambridge had decided to adjourn selection of officials if the traditional date fell on a Sunday.[5] Richard Stock, the Feoffee for Impropriations, persuaded some City Companies to postpone their feasts from Monday to Tuesday, so that the Lord's Day should not be abused by the preparations.[6] The Six Clerks used to do official business and take fees on Sundays; but they reformed after a fire in their office in 1621, which they recognized as a judgment on them. Henceforth the doors were kept closed on the Sabbath.[7] Sir Augustine Nichol's "forbearing to travel on the Lord's Day wrought a reformation" on some of his fellow lawyers.[8] Thomas Gataker persuaded the lawyers of Lincoln's Inn to stop seeing clients on Sundays: his main argument was the necessity of setting a good example to the lower orders.[9]

1. N.R.S., II, pp. 82, 95–6.

2. F. Higham, *Catholic and Reformed* (1962), pp. 75–6.

3. Ed. J. G. Nichols, *Diary of Henry Machyn* (Camden Soc., 1848), p. 390.

4. Levy, *Dor Sabbath in England*, pp. 190–1.

5. *V.C.H. Cambridgeshire*, III, p. 16.

6. Fuller, *Worthies*, III, p. 468. But under-officers of the Eastland Company were expected to attend on the Governor or his deputy on Sundays just as on any other day (R.K.W. Hinton, *The Eastland Trade and the Common Weal*, 1959, p. 55).

7. Halliwell, *The Autobiography and Correspondence of Sir Simonds D'Ewes*, I, p. 210.

8. D. Lloyd, *State-Worthies* (1766), II, pp. 245–6.

9. T. Gataker, *A Discours Apologetical* (1654), pp. 16–17; cf. Coke, *I*

In a case of 1611 Sunday was held to be a *dies non* for the
sitting of courts or the meeting of public bodies.[1] Whereas
normally men robbed by highwaymen could sue the local
authority for the amount they had lost, no action would lie if
the robbery took place on a Sunday.[2] Even in 1633 the judges
were enforcing the Act of 1627 against driving cattle on Sundays.[3]

Things were different at Court. Edward VI directed that, as
a point of principle, the Council should meet to transact business on Sundays and the Secretary should report to him on
Sunday evenings. Elizabeth's ministers wrote despatches on
Sundays, and in 1559 the Queen herself went to a great banquet
on a Sunday. In 1599 a tilting match for the aristocracy was
held in London that day.[4] Burghley had thought it desirable
that "Sundays would be both by order and example more
strictly kept";[5] and in 1603 James issued a proclamation to this
effect. Nevertheless, in 1608 a masque was performed at court
on a Sunday.[6] The year before the King had aroused un-
favourable comment by travelling on a Sunday.[7] Sir George
Bolles, Lord Mayor in 1617, prohibited all carriage traffic in
time of service, and on one occasion James's coaches were
stopped as they passed through London in preparation for a

Institutes, p. 135; William Noy, *Principal Grounds and Maxims of the
Common Law* (1821), p. 2. For Heylyn's sneers at lawyers who had con-
scientious scruples about working on Sundays, see his *History of the
Sabbath*, in *Historical and Miscellaneous Tracts*, I, p. 490.

1. "The Law and Sunday", article in *The Times*, 23 January 1953.

2. John Clavell, *A Recantation of an ill ledde life* (1628), p. 27. Clavell,
a highwayman reprieved at the coronation of Charles I, advised travellers
not to ride on Sundays:

> "*For then the roads are quiet, and they know*
> *None ride but those have great affairs to do;*
> *Which to effect, 'tis thought, they have about them*
> *Great store of coin, and this makes thieves misdoubt them*".

3. Ed. T. G. Barnes, *Somerset Assize Orders* (Somerset Record Soc.,
1959), p. 66. This, however, was before Laud had tamed C. J. Richardson. See p. 40 above.

4. Buckle, *Miscellaneous and Posthumous Works*, II, p. 507, III, p.
161.

5. C. Read, *Lord Burghley and Queen Elizabeth* (1960), p. 120.

6. Whitaker, *op. cit.*, p. 70.

7. *Letters of John Chamberlain*, I, p. 245.

journey on the following day.[1] James was gracious to Bishop Davenant, who refused to travel on Sunday when called at short notice to preach at Court, and so arrived a day late;[2] but he sharply reproved Bishop Bayley for the Sabbatarianism expressed in *The Practice of Piety*.[3] Not only did courtiers profane the Sabbath, but public spectacles at Court kept people away from afternoon sermons, as when the Russian Ambassadors were given audience in 1628.[4] James's Privy Council met every Sunday morning, as Elizabeth's had done. This continued until Laud persuaded Charles to alter the time to Sunday afternoon.[5] Privy Councillors were sworn on Sundays, in 1628 as in 1592.[6] In 1636 great clamour was aroused when Davenant's masque, *Britannia Triumphans*, was acted at Court, by the King and his lords, on a Sunday.[7]

By contrast, the House of Commons refused in 1604 to have a conference with the Lords on a Sunday, the day suggested by the House in which the bishops sat.[8] The Long Parliament's Council of State met every day *except* Sunday. When in August 1641 Parliament felt it to be necessary to sit on a Sunday in order to transact urgent business before the King's departure for Scotland, the two Houses issued an explanation and apology, and insisted that their example was not to be followed.[9] At the same time it was noted by the Venetian Ambassador, as evidence of a crisis situation, that work on the City's fortifications was continued even on Sundays.[10] It took

1. Jordan, *The Charities of London*, pp. 380–1. Levy, *Der Sabbath in England*, p. 201. In 1619 the preacher at Paul's Cross dedicated his sermon to the Lord Mayor of London, Sir Sebastian Harvey, who had had "a singular care of God's Sabbath" (Stephen Denison, *The New Creature*, 1619, Sig. A 3v).

2. Fuller, *Worthies*, II, p. 360.

3. Ed. T. Birch, *The Court and Times of James I*, II, pp. 265–7; *Letters of John Chamberlain*, II, p. 387.

4. D'Ewes, *Autobiography and Correspondence*, II, p. 196. "A horrible profanation", D'Ewes thought it.

5. *Aulicus Coquinariae* (1650), in *Secret History of James I*, II, p. 143.

6. Buckle, *Miscellaneous and Posthumous Works*, III, p. 332; D'Ewes, *Autobiography and Correspondence*, II, p. 202.

7. Sir W. Davenant, *Works* (1872), II, p. 247.

8. Gardiner, *History of England*, I, p. 173.

9. Whitaker, *op. cit.*, pp. 144–5; *C.J.*, II, p. 245; cf. p. 837.

10. *C.S.P.*, *Venetian, 1642–3*, p. 256, quoted by Pearl, *London and the Outbreak of the Puritan Revolution*, p. 264.

the severe shock of Joyce's seizure of Charles I from Holmby House to make Parliament sit through the first Sunday of June 1647, and again after evening service on the Sunday following.[1] The conservative group in the Barebones Parliament met on a Sunday to plot its dissolution.[2] The Parliament of 1654 had a brief opening session on Sunday, to the indignation of Presbyterians; and in the same year Johnston of Warriston heard, with some disapproval, that Cromwell's Council met on the Sabbath. Johnston himself had stayed away from kirk service in 1643 when negotiating with Sir Henry Vane for the Solemn League and Covenant.[3] After the Restoration the Privy Council normally abstained from Sunday sessions, though an exception was made in the crisis of 1679.[4]

The sabbatarian activities before 1640 of local government authorities, of the House of Commons, and of numerous individuals of standing and responsibility, suggest that there was more here than mere doctrinal Puritanism. As with the objections of the City Fathers to stage plays, a powerful motive was dislike of the disorder to which Sunday sports and drinking, or theatrical performances, often gave rise.[5] When in 1643 the Lord Mayor of London was asked by Parliament to enforce the statutes on Sunday observance, he was especially careful to obey in respect of those whose breach led to noise or nuisance.[6] But there was also a strong social case for enforcement of Sunday rest. This has been obscured by historians who repeat contemporary propaganda emphasizing the "killjoy" side of Sabbatarianism.[7] Had there been no administrative action by J.P.s and municipal authorities and no legislation

1. Ed. A. F. Mitchell and J. Christie, *Records of the Commission of the General Assembly of the Church of Scotland* (Scottish History Soc., 1892–1909), I, p. 586. Ironically enough, it was on this Sabbath that the Commons, desperate for allies, voted the prentices a holiday on the first Tuesday of every month, to compensate for loss of saints' days (see p. 191 below).

2. E. R. Turner, *The Privy Council in the 17th and 18th centuries* (Johns Hopkins University Press, 1927), p. 303.

3. A. Johnston of Warriston, *Diary* (Scottish History Soc., 1911–40), II, p. 310, III, p. 22.

4. Turner, *op. cit.*, pp. 384–5, 425. See pp. 208–9 below.

5. See pp. 183–4, 195 below.

6. Whitaker, *op. cit.*, p. 143.

7. See pp. 26–7 above.

against Sunday work, the competitive pressure on some employers and some of the self-employed poor to work a seven-day week for some of the time would have been irresistible.

Sabbath-breaking was usually due to economic considerations, said Greenham and many others.[1] "How shall the poor do", John Mayne asked, "which want food and raiment, and cannot provide sufficiently upon the six days? May not they in this case work some part of the day?" (The answer was "No verily"[2]). "No schoolboy", agreed Cawdrey and Palmer, "is so unwilling to go to his book, no galley-slave so unwilling to tug at his oar, as we are all now naturally to wait upon God. . . . All men want wisdom to judge always at the instant when time is convenient for religion, men's minds naturally . . . being full of the world, and thoughts of worldly profits".[3] A competitive atomized society was replacing the communities which had to some degree protected their members. In this society it was the Sabbatarians who looked after the interests of the small craftsmen, apprentices and journeymen, who "would be left remediless under such masters as would both oppress them with labour and restrain them from God's service".[4] The Massachusetts Bay Company insisted that in the puritan promised land all labour should cease at 3.0 p.m. on Saturday. The rest of the day should be spent in catechizing and preparing for the Sabbath.

Sabbatarianism was *popular* with the industrious sort of people. It was disliked, John Sprint tells us in 1607, only by "such as either live in unlawful callings or unlawfully in their honest callings" – fiddlers, for example, stage-players, bear-

1. Greenham, *Workes*, pp. 163–5.
2. John Mayne, *The English Catechism Explained* (3rd. ed., 1623), p. 275. Note that Mayne's view is much stricter than the legislation of Edward VI quoted on pp. 145–6 above.
3. Cawdrey and Palmer, *Sabbatum Redivivum*, pp. 116–17, 126.
4. R. Baxter, *The Catechizing of Families* (1683), p. 285; Whitaker, *op. cit., passim,* esp. pp. 157–8. Mr. Whitaker's elucidation of this point is one of the most valuable contributions of his useful book. It had been made, forcibly, in a pathetic little book, *The Pearl of Days,* which in 1848 won a prize offered for the best essay on the Sabbath by a member of the working class. The author was a labourer's daughter. She argued that the Sabbath limited to some extent the power of employers (p. 27). Cf. a speech which Macaulay made on the Ten Hours Bill, stressing the *economic* advantages to the nation of Sunday rest and study (G.O. Trevelyan *Life and Letters of Lord Macaulay,* 1889, p. 465). See also pp. 199–203 below.

and bull-baiters, usurers.[1] Fuller says that "especially in corporations" people became "a law unto themselves, forbearing such sports as yet by statute permitted: yea, many rejoicing at their own restraint herein".[2] Nehemiah Wallington, a London turner who kept his own shop, began in the sixteen-thirties a large book in which for the next 20 years he recorded "God's Judgments on Sabbath Breakers".[3] There were plenty of Bibliolaters among the puritan Sabbatarians; but there was also a rational case for the Sunday rest. It was the habit of the age to find Biblical texts to justify men in doing what they would have done even if no texts could be found. Indeed George Abbott, in his *Vindiciae Sabbathi* (1641), justified the Sabbath rest by the law of nature as well as by divine command. It is important to remember this popular aspect of Sabbatarianism (at least in the towns) when we read sentimental accounts of those defenders of the old order who wished to retain the traditional rural sports. Take for instance, the Laudian Peter Heylyn. He, unlike the Puritans, was in favour of servants working on Sundays:[4] which Calvin had prohibited[5] and legislation of the sixteen-forties went out of its way to prevent. Take, again, the Rev. John Jegon, whose parishioners testified against him in 1643. He was "a prophaner of the Sabbath day, sending his servants usually on errands: and one day left his wife and servants to bag hops when himself went to evening prayer, and threatened to cudgel his man to it because he argued the unlawfulness of it; and these hops were the same day weighed and carted".[6]

1. J. Sprint, *Propositions, tending to proove the necessarie use of the Christian Sabbaoth* (1607), p. 26. Cf. p. 457 below.

2. Fuller, *Church History*, III, p. 144.

3. N. Wallington, *Historical Notices* (1869), I, pp. xxviii–ix, 49–60; cf. Henry Burton's *A Divine Tragedy Lately Enacted* (1641), *passim*. There was a large literature dealing with judgments on Sabbath-breakers, including Thomas Beard's *The Theatre of God's Judgments* (1599). Its popularity can be judged from the pains which Gilbert Ironside took to refute it in his *Seven Questions of the Sabbath* (1637), pp. 236–45.

4. Heylyn, *History of the Sabbath*, in *Historical and Miscellaneous Tracts*, p. 491; cf. his *Microcosmos* (1629), pp. 702–3.

5. "That servants be indulged with a day of rest, and thus have intermission from labour" (*Institutes of the Christian Religion*, I, p. 339).

6. Davids, *Nonconformity in Essex*, pp. 235–6. Jegon thought it a pity the Bible had ever been translated into English. But cf. Ironside's *Seven Questions of the Sabbath*, p. 269 (Household worship on the Sabbath must not be burdensome to servants); see pp. 464–5 below.

With the Laudian attitude we may contrast that of the Westminster Assembly of Divines, which in November 1644 voted that "the diet on the Sabbath day be so ordered that no servants or others be unnecessarily kept from the public service".[1] This was made law by Parliament two months later. The most passionate defence of the equal right of servants to Sunday rest known to me was written by two members of the Westminster Assembly: "Our adversaries . . . exempt shepherds, diggers in mines, servants (sundry sorts of them at least, as cooks and others. . . .) from any necessity of constantly observing the public worship. . . . Will they say that servants and inferiors are not members of the church?"[2]

IV

The suggestion is that there were social as well as religious reasons for Sabbatarianism in our period; that the opposition to it of king and bishops developed late, and was also social in its motivation: and that the question of Sunday sports was secondary to that of Sunday labour. If the traditional sports were popular in the countryside, the Sabbath rest was popular with the industrious sort, especially in the towns. Two modes of life, with their different needs and standards are in conflict as England moves out of the agricultural Middle Ages into the modern industrial world.

Nevertheless, the determination of English Puritans to prevent some forms of pleasure on Sunday does call for explanation. The fact that men laboured for their full six days and rested the seventh would seem to justify them in claiming a right to recreation on Sunday.[3] The English puritan attitude is generally dated from and attributed to *The Doctrine of the Sabbath*, published in 1595, and written by Dr. Nicholas Bownde. His doctrine, wrote Rogers in 1607, "had taken deep impression in men's hearts, and was dispersed (while our watchmen were otherwise busied, if not asleep) over the whole kingdom".[4] Influential though Bownde's book undoubtedly

1. J. Lightfoot, *Works* (1824), XIII, pp. 328–9.
2. Cawdrey and Palmer, *Sabbatum Redivivum*, pp. 258–60. They were criticizing especially Gilbert Ironside.
3. See pp. 168, 175–6, 192 below.
4. T. Rogers, *The Faith, Doctrine and Religion, professed and protected . . . in England*, Sig. C 2v. Rogers was Bancroft's chaplain, and his book

was in publicizing the attitude, it would not have been so effective had there not already existed a pre-disposition to accept it.[1] Respect for the Sabbath was part of the common protestant heritage, summed up in the *Homily of the Place and Time of Prayer*.[2]

In 1575 Bishop Cooper of Winchester had ordered the suppression of "church ales, May games, morris dances and other vain pastimes".[3] Eleven years later Robert Hamond of Bobingen was alleged to have said that it was as good to steal a horse as play lawful games on the Sabbath: for which he had to account for himself in the ecclesiastical court.[4] The Dedham Classis in 1583 was anxiously discussing Sabbath observance; it decided to ask for advice from "some godly men in Cambridge".[5] At Cambridge from 1578 onwards, before either Greenham or Bownde, and probably influencing both of them, Lancelot Andrewes delivered lectures on the Ten Commandments, in which he insisted on the strictest observance of the Fourth Commandment. Keeping holy the Sabbath day he held to be part of the moral, not the ceremonial law. But these lectures were not published until 1630. The Laudians had some difficulty in laughing them off when the King's Book of Sports had said the opposite. In Andrewes's visitation articles of 1619 and 1622 there were still searching questions about Sunday observance.[6]

---

was published a year after a revised and enlarged edition of Bownde's *True Doctrine* had appeared. For an early example of Bownde's influence, see *The Diary of Lady Margaret Hoby* (ed. D. M. Meads, 1930, pp. 62, 243) where "bond of the Sabbath", which the editor could not identify, is Bownde. This was in 1599. See also R. Cawdrey, *A godly forme of Household governement* (1614), Sig. B 3–C 5, pages which derive largely from Bownde. (Cawdrey's book was first published in 1600.)

1. Gilbert Ironside was wrong when he said that Sabbatarianism was unknown to the Marian martyrs, but more correct when he added that by 1637 "all religion" is (for Puritans) "reduced to this one head, the observation of the Sabbath" (*Seven Questions of the Sabbath*, Sig. B lv–B 2).

2. Cf. also the Injunctions of 1547, quoted on p. 166 below.

3. M. C. Bradbrook, *The Rise of the Common Player* (1962), p. 142.

4. Hale, *A Series of Precedents and Proceedings*, p. 187. Bishop White of Ely was still endeavouring to counter similar arguments 50 years later (F. White, *A Treatise of the Sabbath-day*, 1635, p. 246).

5. Usher, *The Presbyterian Movement in the Reign of Elizabeth*, p. 30.

6. P. A. Welsby, *Lancelot Andrewes* (1958), pp. 23–9, 224. Bishop

But, as in so many other respects, the fifteen-nineties seem to have witnessed a shift of emphasis. One of the most influential Puritans of his generation, Richard Greenham, published his *Treatise of the Sabbath* in 1592. In this work, with which Lancelot Andrewes may have collaborated, Greenham insisted that Sunday should be wholly given up to meditation and spiritual exercises: there should be no labour and no feasting. "No book in that age", said Fuller, "made greater impression on people's practice".[1] Its significance has been obscured for historians because the content of Greenham's book was summed up and elaborated by his step-son, Nicholas Bownde.

So when Bownde published his notorious book in 1595, he was only extending a thesis on which there had previously been considerable agreement. His position, like that of Greenham, was substantially that of Calvin.[2] The fact that Calvin had played bowls on Sunday worried some of the more zealous Sabbatarians, who did not approve of bishops who in this followed Calvin's example.[3] For Calvin the Sabbath was not merely a rest-day for servants, but also the day on which "believers were to cease from their own works, and allow God to work in them; . . . a stated day on which they should assemble to hear the law and perform religious rites, or which, at least, they should specially employ in meditating on His works, and be thereby trained to piety. . . . The Sabbath was appointed for no other purpose than to render [men] conformable to their Creator". A carnal cessation from labour is therefore insufficient.[4] "The principal end then of rest", said

White, in his *Treatise of the Sabbath-day*, tries to explain Andrewes away.

1. Fuller, *Church History* (1842), III, pp. 132, 134.

2. For Greenham and Calvin, see Greenham's *Workes*, pp. 809–12, 839–42.

3. The practice of Geneva was quoted against excessive Sabbatarianism, e.g. by Laud (*Works*, II, pp. 252–5); by the translator of John Prideaux's *The Doctrine of the Sabbath* (1634), in his Preface (Sig. B 3); and of course by Heylyn, *History of the Presbyterians*, p. 27. Cf. Marchant, *The Puritans and the Church Courts in the Diocese of York*, p. 37. Lady Brilliana Harley thought that it was because Calvin "was so earnest in opposing the popish holy days that he entrenched upon the holy Sabbath" (*Letters*, p. 63). Baxter was also a little uneasy in his attempts to explain away Calvin's and Beza's laxness (*Works*, XIII, p. 451). Aylmer played bowls on Sunday afternoons. The practice was defended by Bishop Cooper in his *Admonition*, pp. 43–4.

4. Calvin, *Institutes*, I, pp. 339–41; cf. p. 258.

Bownde, "is that we might wholly in soul and body without all let and interruption attend upon the worship of God". Refreshment of the body is only a secondary cause of the Sabbath rest; though Bownde shrewdly pointed out to employers that granting one rest day a week is to their economic advantage.[1]

Let us return for a moment to the Injunctions of 1547. These declare: – "Like as the people be commonly occupied the workday with bodily labour for their bodily sustenance, so was the holy day at the first beginning godly instituted and ordained that the people should that day give themselves wholly to God". Sunday, that is to say, should be the day of spiritual labour, for spiritual sustenance. But "in our time, God is more offended than pleased, more dishonoured than honoured upon the holy day, because of idleness, pride, drunkenness, quarrelling and brawling".[2] People think they have sufficiently honoured God if they go to church, "though they understand nothing to their edifying". The conclusion is significant. "Therefore all the king's faithful and loving subjects shall from henceforth celebrate and keep their holy day according to God's holy will and pleasure, that is, in hearing the Word of God read and taught, in private and public prayers, [good works] . . . and godly conversation".[3]

We should abstain from outward or bodily works on the Sabbath, said Bullinger, "but so that we should have the leisure to attend unto our spiritual business. For that cause is the outward rest commanded, that the spiritual work should not be hindered by bodily business".[4] This formulation was accepted even by Whitgift, who indeed at the instance of the 1586 Convocation had ordered all his clergy to buy Bullinger's *Decades* and study them constantly.[5] Tyndale had put it even more forcefully in replying to some rather pedantic arguments of Sir Thomas More's. "We be lords over the Sabbath" he asserted, and might change it to any other day of the week, or have two Sabbaths every week *if one was not enough for teach-*

1. Bownde, *op. cit.*, (1606), pp. 129–30 (expanded from pp. 57–8 of the 1595 ed.) and p. 174.
2. This phrase is echoed in the *Homily of the Place and Time of Prayer*. The same point had been made in *The King's Book*, in 1543.
3. Cardwell, *Documentary Annals*, I, pp. 15–16.
4. Bullinger, *Decades*, I, p. 255.
5. Whitgift, *Works*, II, p. 588; cf. p. 565.

ing the people.[1] Recalling what puritan ministers said about the ignorance and need for discipline of the majority of the population, and of the need for constant vigilance over themselves by the elect, their attitude towards the Sabbath becomes clear. It was the day for edification, for education.

Bownde's book plays the familiar puritan trick of returning to the Bible as a means of criticizing those mediaeval institutions and ceremonies of which he and his like disapproved. Since they were not to be found in the sacred Scriptures, they must be got rid of. Saints' days are of human institution. God sanctified the Sabbath only. Some contemporaries saw that this was an attack on the authority of the church as an institution.[2] "Topical or probable arguments", said Bishop White of Ely, "either from consequence of Scripture or from human reason, ought not to be admitted or credited against the consistent testimony and authority of the ancient Catholic Church on the Sabbath".[3] Otherwise how should the authority of the Church stand in other matters? A door would be opened to all kinds of democratic criticism. "It cannot go well with the Church unless due subordination . . . be maintained and observed; and then men of meaner judgment and capacity submit themselves to such as are able to govern and direct them".[4]

By the fifteen-nineties theological unity and respect for Calvin were declining among English Protestants.[5] Bownde's treatise was suppressed, with the usual inflationary effect an sales. A second edition, "enlarged with answers to objections" was published in 1606, dedicated to John Jegon, Bishop of Norwich. (The first edition, rather less happily, had been dedicated to the Earl of Essex). The "Epistle Dedicatory" contains a laboured defence of Bownde's respect for "the governors of the church and commonwealth". It may be lawful, he concedes, for such governors to break the Sabbath, in peace or in war, for reasons best known to themselves: and

1. W. Tyndale, *An Answer to Sir Thomas More's Dialogue, The Supper of the Lord* (Parker Soc., 1850), p. 97.

2. T. Rogers, *op. cit.*, Sig. C 2–3.

3. Francis White, *A Treatise of the Sabbath-day* (1635), p. 15; cf. pp. 95, 104.

4. *Ibid.*, pp. 309–10, citing the recantation of Theophilus Brabourne, for whom see p. 197 below.

5. See pp. 485–90 below.

the people ought to obey superiors' orders, even if they involve Sabbath-breaking, without asking questions.[1] Among the enlargements apparently made in answer to criticisms occurs the oft-quoted passage in which Bownde allowed feasts to be given on the Sabbath by "noblemen and great personages". He goes on, however, to say that lords, knights and gentlemen must whenever possible leave their families free to go to church, working a shift system if they live in towns where there is more than one service: so they will "provide for the glory of God, and yet not altogether neglect the convenient furniture of their tables".[2] Too much emphasis should not be laid on this concession. It may only be evidence of what the rulers of Bownde's society insisted on his saying, rather than of what he would have ideally wished to say.[3]

It was the popular festivals to which Bownde and his like mainly objected. "They that be wealthy . . . have greater liberty than others", said Bownde: his task, as he conceived it, was "to speak to the poorest".[4] (George Hakewill made what would seem today the obvious point, that if anyone had a right to recreation on Sundays to refresh their spirits, it was rather "tradesmen and husbandmen" than "gentlemen, who for the most part make every day holiday in following their sports".[5])

The view that, after public worship on Sunday, "men have liberty either to give themselves to labour, or to honest pleasures and recreations . . . doth quite abolish one of the commandments of the Decalogue", declared Perkins. He was no less severe to "the common sort" who argued that they could not maintain themselves and their families if they must abstain from work the whole day.[6] The Sabbath, for the Puritans, was

1. This appears to conflict with the argument of the text at pp. 183–5 of the 1606 edition.

2. N. Bownde, *The True Doctrine of the Sabbath* (1606 ed.), pp. 211–12. The passage is an expansion of pp. 105–6 of the 1595 ed.

3. Cf. Heylyn, cited on p. 162 above.

4. Bownde, *op. cit.* (1606), p. 143. He is speaking of labour at harvest-time. Cf. pp. 130–1 above.

5. G. Hakewill, *A Short, But Cleare, Discourse of the . . . Lords-Day* (1641), p. 36. Baxter also observed that students, lawyers and gentlemen, unlike the poor, could afford to take exercise on week-days (*The Divine Appointment of the Lord's Day*, in *Practical Works*, 1830, XIII, pp. 445–6).

6. Perkins, *Workes*, II, pp. 109–11; cf. Greenham, "The Lord giveth six days to work and but one to serve Him" (*Workes*, p. 810).

the day on which men should be educated in their religious and social duties, the day of preaching, catechizing, indoctrination. It was a sin to work on that day, or indeed on any day of the week when labour would conflict with spiritual duties.[1] "I zealously kept the Sabbath", wrote Mary Proude of her childhood in the sixteen-thirties, "not daring to eat or be clothed with such things as occasioned much trouble or took up much time on that day, which I believe ought to be devoted to hearing, reading and praying".[2] The Sabbath was not a day of leisure, on which it was lawful to waste time: it was a day for a different kind of labour, for wrestling with God. The whole of Bownde's Second Book (i.e. half the treatise) is devoted to the use of the Sabbath for meditation and edification. "It is a notable abuse of many", said Perkins, "to make the Lord's Day a set day of sport and pastime, which should be a day set apart for the worship of God and the increase in duties of religion". Heads of households were especially to blame for conniving at this abuse in their servants and employees.[3] Everyone, Turk, papist or other pagan, "ought to be compelled to conform himself to the outward service of the true God", wrote Penry in 1587. This service necessarily included listening to sermons.[4] John Cotton taught – in 1614, before he left England – that it was not lawful to let the Sabbath pass without hearing two sermons.[5]

Of course the mass of the unregenerate wished to pass the seventh day in idleness and debauchery, but that was because they were unregenerate. It should not be left to them to choose. They should be compelled to come in and be edified. Adam, even in Paradise, "was to set one day apart from all works of

1. White, *op. cit.*, pp. 227, 231.

2. L. V. Hodgkin, *Gulielma, Wife of William Penn* (1947), p. 7.

3. Perkins, *Workes*, I, p. 775. Substantially the same view was held by Bishop Hooper (R. Cox, *The Literature of the Sabbath Question*, 1865, I, pp. 136–7); by Robert Browne (*Writings of Harrison and Browne*, p. 329); by George Widley (*The Doctrine of the Sabbath*, 1604, pp. 72–4); by William Gouge (*Commentary on Hebrews*, I, p. 305); by Samuel Rutherford (*Letters*, ed. A. Bonar, 1894, p. 522); by Baxter (*The Reformed Pastor*, 1655, p. 82). *The Shorter Catechism* extended the prohibition on work to "unnecessary thoughts, words or works about wordly employments or recreations" (1897, pp. 10–11).

4. Penry, *Three Treatises*, pp. 60, 155.

5. Venables, "The Primary Visitation of the Diocese of Lincoln" p. 51.

his vocation, that he might wholly addict himself to religious and holy exercises". For fallen man the necessity was far greater. "It were better to leave our work undone, upon the days allowed for our labour, than God's work, on God's day, appointed for His service".[1] The Sabbath is the market-day of the soul, on which we lay in spiritual food for the following week; a day "that doth saints enrich". So said Bownde's son-in-law, John Dod; so said Gataker, Palmer, Geree and very many others.[2] Sabbath meditation was above all necessary for the industrious sort, who would otherwise devote themselves to worldly occasions and be in danger of having their hearts "corrupted and glued to the world".[3] It was this aspect of reading and meditation which the 1645 ordinance for Sabbath observance especially emphasized.

Hence (among other reasons) attendance at church on Sundays was compulsory, in England as in Geneva and Zurich. The heavy stress on catechizing is part and parcel of this desire to use the Sabbath for edifying and instructing the lower orders. "We be enjoined to it. . . . We have law to enforce them to come to be instructed by a book": so said the Rev. Robert Lewis during a discussion in the Dedham Classis in 1584.[4] If servants were to be educated and disciplined at all, Sunday was the only day on which the job could be tackled. William Kiffin tells us how he and his fellow apprentices "had no opportunity of converse but on the Lord's Day". They used to meet for religious discussion an hour before the 6 o'clock morning lecture.[5] For many of the industrious sort, a Sabbath passed in such exercises would indeed – in John Preston's unexpected phrase – be "kept with delight".[6]

1. Dod and Cleaver, *Ten Commandements*, pp. 120, 131.
2. H. C. Porter, *Reformation and Reaction in Tudor Cambridge* (1958), p. 224; T. Gataker, quoted in the epigraph to this chapter; H. Palmer, *Memorial of Godlinesse and Christianitie* (2nd ed., 1645), p. 20; J. Geree, *The Character of an Old English Puritane* (1646); W. G., *The Sabbaths Sanctification* (1641), p. 39. Cf. *A Garden of Spirituall Flowers* (1643), Part II, p. 175; J. Mason, *Spiritual Songs* (10th ed., 1718), p. 35. First published 1683.
3. A. Hildersam, *CLII Lectures Upon Psalme LI* (1635), p. 320.
4. Ed. Usher, *The Presbyterian Movement under Queen Elizabeth*, p. 90.
5. W. Orme, *Remarkable Passages in the Life of William Kiffin* (1823), pp. 11–12.
6. Preston, *The Saints Qualification* (2nd ed., 1634), p. 66. The phrase recurs in a Parliamentary ordinance of January 1645: see p. 191 below.

V

Just as the doctrine of the dignity of labour made some of the industrious sort ask questions about rentiers, so Sabbatarianism might stimulate a critical independence in prentices and journeymen. This appears from an illuminating controversy between Edward Brerewood, Professor of Astronomy at Gresham College, and Nicholas and Richard Byfield. Brerewood accused Nicholas Byfield, lecturer in Chester, of having by his preaching encouraged an apprentice to refuse to obey his master when ordered to perform household duties on the Sabbath. The apprentice was Brerewood's nephew, and the Professor was himself liable to suffer if the indenture of apprenticeship was broken, since he had gone surety for his nephew. So Brerewood refuted Byfield's thesis in a powerful argument, which must have delighted the hearts of City employers. The law of nature, he declared, binds servants to obey their masters: "which law of nature the laws of God dissolve not". The commandment to observe the Sabbath was given to masters: it was not given, was indeed not fit to be given, to servants, who "do not need to be commanded to take their ease on the Sabbath". Servants are not *homines juris sui*, nor *operum suorum domini*: they are but their masters' living instruments.[1] If the master gave wrongful commands, the sin was his, not the servant's: the duty of the latter was to obey without question. He might complain to lawful authority, "to whom the oversight of laws belongs". But even lawful authority might not order a servant to disobey: it might only tell the master not to lay such commands on him. In any case the commandment to obey the Sabbath had been in part revoked by the teaching of Jesus; "the Apostles knew full well that to tell servants to disobey their masters was not the way to propagate the Gospel". Sunday observance rests on the canons of the church and the edicts of the prince: the authority of employers is something far more fundamental. The dregs of Byfield's doctrine, Brerewood thought, could lead to "nothing but disturbance and sedition both in church and commonwealth".[2]

1. The Levellers were to refuse the franchise to servants on precisely these grounds: see C. B. Macpherson, *The Political Theory of Possessive Individualism* (1962), Chapter III, *passim*.

2. E. Brerewood, *A Learned Treatise of the Sabbath* (1636); *A Second Treatise of the Sabbath* (1637), *passim*. First published 1630 and 1632 respectively.

Richard Byfield, replying for his dead brother, asserted that the Fourth Commandment was for servants no less than for masters. They were not merely chattels, subordinate to the will of their lords: servants too were responsible human beings with rights and duties. "As thy servant, he is not thine in thy . . . servile works that day [the Sabbath], but the Lord's freeman, yet thy servant that day by thee to be injoined to the Lord's work, God's servant to be free from thy works". "The servant is not to fulfil the boundless and unlawful puttings forth of that [his master's] power. . . . The servant remaineth no less in his master's power, but to higher ends, but more free to God's service, while the master may not call him off by unjust exactions. And so far is this from occasioning any disobedience that it occasioneth, and properly effecteth in the servant's heart, a conscionable, and produceth in his life an entire and single-hearted, obedience to his master as to the Lord".[1]

The reasoning is tortuous, but the tendency is clear: under certain circumstances the servant can refuse obedience to his master. We recall the manservant whom the Rev. John Jegon threatened to cudgel because he argued the unlawfulness of labouring on Sunday;[2] and there were maid-servants in Hertfordshire who had conscientious scruples about washing dishes or cleaning kitchens on the Sabbath.[3] Respectable Presbyterians like Cawdrey and Palmer asked in 1645: what are servants to do when masters charge them to stay at home during service, and threaten or beat them – "cases . . . which are every day one where or another"? Even servants and in-

1. Richard Byfield, *The Doctrine of the Sabbath Vindicated* (1631), pp. 6–7, 44–5, 187–9. Nicholas Byfield's *Posthume Works*, it is perhaps not irrelevant to note, were published in 1623 with a preface by William Gouge, the Feoffee for Impropriations. Byfield had a considerable influence among the radical Puritans: see for instance Johnston of Warriston's *Diary* (Scottish History Soc., I, p. 104 and index).

2. See p. 162 above.

3. Ed. W. Le Hardy, *Hertfordshire County Records*, V (1928), p. 249. This point was made clearly in *The Pearl of Days* (see p. 161 above). The Sabbath rest was essential not only for health and cleanliness but also for the strenuous spiritual activity necessary if members of the working class were to improve themselves and others. The Sabbath alone gave them leisure and the moral force to make themselves heard. Without the Sabbath the workers would be ignorant indeed, potential slaves of despots, tools of crafty politicians, or followers of superstitious zealots. It was essential for the liberty of the working man and his wife (pp. 34–46, 59, 66–9, 74).

feriors, the two divines concluded, were bound to observe God's commandment, "notwithstanding any opposition of men, masters, parents and others".[1]

Both Brerewood and Byfield were aware that such teaching had political consequences. Byfield argued that Brerewood had been refuted in advance by Greenham, and carefully defended his brother's doctrine from the charge that it encouraged social insubordination. On the contrary, denial of their moral responsibility "casts servants (and by the same reason all inferiors) under an insupportable burden, which hath always (through man's corruption) caused rebellion and disturbance. Secondly, it taketh them from under the command of their prince and country: for if God may not command them to His service, because as you say it is against the law of nature: how may princes command them to their occasions?" The transitions are historically accurate: loyalty to the national state first challenged absolute subordination to the immediate feudal lord; then the puritan concept of overriding obedience to God rather than man threatened all loyalties within the framework of existing society. For any master, said Byfield, "by nature is ready to prefer his humour, pride and profit before the fear of sin".[2] "The only fear of God's displeasure hazardeth us upon your Majesty's", a deprived minister assured James I in 1605.[3] It was no sectarian radical, but John Pym's friend Richard Sibbes who wrote "When we become Christians to purpose, we live not exempt from all service, but only we change our lord". "Ambitious men study accommodation of themselves to the humours of those by whom they hope to be raised; and shall not we study application of ourselves to Christ, by whom we hope to be advanced?" He summed this aspect of Puritanism up in the phrase "new Lords, new laws".[4]

The danger here, the possibility that the whole controversy might have intellectually liberating effects, was acutely felt by conservatives. For the negative arguments of both sides made their mark. The radicals attacked the authority of the

1. Cawdrey and Palmer, *Sabbatum Redivivum*, pp. 258–60.

2. R. Byfield, *op. cit.*, pp. 92–3, 181–2. Mr. Whitaker shrewdly noted that there was "no room for democratic ideas" in Brerewood's theory (*op. cit.*, p. 79). Cf. Greenham, *Workes*, pp. 231, 374.

3. John Burges, quoted by Babbage, *Puritanism and Richard Bancroft*, p. 382.

4. R. Sibbes, *The Bruised Reed* (1838), pp. 11, 40, 103.

Church, the conservatives attacked irrational Bibliolatry in things indifferent.[1] Thus Theophilus Brabourne argued that to regard the Sabbath as only ceremonial opened the door to Anabaptistry: if the Sabbath rest was not absolutely binding on believers, because instituted by divine command, then the master and mistress in a godly household might treat it as an ordinary working day for themselves, whilst strictly enforcing Sabbath observance on their unbelieving servants.[2] This neat illustration of the economic consequences of antinomianism roused the wrath of Bishop White: but he had no very satisfactory answer.[3]

It was the uncomfortableness of discussing such matters in public that made so many conservatives fear toleration and free discussion. The greatest of them all, Thomas Hobbes, had taken the point, though he twisted it to serve his own highly unorthodox anti-clerical purposes. In 1636 he wrote to a correspondent, apropos of Heylyn's *History of the Sabbath*, expressing apprehension lest books of that kind "put such thoughts into the heads of vulgar people as will confer little to their good life. For when they see one of the ten commandments to be *jus humanum* merely (as it must be, if the church can alter it) they will hope also that the other nine may be so too. For every man hitherto did believe that the ten commandments were the moral, that is an eternal, law".[4] Here we have summed up the whole paradox of Hobbes's political thought. He was of the saints' party against clerical authoritarianism, and he knew it, though on political matters he opposed them. But what was Hobbes to say positively? If the church cannot tell us what is the moral law, who can? Leviathan, answers Hobbes. But then Leviathan can change "the moral, that is an eternal, law"? Hobbes would shrug his shoulders at that and say that we do not always do everything that we can: sovereigns

1. Cf. those who used arguments drawn from the new geography to show that in the polar regions days might be several weeks long (White, *op. cit.*, pp. 178–9).

2. T. Brabourne, *A Defence of the Most Ancient, and Sacred Ordinance of God, the Sabbath Day* (1632), pp. 13–14, 619. Cf. T. Adams, *The Happiness of the Church* (1619), I, pp. 226–7. See pp. 203–6 below.

3. White, *op. cit.*, p. 131. It also illustrates the Puritan assumption that servants are likely to be ungodly; and shows the pressure on small masters towards unremitting labour which Sabbatarian legislation tried to check.

4. Peck, *Desiderata Curiosa* (1779), p. 218.

must learn to act rationally no less than subjects. Meanwhile the clergy should not make extravagant claims which provoke embarrassing retorts. But the door is opened wide. There is no half-way house between complete intellectual submission and complete rationalism. Neither the divine right of kings nor the sovereign Leviathan could restore what Luther had unwittingly and unwillingly overthrown – authority in matters of faith. Four and a half centuries have failed to find a *via media* that will stand honest intellectual examination.

Dangers lurked in unlimited discussion of sabbatarian doctrine by the lower classes, dangers of which the Laudians were most conscious before 1640, but which came to the notice of orthodox Puritans during the interregnum. It may have been from awareness of the ambivalence of their teaching that the preachers stressed so heavily family worship on the Sabbath, under the guidance of heads of households.[1]

"Why is the charge of keeping the Sabbath more especially directed to governors of families?" asked *The Larger Catechism*. The reply was that they had a dual obligation, to observe the Sabbath themselves and to see that their dependants were free to do so.[2] The model head of a family took – literally took – his children, servants and neighbours to church with him on that day.[3] After service servants must not be called upon to work.[4] William Gouge had no supper on Saturday evenings, so that his servants were not kept up late; and no servant stayed at home to prepare a meal on Sundays.[5] But the duties of the head of the household were positive too. "Where is the master", Philip Stubbes asked, "that hath had a conscience to restrain his servants from this impiety [of going to plays], or the servant

1. See Chapter 13 below.
2. *The Larger Catechism*, p. 163.
3. For the theory see Grindal, *Remains*, pp. 137–8; W. H. Frere and W. P. M. Kennedy, *Visitation Articles and Injunctions* (Alcuin Club Collections, XVI), pp. 266, 288; Perkins, *Workes*, III, p. 699; Bownde, *op. cit.* (1606), pp. 448–54, 458–9; Dod and Cleaver, *Ten Commandements*, pp. 145–6; *Directions of the General Assembly concerning Secret and Private Worship*, p. 9. For the practice, see Hinde's *Life of John Bruen*, quoted in *The Journal of Nicholas Assheton* (ed. F. R. Raines, Chetham Soc., 1848), pp. 3–4.
4. Bullinger, *Decades*, I, pp. 257–8, 262–3; Grindal, *Remains*, pp. 137–8.
5. Thomas Gouge, *A Narrative of the Life and Death of Doctor Gouge* (1655), in W. Gouge, *A Commentary on Hebrews*, I, pp. vii–viii.

again that hath . . . well accepted his master's or mistress's restraint being made unto him, and which hath not rather burst out into ungodly and disobedient speeches, murmuring that because he hath wrought all the week, therefore he should have liberty to do what he list on the Sabbath?"[1] Heads of households were held responsible for their servants' absence from church: or if they played in the streets or walked in the fields.[2]

The puritan ideal was that men, women and children should be persuaded or compelled to come to church, should hear a sermon there expounding wholesome doctrine; and that then the rest of the day should be passed in repetition and discussion of the sermon, in spiritual instruction, in education.[3] Both *The Practice of Piety* and *The Whole Duty of Man* envisaged the intervals not occupied in public worship as spent "privately at home in praying with and instructing our families". "Let no man think that a bare rest from labour is all that is required of him on the Lord's Day, but the time which he saves from the works of his calling he is to lay out on those spiritual duties".[4] "Those families where there is no repeating of the Word preached", wrote Anthony Burges, "do plainly discover that they regard not the retaining of it in their hearts".[5] An ideal order was enforced in his family by the Rev. Herbert Palmer, Master of Queens' College, Cambridge under the Long Parliament, and co-author of a treatise on the Sabbath which I have frequently quoted. All members of his household attended public worship and family prayers. In the evening "he required of all his servants, and the young gentlemen that sojourned with him, an account of such portions of Scripture

1. P. Stubbes, *The Anatomie of Abuses* (ed. F. J. Furnivall, 1879), p. 81; Bownde, *op. cit.* (1606), pp. 448–63. Cf. p. 163 above.

2. Hill, *Lincoln*, pp. 99–100 (1572, 1584); *Yorkshire Archaeological Soc. Miscellany*, VI (1953), pp. 24–5.

3. *Reliquiae Baxterianae*, I, pp. 83–4; cf. J. Bunyan, *Works* (1860), III, p. 600, on Sabbath observance as a test of "the hearts and inclinations of *poor* people" (my italics). Cf. Baxter's Preface (1672) to *The Lords-Day* (a translation of Thomas Young's *Dies Dominica*, 1639), Sig. A 4–5.

4. Bayley, *The Practice of Piety*, pp. 270–2; *The Works of The . . . Author of the Whole Duty of Man*, pp. 18–19; cf. p. 44. Dr. Johnson included the instruction of his family as well as church-going, reading and meditation in a programme for Sabbath observance which he drew up in 1755 (Boswell, *Life of Johnson*, Everyman, ed., I, p. 184).

5. A. Burges, *The Doctrine of Original Sin* (1659), p. 267.

as had been read in public; and as they recited particular passages thereof, he gave brief expositions of them, and observations from them; pressing them to meditate in private of what they read in public". Palmer packed his servants off to bed early on Saturday night and would eat nothing on Sunday whose preparation kept them from church.[1]

The village of Barnsley, near Cirencester, came as near to perfection in these respects as is possible in a sinful world. When John Taylor visited it in 1652 he found that little children were not suffered to walk or to play, and two women who had been to both morning and afternoon services were put in the stocks for walking in the fields for recreation.[2] But even Barnsley could not compare with Aberdeen. There on Tuesday, Thursday and Saturday afternoons all shops were shut, and the people were compelled to attend lectures. On Sundays the highways were watched for absentees from church.[3] In Scotland the presbyterian discipline really took root, sometimes with curious consequences. Thus in April 1646, at the height of critical negotiations between Charles I, the Scots and the English Parliament, Balmerino, travelling to Newark with an urgent message from London, halted when 13 miles short of his destination in order not to travel on the Sabbath.[4]

VI

The traditional sports in the countryside, and plays in the towns, were the main rivals to religious education on Sundays. Twenty-five years before Bownde wrote, a preacher at Blandford said that "the multitude" call Sunday "their revelling day, which is spent in bull-baitings, bear-baitings, bowls, dicing,

1. S. Clarke, *The Lives of Two and Twenty English Divines* (1660), p. 227; H. Palmer, *Memorial of Godliness and Christianity* (11th ed., 1681), Sig. A 8; cf. p. 114, and *The Necessity and Encouragement of Utmost Venturing for the Churches Help* (1643), pp. 38–9. Palmer was a supporter of presbyterian government (Clarke, *op. cit.*, p. 229). For his refusal to read the 1633 Declaration of Sports see p. 193 below.

2. John Taylor, *A Short Relation of a Long Journey* (1652), p. 23. I fear that Taylor, no friend of Puritans, may have had his tongue in his cheek.

3. J. Spalding, *Memorialls of the Trubles in Scotland and in England* (Spalding Club, 1850–1), II, pp. 226–7. Cf. p. 160 above.

4. Ed. J. G. Fothcringham, *The Diplomatic Correspondence of Jean de Montereul and the brothers de Bellièvre* (Scottish History Soc., 1898–9), I, p. 185. There are parts of Scotland to-day in which his behaviour would be thought merely right and proper.

carding, dancing, drunkenness and whoredom, inasmuch as men could not keep their servants from lying out of their houses the same Sabbath day at night".[1] Ten years later, fully in the spirit of the Injunctions of 1547, the translator of Calvin, Beza and Ovid complained that "the Sabbath days and holy days ordained for the hearing of God's Word to the reformation of our lives . . . is spent full heathenishly, in taverning, tippling, gaming, playing and beholding of bear-baitings and stage-plays, to the utter dishonour of God, impeachment of all godliness, and unnecessary consuming of men's substances, which ought to be better employed".[2] This particular point should be carefully borne in mind when considering the puritan attitude to the stage and its appeal for the industrious sort of people.

Bownde had devoted a good deal of attention to the way in which the traditional sports lured countrymen away from their devotions. The village maypole, Richard Baxter tells us, was near his father's house at Eaton Constantine, "so that we could not read the Scriptures in our family without the great disturbance of a tabor and pipe and noise in the street". Baxter often wanted to join the revellers, but he was put off by their calling his father a Puritan. The phallic maypole was for the rural lower class almost a symbol of independence of their betters: Baxter's father "could not break the sport", even though the piper was one of his own tenants.[3] In Lincoln, in 1584–5, when the city fathers had introduced an exceptionally strict régime of Sabbath observance, the opposition encouraged the setting up of maypoles and the playing of May games.[4] In 1588 the authorities of Shrewsbury prohibited the traditional maypole, and several members of the Shearmen's Gild ("recruited from the poorer elements of the population", notably from Wales),

1. Ed. J. Harland, *The Lancashire Lieutenancy under the Tudors and Stuarts* (Chetham Soc., 1859), II, p. 218. Note once more the emphasis on household discipline.

2. A. Golding, *A Discourse upon the Earthquake* (1580), in L. T. Golding, *An Elizabethan Puritan* (New York, 1937), pp. 194–5. Any number of similar utterances could be quoted. Cf. Anthony Munday, *Second and Third Blast of retrait from plaies and Theatres* (1580); P. Stubbes, *The Anatomie of Abuses*, pp. 323 sqq.; E. K. Chambers, *The Elizabethan Stage* (1923), I, p. 255, IV, p. 307. Cf. p. 182, note 6 below.

3. *Reliquiae Baxterianae*, I, p. 2. Hobbes as well as the Puritans noted the phallic significance of the maypole (*Leviathan*, Everyman ed., p. 363).

4. Hill, *Lincoln*, pp. 99–104.

were sent to jail for trying to defend it.[1] In Stratford-on-Avon in 1619 popular libels were distributed, attacking the puritan ruling group and calling for maypoles. The Puritans were described as economic oppressors, twisters of the law.[2]

In New England in the sixteen-twenties, when the servants of one settlement revolted against their masters and "maintained (as it were) a school of atheism", on May Day they erected ("with the help of savages", with whom they were on friendly terms) a goodly pine tree 80 feet long as a maypole. The godly rulers of the neighbouring settlement "saw they should keep no servants, for Morton [the leader of the revolt] would entertain any, how vile soever, and all the scum of the country or any discontents would flock to him from all places, if this nest was not broken". The other English would "stand in more fear . . . from this wicked and debauched crew than from the savages themselves". Broken the nest accordingly was, and the offending maypole cut down; but it had been a challenge to the social order that the puritan discipline was trying to establish.[3] Thomas Morton, it is perhaps superfluous to add, was a royalist during the civil war. It is one of history's little ironies that the liberty poles of the American Revolution descended from the maypole.

In Guildford in James I's reign a maypole was pulled down in contempt, although it had the King's arms on it: and the mayor refused to allow it to be put up again. "If it had the picture of any saint", wrote the Earl of Nottingham about this incident, "I should mislike it as much as any; but the arms of his majesty, or any other arms of noblemen or gentlemen, I do not see but that it is lowable".[4] In 1642 a maypole was set up in Ludlow as a political symbol.[5] Two years later Parliament

1. T. C. Mendenhall, *The Shrewsbury Drapers and the Welsh Wool Trade in the 16th and 17th centuries* (1953), pp. 43–4; see my "Puritans and 'the Dark Corners of the Land' ", pp. 82, 97–8. In such corners quarrels about maypoles and Sunday sports were especially frequent: see e.g. pp. 180, 183–9 below; *Elizabethan Government and Society* (ed. Bindoff, Hurstfield and Williams), p. 271; Hart, *The Country Clergy*, pp. 44–5.

2. C. J. Sisson, *Lost Plays of Shakespeare's Age* (1936), p. 192.

3. W. Bradford, *History of Plymouth Plantation* (Massachusetts Historical Soc. Collections, 4th Series, III), pp. 237–43; J. H. Lawson, *The Hidden Heritage* (New York, 1950), pp. 522–3.

4. *H.M.C., Seventh Report, Appendix*, I, p. 675.

5. *Letters of Lady Brilliana Harley*, p. 167.

ordered the destruction of maypoles in every parish in England. In at least one parish in Essex in 1647 people were still "hankering after the sports and pastimes which they were wonted to enjoy", although "they are in many families weaned from them".[1] In 1648 at Bury St. Edmunds the townsmen, encouraged by the local gentry, "ran horribly mad upon a maypole".[2] At Wolverhampton a maypole was set up in 1653 to celebrate the dissolution of the Rump.[3] And in 1660 a maypole was erected on May Day in royalist Oxford "to vex the Presbyterians and Independents", and was protected by "the mob" when the Vice-Chancellor and his beadles came to cut it down. On May 31 a dozen were set up, and the cowed Puritans did nothing about them.[4]

The Restoration brought back "maypoles in abundance", as well as morris dances, "not seen of twenty years before".[5] In 1661 Adam Martindale in his Cheshire parish was affronted by a rabble of profane youths who set up a maypole on the way to his church. Martindale preached against it, explaining that "many learned men were of opinion that a maypole was a relic of the shameful worship of the strumpet Flora in Rome", but to no effect. Mrs. Martindale and three other women then cut down the obnoxious symbol in the night. It was put up again, "but it was such an ugly thing, so rough and crooked, as proclaimed the folly and poverty of those that set it up".[6] Folly and poverty: the class note again.

Nor should we lightly dismiss the recurrent emphasis on paganism in discussing the maypole and the traditional sports. Some of Philip Stubbes's more hysterical passages deal with this subject.[7] Bishop Corbett wrote an "Exhortation to Mr.

1. Smith, *Ecclesiastical History of Essex*, p. 216.

2. A. Everitt, *Suffolk and the Great Rebellion* (Suffolk Records Soc., 1960), p. 94.

3. M. Ashley, *The Greatness of Oliver Cromwell* (1957), p. 270.

4. G. Davies, *The Restoration of Charles II* (1955), p. 345.

5. Ed. R. Parkinson, *The Autobiography of Henry Newcome* (Chetham Soc., 1852), p. 121; cf. A. Kingston, *Hertfordshire during the Great Civil War* (1894), pp. 101–2.

6. Ed. R. Parkinson, *The Life of Adam Martindale* (Chetham Soc., 1845), p. 157. William Bradford also referred to the goddess Flora in relation to Morton's maypole (*History of Plymouth Plantation*, Massachusetts Historical Soc. Collections, 4th Series, III, p. 237). It was "the rout and rabble of the world" that favoured maypoles, said Thomas Hall in his *Funebria Florae* (2nd ed., 1661), p. 19; cf. p. 4.

7. P. Stubbes, *The Anatomie of Abuses*, Part I, p. 149.

John Harrison, minister in the parish of Bewdley, for battering down the vanities of the Gentiles, which are comprehended in a May-pole". The point of the joke was that the poem purported to be written by "a zealous brother from the Blackfriars", where William Gouge had his church.[1] The ordinance of 8 April 1644 for the better observance of the Lord's Day described maypoles as "a heathenish vanity". In Hungary too in the sixteen-forties the Puritan John Tolnai Dali denounced the celebration of days other than Sunday as "devil-born heathenism".[2] An understanding of this point will help us to grasp the consistency of many puritan attitudes. The traditional sports clearly were survivals of pre-Christian fertility rituals: May Day celebrations still reputedly produced their crop of bastards in seventeenth-century England. Mediaeval catholicism had subsumed much of the older religion, but from the fifteenth century onwards Christianity had gone over to the offensive against witches in an attempt finally to eradicate the degenerate remnants of the rival cult.[3] The campaign against the traditional sports linked up with the campaign against witches.

Sabbatarianism was believed to be a post-reformation product. "If popery will have gross ignorance and blind devotion continued among its miserable captives, let it [Sunday] be made (like the other festivals) a merry and a sporting Sabbath".[4] Yet in fact both Sabbatarianism and persecution of

1. Ed. J. A. W. Bennett and H. R. Trevor-Roper, *Poems of Richard Corbett* (1955), p. 52. The title of Hall's *Funebria Florae* speaks for itself. See esp. pp. 7–9.

2. L. Makkai, "The Hungarian Puritans and the English Revolution", *Acta Historica*, V (Budapest), p. 26; A. Pirnát, *Die Ideologie der Siebenburger Antitrinitarier in den 1570er Jahren* (Budapest, 1961), chapter 4 *passim*.

3. See Margaret Murray's *The Witch-Cult in Western Europe* (1921); and more recently, Alan Macfarlane, *Witchcraft in Tudor and Stuart England*, (1969).

4. T. Shepard, *Theses Sabbaticae, Or, The Doctrine of the Sabbath* (1649), Sig. A 2v–A 3v. Shepard knew what he was talking about. He was born on Guy Fawkes Day, 1605, the son of a grocer's apprentice and a grocer's daughter. He escaped from "a most blind town and wicked corner" in Northamptonshire which celebrated riotous Whitsun ales, first to Emmanuel College and ultimately to New England (J. A. Albro, *Life of Thomas Shepard*, Boston, 1870, pp. 12–23). For another parallel drawn between popery and paganism see *An Answer to a Romish Rhyme*, by J. Rhodes (1602), which says that Englishmen detest alike "your May-game pastimes . . . and your popish saints" (ed. E. Farr,

SOCIETY AND PURITANISM

182

witches are to be found among catholics. "When we come across 16th or 17th century clerics dealing with popular sports", wrote Dr. Coulton, "it would be very difficult to decide on internal evidence whether the writer was on the Roman or the non-Roman side".[1] The Jesuit party among the English catholics seems to have disliked some of the sports which the Puritans described as popish.[2] Yet protestantism, and especially Puritanism, like Lollardy before them[3] went furthest in rejecting all kinds of magic and attacking those survivals of the old rituals whose existence had so long been tolerated. In this popular radical Puritanism unwittingly prepared the way for the modern scientific attitude, as well as helping to eradicate habits which unfitted men for an industrial society.[4]

In Edward VI's reign an attempt had been made to abolish wakes, since they led to idleness, drunkenness and brawls.[5] But Elizabeth licensed Sunday games, although more cautiously than her successors.[6] In 1585 a clergyman who maintained

Select Poetry, Parker Soc., 1845, II, p. 276). See also Buckle, *Miscellaneous and Posthumous Works*, II, pp. 138–9, 693.

1. G. G. Coulton, *Medieval Panorama* (1945), p. 613; cf. E. G. Rupp, *Studies in the Making of the English Protestant Tradition* (1947), p. 39.

2. T. G. Law, *Jesuits and Seculars in the Reign of Queen Elizabeth* (1889), pp. liv, 18–19; ed. Law, L. Vaux, *Catechism or Christian Doctrine* (Chetham Soc., 1885). First published in 1583.

3. The Lollards' petition to Parliament in 1395 attacked as "necromancy" popish exorcisms and the blessing of inanimate objects. Their articles were nailed to the door of St. Paul's cathedral for the benefit of London citizens (G. M. Trevelyan, *England in the Age of Wycliffe*, 1906, pp. 328–9). I owe this point to Professor A. G. Dickens.

4. For an excellent example of a Puritan using scientific methods in witch-hunting, see I. Mather, *An Essay for the Recording of Illustrious Providences* (1890), pp. 188–94 and *passim*: first published 1684. Mather very carefully assessed all the evidence when witchcraft was alleged, setting on one side every phenomenon which could be explained by natural causes or human duplicity or error: what remained inexplicable he accepted as the operation of the devil.

5. A. G. Dickens, *Lollards and Protestants in the Diocese of York, 1509–1558* (1959), p. 180.

6. Cardwell, *Documentary Annals*, I, pp. 311–12. But contrast a Government *Admonition* of 1580, to be read as a Homily. This deplores the fact that Sundays and holy days, which should be "for the special occupying of ourselves in all spiritual exercises" are in fact spent to "the utter consuming of men's substances, which ought to be better employed" (Strype, *Annals*, II, p. 668). Cf. also Shaw: "All through Elizabeth's reign the civil power had attempted both by legislation and

in a sermon before the University of Cambridge that plays and sports were unlawful on Sundays had to account for himself before the Vice-Chancellor.[1]

By about the time of the Armada, a puritan memorandum speaks of "wakes, ales, greens, May games, rush-bearings, bear-baits, dove-ales, bonfires, and all such manner unlawful gaming, piping and dancing . . . in all places freely exercised upon the Sabbath; by occasion whereof it cometh to pass that the youth will not by any means be brought to attend the exercises of catechizing in the afternoon; neither the people to be present at the evening service".[2] Stubbes and a score of puritan propagandists could be quoted for the charge that men "could not keep their servants from lying out of their own houses" on Sunday nights.[3]

There were thus police arguments against permitting some of these jollifications. In 1550 the Lord President of the Council in the Marches instructed J.P.s to prevent assemblies or games during divine service; and 32 years later one of the four penal statutes the Council in the Marches was allowed to execute was that against unlawful games – especially prevalent in Wales.[4] The motive for issuing the original Book of Sports in 1618 was the action of the Lancashire J.P.s who in 1616 had issued a comprehensive series of orders against violation of the Sabbath, and required the clergy to read them from the pulpit once a quarter.[5] Sir Ralph Hopton, later royalist commander in the South-west, was one of the many Somerset J.P.s who protested against the revocation of the judges' order forbidding sports: the revocation was, they said, "to the great prejudice of the peace, plenty and good government of the county".[6]

Mr. Barnes has discussed church ales at length, and the fact that the frequent prohibitions of them in Somerset from 1594 to 1632 were mostly made in the interests of law and order. At the

by proclamation to put down the more brutal sports" (*V.C.H. Lancashire*, II, pp. 61–2).

1. Buckle, *Miscellaneous and Posthumous Works*, III, p. 160.

2. G. H. Tupling, "The Causes of the Civil War in Lancashire" *Trans. Lancashire and Cheshire Antiquarian Soc.*, LXV, p. 9.

3. See pp. 177–8 above, 187 below.

4. P. Williams, *The Council in the Marches of Wales under Elizabeth I* (1958), pp. 38–9, 53.

5. Tupling, *op. cit.*, p. 10.

6. H. A. Wyndham, *A Family History* (1939), I, p. 171.

assizes of 1632 "many" were indicted for murdering illegiti-
mate children conceived after Church ales,[1] and the J.P.s
"earnestly importuned" the judge to make an order against
Sunday sports, which again the clergy were instructed to read
to their parishioners. It was this instruction which caused
Laud's intervention, and the disgrace of Chief Justice Richardson. The matter then passed into high national politics; and
Mr. Barnes has shown how it was also involved in county
disputes. He is perhaps too anxious to emphasize the personal
element in the quarrel, in which "these great concerns could be
used to belabour one's opponent". The concerns did not cease
to be great because they were so used. On the contrary, they
could be used because many people felt strongly about them,
for religious reasons as well as those affecting law and order.[2]

The village sports which the church patronized, indeed, were
rather different from the activities indulged in by folk dancers
to-day. Gardiner has been sneered at for saying that wakes not
infrequently ended in "indulgence of the lower passions"; but
he glossed this two sentences later by reference to two man-
slaughters committed at a Devon wake in 1615;[3] and he might
have referred to bastards conceived on the Sabbath after the
festivities. In 1600 the Devon magistrates had prohibited
church ales and similar entertainments, saying coyly that
"many inconveniences, which with modesty cannot be
expressed", had resulted from them.[4] A witch in Ben Jonson's
Masque of Queenes killed an infant:

> "*A piper it got, at a church-ale.
> I bad him again blow wind in the tail*".[5]

A character in Cartwright's *The Ordinary* referred more
directly than the Devon magistrates to "a great belly caught at

1. Professor Barnes, following Prynne, states that children were conceived *at* Church ales. This might have been difficult: I have ventured to
amend to "after".
2. T. G. Barnes, "County Politics and a Puritan Cause Celèbre:
Somerset Churchales, 1633", *T.R.H.S.*, 1959, pp. 103–22; *Somerset
Assize Records, passim.*
3. Gardiner, *History of England*, VII, p. 319.
4. Order Book I, 1592–1600, County Record Office, Epiphany, 1599–
1600. I am indebted for a transcript of this to Mr. R. L. Taverner, who
quotes it in his *History of All Saints Church, Okehampton*, p. 13.
5. Jonson, *Works* (ed. C. H. Herford and P. and E. Simpson), VII,
(1941), p. 291.

a Whitsun-ale".[1] In Somerset, five years after Charles I's Book of Sports was issued, the grand jury had the courage to present the high price of corn as being due to bull-baitings "under the pretence of helping some poor man, who brews about 30 or 40 bushels of malt and spends it all at one of these meetings".[2] We must be very careful not to sentimentalize ye olde morris dances of Merrie England.

In this respect, then, as well as in its anti-pagan aspect, the puritan attack on Sunday sports should be seen as part of an attempt to impose the ethos of an urban civilization on the whole realm, especially its dark corners.[3] In Lancashire, we learn, four years before James's momentous visit, piping "put down preaching. . . . For one person which we have in church . . . every piper (there being many in one parish) should at the same instant have many hundreds on the greens".[4] Thomas Mun had a very cautiously-worded reference (he might well be cautious in the sixteen-twenties) to "piping" among the forms of idleness which handicapped England in competition with the Dutch.[5] Somerset, like Lancashire, was an outlying but a clothing county, in which Sabbatarianism had the support of the industrious sort of some at least of the gentry.

The traditional sports had their non-clerical defenders in the early seventeenth century. The poet-laureate wrote a provocative poem to "my jovial good friend Mr. Robert Dover, on his great instauration of his hunting and dancing at Cotswold". In this Johnson observed that

1. Act V, scene iii, in Dodsley's *Select Collection of Old Plays* (1826), p. 255.

2. Barnes, *Somerset Assize Records*, pp. 60–1.

3. See my "Puritans and 'the Dark Corners of the Land' ", pp. 97–8; K. Thomas, "History and Anthropology", *P. and P.*, No. 24, p. 8. Cf. pp. 58–60 above.

4. W. Harrison, *The Difference of Hearers* (1614), Sig. A 6–A 9: recusants were the greatest maintainers of this impiety. Cf. Yapton, Sussex, where a fiddler took 30 to 40 persons every Sunday out of the parish to dances (ed. Hilda Johnston, *Churchwardens' Presentments* (*17th Century*), *Part I, Archdeaconry of Chichester*, Sussex Record Soc., XLIX, p. 66). For further examples from Wales, see my "Puritans and 'the Dark Corners of the Land' ", pp. 81–4. Cf. also a scornful reference by Bancroft's chaplain to excommunication for May games and Robin Hood matters in Scotland (T. Rogers, *The Faith, Doctrine and Religion professed and protected . . . in England*, 1681, p. 196).

5. See p. 122 above.

> *"thy games*
> *Renew the glories of our blessed James:*
> *How they do keep alive his memory,*
> *How they advance true love and neighbourhood,*
> *And do both church and commonwealth the good*
> *In spite of hypocrites who are the worst*
> *Of subjects; let such envy till they burst".*[1]

In *The Sad Shepherd* Jonson defended the traditional sports against accusations of "paganism" from "the sourer sort". Far and away the best expression of this point of view was given by Carew in his *Survey of Cornwall*. Church ales promoted Christian love, "the conforming of men's behaviour to a civil conversation, compounding of controversies, appeasing quarrels, raising a store which might (!) be converted to poor relief and repairing highways ... and commendable exercises". Carew replied at some length to this argument, which he reported but did not accept.[2]

When in 1637 the Bishop of Hereford succeeded in having the circuit judges' order against clerks' ales recalled, the reasons he gave were (i) Ales brought the people more willingly to church; (ii) they tended to civilize them and to compose local differences; (iii) they increased love and unity, being of the nature of feasts of charity; (iv) they brought rich and poor together.[3] The emphasis is on a social cohesion and solidarity which were fast losing their reality. The Bishop's agreeable picture of Sundays spent in love, unity and drinking might well conflict with the puritan stress on Sabbath religious education and on the inculcation of an individualist morality.[4] The difference in outlook is revealed in the complaint that Bishop Pierce forbade the preaching of sermons at times which hindered the selling of church ale.[5]

Though the respectable and the godly alike disapproved of the rural sports, the first two Stuart Kings went out of their way to encourage them. The Books of Sports of 1618 and 1633 must

1. B. Jonson, *Poems* (Muses ed.), pp. 313–14.
2. Carew, *A Survey of Cornwall*, pp. 187–91.
3. J. Christie, *Some Account of Parish Clerks* (1893), p. 174.
4. See pp. 431–3 below. For a defence of May games and morris dances by a spokesman of the hierarchy, see Ironside, *Seven Questions of the Sabbath*, pp. 271–5.
5. Nalson, *An Impartial Collection*, II, p. 413. See pp. 412–13 below.

have seemed profoundly, satanically wicked to Puritans, and to many of the industrious sort of people, just because they appealed to all that was unregenerate, popish and backward-looking in man, to all the bad side (from their point of view) of popular tradition, which it was the function of preaching, discipline and Sabbatarianism slowly and painfully to eradicate. The magistrates should have co-operated in this: and at the local level, as we have seen, J.P.s and civic authorities in many parts of England were trying to do so. But kings and bishops, so far from joining in this civilizing process, were pandering to the very worst instincts of natural man. As Prynne asked, "What could Beelzebub, had he been the Archbishop, have done more than in publishing the book against Sunday?"[1]

"The public toleration of the profanation" of the Lord's Day authorized by the Book of Sports seemed to two divines of the Westminster Assembly "one main cause of those national judgements, under which this land groans. . . . Our prosperity hath begun to wither, and our miseries to grow upon us, ever since".[2] Among other inconveniences, Charles I's Book of Sports made "masters of families complain exceedingly they cannot contain their servants from excursions into all profane sports and pastimes on the Lord's Day".[3] In 1660 a minister attributed to May games most of the evils which royalists had blamed on sermons twenty years earlier. They made "the servant contemn his master, the people their pastor, the subject his sovereign, the child his father", and taught "young people impudency and rebellion".[4] Defoe wrote long after the event, but he was undoubtedly expressing the convictions of decent middle-class folk, then and earlier, when he echoed Prynne to say that Charles I "had the misfortune to be the first king of England, and perhaps in the world, that ever established wickedness by a law".[5]

1. Windebanke's notes on the examination of Prynne, quoted by the editor in N. Wallington, *Historical Notices*, II, p. 304. Laud was with James when he passed through Lancashire in 1618.

2. Cawdrey and Palmer, *Sabbatum Redivivum*, Sig. A 2v.

3. Reyce to Winthrop, 9 September 1636, *Massachusetts Hist. Soc. Collections*, 4th Series, VI, p. 408. See p. 433 below.

4. T. Hall, *Funebria Florae*, p. 14.

5. Ed. H. Morley, *The Earlier Life and Works of Daniel Defoe* (1889), p. 166. Cf. p. 195 below.

VII

Gardiner argued that stricter Sabbatarianism would have won its way to acceptance gradually and unobtrusively if James had not forced the issue (or had not allowed the Lancashire Puritans to force the issue upon him).[1] In a sense this may be true. But it obscures, surely, the whole social context. James, that sharp intellectual, wished to define the position about Sunday work and games for exactly the same reason as lod him to define his theory of the prerogative. Otherwise the position was going by default. It was to the interest of Puritans and those who controlled local government, quietly to assume that everyone agreed with them, and meanwhile to establish precedents. It was to the interest of the government to define positions before it was too late, since it would necessarily do the defining. By doing so in this case, however, James underlined the monarchy's identification with the less economically advanced areas of the North and West (from which its support was to come in the civil war), and its alienation from the values of the industrious sort of people. The kindest thing Sir Arthur Throckmorton could find to say about the 1618 Book of Sports was that "his Majesty from his wisdom [is] countenancing many things in the remote places of his realm which he will not do in the centre of his kingdom, for many things may become the borders and skirts . . . which will disgrace the heart of the garment".[2]

James himself gave three reasons for issuing the Declaration. First, men would associate the traditional sports with popery, and become disaffected to the state Church if they were deprived of them;[3] secondly, "the common and meaner sort" would be debarred "from using such exercises as may make

1. Gardiner, *History of England*, III, p. 248.
2. A. L. Rowse, *Ralegh and the Throckmortons* (1962), p. 302.
3. The evidence on this point is contradictory. One suggestion was that James was incited to issue the Book of Sports in the first instance by the catholic gentry of Lancashire (Gardiner, *History of England*, III, pp. 248–9). Barwick on the other hand says that papists tried to keep people from church by dancing and other recreations, and that this led Morton, Bishop of Chester, to help James to draft the Declaration of Sports (J. Barwick, *A Summarie Account of the Holy Life and Happy Death of . . . Thomas, Late Lord Bishop of Duresme*, 1660, pp. 80–3; cf. J. Tait, "The Declaration of Sports for Lancashire" *E.H.R.*, XXXII, pp. 561–8).

their bodies more able for war"; thirdly, they would go in disgust into alehouses, and there indulge in "a number of idle and discontented speeches".[1] James's reasons, it will be observed, were all concerned with the maintenance of the state and its authority. Since they were intended for publication, the reasons given may not have been those really operative; but they had to appear plausible. Bishop Pierce, a few years later, elaborated upon James's third point. Some of his clergy assured him that men deprived of "their honest and lawful recreations upon Sundays after evening prayer . . . would go either into tippling houses, and there upon their ale-benches talk of matters of the church or state, *or else into conventicles*".[2] Prynne confirmed this from the opposite point of view by saying that afternoon sermons were prohibited in order to enable "the profane vulgar . . . to dance, play, revel, drink and profane God's Sabbaths".[3]

After the Restoration, much the same antithesis between the liberty allowed to Sunday sports and the suppression of conventicles was made by the Quaker, Samuel Fisher:

"Are not the multitudinous meetings, conventions and musterings together of rude, wild, wicked people to drinking and revellings, wakes and Whitsun ales, May-games and morris dancings . . . [etc.], where they kindle and inflame one another in lust, wantonness and wickedness as charcoal in heaps by their numbers, and thrive in swearing, whoredom, dissoluteness and all manner of debauchery and profaneness, much more inconsistent with the nation's safety, disturbing its peace . . ., affronting our established religion . . ., than for the people that fear the Lord to meet together to worship God in spirit and truth, and to preach up the power of godliness that would bring people out of all these ungodly courses to

1. Gardiner, *Constitutional Documents of the Puritan Revolution*, pp. 100–1.
2. Prynne, *Canterburies Doome*, p. 151 — 137 — my italics. Pierce's letter, and some of his sentiments, had been prompted by Laud: see his *Works*, VI, p. 319. For a more considered defence of the Book of Sports on social grounds, see Heylyn, *History of the Presbyterians*, pp. 389–90.
3. Prynne, *Newes from Ipswich* (1636), Sig. A 2; cf. *Canterburies Doome*, pp. 154, 373, 382; *Reliquiae Baxterianae*, I, p. 233. (I refer to *Newes from Ipswich* as Prynne's, though this is not certain. See W. M. Lamont, *Marginal Prynne*, 1963, pp. 38–9. The authorship does not affect my argument).

that grace of God in themselves that teaches to live godly, righteously and soberly in this world?"[1]

Without sports, governments thought before 1640, men would become militarily useless. We may perhaps compare with this line of argument the traditional governmental opposition to enclosures, which was similarly largely motivated by military considerations, although it has been given other explanations by sentimental historians. But what of the other arguments? Without sports to distract them, men would become seditious papists or seditious nonconformists, or they would go into ale-houses in order to talk sedition there. What a picture of the government's confidence in the people it ruled over! Yet those indeed were the alternatives: and that is why the controversy over the way in which Sundays were to be spent became more acrimonious from the fifteen-nineties. Dr. Rowse has suggested that this is evidence of a sharpening class differentiation. He rightly instanced the drawing away of the urban middle class from the life of the people in the country-side,[2] but it goes deeper than that. From the end of the sixteenth century the government was more and more losing the confidence of the politically effective groups in the country. It was apprehensive of any popular assemblies for educational or discussion purposes. Either on ale-benches or in conventicles, wherever two or three were gathered together, even to worship their God, especially to worship their God, the government was likely to be criticized. The lead in such discussions would be taken not by parsons but by educated, independent laymen who could not be controlled. Far better to make such meetings impossible, or at least do nothing that would help to provide an audience.

A further defence of his Declaration, which was made by James in 1624 and appears to have been an afterthought, was that strict Sabbatarianism would allow "no recreation to the poor men that labour hard all the week long".[3] The 1633 Book of Sports also emphasizes the need that "the meaner sort who labour hard all the week" have of recreation to refresh their spirits.[4] The Puritans countered this argument by saying that

1. S. Fisher, *An Answer to Dr. John Gauden*, p. 23, in *The Testimony of Truth Exalted* (1679).

2. A. L. Rowse, *The England of Elizabeth* (1950), p. 182.

3. Gardiner, *History of England*, V, p. 234.

4. Gardiner, *Constitutional Documents*, pp. 99–101.

"if men will allow their servants recreation", they should allow it out of their working time. For "recreation belongs not to rest, but to labour, and it is used that men may by it be made more fit to labour, and therefore it must be granted on days of labour", and not on the Sabbath.[1] This argument was not wholly disingenuous. When the Westminster Assembly decided that in the Directory for the Sabbath day something should be said against wakes, church ales and observance of holy days, it was careful to add that some course must "be thought upon for the relief of servants".[2] Wakes and church ales, along with labouring, travelling and crying of wares on the Sabbath, were made illegal by Parliamentary ordinance in April 1644. Nine months later another ordinance insisted that servants were not to be unnecessarily detained from church, and were to be given time for reading, meditation, discussion, etc., so that they accounted the Sabbath a delight.[3] On 8 June 1647 another ordinance established every second Tuesday in the month, in lieu of saints' days, as days of "recreation and relaxation" for scholars, prentices and other servants; this became a sort of bank holiday on which shops and warehouses were closed.[4] So something at least was done to give more leisure. But that must have seemed secondary to most ministers. "Is it their bodies or their minds that need recreation?" Baxter cried.[5]

The Duke of Newcastle, that outspoken defender of the old order, thought that too much education bred rebellion, but that the traditional rural sports "will amuse the people's thoughts, and keep them in harmless action, which will free your majesty [Charles II] from faction and rebellion".[6] Bishop Sanderson put forward a more sophisticated defence of Sun-

1. White, *A Treatise of the Sabbath-day*, p. 234.
2. Ed. A. F. Mitchell and J. Struthers, *Minutes of the Sessions of the Westminster Assembly of Divines* (1874), p. 3.
3. Cf. Preston, quoted on p. 170 above.
4. This ordinance was passed by the presbyterian majority in Parliament when the Army was preparing to advance on London. So the state of opinion among the lower orders may have had something to do with its timing. The Independents strengthened it on 28 June. See pp. 159–60 above.
5. Baxter, *Practical Works*, XIII, pp. 445–6; cf. p. 429.
6. A. S. Turberville, *A History of Welbeck Abbey and its owners* (1938), I, pp. 174–6; S. Strong, *A Catalogue of Letters . . . at Welbeck*, pp. 223–7. Newcastle's view that merriment was an antidote to heresy and rebellion was shared by at least one English catholic (J. W. Stoye, *English Travellers Abroad, 1604–67*, 1952, p. 191).

day sports for the lower orders, but he clearly had the same essential considerations in mind: "Walking and discoursing, with men of liberal education, is a pleasant recreation; it is no way delightsome to the ruder sort of people". For the latter those sports are "the meetest to be used, which give the best refreshing to the body and leave the least impression in the mind".[1]

The thoroughness and consistency of pre-revolutionary government policy on this matter is shown by the fact that Laud in his capacity of censor deleted references in Sibthorpe's notorious assize sermon to idolators and Sabbath-breakers, and changed the word Sabbath wherever it occurred.[2] Laud also amended Joseph Hall's *Episcopacie by Divine Right Asserted*, in order to make it more anti-Sabbatarian.[3] Dr. Samuel Baker, one of the Bishop of London's chaplains, censored a passage in Dr. William Jones's commentary on the Epistle to the Hebrews which dealt with Sabbath observance, before the book was licensed for publication in 1635. The offending passage, on Hebrews iv, 4, began "Here we are to learn that we are to occupy ourselves in a serious contemplation of the Sabbath day . . .". "All this wholesome doctrine", commented Sir Edward Dering, "was expunged lest it should mar a ball, a wake or a morris dance upon the Lord's Day".[4] George Walker's *Doctrine of the Sabbath* was regarded by the High Commission as too dangerous a book to be published.[5] In contrast with James's I's concern for military training, Milton believed that the effect, if not the intention, of the bishops' plucking men "from their soberest and saddest

1. Sanderson, *Eight Cases of Conscience Occasionally Determined* (1674), p. 17.

2. Prynne, *Canterburies Doome*, pp. 245–6.

3. Hall, *Works* (1837–9), XII, p. 455; Laud, *Works*, VI, p. 577.

4. Lambeth MS. 943, ff. 735–6. Dering's speech, prepared in 1641, was apparently never delivered, but the material in it was used later by Prynne in *Canterburies Doome* (p. 337, and see pp. 255–349 *passim*). Most of the suppressed passages in Jones's *Commentary* attacked popery, but some dealt with the arbitrary power of kings (*ibid.*, pp. 290–1). For all this mangling, Dr. Jones's book ran to over 700 folio pages when it was finally published, with eminently safe dedications to the Earl of Holland and Sir Thomas Jermyn.

5. Information from Miss M. D. Slatter's unpublished Oxford B.Litt. thesis "A Biographical Study of Sir John Lambe" (1952), p. 161. For another example of the censorship exercised against an expression of opinion about the Sabbath, see *H.M.C., Third Report, Appendix*, p. 44.

thoughts, and instigating them by public edict to gaming, jigging, wassailling and mixed dancing" on the Sabbath was to "prepare and supple us either for a foreign invasion or domestic oppression". Sundays should be set apart, Milton continued in wholly conventional puritan manner, "to examine and increase our knowledge of God, to meditate and commune of our faith, our hope, our eternal city in heaven, and to quicken withal the study and exercise of charity".[1]

Everybody knows the story of the London minister who read the Declaration of Sports, then read the ten commandments, and told his congregation "You have heard now the commandments of God and man. Obey which you please".[2] Whether true or not, the story was certainly *ben trovato*. After 1618 such strong objections had been raised by the clergy, led by Archbishop Abbot, to reading James's Declaration in church that he withdrew the order.[3] More than one minister preached against the Declaration.[4] Another was suspended for praying publicly that "the King's heart may be turned from profaneness, vanity and popery", in a sermon against profanation of the Sabbath.[5] Prynne exaggerated when he said that hundreds of the clergy were suspended for not reading the Declaration of 1633; but there is again much evidence of opposition, and of ministers getting into trouble because of it. John White of Dorchester refused to read the Declaration. So did Herbert Palmer, whom I have so often quoted on sabbatarian questions. In the deaneries of Buckingham, Wycombe and Wimborne the Declaration was read by very few incumbents, "and they slandered as time-servers", whilst those who refused to read it were applauded. Three were suspended for refusing, including Thomas Valentine of Chalfont St. Giles, later of the Westminster Assembly. He promptly got himself absolved, apparently by Bishop Williams. Gerrard Dobson at High Wycombe, twenty-four of whose

1. Milton, *Prose Works* (Bohn ed.), II, pp. 401–2.
2. A letter-writer in *Strafforde's Letters and Dispatches*, I, p. 166, attributes the remark to "Dr. Denison", presumably the Stephen Denison mentioned on p. 159 above.
3. Fuller, *Church History of Britain* (1842), III, pp. 270–4.
4. *C.S.P.D., 1611–18*, pp. 608–9; cf. *Montagu MSS.* (H.M.C.), pp. 94–5.
5. *V.C.H. Worcestershire*, II, pp. 57–61; cf. *V.C.H. Somerset*, II, p. 43.

parishioners had just protested against the financial effect on him of the suppression of the Feoffees for Impropriations, preached against the Declaration.[1] In Wren's diocese of Norwich 17 refused to read it.[2] Bridge, Burroughes and Samuel Ward were suspended, and went into emigration. The Bishop of Oxford rejected an ordination candidate because he gave an unsatisfactory answer to a question about the Book of Sports: it had become a shibboleth to distinguish friends from foes.[3] Even among those who read the Declaration there were many like the Northamptonshire minister who "concluded that the orders of a Christian King must be lawful and therefore had obeyed"; but whose conscience remained troubled.[4] It was the quantity and quality of the opposition to the Book of Sports that made Gilbert Ironside write his *Seven Questions of the Sabbath*.[5]

The prelates were trying to destroy the Sabbath by the Book of Sports, said Prynne.[6] Encouragement of Sunday sports by bishops and court, Tom May tells us, made many not very godly men see unsuspected virtues in Puritanism, and increased the divergence in outlook between "court" and "country".[7] Puritanism and Sabbatarianism were forced by

1. Summers, *op. cit.*, pp. 104–11; *V.C.H. Buckinghamshire*, I, p. 322; Brinkworth, "The Laudian Church in Buckinghamshire", pp. 39, 50; L. J. Ashford, *History of . . . High Wycombe . . . to 1880* (1960), p. 121.
2. Tanner MS. 314, f. 146. I owe this reference to Mr. Boorman.
3. Hart, *The County Clergy in Elizabethan and Stuart Times*, p. 122; cf. Whitaker, *Sunday in Tudor and Stuart Times*, p. 131.
4. M. H. Curtis, *Oxford and Cambridge in Transition, 1558–1642* (1959), p. 210. For examples of refusals, see Rushworth, *Historical Collections*, II, pp. 301, 459–62; *C.S.P.D., 1633–4*, p. 540; *1634–5*, pp. 2, 355; *1635*, pp. xliv, 195, 201, 208, 215, 221; *1635–6*, p. liv; Prynne, *Canterburies Doome*, p. 154; Fuller, *Church History*, III, p. 378; W. Maitland, *History of London* (1756), I, pp. 298, 301; *H.M.C., Fourth Report, Appendix*, p. 49; *Montagu MSS.* (H.M.C.), pp. 94–5; *Massachusetts Historical Soc. Collections*, 4th Series, VI, p. 411; T. Rees, *A History of Protestant Nonconformity in Wales* (2nd ed., 1883), pp. 43, 47; Whitaker, *op. cit.*, pp. 131–2; *V.C.H. Gloucestershire*, II, p. 34; G. Soden, *Godfrey Goodman, Bishop of Gloucester* (1953), pp. 198–9, 244; Everitt, *Suffolk and the Great Rebellion*, p. 110; *A 17th Century Miscellany* (Kent Archaeological Soc., 1960), p. 128; Marchant, *The Puritans and the Church Courts in the Diocese of York*, pp. 81–4, 97–8 196, 244.
5. Ironside, *op. cit.*, Sig. B 3–3v.
6. Prynne, *Newes from Ipswich* (1636), Sig. A 2–3.
7. T. May, *History of the Parliament* (1647), pp. 23–4.

government and hierarchy on many of the industrious sort who were interested mainly in law and order, good government and decent working conditions. But the puritan association allowed moral overtones. Fuller tells us that many moderate men thought the Declaration of Sports was a principal cause of the civil war.[1]

The opposition, contemporaries assure us, was most clamorous in the dioceses of Norwich and Bath and Wells – the clothing areas. Most significant from the government's point of view was the discovery that a vicar in Somerset, accused of circulating books against profanation of the Sabbath, had obtained them from John Ashe, "the greatest clothier in England". For Ashe had received a bulk delivery of 200 copies from Henry Burton in London.[2] There was clearly a considerable degree of organization here. This reinforces the point that opposition to sports and emphasis on Sabbath observance was not merely a fad of Puritan ministers or lay cranks: it was shared by a responsible gentleman like Ashe, of an old parliamentary family, who himself 6 years later was to lead the yeomen and clothiers of his county into the field against the King. Nehemiah Wallington was probably not the only craftsman to note in his journal "the judgements of God among us this year, 1634, since the book of liberty for breach of the Lord's Day came forth".[3] For their various reasons, similar attitudes were shared by most M.P.s, by J.P.s of many counties, by municipal authorities, by judges. It was a matter of political order, security, discipline: not merely a fad.[4]

1. Fuller, *Church History*, III, pp. 378–9; cf. p. 188 above. Fuller was the nephew of the Sabbatarian Bishop Davenant. See p. 159 above.

2. *H.M.C., Third Report, Appendix*, p. 191; Fuller, *Church History*, III, p. 378; *Massachusetts Historical Soc. Collections*, 4th Series, VI, p. 447. Ashe also distributed *Newes from Ipswich*.

3. Wallington, *Historical Notices*, I, pp. 53–60.

4. In 1788 (significant year), a French employer wrote to the Archbishop of Laon saying that the only way in which he could prevent his workers having orgies on saints' days and Sundays was to make them work. The archbishop did not reply, the reason being, the employer thought, that as a dignitary of the Church he could not approve, but as an intelligent man and lover of order he could hardly disapprove (J. Bruhat, *Histoire du Mouvement Ouvrier Français*, I, Paris, 1952, p. 89).

VIII

There is a final point worth mentioning, though full consideration of all its implications would take us far afield. In May 1621 the House of Lords, with the Archbishop of Canterbury as their spokesman, criticized Coke's bill for the Sabbath, and "would have the word Sabbath put out, because many were inclined to Judaism and dream that the Jews shall have regiment and kings must lay down their crowns to their feet. Therefore it should be styled the Lord's Day, commonly called Sunday". One reason for this fear of "opinionists concerning the terrene kingdom of the Jews"[1] was the Star Chamber prosecution, in 1618, of John Traske, for maintaining that the Jewish Sabbath (i.e. Saturday) ought to be observed, and no work done on that day. He had a following in London, and admitted that he had tried to convert people to his opinion.[2] Despite a recantation, he was fined and imprisoned. Mrs. Traske, who seems to have been more determined than her husband, was later in prison for 11 years "for keeping Saturday for her Sabbath", and was only released by the approach of the Long Parliament.[3]

Another reason was the publication in 1621 of *The Worlds Great Restauration or the Calling of the Jews*. This work was written not by a religious maniac, but by Serjeant Sir Henry Finch, a lawyer of eminence whose treatise expounding the common law was only superseded by Blackstone and Austin, the *Dictionary of National Biography* tells us. Finch's book was published by our old friend William Gouge, later a Feoffee for Impropriations. It spoke, among many other

1. N.R.S., II, p. 397, IV, pp. 377–8.
2. Bacon, *Works*, XIII, p. 315, XIV, p. 67; Birch, *Court and Times of James I*, II, p. 65; Welsby, *Lancelot Andrewes*, p. 232, and references there given. Andrewes made a speech against Traske. Saturday-Sabbatarianism is said to have been founded by Robert Dogs, "a coal-man in London" (L. Magalotti, *The Travels of Cosmo III, Grand Duke of Tuscany, through England in 1669* (1821), pp. 445–6). In 1617 Bishop Morton of Chester advised James I to observe "all such kind of people as are said to incline to a kind of Judaism by neither eating meat nor suffering others to dress it on the Lord's Day", quoted by J. Tait, "The Declaration of Sports for Lancashire", *E.H.R.*, CXXV, p. 565. Two years later James himself urged the University of Cambridge to check and reform "any fanciful conceit savouring of Judaism" (Curtis, *Oxford and Cambridge in Transition*, p. 172).
3. *C.S.P.D.*, *1639*, pp. 466–7.

things, of God's "justice in executing judgement, tumbling down the enemies of God's people, notwithstanding all their might".[1] Both Finch and Gouge were imprisoned until they retracted such dangerous views, and the book was suppressed: but the government was clearly alarmed. In June 1621 Laud preached a sermon at court against the "error of the Jews", that "Christ's kingdom should be temporal".[2] Theophilus Brabourne, in a book published abroad and smuggled into England in 1632, also upheld the Jewish Sabbath, and argued that Sunday should be an ordinary working day. He was degraded from the university, excommunicated, fined £100, and sent to prison until he should make public submission, which he had apparently done before 1635.[3] Hamon L' Estrange said that "a potent tendency in many to Judaism" (and he cited Brabourne as an example) was one of the reasons for issuing the 1633 Book of Sports.[4] The Sabbath in New England, it is perhaps not irrelevant to recall, ran from sunset to sunset – the Jewish custom.[5]

Governmental fears seem far-fetched. But political theories were still almost always expressed in religious terms. Descriptions of God's judgements upon His enemies might often be a way of calling upon God's people to execute those judgments, even if not consciously so intended by the writer. Many Puritans regarded themselves as the chosen people, and their reliance upon Old Testament texts is notorious. "Judaizing" meant, among other things, looking back to the customs and traditions of a tribal society, still relatively egalitarian and democratic; its standards and myths could be used for destructive criticism of the institutions that had been built up in mediaeval society. Long before 1621 Whitgift had told Cartwright that he did "Judaizare, 'play the Jew' ".[6]

The phrase became hackneyed. In Hampden's case in 1638

1. Finch, *op. cit.*, p. 105; Gouge, *Commentary on Hebrews*, I, pp. ix–x.
2. Laud, *Works*, I, pp. 1–29, esp. pp. 16–20.
3. T. Brabourne, *A Defence of . . . the Sabbath Day* (2nd ed., Amsterdam, 1632); cf. *A Discourse upon the Sabbath Day* (1628); *C.S.P.D., 1634–5*, pp. 126 sq.; F. White, *A Treatise of the Sabbath-day*, pp. 309–10.
4. H. L'Estrange, *The Reign of King Charles* (1656), pp. 128–9. L'Estrange himself had published a sabbatarian treatise in 1641, *Gods Sabbath before and under the Law and under the Gospel*.
5. R. Cox, *The Literature of the Sabbath Question* (1865), I, pp. 252–3.
6. Whitgift, *Works*, I, p. 271.

Sir Robert Berkeley declared that it was "a kind of judaizing opinion, to hold that the weal public must be exposed to peril of utter ruin and subversion, rather than such a charge... may be imposed by the King upon the subject, without common consent in Parliament".[1] Here the word "judaizing" clearly had political as well as theological connotations. So it had when Heylyn said the Puritans hoped "to bring all higher powers whatever into an equal rank with the common people, in the observance of their Jewish Sabbatarian rigours".[2] In May 1643 Sir Humphrey Mildmay said that Cheapside Cross was taken down "by the Jews".[3]

There were many converging reasons for Sabbatarianism, affecting diverse social groups: police and security considerations; opposition to pagan survivals; dislike of brawls and bastards; economic protection for the small man; Old Testament Bibliolatry, with its roots in yearnings for the more equal society there depicted and with its sub-revolutionary overtones. When in 1641 the House of Commons instructed the Lord Mayor of London to enforce legislation against labour on Sundays, it does not appear that there was much opposition. The burning of the Book of Sports in the City three years later must have been welcomed by erastian as well as puritan supporters of Parliament among the gentry and the industrious sort, though not perhaps by the lowest social groups. Responsibility for the Declaration of Sports furnished one of the charges on the basis of which Laud was accused of high treason. In the ordinance of 20 October 1645 concerning suspension from the Lord's Supper, by far the largest part deals with rules for keeping the Sabbath. In 1646 the judges on the Western circuit were instructed to enforce Sabbath observance. The Parliamentary armies had finally overcome the Book of Sports in Somerset.[4] An act for the observation of the Lord's Day was one of the bills which Charles I accepted in the Isle of Wight treaty.[5] The culminating act of June 1657 dealt

1. Gardiner, *Constitutional Documents*, p. 120. For other examples of accusations of Puritan "Judaizing", see P. N. Siegel, "Shylock and the Puritan usurers", in *Studies of Shakespeare* (Miami, 1952), pp. 131–2.
2. Heylyn, *History of the Sabbath*, p. 490.
3. Ed. P. L. Ralph, *Sir Humphrey Mildmay* (Rutgers University Press, 1947), p. 164.
4. Barnes, *Somerset Assize Orders*, p. xxii.
5. Peck, *Desiderata Curiosa* (1779), p. 407.

elaborately with the prevention of labour on Sundays. The prohibition of Sunday travel during the interregnum was dictated by economic and security considerations at least as much as by religious: it was repeated by the Cavalier Parliament.

Public opinion, then, among all but the highest and lowest classes, seems to have been with the Sabbatarians. In 1646, we are told, the authorities allowed men to open or close their shops on saints' days as they pleased; but disorder was caused by those who kept their shops open.[1] Many examples could be given of local authorities availing themselves of the changed atmosphere to reimpose orders for Sabbath observance. In the 'forties the House of Lords sometimes lagged behind the Commons in sabbatarian enthusiasm.[2] It was the radical Barebones Parliament which resolved to bring in a bill "for taking away holidays and the observation of those days which are not juridical".[3] A legal book published in 1655 summed up the state of the law by saying that no day ordinarily should be kept holy except Sunday and November 5.[4] Events had moved fast and far since Laud's time.

IX

We are now perhaps in a position to ask the question which must occur to anyone who considers English and Scottish Sabbatarianism: Why did nothing like the English Sunday establish itself in any continental Calvinist country? What were the peculiar British conditions that ensured the survival of so gloomy an institution? In 1563 Archbishop Parker had noted that the French and Dutch protestant refugees settled at

1. [Anon.], *Anti-Toleration* (1646), pp. 31–2.
2. A bill of May 1641 against draymen and lightermen unloading on Sundays stuck in the Lords after passing the Commons; and a resolution of the Commons of 8 September of the same year, for afternoon sermons and against Sunday dancing and sports, also got no further (Whitaker, *op. cit.*, pp. 144–6).
3. *C.J.*, VII, p. 343. The members of this Parliament, one of them claimed, were men of small yet free estates—i.e. more representative of the industrious sort of people than their predecessors (L.D., *An Exact Relation of the Proceedings and Transactions of the Late Parliament* in *Somers Tracts*, 1748–51, X, p. 95).
4. W. Sheppard, *A View of the Laws and Statutes of the Nation Concerning the Service of God or Religion* (1655), pp. 5, 8.

Sandwich were as godly on the Sabbath as they were industrious on week-days: a fact to which he appears to have objected
less than later archbishops were to do.[1] But French, Dutch,
Swiss and Hungarian Sunday observance was not as strict as
that advocated by the English and Scottish Puritans.[2] In the
Netherlands, precisely during our period, ministers were complaining of "the difficulty of reclaiming the country people on
the Sundays either from the sports or from their work". The
Synod of Dort recommended afternoon catechetical sermons
as well as morning sermons, and resolved to seek the help of
the magistrate.[3] The great neglect of observing the Lord's
Day in Holland was very grievous to the Pilgrim Fathers, and
was one of the reasons which decided them to emigrate to
America.[4] Attempts to improve Sunday observance at
Rotterdam in the sixteen-thirties were successfully sabotaged
by the brewers. Travellers from Sir William Brereton in 1634
to Ralph Thoresby in 1678 were shocked at the laxity of
Sunday observance in the Netherlands.[5] In every other
European country the Calvinists were defeated, and so had
no opportunity to impose on the masses of the people a type
of Sabbath about which at least the rural poor were unenthusiastic. Bulstrode Whitelocke was outraged by Sunday behaviour
in *Lutheran* Sweden. He hoped rather bleakly that the recent
English reformation of the Lord's Day might be imitated there,
and he persuaded Queen Christina to discontinue Sunday balls
at court – at least so long as Whitelocke was there.[6]

In 1652 a French translation of the Leveller Agreement of
the People was published in Bordeaux by the radical rebels of
the Ormée. One article of the manifesto which accompanied it
called on magistrates to enforce strict Sabbath observance.

1. Strype, *Life of Parker*, I, p. 276.
2. For Sabbatarianism in sixteenth-century Hungary see A. Pirnát,
Die Ideologie der Siebenbürger Antitrinitarier in den 1570er. Jahren
(Budapest, 1961), *passim*.
3. John Hales, *Letters from the Synod of Dort* in *Golden Remaines*
(1659), pp. 3–4.
4. Nathaniel Morton, *New England's Memorial* (1669), in *Chronicles
of the Pilgrim Fathers* (Everyman ed.), p. 9.
5. Ed. E. Hawkins, *Travels . . . by Sir William Brereton* (Chetham
Soc., 1844), pp. 6, 10–11; R. Thoresby, *Diary* (ed. J. Hunter, 1830),
I, pp. 17–18.
6. Whitelocke, *A Journal of the Swedish Embassy* (1855), I, pp.
287–8, II, p. 267.

This was not a demand which the Levellers put forward in England, since there the danger was excessive Sabbatarianism rather than inadequate Sunday rest. We are left wondering whether the insertion of this clause in the manifesto was a genuine local demand, springing from the same needs of the industrious sort of people (the main supporters of the Ormée), as Sabbatarianism did in England before 1640.[1] When the next major European revolution came, in France, the revolutionaries attacked religion as such: but it is not altogether without interest that in 1789 the *cahier* from protestant Nimes demanded the abolition of all but the most important church festivals, and their transference to Sunday.[2]

The younger Matthew Wren, son of the Bishop of Ely, made an attempt to answer the question why "the faction in England should be so rigid in observing the Sabbath, when the men of Geneva and Holland, from whom in almost all things they took their pattern, are so extremely loose in that point".[3] His answer is too partisan to be entirely satisfactory: "because under this pretence they kept the people to sermons, expositions, repetitions and such-like exercises, which were the most useful tools they could employ in their design".[4] But this explanation does contain the essential truth that strict Sabbath observance helped the Parliamentarians, through the ministers, to educate, discipline and control their humbler supporters.

The reasons for the peculiar British Sunday are to be sought, it is suggested, in the peculiar economic and political development of England. In England commerce, industry and an urban way of life established themselves on a national scale

1. H. N. Brailsford, *The Levellers and the Puritan Revolution* (1961), pp. 688–9. The former Leveller Sexby was in Bordeaux at the time, and almost certainly had a hand in drafting this manifesto.

2. A. Soboul, *1789* (Paris, 1939), pp. 62, 75.

3. Thomas Shepard also asked "Why the Lord Christ should keep his servants in England and Scotland to clear up and vindicate this point of the Sabbath, and to welcome it with more love than some precious ones in foreign churches?" But he produced no sociological answer. It was one of several "discoveries by the British nation which modesty and humility would forbid all sober minds to make mention of now"; and Shepard attributed it to "God's free grace" (*Theses Sabbaticae*, Sig. A 2v–A 4).

4. M. Wren, *Of the Progress of the Revolutions in England*, in *Collectanea Curiosa* (ed. J. Gutch, 1781), I, p. 237; cf. also Heylyn, *History of the Presbyterians*, pp. 407–8.

earlier than anywhere else in the world except the Netherlands. And in the Netherlands the circumstances of the Revolt put control securely in the hands of the "natural rulers" of town and countryside; in any case there was no expansion of *industrial* capitalism in the northern Netherlands comparable with that which took place in England. In England the industrious sort of people faced unprecedented possibilities of advance. But they needed both protection from overwork and a new ethic, for themselves and for their employees as well. Such men seem to have been sympathetic to Sabbatarianism and hostile to the traditional sports, as they were to the older magical and sacramental modes of thought, whether papist or pre-Christian. The old ruling class and its spokesmen among the hierarchy, on the other hand, encouraged the traditional sports (a harmless, non-political form of recreation for the lower class), at least from the turn of the century, when the challenge to the old order was becoming marked. The proponents of the new ideas, in addition to their concern for the weekly rest for small business men and their workers, wished to extend preaching, and to see the Sabbath spent in "reading, meditation, repetition of sermons (especially by families), catechizing" and good works.[1]

The abolition of saints' days, then, was part of the attack on the old social and economic order: the regular weekly rest became common to all modern industrial communities. In mediaeval society religious festivals measured out the seasons of the year: in the modern world it is no longer the saints in whose honour holidays are celebrated: the Church has yielded place to the less personal institutions which give their name to bank holidays. The fight for Sabbatarianism and against rural sports was an attempt to extend the concern for labour discipline from the South and East of England into the dark corners of the North and West.

Sunday as a day of religious instruction is a peculiarly British phenomenon because of the use made of it by the Puritans during the five decades after the suppression of the classis movement. It was on the Sabbath, particularly in households and in the sectarian congregations, that unity and discipline under the leadership of heads of families was won. "Wren's

1. Ordinance of 4 January 1645, C. H. Firth and R. S. Rait, *Acts and Ordinances of the Interregnum* (1911), I, p. 599.

man", Dr. John Pocklington, said of the Puritans: "They must gain elbow room for their Sabbath's exercise, or preaching falsely so called; being for the most part (as their hearers will justify) but violent discourses and personal invectives against the present state and settled laws of the land, with the governors".[1] Sunday was "the training day of military discipline, by which the Church of Christ is unto the Synagogue of Satan . . . terrible as an army with banners; which, if it should not be well united, and often exercised, the powers of darkness would be mightily exalted".[2] The men of Cromwell's army must have owed much to moral lessons taught on the Sabbath: they helped to hold the parliamentarians together through the civil war. After it had been won, serious steps were taken to extend this use of the Sabbath to the dark corners of the land, and to social strata which the pre-revolutionary church had almost certainly neglected. Parliament's ordinance of 8 April 1644 insisted that J.P.s should see that rogues, vagabonds and beggars attended church. Nine months later legislation similarly provided that servants were not to be unnecessarily detained from church. The repeal in 1650 of the statutes on compulsory church attendance would reduce the effectiveness of these ordinances, but by that date the sects were catering more seriously for the lower classes in society.[3]

Some of the sects went beyond Sabbatarianism. It had always been especially the conservatives, the disciplinarians, the Presbyterians, the enemies of free discussion, who idolized the Sabbath. The radical protestant tradition refused to attribute sacredness to externals, whether ceremonies, places or times; and this could be turned against the Sabbath. "If anywhere the day is made holy for the mere day's sake", said Luther, "then I order you to work on it, to ride on it, to feast on it, to do anything to remove this reproach from Christian liberty".[4] Calvin was said to have held that the seventh day's

1. J. Pocklington, *Sunday No Sabbath* (1636), p. 7. This book was condemned to be burnt by the House of Lords in 1641 (Wallington, *Historical Notices*, I, p. 137). Cf. *The Character of an Oxford Incendiary* (1643), in *Harleian Miscellany* (1744–56), V, p. 471.

2. John Ley, *Sunday a Sabbath* (1641), Sig. C 4. Ley was a minister in Cheshire, where he had ample evidence of the activities of the Synagogue of Satan.

3. See pp. 458–9 below.

4. Quoted by F. Cox and H. Seekings, *Our English Sunday* (1920), p. 57.

rest could be held on any day: its transfer to Thursday was discussed in Geneva.[1] In England Tyndale thought the Sabbath could be celebrated on any day.[2] Robert Barnes had said in 1531 "for the Christian every day is a Sabbath and a festal day, and not only the seventh day".[3] John Etherington was accused in the sixteen-twenties of making the same point. The Sabbath should be observed only because this was the law of the land; but no one who had conscientious scruples about its observance should be coerced.[4] In 1623 a Sussex man was saying that "the people need not be so strict and careful in keeping the Sabbath day, for it is abolished, and that every day in the week is a Christian's Sabbath".[5] A pamphlet of 1636 would permit moderate recreation on Sundays, but always according to a man's own conviction, "lest he sin against his own conscience".[6]

Consciences however differed. Even Gilbert Ironside, in a treatise dedicated to Laud, made the dangerous admission that outward worship in public congregations would not have been required in the state of innocence.[7] Sir Henry Vane thought the Sunday Sabbath was of magisterial institution, and observed it for that reason only.[8] Roger Williams, on the other hand, was of the opinion "that the magistrate might not punish the breach of the Sabbath, nor any other offence which was a breach of the First table".[9] Some men are now cold to external Sabbath observance, Thomas Shepard noted in New England in 1649, "because the internal and spiritual Sabbath

1. Pocklington, *op. cit.*, p. 8.

2. See p. 166 above.

3. Quoted by E. G. Rupp, *Studies in the Making of the English Protestant Tradition* (1947), p. 39.

4. J. Etherington, *The Defence of John Etherington against Stephen Denison . . . which he having now opportunitie . . . thought needful to publish* (1641), pp. 30, 35. Etherington had been imprisoned by the High Commission from 1626 to 1629. Cf Greenham, *Works*, p. 374, and Brabourne, quoted on p. 174 above.

5. H. Johnstone, *Churchwardens' Presentments*, . . . *Archdeaconry of Chichester*, p. 66.

6. [Anon.], *A Soveraigne Antidote Against Sabbatarian Errours* (1636) quoted by A. French, *Charles I and the Puritan Upheaval* (1955), p. 269.

7. Ironside, *Seven Questions of the Sabbath*, p. 8.

8. W. W. Ireland, *The Life of Sir Henry Vane the Younger* (1905), p. 443.

9. T. Prince, *A Chronological History of New England* (1736), in Arber, *An English Garner*, II, p. 583.

is all in all".[1] John Saltmarsh shocked conservatives by saying "The Christian knows no Sabbath but the bosom of the Father".[2]

In 1641 George Wither had said that the Sabbath was to be spent "with a sanctified pleasure . . . even to the use of bodily labours and exercises wheresoever (without respect to sensual or covetous ends) a rectified conscience shall persuade us that the honour of God, the charity we owe to our neighbours, or an unfeigned necessity requires them to be done".[3] That already left a good deal to the rectified conscience, and it is not surprising that in 1653 Wither urged that Parliament should follow the example of the Venetian Senate and meet on Sundays as well as other days.[4] Milton carried the argument further. "It is not the formal duty of worship, or the sitting still, that keeps the holy rest of Sabbath; but whosoever doth most according to charity, whether he works or not, he breaks the holy rest of Sabbath least".[5] "If I observe the Sabbath in compliance with the Decalogue, but contrary to the dictates of my own faith, conformity with the Decalogue, however exact, becomes in my case a sin and a violation of the law".[6] It was always wrong to limit Christian freedom by inventing imaginary sins, or to burden life with laws and prohibitions not imposed by the Gospel. In the *Christian Doctrine*, with unusual historical sense, Milton argued that the seventh day rest had been needed only under slavery: the condition of hired servants, "who are now generally employed", was much easier.[7] Milton's approach would have left everything to the individual conscience – whether one went to church or not, whether one worked on the Sabbath or not.

Thomas Ellwood, arrested in 1660 for travelling on a Sunday, confused the constable who arrested him by using similar arguments.[8] In the cruder mind of Roger Crab, a plebeian

1. Shepard, *Theses Sabbaticae*, p. 2.
2. Quoted in S. Rutherford, *A Survey of the Spirituall Antichrist* (1648), p. 229.
3. G. Wither, *Hymns and Songs of the Church* (1856), p. 216.
4. Wither, *A Poem concerning a perpetuall Parliament* (1653), in *Miscellaneous Works* (Spenser Soc.), III, p. 60.
5. Milton, *Prose Works* (Bohn ed.), I, p. 455.
6. *Ibid.*, V, p. 3 (*Christian Doctrine*).
7. *Ibid.*, V, p. 67.
8. T. Ellwood, *Life* (1906), p. 66; cf. p. 141.

anti-Sabbatarianism expressed itself by working on Sunday as on any other day. He was put in the stocks for it and for telling the J.P.s that "the Sabbath was an abominable idol". He parodied the traditional phrase by refusing to "observe the market-day" of "the old jade".[1] The Diggers in 1649 symbolically began to cultivate St. George's Hill upon a Sunday. This assertion of Christian liberty took the same form as when James I's Privy Council met on a Sunday; but the motive behind it was rather different, as was the publication of No. 1 of *Mercurius Aulicus* on Sunday, 1 January 1643.[2] Gerrard Winstanley indeed would have transformed Sabbath observance in his Utopia. It is "very rational and good" that "one day in seven be still set apart" for fellowship and rest. But services are to be replaced by lectures on current affairs, history and the natural sciences.[3] So the puritan Sabbath would be completely secularized, and yet its two essential functions of giving an opportunity for rest from labour and for education would be retained.[4]

X

The freedom of the revolutionary decades allowed men to explore the libertarian aspects of Sabbatarianism which Brerewood had so presciently attacked. " 'Tis liberty, liberty, liberty, that wicked men long for": on this point many men had come to agree with Richard Baxter and Thomas Hall by the end of the sixteen-fifties.[5] Fear of the radicalism and irreligion

1. R. Crab, *Dagons-Downfall* (1657), pp. 3, 24–8; cf. p. 9. Cf. also "the old gentlewoman" whom Henry Newcome met in 1651. "On the Lord's Day" she "pulled out her sewing and said, 'Why might she not sew on that day as well as another?' ". She was a sectary (Newcome, *Autobiography*, Chetham Soc., 1852, p. 32). Some early Quakers also worked on Sundays.

2. J. Frank, *The Beginnings of the English Newspaper, 1620–60* (Harvard University Press, 1961), p. 33.

3. G. Winstanley, *The Law of Freedom* (1652), in G. H. Sabine, *The Works of Gerrard Winstanley* (1941), pp. 562–4. Hobbes, like Winstanley, seems to suggest using the Sabbath for political education (*Leviathan*, Everyman ed., p. 181).

4. Even good people, Oliver Heywood observed in 1664, "do not sanctify the Sabbath as they ought", but "read histories, books" (ed. J. H. Turner, *Autobiography, Diaries, etc., of Oliver Heywood* 1882–5, III, p. 19).

5. Baxter, *The Holy Commonwealth* (1659) pp. 92–4, 226–31; Hall, *Funebria Florae*, p. 4.

shown by the lower orders, not all of whose consciences were rectified, increased respect for the puritan Sabbath among the propertied classes, and reduced anti-Sabbatarianism among the respectable. Already an act of Cromwell's second Parliament in August 1657 went some way towards repealing the Act of October 1650 by insisting that the permission of a J.P. was necessary to avoid a fine for absence from a place of worship on Sunday. But the gentry's dominance was only to be re-established by restoration of the episcopal state Church under Parliamentary control.

Sabbath observance, Baxter held, was necessary to keep up the solemn worship of God and the public owning and honouring of him in the world. "If all men were left to themselves, what time they should bestow in the worshipping of God, the greatest part would cast off all, and grow into atheism or utter profaneness, and the rest would grow into confusion". The lamentable ignorance of "the generality" called urgently for strict observance of the Sabbath. Tenants and labourers, carters and carriers and abundance of tradesmen, live in such poverty that on week-days they can hardly spare time to meditate on their eternal welfare: and still less so their children and servants. "They are fain to rise early and hasten to their work, and scarce have leisure to eat and sleep as nature requireth; and they are so toiled and wearied with hard labour, that if they have at night a quarter of an hour to read a chapter and pray, they can scarce hold open their eyes from sleeping". The tyranny of masters made rest for their bodies and an opportunity for the good of their souls welcome. The overworked minister had no time to give them all the attention they required: they *must* attend public worship on Sundays and be compelled to meditate in their households, if England were to remain a Christian country.[1] God, wrote ex-Lord Chancellor Clarendon, demands "a tenth of our substance, and a seventh (which is more strict) of our time".[2] From Baxter to Clarendon the ranks were being closed. Samuel Fisher in 1660 looked far ahead when he objected to "our

1. Baxter, *Practical Works*, XIII, pp. 458–63.
2. Clarendon, *Essay of Life*, in *A Compleat Collection of Tracts* (1747), p. 92. Whether consciously or not, Clarendon was almost quoting Richard Greenham, (see p. 168, note 6 above) and George Hakewill (*Short . . . Discourse of the . . . Lords-Day*, 1641, p. 6).

poor still bepoped people" keeping a best suit for wear on Sundays.[1]

The emphasis is now less on harmonious Sabbath discussion within the family, more on discipline imposed from above. "The profanation of the Lord's Day by open sports and pastimes is by the civil part of the nation accounted scandalous", said John Corbet in 1660;[2] and by now "the civil part of the nation" were those who counted. Kings and bishops had to follow them. After some prodding by the House of Commons, Charles II's Worcester House Declaration of October 1660 promised "to take care that the Lord's Day be applied to holy exercises, without unnecessary divertisements"; and so by implication abandoned his father's Book of Sports.[3] In 1662, again in response to a request from Parliament, Charles wrote to the Archbishop of Canterbury calling "for the better observing of the Lord's Day, much neglected of late" and insisting that churchwardens should present all who indulged in unlawful sports or exercises on the Sabbath. The clergy were to exhort parishioners to frequent divine service on Sunday. Offenders who resorted to taverns or used unlawful games were to be "carefully looked after".[4] J.P.s increasingly took over the enforcement of Sunday observance – e.g. by suppressing ale-houses which allowed tippling on the Sabbath.[5] After 1660, by contrast, it proved increasingly difficult for the church courts to stop men working on saints' days.[6] In 1662 too the Bishop of London issued a very strict order against boats travelling on Sunday; next year, at the

1. S. Fisher, *The Rustics Alarm to the Rabbies*, in *The Testimony of Truth Exalted* (1679), pp. 571–2.

2. J. Corbet, *The Interest of England in the Matter of Religion* (1660), quoted in *Crisis in English History, 1066–1945* (ed. B. D. Henning, A. S. Foord and B. L. Mathias, New York, 1949), p. 268.

3. *L.J.* XI, p. 180.

4. Cardwell, *Documentary Annals*, II, p. 258. Cf. Eachard's tart observation: "Truly, if religion and the worship of God consisted only in negatives, and that the observation of the Sabbath was only not to be drunk . . .". (*Grounds and Occasions for the Contempt of the Clergy*, 1670, in Arber, *An English Garner*, VII, p. 312.)

5. Ed. S. C. Ratcliff and H. C. Johnson, *Warwickshire Quarter Sessions Order Book, 1657–65* (Warwick County Records, 1938), pp. 148–9; M. S. Gretton, *Oxfordshire Justices of the Peace in the 17th century* (Oxfordshire Record Soc., 1934, pp. 9–10, 22–3, 51–2).

6. *V.C.H. Wiltshire*, III, pp. 46–7; cf. G. M. Trevelyan, *Social History of England* (1945), p. 231.

House of Commons' request a proclamation was issued against Sunday travelling in general. Bills for Sunday observance passed the Commons in the Convention Parliament, and several times in the Cavalier Parliament, before finally the Act of 1677 summed up the legislation of the interregnum which prohibited Sunday work.[1] "Preaching and sitting on Sundays" had become, and long remained, "the religion of England".[2]

A Frenchman's description published in 1672 said "there is no kingdom wherein Sunday is better observed . . .; for so far from selling things on that day, even the carrying of water for the houses is not permitted; nor can anyone play at bowls or any other game, or even touch a musical instrument, or sing aloud in his own house, without incurring the penalty of a fine".[3] Sunday sittings of Parliament in 1679 were a sign of the gravity of the crisis in that year. A rumour that William of Orange habitually hunted on Sundays was deliberately spread by the French Ambassador in the following year in order to discredit the Prince.[4]

It was the social rather than the religious aspect of Sabbatarianism that had triumphed. When a pirate crew mutinied in 1681, their nominee as captain not only had a brisker way with prisoners but also saw that the Sabbath was observed as a day of rest.[5] Shortly after 1688 the great merchant Thomas Papillon drafted a memorandum in which he declared "There is no such way to preserve this kingdom against the common enemy, to wit France and Rome, as that the government do effectually take care to suppress all Sabbath profanation, and

1. W. B. Trevelyan, *Sunday* (1902), p. 73; Whitaker, *Sunday in Tudor and Stuart Times*, pp. 188–97.

2. J. Evelyn, *A Character of England* (1659), in *Miscellaneous Writings* (1825) p. 153. The striking phrase, as we might have guessed, is not Evelyn's own. See the passage from Milton's *Colasterion* (1645) quoted on p. 205 above.

3. Buckle, *Miscellaneous and Posthumous Works*, II, p. 220; cf. III, p. 536. The phrases were repeated by another French visitor in 1727, who attributed the English Sunday to legislation of the Commonwealth, and noted that card-playing was also strictly forbidden,"at least for the citizens and common people" (Mme Van Muyden, *A Foreign View of England in the Reigns of George I and George II*, 1902, p. 322).

4. J. R. Jones, *The First Whigs* (1961), pp. 66, 151.

5. P. K. Kemp and C. Lloyd, *The Brethren of the Coast* (1960), p. 48.

all drunkenness, swearing and debauchery".[1] The societies for the reformation of manners founded in William III's reign set themselves precisely this patriotic task, now that the government was no longer under the influence of France and Rome.[2] That aspect of Laudianism was as dead as a door-nail. It was bishops who warned George I that official support of "infamous" sports had brought on the civil war, and might do so again.[3] Bishops were now one with the civil part of the nation. So there was no need for the alliance between gentry and Puritanism after 1660: henceforth nonconformists are drawn almost exclusively from the industrious sort of people.

Addison, as so often, can sum up. "If keeping holy the seventh day were only a human institution, it would be the best method that could have been thought of for the polishing and civilizing of mankind: . . . a stated time in which the whole village meet together with their best faces and in their cleanliest habits, to converse with one another upon indifferent subjects, hear their duties explained to them, and join together in adoration of the Supreme Being. . . . As Sir Roger is landlord to the whole congregation, he keeps them in very good order, and will suffer nobody to sleep in it besides himself. . . . He . . . sometimes stands up when everybody else is upon their knees, to count the congregation, or see if any of his tenants are missing. . . . The authority of the knight . . . has a very good effect on the parish, who are not polite enough to see anything ridiculous in his behaviour". In the next village, where parson and squire are at loggerheads, the squire has made all his tenants atheists and tithe-stealers.[4]

That is an idyllic and an idealized picture; it is also a picture of the puritan Sabbath without Puritanism. The traditional sports have gone. Church attendance is enforced neither by church courts nor by a presbytery, but by the squire. Jehovah has become the Supreme Being. The puritan revolution has been defeated, but some of the social programme which accompanied its religious fervour has been taken over. (Some, though not all: there is less emphasis on discussion than a

1. A. F. W. Papillon, *Memoirs of Thomas Papillon* (1887), p. 376.
2. D. W. R. Bahlman, *The Moral Revolution of 1688* (Yale University Press, 1957), *passim*.
3. N. Sykes, *Edmund Gibson* (1926), p. 190.
4. *The Spectator*, No. 112 (9 July 1711). Cf. the passage from Mandeville quoted as epigraph to this chapter.

radical Puritan would have wished). And Addison's picture is explicitly rural: such harmony could no longer even be imagined in the towns, where the traditional anti-Sabbatarianism of the lowest classes had been reinforced by the principled anti-Sabbatarianism of the more radical sectaries. Only in the villages was there still a single religious community embracing the whole civil community.

Chapter Six

Discipline, Monarchical, Aristocratical and Democratical

He thought God had left a rule in His Word for discipline, and that aristocratical by elders, not monarchical by bishops, nor democratical by the people.

John Geree, *The Character of an Old English Puritane* (1646), p. 4.

The Parliament of England cannot have on earth so strong pillars and pregnant supporters of all their privileges as free protestant assemblies established by law and kept in their full freedom from the lowest to the highest, from the congregational eldership to the general synod of the nation. No such bars as these are imaginable against tyranny or anarchy; they are the mightiest impediments both to the exorbitancy of monarchs, which has been and is our misery, and to the extravagancy of the common multitude, attempting to correct and subject all Parliaments to their own foolish desires – which is like to be the matter of our next exercise and trouble.

R. Baillie, *A Dissuasive from the Errors of the Time* (1646), Epistle Dedicatory.

I

THE discipline advocated by the Puritans[1] was something quite novel, unknown to Roman canon law. It concerned itself, to outward appearances, exclusively with the safeguarding of the sacrament and a censorship of conduct. Yet to this discipline, however novel and however apparently

1. See Tawney, *Religion and the Rise of Capitalism* (Penguin ed.), pp. 191–205.

restricted, the greatest possible importance was attached. It was heavily emphasised by Bucer in Cambridge in Edward VI's reign, and it appeared as one of the four marks by which the true Church is discerned in the catechism of 1553.[1] Together with true preaching and right administration of the sacraments, discipline was given as one of the three notes of the Church in the Scottish Kirk's Confession of Faith in 1560.[2] The same three "true marks of Christ's Church" were laid down by Richard Fitz's "Privy Church" in London in 1567, discipline being explicitly contrasted with "the filthy canon law".[3] They reappear in the 1572 *Admonition to Parliament*.[4] Yet discipline, "the sinews of religion", was utterly lacking in the Elizabethan Church, Humphrey and Sampson complained to Bullinger in 1566.[5] (We may note, all through, the foreign connections of the early advocates of the discipline: it is one of the few components of English Protestantism which is not to be found in the popular native heresy, Lollardy). An exact and perfect platform of church government is prescribed in the New Testament, Udall tells us, and to swerve from this is unlawful.[6] The Brownists urged the lack of a satisfactory

1. Ed. H. Robinson, *Original Letters relative to the English Reformation* (Parker Soc., 1846–7), II, p. 544; ed. J. Ketley, *The Two Liturgies . . . with other Documents . . . in the Reign of Edward VI* (Parker Soc., 1844), p. 513. Discipline as a note of the Church had the authority of Luther as well as of Calvinists and Zwinglians (see p. 242–3 below, and cf. Tyndale, *Expositions and Notes on Sundry Portions of the Holy Scriptures* Parker Soc., 1849, pp. 219–20).

2. J. Knox, *History of the Reformation in Scotland* (1832), p. 215. (The note which was not repeated in the Scottish Confession of Faith was "brotherly love"). Bancroft was therefore wrong in saying that discipline as a note of the true Church was invented by Cartwright and Travers upon Beza's authority (*Dangerous Positions*, 1640, pp. 42–3; cf. *Tracts ascribed to Richard Bancroft*, p. 109; Heylyn, *History of the Presbyterians*, p. 41).

3. Burrage, *Early English Dissenters*, II, p. 13.

4. W. H. Frere and C. E. Douglas, *Puritan Manifestoes* (1907), p. 9.

5. Ed. H. Robinson, *The Zurich Letters* (Parker Soc., 1842–5), I, p. 164. Cf. Beza to Bullinger, 3 September 1566, *ibid.*, II, pp. 128–9, contrasting the popish system of discipline with that of lawfully appointed presbyteries.

6. J. Udall, *A Demonstration of Discipline* (1880), pp. 65–7. First published 1588. There is a full statement of the significance of discipline in the 1571 Preface to *The Reformation of the Ecclesiastical Laws* (ed. Cardwell, 1850, pp. xix–xxvii). Cf. Bancroft's *Dangerous Positions*, pp. 43–4, for further illustrations of the importance attached to discipline.

discipline in the English Church to justify separation.[1] Thomas Rogers said that the Brownists "make discipline (and that too of their own devising) such an essential argument of the visible Church, as they think where that is not, the magistrates there be tyrants; the ministers, false prophets; no Church of God is; anti-Christianity doth reign".[2]

"Discipline", declared Leighton, "is the chief commander in the camp-royal of God".[3] Bacon pointed out the political consequences of this emphasis when he wrote: "It is very hard to affirm that the 'discipline', which they [the Puritans] say we want, is one of the essential parts of the worship of God: and not to affirm withal that the people themselves, upon peril of salvation, without staying for the magistrate, are not to gather themselves into it".[4] Whitgift thought that Cartwright's conception of discipline smelt of anabaptism.[5]

This heavy emphasis on discipline had social and political implications. Some valuable hints given by S. R. Gardiner – not the most sociological of historians – may help us here. "Every new social class as it rises into power", he wrote, "needs, in proportion to its previous ignorance, a strictness of discipline which becomes unnecessary as soon as it has learned to bear lightly the responsibilities of its new position. . . . In Scotland it was by the Presbyterian clergy that the middle classes were organized, and the organization thus given enabled them to throw off the yoke of the feudal nobles and ultimately to assert their own predominance. . . . Men learned to act together in the church courts, where they were not overshadowed, as they were in their single House of Parliament, by great lords and ministers of state. It was not an education which would encourage variety of character. . . . But if the system bred no leaders of thought, it bound man to man in an indissoluble bond. . . . The clergy . . . strove by means of church discipline, enforced in the most inquisitorial

1. Ed. A. Peel and L. H. Carlson, *The Writings of Robert Harrison and Robert Browne* (1953), pp. 31, 212–13, 447, 453, 460, 464, 513.

2. T. Rogers, *The Faith. Doctrine and Religion professed and protected in . . . England*. p. 98.

3. A. Leighton, *Sions Plea against the Prelacie* (? Holland, 1628), p. 110.

4. Bacon, *An Advertisement touching the Controversies of the Church of England* (1589), in *Works*, VIII, p. 87.

5. Whitgift, *Works*, I, pp. 185, 290; III, pp. 552–4.

manner, to bring a whole population under the yoke of the moral law. . . . The Scottish system was not a rule for those alone who sought counsels of perfection, whilst the mass of mankind was left to content themselves with a lower standard of morality. In Scotland there was to be parity of moral law as there was to be a parity of ministerial office. The fierce ruffians who in the sixteenth century had reddened the country with the feuds of noble houses, the rude peasants who wallowed in impurity, were made to feel the compulsion of a never-resting, ever-abiding power, which pried into their lives and called them to account for their deeds as no lay government, however arbitrary, could venture to do. Therefore the Scottish people has rightly venerated as its saviours those to whom it is mainly owing that even in that race after material wealth which set in amongst a people whose soil was poor and whose climate was ungenial, it has ever kept in honour the laws of righteousness."[1]

Allowing for the somewhat old-fashioned language, that makes the most important points. The presbyterian organization helped "the middle classes . . . to throw off the yoke of the feudal nobles" and establish the rule of lower social types, who gained their political experience in local presbyteries. Presbyterianism rejected the dual morality of monastic Catholicism: its discipline was applied to the whole population. Kings themselves were not exempt from discipline and excommunication.[2] This discipline could be effectively enforced only by a body with the supernatural prestige of the Church. The victory of the new social groups justified itself by leading to material prosperity, and the discipline became superfluous once their rule was securely established: but it left an ineradicable mark on national ways of thought.

The economic transformations of our period did not revolutionize men's thinking overnight. For a long time the industrious sort of people fumbled for a new ethos: it took time for these groups to realize their common interests, and that these interests were being formulated in a body of ideas and a disciplinary system by Calvin and others. But as more of them came to this realization, so they felt the need for an

1. Gardiner, *History of England*, VIII, pp. 308–9; *History of the Great Civil War* (1901), I, pp. 226–7.
2. Cf. Bancroft, *Dangerous Positions*, pp. 49–50, quoting Cartwright.

organization which would confirm and comfort them in their beliefs, and help them to work together for the imposition of their set of ideas, their new conception of discipline. upon society through the Church. The puritan movement, it may be suggested, is always groping towards a form of organization which will fulfil the functions of a political party, to remake society as God wished to see it. Those aspects of the discipline which they most prized were those which had existed in the primitive Church whilst it was still an underground organization.[1]

Discipline, like charity, begins at home: the first significance of the Calvinist system was its effect on the moral characters of its advocates, in preparing them both for intense and devoted activity in all spheres of life, and for actions requiring great political courage. This point was well put by Professor Knappen: – "If the Calvinists eventually became more diligent in business than their fellow-Christians, the historian, in accounting for this fact, might do well to pay more attention to their peculiar system of church government and discipline, and less to their doctrine of predestination, which was held in common by most of their protestant contemporaries". "An iron discipline it was; but, when allowed to operate, it produced men of the same quality, capable of standing up to crowned monarchs without flinching".[2] Professor Jordan had similarly suggested that Calvinism's psychological contribution in giving the "rising middle class" a sense of status, in ridding them of their feeling of inferiority, was probably more important than "the incidental contributions which Calvinism made to the acquisitive philosophy" in accounting for "the amazing rapidity with which Calvinism spread through the trading and industrial groups".[3] Stoughton in 1604 "on the behoof and in the defence of the common people of England" testified and protested that "we are not yet become so ignorant, rude and barbarous" as to "hazard all our birthrights

1. This point was made by Whitgift (*Works*, I, p. 391; III, pp. 166, 180); in *Tracts ascribed to Richard Bancroft*, pp. 109–10; and by Calybute Downing, quoted on p. 225 below. Hence elders might be permitted in time of persecution, as under Mary.

2. Knappen, *Tudor Puritanism*, pp. 92–4. Cf. Haller, *The Rise of Puritanism*, Chapter IV.

3. W. K. Jordan, *The Development of Religious Toleration in England 1603–40* (1936), p. 203.

upon the skill and ability of such a mass of hirelings" as the established clergy. There were plenty of "men of occupations", the sort who were already churchwardens, who could be elders or "lay aldermen (as they call them)". "If then the common people be foolish and ignorant, if they do err and be irreligious, they may justly challenge the Lords Spiritual of unkindness and want of love", since they were most to blame for the ignorance. In any case, he argued, this alleged "backwardness of the people in the truth of religion . . . can be no good plea in bar to take from the people of God their right, interest and freedom" to choose their own ministers.[1] The phrases almost anticipate those of the Levellers, and may indeed conceivably have influenced them, since Stoughton's pamphlet was reprinted in 1642.

"To discipline must all the estates within this realm be subject, as well rulers as they that are ruled; yea, and the preachers themselves, as well as the poorest within the Kirk". So said *The First Book of Discipline*.[2] Paradoxically, the strict discipline which helped to weld Scotland into a nation, and which seems so tyrannical to us, was liberty for those whose economic and political activities flourished under national unity and peace. Heylyn referred to "the great contentment which it gave the common people to see themselves entrusted with the weightiest matters in religion: and thereby an equality with, if not (by reason of their numbers, being two for one) superiority above their ministers".[3]

But the church contained "two sorts of people": the godly minority and the unregenerate mass. So Foxe and Bullinger taught in the 16th century: so William Bridge reminded Parliament in 1643.[4] Puritanism is thus a two-faced theory. To the elect, those who accept the new ideas, those who wished God's will (as interpreted by Puritans) to prevail, it brought

1. W. Stoughton, *An Assertion for true and Christian Church-Policie* (Middleburgh, 1604), pp. 238–47, 193–5, 383–4. See p. 228 below. For Stoughton, a protégé of the Puritan Earl of Huntingdon, see P. Collinson, *Letters of Thomas Wood, 1566–1577* (Bulletin of the Institute of Historical Research Special Supplement, No. 5, 1960), p. x.

2. In J. Knox, *History of the Reformation* (1832), p. 508.

3. Heylyn, *The History of the Presbyterians*, pp. 10–11.

4. J. Foxe, *Acts and Monuments* (n.d., ed. J. Pratt), I, p. 88; Bullinger, *Decades*, V, pp. 7–8, 11–17; W. Bridge, *A Sermon Preached before the House of Commons* 29 November 1643, pp. 25–6.

self-confidence, energy, enthusiasm in the performance of their providential tasks. The discipline in Scotland was, in its origins, a form of opposition organization, by which laity and lesser clergy set themselves free from the hierarchy.[1] But to the mass of the population, the unregenerate, discipline turns a harsher face: for them it was not quite so clearly liberating.[2]

II

What was discipline? "There is not that thing in the world of more grave and urgent importance throughout the whole life of man, than is discipline", wrote Milton in 1641. "The flourishing and decaying of all civil societies, all the movements and turnings of human occasions are moved to and fro upon the axle of discipline. . . . Nor is there any sociable perfection in this life, civil or sacred, that can be above discipline; but she is that which with her musical cords preserves and holds all the parts thereof together. . . . Discipline is not only the removal of disorder, but if any visible shape can be given to divine things, the very visible shape and image of virtue".[3] Education and discipline have the same function: to liberate us from the naturally sinful state. In *Comus* it was the rod of discipline which freed men from the sorcerer's enchantments.[4] Milton's own ambivalent attitude towards the discipline is of peculiar interest, for our purposes, just because he had grasped its necessary connection with a social order. His support for and vigorous defence of a presbyterian discipline in 1641–2 arose from his sense of the need for tight organization and solidarity among those who wished to remove disorder; and from his conviction that it would enhance the dignity of those laymen who administered it. "The exclusion of Christ's people from the offices of holy discipline through the pride of a usurping clergy causes the rest to have an unworthy and abject opinion of themselves". Experience of governing the Church will open the eyes of the man who enjoys it "to a wise and true valuation of himself". Milton insisted that the functions of

1. G. Donaldson, *The Scottish Reformation* (1960), pp. 80–1, 107, 130, 138–9.

2. See pp. 234–41 below.

3. Milton, *Prose Works* (Bohn Edition), II, pp. 441–2.

4. Rosamund Tuve, *Images and Themes in Five Poems by Milton* (Harvard University Press, 1957), pp. 132, 152.

church government ought to be free and open to any Christian man, but the qualifications which he adds, and the context, make it clear that he was thinking primarily of the industrious sort of people, of heads of households.[1] As long as "virtue" was thought of in negative terms, as that which the Laudian régime made impossible, the presbyterian discipline seemed to offer the most hopeful alternative. Milton learnt better later, and his change of heart should serve as a warning for us in the earlier period. It is possible that men who advocated presbyterian discipline with great enthusiasm before 1640 were in fact thinking more of what it would get rid of than of what it would establish.

That shrewd social scientist, Adam Smith, grasped the connection between religious discipline, self-discipline and labour discipline. There have been two moralities in every civilized society, he explained: the loose system adopted by the people of fashion, and the strict or austere system, which is "admired and revered" by the common people and adopted by "the wiser and better sort of the common people". For "the vices of levity are always ruinous to the common people, and a single week's thoughtlessness and dissipation is often sufficient to undo a poor workman for ever". It is more difficult for men of fashion to be ruined by dissipation, and they are apt to consider the liberty of indulging in some degree of excess without censure or reproach as one of the privileges of their station. But "the wiser and better sort of the common people" detest those vices which are so immediately fatal to them and their employees: they support the strict system of morality because it conforms to their economic interests. "A man of low condition", whose conduct is subject to scrutiny and censure as long as he remains in his village, is lost once he emigrates to a city, unless he joins one of the austere religious sects. In such a sect he "acquires a degree of consideration which he never had before", and his conduct is subject to careful supervision. In these sects "the morals of the common people have been almost always remarkably regular and orderly".[2] The non-conformist congregations were all that there was to replace the local communities as custodians of moral standards once the

1. Milton, *Prose Works* (Bohn ed.), II, pp. 495–6. Cf. pp. 455–63 below.
2. A. Smith, *The Wealth of Nations* (World's Classics), I, pp. 432–4.

villages had been disrupted by enclosure and growing class divisions.

For us, as for Milton, the essential fact about the Calvinist disciplinary system was that it brought a new kind of layman into the government of the Church. 37 Hen. VIII cap. 17 had allowed laymen who were doctors of civil law to exercise ecclesiastical jurisdiction. But such men were part and parcel of the State machine. A presbyterian system would have meant that local laymen without specialized legal training sat in judgment side by side with ministers. In Scotland, so often cited as a priest-ridden country, lay elders in fact exercised control on important issues. Indeed a petition to Parliament in 1576 suggested that introduction of "the true discipline" would improve the quality of English ministers.[1] "The reason of setting up ruling elders", Charles I recognized, "was to curb the ministers".[2] Elders were elected: ministers nominated. Yet English Calvinism was even more Erastian than Scottish. The threat of "a pope in every parish" was never a real one. One of the earliest propagandists to raise this bogey simultaneously criticized Swiss Calvinists for tolerating the supremacy of a layman, and spoke far more realistically of the "Popelike authority" which every *presbytery* would enjoy in its own parish.[3]

III

The Calvinist system, then, gave organizational form to that priesthood of all believers which Luther had preached. But granted the structure of society in the sixteenth and seventeenth centuries, it was inevitable that the laymen who co-operated with ministers in running churches, the elders, would – in the first instance at least – be the better-off and middling members of the congregation. This point was obvious to contemporaries, and has been accepted by historians. Some governors, said

1. Babbage, *Puritanism and Richard Bancroft*, p. 16.
2. Conversation with Sir Henry Herbert in 1639, in *Epistolary Curiosities; Series the First* (ed. Rebecca Warner, 1818), p. 198.
3. *Tracts ascribed to Richard Bancroft*, pp. 48, 79. Professor Strider suggests that the actual phrase "a pope in every parish" was first used by George Digby in the House of Commons in February 1641 (R.E.L. Strider, *Robert Greville, Lord Brooke*, Harvard University Press, 1958, p. 205). But Bishop Hall had written the year before of "a pope and his conclave of cardinals within his own parish", in *Episcopacie by Divine Right* (1640), in *Works*, X, p. 260.

even Robert Browne, "must have parentage and birth".[1] Henry Barrow made a precisely similar if less sympathetic analysis. Elders, he declared, would be "but of the wealthiest, honest, simple men of the parish, that shall sit for cyphers dumb by their pastor, and meddle with nothing". The people will get only "the smoky, windy title of election" of their ministers.[2] After these criticisms from the left, as it were, we may quote one from the right which is in agreement: "the chief men of every parish (except there be some notorious cause to the contrary), must bear the office of eldership".[3] But in most parts of seventeenth-century England, "the chief men of every parish" were the squire and those whom I have called the industrious sort – yeomen, merchants and richer artisans. In mediaeval society the dominance of the landed aristocracy over the Church had been maintained by the ascendancy of the lord of the manor over the parish priest; by the fact that monasteries and great ecclesiastical functionaries were also feudal landlords; and by the integration of the ecclesiastical into the civil hierarchy of the state. The mediaeval rivalries between Church and state never threatened the fundamental stability of the feudal social order. The introduction of the Calvinist discipline in our period would have challenged the stability of the old order, because it would have sapped from below the dependence of the Church on the monarchy and aristocracy, and would have created a Church closely linked with those classes which took the lead in parliamentary opposition. It would have pushed aside the bishops nominated by and dependent on the Court and replaced them by ministers and elected representatives of the gentry and the industrious sort of people.[4]

1. R. Browne, *A Booke which sheweth the Life and Manners of all True Christians* (1582), in *The Writings of Robert Harrison and Robert Browne* (ed. A. Peel and L. H. Carlson, 1953), p. 330.
2. H. Barrow, *A Brief Discoverie of the False Church* (1590), in *The Writings of Henry Barrow, 1587–90* (ed. L. H. Carlson, 1966), pp. 561–2.
3. *Tracts ascribed to Richard Bancroft*, p. 41. Cf. *A Petition presented to Parliament from the County of Nottingham* (1641), signed by 1,500 gentlemen and yeomen, which asked for every particular church to be allowed "its own right of ordinary discipline within itself . . . by the judgment of the presbyters with concurrence of the congregation (either at large or contracted into some few chosen persons)" (p. 24).
4. Ed. A. Peel *Tracts ascribed to Richard Bancroft*, pp. 41, 45–6.

Hooker's account of the origins of the Genevan discipline is a shade malicious, but it dwells on just the social points we are discussing. Calvin "ripely considered how gross a thing it was for men of his quality, wise and grave men, to live with such a multitude, and to be tenants at will under them, as their ministers, both himself and others, had been. For the remedy of which inconvenience he gave them plainly to understand that, if he did become their teacher again, they must be content to admit a complete form of discipline". This discipline was to be administered in part by elected lay officers. "Some of the chiefest place and countenance amongst the laity" disliked the scheme, thinking the introduction of laymen "was but to please the minds of the people, to the end they might think their own sway somewhat". The civil authorities tried ("with strange absurdity", says Hooker) to reserve final judgment in matters of authority to themselves. But Calvin stuck to his insistence on an independent ecclesiastical jurisdiction, realizing, in Beza's words, "how needful these bridles were, to be put in the jaws of that city".[1] "It may justly be feared", Hooker reflected, "whether our English nobility, when the matter came in trial, would contentedly suffer themselves to be always at the call, and to stand to the sentence, of a number of poor mean persons assisted with the presence of their poor teacher".[2]

Hooker, as so often, expressed a deep social truth. As early as 1550 Bucer was writing from Cambridge to Calvin, saying that a chief obstacle to the introduction of true discipline was the existence among the nobility of some "who would reduce the whole of the sacred ministry into a narrow compass, and who are altogether unconcerned about the restoration of church discipline".[3] If that was true in Edward's reign, how much more so under Elizabeth. Leicester and groups of the country gentry favoured associating godly M.P.s with the episcopal government of the Church; but they were less enthusiastic about introducing the full presbyterian discipline.[4]

1. Hooker, *Laws of Ecclesiastical Polity*, I, pp. 83–9. See also Heylyn, *History of the Presbyterians*, p. 40.
2. Hooker, *op. cit.*, I, p. 128.
3. *Original Letters relative to the English Reformation* (Parker Soc. 1846–7), II, p. 544.
4. Ed. Collinson, *Letters of Thomas Wood*, p. xxxvii; contrast a letter of 1576 from Wood to Leicester, saying that want of discipline meant the overthrow of the whole building (*ibid.*, p. 29).

"We retain in some measure the moral discipline", wrote Bishop Cox apologetically to Rodolph Gualter in 1574; "but should anyone seek to compel our great men to submit their necks to it, it would be much the same as shaving a lion's beard".[1] We note the democratic tendency Cox thinks Gualter will expect there to be in the discipline.

The link between the godly and men of property was made deliberately. Thus a puritan petition of 1585 asked the Queen that "grave and godly men of worship" or J.P.s should be associated with bishops in trying ecclesiastical causes; and *Certaine points concerninge the policie and government of the Ecclesiastical State* (1586) urged that discipline should be exercised by "a convenient number . . . of the most religious, godly and virtuously disposed parishioners, joined (as near as might be) with the best [for] countenance, credit, and ability in that place".[2] Stoughton, writing in 1604, agreed that "men of occupations" would be chosen elders and deacons. This, however, would cost the parish nothing, since "as well in country parishes, as in cities and towns . . . we have many able, wealthy and substantial persons, who have given their names unto Christ". None need be elected to such offices who would depend upon relief and support from the common purse, any more than parishes have to contribute to the maintenance of churchwardens ("who carry a semblance of governing seniors") or collectors for the poor ("who jostle out the deacons"). Stoughton went on to ask the King to allow resident preaching ministers to be assisted in the execution of spiritual justice by "other godly and faithful knights, esquires, gentlemen, citizens, borough-masters or other chief men of the same parish".[3] In exactly the same spirit the Root and Branch Petition wanted episcopal authority to be wielded by lay commissioners.

In fact when a presbyterian system came to be set up in the sixteen-forties, it horrified the Scots by its erastianism: nominated laymen enjoyed a majority over ministers at all levels. In Lancashire (the area about which we are best informed, because there seems to have been most presbyterian enthusiasm

1. *Zurich Letters*, I, p. 307.
2. G. W. Prothero, *Select Statutes and Other Constitutional Documents, 1558–1625* (1906), p. 219; ed. A. Peel, *The Seconde Parte of a Register* (1915), II, p. 20.
3. W. Stoughton, *An Assertion for true and Christian Church-Policie*, pp. 193–5, 383–4.

there), the lead was taken by three ministers and "diverse gentlemen and tradesmen in and about Manchester". Gentlemen seem to have predominated over yeomen in the Lancashire classes.[1] Baxter in Kidderminster benefited from "the countenance and presence of three justices of the peace". He subsequently proposed that magistrates should be exempt from "open personal rebukes, or disgraceful censures, or excommunications".[2] The peers, wisely, stood on their traditional privilege of having their chaplains and families exempt from the new ecclesiastical discipline, as they had been from the old.[3] Independency, with its emphasis on the congregation as the unit of discipline and its denial of hierarchical control, would have led even more than Presbyterianism to a dominance of the industrious sort and their allies among the gentry over their congregations, in the same way that the abolition of Star Chamber led to the dictatorship of J.P.s in local government.

Such then were some of the social and political implications of discipline. From the fifteen-nineties, with increasing tension between hierarchy and Puritans, the revolutionary potentialities in the discipline began to be emphasized by conservatives. Richard Cosin, Dean of the Arches, published in 1592 a tract which was designed to capitalize the conspiracy of the lunatic Hacket and his disciples Coppinger and Arthington. Cosin emphasized that supporters of the discipline thought that lawful kings might be deposed and advocated a right of resistance to magistrates who did not govern well.[4] The next year saw the publication of Bancroft's *Dangerous Positions* and *Survey of the Pretended Holy Discipline*, as well as of Hooker's subtler social analysis.[5] Thomas Bilson made similar points in

1. Ed. R. Parkinson, *The Life of Adam Martindale*, p. 62; W. A. Shaw, *A History of the English Church during the Civil Wars and under the Commonwealth* (1900), II, pp. 393–8.

2. *Reliquiae Baxterianae*, I, p. 402; II, pp. 113, 129–30. This last suggestion was too much even for post-Restoration bishops. The "erastianism" of the presbyterian system as established in England (e.g. the nomination of elders by the House of Commons) may be compared with the system at Geneva in Calvin's day, when some of the elders were nominated by the Council, others by the pastors.

3. R. Baillie, *Letters and Journals* (1775), II, p. 149; cf. my *Puritanism and Revolution*, p. 45.

4. R. Cosin, *Conspiracy for Pretended Reformation, viz. Presbyterial Discipline* (1699), pp. 179–80.

5. See pp. 165–7 above.

the same year. "In popular states and persecuted churches", he wrote, "some pretence may be made for that kind of discipline; in Christian kingdoms I see neither need nor use of lay elders".[1] Bilson, who got his bishopric three years later, subsequently gained an unsavoury reputation and was not the most disinterested of theorists; but the same point of view was expressed by Gabriel Harvey, also in 1593: the Genevan discipline suited a town of "mean merchants and meaner artificers", or "any like popular town . . . where democracy ruleth the roost". But it was wrong to "build a reformation . . . upon a popular foundation, or a mechanical plot".[2] Archbishop Hutton in 1604 said something very similar.[3] Calybute Downing was not altogether hostile to the Genevan discipline. He wrote: "This form of government may be of good use in some states at some times, as in a popular state where those lay elders may be both church and city burgesses", or "in time of tumult". He gave the following remarkable account of what would have been the effects of its introduction in Elizabeth's reign:

"It must necessarily have conferred ruins upon our schools of learning and hospitals of charity, razed the foundations of our churches, confounded divisions of parishes, changed the right and custom of paying tithes, with many such miserable inconveniences, which were so in the Apostles' time of miseries, of persecution". So the State did not risk introducing the discipline, and had subsisted, even if not in the height of health which that government promised, yet reasonably well.[4]

Joseph Hall may have read Bilson and Downing: he wrote in *Episcopacie by Divine Right Asserted:* "When some new state is to be erected, especially in a popular form, or a new city to be contrived, with power of making their own laws, there

1. T. Bilson, *The Perpetual Government of Christs Church* (1593), pp. 213–14. Lord Keeper Puckering made analogous points in the same year (Strype, *Annals*, IV, pp. 197–8).
2. G. Harvey. *Pierce's Supererogation* (1593), quoted by C. S. Lewis, *English Literature in the Sixteenth Century, excluding Drama* (1954), pp. 353–4.
3. Babbage, *Puritanism and Richard Bancroft*, p. 58.
4. Calybute Downing, *A Discourse of the State Ecclesiasticall of this Kingdome, in relation to the Civill* (2nd ed., 1643), pp. 13–20. Cf. George Downame, *A Defence of the Sermon preached at the consecration of the L. Bishop of Bath and Welles* (1611), p. 166; a popular state could not endure the government of a bishop.

might, perhaps, be some possibility of complying, in a way of policy, with some of the rules of this pretended church-government. Yet certainly in a monarchical state, fully settled, and a kingdom divided into several townships and villages, some whereof are small and far distant from the rest, no human wit can comprehend how it were possible, without an utter subversion, to reduce it to those terms". In Scotland, the good bishop warned, nobles could be treated as if they were inferior to their chaplains. "Upon their consistorial bench their peasantly tenant is as good as the best of them; . . . if they look away to be so matched (which T. C. [Cartwright] suggests) they disdain not man but Christ".[1] It was indeed an observed fact that the most prominent states in which non-episcopal Churches existed were republics – Switzerland, the Nether-lands. Scotland, the apparent exception, proves the rule, for the tussle between Presbyterianism and episcopacy was one in which the power of the monarchy was thrown whole-heartedly behind the bishops.

Paul Bayne saw in its equalizing effects a principal ad-vantage of the discipline: "Do not men stand upon their out-ward excellencies, as their wealth, honours, high places, even before God? . . . To have the more liberty from serving God so strictly and precisely as meaner men do? Do they not think that, in regard of their riches and high places, they need not pray so much, be so careful of an exact sanctifying of the Sabbath? . . . Do they not, upon these things, scorn the minister and his admonitions, being ready to say, 'What a sauce-box he is to meddle with me, and why should I be under his control or do as he will? I will not: but as I have done, so will I do' ".[2] Bayne died in 1617, but his full treatise was not published until 1643. Already by then the great ones were feeling the pinch of discipline. We may contrast with Bayne's puritan vision of a more democratic order the Laudian Bishop Montagu's rules for communicating, issued in 1639. The congregation should form into ranks, with "the best of the parish" actually kneeling at the altar rails, and the others behind them in order of social precedence.[3] Those who be-

1. J. Hall, *Works*, X, pp. 259–60.
2. P. Bayne, *An Entire Commentary upon the whole Epistle of St. Paul to the Ephesians* (1866), p. 233.
3. Prynne, *Canterburies Doome*, p. 100.

lieved in the equality of man before God might well refuse to come up to the altar and kneel in this humiliating worldly subordination at the moment of celebrating their religion's greatest mystery. There was an element of social protest in almost every puritan attitude. "Discipline" was not something abstract. It was very concrete indeed. The issues involved were social and economic as well as religious and moral. The all-important questions were, What kind of discipline? Administered by and for whom?

Such social analyses suggest that the conflict was not between laymen and clerics in the simple fashion in which it is often presented; but between two different social groups among the laity. For an example of such a conflict between laymen, take the case of the Rev. John Carter. The majority in his congregation at Bramford, Suffolk, approved of him so much that they augmented his stipend. But about 1615 "there arose up a generation of malignant spirits, who were haters of a plain, powerful and searching ministry. . . . These were the gentry and chief of the parish", and by invoking the authority of the bishop they were able to drive Carter away to a more congenial parish on the outskirts of Ipswich.[1] The really big bourgeoisie in the cities, and the gentry in the countryside, though economically very powerful and invaluable as patrons of puritan ministers, were numerically insignificant. Those whose numbers counted, whose co-operation was essential if any presbyterian or congregational system was to work, were the industrious sort of people, employing a handful of journeymen and apprentices, who were struggling (often with the aid of the puritan virtues of thrift and industry) to enrich themselves, to lift themselves above the mass of the population. It was to this class that Puritanism, in the widest sense of the word, appealed. It was a large class, covering men of varying degrees of wealth, but it can be distinguished, as a social group, by the economic independence of its members and the fact that all of them have their feet on the ladder which leads to prosperity, though few would retain their foothold.

The variations in wealth of the members of this class account for the diverse descriptions of it by contemporaries, who according to their point of view may emphasize either the

1. S. Clarke, *A Collection of the Lives of Ten Eminent Divines* (1662), pp. 3–6.

wealth of Puritans and ruling elders, or describe them as
the dregs of the people – "John a Nokes and John a Stiles, the
elders: Smug the smith, a deacon", wrote Joseph Hall with a
propagandist's license.[1] In any congregation it was likely to be
the richer members who dominated: but in some the richest
would be quite small people. "Considering the sinister affections of the people" it would be all too easy, Bancroft feared,
for this leading nucleus to carry congregational elections (if
they were ever established) against those whom the hierarchy
would wish to see elected.[2] We must also recollect the speed
with which economic differentiation was proceeding among the
industrious sort, with an upper group rapidly increasing in
numbers and self-confidence. In the fifteen-eighties men might
reasonably ask themselves "Where shall we have fit men for
elders?"[3] Two generations later, that, at least, gave no cause
for worry. Even in 1604 Stoughton could declare confidently
that the election of elders would not be made by the basest of
the people, any more than that of officers in cities and corporate towns: whatever the electoral forms, *de facto* the
better sort would be chosen, "the chief fathers, ancients and
governors of the parish".[4] In the decades before 1640 many
of the English gentry were already deeply engaged in production for the market, or had interests in commercial ventures of
one kind or another. Gentlemen were likely to dominate a
Calvinist disciplinary system in so far as they were able to co-
operate with the well-to-do yeomen and farmers in their
villages. As landlords and employers, as educated men, their
influence over the mass of the population would, at least in the
first instance, have been decisive – once the political power of
the hierarchy and its courts had been broken. In short, such a
disciplinary system would have more faithfully reflected the

1. J. Hall, *Works*, X, p. 259. The words recall those which Sir John
Oglander used to describe the Committee which ruled the Isle of Wight
after 1642 (ed. F. Bamford, *A Royalist's Notebook*, 1936, pp. 105–6, 110,
129).

2. *Tracts ascribed to Richard Bancroft*, p. 83. Note – as many ecclesiastical historians fail to do – this recognition, normal among the franker
bishops, that their Church was unpopular with the mass of the English
people.

3. Harrison, *A Little Treatise uppon the first Verse of the 122 Psalm*
(1583), in *Writings of Harrison and Browne*, p. 117.

4. Stoughton, *An Assertion for True and Christian Church-Policie*
pp. 193–5, 246–7.

social structure of England, would have given a predominant influence to the men of new wealth. They could not exert such influence over the Anglican establishment so long as it was independent of parliamentary control. "Lay elders from their ends create their God", sang Sir John Denham sardonically.[1]

It was this ability to reflect present social reality, as opposed to ossified political institutions which reflected *past* reality, that made a Calvinist disciplinary system so dangerous to the old order, and gave it its peculiar flexibility. Though originally and best adapted to the needs of a rising urban middle class (as in Geneva, the Netherlands, parts of France, England), it could also be used by gentlemen to ensure their predominance in a war of national liberation into which they wished to draw the masses of the population (e.g. in Scotland, parts of France, Transylvania). Lord Lindsay gave an agreeable instance of the adaptation of the presbyterian system to an Indian village community;[2] and it appears to be equally well suited to the needs of disintegrating tribal society in parts of Africa to-day. It is perhaps legitimate to compare the soviet system which, originally evolved as a form of organization by and for the working class in the most advanced industrial centres of Russia, was subsequently adopted by communities at a much earlier stage of social development.

In pre-revolutionary England the introduction of the discipline would have been equivalent to a change of government at all levels. If Elizabeth were thus to "innovate the whole government of the Church", Bancroft warned her, "she must submit herself and her sceptre to the fantastical humours of her own parish governors". The sword would be delivered from the prince's hands and committed "to the discretion of the common sort, to displace noblemen, gentlemen, wise, learned and discreet men, and commit the whole government of the Church to master pastor and his ignorant neighbours".[3] "They that seek to bring parity . . . into the Church", said Lancelot Andrewes, "do we not know their second position? . . . The Church is the house, the commonwealth but the hangings. The hangings must be made to fit the house, that is the commonwealth fashioned to the Church".[4]

1. Sir J. Denham, *Poems* (1807), p. 27.
2. A. D. Lindsay, *The Modern Democratic State* (1943), I, p. 68.
3. *Tracts ascribed to Richard Bancroft*, pp. 47, 93.
4. Andrewes, *XCVI Sermons* (1841–3), IV, p. 304.

Once the central authority of what Archbishop Parker called "the state-ecclesiastical"[1] had been overthrown, the parishes would administer themselves under the supervision of the men of property on the spot:[2] national co-ordination would be secured through the pyramid of consistories and synods and through the overall supervision of the House of Commons – the elected representatives of the men of property. The means of enforcing the new standards of behaviour, in the Netherlands and Scotland, were (a) education, including preaching and catechizing; (b) economic pressure – poor relief; (c) social pressure and disfranchisement – excommunication.

IV

There were, then, good reasons why before 1640 the discipline appealed to small employers in town and country, why "half a dozen artisans, shoemakers, tinkers and tailors, with their preacher and reader" might hope to "rule the whole parish", sometimes in alliance with a local gentleman or merchant.[3] This alliance of the industrious sort with those men of bigger property whom the House of Commons represented disintegrated after the breaking of the power of the hierarchy: but so long as that existed there was a real union of interest; the demand for discipline was one expression of this common interest. "It is far from our purpose", the Grand Remonstrance declared, "to let loose the golden reins of discipline and government in the Church".[4]

In Elizabeth's reign an attempt was made to side-step the hierarchy of courts and to build up a new state-ecclesiastical from below, within the old political framework. We can see the conflict between the two rival disciplinary authorities raging especially around the oath *ex officio*.[5] The Puritans disliked this oath under all circumstances; but they particularly re-

1. Parker, *Correspondence*, p. 445 (Parker to Burghley, 3 November 1573).

2. We may perhaps compare the automatic domination of the French National Guard by the bourgeoisie in 1789.

3. Bancroft, *Dangerous Positions*, p. 44. Cf. my *Puritanism and Revolution*, p. 229.

4. Gardiner, *Constitutional Documents of the Puritan Revolution*, p. 229.

5. See Chapter 11 below.

sented the practice of putting elders upon oath in order to force them to expose the underground consistorial organizations. "The hedge which the Lord Himself hath set about ecclesiastical elders to keep their credit from the breaking in of slanders, by this oath is cast to the ground and slanderers and false suggesters are suffered underhand by informing an apparitor or a pursuivant to call the credit of a minister into public question".[1] How could the new discipline be built up, and the prestige of the new governors of the Church be maintained, under these circumstances?

A national disciplinary system run by congregational elderships would, then, have given a far greater share in government to the industrious sort. If the transition to a disciplinary system controlled by Parliament could have been made peacefully, without social turmoil, no doubt this class would have been able to maintain its predominance over aristocracy and lower orders alike. But there was no guarantee that the transition would be peaceful; and it was here that opponents of the discipline saw their best chance of disrupting the heterogeneous alliance of its advocates. The discipline threatened the old order because of its democratic tendency; at the same time those of the rich who believed they would remain in control of such a system were running a grave risk of themselves being pushed out by the smaller men, who might not for ever be satisfied with "the smoky, windy title of election", but might follow the Brownists in asking for fuller democracy.

The point was made, with considerable urgency, in a pamphlet of 1641 attacking the presbyterian discipline on the grounds that it "must necessarily produce an extermination of nobility, gentry and order, if not of religion". It was all very well, said the baronet who wrote the pamphlet, to plead that "the prime gentleman in every parish shall be perpetual elder and have a negative voice". It is instructive to note that such arguments were used to overcome the gentry's repugnance to the discipline; but Sir Thomas Aston was not convinced. By such means "the gentry will . . . make a shift to keep the clergy humble, and the vulgar low enough. But if we must look for new elections every year, what must this produce but a little civil war in every parish?" In Scotland the gentry can rule easily enough through a presbyterian system, since there the

1. Ed. A. Peel and L. H. Carlson, *Cartwrightiana* (1951), p. 38.

common people are vassals to their lords. But in England, if "the inferior sort of people" once find "their power in popular election of elders", they "will rather exclude both nobility and gentry". "The empty name of liberty, blown into vulgar ears, hath overturned many gentlemen: how much more prevalent and dangerous must it be when enforced as a religious duty to disobey authority?" It will soon lead on to a claim to share the earth equally. The petition which roused Sir Thomas's fury had suggested that a congregational discipline "would learn landlords more compassion".[1] The gentry, said Jeremy Taylor a few years later, after watching presbyterianism in action, might be "little better than servants" under it.[2]

In fact the attempt to build a presbyterian system in England was made in conditions of revolutionary civil war, when all authority was being called in question. So it proved impossible to "keep the vulgar low enough". The erastian structure so carefully devised by the Long Parliament to prevent the tyranny either of priests or of lower orders broke down, and "the people" found in the sectarian congregations the organs of democracy which the presbyterian system promised but did not give. The breakdown of the presbyterian system, of a persecuting State Church, created problems in relation to the lower orders. Hugh Peter was acutely aware of these, and it helps to explain his heavy emphasis on preaching: "What you have gotten by the sword must be maintained by the Word, I say the Word, by which English Christians are made. In other countries, discipline makes them so, drives them into a church together, and then dubs them Christians".[3] In the fine optimism of 1646 Peter believed that more rational processes would work. His words help us to grasp the dual function of discipline.

We may compare the attempt to build up a new disciplinary system from below with the Calvinist attitude towards rebellion. Save in very exceptional circumstances, Calvinists thought rebellion was never justified unless it was called for by "the magistrate". "The people" must be led by their social betters, the "many-headed monster" must take no independent

1. Sir Thomas Aston, *A Remonstrance against Presbytery* (1641) Sig. b 4, I 4v – M 4v.

2. J. Taylor, *The Whole Works* (1836), II, p. 37.

3. H. Peter, *God's Doings and Man's Duty* (1646), pp. 43–4.

political action, lest it indulge in anabaptist "excesses" such as had thrown German Lutherans into the arms of the princes. The Calvinist discipline arose after Münster had sent a thrill of horror through the respectable classes all over Europe.[1] As interpreted in Scotland, France and the Netherlands, Calvinist political doctrine meant that the lesser authorities in the State could summon the people to revolt against the sovereign. These lesser authorities – the J.P.s, the town corporations, the members of the House of Commons – would be drawn from the same social groups as the elders. A revolt led by them was the only type of revolt that could be justified, because it would be relatively orderly, involving the substitution of one propertied ruling group for another. The absolute enemy for Calvinists was a merely popular, democratic revolt, without tarrying for the magistrate.[2] For this would lead to "anarchy", to the rule of "the many-headed monster", to license for the ungodly to behave and believe as they wished: it would threaten the overthrow of all social subordination and all discipline. Hence separatism, for the true presbyterian Calvinist, was analogous to anarchical rebellion: it was a denial of existing authority on no better grounds than a subjective belief that such authority was ungodly. That was an inadequate reason either for leaving the Church or for revolting against the magistrate.[3] Here we have one of the fundamental causes of divergence between Presbyterians and sectaries from 1644 onwards, and indeed of ultimate presbyterian acquiescence in the restoration.

Separatism had direct political implications, especially where the franchise was dependent on church membership, as was so often the case in *émigré* congregations in the Netherlands and New England. For full church membership was not automatically given to all members of the community, but only to those who satisfied the existing congregation of their

1. At Zurich too Zwingli's conflict with the Anabaptists and other radicals led him to see positive advantages in ecclesiastical discipline (N. Birnbaum, "The Zwinglian Reformation in Zurich", *P. and P.*, No. 15, p. 35). Similar effects were obtained by Luther's establishment of a Consistorial Commission, composed of two theologians and two jurists, and headed by the prince (E. H. Erikson, *Young Man Luther* 1959, p. 232).

2. Cf. the passage from Bacon quoted on p. 214 above.

3. Peel and Carlson, *Cartwrightiana*, pp. 204, 228, 253.

godliness. On the *Mayflower* the church covenant was devised as a means of excluding unruly servants from the vote, and from the earliest days in Massachusetts church government was controlled by a small minority.[1] A Lancashire petition of 1646 asked that all those who did not submit to the established presbyterian discipline should be removed from and kept out of all places of public trust.[2] Baxter recommended that "none but church members may govern or choose governors".[3] Once established, a church membership franchise was a method of maintaining the dominance of a given social outlook. In the same way, so long as there was a single national Church, exclusion from the sacrament was a means of bringing pressure to bear on the undisciplined, or of ostracizing the recalcitrant and the undesirable.[4] I Ed. VI cap. I had deprived the clergy of this powerful and traditional weapon by laying it down that the sacrament should not, "without lawful cause, be denied to any person that will devoutly and humbly desire it". It was the urgent desire of the presbyterian preachers to recover this power, so essential to the maintenance of a local discipline. But just as they recovered it, the *de facto* establishment of religious toleration caused their most powerful weapon to break in their hands.[5]

v

The other face of discipline was turned towards the lower orders, often equated with the ungodly. Similarities have been noted between the Calvinist view of natural man and Hobbes's view of man in the state of nature. Hobbes's state of nature is bourgeois society with the policeman removed: Calvinist fallen man can only be reduced to civil subordination (failing regeneration) by an imposed discipline. The High Anglican conception of "natural law", of the "reasonableness" of man,

1. E. S. Morgan, *The Puritan Family* (Boston, 1944), pp. 93, 117.
2. *L.J.*, VIII, p. 470.
3. Baxter, Letter to John Swinfen, 17 February 1659, in R. Schlatter, *Richard Baxter and Puritan Politics* (Rutgers University Press, 1957), p. 64; cf. *A Holy Commonwealth* (1659), pp. 218–19, 249–51.
4. Cf. Herbert Palmer, *A full Answer to A Printed Paper, Entituled, Foure serious Questions concerning Excommunication* (1645), *passim.* For example, see *Minutes of the Manchester Presbyterian Classis* (ed. W. A. Shaw, Chetham Soc., three vols., 1890–1), *passim.* See pp. 283–4 below.
5. See pp. 355–6 below.

takes for granted the preservation of the state and the old type of social subordination. The Calvinist emphasis on sin and the need for discipline links up with the opposition's wish to scrap the traditional hierarchical machinery of the Church and replace it with a new disciplinary organization. Hence the distrust of mere reason by Puritans, at least until the new order was built. Natural man cannot be left to himself, nor to the traditional institutions: he must be subordinated to a new discipline and leadership, to the control of the regenerate.[1]

The need for discipline, and for a discipline organized and imposed by a minority, was succinctly expressed by Penry, though he is merely stating what all orthodox Calvinists would have accepted. Man is sinful; he is by his nature an enemy of God, a rebel and a traitor: he cannot understand and consequently cannot will the things acceptable to God. Only the enlightened elect are capable of fighting against the sins and corruptions of the mass of humanity. Hence it is the divine will that they should be in a position of power over the unregenerate many.[2] Once we complement this theoretical proposition by the fact that elders were drawn from the propertied classes, the social consequences are clear.

In sixteenth-century England economic change was accompanied by acute distress affecting many smaller men of the industrious sort. Some were no doubt driven to despair: others would look to the Church as the traditional source of guidance and consolation. In one sense they would look in vain. Nothing had filled the void left by the abolition of confession and penance as a means of consoling and guiding the masses of the population.[3] It was all very well for Calvin and the puritan preachers to adjure their public to substitute daily scrutiny of their own conduct for confession in the lump at long intervals;[4] but that demanded a degree of self-consciousness and conviction, a desire for salvation, which the many had not yet got,

1. Cf. P. Miller and T. H. Johnson, *The Puritans* (New York, 1938), pp. 51–3.
2. Ed. A. Peel, *The Notebook of John Penry*, 1593 (Camden Soc., 1944), pp. 17–20. Cf. *Cartwrightiana* (ed. Peel and Carlson), pp. 171, 228.
3. This point was made by Burnet, *History of the Reformation*, III, 87. Cf. Greenham, *Workes*, p. 359.
4. J. Calvin, *The Institutes of the Christian Religion* (transl. H. Beveridge, 1949), I, pp. 549–54.

and on Calvin's own definition were not likely to get. Only the
few kept diaries and spiritual journals. A Milton could discipline *himself* to act "as ever in his great Taskmaster's eye".
Dod and Cleaver hoped to convince a servant that he should
work diligently "not because his master's eye is upon him, but
because God's pure eyes behold him, either to punish him, if he
do not his duty, or to reward him, if he do it faithfully. This is
the chief point at which servants must aim". Unless they "serve
God in their labours, . . . their obedience can never be constant,
but will be by fits and starts, and hang only on the master's
eye".[1] But this was setting standards high. How many servants
were likely to accept this advice? Yet God remained a Taskmaster, even for those who would not discipline themselves. An
external discipline was needed to help employers in the task of
making servants worship God by diligence in their calling.

It might sometimes occur to the Puritan to ask why it was
worth bothering about the unregenerate at all. John Preston
gave him his answer. A captain does not execute all offenders
for a general fault in his army, for that would destroy the army.
So God does not punish men as often as they deserve death, or
the Church would cease to exist.[2] The ungodly multitude, in
other words, is necessary to society: the same reminder had
to be given to the vengeful landlords after the defeat of Ket's
rebellion in 1549. In any case, the object of the discipline was
to encourage others. When Baxter asked himself whether public personal reprehension did any good, he replied first that it
was God's ordinance; and secondly that "the principal use of
this public discipline is not for the offender himself but for the
Church". Neglect of discipline might make men think themselves saved when they were not: and might make the scandalous think their sin tolerable.[3] Moreover some of the
multitude, the preachers reminded their congregations from time
to time, might even be capable of learning: "If we restrain them
from gross profanations upon His holy day . . . they may come
at length to think His Sabbath a delight. If we keep them from

1. Dod and Cleaver, *Ten Commandments*, pp. 190–1. It is highly
probable that Milton had either read this popular work, or at least
heard sermons based upon it.
2. J. Preston, *Paul's Conversion, or the right way to be saved* (1637),
p. 266; *The New Covenant, or the Saint's Portion* (5th ed., 1630), p. 535.
3. Baxter, *The Reformed Pastor* (1956), pp. 61–4. First published
1656.

swilling and gaming and revelling and rioting and roaring the while, God may frame them ere long to a sober and sanctified use of the creatures".[1] Not an extravagant hope: but a hope. William Crashawe discovered here the pleasing idea that emigration to North America (under godly pastors) might be good for the souls of emigrants, as well as for the pockets of their employers. "The basest and worst men, trained up in severe discipline, sharp laws, a hard life and much labour, do prove good members of a commonwealth". "The very excrements of a full and swelling state", put under firm discipline in a new country, "wanting pleasures and subject to some pinching miseries" will become new men.[2] The social function of discipline could hardly have been stated more clearly.

The puritan complaint was that the existing ecclesiastical hierarchy was not active enough in imposing the new discipline, the sense of the necessity and dignity of labour, upon the mass of the population. "In the primitive church", the Commination service began, "there was a godly discipline" of public penance to the discouragement of others. "Instead whereof, until the said discipline may be restored again (which is much to be wished)", cursing had to do duty instead. The repeated attempts made after the Reformation to establish a disciplinary *system*, based on an agreed revision of ecclesiastical law, produced no results, largely because of the disagreements about the exact function of discipline here analyzed. In the fifteen-seventies and -eighties the Puritans tried to have either *The Reformation of the Ecclesiastical Laws* or the Scottish *Book of Discipline* adopted by Convocation or imposed by Parliament.[3] The other side began to produce its rival system only in the seventeenth century, when *Bishop Overall's Convocation Book* was equally abortive.

A learned student of the period declared that the discipline

1. R. Sanderson, *XXXV Sermons*, p. 283. With the assumption of two levels of rationality in the two classes, cf. the admirable analysis in C. B. Macpherson, *The Political Theory of Possessive Individualism* (1962), pp. 221–38.

2. W. Crashawe, *A Sermon Preached . . . before . . . Lord La Warre, Lord Governour and Captaine General of Virginea* (1610), quoted in Perry Miller, *Errand into the Wilderness*, pp. 131–2.

3. Cardwell, *The Reformation of the Ecclesiastical Laws*, Preface; Strype, *Life of Parker*, II, pp. 62–4, 455; Frere, *The English Church in the reigns of Elizabeth and James I*, pp. 164–5, 195–6. See p. 290 below.

of church courts was as rigorously exercised throughout the years 1558–1640 as in any previous period.[1] But that did not meet the demands of those who wanted a new type of discipline. A petition to the Parliament of 1584 called for the suppression of blasphemy, looseness of life, bribery and offences against good doctrine; it asked simultaneously for more generous poor relief (at the expense of bishops and cathedral clergy) and for a sharper law against fornicators "than is only to stand in a white sheet as the manner is now".[2]

There was the rub. If discipline was to be made more rigorous, who was going to enforce it and against whom? Discipline, under the existing system, could only be administered by bishops and the hierarchy of ecclesiastical courts. But Peter Wentworth was not the only member of Parliament who did not want to make the bishops popes. We may recall the bill introduced into the Parliament of 1571 which would have restrained ordinaries from commuting penance without the advice of two J.P.s.[3] The Puritans wanted lay participation and control.

There was no escape from this dilemma within the framework of the old régime. Until the whole hierarchy of church courts, and the power of bishops, had been destroyed, the puritan opposition saw no existing coercive authority whose hands it dared strengthen. Yet they made demands for the enforcement of discipline which could not become effective without the co-operation of the state power. Bishop Cooper, with his sharp eye for chinks in his enemies' armour, emphasized that the present discipline, imposed by existing laws and courts, however unsatisfactory they might be, was more effective than a discipline which had behind it only the sanction of excommunication. "It will be of most men contemned, and of . . . small force . . . to bring to effect any good amendment of life. . . . The looseness of these days requireth discipline of sharper laws by punishment of body and danger of goods".[4]

The Bishop of Winchester was quite right. In the fifteen-

1. Hale, *A Series of Precedents and Proceedings*, p. xliii.

2. Strype, *Annals*, III, part ii, pp. 278–302.

3. Sir J. E. Neale, *Elizabeth I and her Parliaments, 1559–81* (1953), pp. 205, 209.

4. T. Cooper, *An Admonition to the People of England*, p. 69. See pp. 343–4, 357 below.

eighties the Dedham classic discussed not only church attendance, catechizing and the provision of universal education, but also arbitration in disputes, restraint of disorders, the good government of the town, poor relief and the provision of work for the unemployed. At every point it found that its orders could be enforced only with the co-operation of the magistrate. The minute book is full of references of problems to J.P.'s, to the Court leet, to the bishop, to the constables (for poor relief).[1] The classis looked hopefully to parliament; but the magistrate could not co-operate fully in enforcing discipline of the Dedham type unless state power was transferred to new hands. The hierarchy's counter-attack in the fifteen-nineties seemed to put such a transfer beyond the bounds of possibility. Baxter wrote in 1664 that in fifty years (*"except in the space when bishops were down"*) he never saw anyone do public penance for scandalous crimes, and had heard of only two in Worcestershire that stood in a white sheet for adultery. His echo of the puritan petition of 1584 registers the failure of this approach to the problem before 1640.[2] But it also registers the transvaluation of social values which was achieved during the revolutionary decades. In 1670 a clergyman still recalled with horror the dreadful days of the interregnum when landlords became "slaves to tenants; . . . while the surplice [was] cut into a white sheet for the gentlemen to wear upon the stool of repentance".[3]

Supervision, control, education, examination, punishment: these are what the preachers meant by discipline. It was only gradually that they came to realize that they were challenging the whole ecclesiastical order. Richard Baxter thus describes his state of mind just before 1640: "Discipline I wanted in the

1. Ed. R. G. Usher, *The Presbyterian Movement in the Reign of Queen Elizabeth, passim,* esp. pp. 53–7, 100–2. Mr. Usher is right to say that inability to get its orders enforced was a principal cause of the failure of the classis; but he makes an unwarranted assumption when he argues that "in the last analysis it meant that the people refused to support it" (p. 62; cf. p. 46). That may have been the case: but it is not proved by the facts which Mr. Usher presents.

2. *Reliquiae Baxterianae,* I, p. 397; cf. p. 238 above.

3. [T. Pittis], *A Private Conference between A Rich Alderman and A Poor Country Vicar* (1670), p. 131. The horror was no doubt overdone to make aldermen's flesh creep at the parallel prospect of becoming "servants to their own apprentices". To avoid this they should elect "gentlemen of worth" to Parliament.

church, and saw the sad effects of its neglect. But I did not understand that the very frame of diocesan prelacy excluded it, but thought it had been only the bishops' personal neglects".[1] "It is not what Laud did that Baxter seems to complain of", noted Professor Grierson acutely, "so much as what he would not allow them, the parish pastors, to do, viz. to exercise a moral discipline co-extensive with the parish".[2]

It was more than "the bishops' personal neglects". The courts of the established Church had their own standards of discipline, inherited from before the Reformation: the only difference was that they administered the laws, say, against usury with less consistent vigour than their predecessors had done. But as the mediaeval standards and assumptions informing the law got increasingly out of touch with those that prevailed among the congregations, so the disciplinary system of the hierarchy came to be regarded as something alien, imposed from outside, from on top. A great part of the strength of the puritan conception of discipline was that it would have restored a local immediacy to the censures of the Church. Instead of an anonymous lay chancellor administering from a distance an obsolete law, the minister and the elders of the parish would have spoken paternally to and for the congregation about matters on which both parties had first-hand knowledge. In Scotland "the fostering of the kirk session as an instrument of discipline reinforced the emphasis on the parish".[3] In England something of this local immediacy was obtained by working the poor law through the parish: overseers of the poor performed functions which Presbyterians would have wished to see entrusted to elders and deacons. The failure to agree on a system of ecclesiastical discipline helped the secularization of the parish: J.P.s supervised poor relief.[4]

A parochial discipline would have been vigorous because novel, because engaged in *imposing* standards painfully worked out and passionately believed in. The weakness of the presbyterian discipline sprang from this novelty, and from the fact that not all members of the community accepted the new

1. *Reliquiae Baxterianae*, I, p. 14; cf. pp. 32, 141–3, 396–404.
2. H. J. C. Grierson, *Cross Currents in English Literature of the 17th century* (1948), p. 185.
3. Donaldson, *The Reformation in Scotland*, p. 81.
4. See Chapters 7 and 12 below.

standards. The homogeneous community which the presbyterian system assumed was ceasing to exist. The heavy Calvinist emphasis on the sinfulness of the mass of humanity, indeed, expresses this lack of unity of outlook within congregations, just as it justifies the insistence on discipline. The theology and the discipline are inseparable parts of the same world outlook. When both the discipline and Calvinist theology lost their grip in the conditions of relative freedom of the sixteen-forties, the sects formed new voluntary communities. In them the emphasis moved away from discipline to social services and communal self-help, just as the theological emphasis shifted from the eternal decrees to the perfectibility of man.

VI

Professor Haller, in an admirable piece of social analysis, has shown how perfectly the theology of the Puritan preachers fitted the needs of a revolutionary class. It did so in spite of its inherent contradictions, *because* of its inherent contradictions, because the preachers concentrated on influencing their hearers to activity here and now, and did not speculate about possible logical conclusions which might be drawn from their arguments. He is speaking of the period before 1640:

"The Puritan preachers were at this time innocent of any intention of laying down a theory of natural rights as a basis for a democratic society. They were absorbed in their immediate object, which was to instill in the minds of country gentlemen, merchants, lawyers and their followers the idea that, over against the carnal aristocracy which ruled the world, there was an aristocracy of the spirit, chosen by God and destined to inherit heaven and earth. Their sympathetic hearers were quite capable of observing for themselves how the carnal men in control of government were running the country. Thus the preachers were in effect organizing a discontented minority into an opposition. . . . At the moment, therefore, the restriction of salvation in the hereafter to a limited number of souls chosen out of all the rest by God alone . . . was certainly sound political psychology. Practical men in considerable numbers can be persuaded to commit themselves to fight for a faith and a programme when they can be induced to believe in the inevitability of a favourable outcome. If, however, some are predestined to win, some must be equally sure to lose. If any are elect, others must be damned. The certainty of election and reprobation was, then, an indispensable theme in the argument of Puritan preachers prior to 1640". Professor Haller notes the contradictions: the preachers needed the support of numbers if the Revolution was to be successful: that is, they needed the support of the reprobate. Hence the necessity of discipline for the whole of society so that the ungodly multitude should not get entirely out of hand even if called upon to take limited political action as the allies of the godly. Yet the theory of justification by faith could by its very nature never appeal to more than the minority of those who believe themselves to be the elect: Calvinism broke down when the Revolution established freedom of discussion.[1] And many of the gentry, whose attitude towards discipline had always been ambivalent, came to see a restoration of the episcopal Church as the only way to restore social subordination.

VII

The preachers were in general agreement about ignorance of Christian duties among the masses, and the consequent need for rigorous control and re-education.[2] When John Dury was appointed a preacher at Winchester in 1646, he declared that he had scarcely ever met with people of less knowledge than his congregation, both old and young being as if they had never heard of Christ.[3] John Shaw at Cartmel, Lancashire, found a man of about 60 years old who had heard of Jesus Christ only as a character in a Corpus Christi play.[4] The remedy of both Dury and Shaw was to catechize. They found their parishioners regular in attendance and attentive at catechism: only the aged were unwilling to abandon their accustomed ways. But Baxter at Kidderminster a few years

1. Haller, *The Rise of Puritanism*, pp. 168–9; *Liberty and Reformation in the Puritan Revolution*, pp. 105, 122 and *passim*.
2. In the fifteen-eighties the Dedham classis took measures to ensure that every child in the town was taught to read, and set up a school (Usher, *The Presbyterian Movement in the Reign of Queen Elizabeth*, p. 100) Cf. p. 57 above.
3. G. H. Turnbull, *Hartlib, Dury and Comenius* (1947), p. 253.
4. J. Shaw, *Life*, in *Yorkshire Diaries and Autobiographies in the 17th and 18th centuries* (Surtees Soc., 1877), pp. 138–9. See pp. 91, 105–6 above.

later discovered that nearly two-thirds of the parish stayed away from church out of "very fear of discipline". (That is why the stricter sort could never have tolerated a voluntary system in religion.) For Baxter the division was a social one: religious knowledge was a function of class. Those few at Kidderminster who utterly refused to be catechized were "beggars at the town's ends". Baxter later gave a generalized description of our "industrious sort of people": "Among merchants, mercers, drapers and other corporation-tradesmen, and among weavers, tailors and such-like labourers, yea among poor nailers and such-like, there is usually found more knowledge than among the poor enslaved husbandmen". "In most places there are a sober sort of men of the *middle rank*, that will hear reason, and are more equal to religion than the highest or the lowest usually are".[1] Milton was another who found religious and political sense strongest in the middle sort.

There is no evidence that the lower orders had ever shared their betters' enthusiasm for the Calvinist discipline. Such discipline as had been advocated by the popular heresies, including Lollardy and English Anabaptistry, had been entirely voluntary: if only because such movements had had to function illegally. But Protestantism itself was always ambivalent in its attitude towards discipline. The original Lutheran impulse was a liberation of individualism: it was only after the Anabaptists had carried Christian liberty further than he wished that Luther belatedly added discipline as a note of the Church.[2] It was after Münster that the Calvinist disciplinary system achieved its successes. So the two conceptions of discipline polarized: the Calvinist view of the necessity of subjecting the unregenerate, in order that their open viciousness should not reflect on the glory of God; the sectarian view that one must separate from the unregenerate, refuse to communicate with them. This necessarily led to the view that the only sanctions the Church should wield were spiritual censures, and that within the true Church the people could not surrender their authority to elders. That would be

1. *Reliquiae Baxterianae*, I, pp. 91, 85, 89; Baxter, *The Poor Husbandman's Advocate* and *Christian Directory*, quoted in R. B. Schlatter, *The Social Ideas of Religious Leaders, 1660–88* (1940), pp. 159–60. My italics.

2. E. G. Rupp, "Luther and the Doctrine of the Church", in *Atti del X Congresso Internazionale di Scienze Storiche* (1957), p. 469.

"dissonant . . . to true faith and piety, . . . consonant unto the papists' implicit faith". So John Robinson anticipated Rousseau's view of the impossibility of representative government.[1] Spiritual censures, Burroughes told the Westminster Assembly, with unpopular logic, "will remedy evils if men be conscientious"; acts of jurisdiction "will not do it if they be not conscientious". "To set up government and discipline before this [spirit of the Gospel] comes into the soul", Walter Cradock thought, "truly it is to build castles in the air".[2]

The classes which Parliament represented were, in the early years of the Revolution, virtually unanimous in preferring the former conception of discipline. "A church government we must have", said Sir Edward Dering in June 1641. "This is (within these walls, for ought I hear) on all hands agreed upon".[3] But already different views could be heard outside the walls. The demand for discipline came to be closely associated with Presbyterianism; opposition to religious toleration and the Scottish alliance went together. Cromwell told his superior officer he could as soon draw his sword against the Scots as against any in the King's army because of the way they carried themselves, "pressing for their discipline".[4]

The presbyterian disciplinary system never functioned satisfactorily because no state power enforced its censures. What ministers needed was a power of the keys which would impose real inconvenience and a social stigma on those excommunicated. Mr. Cant, for instance, gave no communion to the town of Aberdeen for two years, until they were well catechized.[5] He was able to do this because his parishioners had nowhere else to go. In England religious toleration and the repeal of the statutes for compulsory church attendance meant that an excommunicated person, at least in urban parishes, simply went to another church. But in the countryside exclusion, or the threat of it, was still a powerful weapon in the

1. J. Robinson, *Works* (ed. R. Ashton, 1851), III, p. 34.
2. J. Burroughes, *A Vindication of Mr. Burroughes against Mr. Edwards his foule aspersions* (1646), quoted in B. Gustafsson, *The Five Dissenting Brethren* (Lund, 1955), p. 50. W. Craddock, *Mount Sion* (1649), p. 292, quoted by G. F. Nuttall, *The Welsh Saints, 1640–60* (1957), p. 28.
3. *A Collection of Speeches made by Sir Edward Dering* (1642), p. 69.
4. Abbott, *Writings and Speeches of Oliver Cromwell*, I, p. 290.
5. J. Spalding, *Memorialls of the Trubles in Scotland* (1840), II, p. 156.

hands of a minister and co-operative elders. Even in the politically unpropitious circumstances of 1656 Henry Newcome could rejoice that in his Cheshire parish "the scandalous and grossly ignorant are kept back. And though the good are the lesser party", he confessed to Baxter, "yet the other party is kept under more than heretofore".[1] But in order to be an effective sanction excommunication demanded an exclusive national Church, and the co-operation of the civil authorities.[2]

In 1658 two judges of assize declared that it would be lawful for parishioners to refuse tithes to incumbents who would not baptize their children, or refused to administer the sacrament "to all but the ignorant and scandalous".[3] Men were anxious enough not to pay tithes anyway; so this put an intolerable obstacle in the way of those trying to reconstruct a disciplinary system. Baxter, whose Worcestershire Association was just such an attempt to build up a disciplinary system from below, made desperate attempts to win state support. In September 1656 he wrote to Sir Edward Harley suggesting that the Parliament of which Sir Edward had just become a member should pass an act declaring that those clergy "who neglect all discipline (while they own a pastoral charge) and . . . omit private instruction and catechizing . . . should be enumerated . . . to be negligent". He listed the difficulties in the way of discipline – the rage of the censured, the backwardness of the flesh, jealousy of ministerial tyranny. His main concern was to remove these and to "deal as severely with them that are remiss in discipline as with them that are vigorous". When the next Parliament met he returned to the charge in a letter to John Swinfen. He was anxious for Presbyterians, Independents and others to agree between themselves on a discipline to be settled by State action. Things would not be well until pastors were forced to exercise discipline; "the non-exercise of it

1. Newcome, *Autobiography*, p. 327. Jeremy Taylor, on the other hand, objected on principle to excommunication of scandalous persons by "single presbyters". Excommunication was lawful only when performed by the properly accredited officers of a state church (*The Great Exemplar*, in *The Whole Works*, 1836, I, p. 312).

2. See Chapter 10 below.

3. Ed. C. H. Firth, *Clarke Papers*, III, pp. 164–5; H. A. Wyndham, *A Family History* (1939), I, p. 258. Many radicals had said that ministers who did not do their job should not be paid: but it was new for judges to agree with them.

continueth the Independents' withdrawing more than any distance in principals". Once the discipline was settled, none but church members should govern or choose governors.[1] Discipline, Francis Osborn observed in 1658, "is the same thing in the church as law in the state, can no more be spared than government itself".[2] We can see here the growing fear of social insubordination which led Baxter in April 1660 to tell the House of Commons "the question is not whether Bishops or no but whether discipline or none".[3] This anxiety helped to reconcile to the restoration of the Anglican hierarchy many less sincerely religious men than Baxter; for the Anglican system restored by Parliament, imperfect though it was, had at least some coercive power behind it; at least there was a single national state Church. And now this Church had no High Commission; it was subordinate to Parliamentary control. The Clarendon Code was imposed by Parliament.

VIII

Before 1640 most Englishmen, when they thought of Presbyterianism, thought of Scotland. In Scotland it was the landed class that (when it wished to rouse the nation in defence of its Reformation plunder) took the lead in and dominated the presbyterian movement. But as seen from England there could be no doubt that the Scottish system of "free yearly election of deacons and elders",[4] ensured the preponderance of laymen of property, and that it put a very powerful weapon at their disposal for bringing pressure to bear on the civil government. Charles I at once objected to the preparations for the General Assembly of 1638 when he saw that the Scottish leaders were appointing laymen to sit in presbyteries, which they had not done for 40 years: and that laymen were equal in numbers to the ministers. It was, he said, "a preparative very dangerous, where presbyteries had many nobles and gentlemen of power and command amongst them; . . . these ruling

1. Schlatter, *Richard Baxter and Puritan Politics* pp. 51–4, 64–6.
2. Osborn, *Advice to a Son*, Part 2, in *Miscellaneous Works*, I, pp. 200–1. Cf. *Political Occasions of the Defection from the Church of Rome*, *ibid.*, p. 67.
3. Baxter, *A Sermon of Repentance* (1660), p. 43.
4. *The First Book of Discipline*, in Knox's *History of the Reformation* (1832), p. 505.

elders would rule all". The Scots replied, truthfully, that the ministers were already heavily outnumbered by lay elders in the parishes (as they had been at Geneva, from the earliest days of Calvin's sway there), and that it was not right "for to debar gentlemen of breeding and parts for to admit for assessors to ministers mean men, every way to them inferior".[1] (Both sides agreed on that point, Charles demanding whether it was right that laymen, "many of them ignorant mechanics" should "sit in the highest ecclesiastical judicatory?"). In fact laymen did control the Assembly, and had a decisive voice in excluding non-covenanting ministers. The latter even protested against the "heavy yoke of overruling elders".[2] When Charles's representative, Hamilton, failed to have the laymen ejected, he dissolved the Assembly, so vital did he feel the point to be, both in itself and as an example for England.

There were in fact two ways in which the machinery of the Church could be subordinated to the control of the dominant social classes in lay society. The first, the Scottish way, may be called control by infiltration: laymen take over effective sway of the ecclesiastical disciplinary machine at the lower levels. After that, in the inevitable struggle with the civil power, the population can be rallied to the cry "the Kirk is in danger", "seeing the cause of God's true religion and His Highness's authority are so joined as the hurt of one is common to both; and that none shall be reputed as loyal and faithful subjects to our Sovereign Lord or his authority but shall be punishable as rebellers and gainstanders of the same, who shall not . . . make profession of the said true religion".[3] Control by infiltration was the easier in Scotland since there no such profound social revolution was involved as in England: only the throwing off of alien domination.

The other way was the English way. Here the attempt at a

1. J. Gordon, *History of Scots Affairs* (Spalding Club, 1841), I, pp. 104–5. Only 12 years later the General Assembly Commission, in a review of national sins, referred to partiality in the administration of discipline and respect of persons; "offences and scandals in meaner persons are taken notice of, challenged and censured, [but] not the like Christian freedom and faithfulness and zeal used towards such as are more eminent for wealth, place or dignity in the world" (*Records of the Commission of the General Assembly*, III, p. 147, 29 November 1650).

2. Gordon, *op. cit.*, II, p. 35; I, pp. 120–1, 169.

3. The Scottish National Covenant of 1638, in S. R. Gardiner *Constitutional Documents of the Puritan Revolution*, p. 129.

Scottish solution was defeated in Elizabeth's reign, and in 1640–1 control was secured by revolution, by conquest of political power and the subordination of the Church to the sovereignty of Parliament. Thereafter, though this was not at once realized by everybody, Presbyterianism had lost its usefulness for the main body of the propertied parliament-arians, and become the shibboleth of a group of ministers. When a presbyterian system was established as the price of the Scottish alliance, it was riddled with safeguards for lay control, and once the Scottish army withdrew the system collapsed. The Westminster Assembly's Directory for Worship was accepted by Parliament; its Directory for Admonition, Excommunication and Absolution never got beyond the stage of discussion.[1] This perhaps confirms Professor Haller's suggestion that the driving force behind Presbyterianism was the desire of a discontented minority to remould society and the state on lines more favourable to their needs. The religious Presbyterians, the ministers, were left stranded when condi-tions were established for achieving this main object by direct political action: 1660 showed the completeness of their isolation. The Restoration was mainly the work of that group of laymen whom we call "Presbyterians": yet doctrinal Presbyterianism was dismissed into a wilderness from which it never returned in its old glory.

IX

The reluctance of the multitude to accept discipline pro-duced one manifestation of what is usually known as puritan hypocrisy. If the ungodly many would not be good (and by definition this was impossible for them), then at least they could pay lip-service to standards they could not themselves attain. "Lewd sons and servants", said Thomas Taylor, must be brought "to the means and outward conformity, to submit themselves both to the public worship of the Sabbath and private duties in the family; so was Cain himself so long as in *Adam's* house".[2] Make your family "at least visible saints", said Daniel Cawdrey in 1656, with a significant debasement

1. C. V. Wedgwood, *The King's War, 1641–7* (1958), p. 511.
2. T. Taylor, *Works*, p. 119: cf. T. Goodwin, *Works*, 111, pp. 496, 525–8.

of vocabulary; "that is, apparently religious, though perhaps secret hypocrites".[1] The profane ungodly presumptuous multitude, wrote Baxter, "will not be persuaded to be at so much pains for salvation as to perform the common outward duties of religion".[2] But a standard could be set up and respected, outwardly at all events, even by those who were not worthy of it.

This is what Philip Henry meant when, looking backwards, he used to say: "During those years between '40 and '60, though on civil accounts there were great disorders, and the foundations were out of course, yet, in the matters of God's worship, things went well; there was freedom and reformation, and a face of godliness was upon the nation, though there were those that made but a mask of it . . .".[3] Mrs. Baxter, too, learnt the social value of a "face" of godliness. At the beginning of her married life she refused to take family prayers in her husband's absence, through an excessive scruple and fear of hypocrisy. "But of later years", Richard Baxter wrote, "when she saw me and others too sparing in profitable speech to young and ignorant people, she confessed that she saw her error, and that even an hypocrite, using but the words and outside of religion, was better to others than silence and unprofitable omission was".[4] This point of view was common to all conservatives after 1660, whether bishops or nonconformists.[5] One of Baxter's own arguments in favour of strict Sabbath observance was that "it will make men to be in some sort religious whether they will or not: though they cannot be truly religious against their will, it will make them visibly religious".[6] In New England in the same period the uses of

1. D. Cawdrey, *Family Reformation Promoted* (1656), p. 54. This sermon was based on material left by Richard Cawdrey, the author's father (*ibid.*, Sig. A 2v). Cf. the remark made by Cutbeard, a barber pretending to be a canon lawyer in Ben Jonson's *Epicoene*: vows of chastity are "taken away among us, thanks be to discipline" (Act V, scene i).

2. Baxter, *The Saints Everlasting Rest* (1651), Part III, p. 86.

3. M. Henry, *The Life of the Rev. Philip Henry* (1825), p. 89.

4. Baxter, *A Breviate of the Life of Margaret Baxter*, in J. T. Wilkinson, *Richard Baxter and Margaret Charlton* (1928), pp. 136–7.

5. Simon Patrick, *A Treatise of Repentance* (1841), p. 178. First published in 1686.

6. Baxter, *Practical Works* (1830), XIII, p. 459. Cf. the reference to "visible saints" on p. 248 above.

hypocrisy were discovered too: at least "hypocrites give God part of His due, the outward man", wrote John Cotton; "but the profane person giveth God neither outward nor inward man". So hypocrites were "serviceable and useful in their callings" so long as they kept up their hypocrisy.[1] As in so many other respects, the social husk of the puritan discipline survived after it had lost its religious kernel.

1. Perry Miller, *The New England Mind: from Colony to Province* (Harvard University Press, 1953), pp. 79–80.

Chapter Seven

The Poor and the Parish

It is a foul disorder in any commonwealth that there should be suffered rogues, beggars, vagabonds; for such kind of persons commonly are of no civil society or corporation, nor of any particular church.... To wander up and down from year to year to this end, to seek and procure bodily maintenance, is no calling, but the life of a beast: and consequently a condition or state or life flat against the rule, that every one must have a particular calling. And therefore the Statute made the last Parliament [1597] for the restraining of beggars and rogues is an excellent statute, and, being in substance the very law of God, is never to be repealed.

William Perkins, *A Treatise of Callings*, *Workes*,
I, p. 755.

I

The tradition that big property-owners should dispense hospitality and relieve the poor goes back a very long way.[1] It is at once ostentation and a form of social insurance: it is the tribute which members of a ruling class pay to surviving ideals of a more equal society, memories of which, or legends about which, haunt so many mediaeval movements of social protest.[2] The tradition remained that hospitality was a duty incumbent

1. In this chapter I am indebted to Professor R. Pascal's *The Social Basis of German Reformation* (1933), especially Chapter 4; cf. Paul Baran, "Economic Progress and Economic Surplus", *Science and Society*, XVII, p. 303.
2. A. L. Morton, *The English Utopia* (1952), Chapter I; N. Cohn, *The Pursuit of the Millennium* (1957), *passim*; cf. my *Puritanism and Revolution*, pp. 50–9.

upon the very wealthy. The derivation of our word "generous" from the Latin word meaning "well-born", "noble", is suggestive. In mediaeval society this duty may not have been regularly observed; its operation was no doubt restricted and selective; but the acceptance of it, at least as a theoretical concept, helped to smooth the workings of that brutal society, to blunt the edge of class hostility on each side. Even in the seventeenth century manorial lords were by the customs of many parishes still deemed to have a special duty to maintain the poor of those parishes.[1] Edward Nicholas, a landlord with a social conscience, vowed in 1629 to give the poor 5 per cent from his government official salary, 6 per cent from leases for years or lives, 8 per cent from rents and the interest on loans.[2] The grading is interesting: he clearly felt that he had special obligations as a landowner, as well as a guilty conscience about usury.

A parallel process took place in the Church. Community of goods in primitive Christianity was soon transformed into financial assistance for the less prosperous among the faithful; and as Christianity became an official religion, the Church was increasingly institutionalized. It became the recipient even more than the dispenser of alms. The process is symbolized by the degradation of the word "charity". It used to be the holiest, of the three, holier than hope or even faith: it has become a crust of bread handed to the poor man at the gate.[3] Adam Smith attributed the decline of clerical charity to the rise of industry, which made available commodities in exchange for agricultural products whose "quantity exceeded greatly what the clergy could themselves consume".[4]

But a tradition remained, and it was in the sixteenth century still a very strong tradition. The monasteries, in particular, were felt to have a dual responsibility for hospitality and almsgiving, as ecclesiastical bodies and as big landowners. But the responsibility was not theirs alone: it was shared with other ecclesiastical properties. Starkey had urged that first-fruits

1. W. E. Tate, *The Parish Chest* (1946), p. 294.

2. D. Nicholas, *Mr. Secretary Nicholas* (1955), p. 71.

3. Cf. E. Troeltsch, *The Social Teaching of the Christian Churches* (transl. O. Wyon, 1931), I, pp. 166–7, 399; C. Caudwell, *Further Studies in a Dying Culture* (1949), p. 62.

4. Adam Smith, *The Wealth of Nations*, (World's Classics), II, p. 442.

should be diverted from the pope to poor relief.[1] Simon Fish demanded tithes for the poor.[2] "It is not lawful for thee to have parsonage, benefice, or any such living", declared Lever, "except thou do feed the flock spiritually with God's word, and bodily with honest hospitality".[3]

"The goods of the church are called the goods of the poor", said Edward VI's Injunctions of 1547: but "at these days nothing is less seen than the poor to be sustained with the same". The remedy was not as drastic as the sweeping preamble would have suggested: it was that all non-resident parsons with incomes over £20 should dispense one-fortieth thereof in charity,[4] – which may give some idea of what hospitality would have been expected to cost them if they had been resident. The 1547 Articles of Visitation inquired whether ministers kept hospitality and relieved their poor parishioners.[5] In the seventeenth century the rector of Fenny Compton paid £1 a year to the poor "in lieu of a drinking" – presumably commutation for an annual party.[6] Spokesmen of the hierarchy did not fail to point to these duties of hospitality and charity when defending their revenues against puritan attack. Thus in 1584 the bishops answered criticisms made in Parliament by pointing out that prices had risen two or three times in the past 50 years, "and yet as great or greater hospitality looked for".[7]

There is no need to attempt to assess here how satisfactorily the monasteries functioned as agencies of poor relief. As the Duke of Norfolk pointed out to Thomas Cromwell in 1537, "the alms that they have in religious houses is the great

1. T. Starkey, *A Dialogue between Reginald Pole and Thomas Lupset*, ed. K. M. Burton (1948), p. 179; of. W. G. Zeeveld, *Foundations of Tudor Policy* (Harvard University Press, 1948), p. 162.

2. S. Fish, *A Supplication of the Poore Commons* (1529), Sig. a 8–b 3.

3. Thomas Lever, *Sermons* (1901), p. 30. First published 1550.

4. Cardwell, *Documentary Annals*, I, pp. 11–12; repeated in Elizabeth's Injunctions of 1559 (*ibid.*, p. 184) and enforced by the Church courts (S. L. Ware, *The Elizabethan Parish in its Ecclesiastical and Financial Aspects*, Baltimore, 1908, pp. 31–2).

5. Cardwell, *op. cit.*, I, p. 45, repeated in the Articles of Visitation of 1559, *ibid.*, pp. 211–12.

6. Ed. S. C. Ratcliff and H. C. Johnson, *Quarter Sessions Order Book, 1657–65* (Warwick County Records, 1938), p. 266; cf. W. Andrews, *Curiosities of the Church* (1890), p. 44. But "a drinking" may have meant a church ale.

7. Cardwell, *op. cit.*, I, p. 433.

occasion" of vagabondage.[1] And they can have done nothing for the deserving poor in the vast majority of parishes where there was no monastery.[2] But the important points for our purpose are that monasteries had in the public eye a function which included relief of the destitute: that many contemporaries hoped that their confiscated revenues would be diverted, at least in part, to charitable purposes; that these hopes were disappointed; and that the two generations after the dissolution saw pauperism on a larger scale than ever before in English history.

The dissolution did not create this problem. As John Hales made his Doctor observe, "The soil is not taken away, but the possession thereof is only transferred from one kind of person to another".[3] Pauperism was the result of many factors – rising population, conversion of arable to pasture, enclosure of common lands, racking of rents, growing dependence of industrial producers on overseas markets, the cutting down of great feudal households. An assessment of 1597 gave the causes of poverty and vagabondage as (i) excessive luxury expenditure, leading to racking of rents and sale of lands; (ii) and (ix) excessive consumption of food by the rich, leading to scarcity and high prices; (iii) oppressive landlords; (iv) usury; (v) cornering corn and holding out for high prices; (vi) wasting of substance at law; (vii) gambling; (viii) breaking up of households, unnecessary dismissals of servants and apprentices; (x) failure to execute the poor law.[4]

The dissolution of the monasteries, then, may have contributed slightly to the vagabond population: in the seventeenth century it was common to attribute the statutes against vagrancy to the fear that wandering ex-monks and ex-friars would spread sedition.[5] But of far greater significance was the fact that pauperism began to increase seriously just after the traditional means for coping with it had been destroyed. How-

1. Quoted in Tawney and Power, *Tudor Economic Documents*, II, p. 301.

2. R. A. R. Hartridge, *A History of Vicarages in the Middle Ages* (1930), p. 156.

3. Ed. E. Lamond, *A Discourse of the Common Weal* (1893), p. 85. First printed 1581.

4. Tawney and Power, *Tudor Economic Documents*, III, pp. 452–4.

5. S. Butler, *Characters and Passages from Note-books* (ed. A. R. Waller, 1908), p. 374; Burnet, *History of the Reformation*, III, pp. 59 398; IV, p. 307.

ever inadequate the monasteries had been in the past, they provided machinery which could have been used and improved, as it was by Colbert in France. In England new machinery had to be improvised in a long and painful series of experiments.[1]

Propagandist though he was, Roderick Mors was to the point: "Your pretence of putting down abbeys was to amend that [which] was amiss in them. It was far amiss that a great part of the lands of the abbeys (which were given to bring up learned men that might be preachers, to keep hospitality and to give alms to the poor) should be spent upon a few superstitious monks which gave not £1 in alms when they should have given £200 . . . But . . . it is amended even as the devil mended his dam's leg (as it is in the proverb) – when he should have set it right he brake it quite in pieces".[2]

The dissolution statutes did in fact lay on the inheritors of monastic lands the obligation of keeping up hospitality, under penalty of a fine of £6 6s. 8d. a month. But the ensuing years saw a general reduction of the old standards of hospitality, despite the increased needs of the poor. "Many for fear of the statute keep up houses", declared a preacher as early as 1545; "but as for the householding, they maintain it so that neither mouse nor sparrow will abide there".[3] In the 1597 Parliament Sir Robert Cecil lamented the inability of many "to keep hospitality". The burden of hospitality, another M.P. in-

1. In Ireland the great Earl of Cork reported in 1631 that he had "set up two houses of correction in dissolved friaries, in which the beggarly youth are taught trade" (*C.S.P., Ireland, 1625–32*, p. 611).

2. [H Brinkelow], *The Complaynt of Roderyck Mors* (Geneva, ?1548), Sig. D iiii. Note the emphasis, so early, on a preaching clergy, which was no doubt one reason why Selden quoted this passage in his *History of Tithes* (*Works*, 1776, III, p. 1339). Starkey and Crowley had also hoped to see preachers, as well as the poor, financed from the spoils of the monasteries (Zeeveld, *The Foundations of Tudor Policy*, p. 162; R. Crowley, *Select Works*, Early English Text Soc., 1872, p. 7). Cf. J. Bale, *Select Works* (Parker Soc., 1849), pp. 485–6.

3. Sermon by William Chedsey, quoted by Haweis, *Sketches of the Reformation*, p. 269. What householding might be is illustrated by the funeral sermon on Thomas Sackville, first Earl of Dorset, preached by his chaplain, later Archbishop of Canterbury: "For more than twenty years, besides workmen and other hired", the Earl fed no less than 200 persons daily. "A very rare example in this present age of ours, when housekeeping is so decayed" (George Abbot, *Sermon preached at Westminster*, 1608, p. 16).

sinuated, fell especially on the gentry, since the nobility neglected their duty. Therefore, he thought, the gentry should be relieved from taxation.[1] "The building of great houses was the bane of good house-keeping in England", declared Camden.[2] Contemporaries disagreed only on the question whether hospitality was "laid abed" when preaching came in;[3] or when impropriations were established;[4] or had "been laid asleep in the grave of Edward Earl of Derby", the great northern potentate who died in 1572;[5] or whether "she gave her last groan among the yeomen of Kent",[6] or had been slain, together with Christmas, at Naseby Fight.[7] All agreed that the lady was dead. Fuller thought it was the ordinance of 1646 which took away bishops' lands and most of English hospitality.[8] The usurer's calling, Sanderson thought, was unprofitable to society for the reason that "he keepeth no hospitality".[9] In this atmosphere the statutes laying special obligations on the owners of monastic lands were easily disregarded, especially as their enforcement was left to J.P.s.

In two propositions Thomas Adams demolished the arguments of those gentlemen who said they needed impropriations "for hospitality's sake". Even if the claim were true, it only showed that "you make the clergy poor that you may make the

1. Neale, *Elizabeth I and Her Parliaments, 1584–1601*, pp. 349, 361; cf. L. C. Knights, *Drama and Society in the Age of Jonson* (1937), pp. 114–16.

2. Quoted in Fuller, *Worthies of England* (1840), III, p. 488; cf. E. Sandys, *Sermons* (Parker Soc., 1841), p. 401; and John Taylor, *The Old, Old, Very Old Man* (1635), p. 13.

3. Davids, *Nonconformity in Essex*, p. 240. Cf. p. 69 above.

4. T. Adams, *The Happines of the Church* (1619), I, pp. 229–30.

5. W. Camden, *History and Annals of Elizabeth, Queen of England* (1625), pp. 316–17; cf. R. Brathwaite, *The English Gentleman* (2nd ed., 1633), pp. 65–8, 132. First published 1630.

6. Fuller, *The Holy State* (1648), pp. 106, 145.

7. *The World is turned upside down*, a broadside ballad of 1646. I owe this reference to Mr. A. L. Morton's "John Lanseter of Bury", *Proceedings of the Suffolk Institute of Archaeology*, XXVIII, p. 45. Cf. John Buxton, "A Draught of Sir Philip Sidney's Arcadia,' in *Historical Essays, 1600–1750 presented to David Ogg* (ed. H. E. Bell and R. Ollard, 1963), p. 70.

8. Quoted by M. Fuller, *The Life, Times and Writings of Thomas Fuller* (1886), p. 188. The view that hospitality was declining dates at least from the early fifteenth century (Buckle, *Miscellaneous and Posthumous Works*, III, p. 459).

9. Sanderson, *XXXV Sermons* (1681), p. 204.

poor rich". But it was not true. "Hospitality was at the same time impropriated from the land, that spiritual livings were impropriated from the church".[1] So completely had the statutes imposing hospitality on inheritors of monastic lands become a dead letter than when they were repealed in 1624 James I could not even get compensation, though most of the landed families in the kingdom must previously have laid themselves open to heavy penalties.[2] The poor lost a palliative without getting a cure. Cobbett, who was responsible for drawing the attention of historians to this aspect of the Reformation, was no doubt wrong when he said that before the dissolution one-third of what was paid in tithes went out on poor relief. But he was more right when he continued "the change of religion, and the transfer of the tithes and of the estates of the monas-teries, caused the tithe-owners and the new abbey land-holders to *neglect* this sacred part of their duty, relieving the poor".[3]

Catholic propagandists suggested that charity had dried up at the Reformation: to which Protestants replied that it had merely taken new directions – into almshouses and education, for instance.[4] Points could be made on both sides. In the York cycle of mystery plays, for instance, performed annually from the fourteenth century till about 1570, when Christ came to divide the sheep from the goats, the decisive test was perform-ance of the seven works of mercy.[5] The Church of England's *Homily of Salvation*, on the other hand, omits charity from the

1. Adams, *The Happiness of the Church*, I, pp. 229–30.

2. Fuller, *Church History*, II, pp. 281, 312.

3. W. Cobbett, *A Legacy to Labourers* (1872), pp. 88–91. There has been a large literature on the subject since Cobbett's day, some of it Catholic-apologetic. Cf. a letter from Gerard Manley Hopkins to Bridges, written at the time of the Paris Commune: "As [the old civiliza-tion] at present stands in England, it is itself in great measure founded on wrecking. But they [the working classes] got none of the spoils, they came in for nothing but harm from it then and thereafter. England has grown hugely wealthy, but this wealth has not reached the working classes". "Horrible to say", he had confessed earlier in the letter, "in a manner I am a communist" (G. M. Hopkins, *Letters to Robert Bridges*, 1935, pp. 27–8). So the tradition of the rights of the community survived in unexpected places.

4. G. Hakewill, *An Apologie or Declaration of the Power and Provi-dence of God* (3rd ed., 1635), Book V, p. 167; Fuller, *Worthies* (1840), I, pp. 52–3. "Hospitals abound, and beggars abound, never a whit the less", wrote Bacon to Buckingham in 1618, regretting the King's decision not to endow university lectureships (*Works*, XIII, p. 324).

5. Ed. Lucy Toulmin Smith, *York Plays* (1885), pp. 508–13.

requisites for salvation. A minister who preached "that alms purge away sin, and good works deliver from death" was sequestered by Parliament in 1644 for being little better than a papist.[1] The James I translation of Hebrews xiii, 2, "be not forgetful to entertain strangers, for thereby some have entertained angels unawares", should more properly be rendered "forget not hospitality", William Gouge thought.[2] Yet Lancelot Andrewes argued that true charity in England, on the contrary, was the *result* of the Reformation.[3] There had been more works of charity in England since the Reformation, wrote Sir Edward Coke in 1614, than in many ages before.[4]

Modern research suggests that this boast was not altogether unjustified.[5] What was ceasing was the distribution of alms to the poor in the traditional indiscriminate way. The new wealthy class expended its surplus in different directions from its mediaeval predecessors. Even a Catholic who left money for charitable distribution in 1584 stipulated that none of the recipients should be vagrants or idlers.[6] The scattering of largesse and the foundation of monasteries (which also scattered largesse) had met the needs of the rulers of one type of society: the endowment of grammar schools and colleges (a *lay* educational system), of sermons and of almshouses and houses of correction (for the impotent poor and sturdy rogues respectively) seemed to the classes which were prospering in the sixteenth and seventeenth centuries more socially useful and more pleasing to God. Professor Trevor-Roper has pointed out that it was the Calvinist bishops – Parker, Grindal, Whitgift, Sandys, Hutton, Pilkington, Abbot – who

1. Davids, *Nonconformity in Essex*, p. 417.

2. Gouge, *Commentary upon Hebrews*, III, p. 271. Nowadays, commented Arise Evans bitterly, "there is a command to the contrary given that strangers should be carried to Bridewell; and if an angel come now, there he shall be lodged" (*An Eccho to the Voice from Heaven*, 1653, p. 3).

3. Andrewes, *XCVI Sermons* (1841–3), V, p. 37.

4. Coke, *10 Reports* (1614), Sig. C iv. Cf. A. Willet, *Synopsis Papismi* (1634), pp. 1220–43; A Hildersam, *CLII Lectures upon Psalme LI* (1635), p. 479; *The Diary of John Milward* (ed. C. Robbins, 1938), p. 231.

5. Cf. Joan Simon, "A. F. Leach on the Reformation, II", *British Journal of Educational Studies*, IV, pp. 47–8; contrast L. Stone's review of Jordan, *E.H.R.*, No. 303, pp. 327–8. See also W. T. MacCaffrey, *Exeter, 1540–1640* (Harvard, 1958), pp. 109–10; Jordan, *Philanthropy in England* and *The Charities of London, passim*; A. L. Rowse, *The Elizabethans and America* (1959), p. 87; and pp. 263, 267–73 below.

6. H. Jenkins, *Edward Benlowes* (1952), p. 4.

founded schools and almshouses: the Laudians were much less generous for these social purposes.[1] When a Protestant did endow indiscriminate distribution of alms it was for a specific purpose, as when Adrian Mott of Braintree gave £100 to invest in land, the profits to be distributed every November 5th, so that Guy Fawkes's treason should never be forgot.[2]

Many were the contemporary jokes about the usurer and the profiteer: "with the superfluity of his usury he builds an hospital and harbours there whom his extortion hath spoiled; so while he makes many beggars he keeps some".[3] "Heaven is not to be had in exchange for an hospital or a chantry or a college erected in thy last will", Donne warned.[4] Cable, in Davenant's *News from Plymouth* (1635) says "I love churches, I mean to turn pirate, rob my countrymen, and build one".[5] "Is it not a great piece of charity to get £500 a year from God, to bestow 20 marks a year on the poor?" Thomas Adams asked about impropriators.[6] The famous Henry Sherfield, Recorder of Salisbury and breaker of stained glass windows, was said to have made six fraudulent conveyances of his estate before finally leaving it to pious uses.[7] Alderman Cambel, a "near, austere, and hard man," in 1642 left £2,000 as a stock to keep idle youths at work in Bridewell and £1,300 for loans at 4 per cent to poor freemen of the Ironmongers' Company.[8] The point was made in Cartwright's poem, "on the death of the right Honourable Viscount Bayning":

1. Trevor-Roper, *Historical Essays* (1957), p. 127. Abbot's charity to Guildford in 1614 was aimed to help in retooling the town's clothing industry so that production could be switched from the old to the new draperies, in which demand was heavier and less erratic (Anon., *Life of George Abbot, Archbishop of Canterbury*, 1777, p. 75).

2. Davids, *Nonconformity in Essex*, p. 290.

3. J. Hall, *Characters*, in *Character Writings of the 17th century* (ed. H. Morley, 1891), p. 131; T. Adams, *Works* (1629), p. 80; *The Happines of the Church*, II, pp. 132–3; R. Burton, *The Anatomy of Melancholy* (Everyman ed.), I, p. 99; Fuller, *Worthies* (1840), I, p. 46; R. Stock, *A Commentary upon the Prophecy of Malachi* (1865), p. 113. Stock died in 1626; this *Commentary* was published posthumously in 1641.

4. J. Donne, *XXVI Sermons* (1660), p. 158.

5. Sir William Davenant, *Works* (1872–4), IV, p. 137. Could this allude to the Earl of Warwick?

6. T. Adams, *Works* (1629), p. 864.

7. Ed. W. Knowler, *Strafforde's Letters and Dispatches*, I, p. 206. For Sherfield see also p. 414 below.

8. E. Browne, *A rare Paterne of Justice and Mercy* (1642), pp. 43, 56 sqq.

> *Nor are his legacies poor men's present tears,*
> *Or do they for the future raise their fears.*
> *No such contrivance here as to profess*
> *Bounty, and with large miseries feed the less;*
> *Fat some with their own alms; bestow and pill;*
> *And common hungers with great famines fill,*
> *Making a hundred wretches endow ten.*"[1]

But one type of charity was neither more nor less "moral" than the other: each might be either pious or prudential, or perhaps both. Francis Trigge assured those who "say it was never merrie world" since the dissolution of the monasteries that "the landlords in those days were glad to seek their tenants; yea, as I have heard, to hire them that should till their grounds and be their tenants. A good tenant was then hard to be found". What had changed was the state of the labour market.[2] Denzil Holles recommended his son to "let thy hospitality be moderate, according to the measure of thy revenues"; but added "many consume themselves with secret vices and their hospitality must bear the blame".[3] John Holles took the advice to heart, and throve to purchase the earldom of Clare. As late as 1691 Mrs. Evelyn discovered that "discreet hospitality assists very much towards governing the nation, for the people are led by the mouth with moderate management, and without a little popularity they are perfect mules and ungovernable".[4] But she was discussing what might be politically necessary, not what was economically desirable. Thought about charity was changing rapidly in the sixteenth and seventeenth centuries, and changing to the detriment of the poor. A bill in the Parliament of 1597 which suggested that relief for the poor should be provided from impropriations and other church livings got no further than the second reading.[5] Charity "was a virtue of old times", declared Thomas Adams, "not so much now in fashion".[6]

1. Ed. R. C. Goffin, *The Life and Poems of William Cartwright* (1918) p. 105.
2. Francis Trigge, *An Apologie or Defence of our dayes* (1589), pp. 11–21, quoted by A. G. Dickens, "An Elizabethan Defender of the Monasteries", *Church Quarterly Review*, CXXX, p. 261.
3. *Portland MSS* (H.M.C.), IX, pp. 4–5.
4. W. G. Hiscock, *John Evelyn and his Family Circle* (1955), p. 158.
5. Sir Simonds D'Ewes, *The Journals of all the Parliaments during the Reign of Queen Elizabeth* (1682), p. 561.
6. Adams, *The City of Peace*, in *Works* (1861–2), II, p. 318.

II

Since machinery for poor relief had to be improvised, it was natural that the Government should look to the parish to undertake it. Relief of the poor was still thought of as a branch of good works, the function of the Church. The state intervened in the first instance (27 Hen. VIII cap. 25) only to forbid alms-giving except through church collections. The penalty for infringing this "nationalization" of charity was a fine of ten times the sum given in the illicit private alms. Ministers and bishops were instructed to exhort men to contribute; publicity was to be used within the parish in order to win popular approbation for the generous rich, public obloquy for the stingy. Church courts compelled those to give who would not do so voluntarily. In Edward VI's reign London abandoned voluntary collections in favour of a compulsory rate, and so provided the model for Elizabethan national legislation. After 1563 recalcitrants were handed over to quarter sessions for punishment by the civil arm.[1] The poor rate became a tax.

So poor relief was originally thought of as a purely parochial problem: each parish was to look after its own poor. If it had too many, they were to be given licences to beg, and packed off elsewhere. Only gradually in the course of the sixteenth century did it come to be realized that this would not do. In 1597 the unit of finance was enlarged to the county; rich parishes had to subsidize those with large numbers of paupers; and the attempt was begun to whip the poor back to their parish of birth.[2]

In the process, the ecclesiastical unit of the parish had been completely fused with the administrative hierarchy of the civil State. Churchwardens and overseers of the poor took orders from J.P.s. The problem of the destitute had become too vast and too formidable to be left to private alms-giving, for repression as well as relief was required. In this as in so many

1. Cardwell, *Documentary Annals*, 1, p. 57; Ware, *The Elizabethan Parish in its Ecclesiastical and Financial Aspects*, p. 41; S. and B. Webb, *The Old Poor Law* (1927), p. 48.

2. Prothero, *Select Statutes and other Constitutional Documents, 1558–1625*, pp. 42–4, 97; Sir W. Holdsworth, *History of English Law* IV, pp. 392–400. The draft act summarized by Dr. Elton in *Econ. H.R.* (Second Series, VI, pp. 55–67), shows that some men had grasped the scope of the problem as early as 1536: but it remained only a draft.

other ways in the Tudor age, the central state power had to step in behind the local semi-autonomous agencies, which had coped with the smaller scale problems of mediaeval England. "This is but a covetous folly", a preacher said of the legal obligation on each parish to support its own poor, "to persuade ourselves that we are not bound in conscience to give anything out of our own parishes".[1] Leviathan had replaced the Good Samaritan.

The poor law was thus a cause as well as an effect of the decline in personal charity: in particular the parson came to feel himself one of many members of a parish, each of whom was rated to poor relief; and no longer the representative of a community, specially endowed by that community to look after the needs of the poor. There was ground for friction in that parishioners might continue to look to the parson for charity after he himself had decided that that attitude was out of date. "The poor come to their [ministers'] houses as if they had interest in them", grumbled Fuller.[2]

III

The growth of capitalist relations in England, then, was accompanied by a new attitude towards poor relief. But this was no peculiarly English problem: it occurred in many continental countries. It was a problem to which the early Protestants devoted a great deal of thought; and the earliest measures for poor relief were taken in protestant countries. Partly this was due to the fact that everywhere a rise in prices followed hard on a secularization of ecclesiastical properties. But the new attitude would have come to the fore even if the price revolution had not precipitated matters: it lies deep in protestant theology. The connection between Protestantism and the rise of capitalism is far more fundamental than the accidental fact that both godly reformers and greedy landlords liked pillaging the Church. The early Protestants also inherited a lower-class heretical tradition of mutual insurance against poverty. "There were no beggars among them", De Thou tells

1. Thomas Drant, *Sermon at St. Mary's Spittle* (1570), quoted by Haweis, *Sketches of the Reformation*, p. 274.
2. Fuller, *The Holy State* (1841), p. 219; cf. *The Historie of the Holy Warre* (1651), p. 38, where Fuller argues that poverty restricted ministers' charity.

us of one branch of the Waldenses.[1]

The reformers justified the dissolution of the monasteries because their inmates were idle and unproductive. Luther attacked monks, friars and beggars in the same breath; part of his original case against indulgences had been that they led to the squandering of men's substance. Christians should "keep back what is needful for their own households" "unless they have an abundant superfluity of means". Relief of a brother in need should have precedence over purchasing a pardon for oneself.[2] At Wittenberg church funds, hitherto devoted to superstitious uses, were diverted to educational grants and interest-free loans to indigent craftsmen. Begging was prohibited, as it was by Zwingli at Zürich, and in Sweden – ineffectively – by Gustavus Adolphus.[3] In Calvinist countries like Scotland and the Netherlands some at least of the spoil of the monastries went to education and the provision of work for the poor.

In Scotland attempts were made to recover episcopal and parochial revenues for poor relief.[4] When John Evelyn was in the Netherlands in 1641 he saw no beggars except lepers, so well were the poor provided for.[5] The more radical reformers hoped that a Calvinist discipline would produce similar effects in England.[6] All over Europe, even in catholic countries, the state or municipal authorities had to intervene to cope with a problem which had become too vast for private charity administered by the Church. The literature of roguery, exposing the deceits of beggars, is common to countries of both faiths. This widely popular literary form may have been "written to soothe the consciences of the wealthy";[7] but the assumption that idleness is voluntary and wicked is shared by it with the severer protestant current of thought.

1. Quoted by Fuller, *The Historie of the Holy Warre*, p. 145.
2. Nos. 45 and 46 of the 95 Theses.
3. R. Pascal, *The Social Basis of the German Reformation* (1933), pp. 95–6, 235–6; M. Roberts, *Gustavus Adolphus*, II (1958), p. 144. Begging was said to have ceased in Calvin's Geneva (S. J. Knox, *Walter Travers*, 1962, p. 26). Cf. the Injunctions of 1547, in Cardwell, *Documentary Annals*, I, p. 18.
4. G. Donaldson, *The Scottish Reformation, 1560* (1960), pp. 64, 197–8.
5. Ed. E. S. de Beer, Evelyn's *Diary*, I, p. 25.
6. See pp. 271–3 below.
7. C. S. Lewis, *English Literature in the 16th Century, excluding Drama* (1954), p. 59.

This is the outlook of a new civilization, consciously com-
batting the standards of value of the old order. "It is most
certain", Bucer had declared, "that such as give themselves
wilfully to the trade of begging be given and bent to all mischief". Consequently, "what other thing do they that nourish
them than maintain and increase the greatest pestilences and
destructions of a commonwealth ?"[1] The sentiments were faithfully echoed by Bucer's royal pupil, Edward VI.[2] "The
Christian", Thomas Taylor tells us, "vows not . . . voluntary
poverty: for the commandment is, Let there be no beggar in
Israel".[3] We must learn how to use riches, Thomas Gouge was
to say, lest we be *tempted* to prefer a state of poverty.[4] The
reversal of values from the mediaeval cult of holy poverty is
complete. And the new values strike at the root of the feudal
order, secular as well as religious. In Marston's *Histriomastix*
(if it is Marston's), a discharged train of serving-men are bid by
their lord

> "*Walk sins, nay, walk; awake ye drowsy drones*
> *That long have sucked the honey from the hives:*
> *Begone, ye greedy beef-eaters, ye are best:*
> *The Calais cormorants from Dover road*
> *Are not so chargeable as you to feed*".

He tells them

> "*In faith, good fellows, get some other trade;*
> *Ye live but idle in the commonwealth*".

And the lord concludes

> "*Broke we not house up, you would break our backs. . . .*
> *A thousand pound a year will so be saved*".[5]

Idleness, unproductive consumption, is the count against
monks, retainers and beggars alike. The employment of industrious labourers, not the maintenance of loyal dependants, is
the way to prosper now. "A man grows rich by employing a

1. Bucer, *A Treatise, how by the Worde of God, Christian mens Almose
ought to be distributed* (1552), p. 8; cf. p. 6.
2. Burnet, *History of the Reformation*, III, p. 290; IV, pp. 85–9.
3. T. Taylor, *Christian Practice*, in *Works* (1653), p. 103.
4. T. Gouge, *A Sermon of Good Works*, in *Works* (1663), pp. 570–1.
5. J. Marston, *Plays* (1934–9), III, pp. 270–1. The satirist could not
resist making the lord end his speech, full of such admirable sentiments,
by ear-marking the £1,000 saved "for revelling and banqueting and
plays".

multitude of manufacturers", declared Adam Smith, "he grows poor by maintaining a multitude of menial servants".[1] Such statements seemed self-evident truths to the scientists of the new order; but they were also value-judgments. Smith realized that he was dealing with a distinction between two historically different social orders.[2] So too did Dr. Johnson, four years before the publication of *The Wealth of Nations*, when he said: "That ancient hospitality, of which we hear so much, was in an uncommercial country, when men, being idle, were glad to be entertained at rich men's tables. But in a commercial country, a busy country, time becomes precious, and therefore hospitality is not so much valued. . . . Promiscuous hospitality is not the way to gain real influence. . . . No, Sir, the way to make sure of power and interest is by lending money confidentially to your neighbours at a small interest, or perhaps at no interest at all, and having their bonds in your possession".[3] Some men even in the early seventeenth century were working their way towards such sociological conceptions; and Puritanism helped them. Hakewill in his denunciation of the excessive luxury of the Romans referred indignantly to "private men . . . casting their largesse among the people", and to their wasting of patrimonies upon idle hangers-on, "excluding their lawful heirs".[4]

IV

The same economic facts which necessitated labour legislation in England were at work all over Western Europe. Everywhere there was economic crisis, bitter class war, a strengthening of the power of the State to curb vagabondage and keep the poor in their place. The lower classes could improve their position only in so far as they were mobile[5] – i.e. in so far as they defeated both their lords and their lords' state. The combination of fierce repression with indiscriminate alms-giving

1. A. Smith, *The Wealth of Nations* (World's Classics), I, p. 369.
2. *Ibid.*, pp. 390–1, 455–61.
3. J. Boswell, *Life of Johnson* (Everyman ed.), I, p. 422.
4. Hakewill, *An Apologie*, pp. 445–7, 471–3.
5. Cf. Lenin on the pre-revolutionary Russian peasantry: "Without the mobility of the population . . . the development of its intelligence and initiative is impossible" (*The Development of Capitalism in Russia* 1899, in *Selected Works*, 1934–8, I, p. 301).

exacerbated the problem. Sir Thomas More pronounced its bankruptcy: "Neither is there any punishment so horrible that it can keep them from stealing which have no other craft whereby to get their living".[1] A century later a pamphleteer estimated that "the fourth part of the inhabitants of most of the parishes of England are miserable poor people and (harvest-time excepted) without any subsidence [?subsistence]".[2]

The sober scholarship of Professor MacCaffrey calculates that in Exeter in the sixteenth century "grinding poverty was the lot of more than half the population". "Learning a craft or purchasing the most elementary tools of a trade were impossible for the children of the poor. . . . The possibility of saving was beyond the hopes of the majority of the community".[3] Wandering away from one's native village in search of work was forbidden without a certificate signed by a J.P. Poor relief in fact subsidized wages.[4] The poor were excluded not only from the parliamentary franchise but also from almost any say in local government. Professor MacCaffrey associates this poverty with the endemic fear of popular revolt which the well-to-do felt. So did contemporaries. The poor are "apt to assist rebellion" or join a foreign invasion, said a pamphlet of 1580: "for having nothing they are desperate".[5] "The poor hate the rich", Deloney agreed, "because they will not set them on work; and the rich hate the poor, because they seem burdenous".[6] In 1619 children were dying of cold in the streets of London.[7]

First the humanists, and then Puritans, began to advocate a new policy which would attempt to ease the transition to new productive methods by providing for the landless impotent poor, by training children to labour, and by schemes for setting

1. Sir T. More, *Utopia* (Everyman ed.), p. 21.

2. [Anon.], *Considerations Touching Trade, with the Advance of the Kings Revenues* (1641), p. 15.

3. MacCaffrey, *Exeter*, pp. 94–5, 116–17, 249.

4. E. Lipson, *Economic History of England* (3rd ed., 1943), III, pp. 475, 486. For an example, see my *Puritanism and Revolution*, p. 221.

5. R. Hitchcock, *A Politic Plat* (1580), in Arber, *An English Garner*, II, p. 159.

6. T. Deloney, *Jack of Newbury*, in *Shorter Novels, Elizabethan and Jacobean* (Everyman ed.), p. 50.

7. Stephen Denison, *The New Creature* (1619), p. 43. A sermon preached at Paul's Cross.

the sturdy poor on disciplined work. Professor Jordan has documented the great effort of private individual philanthropy which aimed at solving the problem of poverty.[1] What was new in the sixteenth century was the concentration of paupers in large cities by industry, the substitution of seasonal complete unemployment for the perennial under-employment of the mediaeval peasant, and the increased chances that men who became too old to work would have no land to support them. Professor Jordan has emphasized the puritan impulse behind the great charitable endowments with which London merchants assaulted poverty and ignorance. It is no accident that it was a puritan family which produced Francis Bacon, the man who more than any one else held out the vision of a co-operative science devoted to industrial production for the relief of man's estate. There is the very closest connection between the protestant ideology of hard work and the economic needs of English society. Labour discipline was vital to the advance of the whole economy.

William Swinderby, a Lollard, said in 1391 that we are "not to give alms to each shameless beggar, strong and mighty of body to get his livelihood". Whoever wittingly gave to such a person "sins as fautor of his idleness".[2] "Foolish pity moving many to make provision at their doors (hoping to do good) "was thought to have increased the problem of poverty in Norwich in 1571.[3] One of Thomas Heywood's sympathetic characters in *If You Know Not Me* made the identical point:

> "*He makes a beggar first that first relieves him:*
> *Not usurers make more beggars where they live*
> *Than charitable men that use to give*".

Many protestant theologians laboured the same point.[4] It was an ultra-royalist clergyman, Clement Paman, who thought that the devout soul should be charitable "even to the loose

1. Jordan, *Philanthropy in England*, and *The Charities of London, passim*; *The Charities of Rural England*, pp. 41, 99, 154; *Social Institutions in Kent*, p. 131.

2. Foxe, *Acts and Monuments* (ed. J. Pratt), III, p. 118.

3. Tawney and Power, *Tudor Economic Documents*, II, p. 318. Cf. pp. 272 note 2, 286-7 below.

4. T. Heywood, *Dramatic Works* (1874), VI, p. 60 (I owe this reference to Robert Weimann's *Drama und Wirklichkeit in der Shakespearezeit*, Halle, 1958, p. 305). Cf. P. Bayne, *Commentary on Ephesians*, p. 295; T. Fuller, *Commentary on Ruth* (1865), p. 29. First published 1654.

and impious".[1] Milton in his *Commonplace Book* collected examples to show that "the most lavish alms-givers are not always truly devout".[2] "The country farmer will tell you", stated a pamphlet of 1656, "these great house-keepers bring all the beggars in a region to his parts, and never a one of these beggars but expect from us some alms, with continual clamour at our doors. Your private gentleman finds the price of provision raised to a third part, and therein suffers".[3]

The constructive protestant alternative to indiscriminate charity was to set the poor on work, to stimulate self-help. This was done at the lowest level by the puritan minister Richard Greenham, who worked out a scheme of co-operative purchasing in his parish, whereby all the poor were able to buy cheap corn in time of dearth.[4] At the national level, Robert Hitchcock thought that "that loathsome monster idleness" could be rooted out by an expansion of the herring industry, provided that the provision of godly preaching were made a first charge on the expanded profits of the industry. The provision was equivalent to ploughing profits back in further investment: it was not just an irrelevant whim.[5] The sense that charity was above all a duty to the commonwealth is a consistent puritan theme. "This is the best charity", said Richard Stock, "so to relieve the poor as we keep them in labour. It benefits the giver to have them labour; it benefits the commonweal to suffer no drones, nor to nourish any in idleness; it benefits the poor themselves". The rich, Stock thought, should reduce expenditure on luxury goods and clothes, on hawks, hounds and gaming, and invest these savings in production.[6] Hard and productive work is of advantage both to the individual and to the community of which he is a member. Interest and duty here coincide.

1. H. Jenkins, *Edward Benlowes* (1952), p. 159.

2. Milton, *Complete Prose Works* (Yale ed.), I, pp. 417–18.

3. [Anon.], *The Surfeit* (1656), quoted in *Reliquiae Hearnianae* (ed. Bliss, 1869), III, pp. 238–9.

4. S. Clarke, *A Martyrologie* (1652), II, pp. 83–4.

5. Hitchcock, *A Politic Plat*, in Arber's *English Garner*, II, pp. 146–53. Hitchcock wanted an itinerant preacher based on each of the eight principal ports, at the generous stipend of £100 a year. Cf. p. 134 above.

6. Stock, *Commentary upon . . . Malachi*, II, p. 56. For other examples of this emphasis, see my "Protestantism and the Rise of Capitalism", in *Essays . . . in Honour of R. H. Tawney* (1961), pp. 31–3.

In England a programme of setting the poor on work was put into effect by legislation embodying the agreed policy of the employing class and the government. But from the end of Elizabeth's reign, as this agreement began to break down at all points, the government resorted increasingly to a policy of regulation, rationing, price-fixing, forced sales and raiding of private stocks. This interference with the free market by a state power which (whatever the monarchy's professions) in fact represented the interests of a narrow oligarchy, backed up by the leaders of the English Church, had, as the Webbs shrewdly pointed out, a great deal to do with turning the lesser landowners against the old régime. Government interference intensified after the alarm caused by the western revolt of 1628–31, and starvation in many places in 1629–30. The evidence does not suggest that this attempt to assuage unrest greatly benefited the poor:[1] but there is plenty of evidence that it irritated the rich and productive. Many were the complaints from their representatives that it had been "found by experience that the raising of wages cannot advance the relief of the poor", but will aggravate unemployment; that the J.P.s' "strict looking to the markets is an occasion that the markets are the smaller, the corn dearer".[2]

What such men resented was not the poor law, which was administered best before 1640 in the areas where opposition was strongest and which supported Parliament in the civil war. Still less was their attitude due to a lack of concern for the problem of poverty, as the labours of Professor Jordan have amply demonstrated. They felt that the government, by its refusal of free play to the forces of supply, demand and competition, was hampering their efforts to solve the problem by expanding production and by private charitable endowment. When all allowances have been made for self-deception and self-regarding motives, it is difficult not to conclude that the opponents of the government had the better case. It was the

1. S. and B. Webb, *The Old Poor Law*, pp. 67–97; Jordan, *Philanthropy in England*, pp. 135–42; T. G. Barnes, *Somerset, 1625–40* (1961), chapter VII.

2. *C.S.P.D.*, *1625–29*, pp. 430–1; *1629–31*, p. 539; *1631–3*, p. 186. (All these are quoted in Lipson, *Economic History of England*, III, pp. 259, 445–6; cf. also p. 440). For resistance to schemes for compulsory apprenticeship, see T. G. Barnes, *Somerset Assize Orders, 1629–40* Somerset Record Soc., LXV), pp. xxix–xxx, 42, 49, 58, 63–4, 71.

philanthropist Samuel Hartlib, taking a very long-term view, who pointed out that "there are fewest poor where there are fewest commons".[1] It was the possibility of the poor maintaining themselves without regular labour that seemed to such reformers to be delaying the advance of the whole economy.

On the other hand, the "impotent" poor did set a serious social problem. The number of unemployed grew as a result both of rising population and of the tendency of the great households to meet inflation by cutting down their staffs, beginning with the less active, and of the increase in the number of wage-labourers who had no agricultural holding to maintain them after their labour had ceased to be profitable to their employers. One of the most popular puritan treatises, *A plain and familiar Exposition of the Ten Commandements* by John Dod and Robert Cleaver, sums up this point: "It is the custom of most men nowadays (so wretchedly covetous are they grown) that they toil their servants while they can labour, and consume their strength and spend them out: and then when age cometh, and the bones are full of ache and pain, and the body feeble and faint, they turn them out of the doors, poor and helpless into the wide world to shift for themselves as they can; and they must either beg or steal or starve, for any relief they shall receive from their masters, in whose service they have spent all their time and strength. And thus it cometh to pass that many become thieves and vagrant beggars through their master's niggardliness that would not do his duty in bestowing some proportionable and competent relief upon them".[2]

1. S. Hartlib, *Legacy of Husbandry* (1655), p. 43. Enclosure contributed to labour discipline. "The use of common land by labourers operates upon the mind as a sort of independence", said the *Board of Agriculture Report on Shropshire* in 1794. Enclosure will make them "work every day in the year", and so secure "that subordination of the lower ranks of society which in present times is so much wanted" (quoted by Dona Torr, *Tom Mann and his Times*, 1961, p. 528).

2. Dod and Cleaver, *op. cit.* (19th ed., 1662), p. 199 (the fifth commandment). The first (unauthorized) edition appeared in 1603, in which this passage was even more strongly worded. (In the edition of 1607 it was almost as quoted above.) The reader who, on the basis of this passage, supposes that the authors cherished a sentimental sympathy for vagrants is asked to suspend judgment until he has read their remarks quoted on pp. 275–6. Note the use, at the beginning of the sentence, of the words "most men", where the meaning is "most employers". For real-life illustrations, see MacCaffrey, *Exeter*, pp. 94–5.

Professor Tawney once summed up the processes we have been describing in a justly famous phrase: "Villeinage ceases but the Poor Laws begin".[1] If he had added "and debt servitude begins", he would have been virtually quoting seventeenth century opinion. For Dod and Cleaver also wrote: "Albeit that villeinage and bondage be not now in use among us, yet imprisonment [for debt] is not altogether out of use. And every one is so far in servitude, and in the creditor's power, as he wanteth ability to pay his debts. He may well be said to be another man's servant whose state and liberty doth stand at another man's courtesy". The moral which the authors drew was "to be good husbands for our estates . . . and in Christian providence for our present condition, if not to get, yet to save, as to preserve our goods, so to retain our freedom".[2] "True freedom", said Gerrard Winstanley in 1652, "lies where a man receives his nourishment and preservation, and that is in the use of the earth".[3] It was not long before the Diggers, from premisses similar to those of Dod and Cleaver, were arguing for the abolition of wage labour altogether; and reform of the debtors' law was a regular demand with all the radicals during the revolutionary period.

v

Part of the attraction of the discipline, then, was in relation to the problem of pauperism. Thomas Cartwright had believed that the multitude of rogues and beggars in England, despite the many excellent laws against them, was due to the absence of deacons. In a properly constituted disciplinary system, he thought, the Church's officers would be able to overcome "riot, adultery, covetousness, pride, idleness, etc", which were the cause of "diseases, beggary, translations of inheritance from the right heirs, needless dearths, seditions, rebellions, (whereof every one is an engine able to pull down the commonwealth)".[4]

1. R. H. Tawney, *The Agrarian Problem in the 16th century* (1912), p. 46; cf. pp. 266–70.
2. Dod and Cleaver, *Proverbs XI–XII*, pp. 101–2; cf. M. H. Dobb, *Studies in the Development of Capitalism* (1946), Chapters 4 and 5, and H. N. Brailsford, *The Levellers and the English Revolution* (1961), pp. 125–9, on the debtor-creditor relationship in industry.
3. Winstanley, *The Law of Freedom* (1652), in *Works* (ed. Sabine) p. 519.
4. A. F. Scott Pearson, *Church and State: Political Aspects of Sixteenth Century Puritanism* (1928), p. 22.

The specific function of deacons should have been to look after poor relief, Bucer had said in advocating their institution, since "it is not possible . . . that any private man should so certainly search out the disposition of the poor as those that be appointed to that office by the church, and daily be exercised with all diligence therein".[1] Deacons, working in conjunction with elders, would really know who were the idle and who were the industrious in the parish: they would be anxious to encourage the latter and discourage the former; they would be able to exercise control by withholding relief from the idle poor;[2] and behind them would stand the powerful sanction of excommunication at the disposal of the presbytery. Legislation, as Cartwright pointed out, was not enough. Rogues and vagabonds still swarmed. Why? For Cartwright the answer was obvious: deacons, elders and the discipline of the primitive Church had not been restored.[3] A pamphlet attributed to Cartwright praised the presbyterian preachers because they "denounce them no brethren" who "are commonly given to idleness by giving over or ceasing their calling".[4] Philip Stubbes, and many after him, observed that the Reformed churches abroad set us a good example in having no beggars.[5]

In England and Scotland alike Presbyterians struggled for the appointment of lay financial officers – deacons – elected

1. Bucer, *A Treatise, How by the Worde of God Christian mens Almose ought to be distributed*, p. 18. Cf. J. Udall, *A Demonstration of Discipline* (1588), ed. Arber (1880), pp. 55–8; Bunyan, *A Discourse of the Building . . . of the House of God*, in *Works*, II, p. 583.

2. Deacons did exactly that at Norwich in 1571 (Tawney and Power, *Tudor Economic Documents*, II, pp. 322–5; Jordan, *Charities of Rural England*, pp. 237–9).

3. Strype, *Life of Whitgift*, I, pp. 131–2. A pamphlet published over a century later put the economic point rather more crudely and directly than Cartwright. Lay elders, it stated, had the duty of presenting "such persons whose vices are the concomitants, or rather the natural consequences, of idleness and luxury" ([Anon.], *St. Paul the Tent-Maker*, 1689, p. 18).

4. *A reproofe of certeine schismatical persons* (1588), in *Cartwrightiana* (ed. A. Peel and L. H. Carlson, 1951), pp. 243–6. Cf. also Henry Arth[ington]'s *Provision for the Poor* (1597), quoted in Tawney and Power, *Tudor Economic Documents*, III, p. 447.

5. P. Stubbes, *The Anatomie of Abuses*, Part III, pp. 45–50; L. Andrewes, *A Sermon Preached at the Spittle* (1588), in *XCVI Sermons* (1841–3), V, p. 436; Burnet, *History of the Reformation*, III, pp. 535–6. Cf. Heylyn's sneer, apropos of Scotland in 1578: "The discipline must be of most excellent use, which could afford a present remedy to so many mischiefs" (*History of the Presbyterians*, 1670, pp. 213–14).

by and responsible to their congregations, who would have handled ecclesiastical revenues. So congregations could have safeguarded themselves against misuse of parochial revenues by a single incumbent; so the great revenues usurped by bishops would have reverted to the purposes for which they were originally intended, poor relief.[1] We can see these simultaneous intentions of relieving the poor and enhancing the importance of the parish at work in the Dedham Classis.[2] We can see something similar in the Parliament of 1597, when "a group of Puritans . . . had made the problem of poverty their concern", and wanted to use impropriations and other clerical livings to solve it.[3]

At the Reformation men so diverse as Starkey, Brinkelow and Crowley had hoped to see the poor, as well as preachers, financed from the spoils of the monasteries.[4] The attempt to use monastic revenues for poor relief, or for education, had failed: nor were episcopal properties used for these purposes in England as the Puritans suggested and as they were in Scotland. Aylmer in 1559 urged bishops to give up their possessions to the Queen in order that schools and a preaching clergy might be provided; but he did nothing to carry out his recommendation when he became a bishop himself.[5] At Exeter the municipal authorities had great difficulty in getting the dean and chapter to fulfil even their legal obligations in the sphere of poor relief; they had to conduct a similar struggle before they could establish a school free from clerical control.[6]

VI

Only after the defeat of the classis movement did the new attitude towards poverty attain full clarity and coherence in

1. Donaldson, *The Scottish Reformation*, pp. 197–8.
2. Usher, *The Presbyterian Movement in the Reign of Queen Elizabeth passim*.
3. Neale, *Elizabeth I and her Parliaments, 1584–1601*, pp. 347–8.
4. Zeeveld, *The Foundations of Tudor Policy*, p. 162; R. Crowley, *Select Works*, p. 7; and see p. 255 above.
5. John Aylmer, *An Harborough for Faithful and True Subjects* (1559), p. 148. But this background may have contributed to the failure of so many bishops to resist the stripping of the property of their sees which the Queen and her courtiers carried out so ruthlessly (see *E.P.C.*, chapter 2).
6. MacCaffrey, *Exeter*, pp. 103, 108, 120–5; cf. Jeremy Taylor's warning of the dangers lying in the wealth of the Church if it is not expended in charity (*The Whole Works*, 1836, I, p. 78).

England, with William Perkins as its chief formulator. I have[*]
tried elsewhere to analyse Perkins's contribution.[1] He was
forced to conclude that the very poor must be wicked, since
"rogues, beggars, vagabonds . . . commonly are of no civil
society or corporation"; "they join not themselves to any
settled congregation for the obtaining of God's kingdom".[2]
Those who were members of no stable community, and their
families, had no access to the means of grace, sacraments and
sermons. They were outside the commonwealth and Church.
Taking a hint no doubt from Genesis iv, 12, where Cain was
condemned to be "a vagabond and a runagate . . . in the
earth", Perkins decided that vagrants "are (for the most part)
a cursed generation".[3] Indiscriminate charity enabled the
idle poor to evade the obligations of living in society. They
should be set on socially useful work, as was in fact done in
Cambridge in Perkins's time.[4] For by diligence in a calling
vagabonds might be restored to community life, to a disciplined congregation, and to the promise of salvation offered
to believers through the Church.[5]

The attitude is conveniently summarized by Dod and
Cleaver: "Another point of honesty is to take order for the

1. See my *Puritanism and Revolution*, pp. 215–38; also a communication by V. Kiernan in *P. and P.*, No. 3.

2. Perkins, *Workes*, (1609–13), I, p. 755; III, p. 191; cf. epigraph to
this Chapter.

3. *Ibid.*, III, p. 191. Genesis iv, 12 is quoted from the Geneva translation, which Perkins used. Sir Walter Ralegh observed that vagabonds
were cut off from God's promises (*History of the World*, 1820, I, p. 154),
and told his son that charity should not be given to them (*Works*, 1751,
II, p. 354). The point was accepted without question by Thomas
Shepard, in his Preface to Peter Bulkeley's *Gospel Covenant* (quoted by
P. Miller, *Errand into the Wilderness*, p. 65). Readers of *The Holy War*
will recollect that in Mansoul the vagabonds sided with Diabolus and
acted as spies for him (Bunyan, *Works*, III, p. 348). Cf. *Puritanism and
Revolution*, pp. 228–31.

4. E. M. Hampson, *The Treatment of Poverty in Cambridgeshire,
1597–1834* (1934), pp. 12, 17, 26.

5. The ordinance of 8 April 1644 instructed J.P.s to send rogues and
vagabonds to church on Sunday: they were to be given their chance.
Strolling players were particularly obnoxious to Elizabethan legislators
and preachers. They often led a wandering, vagabond life; they took no
part in productive activity; and in others they encouraged idleness on
working days, or Sabbath-breaking, or both (R. Weimann, "Zur
Entstehungsgeschichte des elisabethanische Dramas", *Zeitschrift für
Anglistik und Amerikanistik*, IV, p. 213; M. C. Bradbrook, *The Rise of
the Common Player*, 1962, pp. 46–7, 58). See also pp. 492–3 below.

poor in good sort. First for rogues and runagates who, being strong and lusty, make begging and wandering their trade of life; that they be severely punished and set to work: that no maintenance or allowance be given unto them (without punishment, unless they will settle themselves to labour): for so the Apostle speaketh, *He that will not work, let him not eat.* And what more dishonest thing can be in a Christian commonweal than that such men should be permitted? which fill the land with sin, making their life nothing else but a continual practice of filthiness, theft and idleness (which are sins of Sodom), that live without a calling, without magistracy, without ministry, without God in the world; that neither glorify God, nor serve the prince, nor profit the commonweal: but are an unprofitable burthen to the earth or blot to the state, and (as drones) live on other men's labours, and on the sweat of other men's brows. These filthy persons and unprofitable generation, this refuse and off-scouring of the world, must be purged away by the hand of the magistrate, in whose hand there is power, and to whom God hath for this intent committed the sword, that such rotten branches may either be cut off or mended. . . . For the best mercy to such is to help them out of their sin, by giving them [employment or] due correction, till they do content [*sic*] to labour and eat their own bread".[1] The authors (on what authority is not clear) quote Job xxx, 1–8 as the "sentence the Holy Ghost gives of these young and lusty vagrants", that "they were villains, and the sons of villains", who have so defaced the image of God "as that they be not to be compared to the dogs". Neither the Geneva nor the Authorized Version appears to apply this passage to vagabonds. We may contrast that good Protestant, Thomas Lever, who a bare 50 years previously had declared, apropos of beggars, that "the vilest person upon earth is the lively image of almighty God".[2]

The attitude of Dod and Cleaver was well on its way to acceptance in puritan and business circles by the eve of the civil war. Our authors, who assumed that God instituted the market and trade, found it necessary in another of their very

1. Dod and Cleaver, *The Ten Commandements*, pp. 218–20. In the unauthorized first edition (1603), the words in the first square bracket were not present; and the whole passage speaks only of punishment, not of providing work. By 1607 the text was almost as quoted.

2. Lever, *Sermons* (1901), p. 78.

popular works seriously to assure their readers that it was possible for a man to go hungry without this proving that he was a reprobate.[1] "The poor in all places", wrote Hildersam, "are for the most part the most void of grace, and not so miserable in their corporal as in their spiritual state".[2] "Many are poor awhile though labouring", Bayne admitted reluctantly; yet he was sure that "God at length doth bless them", even on earth.[3] George Wither included "indiscreet and fond compassion" for the poor among the passions pilloried in *Abuses Stript and Whipt*, finding men "often erring in their charity".[4] Thomas Heywood regarded refusal of charity to the idle as a specifically puritan attitude.[5] Yet it was more general than that. Thomas Whythorne, writing probably in the fifteen-seventies, noted that people account the poor wicked.[6] A future bishop could argue that if a poor man was idle and untoward "it is alms to whip him". Such persons were "scabs, filth and vermin", "base excrements of the commonwealth". "He that helpeth one of these sturdy beggars to the stocks and the whip and the house of correction not only deserveth better of the commonwealth, but doth a work of greater charity in the sight of God, than he that helpeth him with meat and money and lodging".[7] Another budding bishop, of Calvinist sympathies, wrote: "Thou art very poor: who made thee so? If thine own negligence, laziness, improvidence, unthriftiness, rash engagements, thou hadst reason to bear that burthen which thou hast pulled upon thine own shoulders. . . . If the mere oppression and injury of others, thou shalt the more comfortably run away with this cross, because thine own hand hath not been guilty of imposing it".[8] Heads the rich win, tails the poor lose! "Poverty

1. Dod and Cleaver, *Proverbs*, IX–X, pp. 60–4; XI, pp. 2–3.

2. Hildersam, *CLII Lectures upon Psalme LI*, p. 118.

3. P. Bayne, *Commentary on Ephesians* (1866), p. 294.

4. Wither, *Juvenilia* (Spencer Soc. Reprint), I, p. 132. Cf. also the Proclamation of the English rulers of Scotland on 4 July 1653 (the day the Barebones Parliament met): "Forasmuch as multitudes of vagabonds, masterful beggars, strong and idle persons, are to the great dishonour of God and eminent prejudice of the inhabitants ..." (Firth, *Scotland and the Commonwealth*, Scottish History Soc., XVIII, 1895, p.155).

5. See p. 26 above.

6. Ed. J. M. Osborn, *The Autobiography of Thomas Whythorne* (1961), p. 140.

7. Sanderson, *XXXV Sermons*, pp. 87–97, 197–9.

8. J. Hall, *The Balm of Gilead*, in *Works* (1837–9), VII, pp. 167–8.

is the greatest dishonesty", declared Sir Thomas Roe sardonically.[1] The high priest of the Perkins tradition in New England,
Cotton Mather, was later to say "for those who indulge themselves in idleness, the express command of God unto us is that
we should let them starve".[2]

Such sentiments found a natural echo in the minds of a
certain type of employer and J.P. Francis Trigge noted in 1604
how much more diligent some magistrates were "to see the
poor whipped" than to execute the statute made at the same
time for the maintenance of tillage and rebuilding decayed
farms.[3] "Men are so busy in examining the poor about their
estate and desert", said Robert Allen, "that they can find no
leisure to open their purses or relieve their wants".[4] In the
autumn of 1590 vagrants were being whipped and branded by
the Middlesex Quarter Sessions at the rate of one a day.[5]

VII

But our emphasis should not be merely upon the simpler
economic motives. The new attitude towards charity arose
directly and naturally from the central tenets of protestant

"We are ashamed of poverty", said Archbishop Tillotson, "because the
poor man is despised and almost ridiculous in the eye of the proud and
covetous rich man" (*Sermons*, 1748, IX, p. 111).

1. Sir T. Roe, *Country Newes*, in *Miscellaneous Works . . . of Sir
Thomas Overbury*, p. 174.

2. C. Mather, *Durable Riches* (1695), quoted by E. A. J. Johnson,
American Economic Thought in the 17th century (1932), p. 31. "They
have sculpture against begging but no bread against famishing", was
Thomas Adams's comment (*The Happines of the Church*, ii, pp. 132-3).
It was the kindly Sir Edward Hext who realized that whipping was no
remedy (Tawney and Power, *Tudor Economic Documents*, ii, p. 343; cf.
my *Puritanism and Revolution*, pp. 222, 233). For Hext's own charitable
foundation for the poor, see Jordan, *The Forming of the Charitable
Institutions of the West of England* (Trans. American Philosophical
Soc., New Series, L, Part 8, 1960), p. 56.

3. [F. Trigge], *The Humble Petition of Two Sisters, the Church and
Commonwealth* (1604), Sig. C 3. The same point was made in *Stanleyes
Remedy* (1646, written c. 1606), p. 8, quoted by E. M. Leonard, *The
Early History of English Poor Relief* (1900), p. 243.

4. R. Allen, *The Odoriferous Garden of Charity* (1603), p. 40, quoted
by C. H. and K. George, *The Protestant Mind of the English Reformation,
1570-1640*, p. 158.

5. Leonard, *op. cit.*, p. 71. I owe this reference to Mrs. Joan Simon.

theology – predestination and justification by faith, not by works. The end of belief in Purgatory-pick-purse had economic consequences: a pamphleteer writing in 1635 suggested that the lenient landlords were those old-fashioned men who believed that they could be saved from Purgatory by the prayers of their tenants.[1]

Nor should we be too startled at the apparent severity of many virtuous Puritan ministers. Punishments were savage for all kinds of crime: pain and death were omnipresent in men's lives. Humanitarianism was irrelevant to those who believed in the fixed decrees. No minister whose imagination pictured the mass of the lower orders writhing in eternal torment could regard their poverty and unhappiness on earth as of more than minor significance. He was much more concerned with the social evils of vagrancy, and with the mental and moral attitudes which perpetuated it. But again his approach was primarily theological. The protestant ethic emphasized not the routine good work, but the motive behind it. "If I give alms only for my reputation's sake" – the words are attributed to King James – "these are wicked deeds, because there is *nullum medium*, whatsoever is without faith is sin".[2]

Bishop Bedell, that great admirer of Perkins, was especially praised by his son for his behaviour, whilst rector of an English parish, "towards the beggars, bedlams and travellers, that use to come to men's doors. These he would not fail to examine, mixing both wholesome instructions and severe reproofs. Nor rested he there; but if they had any passes to travel by, he would be sure to scan them thoroughly, and finding them false or counterfeit, his way was to send for the constable, and after correction given according to law, he would make them a new pass and send them to the place of their last settlement or birth. This", the biographer admiringly adds, "made him so well known among that sort of people that they shunned the town for the most part, to the no small quiet and security of him and

1. T. Powell, *The Art of Thriving*, in *Somers Tracts* (1809–15), VII, pp. 204–5. The Crown and members of the ecclesiastical hierarchy, Powell suggested, were also lenient landlords.

2. *Crumms fal'n from King James's Table*, in *Miscellaneous Works of Sir Thomas Overbury* p. 262; cf. J. Preston, *The Breastplate of Faith and Love* (5th ed., 1634), pp. 180, 187. I have discussed this point at greater length in "Protestantism and the Rise of Capitalism", *Essays . . . in Honour of R. H. Tawney*, 1961.

all his neighbours".[1] We may compare the city of Lincoln's
attempt to solve its unemployment problem in 1634 by enact-
ing that henceforth no inhabitant should take upon him or her
to educate any children that were likely to prove chargeable to
the rates, except their own, unless they first gave notice to, and
obtained the approbation of, the mayor and one or more of
the aldermen, on pain of a fine of £5 for each offence.[2]

Sir William Petty's will, not inappropriately, sums up the
new attitude at its most enlightened. "As for legacies to the
poor", he declared, "I am at a stand; as for beggars by trade
and election, I give them nothing; as for impotents by the hand
of God, the public ought to maintain them; as for those who
have been bred to no calling nor estate, they should be put
upon their kindred; . . . wherefore I am contented that I have
assisted all my poor relations, and put many into a way of
getting their own bread; have laboured in public works; and by
inventions have sought out real objects of charity; and I do
hereby conjure all who partake of my estate, from time to time,
to do the same at their peril. Nevertheless, to answer custom,
and to take the safer side, I give £20 to the most wanting of the
parish wherein I die".[3] The logic is impeccable; the bark is
worse than the bite; and Petty, if anyone, had in fact "by
inventions sought out real objects of charity". But the attitude
was to be taken over by business men less reasonable, less
kindly and less inventive than Petty.

Some of the preachers saw the dangers of their own logic.
Lewis Bayly, after denouncing indiscriminate alms-giving to
impudent vagabonds, nevertheless added: "But if thou meetest
one that asketh an alms for Jesus sake, and knowest him not to
be unworthy, deny him not: for it is better to give unto ten
counterfeits than to suffer Christ to go, in one poor saint,
unrelieved".[4] Similarly it was apropos of charity that Richard
Capel urged us to "beware that religion be not made a cover for
our covetousness". "This deceit", he added sorrowfully, "such

1. Ed. E. S. Shuckburgh, *Two Biographies of William Bedell* (1902), p.
19. Cf. Tillotson's funeral sermon on Thomas Gouge in *Sermons* (1748),
II, pp. 100, 103.

2. *MSS. of Lincoln, etc.* (H.M.C.), p. 100.

3. Quoted, naturally enough, in Samuel Smiles's *Self-Help* (1911), p.
252.

4. L. Bayly, *The Practice of Piety* (55th ed., 1723), pp. 293-4.

are most subject to who are religiously given".[1] One believes him. It is worth glancing forward to Richard Baxter's considered answer to the question, "Can one be prodigal in giving to the poor?" for Baxter himself was an extremely generous man, who gave nearly half his income in charity.[2] His reply was, "Yes, when it is blindly done, to cherish idleness in wandering beggars; or with a conceit of meriting in point of commutative justice from God; or when that is given to the poor which should be given to other uses (as in public tribute, maintenance of children, furtherance of the Gospel, etc.) But", Baxter added, "this is a sin that few have need to be restrained from".[3]

John Hales, then, was a rare exception, and by implication acknowledged that he was, when he gently criticized "an intempestive prudence and unseasonable discretion in performing that little good we do, from whom so hardly after long inquiry and entreaty drops some small benevolence. . . . How many occasions of Christian charity do we let slip when we refuse to give our alms unless we first . . . examine the persons, their lives, their necessities. . . ."[4]

To the new view of alms-giving the recipient was almost irrelevant. "It is not the thing given, but the merciful and pitiful heart of the giver . . . that makes our giving to the poor to be alms".[5] Charity is a duty to God and ourselves even more than to our neighbour. In giving to others we must also look after our own estates and families, Joseph Hall, John Downame and Richard Stock all insisted.[6] This attitude was later effectively satirized by the Ranter Abiezer Coppe: "Besides (saith the holy Scripturian Whore) he's worse than an infidel that provides not for his own family. . . . Have a care of

1. R. Capel, *Tentations, their Nature, Danger, Cure* (6th ed., 1658), I, p. 331. First published 1633. Cf. *ibid.*, p. 16, for the pressures of society.

2. H. Newcome, *Autobiography* (ed. R. Parkinson, Chetham Soc., 1852), p. 344.

3. R. Baxter, *Chapters from a Christian Directory* (ed. J. Tawney, 1925), p. 170. First published 1673.

4. J. Hales, *Golden Remaines* (1659), p. 35.

5. Perkins, *Workes*, III, p. 104.

6. J. Hall, *Works*, I, p. 252; J. Downame, *The Plea of the Poor* (1616), pp. 130–8; Stock, *Commentary upon Malachi*, II, p. 59. They might have quoted St. Augustine, who wrote: "He who wishes to give alms in due order, ought to begin with himself, and give alms first to himself" (*Enchiridion to Laurentius on Faith, Hope and Charity*, in *Seventeen Short Treatises of St. Augustine*, 1885, p. 131).

the main chance".[1] Sir Thomas Browne bluntly stated that "I give no alms only to satisfy the hunger of my brother, but to fullfil and accomplish the will and command of my God; . . . for this is still but moral charity, an act that oweth more to passion than to reason". Men guarded themselves against the sin of indulging in indiscriminate alms-giving. The poor existed as objects of the charity of the rich, Browne and many others tell us:[2] but this charity must be reasonable, socially responsible. The assumption, sharply contrasting with early protestant hopes, is that poverty will continue.

Thomas Hobbes thought that what men usually called charity was either "contract, whereby they seek to purchase friendship, or fear, which maketh them to purchase peace".[3] The sage of Malmesbury, one suspects, wrote with his tongue in his cheek; but as the puritan ideal faded in the later seventeenth century the author of *The Whole Duty of Man*, in all seriousness, wrote of charity as a form of social insurance, "a kind of rent charge" which God had laid on landlords' estates. We should give prudently, carefully choosing out the fittest objects of charity, ignoring the slothful and the lewd. Sometimes a seasonable loan, without interest, might stimulate industry in the recipient more than a gift.[4] Such behaviour is economic activity directed to political and social objectives, comparable (in a different field) to the use of famine relief as a weapon against communism after World War I, or Marshall Aid after World War II. For Defoe's complete English tradesman, annual and regular charitable gifts were a part of his balance sheet.[5]

1. A. Coppe, *A Flying Fiery Roll* (1650), in N. Cohn, *The Pursuit of the Millennium* (1957), pp. 366–8.
2. Sir T. Browne, *Religio Medici* (Everyman ed.), pp. 67, 87; cf. W. Penn, *Some Fruits of Solitude* (1693), Part II, No. 287.
3. T. Hobbes, *The Element of Law* (ed. F. Tönnies, 1928), p. 34; cf. p. 31.
4. [Anon.], *The Works of the Learned and Pious Author of the Whole Duty of Man* (1704), I, pp. 138–42; II, p. 72. Cf. Perkins, *Workes*, III, pp. 104–5. There is a vivid discussion of the two types of charity, indiscriminate and selective, mediaeval and modern, in the conversation between Springlove and Randal in Richard Brome's *A Jovial Crew* (1652), Act I, scene i: acted 1641.
5. D. Defoe, *The Complete English Tradesman* (1841), II, p. 21. First published in 1727. Cf. G. R. Cragg, *The Church and the Age of Reason (1648–1789)* (1960), p. 130.

The famous words of the (much later) hymn

> *"Whatever, Lord, we give to Thee*
> *Repaid an hundredfold shall be;*
> *Then gladly, Lord, we give to Thee".*

expressed (for the propertied class as a whole) an observed truth about this world, as well as (for charitable individuals) a hypothesis about the next. A member of the Long Parliament quoted King James as his authority for the statement that "though alms-deeds merit not at God's hands, yet they make Him our debtor according to His gracious promise".[1] The sentiment of the hymn was also expressed by Thomas Gouge in sober prose: "Christian charity rightly performed is the surest way to plenty and abundance, it being usually rewarded with temporal blessings here, as well as with eternal hereafter".[2] Isaac Barrow agreed that "Liberality is the most beneficial traffic that can be; it is bringing our wares to the best market; it is letting out our money to God, Who repays with vast usury: an 100 to 1 is the rate He allows at present, and above a hundred millions to one He will render hereafter".[3]

The Whole Duty went even further, inculcating the duty of charity *to the rich*. "Whenever we can further their profit without lessening our own store, it [charity] requires it of us: nay, if the damage be but light to us in comparison of the advantage to him, it will become us rather to hazard that light damage than lose him that greater advantage".[4] What neater argument to persuade, for instance, villagers to undergo the light damage of loss of common rights in order that an enclosing landlord should enjoy unquestionably greater advantages! Such a morality could only be preached to and by a class for whom the

1. Edward Leigh, *A Treatise of the Divine Promises* (3rd ed., 1650), p. 361. First published in 1633.
2. T. Gouge, *The Surest and Safest Way of Thriving* (1673), p. 9. The statement is very carefully documented at pp. 20–32, ending with the example of the author's own father, the William Gouge so often quoted in these pages: "How wonderfully God blessed, as his ministry, so his outward estate, is . . . well known". The Leveller Richard Overton had taken a rather less charitable view of the elder Gouge's business acumen: see D. M. Wolfe, "Unsigned Pamphlets of Richard Overton", *Huntington Library Quarterly*, XXI, p. 196, and references there.
3. Isaac Barrow, *The duty and reward of bounty to the poor*, in *Theological Works* (1859), I, p. 91; cf. also pp. 55, 79.
4. *The Works of the Author of the . . . Whole Duty of Man*, p. 138.

accumulation of capital had become an absolute good in itself, good not merely for the individual capitalist but (by a happy dispensation of Providence) for society as well because of the productive activity which his capital would set on foot. A more sophisticated age would express this in the formula "Private vices, public benefits". But in the seventeenth century the new morality was too insufficiently established, still too unsure of itself, to admit that society could benefit by vice.[1]

VIII

The administration of poor relief during the years 1640–60 still awaits thorough investigation.[2] During this period experiments were made in the penal withholding of relief: so control of its distribution became a matter vital to power in the parish. Some attempts had been made to use poor relief in this way before 1640. About 1586 the rector of Grimsby was criticized in the Church courts because he gave his alms only "to such as were careful to learn the points of religion".[3] A sixteenth-century suggestion made at Ipswich, that poor relief should be distributed on Sunday afternoons, only to those who had attended service, was not accepted.[4] But the puritan churchwardens of St. Edmund's, Salisbury, decided in 1629 to withhold relief from absentees from church.[5] In 1618 a London merchant had vested in the Skinners' Company the administration of £30 a year for the relief of the poor in Basingstoke, to be paid only to those who should attend the puritan lectures which he had founded in the town.[6]

The interregnum gave new opportunities for the exercise

1. I have strayed beyond my limits in quoting Barrow and *The Whole Duty*, both published after the revolution. But their ideas were only developments of their predecessors', as Mandeville in his turn developed theirs. Fuller in *The Holy State* (1648, pp. 154–5) comes very near to Mandeville's formulation. Cf. p. 469 below.

2. But see A. L. Beier, "Poor Relief in Warwickshire, 1630–60", *Past and Present*, No. 35.

3. Marchant, *The Puritans and the Church Courts in the Diocese of York*, p. 26.

4. Thomas, *Town Government in the 16th century*, pp. 120–1. The author gives no date for this incident.

5. Ed. H. J. F. Swayne, *Churchwardens' Accounts of St. Edmund and St Thomas, Sarum* (Wilts. Record Soc., 1896), p. 190.

6. Jordan, *The Charities of London*, p. 111.

of this kind of control. An Essex minister refused relief to those who did not come to his church.[1] In 1641 the Warwickshire justices awarded 1*s.* a week to Roger Hodgkins on condition that he attended his parish church every Sunday and collected it there.[2] We may compare Bishop Burnet's adjuration to the clergy, to be "strict at least in governing the poor, whose necessities will oblige them to submit to any good rules we shall set them for the better conduct of their lives".[3] That naïve admission came at a date when there was no prospect of a national presbyterian system. the idle aristocracy no longer need fear that discipline would be imposed on them. Only the poor remained, "whose necessities will oblige them to submit", whether the rules imposed on them were good or bad.

What is not clear is the effect of the abolition, during the revolution, of the church courts, and the failure to establish a presbyterian system. Was Sir Matthew Hale right when he described England, about 1659, as "more deficient in their prudent provision for the poor than any other cultivated and Christian state"?[4] Professor Jordan's statistical approach suggests, on the contrary, that there was better provision for the poor after 1640 than in the sixteen-thirties.[5] There were certainly some gains: pressure from Levellers and Major-Generals helped to get charitable funds restored to the poor which had hitherto been misappropriated by ruling oligarchies – e.g. in High Wycombe.[6] The extent to which such funds had been embezzled before 1640, how far they were restored either under Charles I or during the interregnum, and whether they were all lost again with the restoration of oligarchy in 1660 – this would be a fruitful subject for research. A character in Davenant's *News from Plymouth* built his house

1. H. Smith, *Ecclesiastical History of Nonconformity in Essex*, pp. 142–3.

2. Ed. S. C. Ratcliff and H. C. Johnson, *Warwickshire Quarter Sessions Order Book, 1637–50* (Warwick County Records, 1936), p. 106.

3. Burnet, *History of the Reformation*, III, p. xix.

4. Quoted in S. and B. Webb, *The Old Poor Law*, p. 95.

5. Jordan, *Philanthropy in England*, pp. 137–9; *The Charities of Rural England*, pp. 40, 96, 100, 222, 243–4, 274, 288, 341; cf. L. J. Ashford, *The History of the Borough of High Wycombe from its Origins to 1880* (1960), pp. 126, 134–5.

6. W. H. Summers, "Some Documents in the State Papers relating to High Wycombe", *Record of Bucks*, VII, pp. 512–17; Ashford, *op. cit.*, p. 138.

"in that year I was
Collector for the poor, a profitable time,
And I thank heaven, I made good use of it".[1]

Only on rare occasions like 1649–50 do we hear the voice of, for instance, London journeymen weavers denouncing the governors of their corporation for embezzling money intended for the poor;[2] or a pamphleteer speaking of "the poor of England which . . . daily perish in the streets, fields and ditches, defrauded of larger provisions made for them by laws and legacies than any other nation".[3] Nothing, naturally, came of the Leveller proposal that such misappropriation should be prevented in future by allowing the poor to elect their own trustees to manage the revenues intended for them.[4]

By 1660 parochial poor relief worked after a fashion as an entirely lay system, without the support of a national Church. Thanks mainly to the efforts of private charity, and to the removal of restrictions on industry, the problem was no longer so pressing. Henceforth even the pretence of state regulation was abandoned, and each parish went its own way. J.P.s were no longer supervised by the Privy Council. With Privy Council interference, serious attempts to set the poor on work were also abandoned: state policy now concentrated on restricting the mobility of labour.[5] Meanwhile, too, new forms of relationship between congregations and the State were developing. The voluntary principle in religion has affinities with a maturer stage of development of free enterprise, with the free contract

1. W. Davenant, *Dramatic Works* (1872–4), IV, p. 160; cf. Richard Brome, *The Queenes Exchange* (1657), Act II, scene ii. The subject deserves full investigation. Some chance bits of evidence will be found in Strype, *Life of Whitgift*, II, p. 375; ed. J. B. Leishman, *The Three Parnassus Plays* (1949), p. 77; ed. B. Mellor, *The Poems of Sir Francis Hubert* (Hong Kong, 1961), p. xv; Andrew Morton (?Daniel Defoe), *Parochial Tyranny: or, the Housekeepers complaint . . . with a Detection of many abuses committed in the Distribution of Public Charities* (n.d. ?1727); W. Kennett, *Parochial Antiquities* (1695), Preface; T. F. Thiselton-Dyer, *Old English Social Life as told by Parish Registers* (1898), pp. 34–6; Palmer, *Episcopal Returns for Cambridgeshire*, p. 60; Lord Leconfield, *Petworth Manor in the 17th century* (1954), pp. 38–9; G. Huxley, *Endymion Porter* (1959), pp. 228–9; *Life of Master John Shaw*, p. 147.

2. Brown, Bland and Tawney, *English Economic Documents*, p. 311.

3. J. Jones, *The New Returna Brevium* (1650), pp. 48–9.

4. *The Earnest Petition* (1648); H. N. Brailsford, *The Levellers and the English Revolution* (1961), p. 323.

5. Lipson, *Economic History of England*, II, pp. cxlvii–ix.

system. The imposition of discipline on a national scale ceased to be the main problem when capitalism had securely established itself in the economically advanced areas of England; and by then the sects had won a relative freedom for their own autonomous life.

The early sectarian churches recaptured something of the early Christian attitude towards charity, in assisting unfortunate members of their closely-knit underground communities. This did not occur without struggle or recession. In 1557, in the exiled church at Frankfurt, the majority, composed largely of poorer members, are found trying to remove the elders and capture the church machinery. "The church was above the pastor, not the pastor above the church" they said. The issue was the reorganization of poor relief, and the radical group was led by John Hales, whose social views had been too extreme for Edward VI's government. So economic problems, among others, drove lower-class members of the congregation towards separatism, election of ministers, a real congregational control: the rich, equally naturally, saw more advantages in episcopal nomination of ministers or a consistorial discipline.[1] The self-assertion of the lower orders brought discipline itself into discredit with the respectable classes just at the time when it most needed their support, complained George Gifford in 1590: "When the common artificer, the apprentice and the brewer intrude themselves and they will guide the same, being ignorant, rash and heady, what worldly-wise man will not take it that discipline herself is but a bedlam?"[2]

Social services were an important part of the activities of the early sectarian congregations. Bancroft's chaplain in 1607 criticized the Family of Love because they "say they are not bound to give alms but to their own sect".[3] Henry Ainsworth in 1617 distinguished between poor relief, which is "not by the appointment of the church . . . but by the appointment of the magistrate", and the Church's "ecclesiastical collection by their deacons".[4] The Presbyterians of Norwich claimed in 1646 that their clergy had persuaded the city magistrates to double

1. M. M. Knappen, *Tudor Puritanism* (1938), pp. 155–9.
2. G. Gifford, *A Short Treatise against the Donatists of England* (1590), quoted by Knappen, *op. cit.*, p. 311.
3. T. Rogers, *The Faith, Doctrine and Religion, professed and protected in . . . England* (1681), p. 231.
4. B. Hanbury, *Historical Memorials* (1839–44), I, p. 348.

the poor rates; but they admitted that the poor were better off in congregational churches.[1] For a long time the nonconformist sects (particularly the more radical of them – Baptists, Quakers and Muggletonians) maintained this tradition of help to their members, over and above public relief, or to save them from it. Bunyan advised deacons to use relief to encourage industry and discourage idleness.[2] It seemed an especially dirty trick when in 1668 the House of Commons decided that fines on dissenters should be devoted to poor relief, in order to encourage the poor to denounce them.[3]

This activity is what we should expect. The sectarian congregations were drawn largely from the small masters, those economic groups among whom the relations between employer and employee was least depersonalized. Among them the old tradition survived longest, that social security was a right which the community owed to its members, though now the community was voluntary, not geographical.[4] As an individual prospered, he very often ceased to be a nonconformist and joined the established Church. Others, even after the patriarchal bond between employer and worker was weakened, and the congregation's unity had been undermined by economic divisions, would still recognize the usefulness of congregational charity in inducing the poor to belong to *some* church.

1. J. Stoughton, *History of Religion in England* (1881), I, p. 498. On the generosity of the independent churches, see the claims of Mrs. Katharine Chidley in *The Justification of the Independent Churches of Christ* (1641), pp. 43–4. For relief of members by Bunyan's congregation, see G. B. Harrison, *The Church Book of Bunyan Meeting, 1650–1821*, *passim*.

2. Bunyan, *Works*, II, pp. 582–3.

3. Ed. C. Robbins, *The Diary of John Milward* (1938), pp. 252, 282.

4. Dorothy George, *England in Transition* (Penguin ed.), pp. 97–8, 137–8. Cf. also J. K. Fuz, *Welfare Economics in English Utopias* (The Hague, 1952), *passim*.

Chapter Eight

The Bawdy Courts

The division between the clergy and the temporal law is full of great peril to the state, as much as the discontent of the common people against the gentry.

Journal of Sir Roger Wilbraham, 1607, in Camden Miscellany, X (ed. H. S. Scott, 1902), p. 96.

The best and surest tenure by which every freeborn subject holds the right and property of his goods is the law of the land. But let the subject be brought into one of their ecclesiastical courts . . . and be his cause never so just . . . they will tear a man out of all his estate. . . . At those boards . . . how quickly shall they and their whole estates be swallowed up! . . . . And to the end that the civil state may be subservient to the ecclesiastical church, these ecclesiastics have their oar in every boat, and their finger in every pie, where anything may be plucked from the subject. . . . None can be sure that his goods are his own, when all, and more than all, are taken from him at one censure, and that at the will and pleasure of the board, without any and against all law.

[Anon.], Englands Complaint to Jesus Christ against the Bishops Canons (1640), Bv–B2v.

Two leeches they have that still suck and suck the kingdom – their ceremonies and their courts. . . . For their courts, what a mass of money is drawn from the veins into the ulcers of the kingdom this way; their extortions, their open corruptions, the multitude of hungry and ravenous harpies that swarm about their offices, declare sufficiently. . . . Their trade being, by the same alchemy that the Pope uses, to extract heaps of gold and silver out of the drossy bullion of the people's sins. . . . What stirs the Englishman . . . sooner to rebellion, than violent and heavy hands upon their goods and purses?

Milton, Of Reformation in England, in Prose Works (Bohn ed.), II, pp. 402–4.

I

THE Church had its own hierarchy of over 250 courts, which had come down from the Middle Ages, like the rest of the institutional backbone of the State, little modified by the Tudor monarchy. They came under thunderous attack from the protestant reformers, but they emerged unscathed. By 18 Eliz. cap. 7 the special right of the clergy to be tried by their own courts was abolished. Benefit of clergy had previously been abolished for petty treason, murder, felony and various kinds of robbery. It survived, for first offences, as in effect a social privilege, since most sons of the upper and middle classes were sufficiently educated to stumble through the neck verse. Ben Jonson in 1598 thus escaped the penalty for killing a man. In 1613–14, 61 out of 130 persons sentenced to death by the Middlesex Quarter Sessions successfully claimed benefit of clergy and so escaped with a branding.[1] "Many times murderers and notorious thieves are but warmed a little in the hand, because they can read; and another for a sheep or trifle is hanged because he cannot read".[2] A Balliol freshman who knifed another undergraduate in 1624 got off without even having his palm warmed.[3] In addition to being a social privilege, benefit of clergy was also an exclusively male privilege: women had no clergy. But there were curious anomalies. It was solemnly argued in 1631 that a man might have his clergy if he stood mute when accused of rape, but not when accused of buggery, since this was felony by 25 Henry VIII cap. 6.[4]

Such other changes as had resulted from the Reformation did not diminish the power of the ecclesiastical courts. Pro-

1. Ed. W. Le Hardy, *Middlesex Sessions Records*, New Series, I, p. vii; cf. Coke, *10 Reports* (1616), Poulter's Case; *III Institutes*, pp. 114–15; F. Makower, *The Constitutional History of the Church of England* (1895), p. 449; Sir W. Holdsworth, *History of English Law*, III, pp. 299 sqq.; L. C. Gabel, *Benefit of Clergy in the Middle Ages* (Northampton, Mass., 1929), pp. 124–5. The parallel mediaeval privilege of sanctuary was abolished in Henry VIII's reign, except for parish churches and churchyards, which retained it until a statute of 1624. (The London "liberties" of course survived far longer.)

2. [Anon.], *The Laws Discovery* (1653), in *Harleian Miscellany* (1744–56), II, pp. 556–7.

3. H. W. C. Davis, *A History of Balliol College* (revised ed., 1963), p. 113.

4. Rushworth, *Historical Collections*, II, pp. 94–5.

fessor Sykes, indeed, suggested that their jurisdiction, and their tendency to encroach on common-law jurisdiction over the laity, was substantially increased by the statutes of Henry VIII's reign.[1] The right of appeal was transferred from Rome to Canterbury and York. A regular system of visitation and presentment was evolved in place of the more haphazard mediaeval processes; visitations became more frequent and more thorough, leading to complaints in the House of Commons in 1597 of "the covetous use of visitations".[2] The Court of High Commission was introduced as an organ of centralization and over-riding government control, performing similar functions for the Church to those of Star Chamber *vis-à-vis* the civil administration.

Thomas Cromwell, appropriately enough, had stopped the teaching of canon law at the universities. But despite many demands, canon law was neither abolished nor codified: it was deemed to remain in force in so far as it was not repugnant to the statutes of the realm, or to common law.[3] Cranmer had attempted to produce a revised code of canon law, and Parker published this *Reformatio Legum Ecclesiasticarum*, with John Foxe as editor. But Elizabeth stopped Parliament discussing this book, and it never had any authority. There were here vast possibilities of confusion, disagreement and reinterpretation. In a debate on usury in the House of Commons in 1571, Mr. Clarke said that "the canon law is abolished".[4] Marprelate threatened to have a *praemunire* issued against the bishops for erecting canon law above the law of the land, and four years later Nathaniel Bacon suggested that Bishops' chancellors were "so much affected to the canon law that some are affected with the Popish religion".[5] Robert Browne appealed to common law against "certain Popish canon laws, which though the magis-

1. Review in *E.H.R.*, LXXIII, p. 298.

2. B. L. Woodcock *Mediaeval Ecclesiastical Courts in the Diocese of Canterbury* (1952), p. 69; Strype, *Life of Whitgift*, II, p. 375.

3. Ed. Cardwell, *The Reformation of the Ecclesiastical Laws* (1850), Introduction; Burnet, *History of the Reformation*, V, p. 397, Burnet attributed to this failure to produce an ecclesiastical code the slowness and expense of the Church courts, and the weakness of "all church discipline". Cf. Cardwell, *Documentary Annals*, I, p. 436.

4. Sir S. D'Ewes, *The Journals of all the Parliaments during the Reign of Queen Elizabeth* (1682), p. 171.

5. Pierce, *Historical Introduction to the Marprelate Tracts*, pp. 262–3; Neale, *Elizabeth I and her Parliaments, 1584–1601*, p. 283.

trate do tolerate for a time, yet the common good laws of the land are wholly against them".[1] Abolition of canon law was demanded by some Puritans, since it was "wholly contrary to the will of Christ"; it should be replaced as an administrative code by the word of God. Others, more simply, declared that canon law was "already wholly annihilated and made void", "utterly abolished".[2]

II

In what spheres had the Church courts competence? The Canons of 1604 defined the following offences as liable to presentment before the subordinate ecclesiastical courts: "adultery, whoredom, incest, drunkenness, swearing, ribaldry, usury" and any other "uncleanness and wickedness of life", schism, interference with church services or rude and disorderly behaviour in church, defending popish and erroneous doctrine, not communicating at Easter, hindering the execution of the Canons of 1604. Bacon added accusations against ministers tending to their suspension, deprivation or degradation, simony, heresy, blasphemy and Sabbath-breaking.[3] The Church courts also claimed cognizance over perjury, but after 5 Eliz. cap. 9 this was effective only in cases where the perjury had been committed in the ecclesiastical court.[4] Offenders

1. R. Browne, *An Answere to Master Cartwright* (?1585), in *Writings of Harrison and Browne*, pp. 433–4.
2. Barrow, *A Briefe Discoverie of the False Church* (1590), p. 82; Udall, *A Demonstration of Discipline*, pp. 65–6; Milton, *Prose Works* (Bohn ed.), III, p. 432; W. Stoughton, *An Assertion for true and Christian Church-Policie*, Dedication, p. 11, and text, pp. 39–49; *The Gentlemens Demands unto the Bishops* (1605), quoted in T. Rogers, *The Faith, Doctrine and Religion, professed, and protected in . . . England*, p. 236. The general uncertainty of the situation between Reformation and civil war is brought out by F. W. Maitland, *Roman Canon Law in the Church of England* (1898), chapters IV–VI, and in *The Canon Law of the Church of England* (Report of the Archbishops' Commission, 1947), pp. 47–51. In the preparatory discussions for the Hampton Court Conference some Puritans called for codification (Babbage, *Puritanism and Richard Bancroft*, p. 77). They can hardly have liked what they got in the Canons of 1604. And much was still left indeterminate.
3. Bacon, *Works*, X, p. 113. See *A Remonstrance of the Commons of England to the House of Commons* (1643?) for a list of the offences which were now unpunished because of the abolition of Church courts (*Somers Tracts*, 1748–51, VI, pp. 258–9).
4. Under this count Church courts had dealt with debt cases before the Reformation (Woodcock, *op. cit.*, pp. 90–2, 100–8); but during our

under these categories were to be presented by churchwardens to the bishop or his representative, said the Canons of 1604; if churchwardens failed to present, "either through fear of their superiors or through negligence", the duty of presentment fell on the minister.[1]

The Archdeacon's Courts looked after the church fabric, and so were involved in questions affecting rights to pews. They inquired into the doctrine and behaviour of ministers. Laymen might be presented for nonconformity, for failing to attend church regularly, for speaking ill of ministers or church wardens, for not paying church rates. All these offences were regarded as "sins", punishable by exclusion from church or by excommunication; these penalties in their turn had to be redeemed by penance, quite apart from any penalties which the secular courts might inflict.[2]

If we consider a list which Prynne gives of cases taken to the church courts which should properly be tried at common law, it will be observed that nearly all of them affect in one way or another the property of the subject: tithes; probate of wills dividing lands of inheritance; alimony; sequestrating men's goods and livings and depriving ministers of their freehold in their livings; fining men for contempts; impleading them for debts, trespasses, defamations; trials of rights, patronages, glebe lands. Other grievances included compelling men by excommunications to give up suits at common law; stopping prohibitions; persecuting, fining and imprisoning opponents in the High Commission, "the chief use whereof is now only to advance, protect and defend their own usurped ecclesiastical episcopal jurisdiction".[3] It is a comprehensive indictment; and it is a list of abuses to which many of the gentry and the indus-

---

period they no longer exercised effective jurisdiction in this field (Sir W. Holdsworth, *History of English Law*, IV, p. 516). See also Coke, *5 Reports* (1612), p. 9.

1. See especially Canons 109–19. For evidence of "fear of superiors" acting as a deterrent, see pp. 377–9 below.

2. Strafford was accused at his trial of giving to Irish bishops and their lay officials power to arrest and imprison those "of the meaner and poorer sort" who proved refractory to ecclesiastical discipline. His defence was that such powers had been granted by former Deputies to Irish bishops (Rushworth, *The Tryal of Thomas Earl of Strafford*, 1680, pp. 236–40).

3. Prynne, *A Breviate of the Prelates intollerable usurpations* (1637), pp. 250–1; cf. Strype, *Life of Whitgift*, II, pp. 374–5.

trious sort could have subscribed who did not share Puritan objections to bishops on theological grounds. Property was much better looked after at common law. Dr. Lambe, the mayor and burgesses of Northampton had complained to the Parliament of 1621, took upon him "to prove gifts and tries titles of lands". "The bishops", Alford commented, "if we look not to them, . . . will encroach upon all men's rights and lands in England".[1] The church courts even claimed jurisdiction in a case of theft in the sixteen-thirties, when an accusation of sorcery was involved.[2]

The greatest grievance concerned tithes and wills, "for these be matters of profit and in their nature temporal", Bacon advised James I; they were also the most numerous cases.[3] Disputes between parsons and parishioners over tithes and other dues were hotly contested between ecclesiastical and common-law courts.[4] Jurisdiction over probate was also frequently challenged by the common-law courts.[5] Probate actions formed the largest single group of cases heard before the Archdeacon of Huntingdon's court in the years 1590–6: 121 cases out of 418, 26·5%.[6] Testamentary business was an important source of fees, and officials of the church courts kept a close watch on the moribund.[7] Their exactions were "intolerable", said a petition of 1641 against Bishop Wren.[8] A character of a Commissary published in 1631 said "He looks

1. N.R.S., IV, pp. 346–7, III, pp. 260, 433.

2. F. W. Bull, *A History of Newport Pagnell* (1900), p. 109.

3. Bacon, *Works*, X, p. 113.

4. Emmison "Abstract of the Act Book of the Archdeacon of Huntingdon's Court", *Transactions of the East Hertfordshire Archaeological Soc.*, VIII, pp. 28–9 (69 cases out of 418); Stoughton, *op. cit.*, pp. 90–103; Sir Thomas Ridley, *A View of the Civile and Ecclesiasticall Law* (2nd ed., 1634), pp. 148–51. Such cases formed by far the largest group of citations before the Peculiar Court of Wimborne Minster in the sixteen-thirties (J. M. J. Fletcher, "A Century of Dorset Documents", *Proceedings of the Dorset Natural History and Antiquarian Field Club*, XLVII, p. 48).

5. Kennedy, *Elizabeth Episcopal Administration* (Alcuin Club Collections, XXVII), pp. 184, 348, and *passim*; Stoughton, *op. cit.*, pp. 103–6; Ridley, *op. cit.*, pp. 134–8. Laud's views are expressed in his letter to Bramhall of 5 April 1637, in *Hastings MSS*. (H.M.C.), IV, pp. 72–5.

6. Emmison, *op. cit.*, pp. 28–9.

7. E. R. C. Brinkworth, "The Laudian Church in Buckinghamshire", *University of Birmingham Historical Journal*, V, p. 55.

8. Palmer, *Episcopal Returns for Cambridgeshire*, p. 75.

not so much to the performance of the will as the payment of his fees".[1] Bulstrode Whitelocke's father was in trouble in the early sixteen-thirties for preparing a deed of gift to prevent his personal estate being inventoried and discovered by "the harpies of the ecclesiastical court".[2] Coke's "continued malice against the jurisdiction of the church in testamentary matters" was revealed in Sir Edward's own will, which, Sir Henry Marten said, might have served as "a precedent to both men and women how to out the church of all power . . . in their real and personal estates".[3] "Sole probate of wills" was one of the counts against bishops in the Long Parliament's Committee on Church Government.[4] Stoughton urged in 1604 that tithes, wills and matrimonial suits should be handed over to the common-law courts – as they were to be after the abolition of episcopacy.[5] This of course would have had far-reaching effects, especially in tithe causes, since the common-law courts were far more sympathetic to the interests of lay property owners than the church courts, which from time to time tried to help ministers to increase the amount they might collect as tithe.[6] In 1647 a pamphleteer even argued that the abolition of ecclesiastical courts should lead to the abolition of the tithes they sued for.[7]

Ecclesiastical jurisdiction over matrimonial causes – not only marriages, but also contracts, wives not living with their husbands, adultery, bastardy – was a continual source of irritation. Parker wrote to Burghley in 1573 that "the clamorous cry of some needy wives and husbands do compel us to take their matters out of their common bribing courts, to ease their griefs by commission";[8] but not everybody agreed that it was as simple as that. When in 1631 the High Commission fined Sir Giles Alington £12,200 for marrying his niece, many might

1. F. Lenton, *Characterismi* (1631), No. 4.

2. R. H. Whitelocke, *Memoirs, Biographical and Historical, of Bulstrode Whitelocke* (1860), pp. 72–4.

3. Henry Marten Papers, Political and Miscellaneous, Brotherton Library, Leeds, II, ff. 36–7. I owe this reference to the kindness of Professor C. M. Williams.

4. Sir R. Verney, *Notes of Proceedings in the Long Parliament* (Camden Soc., 1845), pp. 5, 12–13.

5. Stoughton, *op. cit.*, pp. 90–106.

6. *E.P.C.*, Chapter 5, *passim*.

7. [Anon.], *The Husbandmans Plea against Tithes* (1647), pp. 62–6.

8. Parker, *Correspondence* (Parker Soc., 1853), p. 450.

think the fine excessive who did not condone the offence.[1] In 1638 a Cambridgeshire couple was presented for not living together, though the husband pleaded that he was a poor man who had been away looking for work.[2] The church courts allowed separation for adultery, but not remarriage. The High Commission was more generous in giving alimony to separated wives than the common-law courts.[3] This did nothing to endear it to the gentry in that exclusively male body, the House of Commons.

Leighton thought that men spent not less than £50,000 per annum on matrimonial suits, and £100,000 on probate of wills; another £100,000, he thought, was "drawn out of the people's purses for visitation fees, pleas and jangling-matters".[4] In the Long Parliament Hyde went so far as to say that the church courts should incur a *praemunire* if they meddled with probate of wills or matrimonial causes.[5] D'Ewes likewise thought Sir John Lambe had incurred a *praemunire* by charging "the freehold of the subjects of England" to pay for organs. "They meddle with property as if we did owe it to them", said Maynard.[6]

Church courts also prosecuted unlicensed medical practitioners (i.e. those who were not graduates of Oxford or Cambridge, and who had not purchased a licence either from a university or from a bishop). This was outside London: in the capital control lay with the College of Physicians. Religious orthodoxy seems to have been as important as skill in procuring an episcopal licence. Surgeons, male or female,[7] midwives

1. See p. 338 below.

2. Palmer, *Episcopal Returns for Cambridgeshire*, p. 50.

3. Bacon, *Works*, XIII, p. 90.

4. A. Leighton, *Sions Plea against the Prelacie* (?Holland, 1628), pp. 121, 263–4. Leighton gives the total as £200,000, not £250,000: so matrimonial suits may be included in the second £100,000. The figures are presumably a mere guess, and are not likely to under-estimate. But they occur in a passage in which Leighton very accurately assessed the value of bishops' lands.

5. W. A. Shaw, *A History of the English Church, 1640–60* (1900), I, p. 91. The laws known as *praemunire* were originally introduced to protect lay rights in ecclesiastical property against the Church.

6. Ed. W. Notestein, *Journal of Sir Simonds D'Ewes* (Yale University Press, 1923), p. 386; cf. p. 447, p. 156.

7. For a female surgeon licensed by the Bishop of Norwich in 1568, see R. S. McConaghy, "The History of Rural Medical Practice", in *The Evolution of Medical Practice in Britain* (ed. F. N. L. Poynter, 1961), p. 124.

and schoolmasters or -mistresses also had to be licensed by a bishop – at a price. Here again the effect of the activities of the courts was to interfere with the free processes of the market, by which men and women sold their skills, real or alleged, to those who wanted to buy them. The church courts frequently used their powers to prevent a deprived puritan minister from earning his living as a doctor.[1]

Like J.P.s, church courts had the power, not shared by the ordinary common-law courts, to order some positive action to be taken, and could insist on their being notified that it had in fact been taken. They were thus administrative as well as judicial bodies: judges and prosecution were often closely associated if not identical. One of the great achievements of the seventeenth century in the secular sphere was precisely the separation of administrative from judicial functions, the prevention of the evolution in England of any system of *droit administratif*: the same end was gained in the ecclesiastical sphere after 1641 by the abolition of High Commission. But the many men who in the early seventeenth century used the law in order to avoid decisions being taken particularly resented this power of the church courts to enforce positive action, and much preferred the dilatory common law with its negative approach. If the integrity of the ecclesiastical courts had been above reproach, there would have been much to be said in favour of this aspect of their procedure in that litigating age. But it was not, as we shall see.

III

In the seventeenth century the courts remained very active, and their activity seems even to have been on the increase under Laud. Down to 1640 the Archdeacon's Court in Oxfordshire and Buckinghamshire sat regularly during term, for many years weekly, and never with intervals of more than three weeks.[2] In 1636 the Court of the Archdeacon of Colchester held 42 sessions at four different towns; in 1639–40 1,800 persons came before the 30 sittings of the Archdeacon of London's Court. Three-quarters of the number were charged

1. For examples, see my *Intellectual Origins of the English Revolution* (1965), Chapter 2 and references there cited.
2. Brinkworth, "The Laudian Church in Buckinghamshire", p. 103.

with misbehaving during divine service, with Sabbath-breaking or non-observance of saints' days.[1] In the Court of the Arches in the sixteen-thirties one judge might hear up to 360 cases *a day*.[2] More modestly, the High Commission heard 80–120 cases a day.[3]

Some fees in church courts were regulated by 21 Hen. VIII cap. 5. But as prices rose this was put out of date, and courts began to increase their fees. In 1585 a bill "pretending only a redress of some exorbitancies in excessive fees, but aiming plainly at the jurisdiction" of church courts, failed to pass thanks to Elizabeth's showing her dislike of it.[4] There was an even tougher fight over a bill introduced into the Commons in 1597 against excessive fees, "which in some places will be proved to be increased from 12*d*. to 20*s*." It was resisted by the bishops on the grounds that the value of the pound had fallen, and that judges and lawyers were dependent for their livelihood on what they got in fees. It was also alleged that the bill was "but a device of some such as seek to overthrow the ecclesiastical government and to create the presbyterian and new platform of popular government". Nevertheless, Whitgift tried to meet criticism by issuing, in Convocation of the same year, a revised table of fees and charges, which was confirmed by the Canons of 1604.[5]

But this did not stop fees being raised. In the Parliament of 1621 a bill was introduced to have the table of 1597 printed *in English* (not Latin), and to allow common-law judges to try and punish those who extorted more than the table authorized.[6] The bill did not pass. In the sixteen-twenties and -thirties the

1. Hale, *A Series of Precedents and Proceedings*, pp. xxxi,liii–iv.

2. Miss Slatter's Oxford B.Litt. thesis, "A Biographical Study of Sir John Lambe" (1952), p. 116.

3. Usher, *High Commission*, p. 260.

4. Heylyn, *History of the Presbyterians*, p. 307.

5. S.P. 16/250/29; Tanner MS. 280, f. 326 (I owe these references to Professor G. E. Aylmer); Strype, *Life of Whitgift*, II, pp. 374–8; D'Ewes, *Journal*, p. 565; Neale, *Elizabeth I and her Parliaments, 1584–1601*, pp. 357–8; Cardwell, *Synodalia*, pp. 324–6; Wilton Hall, *Records of the Old Archdeaconry of St. Albans*, pp. 111–12. See also W. Bohun, *A Brief View of Ecclesiastical Jurisdiction* (1733), pp. 20–8; C. I. A. Ritchie, *The Ecclesiastical Courts of York* (Arbroath, 1956), pp. 185–6, 228–31.

6. N.R.S., II, pp. 388, 442; IV, p. 434; E. Nicholas, *Proceedings and Debates of the House of Commons in 1620 and 1621* (1766), II, pp. 11, 99, 200.

Commission on Fees spent much time considering fees exacted by ecclesiastical courts since 1568–9 – more time apparently than Laud thought proper for such a lay body.[1] That some fees were well worth having is shown by the sharp struggle waged in the early seventeenth century between the Archdeacon of St. Albans and the Bishop of London over their respective rights to issue marriage licences.[2]

Fees had to be paid to officers of the church courts, on pain of ex-communication, whether defendants were found innocent or guilty – which of course put a premium upon malicious suits, especially those started by apparitors and summoners of the courts.[3] From Robert Browne to Milton this was a standing puritan complaint, since the officers of these courts depended on fees for their living.[4] A certificate of discharge, even after acquittal, cost the defendant 13s. 4d., over and above fees to the court and its apparitors.[5] In 1600–1 a man charged with lying with a neighbour's wife, acquitted after compurgation, still had to pay costs of £1 3s. 4d. on pain of excommunication; and in 1640 10 labourers of Tenterden, an old Lollard centre, who had refused to pay tithe on wages, were also acquitted by the church court but had to pay 15s. or 16s. costs each.[6] Prynne alleged that for probate of wills the fees were in his day three to six times what Henry VIII's statute allowed. Alford said they were 20 times the ancient customs.[7] In 1641 the Commissary at Ipswich was accused to the House of Commons

1. G. E. Aylmer, "Charles I's Commission on Fees, 1627–40", *Bulletin of the Institute of Historical Research*, XXXI, pp. 60–2, 66.

2. R. Peters, "The Administration of the Archdeaconry of St. Albans, 1580–1625", *Journal of Ecclesiastical History*, XIII, p. 66. The ensuing correspondence covers the years 1602–15; but the archdeacon went on issuing licences after that date.

3. Ware, *The English Parish in its Ecclesiastical and Financial Aspects*, pp. 52–3.

4. *Writings of Harrison and Browne*, p. 445; *Shirburn Ballads, 1585–1616* (ed. A. Clark, 1907), pp. 306–10.

5. F. D. Price, "Elizabethan Apparitors in the Diocese of Gloucester" *Church Quarterly Review*, CXXXIII, p. 45.

6. J. Lindsay, *Civil War in England* (1954), p. 42; ed. L. B. Larking, *Proceedings principally in the County of Kent* (Camden Soc., 1862), p. 231. Contrast, however, a speech by Nathaniel Fiennes in Nalson, *An Impartial Collection*, I, p. 677. For compurgation see pp. 299–300, 375–6 below.

7. Prynne, *A Breviate of the Prelates intollerable usurpations*, p. 209; N.R.S., VII, p. 508.

of extorting extreme fees, "and would not, though required to it, hang up a table of fees".[1]

IV

What made the Church courts peculiarly obnoxious was their attempt to enforce standards of conduct, which had been appropriate enough to an unequal agrarian society, long after large areas of England had left such a society behind. The common law was busily adapting itself to the needs of the growing business sector in English life.[2] But the church courts persisted in interfering with matters of trade and credit. They punished laymen for working on saints' days, or for not coming to church on New Year's day: the common-law courts tried to prevent them.[3] In 1638 a parson was in trouble with the church courts for exercising the charitable office of midwife without a licence; a petition against Wren 3 years later alleged that his officials insisted on women being presented for teaching in schools.[4] A Londoner had been presented in 1620 for sitting in the same pew as his wife; another man was fined 54s. for wearing a dirty ruff at church.[5] The courts proceeded, often on the basis of mere scandal and gossip, by placing men on oath, with penalties for perjury. Their business was conducted in Latin, a language incomprehensible to most Englishmen. They retained the archaic oath of compurgation, by which men from the locality were called upon to testify not to the *fact* of the accused's guilt or innocence, but to the general *belief* in it.[6] This procedure was still in full swing in the sixteen-thirties. Like everything else in the ecclesiastical courts, compurgation was an expensive business. In 1591 Lewis Billings of Barking, who had failed to secure sufficient local testimony to his innocence, pleaded "he is a very poor man, and not able to

1. Ed. Notestein, *Journal of Sir Simonds D'Ewes*, p. 414.
2. D. O. Wagner, "Coke and the Rise of Economic Liberalism", *Econ. H.R.*, VI, No. 1, *passim*.
3. N.R.S., III, p. 260; IV, pp. 346–7; VII, p. 607; F. W. Bull, *A History of Newport Pagnell* (1900), p. 109; Usher, *Court of High Commission*, pp. 191–2; Skaife, "Extracts from Visitation Books at York", *Yorkshire Archaeological Journal*, XV, pp. 237, 241.
4. Palmer, *Episcopal Returns for Cambridgeshire*, pp. 64, 75.
5. Thiselton-Dyer, *Church Lore Gleanings*, p. 192; N.R.S., II, p. 368.
6. *C.S.P.D., 1635–6*, p. xxxi.

procure his neighbours to come to the court and bear their charges".[1] Comment on that would be superfluous. Fortunately neighbours were sometimes more amenable. A Cambridgeshire lady was dismissed upon purgation for incontinence in 1638, though "we verily believe her to be guilty of the crime, and do marvel at the boldness of the compurgators for taking so rash an oath".[2]

Whatever the advantages of relying on the testimony of neighbours in a genuine community where everybody knows everybody else's business (and even here tale-bearing and malicious gossip must have been encouraged), there is clearly little to be said for it in a modern urban society. The common law was already discarding such antiquated procedures. Having to testify on oath put a severe strain on the consciences of business men who made their money by outwitting their competitors whilst just keeping on the right side of the law: the common-law presumption of innocence until guilt is proved suited them far better. Excommunication, if its redemption by public and humiliating penance in church or at the church porch is enforced, is a much severer penalty in a business community, where "credit" is essential to success, than in a village of subsistence farmers.[3] But in fact penance was often commuted for money, at the discretion of the judges, even in very serious cases. Similarly the well-to-do might get their cases heard *in camera*, or be absolved by proxy.[4] This lent itself to abuse, and not all judges were above suspicion. Barrow attacked the courts for allowing men to buy themselves off

1. Hale, *A Series of Precedents and Proceedings*, p. 205.
2. Palmer, *op. cit.*, p. 65; cf. Ritchie, *op. cit.*, pp. 162–5.
3. See Grindal's directions for penance in his *Remains* (Parker Soc. 1843), pp. 455–7; cf. Brinkworth, "The Laudian Church in Buckinghamshire", pp. 34–5. The one thing that worried William Walwyn about being arrested as a Leveller was that it might have a bad effect on his credit as a silk-merchant (Walwyn, *The Fountain of Slaunder*, 1649, in *The Leveller Tracts*, ed. W. Haller and G. Davies, Columbia University Press, 1944, p. 248).
4. For examples, see F. D. Price, "An Elizabethan Church Official – Thomas Powell, Chancellor of Gloucester Diocese", *Church Quarterly Review*, CXXVIII, pp. 99, 108; "Elizabethan Apparitors in the Diocese of Gloucester", *ibid.*, CXXXIII, pp. 44–5; Hodgkinson "Extracts from the Act Books of the Archdeacon of Nottingham", *Trans. Thoroton Soc.*, XXX, pp. 32–8; A. C. Wood, "Nottinghamshire Penances (1590–1744)", *ibid.*, XLVIII, p. 53; Brinkworth, *op. cit.*, pp. 35–7; Ritchie *The Ecclesiastical Courts of York*, pp. 167–71.

penance for adultery.[1] Penance might also be commuted for social reasons, and this would increase the hostility of small men to courts which were class-prejudiced as well as corrupt and arbitrary.[2] In 1580 one of a series of articles delivered to the House of Lords from the Lower House of Convocation, asking very properly "that there shall not henceforth be used any commutation of penance", felt it necessary (or prudent) to suggest that exceptions might occasionally be made "either for some great value or dignity of the person, or for fear of some desperate event that will follow in the party that should be put to open shame".[3] Sir John Lambe advised James I that commutation of penance "is not only lawful but (by the common law) the ordinary ought to commute *si sit liber homo*".[4] So feudal was society still.

The system of presentment loaded the dice against the poor and middling sort. "Mean persons", it was said in the Parliament of 1597, had to appear "for small causes" at the same time that there was "a toleration of offences in great persons . . . because none doth present them. These mighty men, they make a profession of sin".[5] Only the High Commission seems to have inflicted public and humiliating penance on offenders from the landowning class.[6] In 1641 the *First and Large Petition of the City of London* argued that "the prelates' corrupt administration of justice" was responsible for "the great increase and frequency of whoredoms and adulteries".[7] Milton agreed that vulgar men loved "the corrupt and venial discipline of clergy courts" and hated true discipline.[8]

As public opinion swung against the courts and against

1. H. Barrow, *A Briefe Discoverie of the False Church* (1590), pp. 232–3, in Carlson, *op. cit.*, p. 624.
2. For evidence see Hale, *A Series of Precedents and Proceedings*, pp. 184, 187, 233, 237, 247–8; Kennedy, *Elizabethan Episcopal Administration* (Alcuin Club Collections, XXVII), pp. 329–30; Price, "An Elizabethan Church Official", *passim*; Marchant, *The Puritans and the Church Courts in the Diocese of York*, p. 26; cf. *The Writings of Harrison and Browne*, pp. 47, 445.
3. Strype, *Life of Grindal* (1821), p. 587.
4. N.R.S., VII, p. 607. A bill against commutation of penance had passed in the Commons in 1571.
5. Strype, *Life of Whitgift*, II, pp. 374–5.
6. See p. 338 below.
7. Printed in *Complete Prose Works of John Milton* (Yale ed.), I, p. 982.
8. *Ibid.*, II, p. 279.

penalties for "sin", public penance may even have ceased to be effective. As early as 1587 Penry asked "what it is . . . to pay a little money, or to run through the church in a white sheet? They have made rhymes and songs of this vulgar penance".[1] William Bell, who in 1632 was ' overtaken with drink" whilst performing a penance imposed by the Durham High Commission, can hardly have taken it all too seriously; but he was too poor a man to be worth fining, so the publicity no doubt did him less harm.[2] In theory church courts (the High Commission excepted) could not fine or imprison. In fact there are examples of imprisonment;[3] and court fees and money taken in commutation of penance were difficult to distinguish *de facto* from fines. Theoretically penance could only be commuted if the money paid went *in pios usus* – e.g. for repairs to the local church, or St. Paul's, or for the relief of the poor.[4] Dr. Lambe, the city of Northampton alleged in 1621, when urged to apply to charitable uses money taken for commutation of penance, remarked that charity began at home.[5]

The unpopularity of the ecclesiastical courts was something more specific than "rivalry between laymen and clerics". It resulted from a revolt of the industrious sort of people against the institutions and standards of the old régime. Such men were not likely to be convinced, as Convocation tried to convince them in 1606, that Christ, by the words "Tell it unto the church", had authorized church courts such as existed in England, as the last remedy against an erring and unrepentant brother. For "the Church" now took the form of a distant professional lawyer. But if "*ecclesia*" were translated not "church" but "congregation", what a difference would be made![6]

1. Ed. David Williams, John Penry, *Three Treatises Concerning Wales*, p. 35.
2. Ed. W. H. D. Longstaffe, *Acts of the High Commission Court within the Diocese of Durham* (Surtees Soc., 1858), pp. 31–2; cf. *V.C.H. Gloucestershire*, IV, p. 336; Price, "An Elizabethan Church Official", p. 112.
3. F. S. Hockaday, "The Consistory Court of the Diocese of Gloucester", *Transactions of the Bristol and Gloucestershire Archaeological Soc.*, XLVI, pp. 202–3.
4. Ware, *The Elizabethan Parish in its Ecclesiastical and Financial Aspects*, pp. 19–20.
5. N.R.S., IV, pp. 346–7; cf. p. 354 below.
6. *Bishop Overall's Convocation Book* (1689), pp. 130–1; cf. p. 137. The reference is to Matthew xviii, 17. Many other illustrations could be given

In countless ways the church courts interfered with the free workings of the market. The High Commission rebuked printers for bad work and high prices; money-lenders were cited before the church courts, together with those who allowed their employees to work on saints' days or November 5.[1] The imposition of heavy fines and penances for delivering corn or opening shops on saints' days, even when they coincided with market day, was one of the charges made against Lambe in the 1621 Parliament. His defence, that in Northampton, from which the charge originated, "the holy days are much neglected", and that he might have proceeded against many more shopkeepers than he actually did, misses the main point of the accusation.[2] How could business flourish until this sort of supervision and interference, however spasmodic, had been utterly overthrown? It encouraged spies, informers, corruption and blackmail.[3] It must have been with relish that City business men in 1640 signed the Root and Branch Petition which attacked, among other things, "the pressing of the strict observation of the saints' days, whereby great sums of money are drawn out of men's purses".[4] Alderman Hoyle of York, a member of the Long Parliament to whom this petition was presented, was one of those who had been in trouble with the ecclesiastical authorities for opening his shop "on holy days being fair days and market days".[5]

There were thus many reasons for the industrious sort to dislike the church courts, over and above any possible connection between Puritanism and the rise of capitalism. But

---

of the fact that the differences between the various versions of the Bible (Geneva on the one hand, the official versions leading up to the A.V. on the other) often turned on points of great political and social significance. The marginal note on this passage in Tomson's version of the Geneva Bible is confident that Christ "hath regard to order used in those days, at what time *the elders* had the judgment of church matters in their hands" (my italics). A text was no final court of appeal! Cf. p. 105 above.

1. Hale, *A Series of Precedents and Proceedings*, p. 242.

2. N.R.S., II, p. 368; III, p. 260; VI, p. 473; VII, p. 607. Cf. p. 152 above.

3. Price, "Elizabethan Apparitors in the Diocese of Gloucester" pp. 47–53.

4. Gardiner, *Constitutional Documents of the Puritan Revolution*, pp. 141–2. Cf. p. 154 above.

5. Marchant, *The Puritans and the Church Courts in the Diocese of York*, pp. 77–8; cf. p. 171.

since it is difficult to deny that some such connection existed, it is also important for our purposes that the sharpest edge of the church courts was turned against nonconformists, on whose behalf the Canons of 1604 forbad the lay courts to intervene. Penry put this case: "If we be any wise malefactors, if they [i.e. we] be not true subjects unto our prince, let us be committed over unto the civil magistrates. And let not our enemies both accuse, condemn and punish, against law, equity and conscience, where they are the accusers, judge, the parties and the executors. They should not by the law of this land go any farther than their ecclesiastical censures in matters of religion, and then commit us unto the magistrates".[1] This dual role of the church courts, as public prosecutor and judge, became especially resented as earnest men ceased to attend their parish church when the minister was a dumb dog or an absentee, and went to neighbouring churches in search of spiritual food.[2]

The whole conception of punishing "sin", the violation of accepted norms of behaviour, was coming under question. First because the moral revolution which accompanied the rise of capitalism meant that there was no longer the same stable acceptance of standards of conduct as had been assumed in the Middle Ages. Had men, or had they not, the right to do what they would with their own? Which should prevail when individual rights conflicted with the common good? In the age of enclosure, of rack-renting and of widely extended credit relations, such questions met with no simple and universally acceptable answer. But secondly, the protestant emphasis on the internal forum of the conscience as the final arbiter of what was and was not "sinful" also worked against the imposition of external codes of behaviour on those whose consciences did not accept them. "Inferior authority cannot bind the superior", declared Perkins. But all courts of men are inferior to conscience, the tribunal which God has erected in every man's heart. The contrary, Perkins believed, was a "popish opinion".[3] The two processes are no doubt connected, since Protestantism was trying to establish its new standards in face of the disintegration of the old. But

1. Ed. Peel, *Notebook of John Penry*, pp. 46–7.
2. See pp. 65–6 above.
3. Perkins, *Workes*, I, p. 530.

there is considerable difference between standards founded on the inner voice of the individual, which inevitably tells him different things as the society in which he lives is transformed, and the traditional standards accepted by and imposed in the mediaeval communities.

V

If the church courts had carried out their work with un-impeachable integrity, they would still have been unpopular among the industrious sort. But they laid themselves open to additional attack by the notorious fact that they were extortionate and not incorruptible. "In their courts", wrote the judicious Hooker, "where nothing but singular integrity and justice should prevail, if palpable and gross corruptions be found, by reason of offices so often granted unto men who seek nothing but their own gain and make no account what disgrace doth grow by their unjust dealings unto them under whom they deal, the evil hereof shall work more than they which procure it do perhaps imagine . . .". When disciplinary matters are treated as a mere formality at visitations, "fees and pensions being the only thing which is sought, and little else done by visitations, we are not to marvel if the baseness of the end doth make the action itself loathsome".[1] When the hierarchy's chief defender thus by implication admitted both the abuses of the courts and the carelessness of the bishops, we can understand the violence of the puritan opposition.

Nor was Hooker alone in his censures. Archbishop Parker in 1560 had said that "all the people are . . . pressed with continual visitations and the immoderate exactions of procurations and other burdens".[2] Fifteen years later, despite all his efforts, things were little better.[3] Archbishop Sandys said that visitations were "abused by men of corrupt minds", who "reform not offences, but for money grant licences still to offend".[4] In 1573 the Council too had suggested that episcopal visitations were used only "to get money, or for some other purposes", and not for the maintenance of "godly

1. R. Hooker, *Works* (1836), III, pp. 386–7.
2. Strype, *Life of Parker*, I, p. 142; cf. p. 362.
3. Parker, *Correspondence*, p. 473 (Parker to Burghley, February 1575).
4. Ed. J. Ayre, *Sermons of Edwin Sandys* (Parker Soc., 1841), pp. 247, 122.

order", a charge that Burghley repeated 11 years later.[1] In many parishes the cost of visitations might be a major item in churchwardens' accounts, right down to the civil war. The diocese of Gloucester seems to have been especially corrupt, though this may be an optical illusion resulting from the fact that it has been particularly well investigated.[2]

In 1588 the French Ambassador was prepared to generalize about "an infinite deal of roguery" amongst ecclesiastical judges.[3] The Puritan William Bradshaw benefited twice by a judicious bribe administered on his behalf. Once the Bishop of Coventry and Lichfield was persuaded, by an annual brace of bucks, to license Bradshaw to preach in his diocese, despite his suspension by the Bishop of London: on a later occasion the Bishop of London's Chancellor removed his suspension in return for cash down.[4] A lady in Norwich bribed Bishop Harsnett to give Samuel Fairclough his discharge after reference to that bishop of accusations made against him in the High Commission.[5] In 1621 Sir John Bennett, Judge of the Prerogative Court, was fined £20,000 in Star Chamber for corruption. "He was as corrupt a judge as any in England", Yonge noted in his diary, "for he would not only take bribes of both parties, plaintiff and defendant, but many times shamefully begged them".[6] Damaging allegations were made in Parliament in the same year against Dr. Craddock, Chancellor to the Bishop of

1. Strype, *Life of Parker*, II, p. 346; C. Read, *Lord Burghley and Queen Elizabeth*, p. 294.

2. F. D. Price, "Gloucester Diocese under Bishop Hooper", *Trans. Bristol and Gloucestershire Archaeological Soc.*, LX; "The Abuse of Excommunication and the Decline of Ecclesiastical Discipline under Queen Elizabeth", *E.H.R.*, LVII; "An Elizabethan Church Official – Thomas Powell, Chancellor of Gloucester Diocese", *Church Quarterly Review*, CXXVIII; "Elizabethan Apparitors in the Diocese of Gloucester", *ibid.*, CXXXIII. Cf. Ritchie, *The Ecclesiastical Courts of Yorks*, pp. 174–5.

3. Ed. G. B. Harrison and R. A. Jones, *De Maisse's Journal* (1931), p. 20.

4. S. Clarke, "The Lives of some of our English Divines", in *A Martyrologie* (1652), pp. 117, 126. The time appears to be the reign of James I.

5. Palmer, *Nonconformists' Memorial*, II, pp. 430–1. Cf. the passage from Lodowick Muggleton quoted on p. 346 below.

6. Ed. G. Roberts, *Diary of Walter Yonge* (Camden Soc., 1847), p. 37; cf. N.R.S., III, p. 28. Bennett appropriately spent his leisure composing meditations upon the 51st Psalm (*Letters of John Chamberlain*, II, p. 623).

Durham: among others, that he took a bribe of £20 to let one man off, and then fined him £50.[1]

There were many warnings. In 1582 the Privy Council ordered that the instructions of Parliament in the previous year about commutation of penance should be strictly carried out.[2] Two years later Burghley drafted a memorandum in which he declared that "the covetous exactions of [the bishops'] officers make not only the papistical sort but the good Christian subjects to mislike the order of the ministry".[3] There were attacks on church courts in the Parliaments of 1586 and 1589. In 1593 the outcry against them was so great that the Queen promised that Whitgift would inquire into the state of all the church courts in his province. In 1597 the archbishop observed that the "multitude of complaints" in the last Parliament had endangered the very existence of church courts: their officials must be more circumspect in future.[4] In 1601, in response to further complaints in Parliament, Whitgift sent two circular letters to his bishops, which contain some remarkable admissions. The archbishop declared that "by reason of the often keeping of courts by Commissaries and by the Archdeacon's officials, . . . the subject was almost vexed weekly with attendance on their several courts, to their infinite charge and daily vexation". Churchwardens' expenses in attending courts often cost a parish more than a whole subsidy to the Queen, to say nothing of their own losses "in leaving their day-labour for attendance".[5] Whitgift denounced "the infinite number of apparitors and petty summoners hanging upon every court; two or three of them at once most commonly seizing upon the subject for every trifling offence, to make work to their courts". He feared "the greediness of mean inferior registers and apparitors . . . was . . . rooted in them." Adding "the scandal which groweth by commutation of penances" and by granting marriage licences, Whitgift referred ominously to criticisms in the late Parliament and to

1. N.R.S., VI, p. 402; cf. II, p. 369; III, p. 262; cf. p. 351 below.
2. Wilton Hall, *Records of the Old Archdeaconry of St. Albans*, p. 21.
3. Read, *Lord Burghley and Queen Elizabeth*, pp. 293–4.
4. Strype, *Life of Whitgift*, II, pp. 374–5.
5. Cf. the sad entry at Minchinhampton in 1606: 6*s.* 8*d.* laid out at Gloucester "when we were excommunicated for our not appearing when we were not warned to appear" (Price, "Elizabethan Apparitors in the Diocese of Gloucester", p. 52).

the possibility of "the taking away of the whole or most of those courts".[1] In the same year we find Bancroft inquiring throughout the diocese of London into offences "winked at and suffered", or "unpunished and uncorrected, for money, rewards, bribes, pleasure, friendship, or any other partial respect".[2]

The efforts of Whitgift and his successor, thus stimulated by pressure from Parliament, caused a temporary flurry in the dioceses, but seem to have had little long-term effect. There was further criticism in the Parliament of 1614[3] and Whitgift's words were almost echoed in the charges against Lambe in 1621, of "impertinent vexation in frivolous causes". Lambe, the Northampton city fathers alleged, cited "men and women to his courts upon small or no just occasion, but only to enrich himself and his followers". He kept two courts a fortnight, for the most part in remote places, so that suitors had to travel up to 24 miles to them; and then were detained so long that they had to make the return journey in the dark. (Anyone, including a churchwarden, unwilling to interrupt his business activities to travel long distances, in cases perhaps affecting trivial sums, would have to incur the expense of feeing a proctor.) Causes were delayed, "especially about assessments for the repair of churches", so that a parish might have to pay up to £20, £30 or £40 "before they could have an end of it". Lambe was also accused of countenancing opponents of the city government, and of citing many to his court and there troubling them because they had refused to vote for him in the late parliamentary election.[4] In 1641 among the articles of impeachment against Bishop Wren were sale of the profits of a visitation for £500, and taking excessive fees from churchwardens at visitation.[5]

1. Strype, *Life of Whitgift*, II, pp. 446–52. "Registers" = registrars. Cf. *Somers Tracts* (1748–51), XIV, pp. 349, 377.
2. Kennedy, *Elizabethan Episcopal Administration* (Alcuin Club Collections, XXVII), p. 343. For agitated correspondence revealing the ecclesiastical authorities' fear of Parliament, see Wilton Hall, *Records of the Old Archdeaconry of St. Albans*, pp. 92–3 (1595), 104 (1601), 119–22 (1603); R. Peters, "The Administration of the Archdeaconry of St. Albans, 1580–1625", *Journal of Ecclesiastical History*, XIII, pp. 64–5 (1598, 1601, 1603 : Church courts must not be held too often.)
3. Moir, *The Addled Parliament of 1614*, p. 91.
4. N.R.S., IV, p. 346; VI, pp. 471–5.
5. Rushworth, *Historical Collections*, IV, p. 354. Wren's answer was

In February 1630 Bishop Bedell wrote to his archbishop, using words which anticipate the passage from Milton at the head of this chapter: "Against all the impediments to the work of God amongst us, there is not any one greater than the abuse of ecclesiastical jurisdiction. This is not only the opinion of the most godly, judicious and learned men that I have known, but the cause of it is plain. The people pierce not into the inward and true reasons of things, they are sensible in the purse. . . . Let us preach never so painfully and piously; I say more, let us live never so blamelessly ourselves, so long as the officers in our courts prey upon them, they esteem us no better than publicans and worldlings".[1] Bedell was writing from Ireland, but he specifically included England in the accusation: he was indeed only repeating points made by many English critics.

Seven of the 17 Canons of 1640 aimed at remedying abuses in ecclesiastical courts. And Bishop Goodman testified after the overthrow of episcopacy to the existence of defects which Bedell had pointed to before it: "the intolerable abuse of ecclesiastical jurisdiction, . . . the corruption of the spiritual courts".[2] We may agree with Dr. Rowse that as the industrious sort of people grew out of their "mediaeval nonage, so the church's supervision came to be more and more resented: it was probably a greater cause of its unpopularity . . . than any of the doctrinal issues, which are given so much place in the books".[3]

---

that he had not sold the visitation but farmed out the profits: not for £500 but for £430 (C. Wren *Parentalia*, p. 105).

1. R. Parr, *The Life of . . . James Usher* (1686), II, p. 421. So much importance did Bedell attach to this point that he repeated it almost *verbatim* in a letter to Laud six months later (Shuckburgh, *Two Biographies of William Bedell*, p. 311). Cf. Barrow, *A Briefe Discoverie of the False Church* (1590), pp. 228–33.

2. G. Goodman, *The Two Great Mysteries of Christian Religion* (1653), Preface, Sig. a 3v–4.

3. A. L. Rowse, *The England of Elizabeth* (1950), p. 424. Where I have written "the industrious sort of people", Dr. Rowse has simply "the people". But the social changes which led to resentment of ecclesiastical supervision affected almost exclusively those who had credit and property to lose, and yet were not wealthy or powerful enough to be immune from the attentions of the hierarchy. The very poor could not afford to litigate.

VI

Robert Harrison proposed the abolition of church courts. In 1604 Stoughton recommended that they should become secular, and that the King should appoint civil lawyers to try what had previously been ecclesiastical causes: none of the officers of these courts should have the right to excommunicate. Among the advantages which its author thought would ensue from this scheme was that "the people also in souls, in bodies and in their goods could not but be much comforted, relieved and benefited. . . . They should not be summoned from one end of the diocese unto the other: nor be posted from court to court and from visitation to visitation. The churchwardens and sidesmen of every parish should not upon pain of excommunication be constrained, once or twice in the year, to pay 6d. or 8d. for a sheet of three-halfpenny articles. They shall no longer, out of the common treasury reserved for the poor, bear the charge of their parishes for making bills, visitations and divers other expenses".[1] The "taxations, fees and penalties" of the church courts, Helwys wrote a year or two later, "are without number". If they were abolished, he added temptingly, "the king would stand no need of taxes and subsidies".[2] Such schemes became popular enough for projectors to take them up. One, writing in March 1610, suggested that all processes in the ecclesiastical courts should be sealed with the King's seal and proceed in his name, as at common law; and 8d. to his majesty on every one. What profit would accrue to the Crown if commutation of penance and such matters were to be taken in the King's name![3]

"The humour of the time is grown to be too eager against all ecclesiastical jurisdiction", Bancroft complained in 1605;[4] the evidence bears him out. "You keep your apparitors to go pricking up and down the country . . . that they should cite for your own gains", said a victim in Coggeshall in 1591.[5] In 1616

1. W. Stoughton, *An Assertion for true and Christian Church-Policie*, pp. 80–9; cf. Strype, *Life of Whitgift*, III, pp. 374–8.
2. T. Helwys, *The Mistery of Iniquity* (1935), pp. 21–2. First published 1612.
3. *H.M.C. Third Report, Appendix*, p. 52.
4. Usher, *Reconstruction of the English Church*, II, p. 82.
5. Pressey, "Records of the Archdeaconries of Essex and Colchester", *Trans. Essex Archaeological Soc.*, New Series, XIX, p. 4. Coggeshall was a very radical town.

a man called before the Archdeaconry Court of St. Albans said he cared not if it cost him 40s. in that court, "for there", said he, "I shall learn knavery for it".[1] The people of Northampton, it was alleged in the Commons in 1621, "have been ready to rise against the abuses in the ecclesiastical courts". Lambe countered by denouncing his enemies in the city as "underhand set on and countenanced by greater persons" in the county, "that through me aim at your Majesty's ecclesiastical jurisdiction".[2] Dissatisfaction with church courts was one of the reasons given by Governor Bradford for the emigration of the later Pilgrim Fathers.[3]

In 1632 a Durham gentleman was reported to have said of church courts: "You officers have gotten a trick to call many poor men into your courts, and thereupon to excommunicate them and then to bring them into the court of the High Commission. . . . The king's people and we all do suffer and groan under the burden thereof. . . . Their courts . . . are but bawdy courts, and merely to oppress people and get money for themselves". And he threatened their officers with a Parliament.[4] "The bawdy court" was the felicitously apt name which was popularly given to the spiritual court, used by an Aylesbury lady in 1634, who was congratulating herself that her son was rich enough to appear before it without fear; and by Cambridgeshire litigants in 1639. Critics of the preacher of a visitation sermon at Beaconsfield in 1633 said that "he preached only to bring money to the bawdy court".[5] ("Bastards and bawdy are his chief rents", said Lenton's character of a Commis-

1. Wilton Hall, *Records of the Old Archdeaconry of St. Albans*, p. 218.

2. N.R.S., II, p. 369, VII, p. 608, cf. *The Correspondence of John Cosin* (ed. G. Ornsby, Surtees Soc., 1868), p. 82, for opposition to Church courts in Yorkshire in 1625.

3. W. Bradford, *History of Plymouth Plantation* (Massachusetts Historical Soc. Collections, 4th Series, III), pp. 8–11. Mr. Marchant argues from the silence of the records that Bradford was lying on this point (*The Puritans and the Church Courts in the Diocese of York*, pp. 165–6). I find this unconvincing, especially as the records of the High Commission are missing for the crucial years (*ibid.*, p. 220).

4. Ed. W. H. D. Longstaffe, *The Acts of the High Commission Court within the Diocese of Durham* (Surtees Soc., 1858), pp. 62–4; cf. p. 12 and Usher, *Reconstruction of the English Church*, II, p. 46.

5. Peyton, *Churchwardens' Presentments in the Oxfordshire Peculiars of Dorchester, Thame and Banbury* (Oxfordshire Record Soc., 1928), p. viii; Palmer, *Episcopal Returns for Cambridgeshire*, p. 54; Summers

sary.[1]) "The judge will find faults enough for money", another
Buckinghamshire man said in court in 1637.[2] It was in Ipswich
that the churchwardens of St. Mary at the Tower in 1635
inscribed on the wall, near the place where the Commissary
kept "his bawdy, thievish court", "It is written, My house shall
be called an house of prayer, but ye have made it a den of
thieves".[3] "Cozening lotteries", Harbottle Grimston called the
spiritual courts in February 1641, "where the King's subjects
are deprived of their moneys, and where the judges and inferior
officers do like physicians that always cure themselves though
they destroy their patients".[4] "That cursed court", said Lodowick Muggleton, looking back at Doctors' Commons, "is
merely to betray the people into the hands of their enemies,
and to ruin the estates of poor people". It was used by the
authorities, he thought, to persecute those who could not be
prosecuted by the temporal laws.[5] That opposition to church
courts was not confined to Puritans is illustrated by the play
put on at the Red Bull in 1639 which "scandalized and libelled
the whole profession of proctors belonging to the Court of
Probate".[6]

VII

"Almost all things are saleable in the court of the metropolitan", Laurence Humphrey and Thomas Sampson complained to Bullinger in 1566, referring to the Court of Faculties:
"pluralities of benefices, licences of non-residence, for not

---

"State Papers relating to Beaconsfield," p. 98; Brinkworth, "The
Laudian Church in Buckinghamshire", p. 53.

1. F. Lenton, *Characterismi* (1631), No. 4.
2. R. Gibb, "The State of the Buckinghamshire parish churches in the
16th and 17th centuries", *Records of Bucks.*, VI, p. 164. For complaints
against the Consistory Court at Leighton Buzzard at the same time, see
V.C.H. Buckinghamshire, I, p. 326.
3. Prynne, *Newes from Ipswich*, Sig. B v; Tanner MS. 89, ff. 172–3 (I
owe the latter reference to Mr. D. W. Boorman's unpublished B.Litt.
thesis). The churchwardens had been ordered by the ecclesiastical
authorities to write sentences of scripture on the walls of the church, so
their action was peculiarly witty. They were both excommunicated.
(Note that it was the Laudians, not the Puritans, who were thus defacing
parish churches.)
4. Nalson, *An Impartial Collection*, I, p. 272.
5. L. Muggleton, *The Acts of the Witnesses of the Spirit* (1764), p. 156
(published 1699).
6. Ritchie, *The Ecclesiastical Courts at York*, p. 60.

entering into orders, for eating meat on days forbidden and in
Lent".[1] Licences and dispensations could always be obtained
from the court to do a number of other agreeable things, such
as marrying without banns being called or in Lent, "and all
this for money, and such a sum of money as the poor man
cannot reach unto".[2] Archbishop Grindal denounced his
predecessor at Canterbury for having made the corrupt Court
of Faculties a source of irregular income; but Parker too had
disliked the court and its dispensations, and would have been
prepared to see it abolished.[3] In the Parliament of 1597
"covetous use of dispensations" was discussed "whereby
men's purses, not their manners, are searched into".[4] Yet in
the early seventeenth century Bishop Cotton of Exeter sold
dispensations for marrying in Lent and eating fish on fast
days.[5] The type of dispensation granted may be illustrated by
one which Archbishop Whitgift gave to Sir Edward Coke and
Lady Hatton (and "four others he may name") to eat flesh
upon forbidden days: for this Sir Edward paid 13s. 4d. to the
poor box of his parish.[6] In 1640 it similarly cost the Earl of
Cork one mark to obtain a licence for himself and 11 others
of his household to eat flesh in Lent.[7] Twelve years earlier
Mr. Thomas Cambel fortified his claim to three pews in the
parish church of Stepney by purchasing a faculty from the
Bishop of London. The irate churchwardens, since "their
customary pewage money" was "the only means by which the
. . . church is maintained" had to appeal to the Court of

1. *Zürich Letters, 1558–79*, p. 164; cf. *ibid., 1558–1602*, p. 130 (Beza to
Bullinger, 3 September 1566).
2. A. Gilby, *A Pleasaunte Dialogue betwene a Souldior of Barwicke and
un English Chaplaine* (1581), in Arber's *Introductory Sketch to the Martin
Marprelate Controversy* (1895), pp. 30–3. Cf. Barrow, *A Briefe Discoverie
of the False Church* (1590), p. 228; Strype, *Life of Grindal*, p. 542; Usher,
Reconstruction of The English Church, II, pp. 36, 45.
3. Grindal, *Remains*, pp. 448–50; Parker, *Correspondence*, p. 473;
Strype, *Life of Parker*, II, pp. 258–62.
4. Strype, *Life of Whitgift*, II, pp. 374–5.
5. White, *Lives of the Elizabethan Bishops*, p. 395.
6. *Salisbury MSS*. (H.M.C.), I, p. 33.
7. D. Townshend, *Life and Letters of the Great Earl of Cork*, (1904),
p. 136. The price had not altered by 1661, when Sir Edward Nicholas
bought a similar licence for himself, his wife and ten others to be chosen
by him (*C.S.P.D., 1660–1*, p. 509). Humbler men, however, could get a
licence at a cheaper rate: cf. W. E. Tate, *The Parish Chest* (1946), for one
costing only 4d. in 1619 (p. 155).

Arches – at the expense of the parish.[1]

Mr. Marchant has pointed out how ineffective the church courts in the diocese of York were in ferreting out Puritans, because they had no detective force at their disposal. In default of presentments by churchwardens they had to rely on accidental information or rumour.[2] Until at least the Laudian decade, bishops anxious to enforce anti-Puritan policies would try to get a diocesan commission which would give them the powers of the High Commission.[3] The impression we get is that processes in church courts were above all an irritant for the industrious sort of people – time-wasting, their costs heavy out of all relation to the sums in dispute. The very ineffectiveness of the courts added to their cost, as cases dragged on for years with fees mounting. In 1641 the breakdown of the censorship let loose a flood of complaints against the exactions and delays of church courts, from individual victims and from churchwardens.[4]

When he had difficulty in collecting tithes, fees or other dues, it was always open to the parson to appeal to the church courts. A number of laymen were increasingly unwilling to make such payments, whilst at the same time the majority of ministers were compelled by rising prices to screw out every penny of revenue which they could claim. The result was the litigation of which we have so many complaints during our period.[5] Sums that seemed trivial to a business man might make a great difference to his minister: the latter could suggest that it might be cheaper to pay up in the first instance. There were opportunities here for blackmail by parsons threatening legal pro-

1. G. W. Hill and W. H. Frere, *Memorials of Stepney Parish* (1890–1), p. 126.

2. Marchant, *The Puritans and the Church Courts in the Diocese of York* pp. 92, 106, and *passim*. See pp. 358–60 below.

3. White, *Lives of the Elizabethan Bishops*, pp. 392–3; ed. G. R. Elton, *The Tudor Constitution* (1960), pp. 218–19; Babbage, *Puritanism and Richard Bancroft*, pp. 246–7; R. Mathias, *Whitsun Riot* (1963), p. 39. See p. 337 below.

4. e.g. Richard Bernard, *A Short View of the Praelaticall Church of England* (1641); [Anon.], *The Spirituall Courts Epitomized* (1641); [Anon.] *The Ministers Petition and Remonstrance* (1641); Peter Wentworth, *A Pack of Puritans* (1641), p. 44; *A Petition presented to the Parliament from the County of Nottingham* (1641), pp. 3–4; [Anon.], *The Doctor and Parrator their Mourning* (1641).

5. *E.P.C.*, *passim*.

ceedings. What was unsatisfactory was the lack of clear definition of claims, and their consistent enforcement by a single legal authority.

But though the church courts may in most instances have protected the interests of parsons against laymen, they also bore heavily on the former. In the fifteen-eighties the Rev. John Elliston had to make 10 journeys to London to answer charges brought against him by his parishioners, after seven visits to Peterborough, one to Cambridge, and many to Leicester and Northampton, all at his own expense.[1] When we hear of a minister being excused visitation fees, it is a curate whose stipend is "but 20s. a year", and the year is 1604, when Whitgift and Bancroft were trying to re-erect the Church's defences.[2] Many years later Bishop Bedell complained bitterly of "the greedy gaping for money by the officers and servants of the bishop, without heeding so much the sufficiency or insufficiency of the man as of the money". That was apropos of his entry into holy orders. When he was instituted to a living in the diocese of Norwich, "the demands of the bishop's officers for his instruments were very high", his biographer tells us; Bedell thought it illegal to demand such fees at all. After a vain protest to the officials, Bedell carried the matter to the bishop himself, refused to take the living at that price, and ultimately got it without paying any fees.[3]

Bedell was no better than a Puritan, who was very properly sent out, subsequently, to govern a difficult and unremunerative diocese in Ireland (where among other reforms he abolished a number of fees).[4] But his story may help to throw light on the way in which Puritans were made among the clergy. They suffered little less than laymen from the hierarchy's huge army of officials, part of whose *raison d'être* seemed to be to collect money for their own maintenance. Fees for

1. Ed. Peel, *The Seconde Parte of a Register*, I, pp. 294–5; cf. Marchant, *op. cit.*, p. 173; Babbage, *Puritanism and Richard Bancroft*, p. 246.

2. C. W. Foster, *The State of the Church in the Reigns of Elizabeth and James I* (Lincoln Record Soc., XXIII), p. lxvii.

3. Shuckburgh, *Two Biographies of William Bedell*, pp. 5, 16.

4. *Ibid.*, pp. 106, 112. John Williams looked upon an Irish bishopric as exile (Hacket, *Scrinia Reserata*, II, p. 136). John Boyle was apparently prepared to pay £500 for one in 1617 (Townshend, *The Life and Letters of the Great Earl of Cork*, p. 66), but no doubt the family would benefit by the investment.

ordination ran from £3 to £6[1] – a large sum in relation to the value of many livings. "Orders are not given", declared Nathaniel Fiennes in February 1641, "but in a manner sold, for not only the bishop and his register, but also his usher, his chamberlain, his butler and porter, and almost all his menial servants, must have their fees before the poor clerk with his box full of orders can pass the bishop's lodge".[2] In James I's reign, when the Anglican hierarchy was imposed upon Jersey, the first dean had to pay fees (i) for the royal patent of appointment; (ii) for presentation to the Bishop of Winchester; (iii) for institution by the bishop; (iv) for a commission from the bishop to exercise jurisdiction.[3] Bishops suffered too: it cost Bridgman nearly £500 in fees and expenses to be made Bishop of Chester in 1619.[4]

We can thus appreciate the point when Stoughton, in his account of the advantages of abolishing ecclesiastical courts, claimed that ministers would be "disburdened from all fees . . . for letters of orders; letters of institution; letters of inductions; for licences to serve within the diocese; for licences to serve in such a cure; for licences to serve two cures in one day; for licences to preach; for licences of resignation; for testimonials of subscription; for letters of sequestration; for letters of relaxation; for the chancellor's, register's and summoner's dinners; for archidiaconal annual, and for episcopal triennial, procurations".[5] This caricatures by being comprehensive: but that it caricatures a reality is shown by a letter written by the Laudian John Cosin to the secretary of the Bishop of Coventry and Lichfield in 1619. He is giving useful financial tips about the exploitation of office: "One secret I will tell you, which I must entreat you to make a secret still: 6*d.* apiece you may demand of every one of them [ministers], either licensed or not, for the exhibition of their licences, and keep the profit to yourself, howsoever the register may perhaps challenge

1. [Anon.], *Lord Bishops none of the Lords Bishops* (1640), Sig. G v.

2. Nalson, *An Impartial Collection*, I, p. 759.

3. A. J. Eagleston, *The Channel Islands under Tudor Government, 1485–1642* (1949), p. 137.

4. G. T. O. Bridgeman, *The History of the Church and Manor of Wigan* (Chetham Soc., 1888–90), II, p. 236.

5. W. Stoughton, *An Assertion for true and Christian Church-Policie*, p. 290; cf. Prynne, *A Breviate of the Prelates intollerable usurpations*, pp. 211–15.

it".[1] Leighton suggested that in one way and another the Church courts extracted an average of £100,000 per annum from ministers alone.[2]

Finally, until Dr. Trevor's Case (8 Jac. I), officers of the courts, from the bishop's Chancellor downwards, purchased their places and expected returns on their investment. Even after that date they were usually appointed for life. Their tenure was as much freehold as that of the bishop himself.[3] In consequence bishops had little control over their nominal subordinates, for instance in regulating the fees they demanded. This was a major obstacle to reform of the courts. On the other hand, the officers and other lay dependents of the courts represented a very considerable interest. "It is no small calling", wrote Henry Barrow, "to be but a pursuivant or cursitor of these courts (I say not so of the apparitors and summoners that belong to the commissary's court). Here are all things pleadable and vendible for money, but without money here is no man will open his mouth, be the cause never so just".[4] Men who were anxious to build a new chapel for their Lancashire village in 1635 found that in addition to the bishop's fee of £10 for consecrating it, "his men, like so many Gehazis, keep a racket" so that at least another 5 marks would be needed "before it be finished".[5]

The number of these hangers-on of the Church courts was calculated in 1641 at above 10,000, whose maintenance cost £200,000 a year.[6] "Some have summed them up to the number of 22,000 or thereabouts", Leighton had said. But

1. Ed. G. Ornsby, *The Correspondence of John Cosin*, I, p. 8.

2. Leighton, *Sions Plea against the Prelacie*, p. 121.

3. Sir R. Phillimore, *The Ecclesiastical Law of the Church of England* (2nd ed., 1895), pp. 915–17. Lord Grey said in Parliament in 1589 that bishops were enemies of reform "for that it nearly touched their freeholds" (Neale, *Elizabeth I and her Parliaments, 1584–1601*, p. 228).

4. Barrow, *A Briefe Discoverie of the False Church* (1590), p. 228, in Carlson, *op. cit.*, p. 616. *The Admonition to Parliament* of 1572 had described the Commissary's Court, in a famous phrase, as "a petty little stinking ditch, that floweth out of that former great puddle", the Archbishop's Court (W. H. Frere and C. E. Douglas, *Puritan Manifestoes*, 1907, p. 33).

5. Ed. J. S. Fletcher, *The Correspondence of Nathan Walworth and Peter Seddon* (Chetham Soc., 1880), p. 33.

6. Sir R. Verney, *Notes of Proceedings in the Long Parliament* (Camden Soc., 1845), p. 75; Bernard, *A Short View of the Praelaticall Church of England*, pp. 8–9.

that figure included the "moths, drones and caterpillars" of cathedral and collegiate churches.[1] Such men were bound to be politically prejudiced in favour of the régime whose maintenance was necessary to their existence, like the party members and police forces of a one-party state to-day. One of the few M.P.s to vote against Strafford's attainder in 1641 was George Parry, Chancellor to the Bishop of Exeter.[2] "Such as had lived upon the bishops' persecuting courts", Mrs. Hutchinson observed in her analysis of the line-up in Nottingham in 1642, ". . . were all bitterly malignant".[3] Christopher Feake complained that the royalists included "the prelates and all cathedral men, the Chancellors, Surrogates, Archdeacons, Apparitors, with all that depends upon the hierarchy".[4] Clarendon attributed Chester's firmness for Charles I in the civil war not only to "the virtue of the inhabitants" but also to "the interest of the Bishop and the cathedral men".[5]

VIII

The alliance between heretics and common-law courts goes back at least to Wyclif's time. In 1555 the martyr John Philpot appealed – vainly – from the church to the common-law courts. But now the conflict was coming to be concerned with new issues. It existed at all levels, the lowest level as well as the highest. In 1610 men presented to the church courts in Somerset for playing bowls in the churchyard complained to quarter sessions that the parson had acted out of malice, and asked for remedy. The inhabitants of another parish in the same county asked quarter sessions to protect them against tithe suits brought by their vicar.[6] The existence of the two sets of courts,

1. Leighton, op. cit., p. 121: cf. W. Bohun, A Brief View of Ecclesiastical Jurisdiction (1733), pp. 7–13. By 1733 the average cost of the officers of courts had risen to £40 a year.
2. M. F. Keeler, The Long Parliament, 1640–1641 (American Philosophical Soc., 1954), p. 297. Parry's reputation was not above suspicion – see p. 351 below.
3. Lucy Hutchinson, Memoirs of the Life of Colonel Hutchinson (1846), p. 133.
4. Christopher Feake, A Beame of Light (1659), p. 12.
5. Clarendon, History of the Rebellion and Civil Wars in England, II, p. 469. Cf. T. May, History of the Parliament (1647), I, pp. 113–14.
6. Ed. E. H. Bates, Quarter Sessions Records for the County of Somerset, 1607–25 (Somerset Record Soc., 1907), pp. 26, 60. Cf. Marchant,

in fact, gave endless possibilities of counter-pleading. The editor of *Acts of the High Commission* in Durham noted that "the party proceeded against in one court seems in general to have been the plaintiff in some charge or other against the plaintiff in the other".[1] The situation lent itself to "spoiling" and delaying litigation, and needed to be clarified and rationalized.[2]

The common-law judges claimed jurisdiction in a number of cases involving property rights. Such cases might concern the execution of a will, matrimonial causes, presentation to a benefice, simony, tithes, payment of a church rate, or property in a pew.[3] In 1567 the Bishop of Norwich refused to admit to a benefice a minister alleged to be a common haunter of taverns. The bishop was overruled in the common-law courts, which decided that this was no sufficient cause of refusal.[4] The disposal of seats in church was normally a matter for the spiritual court. But if a custom was alleged by which, time out of mind, the churchwardens had allotted seats without reference to the bishop, the common-law courts claimed jurisdiction.[5] Cases could be removed from church to common-law courts either by a writ of *Quare Impedit*,[6] or by the issue of a prohibition by the common-law judges. This old practice had originated to preserve the profits of justice for the King's courts. But as Whitgift pointed out to the Privy Council in 1598, the church courts had since the Reformation become royal courts too: and so the issuing of prohibitions no longer made sense. In fact the common-law courts were becoming increasingly independent of royal control, just when the church courts were becoming

The Puritans and the Church Courts in the Diocese of York, pp. 180–8; Nicholas, *Proceedings and Debates in the House of Commons in 1620 and 1621* (1766), I, p. 44; ed. C. H. McIlwain, *The Political Works of James I* (1918), pp. 313, 336.

1. Ed. H. W. D. Longstaffe, *The Acts of the High Commission in the Diocese of Durham* (Surtees Soc., 1858), p. 5.

2. For delays see Ritchie, *The Ecclesiastical Courts of York*, pp. 183–5.

3. Peck, *Desiderata Curiosa* (1779), pp. 107–9; Frere, *History of the English Church, 1558–1625* (1904), p. 334; Hale, *Precedents in Causes of Office*, p. 28; Laud, *Works*, VI, pp. 137–8. See above, pp. 291–3.

4. W. Hughes, *The Parsons Law* (1641), I, pp. 60–1.

5. *Ibid.*, II, p. 113, referring to a case of 1634.

6. For *Quare Impedit* see *ibid.*, II, pp. 55–64. Also *C.S.P.D., 1638–9*, pp. 205–6 – a memorandum on remedies to be adopted in the interests of ministers against whom the writ was issued.

more amenable to it: the positions were being reversed, and prohibitions originally used in the interests of royal policy were now being used to oppose it.[1]

Prohibitions were issued most frequently of all in cases concerning tithes. The common-law interest in tithe suits was enhanced by the Reformation. Impropriated tithes were assimilated to lay property: tithe disputes often turned on questions like the exact boundaries of a parish, cognizable at common law: the common lawyers gradually extended their claims to cover all tithe suits. This was liable to affect the results in disputes over *modi decimandi*. The common-law courts, and juries especially, were much more sympathetic to the property interests of tithe-payers, and much less concerned to see that their minister got an equitable tenth, than were the church courts – as Joseph Hall found to his cost at Waltham in James I's reign.[2] In 19 Eliz. the judges of the Queen's Bench decided that tithes were due "as well by the constitution of kings as by the law of God". But the attitude of the common-law courts seems to have hardened from the last decade of Elizabeth's reign.[3]

"Where there is a *modus decimandi*", Coke declared in 1609 on behalf of his colleagues on the bench, "we are of opinion that the parson, vicar, etc., suing for tithes in kind, and thereby seeking to infringe the custom of *modus decimandi* claimed by the parishioners, that this custom ought to be tried by the common law, and not in the ecclesiastical courts".[4] "Were it not for the prohibition", the common-law judges had stated 4 years earlier, the church courts "would soon overthrow all

1. A similar transformation took place in the use of the writ *habeas corpus*; originally intended to enable the king to invade feudal franchises, it was used in the seventeenth century against arbitrary imprisonment by the king.

2. J. Hall, *Works* (1837–9), I p. xxvi. For examples of juries supporting tithe-payers against ministers, see Hughes, *op. cit.* (2nd ed., 1673), II, pp. 282–3; for unsympathetic attitudes towards ministers in cases of pluralism, *ibid.*, I, pp. 98–102. The Quakers after 1660 always tried to get tithe suits removed to the common-law courts. For *modi decimandi* see *E.P.C.*, Chapter V.

3. Hughes, *op. cit.*, II, p. 73; Strype, *Life of Whitgift*, II, pp. 430–6; cf. Usher, *Reconstruction of the English Church*, II, pp. 57–85; Cardwell, *Documentary Annals*, II, pp. 82–105; W. Stoughton, *An Assertion for true and Christian Church-Policie*, pp. 90–103; Ridley, *A View of the Civile and Ecclesiasticall Law*, pp. 148–51.

4. Usher, *Reconstruction of the English Church*, II, p. 245

prescriptions and compositions that are for tithes". They were trying "to work in the spiritual courts more commodity instead of being content with what was usually paid".[1] Bancroft wanted the ecclesiastical courts to have the right "of interpreting all statute laws concerning the clergy": the judges replied that this right belonged to them. In 1606 the Lower House of Convocation petitioned against prohibitions, saying that by them the clergy were "defrauded of their tithes".[2] Now that both church and common-law courts were the King's courts, neither should be subordinated to the other. The clergy were prepared to recognize "prohibitions of law", those which were authorized by statute; but not "prohibitions of fact", "raised up by argument out of the wit of the deviser", based on "quirks and subtleties".[3]

In 1606 it was reported that the King had consented "to put a restraint upon prohibitions"; and in 1610 the Commons petitioned against the recent more sparing grant of them.[4] James won the reputation of being "an enemy to all prohibitions, and an utter stayer of them", though he denied it.[5] But Bancroft's great battle with Coke ultimately ended indecisively. Prohibitions were "beaten down with a club", but they rose again "like hydra's heads".[6] They continued to be issued in tithe disputes right down to 1640, though they were checked in the years of Laud's supremacy. But the problem had been squarely posed by Coke and Bancroft, and in the uproar over Cowell's *Interpreter* the House of Commons had taken its stand with the common lawyers.

In 1616 Coke was dismissed. James had noted in him, said Bacon, "a perpetual turbulent carriage, first towards the liberties of his church and the state ecclesiastical".[7] Coke laid it down in the second volume of the *Institutes* that "the

1. Coke, *II Institutes*, p. 649.
2. *Ibid.*, pp. 601, 618; Cardwell, *Synodalia* pp. 587–8.
3. Ridley, *op. cit.*, pp. 126–7; cf. Downing, *A Discourse of the State-Ecclesiasticall* (2nd ed., 1634), p. 84; M. H. Maguire, "The attack of the common lawyers on the oath *ex officio*", in *Essays in History and Political Theory in Honor of C. H. McIlwain* (Cambridge, Mass., 1936), p. 221.
4. Cardwell, *Synodalia*, p. 589; *A Record of some worthie Proceedings in the House of Commons, . . . 1611, Somers Tracts* (1748–51), XIII, p. 286.
5. McIlwain, *Political Works of James I*, pp. 312–13.
6. Birch, *Court and Times of James I*, I, p. 91; cf. p. 99.
7. Bacon, *Works*, XIII, p. 95.

expounding of statutes that concern the ecclesiastical government or proceedings . . . belongeth unto the temporal judges".[1]
If such views had prevailed, the church courts would have been
unable to deal with the offences of laymen except by admonition. That was to be the final outcome of the struggle; but it
needed a revolution to realize it. In the meantime Coke's
dismissal decided nothing. The dispute was more than
personal. It survived Coke, and flared up again when Laud
rose to power and revived Bancroft's attempt to strengthen
the position of the Church.

IX

So long as Church and State were in fact united, so long as
the ultimate authority lay with the King in Council, the
problems were soluble. The Chamber of the city of Exeter
might deal with cases of bastardy, despite appeals to the
bishop's court and protests by the bishop.[2] Assize courts dealt
with ecclesiastical matters like blasphemy and disputes over
parish clerks. The Lord Keeper in 1633 told the judges as they
departed on circuit that "the advancement of true religion and
suppression of the contrary" was part of their job. "Those that
will not be fed in the church may be fined in the Exchequer".[3]
The Council in the Marches imposed fines for sexual offences.
Whitgift objected, but the fines were a useful contribution to
the court's income: and in any case there was no question of
such a court exercising its power *against* the interest of the
Church. Nevertheless, it is interesting that the church courts
reasserted their rights against the Council after 1637, under
the ascendancy of Laud.[4] So long as the old régime survived,
the central government could always intervene if a challenge
to episcopal jurisdiction became serious. Powerful offenders
could be brought before Star Chamber – e.g. in disputes over
pews[5] – or before the High Commission, which could fine,

1. Coke, *II Institutes*, p. 614.

2. W. T. MacCaffrey, *The City of Exeter, 1540–1640*, p. 98.

3. Ed. T. G. Barnes, *Somerset Assize Orders* (Somerset Record Soc.
1959), pp. xxvii, 57.

4. P. Williams, *The Council in the Marches of Wales*, pp. 96–105, 135.

5. Ed. Gardiner, *Records of Cases in the Courts of Star Chamber and
High Commission* (Camden Soc., 1866), pp. 139–44.

imprison or impose corporal punishment. It was little consolation to a Puritan who was browbeaten by Laud in Star Chamber to reflect that at least he was being tried before a secular court.

In the Council of the Marches Whitgift had regularly been in favour of the severer penalty, laymen for moderation.[1] In 1607 a Kentish minister was sentenced (by Bancroft, Archbishop of Canterbury, among others) to be fined £2,000, pilloried, deprived of his ears, whipped until he confessed, and perpetually imprisoned. His offence was libelling the episcopal government of the Church.[2] Nothing Laud did to Prynne, Burton, Bastwick and Lilburne improved on that.[3]

Laud himself was aware of the legal difficulties of the situation. On a public occasion he had declared that "the time is now come in this kingdom, that the civil courts are as much too strong for the ecclesiastical" as church courts had been for secular courts in papal times, "and may overlay them as hard, if they will be so unchristian as to revenge". And he admitted in a private letter to Wentworth that "the Church . . . is so bound up in the forms of the common law, that it is not possible for me, or for any man, to do that good which he would, or is bound to do. . . . They which have gotten so much power in and over the Church will not let go their hold: they have, indeed, fangs with a witness".[4] The two forms of jurisdiction were in fact mixed up. The old precedents, dating from a period when the Crown strove to control a semi-independent international Church, were now used by the common lawyers in an attempt to deprive the Crown of the church courts as an instrument of government.

Laud, as his letter to Wentworth shows, was determined to cut through legal obstacles and restore the power of the Church. In 1629 he persuaded the King to discourage the

1. P. Williams, *op. cit.*, p. 254.

2. Ed. W. P. Baildon, *Les Reportes del Cases in Camera Stellata, 1593–1609* (1894), p. 341, quoted by Sir Charles Ogilvie, *The King's Government and the Common Law, 1471–1641* (1958), p. 156.

3. When the Commons of the Long Parliament discussed Lilburne's case, men thought there had been no whipping in Whitgift's time – an interesting example of the Long Parliament's retrospective glamourizing of the days of Good Queen Bess (Rushworth, *Historical Collections*, II, pp. 468, 475).

4. Laud, *Works*, I, p. 82, VI, p. 310; cf. p. 330 below.

judges from too easily granting prohibitions. This was apropos the repair of churches at the expense of the inhabitants, a matter in which the ecclesiastical courts would naturally have less regard to prescriptive and property rights than the common-law courts.[1] Prohibitions, Edward Bagshaw told the House of Commons in March 1641, existed "to prevent clergymen from giving judgment in a lay fee".[2] Laud was reported as saying "I will break the back of prohibitions, or they shall break mine". Even before he became archbishop, when the High Commission over rode a prohibition in the case of Sir Giles Alington, Laud had said, "If this prohibition had taken place, I hope my Lord's Grace of Canterbury would have excommunicated, throughout his Province, all the judges who would have had a hand therein. . . . If he would not, I would have done it in my diocese" of London. Later Laud preached damnation "of all who granted prohibitions to the disturbance of the Church's right".[3] He had the enthusiastic support of Charles I. In the famous test case of the communion table at St. Gregory's church, in 1633, Charles by his mere prerogative stopped proceedings in the Court of the Arches and called the case before the Privy Council. The King there laid down the law himself personally, and the Dean of the Arches was commanded to give judgment against the parishioners. In order to have the Privy Council's ruling effectively carried out Sir Henry Marten was replaced as Dean of the Arches by the more compliant Sir John Lambe.[4] Mr. Brinkworth believes that in Buckinghamshire "a remarkably effective tightening up of discipline" occurred after Laud's visitation of his province in 1634. Dr. Marchant notes a similar phenomenon in the diocese of York from about the

---

1. Rushworth, *Historical Collections*, II, pp. 7–8, 28.

2. Nalson, *An Impartial Collection*, II, pp. 365, 403; cf. p. 398.

3. Laud, *Works*, VI, pp. 137–41; Birch, *Court and Times of Charles I* (1848), II, p. 120; Roger Coke, *A Detection of the Court and State of England* (1694), I, p. 351.

4. Rushworth, *Historical Collections*, II, pp. 207, 462–3, 719–20; Cardwell, *Documentary Annals*, II, pp. 185–7; Gardiner, *History of England*, VII, pp. 310–14. Not only was Charles's interference arbitrary, Gardiner comments, but his decision "asserted . . . the right of the bishop to set aside the spirit of the law and the wishes of the congregation at one and the same time". The congregation of St. Gregory's, unfortunately, was composed of "woollen drapers of good quality" (Rushworth, *op. cit.*, IV, p. 59).

same time.[1] From Suffolk we are told that the visitation of 1636 was "the strictest that ever was".[2]

In 1637 Charles promised to take care that no prohibition was issued against the Bishop of Norwich in a case concerning prescriptive rights to property abutting the church at Bury St. Edmunds.[3] Lord Chief Justice Finch apologized abjectly to Laud when he did once screw up his courage to issue a prohibition.[4] The bishops, said Prynne, "have sued out a prohibition against prohibitions themselves". Appeals, he added, were so expensive that they were a remedy worse than the disease. Appeals to the King were referred back to the bishops themselves to consider. So all avenues were blocked.[5] By 1640 the judges of the land were "so awed with the power and greatness of the prelates", the Root and Branch Petition complained, "that neither prohibition, *Habeas Corpus*, nor any other lawful remedy can be had".[6] Men like Falkland and Hyde who were to support the King in the civil war, agreed in denouncing the hindering of prohibitions.[7] Refusal of prohibitions formed articles of impeachment against Bishop Wren and Lord Chief Justice Bramston.[8] Laud himself argued that the number of prohibitions had not decreased under his régime, but the evidence appears to be against him.[9]

X

In 1595 the Archdeacon of St. Albans raised some far-reaching questions when discussing the reform of the church courts. "I am not able to conceive", he said, "how it may be reformed, preserving his Majesty's royal prerogative and the

1. Brinkworth, "The Laudian Church in Buckinghamshire", p. 59; Marchant, *The Puritans and the Church Courts in the Diocese of York*, pp. 44–5, 50–1, 168.

2. Reyce to Winthrop, *Massachusetts Hist. Soc. Collections*, 4th Series, VI, pp. 407–8, 411.

3. Laud, *Works*, V, p. 351.

4. Rushworth, *Historical Collections*, II, pp. 7–8, 28.

5. Prynne, *A Breviate of the Prelates intollerable usurpations*, p. 73.

6. Gardiner, *Constitutional Documents of the Puritan Revolution*, p. 143.

7. Nalson, *An Impartial Collection*, I, p. 769; Clarendon, *History of the Rebellion*, I, p. 504.

8. Nalson, *op. cit.*, II, pp. 365, 403; cf. p. 398.

9. Laud, *Works*, IV, p. 141.

law of the realm already established, because I know not well how far his Majesty's royal prerogative doth extend as against the common law of the land".[1] Throughout our period challenges were issued from time to time to the right of bishops to hold courts in their own names, without a commission under the great seal. Church courts, it was said in Cawdrey's Case (1591), were the King's courts, just as a court leet held in the name of the lord of the manor was the King's court.[2] In 1604 Stoughton printed "Speeches used in Parliament by Sir Francis Knollys", denying that bishops had any prescriptive right to hold courts; and Stoughton argued that it was an infringement of the Act of Supremacy for them to do so without a commission under the great seal.[3] The Attorney-General seems virtually to have admitted in 1606 that the bishops might risk penalties by acting otherwise than in the King's name.[4] Stoughton's point was repeated by Leighton in 1628, by Burton in the sermon which got him into trouble, by Prynne throughout his *Breviate of the Prelates intollerable usurpations*, and by Bastwick and Prynne at their trial.[5]

We can see the policy of resistance in action in Bastwick's town, Colchester, in 1636. There, at St. Runwald's church, the clergyman, Thomas Newcomen, had the communion table railed in alterwise, in the approved Laudian manner. Samuel Burrows of the parish refused to come up to this altar for the sacrament, and was presented by the churchwardens, at Newcomen's instance, for not receiving. He countered by indicting Newcomen at quarter sessions; the grand jury threw out the indictment. The next move was to have Burrows excommunicated by the bishop's Commissary, Dr. Aylett. This was done on grounds of non-appearance in court, though Burrows claimed that his presence there could be proved by

·1. Wilton Hall, *Records of the Old Archdeaconry of St. Albans*, pp. 92–3.

2. Coke, *5 Reports* (1612), p. 39; *IV Institutes* (1648), p. 321. See pp. 338–9 below.

3. W. Stoughton, *An Assertion for true and Christian Church-Policie*, Appendix, and pp. 49, 53; cf. Strype, *Life of Whitgift*, II, pp. 50–5.

4. *C.J.* I, p. 304; ed. D. H. Willson, *The Parliamentary Diary of Robert Bowyer* (University of Minnesota Press, 1931), pp. 145–7; cf. p. 158.

5. Leighton, *Sions Plea against the Prelacie*, p. 26; J. Collier, *Ecclesiastical History* (1852), VIII, pp. 129–31; Prynne, *Breviate*, esp. pp. 83–137; *C.S.P.D., 1633–4*, p. 345.

20 witnesses. When Newcomen published the excommunication next Sunday Burrows contested it on two grounds. First he said it was forged, since none had been granted at the court when he was present. Secondly, it did not run in the King's name and under his seal and by authority derived from him by letters patent (as was required under 1 Edw. VI cap. 2, 1 Eliz. cap. 1 and 8 Eliz. cap. 1). It was therefore legally void, and he could not in loyalty to his majesty obey it.[1] The churchwardens and the constables thereupon were afraid to remove Burrows from church: and Newcomen discontinued the service.

Burrows then returned to the bishop's Commissary, who told him he was an audacious fellow indeed to indict his minister for innovation. "We will take you down in time, and teach you how to indict ministers; I will excommunicate you in all the parishes round about and throughout England". Thus did Aylett make the penal nature of the excommunication clear. Burrows then threatened Aylett with Star Chamber, and he Burrows with the High Commission, of which Aylett was a member.

Burrows continued to try to attend various churches: and he preferred a new indictment against Newcomen. The mayor and recorder of Colchester timidly tried to persuade him to desist or delay, but in vain: the jury of townsmen, "being stout honest men", found it a true bill, and adhered to their verdict despite pressure. So the sessions was adjourned, Newcomen posted off to Laud; and returned with a pursuivant empowered by the High Commission to arrest Burrows, thereby setting the town in an uproar. The jurors appear to have been called before the High Commission too. After Burrow's arrest, the mayor at first refused to obey a writ of *habeas corpus*, pleading that Laud's writ had come first. "This case", said the pamphleteer grimly at the end of his account of it, "is like to be a precedent for all England to follow". And he called upon all parishioners whose ministers had moved their communion tables to indict them, and their bishops too. Ultimately the case was brought up before the common-law judges upon a writ of *habeas corpus*, and they, in a rare moment of independence, dismissed Burrows, declaring "it was a mere cheat

1. This was the legal position advocated a year or two earlier by the "Instructions for Churchwardens" quoted on p. 361 below.

for money".[1] The most significant point in this case was the challenge to the authority of the ecclesastical courts as such.

No doubt in consequence of this challenge, the judges in 1637 were asked for an opinion, and declared that no patent under the great seal was needed to enable ecclesiastical courts to be held and to inflict penalties: and that the statute 1 Ed. VI cap. 2 which enacted the contrary was no longer in force. This statute had indeed been repealed by 1 Mary st. 2 cap. 2 (to which Newcomen appealed), but that in its turn had been repealed by 1 Jac. I cap. 25. The judges' opinion thus had the effect of repealing two Acts of Parliament.[2] However, in reliance on this opinion, the Government issued a proclamation "to settle the minds and stop the mouths of all unquiet spirits, that for the future they presume not to censure his [Majesty's] ecclesiastical courts or ministers in these their just and warrantable proceedings".[3]

This was a great victory for Laud. It was also a victory for the monarchy, to whose advantage it was to establish this pseudo-independence for the Church, to extricate it from "the forms of the common law", over which enemies of the old order exercised too much influence. In 1629 the King had protected Cosin from a charge of denying the royal supremacy. Privately Charles disclaimed the title of Head of the Church: and now he renounced his supremacy in matters of spiritual jurisdiction in favour of the church courts.[4] But this of

1. [Anon.], *A Quench-Coale* (1637), Postscript, pp. 351–6. (This tract was a reply to Heylyn's *A Coale from the Altar*.) See also Laud, *Works*, IV, pp. 118–20; *C.S.P.D., 1637–8*, p. 69; Prynne, *Canterburies Doome*, p. 101; H. Smith, *Ecclesiastical History of Essex*, pp. 66, 413–16. In 1641 Newcomen and others were accused of having "combined and complotted together" against Bastwick (ed. W. Notestein, *The Journal of Sir Simonds D'Ewes*, Yale University Press, 1923, p. 232). Newcomen was very unpopular in Colchester, and he was lynched when in 1642 he tried to leave to join the royal army. His younger brother was Matthew Newcomen, the Smectymnuan, for whom see p. 116 above.

2. Cardwell, *Documentary Annals*, II, pp. 212–17; ed. Gardiner, *Documents relating to the proceedings against William Prynne* (Camden Soc., 1877), p. 88. Cf. Bagshaw's arguments in the House of Commons in February 1641 (Nalson, *An Impartial Collection*, I, pp. 762–4).

3. Sparrow, *A Collection of Articles*, pp. 132–4; R. Steele, *Tudor and Stuart Proclamations* (1910), No. 1752.

4. Ornsby, *Correspondence of John Cosin*, I, pp. 147–52; Gardiner, *History of England*, VII, pp. 46, 129–30; G. Albion, *Charles I and the Court of Rome* (1935), p. 407.

course was no reversion to the mediaeval papalist position. The Church was now visualized as an obedient instrument of the royal Government. At the same time that the power of church courts was vindicated against common-law courts, Laud was attacking the independent jurisdiction of bishops. In 1634 the archbishop asserted his right to hold an over-riding metropolitan visitation, a right that had not been exercised for a century.

"Like the levy of ship-money", said Gardiner, "Laud's claim rested on precedents of undoubted antiquity. Like ship-money, too, it contained the germs of a great revolution".[1] A revival of mediaeval forms, with the full power of a modern state behind them, would indeed have had far-reaching results. It helped to fix the label of "papist" on Laud, since for contemporaries popery meant the absolute monarchies of France and Spain. Laud's models were Wolsey and Richelieu rather than Thomas à Becket.

But in this as in so many other spheres Laud's triumph came too late. In the assertion of the church courts' independent rights of jurisdiction, in the overthrow of prohibitions, property was at stake. So Nicholas Fuller had argued in 1607: and the view had gained wide currency since that date.[2] The position of the Church as a privileged corporation was also involved: Heylyn, in an attack on Henry Burton, described him as "the only clergyman that stands for prohibitions".[3] But the opinion of those who mattered politically was turning against the independent existence of "worms in the body politic". The dispute over prohibitions focussed the vaster issues of property rights, of the relation of Church to State, of state power, of the type of society that was to survive. Such issues could not be decided by judicial pronouncements, whether those of Coke or of the more servile judges of Charles I.

Lawyers and judges, no doubt, were primarily interested in fees, by which the salaries of judges were largely supplemented. Ridley thought that "as emulation between the two laws in the beginning brought in these multitudes of prohibitions, either

1. Gardiner, *History of England*, VIII, p. 107.
2. Usher, *Reconstruction of the English Church*, II, pp. 136–53.
3. Heylyn, *A Briefe and Moderate Answer to the seditious and scanda-lous Challenges of Henry Burton* (1637), pp. 92, 106.

against or beside law, so the gain they bring unto the temporal courts maintaineth them". Common-law judges, he added, "cess not costs and damages in cases of consultation", so as not to deter men from suing out prohibitions.[1] But the Puritanism of the common lawyers was more than just a sordid (or natural) desire for business and fees. Cartwright, like Luther and Calvin, had had a legal training. Thomas Fuller describes how not only young students but even the gravest benchers sat at the feet of Travers, the Temple lecturer who was Hooker's great rival, eagerly making notes.[2] William Stoughton dedicated his *Assertion for true and Christian Church-Policie* to students of the Inns of Court as well as to apprentices. Throughout the sixteen-twenties and -thirties, under the influence of men like John Preston[3] and Richard Sibbes, the Puritanism of the Inns of Court was notorious: the deeper causes which maintained this tradition have never been properly examined. Laud cried to Sherfield, "and such of his profession as slight the ecclesiastical laws and parsons, that there was a time when churchmen were as great in the kingdom as you are now; and let me be bold to prophesy, there will be a time when you will be as low as the church is now, if you go on thus to contemn the church".[4] It was a challenge to mortal combat; and the lawyers accepted it.

It was also a move to put the clock back, in ways which threatened more than the special interests of the common lawyers. However self-interested the lawyers may have been, they were not alone in wanting to remove some kinds of legal business from the control of a Church and Crown whose policy was increasingly out of touch with the commercial spirit of the age. Many of the propertied classes in town and country had the same aims: and so the alliance between House of Commons, Puritans and common lawyers was forged. Church courts declined in effectiveness from about 1639, long before they were abolished, because they had lost the co-operation

1. Ridley, *A View of the Civile and Ecclesiasticall Law*, p. 127: "Consultation is a writ whereby a cause, being formerly removed by prohibition out of the ecclesiastical court . . . to the King's court, is returned thither again" (*Termes de la Ley*, 1641, p. 79).

2. Fuller, *Worthies*, II, p. 54; *Church History*, III, p. 128; cf. I. Walton, *The Life of Mr. Richard Hooker*, in *Lives* (World's Classics), pp. 207–8.

3. For Preston see my *Puritanism and Revolution*, p. 240.

4. Laud, *Works*, VI, p. 20.

of the laity.[1] The alliance sprang from mutual interests; but these interests themselves were all the expression, in various spheres, of the needs of a new class rising within the old framework of society. "Jurisdictive power in the church", said Milton, "there ought to be none at all".[2] Many who were in no religious sense Puritans would have agreed with him.

The ordinance of 9 October 1646 abolishing episcopacy declared that henceforth "all issues triable by the ordinary or bishop shall be tried by jury in the usual course". Eighty years ago John Stoughton suggested that historians had underestimated the significance of the abolition of church courts. The transference of matrimonial and divorce cases to quarter sessions or assizes, "the destruction of the tribunal before which people were liable to be cited for unchastity and other vices not cognizable by common law" was "a considerable judicial and social revolution".[3] With the failure to establish an alternative presbyterian discipline, these matters were left to be decided by the uncontrolled consciences of individuals, at least in so far as J.P.s did not appoint themselves residuary legatees of the church courts. Henceforth sin was distinguished from crime. This must have greatly accelerated an intellectual and moral revolution which the church courts had previously retarded.

This revolution could never be undone. When ecclesiastical jurisdiction was revived after the restoration, a clause was inserted into 13 Car. II cap. 12 to ensure that neither "this act nor anything in it be construed to abridge or diminish the King's supremacy in ecclesiastical matters". The *jure divino* authority of church courts had gone. Prohibitions ceased to be a weapon and became a device for giving effect to the over-riding control and supervision of the judicial system by the common-law judges.[4] Political developments after 1660 ultimately transformed the supremacy of the King over the Church into the supremacy of Parliament over King and Church. So far as the propertied classes whom Parliament represented were concerned, it was a great liberation. By the end of the

1. Marchant, *The Puritans and the Church Courts in the Diocese of York*, pp. 58, 90, 199–203, 303.

2. Milton, *Prose Works* (Bohn ed.), II, p. 488.

3. J. Stoughton, *A History of Religion in England* (1881), I, pp. 473–5.

4. *The Canon Law of the Church of England* (Report of the Archbishops' Commission, 1947), p. 52.

century the church courts could sometimes be so ineffective in forcing churchwardens to present offenders that the voluntary Society for Promoting Christian Knowledge and the societies for the reformation of manners undertook to duplicate their functions. But it was almost exclusively the lower orders whose pleasant vices were punished.[1]

1. D. W. R. Bahlman, *The Moral Revolution of 1688* (Yale University Press, 1957), p. 74.

Chapter Nine

The Court of High Commission

Experience doth show daily that the Church Militant is never so well constructed in any form of policy but that the imperfections of men who have the exercise thereof do with time though insensibly bring in some corruptions.

Draft proclamation postponing the Hampton Court Conference, 1604, by Archbishop Whitgift and Bishop Bancroft, M. H. Curtis, "Hampton Court Conference and its Aftermath", *History*, No. 156, p. 6.

The High Commission court . . . was grown from an ecclesiastical court for the reformation of manners to a court of revenue, and imposed great fines upon those who were culpable before them, sometimes above the degree of the offence had the jurisdiction of fining been unquestionable, which it was not. . . . Thereby the clergy made a whole nation, that is, almost a whole profession, if not their enemy, yet very undevoted to them.

Clarendon, *History of the Rebellion*, I, p. 372.

THIS is not the place to deal fully with the part played by the Court of High Commission in the conflicts leading to the outbreak of the Revolution. But we can hardly discuss church courts without referring to the highest court, whose ultimate punitive power alone prevented ecclesiastical law from being, in the words of Whitgift, "a carcass without a soul".[1]

The High Commission, like Star Chamber, performed a role that was mainly political. It was one of the many instruments of the Tudor State for centralization, for imposing national

1. Strype, *Life of Whitgift* (1822), I, p. 267.

uniformity. It enforced national tests of political loyalty. Its power extended across those boundaries of dioceses by which episcopal jurisdiction was hampered. Its judges were of sufficient eminence to make its decisions effective, at least by seventeenth-century standards. It fined and imprisoned, as the other church courts could not. There was no appeal from its sentences. Through its support of the monopoly of the Stationers' Company, the High Commission enforced the censorship. It could veto the appointment of any master printer.[1] The Commission of 1611 gave the court complete control not only over "heretical, schismatical and seditious" books and pamphlets, but also over "all other books pamphlets and portraitures offensive to the state" or unlicensed.[2]

The High Commission began to function as a regular court from the fifteen-eighties – when the threat from the puritan radicals began to be taken seriously by the Government. Its early activities, and in particular its use of the oath *ex officio* to enforce what was in effect a political test, caused anxiety to some lay members of Elizabeth's privy council: Burghley's letter to Whitgift in 1583, comparing the court's activities to those of the Romish Inquisition, is well known. The archbishop's reply is illuminating. He said, among other things, that the court was necessary because of the solidarity and influential support enjoyed, at least in certain areas, by Puritans; and the oath *ex officio* was essential because common-law procedure was inadequate to overcome the difficulty of collecting enough evidence to secure convictions.[3] A threat to the High Commission contained in a bill passed by the House of Commons in 1585 might reach, Whitgift warned the Queen, "to the overthrow of ecclesiastical jurisdiction".[4] The archbishop, nevertheless, because of the opposition to the jurisdiction of the court, found it convenient to bring "the most sturdy and refractory nonconformists (especially if they had any visible estates)" before Star Chamber;[5] and he suggested that puritan ministers should be turned over to Star

1. *Ibid.*, III, pp. 160–5.
2. See F. S. Siebert, *Freedom of the Press in England, 1476–1776* (University of Illinois Press, 1952), pp. 139–45, and references there recited.
3. Strype, *Life of Whitgift*, I, pp. 318, 322; see p. 373 below.
4. Usher, *The Rise and Fall of the High Commission*, p. 131; cf. pp. 182–3.
5. Fuller, *Church History*, III, p. 187.

Chamber for "some exemplary corporal punishment".[1] Both courts were aspects of the executive government.

In the later decades of the court's existence privy councillors lost Lord Burghley's squeamishness about the Commission's procedural methods; and High Commission and Star Chamber became almost interchangeable. Offenders against the proclamation of 1623 regulating printing were liable to censure by either court. A Northamptonshire minister whose sermons persuaded his parishioners not to pay ship-money was dealt with by the High Commission.[2] Star Chamber, which could inflict severer punishments than fines, imprisonment or deprivation, was normally used in cases involving sedition or wilful resistance to authority, or when the Government wished to have the accused flogged or maimed. When in 1633 Strafford recommended the establishment of a High Commission for Ireland, the uses which he gave for it were, among others, "to countenance the despised state of the clergy; to support ecclesiastical courts and officers; . . . to restrain the extreme extortions of officials, registers and such like; . . . to provide for the maintenance of the clergy, and their residence; . . . to bring the people here to a conformity in religion; and in the way to all these, raise perhaps a good revenue to the crown".[3] In 1638 he again emphasized the financial aspects of the High Commission when he wondered whether the time might not be ripe for setting "the ecclesiastical courts loose again against recusants". His concern was lest the fines to be raised should go "into the purses of a company of catching officers, greedy informers and pursuivants . . . and other ministerial officers of the High Commission".[4]

Contemporaries so diverse in outlook as John Penry, Lord Burghley, the puritan author of *The Practice of Prelates* and the

1. Strype, *Life of Whitgift*, II, p. 20; cf. p. 70.
2. J. R. Tanner, *Constitutional Documents of the Reign of James I* (1930), p. 144; Usher, *High Commission*, pp. 312–13, 328.
3. Ed. Knowler, *Letters and Dispatches of the Earl of Strafforde*, I, p. 188.
4. *Ibid.*, II, p. 159. Cf. the passage from Clarendon quoted as epigraph to this chapter, and Dr. Duck's account to the House of Commons in 1641 of the High Commission's power of fining (Notestein, *Journal of Sir Simonds D'Ewes*, pp. 435–6). Sir Nathaniel Brent spoke in 1635 of some curates in Derbyshire who were "so poor that I doubt no man will prosecute them in the High Commission Court" (*C.S.P.D.*, *1635*, p. xxxviii).

Venetian Ambassador in 1641 all compared the High Commission with the Spanish Inquisition – which was also an instrument of national unification.[1] Historians so far apart as Hume, Lingard and Professor Trevor-Roper have agreed with them.[2] James Morrice alleged in 1589 that the High Commission was unique among tribunals in that its proceedings contained no record of a person convented before it having been declared not guilty.[3] Citations before the Commission had to be paid for by the defendant: he was thus fined even before he had appeared, declared Prynne.[4] The "popularity" which some historians attribute to the court, such as it was, was connected at least in part with its share in the repression of Catholics: the Commission in the North seems to have been less unpopular than that in London,[5] whose activities were directed, from Whitgift's time onwards, principally against protestant sectaries and the underground opposition. But the High Commission was a court like any other, in which matrimonial and testamentary cases might receive rather swifter settlement than elsewhere. The majority of the cases with which the Commission dealt were not started by the Commissioners themselves. Unlike the common-law courts the High Commission could issue positive instructions – e.g. order someone to perform his share of a bargain which he wished to evade.[6]

The over-riding powers of such a court were invaluable to

1. Arber, *An Introductory Sketch to the Martin Marprelate Controversy*, p. 73; Bancroft, *Dangerous Positions*, p. 57; *C.S.P.*, *Venetian, 1640–2*, p. 178.

2. D. Hume, *History of England* (1826), V, p. 232; J. Lingard, *History of England* (1855), VI, p. 122; H. R. Trevor-Roper, *Archbishop Laud*, p. 103. Professor Trevor-Roper appears to limit his comparison to the period of Laud's ascendancy.

3. Pierce. *A Historical Introduction to the Marprelate Tracts*, p. 77; cf. Peel's note in *The Notebook of John Penry* (Camden Soc., 1944), p. xii. "Once within its grasp", said Mr. Bruce of the High Commission, "for anything which was deemed an offence by the authorities in church or state, submission or ruin were the only alternatives proposed" (*C.S.P.D. 1635–6*, p. xxxi).

4. Prynne, *A Breviate of the Prelates intollerable usurpations*, p. 151.

5. Though it was the Durham High Commission which was described in 1634 as "the most wicked court in England" (ed. H. W. D. Longstaffe, *Acts of the High Commission Covrt within the Diocese of Durham*, Surtees Soc., 1858, p. 265.

6. Usher, *High Commission*, pp. 256–8, 284–91, 323. Delaying tactics, however, could also be used in the Commission – *ibid.*, pp. 273–4.

the hierarchy. By the end of Elizabeth's reign bishops were trying to get separate commissions for their own dioceses, as a means of enforcing discipline; failing that, they frequently transferred cases from their own courts to the High Commission in order to ensure a successful prosecution.[1] In Roper's Case (1608) Coke and other judges, not perhaps entirely ingenuously, suggested that the High Commission was undermining the authority of the bishops' courts. The point was repeated later by Bishop Williams.[2] The High Commission was a kind of ecclesiastical supreme court, and also a court of appeal to be used when one suitor alleged that another was trying to play off the various conflicting judicial authorities. A vicar to whom Chancery had ordered the impropriators to pay an augmentation appealed to the High Commission for protection when the impropriators sued him at common law.[3] The High Commission protected churchwardens who presented ecclesiastical malefactors.[4] The Archbishop of York in 1632 attacked the view of the York common lawyers that the High Commission could not "meddle" with a man who was "a prisoner of the King's Bench, removed by *habeas corpus* from York". "If that be avowed for good", he wrote to Laud, "we may give up the High Commission".[5]

Opposition to the High Commission was thus a curious compound of interest and principle. Common lawyers, Puritans and printers disliked the Commission: so, too, did many rich litigants who utilized the law's delays. But it was also opposed by the growing body of lay opinion which resented the moral jurisdiction of clerics, or ecclesiastical censorship, or heavy fines, or all three. Who shall say whether high principle or self-interest prevailed when the printer, Michael Sparke, told the High Commissioners in 1629 that the Star Chamber decree of 1586, regulating printing, on which the Commission's authority to try him rested, directly intrenched "on the hereditary liberty of the subjects' persons

1. *Ibid.*, pp. 99–100; F. O. White, *Lives of the Elizabethan Bishops* (1898), pp. 392–3. Cf. p. 314 above.
2. Coke, *12 Reports* (1658) pp. 45–7; Usher, *Reconstruction of the English Church*, II, pp. 217–18; *High Commission*, pp. 183–4. See also p. 341 below.
3. Usher, *High Commission*, p. 270.
4. See p. 378 below.
5. *Cowper MSS.* (H.M.C.), I, p. 466.

and goods" and was "contrary to Magna Carta, the Petition of Right, and other statutes".[1]

One reason for the unpopularity of the High Commission with the parliamentary class was its power to impose heavy sentences on the sort of person who might expect to escape from the normal judicial processes. In 1611 Sir William Chancey was imprisioned for adultery and refusal to support his wife.[2] Two years later Sir Pexall Brocas did open penance at Paul's Cross in a white sheet after conviction before the High Commission of secret and notorious adulteries with divers women.[3] Twelve years later Sir Robert Howard was excommunicated in the same public place for contempt in refusing to answer in the High Commission to a charge of incontinency with Lady Purbeck, Sir Edward Coke's daughter.[4] In 1631 the Commission over-rode a common-law prohibition to fine Sir Giles Alington £12,200 for marrying his niece.[5] As Clarendon pointed out, this enforcement of equality before the law did not endear the court to those who mattered in seventeenth-century England.[6]

Whitgift had first shown the possibilities of the High Commission. But it was Bancroft who consistently used it as a coercive instrument to enforce uniformity. In Cawdrey's Case (1591), the judges virtually established the High Commission as a proper and lawful court,[7] but they had declared that its authority derived from the royal prerogative and not from the Act of Supremacy; and the prerogative itself was being challenged in the seventeenth century. In 1607 Nicholas Fuller, already a noted opposition lawyer, maintained, in defence of two clients who had refused to take the oath *ex officio*, that the High Commission had no power to put on oath, to imprison or fine. Fuller was at some pains to emphasize the poverty of some of his clients who had been fined by the

1. Siebert, *op. cit.*, p. 140.

2. Usher, *High Commission*, pp. 211–12.

3. R. Gibbs, *A Record of Local Occurrences* (in Bucks.) (1878), I, p. 85. Brocas was a cousin of Sir Robert Cotton.

4. *Letters of John Chamberlain*, II, pp. 607–8.

5. Gardiner, *History of England*, VII, p. 251. Alington eventually paid at least £10,000, so the fine was not just *in terrorem*.

6. Clarendon, *History of the Rebellion*, I, p. 106.

7. Coke, *5 Reports*, pp. 344–5; J. Collier, *Ecclesiastical History* 1852), VII, pp. 162–4.

Commission £20 and £30 apiece. One man, a householder in Fleet St., had been "imprisoned for many days with great irons on him", and than released without any conviction. Fuller added, gratuitously perhaps, that the ecclesiastical jurisdiction was "Anti-christian", and the Commission's procedure "popish". The court forthwith demonstrated its power by imprisoning Fuller and fining him £200. He got a prohibition from the King's Bench: but the sympathy of the common-law judges was counter-balanced by the hostility of James I, and Fuller had to remain in prison until he had paid his fine.[1]

Fuller's speech, however, when published as a pamphlet, caused something of a sensation,[2] and won the support of the House of Commons as well as of the judges. The Commons' Petition of Grievances, presented to the King in July 1610, attacked the High Commission for its excessive penalties, and argued that – Cawdrey's Case not withstanding – the Court drew its authority from the Act of Supremacy. That Act had claimed merely to "restore" ecclesiastical jurisdiction, of which fining and imprisoning was no part. The Commissioners had as much right to "impose utter confiscation of goods, forfeiture of lands" or of life as they had to exercise their present powers. Trifling offenders might be "drawn from the most remote places of the kingdom to London or York", to their grievous inconvenience. The High Commission over-rode other ecclesiastical courts. It punished laymen for criticizing the "simony and other misdemeanours of the clergy", "though the thing spoken be true"; it incited women against their husbands, its agents broke into men's houses: yet the court proceeded on no certain or known rules of law.[3]

The nature of the counts against the High Commission is worth noting. Even Sir Edward Coke, who regarded murder of the Commission's pursuivant as self-defence, was prepared to admit its right to burn heretics.[4] He also granted that any

1. N. Fuller, *The Argument of Nicholas Fuller, . . . in the Case of Thomas Lad and Richard Maunsell* (1641), p. 22 (first published 1607); Gardiner, *History of England*, II, pp. 36–40; Usher, *Reconstruction of the English Church*, II, pp. 136–53; *High Commission*, pp. 33, 134.

2. It was reprinted in 1641.

3. *Somers Tracts* (1748–51), XIII, pp. 281–3.

4. Usher, *High Commission*, p. 208; Frere, *History of the English Church, 1558–1625*, p. 370; ed. J. P. Collier, *The Egerton Papers* (Camden Soc., 1840), pp. 447–8.

clergyman might be examined upon the oath *ex officio*, and laymen in some cases. It was the Commission's claim to fine and imprison, and its attempt to exercise an over-riding jurisdiction, that he regarded as illegal. Coke agreed with the Commons in thinking that, if the bishops' view were accepted, the High Commission might claim jurisdiction over property (legacies, tithes) without limitation of punishment and without appeal.[1]

The High Commission combined the approach and powers of an ecclesiastical visitation, unlimited and without appeal, with the functions and procedures of a court. Coke's attack perhaps delayed the full utilization of these powers, and got them reduced in certain respects. This was especially true of alimony cases, "whereby", Bacon said, "wives are left wholly to the tyranny of their husbands".[2] "The law of England is a husband's law", said a lawyer:[3] it looked after the property rights of heads of families, whereas wives seeking a separate maintenance – as the Commons complained in 1610 – had hitherto looked to the High Commission. But though Coke won such minor triumphs, the visitatorial activities of the Commission which had lapsed under James I were revived by Laud.[4] In the sixteen-thirties the Commission included the most powerful figures at Court and in the Government. It was this extension in the *use* of the Commission's powers that seemed to its opponents an illegal innovation.[5] Even before Laud's advent, so prudent a politician as John Williams, although a member of the Commission, had been chary of attending its sessions. He declared himself dissatisfied in two respects. First, a multiplicity of trivial causes was brought before the Commission, causing the bishops' courts to lose respect (the point

1. N.R.S., IV, p. 348; Coke, *7 Reports*, pp. 20, 49–62, 69, 84–9; *IV Institutes* (1648), pp. 325–35.
2. Bacon, *Works*, XIII, p. 90.
3. Gardiner, *History of England*, VII, p. 252.
4. Elton, *The Tudor Constitution*, p. 218.
5. Usher, *High Commission*, pp. 232–5. Mr. Usher suggested that the cases edited by Gardiner for the Camden Society should be discounted, since they seem to have been selected by the High Commission's opponents with a view to publication (*ibid.*, p. 258). Their genuineness has, however, not been called in question, and Mr. Tatham pointed out that in any event these cases date from 1631–2, before Laud's succession to Canterbury (G. B. Tatham, *The Puritans in Power*, 1913, p. 22).

made by the judges in Roper's Case). Secondly, its sentences were too severe.[1]

After Coke's dismissal in 1616 interference with the High Commission by the common-law courts declined. Judges were appointed whose views, in Mr. Usher's delicate phrase, "were more consonant with the law as the King understood it".[2] Under Laud the chief common-law judges themselves sat on the Commission; opposition from the common-law courts lost its point. Laud had his own ways of discouraging the issue of prohibitions.[3] There was no chance of rectification within the system. Puritan opponents of the court knew that their defiance could produce nothing more than a demonstration, at best. Reform, if any, must come from without: men looked to Parliament, as Penry had done 40 years earlier, to overthrow "this bloody and tyrannous inquisition".[4]

A last attempt to buttress the authority of the High Commission *as a court* was made in 1638, when Charles I reminded the Commissioners that they were authorized by letters patent under the great seal (unlike other Church courts,) and that their use of the oath *ex officio* was parallel to the procedure of Chancery, Star Chamber and the Court of Requests.[5] They were therefore authorized to proceed against any who refused to answer questions upon oath as though they had confessed to the indictment.[6] (This last merely confirmed existing procedure.) At the same time judges of the common and civil law were told not to interfere in the ecclesiastical courts without the permission of the archbishop.[7] Laud's position was as strong as the authority of the government could make it. After the subordination of the judges, Weldon tells us, the very messengers of the High Commission "were countenanced in their abuse and insultings over the gentry". "Every lackey" of the Lords of the Council and of the High Commissioners "might

1. J. Hacket, *Scrinia Reserata* (1692), I, p. 97. See p. 337 above.

2. Usher, *High Commission*, p. 321.

3. See pp. 323–5 above.

4. Quoted in Arber, *An Introductory Sketch to the Martin Marprelate Controversy*, p. 73; Longstaffe, *The Acts of the High Commission in the Diocese of Durham*, pp. 62, 64.

5. He might have added the Admiralty, and the Councils in the North and in the Marches of Wales.

6. Cardwell, *Documentary Annals*, II, pp. 217–20.

7. H. R. Trevor-Roper, *Archbishop Laud* (1940), p. 359.

give a checkmate to any gentleman, yea to any country noblemen that was not in the court favour".[1] It was not long before
the gentry had their revenge.

With the fall of the High Commission in 1641, wrote a
pamphleteer, "the iron teeth of the Beast were knocked out,
and the sting of abused excommunication was plucked out of
his tail".[2] The failure to restore the Beast's teeth in 1660 was
fatal to any attempt to revive the authority of church courts
on anything like the old pattern: and excommunication never
regained its sting. Ecclesiastical jurisdiction became, as Whitgift had predicted, "a carcass without a soul".[3]

1. Sir A. Weldon, *The Court and Character of King James* (1651), p.
207. Cf. the passage from Clarendon cited as epigraph to this chapter,
and p. 75 above.
2. R. Culmer, *Cathedrall Newes from Canterbury* (1644), p. 16.
3. See p. 333 above, 364 below.

Chapter Ten

The Rusty Sword of the Church

Excommunication is the greatest judgment upon the earth, being that which is ratified in heaven; and being a precursory or prelusory judgment to the great judgment of Christ in the end of the world. And therefore for this to be used unreverently, and to be made an ordinary process, to lackey up and down for fees, how can it be without derogation to God's honour and making the power of the keys contemptible? I know very well the defence thereof, which hath no great force: that it issueth forth not for the thing itself but for the contumacy.... But ... the contumacy must be such as the party, as far as the eye and wisdom of the church can discern, standeth in state of reprobation and damnation.

> Bacon, *Certain Considerations touching the better*
> *Pacification and Edification of the Church of England*
> (1603), in *Works*, X, pp. 121–2.

Whereas the grievance pretended was that they [Church courts] had too much power; the truth is, on the contrary, that they could not do their work as they ought, to satisfy the people and to beat down sin, because they had too little. Take their highest and in a manner their only censure, excommunication (terrible in itself). What doth a profane person care for it? Prosecute them with writs *De Excommunicatis Capiendis*, and all the grist that came to their mill would not pay the cost of it. What a coil hath been made to set up consistories of ministers and ruling elders, that should proceed against scandals with rebukes, suspension from the sacrament, open penance, and lastly, as they expound it, "Let him be unto thee as an heathen and a publican". Make the sin liable to imprisonment, to distraining, to a forfeiture, to some loss in his profit, and he will be sure to feel it, and fly from the occasion. Confess the truth: will not many look better to outward honesty if you discipline them in their purse?

> Hacket, *Scrinia Reserata*, II, pp. 44–5.

The fairies have no existence, but in the fancies of ignorant
people; . . . so the spiritual power of the Pope . . . consisteth only
in the fear that seduced people stand in of their excommunications.
. . . It is not the Roman clergy only that pretends the Kingdom of
God to be of this world, and thereby to have a power therein,
distinct from that of the civil state.

Hobbes, Leviathan (Everyman ed.), pp. 382–3.

I

EXCOMMUNICATION, the casting of an offending individual out
from participation in the rites and ceremonies which bind the
community together, is a very old practice, far older than
Christianity.[1] Its necessity, and its effectiveness, derive from
the reality of the community: the story of the breakdown of
excommunication as an effective censure is the story of the
breakdown of the mediaeval communities.

High claims were still made in the sixteenth century. Excommunication, declared the Constitutions of 1597, is *"quasi
nervus quidam ac vinculum"* of ecclesiastical discipline; without
it the whole system of church jurisdiction would collapse. It
could be imposed, the same source tells us, for heresy, schism,
simony, perjury, usury, incest, adultery, "or other grave
crime".[2] The bishops in 1584 had added to this list such lay
offences as piracy, conspiracy against the Government, per-
turbation of the common peace and quietness of Church or
realm, wilful murder, sacrilege, bearing and suborning false
witness, and violent laying of hands upon ecclesiastical
persons.[3] Midwives who practised without the bishop's licence
were liable to excommunication.[4] In 1614 a lady was excommunicated as a common scold and sower of strife, and
more particularly for "misbehaving her tongue towards her
mother-in-law" at a visitation in Bromsgrove.[5] The sentence
was frequently imposed for contempt of ecclesiastical jurisdiction, whether by refusing to appear in court or for refusal

1. Rosalind Hill, "The Theory and Practice of Excommunication in
Mediaeval England", *History*, No. 144, pp. 1–2.

2. Ed. A. Sparrow, *A Collection of Articles . . . of the Church of
England*, p. 251.

3. Cardwell, *Documentary Annals*, I, p. 428.

4. J. H. Bloom and R. R. James, *Medical Practitioners in the Diocese
of London, 1529–1725* (1935), p. 85.

5. Smith and Onslow, *Worcester* (Diocesan Histories), p. 225.

to plead or to pay fees: as when in 1625 Sir Robert Howard was excommunicated "openly at Paul's Cross" for refusing to answer questions about his alleged incontinence. It was also used to enforce payment of tithes.[1] Churchwardens who failed to present, to certify or to appear in court, or who failed to carry out instructions (e.g. about repairing churches, or the position of the communion table), or who refused to take an oath, might be excommunicated.[2]

To Bancroft's legal mind this aspect of excommunication seemed by far the most important. "Excommunication", he declared, "is as lawful as prohibition, for the mutual preservation of both his Majesty's supreme jurisdictions". The one was to restrain the encroachment of the temporal jurisdiction upon the ecclesiastical, the other of the ecclesiastical upon the temporal.[3] Both the bishops and Prynne, in rare agreement, compared excommunication to outlawry, the penalty imposed by the civil courts for refusal to appear or obey.[4] In the Palatine Bishopric of Durham, indeed, excommunication and outlawry went together.[5] But in the business society that was developing the one was as out of date as the other. The common-law courts were adapting themselves to the needs of this society more effectively than the church courts; they did did not do so by reviving or extending outlawry.

There were two types of excommunication – the lesser and the greater. The lesser – suspension *ab ingressu ecclesiae* – was used especially against ministers, as a penalty for contumacy, to enforce appearance before a church court or compliance with its judgements. It was in effect a pecuniary sanction, since an excommunicated clergyman had to pay someone else to

1. Sparrow, *op. cit.*, p. 251; Cardwell, *Documentary Annals*, I, pp. 425–7; *Synodalia*, II, pp. 550–2; C. Jenkins, "Act Book of the Archdeacon of Taunton (1623)", in *Collectanea*, II (ed. T. F. Palmer, Somerset Record Soc., XLIII), *passim*; J. M. J. Fletcher, "A Century of Dorset Documents", *Proceedings of the Dorset Natural History and Antiquarian Field Club*, XLVII, pp. 39, 45. B. L. Woodcock (*Mediaeval Ecclesiastical Courts in the Diocese of Canterbury*, 1952, p. 100) shows excommunication being used before the Reformation to enforce payment of debts. For Howard, see p. 338 above.
2. Hale, *Precedents in Causes of Office against Churchwardens*, *passim*.
3. Cardwell, *Documentary Annals*, II, pp. 104–5.
4. *Ibid.*, I, pp. 425–6; Prynne, *A Breviate of the Prelates intollerable usurpations*, p. 142.
5. Bohun, *A Brief View of Ecclesiastical Jurisdiction*, p. 16.

take his Sunday services.[1] The greater excommunication was imposed for continued contumacy, for wilfully standing excommunicate, or for associating with excommunicated persons. Lambe was accused in 1621 of excommunicating men for keeping company with excommunicated persons, even though they were ignorant of the fact; and of taking excessive fees for absolution. He replied that "the law warrants this proceeding", and that the excommunicate in question was a notorious whoremaster and recusant.[2] The Long Parliament was told of "a son that was excommunicated only for repeating a sermon to his father", the latter being excommunicate. The son remained excommunicate for 6 years, and had to give up his trade in Leicester and seek a livelihood elsewhere. He was absolved only after petitioning Parliament.[3]

The excommunicated person could not buy or sell, could not be employed,[4] could not sue or give evidence in the courts (and so could not recover debts), could not give bail, make a will or receive a legacy, or serve as administrator or guardian. All these, it will be observed, are *economic* penalties: what Bishop Hacket called discipline by the purse. In particular it might be a very grave handicap to a business man to be disenabled from suing. Lodowick Muggleton on one occasion thought a case had been brought against him in the spiritual court with the sole purpose of getting him excommunicated so "that I might not have the benefit of the law against them". But he "spent money in that court, and kept off their excommunication and proceeded in the common law".[5] "Many are more afraid of excommunication, for that they can prosecute no action, than of imprisonment", declared Whitgift in 1585.[6] The usurer in Dryden's *The Spanish Friar* confirmed this: "If I am excommunicate I am outlawed, and there is no calling in

1. Marchant, *The Puritans and the Church Courts in the Diocese of York*, p. 222; for examples, *ibid.*, pp. 98, 197.

2. N.R.S., VI, p. 472; cf. VII, p. 607.

3. Nalson, *An Impartial Collection*, I, p. 759; *C.S.P.D., 1640–1*, pp. 305–6. See p. 453 below for Jacob Bothomley.

4. See Peyton, *Churchwardens' Presentments in the Oxfordshire Peculiars of Dorchester, Thame and Banbury*, p. 284, for an employer of King's Sutton, Oxfordshire, presented in 1609 for giving employment to an excommunicate.

5. L. Muggleton, *Acts of the Witnesses* (1764), p. 154.

6. Strype, *Life of Whitgift*, I, pp. 360–1; III, p. 129; cf. Penry, *Three Treatises*, pp. 35–6.

my money".[1] Humbler men might be deprived of the possibility of earning altogether. No one was supposed to eat with an excommunicate, or to receive him into his house.[2] "So long as England is Christian", said the House of Commons in 1645, "he that shall be ejected from Christian communion will have little countenance in any civil conversation, and less capability of any employment or preferment either in church or state".[3] Some Puritans – e.g. Thomas Taylor – wished excommunication to be a purely spiritual censure, without economic penalties. Taylor thought it was lawful to buy and sell with an excommunicate;[4] but in this he was certainly unorthodox.

Either type of excommunication could be redeemed by penance, but freeing oneself from the greater excommunication involved the payment of heavy fees. If obdurate, the offender might be handed over to the High Commission, which had power to fine and imprison. Alternatively, if the excommunicate had not submitted within 40 days, the secular power might be invoked. If Chancery issued the writ *De excommunicato capiendo*, sheriffs and all subordinate officers were expected to seize the excommunicate and commit him to gaol until he submitted to the laws of the Church and was absolved. The writ was returnable in the Court of King's Bench: sheriffs were to be amerced if the writ was not duly returned (5 Eliz. cap. 23). The lay arm, however, was not often called upon, partly because it was expensive and slow, partly because of the growing hostility (and consequent slackness) of sheriffs and their officers, and of the reluctance of common-law judges to co-operate.[5] In 1570 the Bishop of St. David's complained that 200 persons in his diocese stood excommunicate for immorality, but the sheriff would not execute the writs against them. Eight years later he suggested that the

1. *Act 2*, scene 3 (1681).
2. Coke, *I Institutes*, p. 133v; T. Rogers, *The Faith, Doctrine and Religion professed and protected in . . . England*, pp. 193–6.
3. *Portland MSS*. (H.M.C.), I, p. 297. In Scotland excommunication might involve loss of civil rights altogether.
4. Taylor, *A Commentary upon the Epistle . . . to Titus*, p. 513. Taylor died in 1633. See also pp. 356–7, 365–9 below.
5. Strype, *Annals*, I, part i, pp. 460–1, 466–7; *Life of Whitgift*, I, p. 267; Ware, *The Elizabethan Parish in its Ecclesiastical and Financial Aspects*, pp. 46–9; Price, "The abuses of excommunication and the decline of ecclesiastical discipline under Queen Elizabeth", *E.H.R.*, LVII, pp. 112–15. Cf. pp. 358–60 below.

Council in the Marches should intervene in a case of incest, since its authority was more respected than that of the church courts. The Council sent a special commission into the see, and rebuked the bishop for failing to punish bigamy and whoredom, which it thought occurred too frequently in his diocese.[1] The bishop had a right to feel aggrieved, since he claimed he was in the habit of excommunicating 500 people a year for immorality.[2] The inadequacy and expense of the civil arm in enforcing excommunication meant that serious cases were normally brought before the High Commission. Without the backing of the secular sword, lesser ecclesiastical censures became – until the Laudian revival – increasingly an irritant rather than an effective sanction.

II

The system had been under attack at least since the days of Wyclif. Luther had said that bishops who excommunicated over money matters should not be obeyed. Archbishop Grindal suggested that excommunication was used too frequently, but found himself opposed by the other bishops. Grindal thought that in place of excommunication bishops should have the right to imprison those who refused to appear for trial: so even his object was hardly to lessen ecclesiastical interference with laymen.[3] Marprelate accused the bishops of profaning excommunication "by excommunicating alone in their chamber, and that for trifles: yea, before men's causes be heard". He was only repeating a point made in the *Admonition to Parliament* of 1572.[4] 5 Eliz. cap. 23 laid it down that excommunication should be valid only for heresy or erroneous doctrine, for refusal to have a child baptized, to receive communion or to attend church, or for incontinency, usury, simony, perjury *in the ecclesiastical courts*, or idolatry.

1. P. Williams, *The Council in the Marches of Wales*, pp. 101–2.
2. D. Williams, *A History of Wales*, p. 74. This was nothing compared with the good old days of the fourteenth century, when half Christendom was under sentence of excommunication; or the times when Gregory VII excommunicated unto the seventh generation (Troeltsch, *Social Teaching of the Christian Churches*, 1931, I, p. 391).
3. Strype, *Life of Grindal*, pp. 385–7; Grindal, *Remains*, pp. 451–5.
4. Ed. Arber, Martin Marprelate, *The Epistle*, p. 35; Frere and Douglas, *Puritan Manifestoes*, p. 17.

Parliament and Puritans alike continuously opposed the use of excommunication for trivial and procedural offences.[1] In 1587 the bishops assured Parliament that men were not excommunicated "for twopenny causes" but "for not obeying the law process and judge".[2] After further protests in Parliament, the Constitutions of 1597 insisted that excommunication should be pronounced in person by the archbishop, bishop, dean, archdeacon or prebendary, and not by deputy.[3] A French Ambassador was presumably reporting current gossip when, in the same year, he noted a certain lightheartedness in use of the sentence "for petty theft and trivial causes".[4] The complaints against excommunication for trifles and by lay officials were repeated in the Millenary Petition, and in Parliament in 1606 and 1610. The Canons of 1640 again laid it down that excommunication and absolution were to be pronounced only by priests.[5] Excommunication was used to enforce unpopular ceremonies; under Laud churchwardens were excommunicated for backwardness in railing in communion tables.[6] A whole parish might be excommunicated for neglecting to obey the orders of the courts – and had to pay stiff fees, and travelling expenses for its officers, before it was absolved. Thus in 1592–3 Shrewsbury Abbey parish had to pay a fine of £1 and 5s. 10d. costs.[7]

The main complaint was always that the spiritual censure of excommunication was too lightly used as a mere aid to procedure in the church courts. It was employed, said Henry Barrow, "for contumacy, as for not obeying their summons, or for not satisfying the judgement of their courts, namely for not paying the[se] ravenous [vultures, these] officers their fees, or not paying the mulcts that are inflicted. . . . It most commonly

1. Strype, *Life of Whitgift*, I, pp. 352–3.

2. Cardwell, *Documentary Annals*, I, pp. 425–6.

3. Strype, *Life of Whitgift*, II, pp. 374–5; Sparrow, *A Collection of Articles*, p. 251.

4. Ed. G. B. Harrison and R. A. Jones, *De Maisse's Journal* (1931), p. 20.

5. Cardwell, *Synodalia*, pp. 410–11.

6. *A Petition . . . from the County of Nottinghamshire* (1641), p. 7; [Anon.], *A Lordly Prelate* (1641), p. 3. See p. 361 below.

7. W. A. Leighton, "Notes relating to the Abbey Church Estate, Shrewsbury", *Trans. Shropshire Archaeological and Natural History Soc.*, I, p. 62.

ariseth [but] about these money matters".[1] The hierarchy's answer was always that excommunication, "being the bond and sinew of authority and discipline ecclesiastical", could not be abolished if the courts were to continue to function effectively. "No man is excommunicated for the value of 12*d*. nor for any sum, but for contemning authority, for disobeying of process, for refusing to answer according to law, etc." Absolution was automatic once the excommunicate submitted.[2] "The less the thing was that was commanded, the greater was the contempt", "a gentleman of the civil law" told the House of Commons in 1641; "the excommunication was not for the thing, but for the contempt." "The greater is the cruelty", Fiennes retorted, "to lay command upon so small a matter" ("for a pig, or for an apple"), "that draweth after it so deep a censure as to cast a man down into hell".[3] It was in 1644 that Bishop Hall, wise after the event, admitted that "the dreadful sentence of excommunication hath too frequently and familiarly passed upon light and trivial matters".[4]

Criticism of the use of excommunication for procedural purposes, irresistible though it seems to us to-day, was in fact, as the bishops very well realized, an attack on the church courts as such, on the whole system of an ecclesiastical discipline "beating down sin", enforcing what seemed to many men out-of-date standards of behaviour. Many who were not Puritans at all objected to "discipline by the purse". Absolution could be received by proxy, provided the fees were paid. When the male guilty party stood proxy for the woman being absolved for incontinence, the spiritual significance of the ceremony was perhaps liable to be obscured.[5]

"The power of this excommunication is of another especial use of profit", wrote Helwys, "in that by the power thereof are brought in all duties, tithes and court fees".[6] The House of

1. H. Barrow, *A Briefe Discoverie of the False Church* (1590), pp. 240–1 in Carlson, *op. cit.*, p. 636. The words in square brackets were omitted in the reprint of 1707 (p. 360).

2. Strype, *Whitgift*, I, pp. 352–3, 359, 375; cf. III, pp. 53–7, 122–3, 128–30.

3. Nalson, *An Impartial Collection*, I, p. 759; cf. the remarks of Bacon cited as epigraph to this chapter, and G. Wither, *Juvenilia*, I, p. 308.

4. Hall, *A Modest offer to the Assembly of Divines*, in *Works*, X, p. 436.

5. Price, "The abuses of excommunication and the decline of ecclesiastical discipline under Queen Elizabeth", *E.H.R.*, LVII, pp. 107–8.

6. Helwys, *The Mistery of Iniquity*, p. 20.

Commons petitioned against this abuse in July 1610, declaring that "excommunication is the heaviest censure for the most grievous offences which the church doth retain, yet exercised and inflicted upon an incredible number of the common people by the subordinate officers of the jurisdiction ecclesiastical, most commonly for very small causes, grounded upon the sole information of a base apparitor, in which case the parties before they can be discharged are driven to excessive expense for matters of very small moment, so that the richer break through more heinous offences and escape that censure by commutation of penance".[1]

This financial aspect of excommunication was not the least of its opponents' grievances. The Dean and Chapter of St. Paul's had the authority of the Bishops of London for excommunicating tenants who failed to pay their rents.[2] In 1624 Samuel Harsnett, Bishop of Norwich, was accused of having "excommunicated many, and would not absolve them under £20 apiece". What was worse, the diarist added in a shocked postscript, "the King commended him for it, in his speech at the dissolving of the House, and willed all the bishops to do the like".[3] Dr. Parry, the Bishop of Exeter's Chancellor, was accused about 1629 of abusing his power of excommunication for the sake of fees.[4] Bishop Bedell, his biographer records, was grieved by "the frequent prostitution of that solemn and dreadful sentence of excommunication, which with them (as it were) was become nothing else but an engine to open men's purses".[5] The point was repeated by George Wither and many puritan propagandists.[6] A churchwarden of Leicester who refused to remove an excommunicated person from church was himself excommunicated by Sir John Lambe, we are told, and

1. In Tanner, *Constitutional Documents of the Reign of James I* (1930), pp. 79–80. Note the ominous word "retain". This Petition repeats the substance of the petition presented to the Parliament of 1584, quoted on p. 238 above.

2. *H.M.C. Ninth Report, Appendix*, I, p. 69.

3. Yonge, *Diary*, p. 75.

4. *C.S.P.D., 1629–31*, p. 426. Parry was M.P. for St. Mawes, Cornwall, in both Parliaments of 1640. He was knighted at Oxford in 1644, and Herrick wrote a poem to him (Herrick, *Poetical Works*, ed. L. C. Martin, 1956, p. 564). See p. 318 above.

5. Shuckburgh, *Two Biographies of William Bedell*, p. 75; cf. Price, *op. cit.*, pp. 111–12.

6. Wither, *Juvenilia*, I, p. 307; [Anon.], *Lord Bishops none of the Lords Bishops* (1641), Sig. D 3v; Nalson, *op. cit.*, I, p. 759; cf. Marchant, *The Puritans and the Church Courts in the Diocese of York*, p. 25.

was not absolved until he had paid £5 10s. 0d. to the proctor, in addition to having to attend at a court 12 miles from Leicester 30 times between June 1634 and December 1635.[1] We may compare the accusation made in the House of Commons in November 1641 that Dr. Fuller, among many other enormities, including denying property and equating Anglican and Roman doctrine, had demanded excessive fees for burials, and had excommunicated several of his parishioners for not paying their whole duties.[2]

Fees from commutation of penance went to pay the officers of the church courts: this was apt to give excommunicates uncharitable thoughts of the whole system.[3] Men of weaker faith might be absolved "without fees, upon condition of appeaching other delinquents to bring more fees". Absolution might be withheld, even after penance had been done, from those who were too poor to pay their fees, "whereby many poor people have been kept excommunicate to their deaths, without other fault than want of money".[4] Ames quoted Lancelot Andrewes, though maliciously translating from the decent obscurity of a learned language in which the bishop's strictures had been veiled: "Church censures nowadays do only touch the purse. Evil doers when they have paid their fee return scot-free. If no money, then have at the offenders with the episcopal sword."[5] "Fornication and adultery are committed many times for 4s.", complained a pamphlet of 1641.[6] "The richer may commute for money", said Richard Bernard in the same year, "but the miserable poor . . . cannot be freed from their courts without money though they beg for it, but must . . . be . . . given over to the devil for non-payment of money".[7] Ex-

1. *C.S.P.D.*, *1640–1*, pp. 304 sqq.

2. Ed. W. H. Coates, *Journal of Sir Simonds D'Ewes* (Yale University Press, 1942), p. 81; cf. Robert Judd, *Fourtie Articles in the High Court of Parliament against William Lang* (n.d. ?1641), for charges against a parson who vexed his parishioners with frivolous suits and excommunicated them with lavish abandon.

3. *Reliquiae Baxterianae*, I, p. 397.

4. *A Petition . . . from the County of Nottingham*, p. 7.

5. W. Ames, *A Fresh Suit against Human Ceremonies in Gods Worship* (? Rotterdam, 1633), p. 421. The quotation is from a sermon preached by Andrewes before Convocation.

6. [Anon.], *A Lordly Prelate*, p. 3.

7. R. Bernard, *A Short View of the Praelaticall Church of England* (1641), p. 14.

communication, Thomas Taylor agreed, "is daily turned into an idle scare-crow, sold and bought at a vile price".[1] Mr. Brinkworth, on the whole prepared to see more good in seventeenth-century church courts than most researchers, nevertheless concluded that in Buckinghamshire in the sixteen-thirties there is no instance of money offered for commutation of penance being refused:[2] so only the poor were liable to atone for their sins by being publicly exhibited in a white sheet. In March 1638 two Cambridgeshire women on poor relief were recorded as remaining excommunicate "for want of money to defray their charge of the court".[3]

Nor was it only laymen who suffered, as we are reminded by the entry in the parish register of Wootton Courtney made in 1629 by the minister. He bitterly regretted that he had proceeded with the excommunication of two parishioners for arrears of tithes, for the amount which he had recovered was quite inadequate to pay the fees demanded by the officials of the Archdeacon's Court.[4] Many of the lower clergy might agree with lay opponents of the hierarchy in seeing the complex of church courts as an intolerable incubus, serving no useful purpose to anyone except its own officials.

The Root and Branch Petition summed up many grievances of Londoners. Excommunication, "the last and greatest punishment which the church can inflict upon obstinate and great offenders", was used frivolously, either as a punishment "for doing that which is lawful . . . as working or opening a shop upon a holiday", or as a penalty for merely procedural offences. The prelates and their officers "have made it, as they do all other things, a hook or instrument wherewith to empty men's purses, and to advance their own greatness". It "is seldom or never used against notorious offenders, who for the most part are their favourites".[5]

1. T. Taylor, *Commentary upon Titus*, p. 517.
2. Brinkworth, "The Laudian Church in Buckinghamshire", p. 35. Examples are given on pp. 35–7. Cf. Price, *op. cit.*, *passim*, and Ritchie, *The Ecclesiastical Courts of York*, pp. 167–8, 171.
3. Palmer, *Episcopal Returns for Cambridgeshire*, p. 51.
4. J. C. Cox, *The Parish Registers of England* (1910), p. 112.
5. Gardiner, *Constitutional Documents of the Puritan Revolution*, p. 142.

III

The complaint throughout is twofold: humbler men were subject to vexatious penalties whilst the richer got off; but wider questions of church government were also involved. The bishop had to supervise hundreds of parishes, whose inhabitants he could not know personally. Discipline, the Puritans thought, should be administered parochially by the "physician of souls", the minister, and his natural advisers among the propertied of the parish. Instead men were hauled off (at considerable expense, to themselves) to distant courts on the information of "a base apparitor", who was a lay official: and there they were tried by the "subordinate officers" of the bishop, laymen again; or the parish was visited by lay officials from outside, who were understandably unpopular with the local community. Professor Notestein quotes an agreeable instance from the parish of Bishop's Stortford, where in 1634 the churchwardens voted 5s. to be paid to the bellringers for *not* ringing the bells when the bishop's Chancellor arrived, and 2s. 6d. for ringing them on the day he went away![1]

In the presbyterian view no laymen except elders – who were sacred officers of the Church, not properly laymen at all – should have anything to do with ecclesiastical government.[2] Elders and the minister watched over and knew their congregations: their discipline would be intimate and well-informed. Distant officials of ecclesiastical courts could merely administer a cold and formal law, enforcing external observances, not a paternal discipline. It is a matter of local society, under its "natural rulers", asserting its independence against the alien demands of a distant state machine: we may compare the hostility of the J.P. class to the prerogative courts, which they also overthrew as soon as the Long Parliament met. But opposition to the Church courts had this "popular" basis in that it drew upon the traditional community sense of the parishes.

1. Notestein, *The English People on the Eve of Colonization* (1954), p. 248.

2. Cf. Udall, *A Demonstration of Discipline*, pp. 36–40; Bacon; *Works*, X, pp. 109–14; Shuckburgh, *Two Biographies of William Bedell*, pp. 122–4; Prynne, *A Breviate of the Prelates intollerable usurpations*, p. 214; *Reliquiae Baxterianae*, I, pp. 141–3, 396–404. For the bishops' defence of the jurisdiction of laymen, see Cardwell, *Documentary Annals*, I, pp. 427–9.

Puritan ministers had wider ambitions than the merely negative reaction of laymen to the church courts. They also wanted to obtain power to exclude from communion those whom they regarded as being in a state of sin.[1] This could be a serious penalty where the parish was still a real community, and where belief in God was still more than conventional. It lost some of its significance when imposed by a distant church court, associated in the public mind with the governmental machine. The object of the puritan ministers was to restore it to reality by giving the minister the right to exclude. Thus the attitude of the puritan ministers before 1640 was complex. On the one hand they wished to strengthen the local authority, to restore to the minister (but in conjunction with elders) some of the powers that had been lost since confession, penance and absolution were abolished. The *Admonition to Parliament* of 1572 wished to see excommunication restored to its former force.[2] But at the same time the ministers, and still more their lay supporters, wished to reduce the power wielded by the hierarchy in the matter of excommunication. Experience taught them that the lay courts were more amenable to outside pressure than the ecclesiastical courts. One of the points which appears to have been provisionally agreed at the Hampton Court Conference was that "civil excommunication now used is declared to be a mere civil censure; and therefore the name of it is to be altered; and a writ out of the Chancery, to punish the contumacy, shall be framed". In 1610 Parliament was pressing the same point.[3] Bancroft, on the other hand, complained in 1605 that persons imprisoned upon the writ *De excommunicato capiendo* were released by judges of the temporal courts without satisfaction being made to the ecclesiastical courts, "where certain lawful fees are due".[4]

Here indeed is a vital distinction between the puritan ministers and those laymen who at one time supported them in mutual opposition to Laud, like Milton, Selden and White-

1. Cf. Burnet, *History of the Reformation*, III, pp. 264–5; [H. Palmer], *A Full Answer to A Printed Paper, Entituled, Foure Serious Questions concerning Excommunication* (1645), *passim*.

2. W. H. Frere and C. E. Douglas, *Puritan Manifestoes*, pp. 17–18.

3. Cardwell, *A History of Conferences*, p. 215; Gardiner, *History of England*, II, p. 85; Curtis, "Hampton Court Conference and its Aftermath", *History*, No. 156, pp. 9, 12.

4. Cardwell, *Documentary Annals*, II, pp. 100–1.

locke. In August 1645 the Westminster Assembly demanded
that presbyteries should be allowed to exclude from the
sacrament even persons not included in the categories laid
down for this purpose by Parliamentary ordinance. This led to a
general attack on excommunication. "No divine can show that
there is any such command as this to suspend from the
sacrament", Selden told the Commons on 3 September. Excommunication, he added, is a human institution dating from
two centuries after Christ; it was imitated from the heathen.
Whitelocke in the same debate said "the best excommunication is for pastors, elders and people to excommunicate sin
out of their own hearts. . . . A church may be a good church",
he added with an irony that can hardly have been unconscious,
"though no member of it hath ever been cut off".[1] Parliament
refused to give ministers the discretionary power asked for.
The House of Commons, in its Declaration on Church Government of 28 October 1645, stated: "We can in no wise admit
that Christ hath invested the presbyteries with an arbitrary
power to keep from communion . . . whomsoever they shall
judge unworthy, and that the magistrate ought to confirm
such a power to them by his civil authority. . . . It is a maxim
amongst all wise law-makers to leave as little arbitrary as
may be".[2] Here we see some of the reasons for the stubborn
support given by men of property to the common law, against
old priests and new presbyters alike: they knew where they
and their property were at common law. In March 1646 an
ordinance insisted that in case of dispute arising over exclusion
from the sacrament, Parliamentary commissioners should act
as a court of appeal. The Westminster Assembly protested, but
was promptly put in its place.[3]

But many puritan ministers had advanced to the conception of excommunication as a non-material sanction. "Excommunication", a group of them wrote from prison to
Burghley, ". . . depriveth a man only of spiritual comforts, . . .
without taking away either liberty, goods, lands, government,
private or public whatsoever, or any other civil or earthly
commodity of this life".[4] Whether the ministers would have

1. Whitelocke, *Memorials of the English Affairs* (1853), I, pp. 503–5.
2. *Portland MSS.* (H.M.C.), I, pp. 297–8.
3. Milton, *Complete Prose Works* (Yale ed.), II, p. 126.
4. Strype, *Annals*, IV, p. 124. Cf. Thomas Taylor quoted on p. 347
above.

been so other-worldly if their lay supporters had controlled the machinery of State is perhaps another matter: certainly excommunication was very much a civil sentence in Scotland. In Geneva, however, Thomas Taylor reassured his readers, excommunication was used very sparingly, "the pastors restoring offenders by the spirit of meekness".[1] Richard Sibbes contrasted preaching with discipline by excommunication: "Other courses to punish men in their purse, or imprison them, or the like, may subdue them to outward conformity; but if we would bring their souls to heaven, let us endeavour to enlighten their understandings".[2]

Bishop Cooper saw here a suitable weak spot for the insertion of a wedge. He attacked the Puritans of his day for crying for "discipline by excommunication only" – i.e. by ecclesiastical censures, not backed up by the civil power. He let several large cats out of the bag when he argued that such discipline would be ineffective and laughed at: "Experience teacheth that men of stubbornness will not shun the company of them that be excommunicated, and then must they be excommunicated for keeping of company with them, and so will it fall out, that more will be excommunicated than in communion". In fact, the good bishop is arguing, the Church has no hold over the people, and can only maintain its position through the coercive machinery of the state, just as ministers during the interregnum were convinced that the abolition of tithes in favour of voluntary contributions would mean starvation for the clergy. Men fear "punishment of body and danger of goods", Cooper thought, more than excommunication. Like Hacket two generations later, after the overthrow of the state-ecclesiastical, Cooper favoured discipline by the purse.[3]

The spirit of the age, in fact, was making against the imposition of ecclesiastical penalties in spheres of activity which were increasingly felt to have their own laws and standards, different from those of the mediaeval Church.

1. T. Taylor, *Commentary on Titus*, p. 517. Control of excommunication had in fact been a matter of bitter dispute between Calvin and the secular magistrates of Geneva, a dispute which Calvin ultimately won.

2. R. Sibbes, *Beames of Divine Light* (1639), pp. 271–3. Cf. Hugh Peter, quoted on p. 232 above.

3. Cooper, *Admonition*, p. 69; cf. Hacket, epigraph to this chapter, and *Reliquiae Baxterianae*, I, p. 403.

Oxford and Cambridge universities renounced their right to excommunicate in temporal causes in 1534; the last example of the use of his power of excommunication by the Chancellor of Oxford occurred in 1592.[1] As men discarded the old standards they ceased to respect the hierarchy's attempts to "beat down sin". The appeal to individual consciences against authority is in effect an appeal to the standards of contemporary lay society, in which those consciences have been formed, against the old-fashioned coercive power of the state-ecclesiastical. It was easy to rouse indignation when excommunication was used to extort money for procedural offences and when the rich could buy themselves off.

IV

Lay society was in revolt against excommunication: but we should not necessarily assume from criticism of it, and from episcopal complaints of its ineffectiveness, that excommunication had everywhere lost its force. Mr. Ware, after considering examples of men wilfully standing excommunicate for long periods, nevertheless concluded that the sentence was a most effective means of coercion in Elizabeth's reign.[2] Mr. Price, on the other hand, argued that it was relatively inefficient in the diocese of Gloucester, where defendants rarely appeared in court, even when innocent, were repeatedly cited for the same offence, and stood excommunicate for long periods, though absolution could be had for as little as 1s.[3] This view is confirmed by much other evidence, dating especially from the end of Elizabeth's reign and the pre-Laudian Stuart period. Mr. Ritchie found that every tenth litigant in the church courts at York was excommunicated, and concludes that the sentence had lost any religious significance it may once have had.[4] In 1601 the official of the court of the Archdeacon of St. Albans

1. *V.C.H. Cambridge*, III, pp. 174–5; M. H. Curtis, *Oxford and Cambridge in Transition, 1558–1642* (1959), p. 31.
2. Ware, *The Elizabethan Parish in its Ecclesiastical and Financial Aspects*, pp. 49–50; cf. Brinkworth, "The Laudian Church in Buckinghamshire", pp. 33–4.
3. Price, "The Abuses of excommunication and the decline of ecclesiastical discipline under Queen Elizabeth", *E.H.R.*, LVII, pp. 106–14; cf. P. Williams, *The Council in the Marches of Wales*, pp. 101–2.
4. Ritchie, *The Ecclesiastical Courts of York*, p. 187.

explained to his bishop that for want of assistance to back up his jurisdiction ("which cannot be obtained without greater charge to us than the whole benefit of this office will sustain") "divers persons, the greater part of whom are poor and wilful" remained excommunicated. The bishop rather helplessly asked that some course should be thought of "for their further speedy correction", which would satisfy and stop the mouths of critics of church courts.[1] But it was not so easy. In part this was a reflection of the ineffectiveness of *all* sixteenth-century administrative and judicial processes. Quarter sessions had similar difficulties in getting offenders to appear. And there must have been much local variation depending on accidents of personality. But the Bishop of London whom we have just mentioned was Bancroft: few are likely to have been more efficient than he.

Recusants, Bishop Overton of Coventry and Lichfield noted sadly in 1582, were glad to be excommunicated, since they did not intend to come to church anyway: it saved them from having to pay a fine.[2] This must have helped considerably to discredit excommunication. There is a great deal of evidence in our period that excommunication was simply disregarded. Although it was "the only bridle the law yieldeth to a bishop", one of them complained in 1596, "either side" utterly despised excommunication.[3] "Our excommunications of recusants are utterly by them contemned", said Bancroft in 1610.[4] Dowsabell Taylor of Bilton, Yorkshire, had stood excommunicate for some 7 years in 1619.[5] William Gresham, Esq., of Hampton, stood wilfully excommunicate for about 6 years before he paid (in 1624), a rate of 7s. for building a churchyard wall.[6] Many fishermen, it was alleged in the Commons of 1621, died excommunicate because they could not, or would not, pay tithes of fish which they believed to be illegal.[7] Within the diocese of

1. Wilton Hall, *Records of the Old Archdeaconry of St. Albans*, p. 104.

2. Strype, *Annals of the Reformation*, III, part ii, p. 217.

3. *Hatfield House MSS.* (H.M.C.), VI, p. 266. The bishop was Bilson of Worcester.

4. Cardwell, *Documentary Annals*, II, p. 124.

5. Skaife, "Extracts from Visitation Books at York", *Yorkshire Archaeological Journal*, XV, p. 228; there are other examples of later date on p. 232.

6. Hale, *Precedents in Causes of Office*, p. 53.

7. N.R.S., II, p. 136; IV, p. 104; V, p. 253.

Hereford, its bishop reported in 1638, many remained excommunicate for long periods, often for non-payment of fees which they could not afford.[1] We should never forget poverty as a possible cause of what appears at first sight to be wilful or principled disregard of church sentences.[2] Ames gives an example of a citizen of Leicester who backslid and abandoned his convictions in consequence of the economic pressure of excommunication.[3]

The effectiveness of excommunication no doubt varied from diocese to diocese and bishop to bishop: there is a field for research here. Yet *potentially* its powers were great. Dr. Price argued that the very ineffectiveness of the sentence added to the grievance: people were pestered by an organization which was powerless to impose real discipline or to keep ecclesiastical order, but whose authority served merely to irritate and hit men's pockets. Disrespect and obstinacy naturally resulted:[4] and, we might add, speculation about the justification of the whole inquisitorial system. "Is nothing amiss?" asked Bacon in 1589. "Can any man defend the use of excommunication as a base process to lackey up and down for duties and fees? it being a precursory judgment of the Latter Day".[5] Excommunication, said Williams with the experience not only of a bishop but also of a Lord Keeper, was "the rusty sword of the church".[6] The sword would have to be thrown away unless a Bancroft or a Laud succeeded in his efforts to sharpen it.

Laud was a strong upholder of the clergy's right to "a coercive power", though he recognized that this was challenged by lay opinion in his day.[7] He insisted on churchwardens providing, at the expense of the parish, "a convenient large sheet or white wand . . . to be used at such times as offenders are

---

1. Laud, *Works*, V, p. 358. For other examples of large numbers of persons standing excommunicate for long periods see Jenkins, "Act Book of the Archdeacon of Taunton", *passim*; H. Johnstone, *Churchwarden's Presentments* (Sussex Record Soc., 1947–8), *passim*; A. J. Willis, *A Hampshire Miscellany*, I (1963), *passim*.
2. Cf. *A Petition . . . from the County of Nottingham*, p. 7.
3. W. Ames, *A Fresh Suit against Human Ceremonies in Gods Worship*, Sig. e.
4. Price, "The Abuses of Excommunication", *E.H.R.*, LVII, p. 108.
5. Bacon, *Works*, VIII, p. 88.
6. *Cabala* (1654), I, p. 103.
7. Laud to Bramhall, May 1635, in *Hastings MSS.* (H.M.C.), IV, p. 67.

censured for their grievous and notorious crimes".[1] His attempts to tighten up ecclesiastical discipline led to longer lists of excommunicates appearing in the parish records. Thus at the small town of Bingley in Yorkshire, 24 persons were excommunicated in 1639.[2] In the archdeaconry of Nottingham there were 82 penances in 1637, 94 in 1638; the figures in the fifteen-nineties and sixteen-twenties had never exceeded 60.[3] Secretary Windebanke thought that one of the great advantages of a restoration of Catholicism in England would be that the pope could excommunicate the King's enemies if they proved unruly.[4]

But by Laud's and Windebanke's time it was no longer merely a matter of men disregarding excommunication: there was an organized campaign against the authority of church courts,[5] which included deliberate inculcation of contempt for their ultimate sanction. Propagandists advocated wilful refusal to regard citations to ecclesiastical courts, on the grounds that they were held in the bishops' name, not in the King's. "If they excommunicate you, it is void: you may go to church notwithstanding. . . . If all subjects will take this course . . . they will soon shake off the prelates' tyranny and yoke of bondage under which they groan through their own defaults and cowardice".[6] But it was not void so long as Laud was virtual prime minister as well as Archbishop of Canterbury. In 1637 the churchwardens of Beckington, Somerset, who had refused to place their communion table altarwise, were thrown into prison for a year, as excommunicate persons, until they publicly admitted their grievous offence to Almighty God.[7]

1. Laud, *Works*, V, p. 450.

2. J. C. Cox, *The Parish Registers of England* (1910), pp. 112–13; W. E. Tate, *The Parish Chest* (1946), p. 149; cf. Brinkworth, "The Study and Use of Archdeacons' Court Records", *T.R.H.S.*, 1943, p. 112.

3. A. C. Wood, "Notts Penances (1590–1794)", *Trans. Thoroton Soc.*, XLVIII, p. 53.

4. Gardiner, *History of England*, VIII, p. 139.

5. See pp. 326–8 above.

6. *C.S.P.D., 1633–4*, p. 345 ("Brief Instructions for Churchwardens and others to observe in all episcopal or archidiaconal visitations and spiritual courts"). This paper is different from the *Brief Instructions for Churchwardens* printed by Prynne as an appendix to his *Breviate of the Prelates intollerable usurpations*, for which see pp. 381–2 below.

7. Prynne, *Canterburies Doome*, p. 97.

V

In the last resort it was state power that mattered. "Men do not care for excommunication, because they are shut out of the church, or delivered up to Satan", Selden observed, "but because the law of the kingdom takes hold of them".[1] This was Hacket's discipline by the purse again. The issues were political, though they seemed to be moral as well. Selden indeed told the Assembly of Divines that excommunication was a human invention taken from the heathens, an innovation used by the popes for their private quarrels: he favoured its total abolition.[2] If Selden had wanted an English example of political use of excommunication he might have instanced the fact that, in voting a clerical subsidy in 1640 (after the dissolution of the Short Parliament), Convocation threatened those who should refuse to pay with suspension and excommunication.[3] Soon after, Bishop Prideaux of Worcester is said to have excommunicated all in his diocese who should take up arms against the King.[4]

Henry Parker, more simply, thought that by excommunication princes and people had been sacrificed to bloodthirsty priests under pretence of obedience to the church. "If . . . spiritual supremacy rest in any one, that one must be unpunishable".[5] That Hobbist remark furnished one of Parker's principal arguments for lay sovereignty, since by the time he wrote any danger of royal absolutism appeared to have been left behind. Excommunication, Theophilus Brabourne wrote in 1660, is the task of the lay magistrate.[6]

To many laymen the issue seemed as clear and simple as to

1. Selden, *Table Talk*, p. 69; cf. Usher, *The Rise and Fall of the High Commission*, pp. 182–3.
2. Rushworth, *Historical Collections*, VI, p. 203. Selden's argument is taken from Erastus. It is noteworthy that Erastianism, properly so called, originated in Erastus's protest against clerical excommunication. See H. H. Henson, *Studies in English Religion in the 17th century* (1903), pp. 132–52.
3. Cardwell, *Synodalia*, p. xiii.
4. J. B. Marsden, *The History of the Later Puritans* (1852), p. 40.
5. H. Parker, *The True Grounds of Ecclesiastical Regiment* (1641), pp. 70–1.
6. T. Brabourne, *A Defence of the Kings Authority and Supremacy* (2nd ed., 1660), p. 1. Brabourne denied being an Erastian, although he admitted that many readers of his works called him one (*ibid.*, p. 4).

Parker: the liberation of men from the tyranny of priests. In 1640 soldiers who pulled down communion rails at King's Walden, Herts, also brought an excommunicated person into the church and forced the minister to conduct the service in his presence.[1] For others, excommunication still seemed a necessary means of preserving social discipline. Thus the Kentish Petition of 1642 demanded that if the coercive power of ecclesiastical courts by way of excommunication either had been or should be abrogated, then there should be "some other power and authority speedily established for the suppressing of the heinous and now so much abounding sins of incest, adultery, fornication and other crimes, and for the recovering of tithes, repairing of churches, probate of wills, church assesses, ... and especially for ministers who neglect the celebrating of the holy communion and of parishioners for not receiving".[2]

Baxter before 1640 disapproved not of excommunication but of the "promiscuous giving of the Lord's Supper to all ... that are not excommunicate by a bishop or chancellor that is out of their acquaintance".[3] He objected, that is, not to the sentence itself, but to the persons by whom and the manner in which it was imposed: and he wished, like many Presbyterians, to enhance the minister's control over his flock by allowing him to withhold the sacrament from them. The other side also objected to excommunication being wielded by persons whom they regarded as socially undesirable. The University of Oxford in 1647, as one of its objections to the Directory, said it was not fully satisfied to leave "so much power in so many persons, and those, many of them, of mean quality, for the keeping back of thousands of well-meaning Christians from the benefit and comfort of the blessed sacrament".[4]

The experience of the revolutionary epoch was to prove that Bishop Cooper had been right: once the Church lost the whole-

1. A. Kingston, *Hertfordshire during the Great Civil War* (1894), p. 6.
2. Quoted in J. M. Kemble's Introduction to Sir R. Twysden's *Certaine Considerations upon the Government of England* (Camden Soc., 1849), p. lii.
3. *Reliquiae Baxterianae*, I, p. 14; cf. pp. 85, 92, 142, 233, 396-7. Samuel Torshell, who like Baxter accepted bishops before 1640, similarly disapproved of "their wanton and profane abuse of the high and dreadful censure of excommunication" (*The Hypocrite Discovered*, 1644, Epistle Dedicatory to the Westminster Assembly).
4. *Reasons of the Present Judgment of the University of Oxford*, in I. Walton's *Life of Sanderson* (1678), II, p. 246.

hearted backing of the State its thunders ceased to terrify. "What will your censure do?" a pamphleteer was asking in 1645. "It will shame a few whores and knaves. . . . A boy in the streets can do as much".[1] The restoration of the Church in 1660 brought a short-lived change. It had been made possible because men like William Prynne feared that the presbyterian clergy wanted power to exclude all classes of society from communion; and because clergymen like Richard Baxter thought the reimposition of discipline on the lower orders worth purchasing even at the price of a restoration of episcopacy.[2] But the Church's scope was very much restricted after 1660. The number of penances imposed by the Archdeacon of Nottingham's court in 1662 was less than one quarter of those in 1638.[3] Just after the Restoration a Wiltshire man said "he cared not for the court nor power of it, it was but excommunication".[4] Men complained in Parliament in 1668 that churches could not be repaired so long as the ecclesiastical courts had no other sanction than excommunication, "which was of no force at all with some men, especially those who did willingly absent themselves from church".[5] A few years later, when the church courts were trying to help a Nottinghamshire rector to collect tithe on wages, the employers urged their workers to resist, since the worst penalty that could be imposed was excommunication, "which was only their not going to church".[6] They did resist, and did not pay the tithe.

Discipline by the purse, the old conception, had almost by definition been directed against men who had some property; but in the new dispensation after 1660 discipline of the lower orders seems to have been the main function of the church courts. Deprived of a High Commission, it was difficult for them to do much against "the rich and influential". Presentments and excommunication in the period 1660–88 came to be directed especially against nonconformity, to the exclusion of

1. W. Hussey, *A Plea for Christian Magistracie* (1645), Dedication.

2. W. M. Lamont, *Marginal Prynne* (1962), pp. 195–200; see p. 246 above.

3. A. C. Wood, "Nottinghamshire Penances (1590/1799)", *Trans. Thoroton Soc.*, XLVIII, p. 53.

4. A. Whiteman, "The Re-establishment of the Church of England, 1660–3", *T.R.H.S.*, 1955, p. 118; cf. *V.C.H. Oxfordshire*, I, p. 49.

5. Ed. C. Robbins, *Diary of John Milward* (1938), p. 240.

6. J. A. Venn, *Foundations of Agricultural Economics* (1923), p. 107.

other offences. "It is probable", Dr. Whiteman concludes ". . . that the gradual growth of toleration after 1689, and the consequent lack of interest even in reporting dissent, had much to do with the decay of presentments and their development into a farcical routine whereby a report of *omnia bene* was almost automatic".[1] By 1670 "a poor country vicar" was arguing for the use of the secular arm even against nonconformists, because the church courts would make themselves much too unpopular if they tried to cope with them as they deserved.[2] In the long run the true residuary legatee of the church courts as disciplinary organs for the lower ranks of society came to be the J.P.s, their power no longer fettered by a central authority with different social ideals. The attempt to tax the pleasant vices of the rich was abandoned; the J.P.s took over, not without relish, the punishment of drunkenness and of the propagation of bastards by those below a certain income level.

VI

Before 1640 only a very few, mostly sectaries, saw the obverse of the point made by Bishop Cooper: that with the end of state support for a persecuting Church, excommunication might again become a real spiritual penalty in a voluntary congregation.[3] One does not think of Calvin primarily as a democratizer of church discipline; but consider this passage from the *Institutes* in the light of Oxford University's protest quoted above: "The legitimate course to be taken in excommunication . . . is not for the elders alone to act apart from others, but with the knowledge and approbation of the Church, so that the body of the people, without regulating the procedure, may, as witnesses and guardians, observe it and prevent the few doing anything capriciously".[4] That is a very

1. Whiteman, *op. cit.*, pp. 118, 122–5, 131.
2. [T. Pittis], *A Private Conference between A Rich Alderman and A Poor Country Vicar* (1670), pp. 232–8.
3. Cf. Anne Stubbe's letter to Cartwright in 1590, in *Cartwrightiana* (ed. Peel and Carlson, 1951), pp. 61–2; John Smith's *Last Book*, printed as an Appendix to chapter VI of R. Barclay's *The Inner Life of the Religious Societies of the Commonwealth* (1876), p. xii; Roger Williams, *The Bloudy Tenent of Persecution* (Hanserd Knollys Soc., 1848), p. 80; cf. pp. 346–7, 356–7 above.
4. Calvin, *Institutes*, II, p. 457.

cautious *via media*, aimed no doubt at making the domination of an oligarchy acceptable to the mass of the congregation. But considered as a criticism of attitudes like that of Bishop Cooper and Oxford University, it is revolutionary and democratic indeed, since it presupposes not merely discipline of the people but also *for* the people, and if not *by* them at least with their passive participation. Given the separation of the Church and state (which of course Calvin did not envisage) it makes ecclesiastical discipline the harmless thing it has become in protestant countries to-day.

Henry Barrow, for instance, was taking Calvin's position only a very little further when he wrote: "This power of excommunication, election, ordination, etc., is not committed into the hands of one particular person [as the Pope and his natural children our Lord Bishops now use it]; nor yet into the hands of the eldership only, or of the pastors of many particular congregations (as the reforming preachers would have it) so much as it is given and committed to the whole church, even to every particular congregation, and to every member thereof alike".[1] So long as men thought in terms of a single state Church, the idea of excommunication by the congregation rather than from above had disturbing political implications, as governing persons in the sixteenth century were well aware. When Barrow was asked in 1586 whether a presbytery may excommunicate the prince, he replied "the whole church may excommunicate any member of that congregation, if the party continue obstinate in open transgression. . . . There is no exception of persons".[2] This fear underlay James I's attitude towards Presbyterianism. First the decision of sectaries to contract out of the state Church, and then the separation of the Church from the state, marked a change which had revolutionary implications for society, not least in its effect on excommunication. The early Brownists advocated separation from all churches where excommunication was not an effective sentence.[3] The early Independents also thought of excommuni-

1. H. Barrow, *A Briefe Discoverie of the False Church* (1590), p. 242, in Carlson, *op. cit.*, p. 638. The 1707 ed. omits the passage in square brackets (p. 362).
2. *The Examination of Henry Barrowe, John Greenwood and John Penrie before the High Commission and Lords of the Council* (1586), *Harleian Miscellany* (1744–56), IV, p. 340.
3. J. Waddington, *John Penry* (1858), p. 53.

cation as a spiritual sanction.[1] The records of the early Baptist Churches deal with little except excommunication.[2] Excommunication from a voluntary congregation is something like expulsion from a political party to-day. It has lost all that aroma of financial exploitation which clung round the courts of the established Church. The members of the congregations decide for themselves what is sinful and what is not. Excommunication has lost any possible political implications.

Milton – who so often carried Calvin's logic to lengths which would have startled Calvin – was shocked at the prelatical prostitution of excommunication "to prog and pander for fees, or to display their pride and sharpen their revenge, debarring men the protection of the law; and I remember not whether in some cases it bereave not men all right to their worldly goods and inheritances". With this he contrasted "the evangelical and reformed use of this sacred censure", which would not invade "worldly possession, which is the rightful lot and portion even of wickedest men".[3]

Between Cooper and Milton the wheel has turned full circle. The one sees no possibility of maintaining the Church's position save by threatening property: the other starts from the sanctity of property to reduce the Church to merely spiritual functions. Discipline by the purse had been a profoundly paternal conception. Standards were imposed, and sin was beaten down, from above. Whatever one may think of the sanctity of property as a political concept, at least it ensured that the property owners were treated as free men, fully responsible for their own actions. To that extent it marked an advance. For the industrious sort of people the property issue, and attitudes

1. For the influence on the Independents of Acontius's *Stratagemata* (1565), translated into English by John Goodwin, see B. Gustafsson, *The Five Dissenting Brethren* (Lund, 1955), pp. 100–5.

2. See for example *Records of the Churches of Christ gathered at Fenstanton, Warboys and Hexham* (ed. E. B. Underhill, Hanserd Knollys Soc., 1854), *passim*; cf. G. H. Williams, *The Radical Reformation* (Philadelphia, 1962), pp. 485–99. The Mennonites on the Continent had from the middle of the sixteenth century emphasized the importance of excommunication as a spiritual sanction whilst denying the right of the secular power to intervene in such matters.

3. Milton, *Prose Works* (Bohn ed.), II, pp. 413–14; cf. W. Dell, *The Way of True Peace and Unity in the true Church of Christ* (1651), in *Several Sermons and Discourses* (1709), pp. 235–6, 306–7.

of mind towards it, may well have played a bigger part (though often no doubt unconsciously) than historians have recognized in determining men's reactions not only towards the jurisdiction of church courts but also to the very idea of punishing "sin" and to the whole conflict of standards symbolized by the two extremes of Cooper and Milton. Within a hundred years of Cooper's book the opposite doctrine to his had become orthodox. "The end of a religious society", wrote Locke, selling the pass by the word "a", ". . . is the public worship of God, and by means thereof the acquisition of eternal life. All discipline ought therefore to tend to that end, and all ecclesiastical laws to be thereunto confined. Nothing ought, nor can be transacted in this society relating to the possession of civil and worldly goods. No force is here to be made use of upon any occasion whatsoever: force belongs wholly to the civil magistrate, and the possession of all outward goods is subject to his jurisdiction. Excommunication neither does nor can deprive the excommunicated person of any of those civil goods that he formerly possessed".[1] That simple formulation summed up the achievements of a century of struggle.

In the mental processes which led men from Cooper's position to Locke's, the protestant emphasis on conscience, on men's inner motives for which they alone were responsible to God, was of the greatest significance. The jurisdiction of the protestant hierarchy was undermined by the fundamental doctrines of Protestantism. Perkins had argued that conscience was a higher authority than any Church court: courts had no "constraining power to bind conscience, and that properly as God's laws do".[2] On the very eve of the civil war Henry Parker kicked punishment for sin upstairs into the after life, and put before the defenders of excommunication propositions to which they could find no answer: "In case of utter impenitence and open perverseness, heaven is shut without the minister's power: and in case of feigned penitence, the minister's key cannot open effectually, though he discern not the fraud: and in case of true penitence, if the minister be mistaken, yet heaven

1. John Locke, *A Letter Concerning Toleration*, in *Works* (1727), II, p. 237.
2. Perkins, *Workes*, I, pp. 528–30. See p. 304 above.

will not remain shut".[1] So the priesthood of all believers put down the priests from their judgment-seat; and ushered in a secular, Erastian society, in which sin was no longer defined and punished by public authority.

1. Parker, *The True Grounds of Ecclesiastical Regiment* (1641), p. 69.

Chapter Eleven

From Oaths to Interest

The safety of the King himself, . . . every man's estate in particular, and the state of the realm in general, doth depend upon the truth and sincerity of men's oaths. . . . The law and civil policy of England, being chiefly founded upon religion and the fear of God, doth use the religious ceremony of an oath, not only in legal proceedings but in other transactions and affairs of most importance in the commonwealth; esteeming oaths not only as the best touchstone of trust in matters of controversy, but as the safest knot of civil society, and the firmest band to tie all men to the performance of their several duties.

> [Anon.], *The Case of Concealment or mentall reservation* (1614), Ellesmere MS., quoted by M. A. Judson, *The Crisis of the Constitution* (Rutgers University Press, 1949), pp. 51–2.

"Nay, but there is more to be done", replied the duenna; "for we must exact another oath of him. . . ."

"He is so good", said one of the slave girls, "that he won't grudge taking as many oaths as we like".

> M. Cervantes, *The Jealous Estramaduran*, in *Exemplary Novels* (translated by W. K. Kelly, 1881), p. 352.

I

CLOSELY connected with opposition to the jurisdiction of the ecclesiastical courts was opposition to being compelled to take an oath. Refusal on principle of all oaths was more common among sectaries than among those whom I have defined as Puritans; but many even of the respectable Puritans objected to some oaths, and the whole subject has a certain interest for our purposes. Too often opposition to oaths is treated as if it were merely a personal idiosyncrasy of Lilburne and the early Quakers. But like many other symbolic gestures of radical Protestantism, the rejection of oaths contains an important social protest. Refusing to remove one's hat before higher authority was a way of asserting human equality: so was the objection to priests wearing distinctive vestments. The destruction of communion rails by soldiers in the reluctant army collected to fight against the Scots in 1639-40 had a similar symbolic significance, even if the troops were not all fully aware of it: by denying the special sanctity of the altar they were denying the miracle of the mass and the peculiar mediating role of the priest, and so proclaiming the priesthood of all believers, that revolutionary protestant anticipation of the equality of man. Refusal of oaths was more complex. But it too was a form of popular protest, with a very long history. It occurred among all those mediaeval heretics – Bogomils, Albigensians, Lollards, Taborites – who denied the authority of the state. Refusal to swear was an act of anarchism, proof presumptive of heresy for St. Thomas More.[1] A learned Quaker like Samuel Fisher was conscious of this continuity stretching back through the Marian martyrs to the Lollards.[2]

"Oaths", a learned member of the Assembly of Divines declared against the Anabaptists, "are necessary for the execution of the magistrate's office and the preservation of human society. For without such oaths the commonwealth hath no surety upon public officers and ministers; nor kings upon their subjects; nor lords upon their tenants; neither can men's titles be cleared in causes civil, nor justice done in causes criminal; nor dangerous plots and conspiracies be discovered against the state".[3] This passage conveniently sums up the two main ways in which oaths were traditionally used: (i) as a means of ensuring obedience of tenants and subjects, an oath of loyalty or non-resistance; (ii) in judicial procedure, an oath to tell the truth. An odour of sanctity was made to surround each type of oath, because each was socially necessary.

1. Coulton, *Mediaeval Panorama* (1945), pp. 465-70, 707.
2. S. Fisher, *The Testimony of Truth Exalted* (1679), pp. 811-13. The Levellers also were conscious of their ancestry, which both they and the Quakers no doubt had learnt from Foxe.
3. Daniel Featly, *The Dippers Dipt* (1646), p. 142.

In days of inadequate communications and a rudimentary
state machine, the first type of oath was essential to social
cohesion and subordination. The second type was as necessary
to early judicial procedure as was torture. "Torture is used for
discovery, and not for evidence", said Bacon.[1] Sir Francis
Walsingham, in a letter which Bacon may have drafted,
declared that the administration of justice depended on the
taking of oaths.[2] The truth of this is confirmed by a puritan
petition to Parliament in 1586, which said that the oath *ex
officio* "to a conscience that feareth God is more violent than
any rack to constrain him to utter that he knoweth, though it
be against himself and to his most grievous punishment".[3] Dr.
Gooch, Master of Magdalene College and a civil lawyer of
eminence, explained in the Parliament of 1621 "that taking of
an oath is incident to all jurisdiction is proved thus: proof is
necessary to all judicature, I mean such proof as may satisfy
the judge; and the most substantial proof is by oath".[4] With an
undeveloped police system and strong local loyalties, it was
often impossible to get evidence except from the suspect himself, or from his neighbours or associates, under compulsion to
tell the truth. This consideration continued to apply even when
economic changes were breaking up local communities and
the Tudor state was building up a national authority of increasing efficiency.

Refusal of oaths was thus the traditional means by which
the lower orders safeguarded themselves against trickery or
pressure aimed at forcing a confession from them.[5] Experience of our own day has perhaps made us more sympathetic
to the dilemma of men thus faced with the alternatives of
incriminating themselves and perhaps their friends and
associates, or committing perjury, or refusing to swear at all.
As the petition of 1586 reminds us, the oath was only valuable
to the authorities against conscientious offenders, those most
likely to withstand torture. Real criminals would presumably
not stick at a little perjury.

1. Bacon, *Works*, X, p. 114.
2. *Ibid.*, VIII, pp. 96–101; Burnet, *History of the Reformation*, III,
p. 535.
3. Ed. A. Peel, *The Seconde Parte of a Register*, II, p. 82.
4. N.R.S., IV, p. 310.
5. H. N. Brailsford, *The Levellers and the English Revolution* (1961),
pp. 82–3.

In 1583 Whitgift defended the oath *ex officio* on the ground that it was difficult to get witnesses against sectaries, since there was no fine from which informers could be rewarded. Nonconformists worked underground and could not be convicted by witnesses, though never so well known. Sects could not be stamped out thoroughly and quickly unless their members could be put on oath and forced to incriminate themselves. "If the chief gentleman in the parish, or most of the parish, be so affected, nothing will be presented, as experience teacheth".[1] As an example we may cite the evidence which William Perkins gave, on oath, in 1591, about the presbyterian assembly in Cambridge 2 years previously. He would hardly have given this information if he could have avoided it. In 1588 Whitgift had told one of the Marprelate suspects that by refusing to answer on oath he had confessed himself guilty. It was the general practice of the High Commission to account refusal of the preliminary oath sufficient proof that an accused person was obdurate and disobedient.[2] In the same way J.P.s would normally try to extort a confession from the humbler suspects whom they examined: when dealing with simple folk it was the easiest method of procedure. This was, of course, in sharp contrast with the procedure of the common-law courts, which catered for the propertied classes. Many opponents of procedure by oath in Star Chamber or High Commission had no qualms about using it themselves as Justices investigating the misdemeanours of the lower orders.[3] In just the same way men shocked by the savage sentences imposed by Star Chamber on gentlemen regularly imposed similar sentences on those who were not gentlemen.[4] There was nothing shamefaced about the existence of different laws for rich and poor in our period.

1. Strype, *Life of Whitgift*, I, pp. 318, 322. We may perhaps compare the procedure of senatorial committees in the U.S.A. in the nineteen-fifties: the inquisitorial method of procedure, says a legal authority, is that best adapted to the needs of social repression (J. P. H. E. Esmein, *A History of Continental Criminal Procedure*, transl. J. Simpson, Boston, 1913, p. 8).

2. H. C. Porter, *Reformation and Reaction in Tudor Cambridge* (1958), pp. 192–3; Peel, *The Seconde Parte of a Register*, II, p. 257; Usher, *High Commission*, p. 248.

3. Notestein, *The English People on the Eve of Colonization*, p. 213; Barnes, *Somerset, 1625–40*, pp. 56–7.

4. R. R. Reid, *The King's Council in the North* (1921), p. 436.

Gentlemen ought not to be whipped, Sir Edwin Sandys had told the House of Commons in 1621 – not even Floyd. A bill prohibiting the whipping of gentlemen passed both Houses of this Parliament, but never became law.[1] It was rare, Prynne correctly reminded his judges, for gentlemen or barristers to lose their ears unless the penalty was specifically laid down by statute.[2] D'Ewes, Fuller and Clarendon all agree that this social aspect of Prynne's punishment helps to explain the outcry against it.[3] In their discussion of Lilburne's case, the Commons of the Long Parliament observed that it had often been resolved, "even in the Star Chamber", that no gentleman was to be whipped for any offence whatsoever. Whipping was a "slavish punishment".[4] Hence Lilburne's insistence, often misunderstood, on being described as a gentleman in his indictment. If a man could show that he had been incorrectly described in a writ, the writ could be abated;[5] and his social class might make all the difference to the punishment.[6] Sir Henry Wotton in 1618 was shocked at the Venetian republic's failure to observe class distinctions in punishment.[7] Miss Wedgwood aptly juxtaposed two cases of 1637. In one, two nobles who had fought in the street were reprimanded by the Council; in the other the Council reversed a jury's acquittal of two draymen who had spoken rudely to a peer after a collision with his coach. "The saucy fellows were flogged and sent to Bridewell by direct order of the Council, which severe and high-handed action in defence of the social order called forth no protest

1. Gardiner, *History of England*, IV, p. 121.
2. Gardiner, *Documents relating to the proceedings against William Prynne*, p. 51. In 1602 a barrister lost his ears for libel (M. C. Bradbrook, *The Rise of the Common Player*, 1962, p. 296).
3. D'Ewes, *Autobiography*, II p. 205; Fuller, *Church History* (1842), III, p. 386; Clarendon, *History of the Rebellion*, I, p. 126.
4. Rushworth, *Historical Collections*, II, pp. 468, 475.
5. Coke, *II Institutes*, p. 596.
6. Cf. the succinct verdict of the Middlesex Quarter Sessions on a man convicted of stealing goods to the value of 11*d.* in 1614: "No goods: to be whipped" (ed. W. Le Hardy, *Calendar of Sessions Records*, Middlesex Sessions Records, New Series, II, 1936, p. 39). It was no use trying to fine a poor man. For examples of differential treatment for a gentleman, even when accused of high treason, see *John Gerard: The Autobiography of an Elizabethan* (transl. P. Caraman, 1951), pp. 67, 117.
7. L. P. Smith, *Life and Letters of Sir Henry Wotton* (1907), I, p. 156.

from anyone".[1] The House of Lords in 1642 had no hesitation about ordering a tailor to be whipped and imprisoned for life for scandalizing some of their members.[2] It was the Levellers who denounced whipping as "fit only for a slave or a bondman".[3]

We must recall the frequency with which this society resorted to oaths of one kind or another. In 1649 a judge could take it for granted that members of a London jury had often functioned as jurors before, and that there was no need to explain to them the sacredness of an oath.[4] A book published in the same year contained 416 pages of oaths which a man might have to take (or had in the past taken), ranging from the oaths of jurors to the Solemn League and Covenant.[5] The sworn jury of presentment and the oath of compurgation were still part of everyday routine. Churchwardens were "sworn to enquire diligently and truly to present", anyone whom "common fame" accused of an offence. The church courts had the duty of proceeding against any person against whom suspicion was "found to be so public that it becometh offensive". A man accused upon common fame could clear himself only by the oath of compurgators; if he failed to persuade or bribe a sufficient number of his neighbours to testify to his innocence, he was held to be guilty.[6]

The common-law courts often objected to the oaths imposed on churchwardens, and granted prohibitions in suits concerning them: but they did not deny the lawfulness of compurgation. Thus in 4 Car. I, when an archdeacon had enjoined compurgation on an alleged railer and sower of discord among his neighbours, a prohibition was granted; but on

1. C. V. Wedgwood, *The King's Peace, 1637–41* (1955), p. 176.

2. *Parliamentary History*, X, p. 414.

3. Petition of 19 January 1649, in D. M. Wolfe, *Leveller Manifestoes of the Puritan Revolution* (New York, 1944), p. 329.

4. *The Tryal of Lt.-Col. John Lilburne* (2nd ed., 1710), p. 127. See also an interesting "Exhortation to be given unto the Jury before the Charge, to consider their Oath" in *The Order of Keeping a Court Leet and Court Baron* (1650), pp. 5–10.

5. [Anon.], *The Book of Oaths and the severall formes thereof* (1649), *passim*.

6. "The judgement of several of the most learned Doctors of the Civil Law" (1590), in Strype, *Life of Whitgift*, III, pp. 232–5; H. Prideaux, *Directions to Church-Wardens* (4th ed. enlarged, 1716), pp. 6, 110; H. Conset, *The Practice of the Spiritual or Ecclesiastical Courts* (1700), pp. 390–6. For compurgation see pp. 298–300 above.

the ground that since the railing was not done in church the case belonged more properly to the court leet than to the spiritual court.[1] Oaths remained an essential part of normal judicial procedure even in the common-law courts. Discussions in 1621 and 1624 on the Commons' power to administer an oath "involved the whole question of the jurisdiction of the House".[2]

II

In 1625 Dr. Turner presented several accusations against the Duke of Buckingham, grounded upon common fame, to the House of Commons. This led to a discussion upon common fame. Dr. Turner found accusations upon this basis warranted both by Roman law and by the canons of the Church. (He did not mention the common law). Sir Thomas Wentworth, Christopher Sherland (the Feoffee for Impropriations), William Noy and other lawyers distinguished between common fame, the general voice, and mere rumour: "if common fame might not be admitted as an accuser, great men would be the only safe men, for no private person dare adventure to enquire into their actions. But the House of Commons is a House of information and presentment, but not a House of definitive judgment": the grand inquest of the nation, in fact. So the House resolved "that common fame is a good ground of proceeding for this House, either by enquiry or presenting the complaint (if the House finds cause) to the King or Lords".[3]

Buckingham argued in the following year that common fame was "too subtle a body . . . to contend with".[4] It was a criticism that might have been extended to the age-old practice of presentment upon common fame, which still flourished in the church courts, was indeed essential to their functioning. In a small homogeneous society jurors and informers could help to maintain conventionally accepted codes of behaviour. But

1. E. Gibson, *Codex Juris Ecclesiastici Anglicani* (1713), pp. 960–1.

2. Ed. W. A. Aiken and B. D. Henning, *Conflict in Stuart England* (1960), pp. 82–3.

3. *C.J.* I, p. 847; Rushworth, *Historical Collections*, I, pp. 217–18. In December 1640 Falkland referred to this discussion in a speech against Strafford. "I have heard, Mr. Speaker (and I think here) that common fame is enough for this House to accuse upon. . . ." (J. Rous, *Diary*, Camden Soc., 1856, p. 108).

4. Gardiner, *History of England*, VI, p. 117. Cf. Ralegh, *History of the World* (1820), I, p. 257.

when the society ceased to be homogeneous, when the codes of behaviour were no longer universally accepted, the system began to be called in question. Fame, said a speaker in the Short Parliament, might spring from small and groundless suspicions, secret whisperings. "If this be fame, their courts shall never want work as long as a promoter hath an ill tongue, or a knave can slander an honest man. . . . I desire the law may punish, not make, offenders; I desire that our words and acts may be subject to the law; I would have thought free".[1] His views were supported next year by *A Petition presented to the Parliament from the County of Nottingham*, signed by 1,500 esquires, gentlemen and yeomen.[2]

In the same year the Long Parliament abolished presentment upon common fame, together with the ecclesiastical jurisdiction itself. (16 Car. I cap. 11 s. 2, renewed by 13 Car. II st. 1 cap. 12 s. 2, cf. s. 4). The fact that this "fair and reasonable" procedure by judicial oaths and purgation was not restored in 1660, Bishop Gibson thought, meant that the Church's power was "greatly diminished and restrained".[3] Sir Michael Foster retorted that what the bishop regarded as "wholesome discipline" had "carried the ecclesiastical jurisdiction to a pitch of tyranny even beyond the . . . oath *ex officio*. . . . It requires a degree of courage and virtue not ordinarily to be met with to be able publicly and effectually to assert the cause of injured innocence against the tide and cry of the times".[4] Here the rights of the individual are squarely posed against the sense of the community, or rather of the central power working through the obsolescent institutions of the community.

The impeachment of Buckingham was quoted in the House of Commons in 1667. He had been impeached, it was said, "because then very high in his Majesty's favour. . . . Great men are to be accused upon common fame, for no particular man dare accuse them. . . . The House of Commons is in the

1. Quoted by M. H. Maguire, "The attack of the common lawyers on the oath *ex officio*", in *Essays in History and Political Theory in Honor of C. H. McIlwain* (Cambridge, Mass., 1936), pp. 202, 228–9.

2. *Op. cit.*, p. 3.

3. Gibson, *op. cit.*, II, p. 965.

4. Sir M. Foster, *An Examination of the Scheme of Church-Power laid down in the Codex Juris Ecclesiastici Anglicani* (1840 reprint), pp. 50–2. Cf. Joseph Hall, who even in 1650 thought that though "every idle rumour must not be believed", still there was "no smoke without fire" (*Works*, VII, pp. 407–8).

nature of the Inquest or Grand Jury . . . because it is their own knowledge that makes it good evidence: otherwise proofs would be needed". In 1680 Sir William Temple opposed condemning Halifax on grounds of common fame for advising Charles II against the Exclusion Bill.[1] Yet until ministers functioned publicly and were responsible to Parliament, it was impossible to bring precise accusations, legally proven, against them.

Common fame and the churchwardens' oath were the links binding local communities and government together.[2] When the interests and desires of those communities (or of significant groups of their members) conflicted seriously with government policy, the imposition of oaths on those who mediated between the two imposed a very severe strain. Churchwardens were continually being presented for refusing to serve, and being excommunicated for not presenting, or for refusing to take oaths. Thomas Adams spoke of churchwardens who failed to present despoilers of the Church, in order to win their favour; but he knew that in so speaking he would be accused of talking "for the profit of the Commissary".[3] A sermon against perjury preached during Neile's visitation of Lincoln in 1614 was "principally tending to the churchwardens".[4]

> *"There are churchwardens, too, I shame to see*
> *How they run into wilful perjury;*
> *Partly in favour, and in part for fear,*
> *They wink at much disorder in a year".*[5]

Wither's lines can easily be illustrated. Laud's Vicar-General found it necessary, during his visitation of Winchester in 1635, to promise that the High Commission would protect from molestation those who presented ecclesiastical malefactors.[6] Churchwardens, after all, might be quite humble people, unable to sign their own names: they could be overawed. Churchwardens generally, a Buckinghamshire parson

1. Ed. C. Robbins, *The Parliamentary Diary of John Milward*, pp. 316, 333–4; M. B. Rex, *University Representation in England* (1954), p. 285.
2. See pp. 415, 427–8 below.
3. T. Adams, *Workes* (1629), pp. 390–1.
4. Venables, "Primary Visitation of the Diocese of Lincoln", p. 49.
5. G. Wither, *Juvenilia*, I, p. 334.
6. Ed. F. R. Goodman, *The Diary of John Young* (1928), p. 107.

reported to Sir John Lambe in 1635, "are wilfully resolved to be forsworn, rather than they will present any justice or gentleman or rich neighbour, be they never so faulty". When ministers took upon them to delate gentlemen, he added sadly, they were liable to persecution.[1] Bishop Wren fined the churchwardens of Dullam, Suffolk, 40s. apiece for permitting Lord Brooke's chaplain to preach a sermon on a Sunday afternoon.[2] In 1637 the churchwardens of Rufforth, near York, dared not present a gentleman who was alleged to have begotten a child on his maid-servant, "he being the lord of the town".[3]

That was fear; favour was perhaps even more frequent. At King's Sutton, Oxfordshire, one of the churchwardens in 1611 was described as "a good fellow, and will not willingly present anything". Five years later the ecclesiastical official "could get no presentments from Banbury nor King's Sutton"; in 1619 the churchwardens at the latter place found themselves unable to define such difficult terms as blasphemer, swearer or drunkard, and therefore dared not present. "As for suspicions", they added when questioned about sexual offences in their parish, "we are loath to trouble our consciences with such uncertainties".[4] The churchwardens of Selsey in 1626 had to present two of their parishioners for living apart though married; but they explained the extenuating circumstances in much detail and with great sympathy, finally committing the case "to your worship's consideration, with as much favour as you may think of it".[5] So local good sense strove to mitigate old-fashioned ecclesiastical law. But it was a thankless task. It was very tempting to report "*omnia bene*" in order to defend the community's liberty against the inquisitorial central power, even when the hierarchy would regard this as "wilful, com-

1. W. H. Summers, "Some Documents in the State Papers relating to Beaconsfield", *Records of Bucks.*, VII, pp. 99–101. For examples see Brinkworth, "The Laudian Church in Buckinghamshire", p. 40.

2. See p. 90 above.

3. Skaife, "Extracts from Visitation Books at York", *Yorkshire Archaeological Journal*, XV, p. 236.

4. Peyton, *Churchwardens' Presentments in the Oxfordshire Peculiars*, pp. 211, 288–9, 294, 299; cf. p. lxx, and Johnstone, *Churchwardens' Presentments* (Sussex Record Soc., 1947–8), pp. xxv, 27, 35; cf. C. W. Foster, "The State of the Church", *Lincs. Record Soc.*, XXII, p. lxvii.

5. Johnstone, *op. cit.*, p. 120, See pp. 152–5 above: churchwardens not presenting men who worked on saints' days.

mon and execrable perjury".[1] "Drunkenness", said Thomas Adams, "uncleanness, swearing, profanation of the Sabbath, go abroad all the year; and when the visitation comes, they are locked up with an *omnia bene*".[2]

There were other loyalties too. Whitgift in 1590 accused a group of Midlands Puritans of deciding that "an oath whereby a man might be tried to reveal anything which may be penal to himself, or his faithful brethren, is against charity, and . . . ought not to be taken".[3] Here we have a new community loyalty, that of the congregation, over-riding that of the old local community: a loyalty all the stronger because the new community was voluntary. Forty years later Prynne elaborated the same point. "What good Christian", he asked, "can or dares take an oath to present . . . his own faithful, painful, conscionable minister, his godly Christian neighbours, kindred, brethren, friends, that are most nearly linked to him, to draw them into trouble, either to the loss of liberty, living, goods (yea, all of them oft times) and that only for their well-doing, at least for that which is not apparently evil? Is this Christianity?"[4]

That this was a statement of an actual problem is shown by the inquiries made in Bishop Wren's visitation articles for Norwich in 1636. He asked for reports whether any person in the diocese had affirmed that men ought not to take the office or oath of churchwarden; or that the oath was unlawfully given, or that it could be disregarded as a mere formality; or that the churchwardens could omit whom they would from their presentments.[5] In return Wren was accused in 1641 of "ensnaring and burdening" the consciences of the chief gentlemen in every parish "by taking the oath for presenting", and

1. *V.C.H. Buckinghamshire*, I, pp. 320–1; cf. Palmer, *Episcopal Returns for Cambridgeshire*, pp. 135–6 – all the churchwardens' returns for Ely in 1622, with one exception, were nil returns.

2. T. Adams, *Works* (1861–2), II, p. 272.

3. Strype, *Life of Whitgift*, II, p. 7; cf. pp. 19–20. Cf. W. Bradshaw, *English Puritanisme* (1605), quoted by Babbage, *Puritanism and Richard Bancroft*, p. 264; Leighton, *Sions Plea against the Prelacie*, pp. 136–7.

4. Prynne, *A Breviate of the Prelates intollerable usurpations*, pp. 235–6. Prynne said that oaths of inquiry originated with Bonner and were revived by Bancroft (p. 233). Cf. *A petition . . . from the County ot Nottingham*, p. 5.

5. Prynne, *op. cit.*, pp. 228–9.

of threatening churchwardens for not presenting.[1]

Pressure on churchwardens greatly increased under Laud and Neile. In the latter's diocese of York "numbers of these officials, who had served their year and probably forgotten about their actions, were suddenly confronted by a prosecution for not having presented defects or offences which had been revealed by their more amenable successors to the Visitors' interrogators, or detected by the Chancellor himself. When they submitted they were usually dismissed with a warning, but there was more than a hint that later defaulters would not escape so easily". There are many examples of refusal to execute the office.[2] The Root and Branch Petition, after complaining of the ruin caused to many families when men were presented to the Church courts for working on saints' days, and that churchwardens were sued or threatened for not presenting, went on to object to "the imposing of oaths of various and trivial articles yearly upon churchwardens and sidesmen, which they cannot take without perjury, unless they fall at jars continually with their ministers and neighbours, and wholly neglect their own calling".[3] The complaint is naïve and almost self-contradictory; but it expresses the real dilemma of men accountable both to a distant Government and hierarchy and to their own society with its very different standards. It is notable that the Petition seems to assume that churchwardens will regard perjury as a lesser evil than giving offence to their neighbours. In these circumstances the effect of imposing oaths was to deprive them of their sanctity, to make them seem a formal ceremony, which could be disregarded in the interests of charity.[4] In 1637 Prynne, from prison, gave churchwardens

1. Palmer, *Episcopal Returns for Cambridgeshire*, pp. 73, 75.

2. Marchant, *The Puritans and the Church Courts in the Diocese of York*, p. 57; for examples, see pp. 70–2, 99, 114, 126, 138–9, 190–2, 197.

3. Gardiner, *Constitutional Documents of the Puritan Revolution*, pp. 142–3. See p. 154 above. Cf. a petition from Kent, also in 1640: Bishops "impose oaths upon churchwardens, to the most apparent danger of filling the land with perjury" (*A Collection of Speeches made by Sir Edward Dering*, 1642, p. 23).

4. These difficulties were not peculiar to England. The accountant for the province of Venezuela wrote to Philip II in 1568 to explain that royal officials had conscientious scruples about examining men on oath about purchases of slaves from English "corsairs". "All we accomplish is to make them perjure themselves" (quoted in R. Unwin, *The Defeat of John Hawkins*, 1960, p. 134). Here too the officials shared the economic interests of the community they were defending.

precise and detailed instructions on ways of evading Laud's regulations about church ornaments;[1] and there is every reason to suppose that his advice was heeded, especially as the political situation after 1638 gave churchwardens the courage to resist.[2]

III

Yet the oath remained a traditionally consecrated religious rite, which was at first unchallenged by most Protestants of respectable social standing. The Book of Homilies, like the Thirty-nine Articles, stressed the lawfulness of oaths required by the magistrate, no doubt with the Anabaptists' heresies in mind: the Homily dwelt on the iniquity of perjury, especially if committed in the law courts. Perjury will be punished in the after life even if offenders escape in this world.[3] This was Calvin's doctrine too, popularized in England by the Geneva Bible.[4] It was shared alike by Archbishop Whitgift, who told a Marprelate suspect that no State could stand "without such answering and swearing",[5] by Lancelot Andrewes[6] and by Joseph Hall. In cases concerning property, said the last-named, "next after written evidence, testimonies upon oath must needs be held most fitly decisive. . . . There cannot . . . be devised a fairer and more probable course" for the exposure of vice "than by discovery upon oaths" of jurors and churchwardens.[7] An opposition business man like Sir Edwin Sandys agreed that "the sacred, the sovereign instrument of justice among men, what is it, what can it be in this world but an oath, being the strongest bond of conscience?"[8]

1. Prynne, "Brief Instructions to Church-wardens", at the end of *A Breviate of the Prelates intollerable usurpations* (1637).

2. Marchant, *op. cit.*, pp. 199–200.

3. *Sermons or Homilies* (1802), pp. 62–4. Perjury was an offence of which the ecclesiastical courts still claimed cognizance (see above, pp. 291–2).

4. Calvin, *Institutes*, I, pp. 334–9; Tomson's edition of the Bible (1603), notes to Genesis xxi, 24, xxiv, 3, etc. The doctrine was fully accepted by *The Reformation of the Ecclesiastical Laws*, pp. 15–16, 216–24.

5. Ed. Peel, *A Seconde Parte of a Register*, II, p. 255.

6. [Anon.], *An Apologie for Sundrie Proceedings by Jurisdiction Ecclesiasticall* (1593), Part III: a defence of oaths, incorporating a Latin determination by Andrewes.

7. Hall, *Works*, VII, p. 407. But see pp. 391–2 below.

8. Sandys, *Europae Speculum*, p. 45.

Hence the horror of the Jesuit doctrine of equivocation, though of course it only theorized what some Puritans of necessity had to do when put on oath. But the formalization of the doctrine seemed to many to challenge the accepted bases of society.[1] Ralegh, who had himself not been strictly veracious when on oath at his trial for high treason, denounced "that cunning perfidiousness and horrible deceit of this latter age, called equivocation". For oaths defend "the life of man, the estates of men, the faith of subjects to kings, of servants to their masters, of vassals to their lords, of wives to their husbands, and of children to their parents, and . . . all trials of right".[2]

The imposition of oaths by the government was an extension of the feudal oath of loyalty, from tenants to subjects. With the fifteenth- and sixteenth-century centralization of the national State, loyalty came to be conceived of as due to the King even against the mesne feudal lord. Almost any of Shakespeare's Historics could be quoted to illustrate the crucial importance attached to oaths. Cardinal Pandulph, the emissary of Rome, persuaded the Kings of France and England to perjure themselves in *King John*, with disastrous results. In *Richard II* the King emphasized the breach of oaths taken to him, especially by Bolingbroke, and presaged ill for the society in which such things are done: the Wars of the Roses followed. The perjuries of the Yorkists are ominously stressed throughout *Henry VI*, Part III; they brought Clarence and Richard himself to bad ends in *Richard III*.

Shakespeare's eye was on his own times. The oaths of allegiance and supremacy were means of reinforcing the new conception of sovereignty, of bringing it home to every free man who had to take the oath. Particularly the oath of supremacy, with its disavowal of papal authority, invoked the most tremendous sanctions in order to enforce a national one-party system, national like-mindedness. In 1563 a second refusal of the oath of supremacy was declared to be high treason and punishable as such. So wavering Catholics were faced with a choice between the supreme penalty in this world, and damnation in the world to come. The oath imposed on all suspect Catholics by the act of 1606, denying the pope's right to depose heretical sovereigns, is generally held to have contributed

1. For equivocation, see Gerard, *Autobiography*, pp. 125–6, 269–70.
2. Ralegh, *History of the World* (1820), II, pp. 416–19.

to the decline of Catholicism in England by dividing its adherents on so important a political issue.[1]

The sanction behind the oath was the universal belief in the
existence of God, and in an after-life in which rewards and
punishments are to be expected. It is another instance of the
importance of this belief to the maintenance of society, of
subordination and of order. The atheist was an anti-social
being, for whose probity there could be no guarantee: this is
one of the essential points of Cyril Tourneur's *The Atheist's
Tragedy* (1611). An oath was something quite different from a
promise, because of the religious form in which it was taken.
Thus Robert Backhouse, describing in print how he had
deceived the royalists in the civil war in a peculiarly unscrupulous manner, excused himself not by saying "all's fair in war"
but by the solemn assurance: "I never passed myself over to
them by any oath or protestation, which alone admits of no
equivocation, and without which they could have no sufficient
grounds of trust".[2] They were fools, in fact, to believe a man's
bare word *not* on oath: it is the child's "Oh, but I didn't promise!"

This seems to us an anti-social attitude: but that is because
we live in a very different society, a society in which exchange of
commodities on credit is a universal phenomenon, in which a
man's word is his bond. In pre-contract society, a man's bond
was his kinsman or members of his community who knew him
intimately. Supernatural sanctions could be effectively invoked
to solemnify contracts and promises, or to enforce feudal
dependence, as long as this was not done too often. But as
trade and industry expanded, contracts and credit transactions
became daily happenings: and this necessitated a new atitude
towards them. The sixteenth-century economic changes shook
the theoretical standards as well as the economic and political
foundations of the old order.

The Reformation worked in the same direction. In the
mediaeval world, where religion for the masses was sacramental and semi-magical, heavily emphasizing the performance of formal works, the important figure had been the

1. Prothero, *Statutes and Constitutional Documents (1558–1625)*,
pp. 40–1, 259.

2. R. Backhouse, *A True Relation of A Wicked Plot . . . against the
City of Gloucester* (1644), in *Bibliotheca Gloucestrensis* (1823), II, p. 323.
See p. 397 below.

priest. He mediated between God and man in the sacraments. He administered oaths, he alone could absolve from them: an oath was almost a sacrament. The reformers attacked the extension of the sacramental aspect of religion beyond baptism and communion. This helped to overthrow the uniquely binding character of oaths. The reformers also attacked the central position of the priest in the scheme of salvation. This included criticism of his power to dispense men's consciences, to do their thinking for them.[1] What mattered was not the form of words which a man had used, but the true intent behind them. "I am not forsworn", wrote Tyndale, "if my heart meant truly when I promised". Indeed an oath is no more sacred than any promise: "Our dealing ought to be so substantial that our words might be believed without an oath".[2] This is part and parcel of the attack on the double standard of morality: a man should pursue his worldly calling to the glory of God no less than actions traditionally regarded as sacred. When the Quakers carried out Tyndale's recommendations, the incidental economic advantages to themselves are well known.

So the puritan-protestant emphasis on the individual conscience, on the purity of a man's motives as seen by himself, created an independent and individualistic attitude of mind which led the radical sectaries to reject state-imposed oaths, whether judicial oaths of oaths or loyalty, in which correct observance of ritual might be more important than inner intention. "The ceremony of an oath they have stood for, without which all other things were accounted of no effect", complained the Quaker Richard Hubberthorne to the newly-restored Charles II.[3] Works of casuistry and guides to godliness, of which puritan ministers wrote so many in the sixteenth and seventeenth centuries, tried to help men to take moral decisions for themselves, and yet at the same time to preserve some sort of control over the workings of the consciences of individuals, to prescribe courses of action for every possible occasion. Jesuit casuistry and equivocation was (among other things) an attempt to deal with similar problems in societies where less was left to the individual conscience: their teachings

1. Cf. pp. 471–2 below.
2. Tyndale, *Expositions of Scripture* (Parker Soc., 1849), pp. 56–7.
3. *A Collection of the Several Books and Writings of . . . Richard Hubberthorne* (1663), p. 269.

were addressed to priests, who alone could loose what the Church had bound.[1]

But even the puritan ministers were fighting a losing battle. Increasingly men were insisting on deciding their moral problems by their own consciences and in the light of lay public opinion around them, and were using these as standards to criticize the traditional solutions of priests. The abolition of the confessional deprived priests of one traditional sanction to back up their advice: they were the more dependent on the power of the church courts. This helped slowly to change men's attitude towards the latter. There came to be less and less reality in the assumption that procedure by oath in the ecclesiastical courts expressed a spiritual and fatherly relation between director of consciences and sinner; there remained a judicial relation between judge and accused, which all too often seemed to be a merely financial relation.

"To decide in the light of lay public opinion around them": this was the decisive factor, and here the economic transformation of society was all-important.[2] In the mediaeval world the relationships between men, and particularly the relationship of subordination, had been expressed by oaths of loyalty. Supernatural sanctions had maintained these relationships, aided by the very present fear of hell so heavily emphasized in the *Homily against Swearing*. But in the new society which was coming into existence in the sixteenth and seventeenth centuries, the relationship of the market, and the veiled subordination of the wage-contract, replaced the direct subordination of the unfree peasant producer. Supernatural sanctions became less necessary in a society in which honesty was manifestly the best policy, in which those who did not keep their covenants made were apt to have difficulties in business relationships. "I will never believe that man whose honesty relies only upon oaths": the words were attributed to King James I.[3] "An oath . . . addeth not a greater obligation to per-

1. W. Gouge, *Commentary on Hebrews*, III, pp. 103–6. Cf. the distinction between "a material oath and a formal oath" attributed satirically to the Recorder in *The Return from Parnassus* (ed. J. B. Leishman, *The Three Parnassus Plays*, 1949, pp. 320, 355).

2. See my *Puritanism and Revolution*, pp. 230–1; "Protestantism and the Rise of Capitalism", pp. 32–3.

3. Overbury, *Crumms fal'n from King James's Table*, in *Miscellaneous Works*, p. 257.

form the covenant sworn", said Hobbes, "than the covenant carrieth in itself, but it putteth a man into greater danger and of greater premeditation".[1] So Hobbes secularized Tyndale. In this world the Quakers, whose yea was yea and whose nay was nay, refused oaths but were to prosper exceedingly. The distinctions between an oath, a vow and a promise, formerly so vital, began to disappear, as Tyndale had wished they should. Hobbes thought the keeping of covenants a law of nature.

IV

Tyndale in 1528 urged judges to "judge and condemn the trespass under lawful witnesses; and not break up into the consciences of men . . . and compel them to forswear themselves by Almighty God . . .or to testify against themselves".[2] The novelty is not in the sentiment, which had been expressed far more violently by those mediaeval heretics who rejected oaths altogether, but in the respectable social position of Tyndale's adherents. It was now no longer merely rebellious peasants and plebeian townsmen but solid and godly men of property who felt threatened by the use of judicial oaths. "The Lord", Cartwright thought, "ordained it a common law in all faults and transgressions, trespasses and sins, that the matter should be established by two or three witnesses". The use of the oath "doth . . . break upon the right of a more ordinary means for trial of truth by witnesses, whose use the Lord ordained and commanded unto us, as often as conveniently it may be had".[3] That God wished them to be tried by common-law procedure was a comfortable thought for many whose consciences were no doubt less clear than Cartwright's. The fire and indignation of Martin Marprelate's pamphlets, and their popularity with the laity, owed a great deal to the use of the oath *ex officio mero* in the ecclesiastical courts, for this had made Whitgift and the bishops hated by many propertied laymen who had no quarrel with their theology.

1. Hobbes, *The Elements of Law*, p. 62.
2. W. Tyndale, *The Obedience of a Christian Man*, in *Doctrinal Treatises* (Parker Soc., 1848) p. 203.
3. *Cartwrightiana*, p. 35; cf. Pierce, *Historical Introduction to the Marprelate Tracts*, p. 80, and Thomas Goodwin, *Works*, V, p. 261: men should not be made to accuse themselves on oath when the accusations against them can be proved by witnesses.

In 1548 it had been made illegal to put a man on oath in tithe suits; and all the efforts of the clergy could not get this reversed. Personal tithes ceased to be paid. Prideaux suggested that examination on oath in such causes was abolished because it led to widespread perjury among dishonest traders.[1] He was writing long after the event; but his assumption that business men would not boggle at a little perjury squares with the views which Tyndale had expressed nearly two centuries earlier, and with what Londoners themselves had said in the Root and Branch Petition.[2] All took it for granted that men would forswear themselves rather than give up what they thought necessary economic and social activities; what was resented was the action of the church courts in forcing them to commit perjury in the attempt to maintain obsolete standards of conduct.

A statute of 1563 insisted that the ecclesiastical judges had jurisdiction over cases of perjury only when committed in church courts. But since Star Chamber had cognizance of perjury committed in other courts, this was little consolation in the Laudian decade. It added one less idealistic reason to the many good ones for wishing to see the supremacy of common law established *vis-à-vis* all other courts. But men of conscience would rather swear not at all than commit perjury. From the same year 1563 onwards the House of Commons refused to allow oaths to be demanded of those charged with subsidy assessments.[3] The Commons objected to "new and needless oaths" imposed on the laity by the Convocation of 1604.[4] Attempts to have oaths against simony imposed on patrons as well as ministers were successfully resisted by the gentry.[5] Even bishops themselves objected to oaths imposed upon and not by the clergy. The Bishop of Lincoln protested in 1582 against commissioners for seeking out concealed church lands who "offered a number of articles to the ministers upon their oaths, very captious and dangerous to answer to, against themselves".[6]

So, principles apart, the use of oaths was declining. The

1. H. Prideaux, *An Award of King Charles I . . . for the Maintenance of the Parochial Clergy*, in *Ecclesiastical Tracts* (1718), pp. 298–300.
2. See p. 381 above.
3. Neale, *Elizabeth I and her Parliaments, 1559–81*, p. 125.
4. Babbage, *Puritanism and Richard Bancroft*, p. 100.
5. *E.P.C.*, p. 66.
6. Strype, *Annals of the Reformation*, III, part i, p. 169.

interests of common lawyers, unscrupulous business men and conscientious Puritans converged to hasten the process. Cartwright thought he was entitled to refuse an oath both by the law of God and by the law of the land.[1] Puritans, declared Bancroft indignantly, refuse for the most part to answer questions "either upon oath or without oath: saying that neither by the laws of God nor man they are bound to answer. Under colour whereof they exempt themselves from the ordinary course held in justice, for criminal causes, throughout all the world".[2] Oaths, Heylyn caustically reminded his readers, were lawful in Geneva.[3]

Refusal to take an oath by the accused was a very effective form of sabotage: it meant that the whole procedure of the court came to a standstill – though he might be imprisoned for contempt until he submitted. Here again the social atmosphere was important. Many a nameless mediaeval heretic must have submitted or perished in jail; but by the seventeenth century opponents of oaths had some solid social backing, and some of them were of sufficient standing to be able to afford to emigrate – like the London minister who in 1639 to Laud's face "boldly undertook to answer that which Bishop Andrewes had written" about oaths, and afterwards "slipped away to the Netherlands".[4]

The Lollards had objected on principle to oaths. Like so much of Lollardy, this passed straight into the tradition which we call Anabaptist. The Anabaptists were the sixteenth- and seventeenth-century equivalent of anarchist. Most of them made a point of conscience of refusing all oaths, though in England some members of the Family of Love thought oaths might be taken and not kept, and one group of Baptists offered in 1614 to take the oath of allegiance as the price of release from prison.[5] Anabaptists were already under attack for

1. Strype, *Life of Whitgift*, II, pp. 74–80; III, pp. 256–8. Cartwright thought it especially unlawful to require such an oath of a minister (H.C. Porter, *Reformation and Reaction in Tudor Cambridge*, 1958, p. 159).

2. Bancroft, *Dangerous Positions*, p. 3; cf. T. Rogers, *The Faith, Doctrine and Religion, Professed and Protected in . . . England*, p. 234.

3. Heylyn, *History of the Presbyterians* (1670), p. 9; Strype, *Life of Whitgift*, II, p. 80.

4. Letter from Laud to Dr. Sampson Johnson, July 1640, in *Bodleian Library Record*, VI, pp. 619–20. See p. 382 above for Andrewes.

5. Burrage, *The Early English Dissenters*, II, pp. 198, 216.

rejection of oaths in Edward VI's reign; article 38 of that King's forty-two Articles, and the last of Elizabeth's thirty-nine Articles, were specifically directed against them. In 1593 John Penry refused an oath proffered him by his ecclesiastical examiners "because it was against conscience and law": protesting at the same time that he held it lawful to take an oath before a magistrate.[1] Here he was differentiating himself from the Anabaptists. In the same year Barrowists were anticipating Lilburne and the Quakers in their principled refusal to take an oath: though one at least of them was prepared to protest before God that all his sayings were true.[2] Robert Browne apparently had no objection to judicial oaths.[3]

The dates should be noted. The emergence of open sectarianism helped to exacerbate the controversy over oaths. After the Marprelate episode Sir Francis Walsingham wrote a letter in which he defined the reasons for the Government's new severity towards those whom "we commonly call Puritans". Among other things he alleged that they were beginning "to make many subjects in doubt to take oaths, which is one of the fundamental parts of justice in this land, and in all places".[4] In the fifteen-nineties there was a flurry of concern in government circles. Committees of lawyers were appointed to report on the lawfulness of oaths. A controversy raged between James Morrice, a common lawyer, and spokesmen of the hierarchy like Richard Cosin and Lancelot Andrewes.[5] At the same time a public campaign was mounted against those who denied the lawfulness of oaths: Cosin made great play with the social subversiveness of the position.[6] So much did men's attitudes towards oaths become a shibboleth dividing conforming Puritans from sectaries that in 1618 Robert Sibthorpe – already with an eye for the prospering cause –attacked "the error of the Anabaptists" by developing the nature of an oath out of Perkins.[7]

Roger Williams held that taking an oath was a religious act,

1. J. Waddington, *John Penry* (1858), p. 124.

2. Burrage, *op. cit.*, II, pp. 32–5; cf. p. 55.

3. *Writings of Harrison and Browne*, pp. 324–7.

4. Burnet, *History of the Reformation*, III, pp. 535–6. The letter may be Bacon's: see pp. 372 above, 488 below.

5. Strype, *Life of Whitgift*, II, pp. 28–32. For Andrewes see p. 382 above, and for Morrice p. 391 below.

6. R. Cosin, *Conspiracy for Pretended Reformation* (1699), pp. 178–9: first published "by authority" in 1592.

7. Maclure, *The Paul's Cross Sermons*, pp. 239–40.

and so ought not to be forced upon anyone. He himself refused to take an oath of fidelity to the civil government of Massachusetts Bay, and urged others to refuse too. The regenerate, he thought, ought not to be forced in their consciences for civil purposes: the unregenerate could not take part in what was an act of religious worship.[1] Even a less radical thinker like the Rev. Richard Ward, in his *Commentary on the Gospel according to St. Matthew*, advised "both magistrates and those who are wronged" to be "very careful not to constrain any offender to swear, if by any other means the matter may be known or decided". His reason appears to be sensible enough: "If he whom we desire should be put to his oath fear the Lord, then he dare no more lie than forswear himself.... If he fear not the Lord, then how will he fear to forswear himself?" But such reasoning did not appear common sense to Laud's licenser: it was dangerous doctrine, which had to be deleted from the book before it was licensed for publication.[2] Nor should we forget the allegation of the common lawyers that the High Commission and its oaths were illegal. Logically this is a distinct point from the lawfulness of oaths in general, but the two got mixed up in men's minds, as we saw in Cartwright's assertion that trial by witness was laid down by God as the normal mode of procedure, and in the distinctions drawn by Penry. Prynne cited both Foxe's *Book of Martyrs* and the Petition of Right against the bishops' claim to impose oaths.[3]

The common lawyers, for their own reasons, also adopted a position of principle in regard to oaths which suited religious opponents of the Government very well. James Morrice, attorney of the Court of Wards, who wrote a treatise against the oath *ex officio*, declared that the oath was against the Word of God, the law of nature, the law of the land and the royal prerogative. He was believed to have advised Cartwright in his refusal of the oath.[4]

1. R. Williams, *The Bloudy Tenent of Persecution* (ed. E. B. Underhill, Hanserd Knollys Soc., 1848), p. xix; Nathaniel Morton, *New Englands Memorial* (1669), in *Chronicles of the Pilgrim Fathers* (Everyman ed.), pp. 103–7; cf. Perry Miller, *Roger Williams* (New York, 1953), pp. 19 25–6.

2. Prynne, *Canterburies Doome*, pp. 255, 329 30. Ward was later to write a vindication of Parliament and a defence of the Covenant.

3. Lamont, *Marginal Prynne*, p. 210.

4. Strype, *Life of Whitgift*, II, pp. 28–32.

"By the laws of England", Bacon had told James I, "no man is bound to accuse himself".[1] No one, the chief justices told the King in 1606, ought to be examined on his secret thoughts and opinions, as opposed to actual words or deeds. Coke later issued a prohibition in the case of two alleged schismatics, on the ground that no free man should be compelled to answer about his secret opinions. "An oath in a man's own cause", said Coke, "is the device of the devil to throw the souls of poor men into hell". In 1610 the King's Bench ruled that no man could be compelled to answer on oath where his answer might show forfeiture of an obligation.[2] And Coke abstracted the maxim "*nemo tenetur seipsum prodere*" from its full context, so as to give an ultra-individualist twist to what had originated in the federation of communities which was mediaeval society.[3] "An oath", wrote Coke with naïve cunning, "is so sacred, and so deeply concerneth the consciences of Christian men, as the same cannot be ministered to any unless the same be administered by the common law, or by some act of Parliament".[4] Just as war is too serious a matter to be left to generals, so the consciences of Christian men are too tender to be left to the spiritual courts.

Under Laud and Neile, with full government backing,[5] there was an extension of the use of the oath *ex officio* just because voluntary co-operation between the central authority and the localities was breaking down. When churchwardens failed to present, and the ecclesiastical authorities wished to prosecute, they had to proceed *ex officio mero*, on grounds of suspicion and rumour: the oath was imposed in the hope of extracting

1. Bacon, *Works*, X, p. 114; cf. N. Bacon, *An Historical and Political Discourse of the Laws and Government of England* (1739), Part II, p. 92. Bishop Hall accepted this position by 1650 (*Works*, VII pp. 408–9).

2. Maguire "The attack of the common lawyers on the oath *ex officio*", in *Essays in History and Political Theory in Honor of C. H. McIwain*, pp. 222–6.

3. Coke, *The Second Part of the Institutes* (1671), pp. 657–8. The full maxim is "*Licet nemo tenetur seipsum prodere, tamen proditus per famam tenetur seipsum ostendere utrum possit suam innocentiam ostendere et seipsum purgare*". Cf. pp. 375–8 above.

4. Coke, *III Institutes* (1648), p. 165; cf. *12 Reports*, pp. 26–9, 131–2. Coke's position, like so many other positions, was elaborated by Prynne: see his *Breviate of the Prelates intollerable usurpations* (1637), pp. 219 sqq.

5. See p. 341 above.

information which might lead to a conviction.[1] Naturally this was unpopular not only with the accused but also with all who resented Laud's attempt to circumvent and over-rule the normal processes. If churchwardens said *omnia* were *bene*, surely they knew best? Resistance to the oath *ex officio* is strictly parallel to the J.P.s' opposition to interference with their local omnipotence, whether by Mitchell and Mompesson's patent under James I, by billeting and martial law in the sixteen-twenties, by the nagging of the Privy Council in the sixteen-thirties, or by Major-Generals in the sixteen-fifties. From Laud to James II those who tried to impose policies on the "natural leaders" of the local communities invariably came to a bad end. "Careful study of the oath *ex officio*" forced Dr. Maguire to the conclusion that "more bitterness arose out of it than historians have hitherto realized".[2] For good and ill, the seventeenth century saw the legal triumph of the principle that no man should incriminate himself, whatever the charge, whatever the court. The old emphasis on denunciation by "common fame", by the community, fades into the background: and the Faustian individual is left free to maintain silence against the genuine outcry of his neighbours as well as against the inquisitorial self-righteousness of church courts or the venal denunciation of informers.

But before 1640 this consummation was still being stubbornly fought for, with a variety of converging arguments. Leighton in 1628 followed Coke in claiming that the oath *ex officio* was "against the law of nature registered in the civil law, '*Nemo tenetur prodere seipsum*' ".[3] Samuel Rutherford used the same argument.[4] We may see the confusion of religious and legal positions, at a slightly less sophisticated level, in the defence put forward by the separatist Abigail Delamar in 1632. The oath *ex officio*, she declared, "is condemned by the law of the land, and I refuse it as an accursed oath, and appeal to the King". She and her fellows "were afraid it was against the subjects' just liberty to be compelled to take this oath, and showed that they would willingly be tried by his Majesty's laws, or by his Majesty or any of his

1. Marchant, *The Puritans and the Church Courts in the Diocese of York*, pp. 191-3.

2. Maguire, *op. cit.*, p. 228.

3. Leighton, *Sions Plea against the Prelacie*, p. 48.

4. S. Rutherford, *Lex, Rex* (1644), Sig. a v.

lords and nobles".[1] Lilburne also used conscientious and religious arguments indiscriminately.

Nehemiah Wallington has recorded for us the real struggle which he had with his conscience when required to take an oath in Star Chamber in 1639.[2] Such men were not frivolous, not merely pedantic, nor were they factious: we should not underestimate the risks they ran, nor the importance of the issues which they felt to be at stake. Those who refused on conscientious grounds to take an oath in the common-law courts might find themselves in very serious difficulties. They could not sue for debts, could not defend their property in court, or give evidence: they could not, in theory at least, prove a will or be admitted to a copyhold. Refusal of an oath in a prerogative court might have incalculable consequences. In the High Commission, it was taken as evidence of guilt. This was not a position to be adopted light-heartedly, least of all by the industrious sort of people, men like Wallington and Lilburne, among whom resistance to oaths seems to have been carried furthest as a point of principle.

During the interregnum principled opposition to oaths was expressed more freely. Even an orthodox divine like Herbert Palmer protested in sermons before the House of Commons against unnecessary oaths imposed by universities and corporations, as well as at inquests.[3] In 1647 the Heads of Proposals, which conspicuously lacked oaths of allegiance, asked for some provision to be made "that none may be compelled by penalty or otherwise to answer questions tending to the accusing of themselves or their nearest relations in criminal causes", and for the abolition or modification of oaths imposed by corporations.[4] Six years later the Barebones Parliament tried to relieve those who scrupled at oaths by an Act abolishing homage, oaths of fealty (an Act originally drafted by the Rump's committee on law reform), oaths upon

1. Burrage, *Early English Dissenters*, II, p. 319.
2. Wallington, *Historical Notices*, I, p. xxxix.
3. H. Palmer, *The Necessity and Encouragement of Utmost Venturing for the Churches Help*, pp. 38, 51–2 (a sermon preached before the House of Commons on 28 June 1643); *The Duty and Honour of Church-Restorers*, pp. 36–7 (preached before the Commons on 30 September 1646).
4. Gardiner, *Constitutional Documents of the Puritan Revolution*, p. 325 (paras. 8, 9).

matriculation, taking a degree, or admission into any corporation, society or company: they were to be retained only for admission to public office.[1] In 1657, at a court of the East India Company, the Anabaptists "would have had the Adventurers obliged only by an engagement, without swearing, that they might still pursue their private trade; but it was carried against them".[2] The Quakers' refusal to take an oath was a handicap to them in their business life: they could not become freemen.[3]

V

There is one further aspect of opposition to oaths which is worth emphasizing: the egalitarian aspect. It was one of the privileges of peers that their word of honour was accepted in lieu of an oath, and therefore they were excused from swearing in court.[4] Noble Roman Catholics were exempt from the oath on matriculation at Oxford. Sons of peers were excused from the oath of loyalty to the Church of England imposed by the Canons of 1640.[5] The Test Act of 1673 was the first occasion on which an oath was statutorily demanded of peers. All "men of quality", all free men, were expected to take the oaths of supremacy and allegiance and the Protestation of 1641;[6] but it was different with judicial oaths.

It was normally only the lower orders whom the J.P.s examined with a view to a sworn confession. "Do magistrates, masters, parents and other superiors ordinarily swear to make good their word to their inferiors?" asked Gouge. "This useth to be exacted of inferiors, as *Gen.* xxiv. 3, but not so of superiors". No freeborn Englishman ought to take an oath *ex officio*, Lilburne told Star Chamber in 1638.[7] It was a stigma of social inferiority, and appeared to be a denial of

1. *Several Draughts of Acts* (1653), in *Somers Tracts* (1748–51), I, p. 502.
2. Evelyn, *Diary* (ed. de Beer), III, p. 201.
3. Lipson, *Economic History of England*, III, pp. 528–9.
4. Hacket, *Scrinia Reserata*, II, p. 151; Isaac Barrow, *Sermon against rash and vain swearing*, in *Works* (1859), II, p. 59.
5. 7 Jac. I, cap. 6; Cardwell, *Synodalia*, I, p. 403.
6. G. F., *Englands Oaths Taken by all men of Quality in the Church and Commonwealth* (1642); cf. Ralegh, *History of the World* (1820), II, p. 419.
7. Gouge, *Commentary upon Hebrews*, II, p. 52; Rushworth, *op. cit.*, II p. 463.

the right to trial by common law which was believed to have
been guaranteed to free men by Magna Carta. "Our English
oaths", said Samuel Fisher, "are imposed upon poor persons
. . . when they come before crooked courts in case of tithes".[1]
As the number of free men increased, refusal of oaths became a
proclamation of human equality. The oath *ex officio*, said
Coke, should only be tendered to laymen in testamentary and
matrimonial causes where no discredit could ensue (an argument which would win the eager assent of business men) "for
laymen for the most part are unlettered, wherefore they may
easily be inveigled and entrapped, and principally in heresy
and matters of faith".[2] The Leveller opposition to the privileges
of peers and to oaths were thus two aspects of a single consistent position.

VI

An oath of allegiance was the means of bringing home
national political transformations to the masses of the population, of involving them to some extent as participators. Each of
the governments which came to power in England in the
revolutionary years tried to buttress its position by securing
national subscription to an oath; with the concomitant that
those who refused the oath were excluded from public
office.

> "*Did not our worthies of the House,*
> *Before they broke the peace break vows?*
> *For having freed us, first, from both*
> *Th'allegiance and supremacy oath,*
> *Did they not, next, compel the nation*
> *To take, and break, the Protestation?*
> *To swear, and after to recant,*
> *The Solemn League and Covenant?*
> *To take th'Engagement and disclaim it,*
> *Enforced by those who first did frame it?*"[3]

In all men might have had to take up to 10 such conflicting
oaths of loyalty between 1640 and 1660, to say nothing of the

1. Fisher, *The Rustickes Alarm to the Rabbis* (1660), in *The Testimony
of Truth Exalted* (1679), p. 441.
    2. Maguire, *op. cit.*, p. 222.
    3. S. Butler, *Hudibras* (ed. Waller, 1905), p. 133.

counter-swearing of the Restoration.[1] And this does not include oaths of secrecy like those which, for example, the Parliamentary Committee for Staffordshire called for from its members "when any business of weight is agitated".[2] In 1659 Milton could think of no better means of uniting Parliament and Army (a difficult task!) than "a mutual league and oath . . . not to desert one another until death".[3]

In these circumstances the casuists were kept busy. Sanderson, a post-Restoration bishop, decided that the Covenant was unlawful, because contrary to the oath of allegiance, whereas he and other royalists were prepared to contemplate the Engagement more favourably.[4] Among "the most common arguments urged for the subscription" of the Engagement, one of Sanderson's correspondents said, was the distinction which we have already met between a promise and an oath. The Engagement "is only a promise, not an oath, and consequently not so obliging the conscience, but only *pro tempore*, whilst the state stands in force".[5] Baxter, post-Restoration dissenter, kept the town of Kidderminster from taking the Covenant, yet also spoke and preached against the Engagement, because he could not think it seemly for those who had taken the Covenant "to play fast and loose with a dreadful oath". "No bonds of society can signify much with such interpreters", said Baxter of Sanderson and his like.[6] It was Anthony Ascham, whose approach to politics was completely secular, who argued: "It is evident that most contracts and oaths made betwixt political or

1. G. Davies, *The Restoration of Charles II*, pp. 361–2. Cf. the Earl of Derby's pleasure at being able, in the remote Isle of Man, to escape this succession of oaths (ed. F. R. Raines, *Private Devotions and Miscellanies of James, Seventh Earl of Derby*, Chetham Soc., 1867, I, p. cxliii). For some of these oaths, see my *Puritanism and Revolution*, pp. 159, 172.

2. Ed. D. H. Pennington and I. A. Roots, *The Committee at Stafford 1643–5* (1957), p. 30.

3. Milton, *Prose Works* (Bohn ed.), II, p. 105.

4. Sanderson, *Eight Cases of Conscience* (1674), pp. 111–12, 121–4. Cf. also his *The Nature and Obligation of Promissory Oaths* (1722), and Sancroft, "Modern Policies", in *Somers Tracts* (1809–15), VII, pp. 169–71.

5. Thomas Washbourne to Robert Sanderson, 7 January 1650, in *The Poems of Thomas Washbourne* (ed. A. B. Grosart, 1868), pp. 39–40.

6. *Reliquiae Baxterianae*, I, pp. 64–5, 408–22. Cf. R. S. Bosher, *The Making of the Restoration Settlement* (1951), pp. 14–15, for casuistry concerning the Engagement.

public persons are made in this political sense, viz. with a tacit condition of holding their possession".[1]

For indeed the enforcing of oaths of allegiance became a self-defeating process. In 1648, too late as usual, Charles I had arrived at the important conclusion that "the laying of oaths upon men (especially such as brought with them a penalty which by the greatness thereof did terrify [men] unto [a compliance] was that which ought to be most tenderly attempted".[2] The more contradictory oaths men took, the less bound they felt by any of them, by a sort of moral Gresham's Law. A royalist song made this point:

> *"They force us to take*
> *Two oaths, but we'll make*
> *A third, that we ne'er meant to keep 'em".*[3]

One royalist boasted that Parliament could not devise an oath which he would not swallow. "Oaths are but snares", said an M.P. in 1657; "times are changeable, and a multiplicity of oaths draw but on to sin. It will but keep out the conscientious, and let in those that make no scruple of any oath".[4] The republican Colonel Hutchinson opposed an oath to exclude Charles II in January 1660, on the same ground that oaths merely multiplied perjuries.[5] The fewer oaths the better, Monck told Parliament next month.[6]

In 1658 Francis Osborn, noting that the revolutionary Netherlands had framed an oath abjuring all those formerly taken to the King of Spain, commented that "they called God Himself to attest that His Name was become of no validity". "No security can be given or taken", he continued, "either

1. A. Ascham, *A Discourse: Wherein is examined, What is particularly lawfull during the Confusions and Revolutions of Government* (1648), p. 28. I owe this reference to the late Dr. Felix Raab's *The English Face of Machiavelli* (1964).

2. F. Peck, *Desiderata Curiosa* (1779), p. 390.

3. *Rump: or an Exact Collection of the Choycest Poems and Songs Relating to the Late Times* (1662), I, p. 235.

4. *Burton's Parliamentary Diary*, II, pp. 279, 290. The second speaker was opposing the proposed oath for M.P.s. Cf. *ibid.*, p. 150, and *A Narrative of the late Parliament* (1657), in *Harleian Miscellany* (1744–56), III, p. 445.

5. Lucy Hutchinson, *Memoirs of the Life of Colonel Hutchinson* (1846), pp. 393–4.

6. G. Davies, *The Restoration of Charles II* p. 277.

singly or reciprocally, between the prince and the people but an oath"; but when they are frivolously multiplied, "the validity of oaths is lost or converted into traps to catch the innocent and unadvised".[1] "Every experience", declared the Rev. Charles Herle in 1642, "tells us that *interests* are better state security than oaths".[2] Herle's argument was that power should be trusted to Parliament rather than to the judges, "rather to many independent men's *interests* than a few dependent men's oaths". This somewhat cynical conclusion of the learned member of the Assembly of Divines was echoed after the Restoration in one of the many poems about the Vicar of Bray. The Vicar sings:

> "*I've took so many oaths before*
> *That now without remorse*
> *I take all oaths the state can make*
> *As merely things of course*".[3]

Wycherly in *Love in a Wood* (1671) made Lucy say to Gripe ("seemingly precise, but a covetous, lecherous old usurer of the City"): "You have broken many an oath for the Good Old Cause, and will you boggle at one for your poor little miss?"[4] Robert Boyle published a *Free Discourse against Customary Swearing* in 1646. He also felt strongly about compulsory oaths: when he was elected President of the Royal Society he declined the office rather than take an oath. John Ray was another eminent scientist who resigned positions of emolument rather than take an oath at which his conscience scrupled.[5]

Isaac Barrow dealt with the problem in his *Sermon against Rash and Vain Swearing*. Oaths, he reminded his congregation, were necessary if society was to ensure the obedience of subjects and soldiers, and the stability of marriage; in legal cases

1. F. Osborn, *Miscellaneous Works*, I, pp. 206–8; cf. *ibid.*, *Essays*, p. 83; II, p. 254.
2. C. Herle, *A fuller Answer to a Treatise written by Doctor Ferne . . .* (1642), p. 14.
3. *The Posthumous Works of Mr. Samuel Butler* (1754), p. 139. The attribution to Butler is highly dubious: the only thing to suggest it is an apparent echo of Butler's favourite *Don Quixote*. Sancho Panza had declared that oaths were "very bad for the health and very harmful to the conscience" (M. de Cervantes, *Don Quixote*, Penguin translation, p. 82).
4. Wycherley, *Love in a Wood*, Act V, scene iii.
5. J. G. Crowther, *Founders of British Science* (1960), pp. 90, 107–8.

affecting the lives, estates and reputations of men there was no comparable security. It followed that "human society will be extremely wronged and damnified by the dissolving or slackening these most sacred bands of conscience: and consequently by their common and careless use; which soon will breed a contempt of them, and render them insignificant, either to bind the swearers, or to ground a trust on their oaths".[1] Indeed perjury, especially after the abolition of Star Chamber, became a serious problem. The Statute of Frauds of 1677 tried to make the common law effective to cope with it.[2]

Samuel Butler noted another consequence of plurality of oaths: hypocrisy. Referring no doubt to the Corporation Act, he said: "As soon as a man has taken an oath against his conscience and done his endeavour to damn himself, he is capable of any trust or employment in the government".[3] This argument proved especially annoying when used by Quakers to ex-Parliamentarian J.P.s who had accepted the Restoration.[4] When the disappointed of right and left, Cavaliers and Quakers, agreed on such a point, times had already changed. "What then can be the end of this swearing?" Roger Coke asked. "Why, 'tis because otherwise the swearer cannot be a member of the corporation; but if I cannot take his word, I'll not take his oath. And he that swears most to get places is least worthy of them".[5] Butler recognized with Herle that in the new Hobbist society oaths had lost their point: "Oaths and obligations in the affairs of the world are like ribbons and knots in dressing, that seem to tie something, but do not at all. For nothing

1. I. Barrow, *Theological Works* (1859), II, pp. 44–9.
2. D. Ogg, "Britain after the Restoration" in *New Cambridge Modern History*, V (1961), p. 313. Cf. Petty, "Of the Preventing the Abuse of Oaths and Ascertaining Testimony", in *Petty Papers* (ed. Marquess of Lansdowne, 1927), II, pp. 204–6.
3. Ed. A. R. Waller, *Characters and Passages from the Notebooks of Samuel Butler* (1908), p. 275. Cf. J. Wilson, *Andronicus Comnenius* (1664), in *Dramatic Works* (1874), pp. 157–8:

Stephanus: *These oaths are dangerous things*
              They conceal enemies and make no friends!
              ... He that's forced to take
              An oath, straight makes a second not to keep it!
Andronicus: *But yet the greater number will swallow it.*
              Oaths are the same to them as rattles to children.

4. Isabel Ross, *Margaret Fell* (1949), p. 34.
5. R. Coke, *A Detection of the Court and State of England* (1694), II, pp. 123–4.

but interest does really oblige".[1] Thorold Rogers observed the interesting fact that the assessment of 1692, for which the assessors took no oath, brought in more than that of 1693, for which they took one.[2] We may compare Voltaire's comment that William Penn's treaty with the Indians of Pennsylvania was both "the only treaty between those people and the Christians that was not ratified by an oath", and the only one that was never infringed.[3]

The more this effective preponderance of worldly interests was recognized, the more resentment grew at the use of religious sanctions for plainly partisan purposes. "If swearing could determine controversies and beliefs", said Roger Coke, "all learning, reasoning and instruction would be at an end; and he that swears most is the best logician and godliest man".[4] The enforcing of oaths by authority was evidence that society was bitterly divided: "reason" could only be relied on when a relative unity had been restored, at least among the educated classes – i.e. after 1688. Already the Engagement of 1649 had recognized the inadequacy of oaths by reducing its demands to a minimum. But in January 1654 Cromwell and his Council observed that "many general and promissory oaths and engagements, in former times imposed upon the people of this nation, have proved burdens and snares to tender consciences, and yet have been exacted under several penalties". They repealed the Act by which those who refused to take the Engagement were denied access to the courts of justice, and so deprived the principal oath of allegiance of its sanction.[5] The Restoration governments tried to set the clock back in this as in so many matters; but in the long run they failed. Samuel Fisher told a pleasing story of a man who, to a Justice's threat "Tell him I will tender the oath to him", replied with the even more menacing words, "Tell him that I will take it if he do".[6] "If we had thought so many of them would have conformed", Arch-

1. Butler, *Characters and Passages from Notebooks*, p. 292.
2. J. E. T. Rogers, *The Economic Interpretation of History* (7th ed., 1909), p. 462.
3. F. M. A. Voltaire, *Letters Concerning the English Nation* (1733), p. 29.
4. R. Coke, *op. cit.*, II, p. 113. On the effects of the civil war period on oaths in general, see *ibid.*, II, pp. 113–27, 218, 335–40.
5. C. H. Firth and R. S. Rait, *Acts and Ordinances of the Interregnum* (1911), II, pp. 830–1.
6. Fisher, *The Testimony of Truth Exalted*, p. 792.

bishop Sheldon is alleged to have confessed, "we would have made [the door] straiter".[1]

In 1657 a Lord Chief Justice had objected to the perjury which a bill for Sunday observance authorized: too much, he thought, was left to the judgment of constables and head-boroughs. The bill passed.[2] But 5 years later the House of Commons rejected a proposal that certificates of exemption from the Hearth Tax, from a minister and at least one church-warden or overseer, and allowed by two J.P.s, should be made on oath.[3] In the initial stages of the Popish Plot men found it hard to believe that a divine like Oates would risk eternal damnation by the sin of wilful perjury: but in the long run the hard swearing on both sides probably did much to discredit oaths as guarantees of truthfulness.[4] In 1690 the ex-Parliamentarian Lord Wharton opposed a bill abjuring the titles of James II, saying "He was a very old man, and had taken a multitude of oaths in his time, and hoped God would forgive him if he had not kept them all; for truly they were more than he could pretend to remember; but should be very unwilling to charge himself with more at the end of his days". The Earl of Macclesfield, an ex-Cavalier, "was much in the same case with Lord Wharton, though they had not always taken the same oaths".[5] That rather weary realism must have expressed the views of many. After 1689 the attempt to impose politico-religious uniformity was abandoned: the long campaign of Quakers and others with conscientious scruples ended in their being allowed to make an unsworn affirmation instead of taking the oath.[6]

The final *reductio ad absurdum* of the traditional position was the Non-jurors' assertion that it would be perjury for men who had taken the oath of allegiance to James II to take a new one to William III.[7] Logically this was irrefutable; but politicians cannot live by logic alone. Sir John Bramston

1. D. Neal, *The History of the Puritans* (1837), III, p. 117.

2. *Burton's Parliamentary Diary*, II, p. 265.

3. *C.J.*, VIII, p. 383.

4. Cf. Evelyn's *Diary* (ed. de Beer), I, p. 27.

5. G. Burnet, *History of My Own Time* (1823), IV, p. 77. Wharton was born in 1613.

6. For the campaign, see A. Lloyd, *Quaker Social History (1669–1738)* (1950) p. 81.

7. Cf. Baxter's attitude to the Engagement, quoted on p. 397 above.

refused the oath to William so long as the cost of refusal was only £2 2s. 0d. a quarter. When the fine was replaced by an obligation to pay double taxes – he took the oath.[1] Many others must similarly have wept and signed. Yet they were the old guard who were most likely to stand for the sanctity of oaths, the traditional bond of social relationships of dependency; they were the last who wished to recognize the new principle that "nothing but interest does really oblige". It is ironical that a backward-looking figure like Thomas Hearne, deprived of his office at the Bodleian Library in 1716 for refusing to take the oath to the Hanoverian dynasty, should be a late victim of procedures surviving from the society which he admired into the new world whose standards he abhorred.[2]

Tillotson in 1681 had declared that the necessity for oaths "is so great that human society can very hardly, if at all, subsist long without them. Government would many times be very insecure", and there could be no substitute, since the obligation of an oath "reaches to the most secret and hidden practices of men, and takes hold of them when no law can".[3] Nevertheless he found it possible to succeed the non-juring Sancroft as Archbishop of Canterbury.[4] When his colleague, John Sharp, Archbishop of York, was asked "How a person who had sworn allegiance to King James could with a good conscience take the same oath to King William?" he replied "The laws of the land are the only rule of our conscience in this matter. . . . If, therefore, King William in the eye of the law be our king, we must in conscience pay obedience to him as such".[5] At a lower social level than Sir John Bramston, the self-appointed lay casuist of *The Athenian Oracle* in the sixteen-nineties gave his readers a similar absolution where really big money was involved. Rash oaths he said, ought to be kept if only inconvenience results, "as suppose you thereby lose some advantages in trade or otherwise"; but need not be kept if they

1. Sir John Bramston, *Autobiography* (Camden Soc., 1845), pp. 372–3.

2. Cf. *Reliquiae Hearnianae* (ed. P. Bliss, 1869), 11, p. 178.

3. J. Tillotson, *The Lawfulness and Obligation of Oaths* (1681), p. 6.

4. For the Hobbist casuistry with which Tillotson and others justified their position, see L. M. Hawkins, *Allegiance in Church and State* (1928), pp. 107–11.

5. MS. life of Archbishop Sharp, "wrote by his son for the use of his grand-children", quoted by Granville Sharp, *A Declaration of the People's Natural Right to a Share in the Legislature* (1774), pp. 15–16.

were originally unlawful, "as the absolute ruining yourself or family".[1] In 1696 Sir Peter Pett wrote sadly to Samuel Pepys after reading the pamphlet *Perjury the National Sinne*: "The author proves his point too well, insomuch that he shows himself perjured too".[2] What was a man to do? The 10 peers who protested against the oath of abjuration in 1702 revived (for the conservative cause) those arguments of Richard Ward's which the Laudian censor had suppressed two generations earlier: "Those who have kept the oaths which they have already taken ought in justice to be esteemed good subjects; and those who have broken them will make no scruple of taking or breaking any others that shall be required of them".[3] This logic led to the eventual abandonment of oaths as a political test, though they survived until the nineteenth century to keep dissenters out of State office.

In the sixteenth and seventeenth centuries the society in which the sworn jury of presentment was a crucial institution in maintaining law and order (and in which oaths were rejected only by heretics and rebels) was yielding place to a business society in which modern laws of evidence were becoming possible. The jury was being transformed from a group of knowing neighbours to a panel of anonymous citizens presumed to be objective because ignorant.[4] In this society oaths lost their force because self-interest obliged. Legal processes themselves, like religion, came to turn less on correct repetition of the appropriate formulae, more on consideration of intention. But *The Life and Death of Mr. Badman* reminds us how slowly the new ethic was establishing itself even in the second half of the seventeenth century. Oaths were still used to bind together the voluntary communities of those who rejected the assumptions of the self-interest society. In the later seventeenth century they helped to maintain honour among highwaymen;[5] and they still played an important part in preserving solidarity among early trade unionists. The oath remains to-day to bind

1. Ed. J. Underhill, *"The Athenian Oracle": a Selection* (1892), p. 172.
2. Ed. J. R. Tanner, *Private Correspondence and Miscellaneous Papers of Samuel Pepys, 1679–1703* (1926), I, p. 113.
3. J. E. T. Rogers, *Protests of the Lords* (1875), I, p. 162. For Ward see p. 391 above.
4. See p. 481 below.
5. Richard Head, *Jackson's Recantation* (1674), in *The Counterfeit Lady Unveiled* (ed. Spiro Peterson, New York, 1961), pp. 162–3.

men to speak the truth in courts, but the sanction behind it now is the unpleasantness of being detected in falsehood, and the legal penalties for perjury, rather than the consideration that "such perjured men's falsehood . . . shall be opened at the last day; . . . and Christ, the righteous judge, shall then justly condemn them to everlasting shame and death".[1]

VII

The supernatural sanction backing the oath of loyalty and the judicial oath – God the supreme overlord – was succeeded in capitalist society by the discovery that it paid a man to make his word his bond because of the rise in social importance of credit, reputation, respectability. God was on the way to becoming the Hidden Hand of Adam Smith, the invisible forces of the market helping those who helped themselves. As a footnote to this we may mark a parallel transformation in the other type of swearing – "vain oaths", expletives, cursing. Swearing, like idleness and royalism, tended to be associated with the highest and lowest classes. Cursing one's inferiors was a form of social arrogance of which the Puritans disapproved. Quarles's "Censorious Man", a Puritan, criticized his opponent who cried up the Book of Common Prayer, honoured not a preaching ministry, adored great ones for preferment, and spoke too partially in favour of authority. Such a man "can hear an oath from his superiors without reproof".[2]

Swearing in the lower classes – a blasphemous reference to the deity, to the Virgin Mary, or an invocation of the Devil – was often an act of protest, of defiance, against something still generally believed in. Swearing was advocated on principle by the Ranters in the sixteen-fifties, as a symbolic expression of freedom from moral restraints.[3] In peasant and catholic countries to-day such oaths retain a good deal of their flavour and power.[4] They survive in industrialized and protestant coun-

1. *Sermons or Homilies* (1802), p. 63.
2. F. Quarles, *Judgement and Mercy* (1807), pp. 128–30.
3. I owe this point to the unpublished Oxford B.Litt thesis of Mr. J. F. McGregor, "The Ranters: a Study of the Free Spirit in English Sectarian Religion, 1648–60" (1969).
4. See Trotsky's sociological analysis of swearing in pre-revolutionary Russia, in I. Deutscher's *The Prophet Unarmed* (1959), pp. 165–6. The Bolsheviks, like the Puritans, opposed "the swearing of masters and slaves" in the name of human dignity.

tries, but as shadows of their former selves, and often the users are unaware of the original significance of swear-words which they employ every day. Blasphemy is no longer a fine art. The live swear-words in such societies are those which offend against something which has much more social reality than God – respectability. Sex and the lavatory have replaced deity, saints and devil as the source of live expletives to-day, because their use breaks a taboo that is still worth breaking. The Cavaliers were familiarly known to their opponents as the "Dammees". ("Court oaths", the vicar of Croft in Lincolnshire thought in 1616, had been "one chief cause" of Prince Henry's untimely death.[1]) On the royalist side Chillingworth noted "horrible oaths, curses and blasphemies" to balance the "pestilent lies, calumnies and perjuries" of the Parliamentarians.[2] When a man died in battle in 1650 with the words "Damn me, I'll go to my King" on his lips, this confirmed the Parliamentarians in their belief that there were Cavaliers in the Scottish army opposing them.[3] In January 1653 the fact that a boatswain was heard to "swear two or three times by his Maker without any provocation" was reported to the Admiralty Committee as presumptive evidence that he was a royalist.[4] So the fighting defenders of the old order paid their last tribute to their type of God – by blaspheming him.

1. W. Worship, *The Patterne of an Invincible Faith* (1616), quoted by M. Maclure, *The Paul's Cross Sermons*, p. 237.

2. W. Chillingworth, *Works* (1838), III, p. 14.

3. *Original Memoirs written during the Great Civil War, being the Life of Sir Henry Slingsby and Memoirs of Captain Hodgson* (1806), pp. 219–20.

4. Ed. S. R. Gardiner, and C. T. Atkinson, *Letters and Papers relating to the First Dutch War, 1652–4* (Navy Records Soc., 1898–1930), III, p. 382. The name "dammee", like the word "cavalier", was applied to soldiers before 1640 (cf. J. Rous, *Diary*, ed. M. A. E. Green, Camden Soc., 1856, p. 78).

Chapter Twelve

The Secularization of the Parish

> A visible communion of saints is of two, three or more saints joined together by covenant with God and themselves. . . . All religious societies except that of a visible church are unlawful, as abbeys, monasteries, nunneries, cathedrals, collegiates, parishes.
>
> J. Smyth, *Principles and inferences concerning the visible Church* (1607), pp. 8–9.

I

IN origin the parish church (except for the chancel, the property of the lord of the manor), appears to have been regarded as belonging to the free parishioners, those share-holders in the village community whose ancestors no doubt helped to build the church. They consequently had the duty of keeping it, or all of it except the chancel, in repair. In the sixteenth and seventeenth centuries responsibility for repairing the chancel rested on the incumbent or the impropriator. Very many churches fell into disrepair during this period: in 1637 all but 9 of 116 rural churches in Buckinghamshire were in a state of serious decay. The evidence suggests that parishioners looked after their part of the church rather better than did ministers. No doubt clerical poverty, and the ability of churchwardens to levy a rate for the repair of the church, help to account for this. The worst offenders appear to have been lay impropriators, whose legal liability for the repair of the chancel was never established, thanks to the vigilance of the common lawyers.[1]

1. *E.P.C.* pp. 142–4; Jordan, *Philanthropy in England*, pp. 314–16.

Each manor was once a petty kingdom in which the church was the seat of administration. The living of Aldeburgh, Suffolk, was a manor: the incumbent enjoyed the profits of the court baron. Hayes, Middlesex, and the rich living of Wigan were also both rectory and manor.[1] In cities and large towns churches were generally the property of the free burgesses. The bells of each church were "the proper goods of the parishioners", the city fathers of Bristol told a royalist general in 1643, and so could not be melted down for cannon.[2]

The parish was still a real social centre. The church was the most substantial and permanent building in most villages: "the stone-house", a Baptist significantly called it.[3] The church was school, storehouse, arsenal, fire-station, and when necessary fortress. For this reason a church was normally the first building to be erected by English colonists in Ireland.[4] The lantern tower of All Saints, York, was a lighthouse for travellers. Churches served as storehouses and fortifications in New England, and during the English civil war: they also did duty as prisons, hospitals, stables. In Dublin St. Andrew's church was the Lord Deputy's stable even in time of peace.[5] Not only the future parliamentarian John Hampden but also the future royalist Sir Edmund Verney mustered trained bands in Beaconsfield churchyard; and the man who denounced them to the ecclesiastical authorities "suffered the spleen of the gentry".[6]

In most parishes the church furnished probably the only

1. Strype, *Life of Parker*, II, p. 156; S. O. Addy, *Church and Manor* (1913), pp. 422–32, 453–6; cf. pp. 1–137, *passim*; G. T. O. Bridgeman, *The History of the Church and Manor of Wigan* (Chetham Soc., 4 vols., 1888–90), *passim*; G. R. Elton, *Star Chamber Stories* (1958), p. 174; Babbage, *Puritanism and Richard Bancroft*, pp. 355–8.

2. Ed. P. Bliss, *Reliquiae Hearnianae* (1869), I, p. 285.

3. Ed. E. B. Underhill, *Records of the Churches of Christ gathered at Fenstanton, Warboys and Hexham* (Hanserd Knollys Soc., 1854), p. 268.

4. D. B. Quinn, "Sir Thomas Smith (1513–77) and the beginnings of English Colonial Theory", *Proceedings of the American Philosophical Soc.*, LXXXIX, pp. 547–8. In Polish the word for "church" is still a derivative of that for "castle", a reminder of the way in which Christianity was introduced by German conquest.

5. Knowler, *Letters and Dispatches of the Earl of Stafforde*, I, pp. 68, 131.

6. W. H. Summers, "State Papers relating to Beaconsfield", *Records of Bucks.*, VII, pp. 103–6; S.P. 16/274/12, a reference which I owe to Miss Doreen Slatter.

library available. The minister of Measham, Derbyshire, in 1634 presented 6 improving books to the parish as the nucleus of a library to be administered by minister and churchwardens.[1] The church was also the news agency, the centre where public and private announcements were made (e.g. about strayed sheep and cattle at Luccombe in Somerset in Charles I's reign), and the forum where communal business matters were transacted. Orders of the manor court were published there. Boxes of evidences were kept in "the lobby at the church". Rents were paid in the church porch. Assessors of the subsidy and overseers of the poor met there: so did vestrymen, coroner's inquests, petty and perhaps quarter sessions. The archdeacon held his court there. In 1641 the Protestation of 11 May was taken by all the citizens of London in their parish churches. Elections took place in the church, churchwardens were sworn there, church rates assessed there. Money was lent by and repaid to churchwardens in the church. Poor relief was distributed, accounts were audited, debtors were ordered to pay their creditors and putative fathers their alimony – all in the church or its porch. Many who were not Puritans might think it inconvenient to rail the communion table in altarwise at the east end of the church. It was too useful for writing accounts on and counting out money. The town plough might be kept in church. At Rye "unruly servants" were whipped there. William Ket was hanged from the tower of Wymondham church after the revolt of 1549. Any transaction that required special solemnity was enacted publicly in the church.[2] In *Oceana* the parish church was used for elections.[3] St. Paul's

1. J. Stevens Cox, *Literary Repository*, No. 4, 1954; cf. T. F. Thiselton-Dyer, *Church-Lore Gleanings* (1891), pp. 284–305; Jordan, *The Charities of London*, p. 36.

2. W. Andrews, *Curious Church Gleanings* (1896), p. 275; J. C. Cox, *Churchwardens' Accounts* (1913) p. 9; Addy, *op. cit.*, pp. 187, 195, 406; E. Trotter, *Seventeenth century life in the country parish* (1919), *passim*; Willcox, *Gloucestershire, 1590–1640*, pp. 234–5; Summers, *op. cit.*, p. 99; ed. W. Cunningham, *Common Rights at Cottenham and Stretham*, *Camden Miscellany*, XII (1910), p. 211; ed. F. R. Raines, *The Journal of Nicholas Assheton* (Chetham Soc., 1848), pp. 56–7; G. Fox, *Journal* (1902), I, p. 92; *Rye Corporation MSS.* (H.M.C.), p. 202; ed. E. H. Bates, *Somerset Quarter Sessions Records* (1907–12), II, pp. 68, 91; W. P. M. Kennedy, *Elizabethan Episcopal Administration*, II, p. 77; Ware, *The Elizabethan Parish in its Ecclesiastical and Financial Aspects*, p. 13; *C.S.P.D.*, *1634–5*, p. 268.

3. J. Harrington, *Oceana and Other Works* (1737), p. 85.

cathedral was a meeting place for business, where bills were posted; a public highway on which men wore their hats; a place where servants were hired; and a playground for children. A scene in Ben Jonson's *Every Man out of his Humour* (1599) is set "in the middle aisle of St. Paul's"; there are similar scenes in Middleton's *Michaelmas Term* (1607), and *Your Five Gallants* (1608).

Churches were used for community amusements. In 1602 players were given 1*s*. not to perform in the church at Syston, Leicestershire.[1] In 1612 at Woburn the curate baited a bear in church; 25 years later, also in Bedfordshire, there were cockfightings on three successive Shrove Tuesdays in Knottingley church, round the communion table. The minister and churchwardens were present.[2] Men smoked in church, and Fynes Moryson was surprised that the Turks thought it wrong "so much as to spit in their churches".[3] The Laudian attempt to reduce the secular activities which went on in churches[4] was undoubtedly an innovation. In 1613 a judge in the London Consistory Court had ruled that rates and assessments should be made, on a Sunday or holy day, in the church or chancel at Hendon, *and in no other place*.[5] The town authorities of Rye claimed in 1637 that they had had the approval of Lancelot Andrewes, when Bishop of Chichester, for using the south aisle of the chancel of their church as an arsenal.[6] Bishop Goodman of Gloucester was surprised to find himself in trouble for giving J.P.s leave to hold quarter sessions in Tetbury parish church when they were driven out of Gloucester by plague.[7] In 1635 the churchwardens of North Collingham were presented for suffering lay juries to meet in the church; three years later the parish of South Leverton had to account for the fact that a school was held in the chancel of their church "and children whipped there".[8] In January 1634 Neile reported that

1. M. C. Bradbrook, *The Rise of the Common Player* (1962), p. 309.

2. *C.S.P.D., 1637*, p. 208; B. Saunders, *The Age of Candlelight* (1959), p. 51.

3. F. Moryson, *Itinerary* (1617), Part III, p. 44.

4. Rushworth, *Historical Collections*, II, p. 77.

5. W. H. Hale, *Precedents in Causes of Office against Churchwardens and others* (1841), p. 39.

6. *Rye Corporation MSS*. (H.M.C.), p. 202.

7. G. Soden, *Godfrey Goodman* (1953), pp. 226–8.

8. R. F. B. Hodgkinson, "Extracts from the Account Books of the Archdeacon of Nottingham", *Trans. Thoroton Soc.*, XXXI, pp. 146, 129.

manorial courts were no longer held in the chapel at Holcombe. His immediate predecessor in the diocese of York, Samuel Harsnett (1628–31), had prohibited the use of churches for social and secular purposes.[1]

One of the charges in Laud's impeachment was that he forbade the Gloucestershire J.P.s to hold a court in church. But in the long run, puritan emphasis on hearing long sermons, making seats in church necessary, may have done more than Laudian theories to stop churches being used for business purposes. It seems to us only right and proper that the ecclesiastical authorities should stop proclamations being made in church about strayed cattle, or courts leet: but this attitude is possible only because the church has ceased to be a real civic centre, and has become a single-purpose building used one day a week only. Its sacred functions are a residuum. The dusty notices fluttering in the porches of country churches to-day are a faint reminder of the days when the real life of the community was focused on its one common centre, as the business life of the City of London focused on St. Paul's, or the university life of Oxford on St. Mary's church before the building of the Sheldonian Theatre.[2]

Most parishes possessed lands or cattle or other funds, as a result of legacies and endowments: though these had frequently been plundered at the Reformation or by Elizabethan courtiers.[3] Such funds or stock often came to be used to finance poor relief, or to provide work for the poor, thus reducing the poor rate. A parish might make loans, with or without interest; or it might invest, for instance in a lottery.[4] Some parishes owned communal dovecotes, bulls or boars, which were often the minister's responsibility; in others a beast was hired for the use of the parish.[5] But the mutual insurance schemes of

1 *C.S.P.D.*, *1633–4*, pp. 443–4; *1629–31*, p. 141.

2. See Evelyn's *Diary* (ed. de Beer), III, p. 385: University acts kept in St. Mary's.

3. Ware, *op.cit.*, pp. 61–4; Cox, *Churchwardens' Accounts*, pp. 294–5; S. and B. Webb, *The Old Poor Law*, pp. 9–10; T. Lever, *Sermons*, p. 82; MacCaffrey, *Exeter*, p. 179. See pp. 284–5 above.

4. Ware, *op. cit.*, pp. 68–9, 76–7; Sir T. Wilson, *Discourse on Usury* (ed. R. H. Tawney, 1925), pp. 126–9; R. R. Sharpe, *London and the Kingdom* (1894–5), II, p. 50.

5. Thistelton-Dyer, *Church-Lore Gleanings*, pp. 264–72; Cox, *Parish Registers* (1910), p. 233; Cox, *Churchwardens' Accounts*, p. 295; Tate, *The Parish Chest*, pp. 185, 299; D. Lysons, *The Environs of London*

the parishes were inadequate to cope with the problems of poor relief set by the economic changes of the sixteenth and seventeenth centuries; and both enclosure and the widening gulf between rich and poor worked against parochial economic co-operation. By 1622 the dovecote at Berwick, Suffolk, was being rented out by the parson.[1]

Many parishes had a "church house" – a community centre or club at which church ales and other parochial functions were held. From the early seventeenth century, as such activities declined, the church house might either become the place where the poor were set on work, or be leased out to poor parishioners. There is an ironical symbolism in this end of "merrie England", of the village community: the community centre becomes the house of correction.[2] More often we hear that the church house is "in the lord's possession", or "lately plucked down", "quite taken down about four to five years ago"; if it survived it was likely to be "in great decay".[3]

Church ales were used to raise money, for the maintenance of the parish clerk, to help a parishioner in financial distress, to raise stocks for the poor.[4] A church ale at Thame in 1636 raised £26 12s. 7d. This was exceptional, but even the £6, £7 or £8 profit that was more normally to be expected was a welcome addition to parish funds which seem always to have been inadequate.[5] "In the poor country parishes", wrote Bishop Pierce in a *Defence of Church Feasting*, "where the wages of the clerk are but small, the people, thinking it unfit that the clerk should duly attend at the church and gain nothing by his

(1792–6), II, p. 56; cf. III, p. 601; E. J. Boddington, "The Church Survey in Wilts", *Wilts Magazine*, XLI, *passim*.

1. Addy, *op. cit.*, p. 409. For parish endowments see Jordan, *Rural Charities*. pp. 148, 190 sq., 246; *Social Institutions of Kent*, Chapter IV.

2. S. and B. Webb, *op. cit.*, p. 141.

3. Robert Gibbs, "The state of the Bucks. Parish Churches in the 16th and 17th centuries", *Records of Bucks.*, VI, pp. 158–67, 245, 252, 256, and *passim*. All these examples are from the visitation of 1637. Cf. G. W. Copeland, "Devonshire Church-houses", *Trans. Devon Assoc.*, XCII, pp. 116–41.

4. Prynne, *Canterburies Doome*, p. 143.

5. S. A. Peyton, *The Churchwardens' Presentments in the Oxfordshire Peculiars of Dorchester, Thame and Banbury* (Oxfordshire Record Soc., 1928), p. lv; J. M. J. Fletcher, "A Century of Dorset Documents", *Proceedings of the Dorset Natural History and Antiquarian Field Club*, XLVII, p. 31.

office, send him in provision and then come on Sunday and feast with him, by which means he sells more ale and tastes more of the liberality of the people than their quarterly payments would amount to in many years".[1] The bishop was a conservative, and may idealize; but there is nothing improbable in such a state of affairs in areas where renders in kind were still common. Aubrey recalled that in Wiltshire there used to be no poor rates: "the church ale at Whitsuntide did their business".[2] The abolition of Easter ales in Salisbury in 1651 made it necessary to consider an increase in the clerk's wages.[3]

Church ales, then, need not always lead to bacchanalian orgies, though those associated with the traditional seasonal festivals often produced the enormities which led J.P.s and others concerned with the maintenance of order to oppose them. Ales were organized by respectable Puritans of the industrious sort: Adam Eyre, as petty constable of Penistone in the West Riding of Yorkshire, was constantly getting up ales to help those of his neighbours who had been unfortunate.[4] Ale played the part in the average man's and woman's diet then that tea does to-day: the nearest modern equivalent to a church ale in a well-ordered parish is a tea-fight at a nonconformist chapel. Church ales thus represented a form of community social insurance. In so far as the new labour discipline aimed at forcing the poor to work through fear of starvation, church ales were a retarding factor, conflicting with the ethic of self-help and rugged individualism which was gaining ground among the employing classes. It may not be altogether a coincidence that the counties in which J.P.s were most opposed to church ales – Somerset, Wiltshire, Dorset, Devon, Worcester, Berkshire, Yorkshire and Lancashire – were also clothing counties.

We must be careful not to sentimentalize the "community" aspects of the parish. It had long been a class-divided group. This is illustrated by the practice of providing two categories

1. Quoted by J. F. Chanter, "The Parish Clerks of Barnstaple, 1500–1900", *Report and Transactions of the Devonshire Association for the Advancement of Science, Literature and Art*, XXXVI, p. 383.
2. Quoted in W. H. R. Curtler, *The Enclosure and Redistribution of our Land* (1920), p. 104.
3. Ed. H. J. F. Swayne, *Churchwardens' Accounts of St. Edmund and St. Thomas, Salisbury* (Wilts. Record Soc., 1896), p. 328.
4. See pp. 183–7 above.

of communion wine – claret for the vulgar, muscatel for the gentry. Its abolition is often attributed to Laud, I do not know on what evidence. Certainly the hierarchy was not always opposed to a two-class system of communicating. Bishop Scambler of Peterborough (1561–85) laid down a rule that at the regular quarterly communion servants should attend at 5.0 a.m., masters and dames at 9.0.[1] But all persons admitted to communion were expected to pay the same sum for their Easter offerings. The pluralist rector of Tenterden at Easter 1640 "did disgracefully put back some poor servants . . . from the receiving of the holy sacrament . . . merely because they would not pay him twelve pence apiece for their offerings, although they had before tendered him their accustomed offerings".[2] At St. Edmunds, Salisbury, superior communion wine was served for masters and mistresses from 1573 to 1629. The ending of the class distinction thus came well before Laud was Archbishop of Canterbury; and the decision was taken by the vestry on the same day as Henry Sherfield was authorized to take down an allegedly superstitious stained glass window – a decision which led to a fierce battle with the ecclesiastical authorities. It seems a fair inference that both decisions were motivated by radical Puritanism.[3] It was Bishop Montagu, a Laudian of the Laudians, who insisted that servants should not presume to approach the altar rails in front of their betters.[4]

We considered above the difficult task which churchwardens had to perform – difficult because dual.[5] On the one hand they were responsible to the ecclesiastical authorities: on the other to the parishioners who had elected them, with the minister's consent. It was often recognized that their functions were semi-political, as in those western parishes which

1. J. E. Vaux, *Church Folk Lore* (1902), p. 64; Swayne, *op. cit.*, pp. 62, 288.

2. Ed. L. B. Larking, *Proceedings . . . in the County of Kent* (Camden Soc., 1862), p. 231.

3. Swayne, *op. cit.*, pp. xxxviii–ix, 190. In 1624 the vestry, with Henry Sherfield present, voted 20s. a year for the clerk to read morning prayer "for the ease of Mr. Thatcher during his time, and likewise for the ease of his successor, being a preacher" (*ibid.*, p. 177). It looks as though the incumbent had scruples about the prayer book which the vestry was prepared to indulge; but only because he was a preaching minister.

4. See p. 226 above.

5. See pp. 378–82 above.

used in the sixteen-thirties to pair a Puritan with an anti-Puritan churchwarden.[1] But the election of churchwardens was rarely so directly political. In many parishes the office went by rotation among the chief houses in the village: by this means in 1635 a woman came to be churchwarden at Moreton-in-Marsh.[2]

In the post-Reformation period parsons and churchwardens were given an increasing number of purely secular tasks. Just as the minister had to

> "*trudge about the town, this way and that way;*
> *Here to a drab, there to a thief*";[3]

so churchwardens looked after the repair of roads and bridges, provided arms and equipment for the musters, collected taxes, and had a host of other local government duties. Yet they remained ecclesiastical officials. They were responsible to the archdeacon for the fabric of the church, and had to report regularly to his court. They were liable to excommunication if they failed to attend, or failed to obey its orders. Churchwardens complained no less than other laymen of excessive fees, costs and delays in the archdeacons' courts: these complaints were no doubt echoed by the parishioners who had to raise the money. There were conflicts of jurisdiction, at the lowest level as at the highest. Men presented in the Archdeacon's Court would complain to quarter sessions: J.P.s began to insist on churchwardens' lists of recusants being presented to them, instead of, or as well as, to the church courts. In 1639 the assize judges gave a ruling in a disputed election of a parish clerk in Wells.[4] As poor relief became a tax, it came under the control of J.P.s, who could order a named pauper to be maintained by assessment. Churchwardens' accounts were submitted to J.P.s. Yet the church courts too would enforce payment of church rates, by excommunication if necessary: the recalcitrant would try to get a prohibition from the common-law courts.[5] These rivalries over jurisdiction con-

1. See p. 24 above.
2. *C.S.P.D.*, *1635*, p. xli.
3. [Anon.], *Gammer Gurton's Needle*, Act IV, scene i (1575).
4. Ed. T. G. Barnes, *Somerset Assize Orders*, p. 41. It should be added that they ruled that the Bishop of Bath and Wells should nominate: this was at the height of the Laudian supremacy.
5. Hale, *Precedents in Causes of Office*, pp. 26–8, and *passim*; see also pp. 318–25 above.

cealed rivalries about policy: they were only ended (temporarily) by the abolition of the ecclesiastical judicial hierarchy, and ultimately by the emergence of quarter sessions as the link between central government and parish.[1]

II

The parish, then, was a unit whose secular administrative importance was growing steadily throughout our period. The main reason for this was that the poor law and poor relief came to be administered by the parish, as economic changes created poverty and vagabondage on a new scale.[2] Parish expenses, especially in relieving the poor, grew. Parish stock was exhausted; ales no longer sufficed. Voluntary collections proved no solution. The dilemma was neatly expressed in West Hanningfield, Essex, in 1596. "The steeple is not repaired", for although the parishioners acknowledged their liability, they could not agree how it should be apportioned. Were the repairs to be financed "by every man's ability, or by every man's lands, or by every man's devotion?" By a property tax, a land rate, or private charity? A compulsory rating system was the device evolved to replace the older financial methods.[3] In 1584 a man in Haverstock refused to pay 5s. to which he had been rated by "the minister and substantial men of the parish for the bells making".[4] In 1618 a group of cottagers in

1. In 1560 the royal Feodary of Lancashire sent a proclamation to the curates of Walton and Liverpool, to be read in their pulpits, warning gentlemen and freeholders to present themselves at Liverpool church with evidences to prove the tenures of their lands. (J. Hurstfield, *The Queen's Wards*, 1958, p. 34). A hundred and three years later the J.P.s of Warwickshire ordered the notice about the Hearth Tax to be publicly read in all churches (ed. M. Walker, with Introduction by P. Styles, *Hearth Tax Returns*, Warwick County Records, 1957, p. xxv).
2. See Chapter 7 above.
3. W. J. Pressey, "Records of the Archdeaconries of Essex and Colchester", *Trans. Essex Archaeological Soc.*, New Series, XIX, p. 21; Ware, *The Elizabethan Parish in its Ecclesiastical and Financial Aspects*, pp. 70-7; Cox, *Churchwardens' Accounts*, p. 291; S. and B. Webb, *The Old Poor Law*, p. 11. In 1653 the freeholders, farmers and cottagers within the chapelry of Baslow, Derbyshire, rated themselves to pay their minister and parish clerk, where previously payments had been in kind. The inhabitants of three other hamlets within the chapelry accepted the new arrangement, but made this agreement conditional on the minister being "godly and preaching" and approved by the parish (Bakewell parish church MSS.).
4. Hale, *A Series of Precedents and Proceedings*, p. 178.

an Oxfordshire village complained that church repairs were being paid for by a compulsory rate rather than by the traditional church ales, and said that the object of this was to force the poor to contribute. The rich were trying to break the older communal customs in order to reduce their own financial responsibility.[1] This possibly throws additional light on hostility to church ales among many of the propertied classes. At all events the assessment and collection of the church rate became a factor of major importance in village life. Presentments for refusing to pay rates became increasingly frequent from the sixteen-twenties. The refusal became a point of principle with Quakers and other sectaries, but its origins may have been more mundane.[2]

The most significant function of the parish thus came to be collection of taxes rather than provision of communal amenities. The Laudian policy added to its already existing burdens. At Bangor in 1636 a rate was levied for church ornaments and repairs, without the consent of the parish, by two churchwardens unprecedentedly nominated by the bishop. Those who refused to pay were excommunicated.[3] At St. Martin's, York, the reluctant churchwardens had to be ordered to levy a rate to pay for "beautifying the church".[4] Bishop Bridgman of Chester certified in January 1637 that he had "brought most of the churches in his diocese to uniformity and decency, whereon the laity have most cheerfully bestowed many thousand pounds".[5] We may reasonably doubt whether the cheerfulness of the gentlemen of Lancashire was entirely spontaneous, since this county was soon to be revealed as the great stronghold of Presbyterianism; and those gentlemen who were not Presbyterians tended to be Catholics. (We may entertain similar doubts about the exceptionally large sums which London merchants contributed to the building and repair of churches

1. Peyton, *Churchwardens' Presentments in the Oxfordshire Peculiars*, p. lv. The village appears to have been Northleigh.

2. H. Johnstone, *Churchwardens' Presentments (17th century), Part I, Archdeaconry of Chichester* (Sussex Record Soc., 1947–8), p. 134 and *passim*.

3. *C.S.P.D.*, *1636–7*, p. 375.

4. Marchant, *The Puritans and the Church Courts in the Diocese of York*, p. 80. For other examples of the high cost of Laudianism, and of objections made on behalf of parishes, see F. Higham, *Catholic and Reformed* (1962), pp. 118–19.

5. *C.S.P.D.*, *1636–7*, p. 410.

in the Laudian decade: they were certainly under strong pressure.[1])

Even in disputes over vestments Puritanism and economics would coincide. Surplices were expensive: one bought for Northill, Bedfordshire, in 1604, cost 28s. 4d. Parishioners, who had to pay for them, were reluctant to replace a surplice even when, as at Salhouse, Norfolk, it was "so rent that it was not decent to be worn", or when as at Great Ryburgh in the same county, the rector was too large to get into it.[2] In Buckinghamshire in the sixteen-thirties, we are told, people "grudged at every penny" taxed for church expenses.[3] The parishioners of Waddesdon complained to the Long Parliament that Sir John Lambe had erected an organ in their church – and imposed a yearly charge of £15 on the inhabitants for the maintenance of an organist.[4] In opposing this they need not all have been actuated by Puritanism. It was only after 1640 that conflicts between puritan standards and financial convenience were revealed. At all Saints, Newcastle-on-Tyne, the tolling of a passing bell was "laid aside" as superstitious. But the loss of fees began to worry the vestry, and in January 1655 – after serious debate – they ordered that the practice should be revived for those who were prepared to pay for it.[5] Superstition was to be rationed by the purse.

"The vestry," wrote Maitland, ". . . is the outcome of the church rate, which in its turn is the outcome of the appropriation of tithes and the poverty of the parochial clergy".[6] As the assessment of rates grew in importance, so did control of the machinery of the parish. Parochial officers had to be men of some substance, since they might have to advance money for parish expenses and recover it later, if they were lucky.[7] Illiterate churchwardens were still to be found "many times in

1. Jordan, *The Charities of London*, *passim*.
2. Hart, *The Country Clergy in Elizabethan and Stuart Times*, pp. 38, 55. For other examples where failure to provide the prescribed apparel seems to have been due to poverty rather than Puritanism, see R. Peters, "The Administration of the Archdeaconry of St. Albans, 1580–1625", *Journal of Ecclesiastical History*, XIII, p. 63.
3. *V.C.H. Buckinghamshire*, I, p. 320.
4. *C.J.*, II, p. 97.
5. Vaux, *Church Folk Lore*, pp. 157–8.
6. F. W. Maitland, "The Survival of Archaic Communities", *Law Quarterly Review*, IX, p. 227.
7. Johnstone, *Churchwardens' Presentments*, pp. xxxiii, 71.

country villages";[1] but the tendency was towards the appointment of men of some standing.

Indeed the general development during our period is towards oligarchy, whether in borough corporations or in country parishes. This follows naturally from the economic changes of the century before 1640. No longer did the borough or manor stand solid and united against the feudal lord or central government, as had so often been the case in 1381, and in rural districts as late as 1549. Even in 1583 we find the inhabitants of a remote northern village taxing themselves to maintain a tithe suit against their vicar.[2] But by the seventeenth century a richer middle class was differentiating itself from the rest of the population, in town and country alike. There were many new demands for expenditure from local authorities, especially on poor relief. Those who contributed most towards such expenditure naturally expected to control it; and the fact that they did contribute more made it difficult to resist their claim.

In 1645 a lady complained that "a few troublesome people" took upon themselves to speak for the whole parish of Chicksands, and were trying to usurp her patronage rights. "I shall ever believe", Sir Samuel Luke replied, "that a single person may sooner err in his judgment than a whole parish".[3] This begged the question, and was an argument whose dangers Luke was soon to appreciate: if ministers and elders might be elected, why not sheriffs, J.P.s, "and all ministers of justice whatsoever", as the Levellers were to demand in 1648?[4]

Local government before the civil war came to be dominated by the richer sort, men who had political ambitions. The officials of the leet, who had been nominated by the lord of the manor, yielded place to churchwardens and other parochial officials who were "elected" – in effect nominated – by "the better sort" of inhabitants, under the supervision of J.P.s. The rate-payer, the householder mattered more than the parish-

1. P. Heylyn, *Cyprianus Anglicus* (1671), p. 278.

2. Ed. J. S. Purvis, *Select 16th century Causes in Tithe* (Yorkshire Archaeological Soc., 1949), pp. 134–6; cf. R. H. Tawney, *The Agrarian Problem in the Sixteenth Century* (1912), pp. 131, 160–1, 244–7, 329–31.

3. Ed. H. G. Tibbutt, *Letter Books of Sir Samuel Luke* (1963), pp. 238, 495.

4. *The Earnest Petition* of 1648; Brailsford, *The Levellers and the English Revolution*, p. 321.

ioner, or even the freeholder: the man who had enough real property, whether freehold, copyhold or leasehold, to be assessed for church rates. But he too was being squeezed out. The church rate was levied by the vestry, which for this reason tended more and more to become "select" and co-optative. "The rich would very unwillingly be concluded by the poor", said Mr. Petty at Putney in 1647:[1] he was speaking of the parliamentary franchise, but his remark was true of any representation whose object was taxation. From the mid-sixteenth century we find groups of richer parishioners formally agreeing to exclude "the rest of the common people", although not the leading families of the parish, who would be consulted on important matters even if not members of the vestry.

Such oligarchies were sometimes corrupt, and often bitterly opposed by many of the excluded parishioners. To strengthen their position, select vestries from about 1590 onwards aspired to have their authority confirmed by a faculty from the bishop. They appealed to the bishops' dislike of democracy, against the "great confusion" which would arise "if the whole parish should be electors"; against election even by "£3 subsidy-men", which would be "popular, and excite the ruder sort to extreme liberty". "The inferior and meaner sort of the multitude of the inhabitants, being greater in number" would "cross the good proceedings for the benefit of the church and parish". Between 1606 and 1626 the bishops of London granted at least 20 faculties to select vestries in City parishes, always using the same formula: "the general admittance of the parish into the vestry" had produced "great disquietness and hindrance to the good proceedings".[2]

The sort of controversy to which this tendency towards oligarchy gave rise may be illustrated from St. Saviour's, Southwark. In 1607 a bill was promoted in Parliament by 1,500 householders of the parish, of whom 200 were subsidy men. Their object was to deprive the 30 vestrymen of the sole power of choosing churchwardens and administering parish finances. It was replied that a select vestry had been settled some 50 years ago. "If the multitude should from time to time

1. A. S. P. Woodhouse, *Puritanism and Liberty* (1938), p. 78.
2. S. and B. Webb, *The Parish and the County* (1906), pp. 184–97; Gibson, *Codex Juris Ecclesiastici Anglicani* (1761), II, pp. 1476–8.

be privy to the stock of the parish, many of the meaner sort would neglect their labour and choose to live on the common stock".[1] The conflict is here between the parish as social security unit and the new conception of the necessity of labour. The excluded parishioners appealed (though unsuccessfully) to Parliament, not to the bishop. Before Laud the Church seems to have had no "social justice" policy which would challenge the rule of urban oligarchies.[2] Embezzlement by town and parish oligarchies of funds intended for poor relief proceeded apace in the century between Reformation and Revolution: the Levellers and Major-Generals were to make more determined efforts to check it than the bishops ever did.[3]

Heylyn tells us that the usurpation of parish authority by select vestries began in London and was imitated in other towns.[4] There is evidence of bishops giving faculties for other parishes around London; and in 1603 a select vestry was instituted at St. Mary's, Reading, which four years later imposed the first church rate ever known in the parish.[5] The bishop's faculty was only confirmatory: its absence did not necessarily mean that a vestry was "open". It might signify only that the select vestry felt completely secure in its authority. St. Edmund's, Salisbury, a lay fee held by trustees on behalf of the parishioners, claimed to be exempt from episcopal jurisdiction. There in 1640 the rector was elected by "the gentlemen of the vestry". At St. Thomas's in the same city it had been decided in the previous year that all past and future churchwardens were automatically to become members of the parish oligarchy.[6]

1. Ed. D. H. Willson, *The Parliamentary Diary of Robert Bowyer* (University of Minnesota Press, 1931), pp. 216-17.

2. But Bancroft in 1609 anticipated something of the rural "social justice" policy attributed to Laud. In a letter whose main object was to defend prerogative jurisdiction against common lawyers, M.P.s and J.P.s, he expressed a wish that "poor people might not have their rents so racked as they are", and that depopulating enclosers might be severely punished. M.P.s, he said, "do for the most part more affect their own designs than the benefit of the commons that choose them" (Strype, *Life of Whitgift*, III, pp. 386–9).

3. See p. 284 above.

4. Heylyn, *Cyprianus Anglicus*, p. 265.

5. S. and B. Webb, *The Parish and the County*, pp. 185–6, 192–4.

6. Rushworth, *Historical Collections*, II, p. 154; Addy, *Church and Manor*, p. 448; ed. Swayne, *Salisbury Churchwardens' Accounts*, pp. xxxi, 208–12, 319.

The tendency then is general. What is significant for our purposes is the alliance which often existed between parish oligarchy and the pre-Laudian episcopal hierarchy. Vestries, said Laud, "were made and suffered first by negligence doubtless, yet being of continuance, we cannot so easily restrain the power which they use".[1] The wish was clearly there if not the power. Opponents of everything that Laud stood for were too securely dug in at, say, St. Stephens', Coleman St., where the select vestry was already opposing both hierarchy and Government in the sixteen-twenties, not unsuccessfully; or at Amersham, where "the dreadful grandees" of the parish successfully sabotaged visitation orders in 1634.[2] Yet at least the hierarchy had no objection to the exclusion of "the rude multitude" and could take financial advantage of it. This point was emphasized by Sir Henry Spelman in his account of what he regarded as an entirely illegal process, in a work published in 1641 but possibly written a few years earlier. Bishops and chancellors – for a fee – would issue sealed instruments to "the masters and chief of the parish", on the authority of which they made orders purporting to bind "the rest of the parish that consented not".[3] In 1635 Star Chamber instituted an inquiry into all London parishes, to ascertain whether they were governed by select vestries or by all the inhabitants, and if the former, by what grant or instruments, and what powers were claimed.[4] One suspects that some fiscal purpose lurked behind this inquiry. At all events, the struggles between democracy and oligarchy within parishes were of direct political significance.

In London, vestries tried to control ward elections by meeting beforehand to decide on a candidate. Capture of the parish was regarded by the Leveller Walwyn as the first round in a political struggle: "An occasion being offered by this honourable Parliament, our minister and parish (James Garlick-Hill, London) being quite out of order, I with others moved for reformation. . . . Our next endeavours were for the whole

1. Laud, *Works*, VI, p. 14.
2. Dorothy Williams, "London Puritanism: the Parish of St. Stephen, Coleman St.", *Church Quarterly Review*, CLX, pp. 468–9; Summers, "State Papers relating to Beaconsfield", *Records of Bucks.*, VII, p. 102.
3. Sir H. Spelman, *De Sepultura*, in *English Works* (1727), I, p. 184; cf. Sir W. Holdsworth, *The History of English Law*, IV., pp. 152–6.
4. I owe this information to Dr. V. L. Pearl, Cf. her *London and the Outbreak of the Puritan Revolution*, p. 55.

ward, wherein, after much labour, we so prevailed that the well-affected carried the choice of alderman and common council men, and all other officers in the ward. My next public business was, with many others, in a remonstrance to the Common Council, to move the Parliament. . . ."[1]

The occasion, it should be noted, was offered by Parliament. The years after 1640 saw a re-establishment of democracy in many parishes: the Restoration brought back bishops and select vestries together. The faculty issued for St. Martin-in-the-Fields in 1662 says frankly that "during the late unhappy times of trouble and disorder", the affairs of the church had been managed by persons admitted in a disorderly manner. "Many persons of quality" were now unwilling to act as a select vestry unless appointed by proper authority. One sees the significance of the Restoration for such people. Not till after 1688 did aspiring parish oligarchies cease to apply to bishops or their chancellors, and turn to other ways of fortifying their position against the rest of the parishioners: not till the nineteenth century was Spelman's assertion of the illegality of bishops' faculties fully vindicated, since by then they were no longer needed.[2]

Because of the increasingly secular nature of the parish, the right to appoint parish clerks was one of the disputed areas. The Canons of 1604 claimed this right for the incumbent. This was, however, an innovation: in 1611 Coke and the whole bench adjudged the Canon contrary to common law, and denied that the incumbent or the ordinary had any right to set aside a clerk chosen by the parishioners. The clerk's was a lay office, and the church courts had no power to deprive a man who executed a lay office.[3] The abolition of the hierarchy's

1. W. Walwyn, *A Whisper in the Ear of Mr. Thomas Edwards* (1646), p. 4, in Haller, *Tracts on Liberty in the Puritan Revolution, 1638–47* Columbia University Press, (1934), III, p. 324.

2. S. and B. Webb, *The Parish and the County*, pp. 194–7; Pearl, *London and the Outbreak of the Puritan Revolution*, pp. 55–6; cf. Evelyn's *Diary* (ed. de Beer), III, pp. 317–18.

3. Coke, *13 Reports*, p. 70; W. Hughes, *The Parsons Law* (1641), II, pp. 115–18. Hughes claimed in the second edition of 1662 that his book – written in 1634 – had been approved in 1636 by the Lord Chief Justice and the Archbishop of Canterbury. One ventures to doubt whether Laud had read the passage on parish clerks: and the fact remains that Hughes's book was not published during Laud's ascendancy, any more than Coke's *12* and *13 Reports* could be.

control during the interregnum saw the triumph of the common-law view.

The revolutionary decades brought other changes. With the
emphasis on congregational hymn-singing, parish clerks ceased to be chosen for their musical skill;[1] but they sometimes
became more efficient at their secular tasks. Parish registers, so
important for proving titles to estates, date from 1536. In the
Aylesbury register, from the end of 1640, "the antique writing
is cast aside, and [entries] are now made in a bold hand-
printed style, as plain as letter press", and quite new.[2] An
improvement in the keeping of accounts is to be noted from
the sixteen-fifties at St. Edmund's parish, Salisbury.[3] It would
be interesting to gather information about the number of
parishes of which this is true. Mr. Tate thinks that registers
were kept better after 1653, when ministers ceased to be responsible for them.[4] But there is evidence to suggest that in the
later seventeenth century, as the secular and financial aspects
of the parish loomed larger, a main consideration in choosing
clerks came to be the avoidance of expense to the parish.[5]

III

The parish, then, had become part of the machinery of
government. In the presbyterian and independent schemes
there was still to be a national Church, though it was to be a
federation of parishes with a greater or less degree of independence. So the sectaries, in refusing to communicate in
parish churches, and still more in advocating their abolition,
were rejecting the State as well as the Church: a fact which
perhaps throws some light on the Government's attitude towards them. Penry, for instance, thought it unlawful to communicate "within any of the parish assemblies of this land, or
in any other public meeting appointed by law".[6] Barrow was
accused of saying that parsonages and vicarages were in name,

1. P. H. Ditchfield, *The Parish Clerk* (4th ed., 1913), pp. 48–9, 92.
2. R. Gibbs, *A History of Aylesbury* (1885), p. 341.
3. Ed. Swayne, *Salisbury Churchwardens' Accounts*, p. 231.
4. W. E. Tate, *The Parish Chest* (1946), pp. 46–7.
5. Ditchfield, *op. cit.*, pp. 49, 52.
6. Ed. A. Peel, *The Notebook of John Penry, 1593* (Camden Soc.
1944), p. 28; cf. pp, 42–3, 86, 89.

office and function as popish and anti-Christian as archbishops and bishops.[1]

This attitude towards the parish became one of the dividing lines between separatist and non-separatist. Henry Jacob, an Independent who just remained within the Church, thought that men should renounce ordinary and constant membership of any "diocesan or provincial church visible political", and "then also of the parishes (as natural parts) depending on them, and on their Lord Bishops"; but he was not prepared completely to sever connection with the political visible Church in England.[2] The ministers in Massachusetts Bay held in about 1629 that the English parish churches were congregational at the core and therefore true churches.[3] This attitude was attacked in 1630 by the separatist Dupper, who called upon the conformist Independents "to detest and protest against the parish churches".[4] The separatist congregationalists' insistence on local autonomy is outlined in William Bartlet's 'Ἰχνογραφια, or a Model of the Primitive Congregational Way (1647). He asked "Whether the Church of England, as it is national, consisting of so many thousand parishes, that are as branches and members of the same, and have no power of government in themselves, but stand under an absolute authoritative ecclesiastical power without them to rule and govern them in the matters of God's worship, be a true church?" His answer was in the negative.[5]

When we reflect on the functions of the parish as a unit of local government and local taxation, the anarchical tendency

1. T. Rogers, *The Faith, Doctrine and Religion professed and protected in . . . England*, p. 213; cf. *Writings of Robert Harrison and Robert Browne*, pp. 206–9, 404–8, 423,536–7; and the epigraph to this chapter.

2. Burrage, *Early English Dissenters*, I, p. 317.

3. P. Miller, *Roger Williams* (New York, 1953), p. 24. For the drift towards parochial independence see *E.P.C.*, pp. 297–302, and pp. 86–90 above. A point which I missed, made by Professor Jordan, is that "Tudor law most wisely left the parish free to manage [poor law administration] in its own way, subject only to the supervision of the local justices, with the result that local tradition and custom were respected and retained" (*Philanthropy in England*, pp. 82–3). Thus the secularization of the parish contributed to its autonomy.

4. Burrage, *op. cit.*, II, pp. 301–2. This was one of the points on which Henry Burton parted company with his fellow-martyr Prynne: see B. Hanbury, *Historical Memorials relating to the Independents* (1839–44), II, p. 409.

5. Quoted in G. F. Nuttall. *Visible Saints* (1957), p. 64.

of this attitude becomes clear. In a way the separatists simpli-
fied their problems by going into exile, for (until they went to
America) they side-stepped the problem set by the existence
of members of the community who were not members of the
Church. The Anglican position was clear enough: all members
of the state were also members of the Church. Since the hierarchy rejected democracy in clerical affairs, this universalism
raised no problems of relations between ruling class and the
mass of the population: the domination of the former was
ensured by the patronage system plus tithes, both in the last
resort backed up by the coercive machinery of Church and
state. The presbyterian system would have maintained this
machinery, but would have modified the structure of the
state-ecclesiastical so as to allow greater influence to those
socially dominant groups who controlled the eldership: at the
same time it would have safeguarded against excessive democracy by rigid discipline and by extensive powers of excluding
the ungodly from the sacraments and so from full church
membership. In New England political control was concentrated in the hands of the minority of church members, in relation to whom the mass of the population existed only to be
ruled. Dr. Nuttall has described the resentment felt by ungodly parishioners during the interregnum at ministers (often
survivors from the episcopal establishment) who tried to
restrict church membership – and so rule of the parish – to
visible saints.[1] This would have re-established oligarchy,
though of rather a different sort, in local government. As in
so many other ways, so here, the battle against clericalism and
for religious toleration was also a battle for political democracy.

The sectarian congregations which developed in the Netherlands, or in England in the relative freedom after 1641, still
could not aspire to rule the state, and yet wished to exist and
develop without interference from state and Church. Hence
the evolution of their negative attitude towards both, an
attitude never quite lost by "nonconformity" or "dissent" (the
words convey the attitude). But a complete rejection of the
State Church had its political and economic implications: excommunication, tithes, poor relief, the franchise, all were
involved.

1. *Op. cit.*, p. 134.

IV

So the political struggle for control of the Church went on at the lowest level – the parish – as well as at the highest. The effective working of the Laudian system demanded the co-operation of parish officials: and conversely the parish could become a focus of local opposition to official ecclesiastical policy. As the functions of the parish became more and more secularized, so the responsibility of parochial officials to the church courts became increasingly irksome. The natural rulers of the parishes were ready to shake off paternal episcopal control.

Good men, Leighton thought, avoided the office of church-warden. For the prelates "cause them to sin most of any of the people". Churchwardens "swear and do they know not what, yea they infringe the laws of the land, being made instruments to afflict God's people".[1] Churchwardens indeed were in a difficult position. Their major loyalty was naturally to the community of which they were permanent members; but during their period of office they were under constant pressure from their ecclesiastical superiors. It was because of the tendency of churchwardens to voice the views of their community, and oppose the wishes of the hierarchy, that the Bishop of Rochester spoke in 1632 of "the power of vestries and church-wardens" as tending "to hatch a lay presbytery". He was referring to the refusal of the churchwardens of St. Austin's parish, London, to remove seats above the communion table in their church, without specific order from the High Commission; "or else we dare not, for the vestry hath ordered it".[2]

After 1641 there was no High Commission to coerce parish-es into ecclesiastical conformity, just as there was no Star Chamber to coerce them into political conformity. Hence-forth parishes were controlled only by quarter sessions and Parliament. Humphrey Prideaux in 1701 observed that altar rails, "being not required by any law" nor in themselves absolutely necessary, cannot be erected without the consent of parish, parson and ordinary. "Since this is a matter which often raises great contests and disturbances", he reflected

1. Leighton, *Sions Plea against the Prelacie*, pp. 136–7; cf. pp. 314–15.
2. C. Stephenson and F. G. Marcham, *Sources of English Constitutional History* (1938), p. 470.

sadly, churchwardens should be careful about taking unauthorized action.[1] In that sentence we can estimate the magnitude of Laud's defeat.

These subsidiary struggles left their mark in political thought and literature: radicals from Gerrard Winstanley to Spence and Godwin looked upon the parish as a potential unit of communal production and self-government, if only it could be set free from the tyranny of the central state power. On the other hand, as Professor Knappen pointed out, the ecclesiastical-political structure of government in England contributed to the *laissez-faire* and individualistic tendencies in puritan thought, to an apparent lack of social responsibility. Why should puritan preachers bother about social questions? They and their allies, the opposition gentry and merchants, had no control over social policy. "There was some point in preaching on matters of individual conduct, because there was a possibility of changing individual lives. But the only effective way to reach the social problem lay through a reorganization of the established church, and a change in its relations with the secular power".[2]

Hence, after the overthrow of the hierarchy, the preachers had little to say to those of the lower orders who felt the need for social reform; the latter were driven to organize themselves in sectarian congregations with a very different theology from the predestinarianism of the orthodox Calvinists, and a very different political and social outlook from that of the conservative supporters of Parliament. After the Restoration J.P.s in some counties refused poor relief to those who did not attend their parish church. It was the sects which carried over into the modern world some of the sense of communal responsibility which was inherited from the mediaeval manor and borough.

1. H. Prideaux, *Directions to Churchwardens* (4th ed., 1716), pp. 40–1.
2. Knappen, *Tudor Puritanism*, p. 416.

Chapter Thirteen

The Spiritualization of the Household

Masters in their houses ought to be as preachers to their families, that from the highest to the lowest they may obey the will of God.
> Geneva Bible, marginal note on Genesis xvii, 23.

Dogberry.   I am a wise fellow, and, which is more, an officer; and, which is more, a householder; and, which is more, as pretty a piece of flesh as any is in Messina; and one that honours the law, go to: and a rich fellow enough, go to: and a fellow that hath had losses: and one that hath two gowns, and everything handsome about him.
> Shakespeare, *Much Ado About Nothing*, Act IV, scene 2.

I

FOR Puritans the lowest unit in the hierarchy of discipline was not the parish but the household. "If ever we would have the church of God to continue among us", wrote Greenham, "we must bring it into our households, and nourish it in our families".[1] "God chargeth the master of the family with all in the family", explained Dod and Cleaver. "Hence . . . it belongs to all governors to see that their children, servants and inferiors whatsoever keep the Lord's day".[2] "All in the family" meant, for upper and middle-class households, considerably more than we should expect to find to-day, since apprentices normally and journeymen sometimes lived with their masters.

1. R. Greenham. *Workes*, p. 799. The same point is made in *A godly form of household government*, by R. Cawdrey, amended and augmented by Dod and Cleaver (1614), Sig. A 2v–A3.

2. Dod and Cleaver, *The Ten Commandements*, p. 145; cf R. Sibbes, *The Soules Conflict* (1635), p. 4.

There might be a dozen in a household in sixteenth-century Exeter.[1] In Sheffield in 1615, of a population of 2,207 only 260 were householders, the rest being dependants or poor.[2] In villages, and in towns developing less rapidly than Exeter, the average size of households was smaller; but there was often a substantial proportion of large households.[3] It seems to have been to the heads of such households that the preachers especially addressed themselves.

"Domestic and family worship is a necessary duty", said two members of the Westminster Assembly, "and as far as it is possible, even moral and natural". God created society not merely for the worldly convenience of its members, "but rather chiefly that they should improve their society one with another to His glory". For everyone needs help from others, and all benefit by "the solemn service jointly presented to God in the family".[4] Yet, one of the authors asked the House of Commons in 1643, "what help have we afforded the church, groaning under the burden of sin, by endeavouring an effectual reformation" of our households?[5] "First reform your own families", Calamy had similarly urged M.P.s in December 1641, "and then you will be the fitter to reform the family of God. Let the master reform his servant, the father his child, the husband his wife".[6] Baxter in 1655 also advised ministers to "get masters of

1. *Patriarcha and other political works of Sir Robert Filmer* (ed. P. Laslett, 1949), pp. 24–5; W. G. Hoskins, "The Elizabethan Merchants of Exeter", in *Elizabethan Government and Society* (ed. S. T. Bindoff, J. Hurstfield and C. H. Williams, 1961), p. 178; B. Little, *The City and County of Bristol*, (1954), p. 328. Cf. *The Household Papers of Henry Percy, Ninth Earl of Northumberland (1564–1632)* (ed. G. R. Batho, Camden Soc., 1962), pp. xxi–iii, for the much greater size of noble households.

2. J. Hunter, *Hallamshire* (1869), quoted by K. Thomas. "Women and the Civil War Sects", *P. and P.*, No. 13, p. 42.

3. P. Laslett and J. Harrison, "Clayworth and Cogenhoe", *Historical Essays, 1600–1750, presented to David Ogg* (ed. H. E. Bell and R. L. Ollard, 1963), p. 166.

4. Cawdrey and Palmer, *Sabbatum Redivivum*, pp. 80–1; cf. D. Cawdrey, *Family Reformation Promoted* (1656), Sig. A 5v: "Families are . . . the hives, out of which do swarm the materials of greater assemblies". Cf. Sig. A 7, pp. 3–4.

5. H. Palmer, *The Necessity and Encouragement of Utmost Venturing for the Churches Help*, pp. 33–4; cf. *The Glasse of Good Providence towards his faithfull ones*, pp. 44–6 (a sermon preached to the two Houses of Parliament, 13 August 1644).

6. E. Calamy, *Englands Looking-Glasse* (1642), p. 31.

families to their duties, and they will spare you a great deal of labour with the rest, and further much the success of your labour. . . . You are like to see no general reformation till you procure family reformation".[1] In the desolate year 1671 he still laboured the same point: "Do you cry out of silent or unprofitable ministers? And do you think that silence and unprofitableness in the governor of a family is no crime?"[2]

Radicals laid equal emphasis on the family unit. In John of Leyden's Münster disobedience to one's master in a household made one liable to the death sentence.[3] One of the original points of agreement among the members of Robert Browne's church was that they "should further the kingdom of God . . . especially in their charge and household".[4] "Be careful to have the Lord purely worshipped in your families", wrote John Penry in 1589. "A farther, and so a master", is bound to bring his children and servants up "in instruction and information of the Lord".[5] Similar views were held by Independents like Philip Nye and Hugh Peter, by George Fox and John Bunyan.[6]

This was part of the protestant inheritance. The religious and disciplinary responsibilities of heads of households towards those under their care was emphasized in Luther's *Short Catechism* of 1529.[7] In England Tyndale similarly stressed their

1. Baxter, *The Reformed Pastor* (1655), p. 59; cf. D. Cawdrey, *Family Reformation Promoted* (1656), Sig. A 7, pp. 3–4.

2. Baxter's letter to the Reader, prefixed to *The Lords-Day* (1672), Sig. A 5, a translation of the Smectymnuan Thomas Young's *Dies Dominica*, originally published in 1639. Cf. also Baxter's *The Catechizing of Families: A Teacher of Householders, How to Teach their Households* (1683), pp. 312–13.

3. G. H. Williams, *The Radical Reformation* (Philadelphia, 1962), p. 371.

4. R. Browne, *A True and Short Declaration* (1584), in *Writings of Harrison and Browne*, pp. 422–3.

5. Penry, *Three Treatises*, pp. 20, 109. Family worship, however, was not enough. Penry spoke slightingly of the "mock-Gods, I mean the common Protestants of this age, who think they do a meritorious work because they entertain the word in their families" (*ibid.*, p. 76).

6. D. Nobbs, "Philip Nye on Church and State", *Cambridge Historical Journal*, V, pp. 53–4; R. P. Stearns, *The Strenuous Puritan* (Urbana, 1954), p. 76; A. Lloyd, *Quaker Social History, 1669–1738* (1950), p. 70; Bunyan, *Works* (1860), II, pp. 555–60; III, pp. 599–615.

7. Printed in *Documents of the Christian Church* (ed. H. Bettenson, World's Classics), pp. 286–7, 292.

religious duties.[1] The Erasmian Richard Whytford published
A Work for Householders in 1531, "directed principally unto
householders or unto them that have guiding and governance
of any company, for an order to be kept both in themself, and
in them that they have in rule and charge". Henry VIII's letter
of 25 June 1535 urged the judges to influence "parents and
rulers of families" to "declare, teach and inform their children
and servants in the spiritualities" of the royal supreme head-
ship of the Church, to the utter extirpation of the Bishop of
Rome's usurped authority. Heads of households were expected
to be sounder theologically on these difficult matters than the
clergy, and so it was to the government's advantage to make
use of them, though the idea had been rejected 18 months
earlier.[2] Thomas Cromwell's Injunctions to the clergy in 1536
instructed them to urge parents to place their children to
learning or some honest occupation. "If they had been well
educated and brought up in some good literature, occupation
or mystery, they should, being rulers of their own family,
have profited as well themselves as divers other persons, to the
great commodity and ornament of the common weal".[3]

The Reformation, by reducing the authority of the priest in
society, simultaneously elevated the authority of lay heads of
households, as intermediaries between the central government
and their own servants and dependents, no less than between
the latter and God. The King's Book of 1543 discussed the
duties of masters and servants in the household.[4] 34 and 35
Hen. VIII cap. 1 allowed merchant householders (as well of
course as noblemen and gentlemen) to read the Bible in their
families, whilst withdrawing this privilege from artificers,
apprentices, journeymen, husbandmen, labourers and women.
Edward VI's and later Injunctions laid upon parents and
employers the responsibility for bringing up the youth in some
virtuous study and occupation.[5] "To have children and servants is thy blessing, O Lord", said a prayer for householders
in the Primer of 1553; "but not to order them according to

1. Tyndale, *Expositions*, p. 36. See p. 451 below.
2. Ed. R. Steele, *Kings' Letters*, II (1904), p. 224; G. R. Elton, *The
Tudor Revolution in Government* (1953), pp. 361–4.
3. H. Gee and W. Hardy, *Documents illustrative of English Church
History* (1896), p. 272.
4. *The King's Book* (1895 reprint), pp. 99–100.
5. Cardwell, *Documentary Annals*, I, pp. 43, 129, 323.

thy word deserveth thy dreadful curse".[1]

"For that every person having house and family is in duty bound to have especial regard to the good government and ordering of the same", 35 Eliz. cap I laid on heads of households the duty of seeing that their children and apprentices went to church, under penalty of a fine of £10 a month.[2] Archbishop Whitgift thought householders "bound of duty as well to instruct their families as the pastor is bound to instruct them".[3] Archbishop Sandys agreed that the "householder that feareth God will, by good order and due consent, keep [his family] in the fear of God".[4] Sternhold and Hopkins's *Whole Booke of Psalms* contains a series of prose prayers for use in private families. Arthur Dent printed family prayers for household use in his best-seller, *The Plaine Mans Pathway to Heaven*; so did Bishop Bayly in his even more popular *Practice of Piety*. The assumption that heads of households would be godly Protestants was thus shared by hierarchy and Puritans alike.[5] It may be significant that in *The Householders Philosophie* translated from the popish Italian of Tasso in 1588, probably by Thomas Kyd, there is virtually no mention of the religious duties of heads of families.[6] We can perhaps trace a new urgency in puritan references to the common protestant tradition from the last decade of the sixteenth century. "It might have been something tolerable in times past", wrote Penry in 1590, "for a sincere professor to have an ignorant, an untaught and an unreformed family": but not since the Reformation. Penry thought it necessary to urge his readers to "show what reformation can do in a whole kingdom by the practice thereof in your own persons and families".[7]

1. Ed. J. Ketley, *The Two Liturgies . . . in the reign of King Edward VI* (Parker Soc., 1844), p. 465.

2. Cf. *V.C.H. York*, p. 151. For the Sabbath duties of heads of households, see pp. 175–7 above.

3. Whitgift, *Works*, II, p. 579.

4. Ed. J. Ayre, *Sermons of Edwin Sandys* (Parker Soc., 1941), p. 265.

5. Cf. Joseph Hall, *Solomon's Oeconomie or government of the Family*, *Works*, VIII, pp. 476–84. *The Plaine Mans Pathway* ran to 25 editions between 1601 and 1640, *The Practice of Piety* to at least 36 between 1612 and 1636 (H. C. White, *English Devotional Literature, 1600–40*, Madison, 1931, p. 13).

6. T. Kyd, *Works* (1901), pp. 231–84.

7. J. Penry, *A Treatise Wherein is manifestlie proved, that reformation and those that sincerely favor the same, are unjustifiably charged to be enemies unto hir Majestie, and the state* (1590), Preface. Two years later

On this point at least, Parliament and the common law were not at variance with the Church. The House of Commons in 1604 asked that all masters of households should be compelled to sign the Thirty-nine Articles – excepting those which dealt with the power of bishops and the Crown over the Church.[1] Coke's list of articles given to high constables for presentment, probably in 1606, contains one which said "All unlawful games, drunkenness, whoredom and incontinency in private families to be reported, as on their good government the commonwealth depends".[2] In 1632 the allegation that 13 maidservants had been begotten with child in the household of William Richman within 14 years was considered by the assize judges, who ordered it to be investigated.[3] Even Laud assumed the same hierarchical devolution, though for him the duty of parents, masters and mistresses was not so much themselves to teach as to send their children, servants and apprentices to church to learn their catechism.[4] And in December 1659, when the Lord Mayor of London was worried about possible disorder, he directed each alderman, with the constable of his ward, to go from house to house and charge all heads of families to see that their sons and servants did not engage in any unlawful design.[5] The household was almost a part of the constitution of the state. When Gregory King made the first serious estimate of the population of England in 1696, he took as his basic unit the household, not the individual.

II

John Major in the early sixteenth century distinguished between "two different ways of life and conduct in Scotland", those of the "Wild Scots" of the north-west, and of the "Householding Scots" of the Lowlands.[6] The family farm or workshop

---

Penry and his fellow prisoners made the need to keep an eye on their families a main argument for asking to be released. "For what is youth without government?" (J. Waddington, *John Penry*, 1858, p. 113).

1. Usher, *Reconstruction of the English Church*, I, p. 349.

2. M. G. Davies, *The Enforcement of English Apprenticeship, 1563–1642* (Harvard University Press, 1956), p. 233.

3. Ed. Barnes, *Somerset Assize Orders*, p. 19.

4. Laud. *Works*, V, p. 446.

5. G. Davies, *The Restoration of Charles II*, p. 181.

6. J. Major, *History of Greater Britain* (Scottish History Soc., 1892), p. 48.

played in the world of early capitalism the part that the great noble household or monastery had played in mediaeval society. It was the lowest unit the heads of which were "active citizens", with independent economic initiative. The master of the household, and no one else, could wear his hat in his own house. It was this piece of traditional social subordination that the Quakers' refusal of hat-honour was to challenge.[1]

The head of a great noble family, or of a monastery, did not exercise his economic control directly over the producers: he worked through a hierarchy of mediators – chamberlains, stewards, bailiffs and the like. His relation with production was indirect and remote. And to look after the spiritual welfare of his immediate underlings the nobleman hired a chaplain. Crashawe observed in 1607 that in families of the great men of this age "many of their inferior officers and servants do scarce ever come to church".[2] But among the industrious sort of people the head of the household had a different relationship to his family. He was in direct personal contact with those who worked side by side with him under his orders. He knew them and could hardly help feeling some responsibility both for their physical and for their spiritual welfare. Calvin himself, in explaining away the text "sell all that thou hast and give to the poor", dismissed voluntary poverty as escapism, and added: "God sets more value on the pious management of a household, when the head of it, discarding all avarice, ambition, and other lusts of the flesh, makes it his purpose to serve God in some particular vocation".[3] Bullinger, no less influential in England than Calvin, agreed that "The Lord mislikes the yawning mouth and folded arms, the signs of sleep which commonly follow the careless man, who doth neglect the state and condition of his house and family". "No parcel of God's law doth bind or bid thee to distribute to other men the wealth which thou thyself dost need as much or more than

1. H. N. Brailsford, *The Levellers and the English Revolution* (1961), pp. 42–6.
2. W. Crashawe, *The Sermon Preached at the Crosse* (1607), pp. 14–15. For the survival of the feudal household and its social and political implications, see a suggestive article by J. Bossy, "The Character of Elizabethan Catholicism", *P. and P.*, No. 21, p. 41 and *passim*. Cf. also L. Stone, "Marriage among the Elizabethan Nobility in the 16th and 17th centuries", in *Comparative Studies in Society and History*, III (1961), pp. 205–6.
3. Calvin, *Institutes*, II, pp. 483–6.

they. It is sufficient for thee to provide that they of thine own household be not a burden to other men's backs".[1] In Geneva, Zürich and London the problems facing the small men were the same: accumulation of capital, oversight of the family business.

"The master oweth to his servant meat, wages, correction, instruction".[2] His educational responsibilities were no less than his responsibility for the physical welfare of those under him. "Doth not every father teach his son, every master his servant?" asked John Hales.[3] How could you, if you were a conscientious head of a household "be careful to teach your children and servants the way of your trades and callings, and neglect to instruct them in the way of life?" "Is weekly catechizing up in every one of your families?" Joseph Alleine continued.[4]

"Every house ought to be ruled by the orders of the skilful, wise and careful householder only", wrote John Udall: "BUT the Church is the house of God, and God is such a householder".[5] "The word 'Father' is an epitome of the whole Gospel", said Sibbes.[6] The theology of Protestantism was patriarchal, reducing the role of the Virgin and of the saints, many of whom were women. The Calvinist God is a God of absolute will and power, Who has laid down His wishes in the form of binding laws. These laws are interpreted by a group of the elect fired by a sense of purpose. God, too, was no respecter of persons: He helped those, and only those, who tried to carry out the wishes of the great Householder.

Bullinger, to the delight of the cynical, pointed out that "the good man of the house, by planting godliness in his family, doth not a little advance and set forward his private profit and own

1. Bullinger, *Decades*, III, pp. 32–3, 58; cf. *Perkins, Workes*, III, pp. 163–4.

2. Sandys, *Sermons*, p. 202.

3. Hales, *Essay Concerning the Power of the Keys*, quoted by J. Tulloch, *Rational Theology and Christian Philosophy in England in the 17th century* (1874), I, p. 242.

4. [J. Alleine], *Christian Letters . . . tending to the Promoting of the Power of Godliness, both in Persons and Families* (1673), p. 40. Written in 1663, from prison, to Alleine's flock at Taunton.

5. Udall, *A Demonstration of Discipline* (ed. Arber), p. 14; cf. p. 65.

6. R. Sibbes, *Works* (1862), V, p. 25, quoted in G. F. Nuttall, *The Holy Spirit in Puritan Faith and Experience* (1946), p. 63; cf. other references, *ibid.*, p. 58.

commodity; for wicked servants are for the most part pickers and deceitful; whereas, on the other side, the godly are faithful, whom in his absence he may trust to govern his house. . . ."[1] Master and journeyman alike were under the great Taskmaster's eye; but so far as journeymen and prentices were concerned the earthly taskmaster did duty both for himself and for God in things spiritual no less than in things temporal.[2] "Servants well instructed in piety", Gouge noted, "are likeliest to prove most profitable, not only to the family, but also to the church and commonwealth". Servants ought for their own good to be stinted of superfluity.[3] The moral conclusion of *The Apprentices Warning-piece* (1641) was "let your study be, first to please your heavenly Master, and then your masters upon earth". It did not seem likely to the author that the two duties would in any way conflict.[4] When William Kiffin played truant in his apprentice days, he was sent back to his master (John Lilburne) by hearing a sermon preached by Thomas Foxley at St. Antholin's on the Fifth Commandment, showing the duties of servants to masters.[5]

"Parents and masters of families are in God's stead to their children and servants"; "every chief householder hath . . . the charge of the souls of his family".[6] The preachers pitched their claims high. So long as a personal relation between employer and employee existed, there was something to be said for this patriarchical attitude. Masters beat their servants, it is true; but

1. Bullinger, *Decades*, I, p. 258. The passage was taken over almost verbatim (though with "loiterers" added to "pickers and deceitful") in *A godly forme of household government: for the ordering of private families*, by R. Cawdrey, amended and augmented by J. Dod and R. Cleaver (1614), Sig. A 4–A 5. It became a protestant commonplace. Cf. J. Preston, *The New Covenant* (5th ed., 1630), p. 171; D. Cawdrey, *Family Reformation Promoted* (1656), pp. 47–9; *The Works of the Author of The Whole Duty of Man*, p. 314.

2. See pp. 442–3 below.

3. W. Gouge, *Of Domesticall Duties* (1626), pp. 372–3.

4. Quoted by L. B. Wright, *Middle-class Culture in Elizabethan England* (1935), pp. 197–8; cf. Joseph Beaumont, *Minor Poems* (1914), pp. 413–14.

5. Ed. W. Orme, *Remarkable Passages in the Life of William Kiffin* (1823), p. 3. Foxley was connected with the Feoffees for Impropriations.

6. J. Mayne, *The English Catechism Explained, . . . Profitable for . . . Householders in their Families* (3rd ed., 1623), p. 278; D. Cawdrey, *Family Reformation Promoted*, p. 23; cf. Cawdrey and Palmer, *Sabbatum Redivivum*, p. 35.

then parents beat their children, and expected highly deferential behaviour from them. Gouge insisted that masters should not be "too frequent and too furious strikers".[1] Mutual participation in family prayers may have contributed to household harmony.[2] Bullinger not only pointed out the economic advantages of having godly servants: he also insisted, like Calvin, that servants must be given rest and leisure.[3] Gouge not only emphasized the necessary subordination of servants to masters; he also declared that God was "the Master of masters. As servants are the Lord's freemen, so masters are the Lord's servants".[4]

In the puritan guides to godliness the duties of a householder to his servants always accompanied the duties of servants to masters. *The Larger Catechism* put out by the Westminster Assembly insisted that governors of families must assist their servants to observe the Sabbath, and not hinder them by giving them work to do.[5] Family religious instruction could also stimulate discussion within the household. "Let the husband with the wife, let the father with the child, talk together of these matters, and both to and fro let them enquire and give their judgments": so Immanuel Bourne, at Paul's Cross in 1617.[6] Roger Clap of Exeter was apprenticed into "as famous a family for religion as ever I knew". The whole household, including a dozen servants, "had a conference upon a question propounded once a week".[7] Such training in discussion was to lead some apprentices further than their well-meaning masters would have wished them to go.

Schücking, indeed, thought he observed a significant softening in attitudes of employers towards their servants, prentices and workmen in protestant countries during the century and a half following the Reformation. He contrasted Tyndale's

1. Gouge, *Of Domesticall Duties*, pp. 342–3, 365. They should not beat their wives at all (*ibid.*, pp. 223–6).

2. See Defoe, *The Family Instructor*, *passim*. Cromwell obviously hoped that a prayer meeting would restore harmony after the fierce debates in the Army Council at Putney in October 1647.

3. Bullinger, *Decades*, I, pp. 257–8.

4. Gouge, *op. cit.*, pp. 321–2, 385.

5. *The Larger Catechism*, p. 163. See pp. 162–3 above.

6. I. Bourne, *The True Way of a Christian* (1622), quoted in Maclure, *The Paul's Cross Sermons*, p. 238.

7. Ed. Alexander Young, *Chronicles of the First Planters of the Colony of Massachusetts Bay* (Boston, 1846), pp. 345–6.

"Thou art his good and possession, as his ox or his horse" with the principle laid down by Gouge or Bunyan, that a workman's employment should be for his own good as well as his employer's. Schücking attributed this change to the fact that sons of gentlemen were becoming apprentices in increasing numbers;[1] but this process probably developed more rapidly, at least in England, after the upheaval of the mid-seventeenth century. Schücking might have added the consideration that the conditions of labour in a small household unit, where the employer worked himself side by side with his employees, made for relations of a not unfriendly kind. The change also relates to the slow but significant humanization of relations between parents and children which took place in the sixteenth and seventeenth centuries.[2] So long as the family farm and the small family business predominated, the patriarchal attitude corresponded to economic realities: it became nauseating only when transferred to the impersonal relations of developed industrial capitalism, dominated by the blind workings of the market.[3]

Perhaps even the protestant recognition of ecclesiastical marriage helped to elevate the prestige of the family in society. The monasteries, nunneries, friaries and chantries disappeared, and the priest, set apart by his celibacy and mediating the sacraments of the universal Church, yielded place to the parson as good family man. Certainly the parson was brought into closer contact with lay reality. John Rogers, whose wife was a thorn in his side, and thereby sent him to God,[4] would understand the domestic problems of his citizen congregations. The changes are subtle and slow, but they are perceptible. "A man that governs his family well", wrote Bunyan, "hath one qualification belonging to a pastor or deacon in the house of God, for he that knoweth not how to rule his own house, how shall he take care of the church of God?"[5]

1. L. L. Schücking, *Die Familie im Puritanismus* (Leipzig, 1929), pp. 133–5.

2. Nuttall, *The Holy Spirit in Puritan Faith and Experience*, pp. 58, 63–4; Stone, "Marriage among the Elizabethan Nobility", *passim*.

3. Defoe in 1724, typically, thought it was the growing immorality of the lower classes which had loosened the patriarchal relationship between employer and employee (*The Great Law of Subordination*, quoted in F. Antal, *Hogarth and his place in European Art*, 1962, p. 12).

4. Ed. G. C. Moore Smith, *Extracts from the Papers of Thomas Woodcock* (Camden Miscellany, XI, 1907), p. 53.

5. Bunyan, *Works*, II, p. 556.

III

Family prayers and family catechizing offered an alternative to public worship, especially when the worship itself left so much to be desired as that of the Laudian Church. "Every master of a household," the *First Book of Discipline* laid down, "must be commanded either to instruct, or cause to be instructed, his children, servants and family in the principles of the Christian religion", without the knowledge of which none would be admitted to communion. Heads of households who failed to carry out this duty were to be visited with ecclesiastical and civil penalties.[1] Catechizing, Cartwright insisted, should be carried on "both at home by the master of the house, and in the church by the minister"; and to the question "Why at home?" he replied succinctly: "Because houses are the nurseries of the church".[2] Domestic catechizing, by fathers and masters in their families, was one of the things insisted on by the divines at the Synod of Dort.[3] The Westminster Assembly voted in 1646 that those who neglected family prayers and family instruction were guilty of sin: the proposition that the sin was scandalous was defeated by only 3 votes. The Assembly published its Shorter Catechism explicitly because "masters of families may need help in catechizing".[4] The good householder, or his wife, would teach servants and apprentices to read.[5] Never any servant came to William Gouge's house, we are told, but gained a great deal of knowledge. There were prayers twice daily, three times on Sundays: there was Bible-reading, and children and servants were catechized. Parents and

1. Knox, *History of the Reformation*, p. 512; cf. *Directions of the General Assembly concerning Secret and Private Worship* (1647), pp. 6–8.

2. *Cartwrightiana*, p. 159.

3. *Mr. Hales Letters from the Synod of Dort to . . . Sir Dudley Carleton*, p. 8, in J. Hales's *Golden Remaines* (1659); cf. *Writings of Harrison and Browne*, pp. 347, 397.

4. Ed. A. F. Mitchell and J. Struthers, *Minutes of the Sessions of the Westminster Assembly of Divines* (1874), pp. 161, 235; *The Shorter Catechism*, p. 30. Cf. *A Solemn Exhortation . . . to the several Churches of Christ within this Province of Lancaster* (1649), in *Minutes of the Manchester Presbyterian Classis* (ed. W. A. Shaw, Chetham Soc., 1890–1), III, p. 373.

5. Ed. C. Jackson, *Yorkshire Diaries and Autobiographies in the 17th and 18th centuries*, II (Surtees Soc., 1886), p. 16.

governors of families, Gouge taught, had an especial duty to be conscionable in catechizing.[1]

Thomas Taylor may perhaps sum up this point: "Let every master of a family see to what he is called, namely, to make his house a little church, to instruct every one of his family in the fear of God, to contain every one of them under holy discipline, to pray with them and for them. . . . The way to frame thee a good servant is, to make him God's servant. . . . How many men go back in their estates, and marvel things thrive so ill, and see not this to be the cause; that suppose themselves be not wicked, yet they suffer their sons or servants so to be, through whose hands the work goeth, and all is in a wane and consumption? . . . Many complain of evil times and general corruption: and many talk of want of discipline in the church, and it were to be wished, not too justly. But thou that [art] a careless master, the times are worse for thee; and all discipline in the church, or good laws in a state, will not mend things till thou mend thy family. If all families, where reformation must begin, were brought in to this discipline, our eyes should see a happy change".[2] Taylor's hope is that reformation will begin in the family and extend to the whole State.

The passage sums up a number of points often repeated by earlier and especially later writers.[3] There was indeed a vast

1. Gouge, *Commentary on Hebrews*, I, pp. vii–iii, 374.

2. T. Taylor, *Works* (1653), pp. 190–2. Cf. *Peter his repentance*, pp. 45–6, in the same volume (separate pagination).

3. e.g. Richard Whytford, *A Work for Householders* (1531 and many later editions); Grindal, *A Form of Meditation, very meet to be daily used of householders in their houses* (1563), in *Remains*, pp. 477–83; E. Dering, *A Briefe and Necessarie Catechisme or Instruction: verie needfull to be knowne of all Householders*, Sig. C–I 4, in *Works* (1614); Dod and Cleaver, *Ten Commandements*, pp. 145–6; N. Bownde, *The Doctrine of the Sabbath* (1595), pp. 260–72; Perkins, *Workes*, III, pp. 698–700; J. Mayne, *The English Catechisme Explained*, pp. 561–9; Bayly, *The Practice of Piety*, pp. 192–6; Sibbes, *The Returning Backslider* (1639), pp. 270–3; W. Gouge, *Of Domestical Duties* (1626), p. 10; *Commentary on Hebrews* (1866), I, p. 374; Paul Bayne, *An Entire Commentary on the Whole Epistle of St. Paul to the Ephesians* (1866), pp. 365–73: first published 1641; R. Stock, *A Commentary upon the Prophecy of Malachi* (1865), I, pp. 44–51; Geree, *The Character of an Old English Puritane*, pp. 3–5; *Directions of the General Assembly concerning Secret and Private Worship* (1647), *passim*; Cawdrey and Palmer, *Sabbatum Redivivum*, p. 191; D. Cawdrey, *Family Reformation Promoted*, Preface and pp. 18–24; Samuel Fairclough, *The Saints Worthinesse* (1653), pp. 17–18; T. Goodwin, *Works*, IV, p. 173; *Works of the . . . Author of*

mass of books published in the sixteenth and seventeenth
centuries which aimed precisely at assisting laymen of the
industrious sort in their semi-priestly duties, a kind of protestant lay casuistry.[1] *The Whole Duty of Man*, its title page
informs us, was "necessary for all families". This popular
treatise almost echoed Thomas Taylor in urging all masters
to endeavour to have their families to be "a kind of church".
But in *The Whole Duty* the appeal has become cruder and more
directly economic. "Besides the eternal reward of it hereafter
. . . worldly business would thrive much the better" for it. The
passage occurs in a discussion of the duties of masters to
servants.[2]

Baxter was later to specialize in this type of literature, designed for the use of "the more intelligent and diligent sort of
masters of families (who would have a practical directory at
hand to teach them every Christian duty, and how to help
others in the practice)".[3] His *Christian Directory* was intended
both for ministers and for "the more judicious masters of
families, who may choose and read such parcels to their
families as at any time the case requireth".[4] In the same way,
his *Poor Man's Family Book* was intended "for poor country
families who cannot buy or read many books". It and its
sequel, *The Catechizing of Households*, was designed to help
heads of families to "do their parts in reading good books to
their households", which "might be a great supply when the
ministry is defective: and no ministry will serve sufficiently

The Whole Duty of Man, pp. 18–19, 44, 125–6; Bunyan, *Works*, II, pp.
555–60; III, pp. 606–15; Baxter, *Christian Directory* (1673), pp. 556–7,
633; W. Penn, *Some Fruits of Solitude*, Part I, Nos. 55–6; Schücking,
op. cit., esp. pp. vi, 84–5; E. S. Morgan, *The Puritan Family* (Boston,
Mass., 1956), pp. 64–85. For an example of a puritan London merchant,
reared on the writings of Greenham and Perkins, whose household was
"nourished upon prayers" and who had a reputation for covetousness
and miserliness, see E. Browne, *A rare Paterne of Justice and Mercy*
(1642), pp. 37, 43.

1. L. B. Wright, *Middle-Class Culture in Elizabethan England* (Chapel
Hill, 1935), esp. chapters VII and VIII; H. H. Henson, *Studies in English
Religion in the 17th century* (1903), Chapter V. See esp. R. Cawdrey, *A
godly forme of household governement*, *passim*.

2. *Works of the . . . Author of the Whole Duty of Man*, pp. 125–6; cf.
p. 440.

3. *Reliquiae Baxterianae*, I, p. 122.

4. Baxter, *Christian Directory*, Advertisements.

without men's own endeavours for themselves and families".[1]

"The priest-like father reads the sacred page":[2] family prayers and family religious instruction helped to induce solidarity in the household,[3] a sense of duty in its dependent members, which the preachers contrasted sharply with the loose behaviour, on Sundays and week-days alike, of under-employed serving-men in great feudal households.[4] At the same time that his responsibility for the moral welfare of his house-hold enhanced the dignity of the father of the family, as Milton noted, the dependence of the rest of the household upon him was increased, including of course that of his wife and children. He was their instructor in matters of conduct. "The church discipline doth not overthrow the authority of the husband in his house, which is of God as well as the other": so Cartwright wrote to his Brownist sister-in-law in 1590.[5] Eve's fall, after all, occurred not merely because she was disobedient to her husband but because she was insufficiently instructed to grasp the importance of the issue.

1. *Reliquiae Baxterianae*, II, pp. 147, 191.

2. Burns, "The Cotter's Saturday Night", *Poems* (World's Classics), p. 61.

3. Or, for that matter between landlord and tenant: see Samuel Palmer, *The Nonconformists' Memorial* (1775), II, p. 179.

4. Bownde, *op. cit.* (1606 ed.), p. 445; Perkins, *Workes*, III, p. 191; cf. p. 435 above.

5. *Cartwrightiana*, p. 73. It is, of course, monstrously one-sided to treat puritan teaching on the family as though it *merely* elevated the male head: radical Puritanism also did much to build up a new and nobler conception of the relation between the sexes. Robert Browne insisted that the authority of the father and husband must rest on agreement and covenant (*Writings of Harrison and Browne*, pp. 334, 342–5). Mrs. Chidley in 1641 thought the husband had no more right to control his wife's conscience than the magistrate had to control his. Both were to obey in civil matters, but conscience could not be coerced (quoted in Milton, *Complete Prose*, Yale ed. I, p. 141). George Fox thought that male dominion belonged to sin, and that in the new life man and wife were equals (E. Fogelklou, *James Nayler*, 1931, p. 140). But this is a large question, on which the reader should consult the Hallers' article "The Puritan Art of Love" in *Huntington Library Quarterly*, V; Schücking, *Die Familie im Puritanismus*; and Milton's *Works, passim*. See also K. V. Thomas, "Women and the Civil War Sects", *P. and P.*, No. 13, and my *Puritanism and Revolution*, pp. 367–94

IV

The point here stressed was effectively put by Professor and Mrs. Haller: "In the society [which the preachers] were helping to shape, the family household, with its extensions in farmstead and shop, and in its relation to religious life, was assuming an importance it had not had in feudal, monastic or courtly society. The preachers described it again and again as a little church, a little state", for which the head of the household was responsible.[1] This social background has since been emphasized by Mr. Laslett, to help to explain the attraction of the patriarchal theory of politics through its long life until finally demolished by Locke.[2] Bodin taught that the family is not only the true source and origin of the commonwealth, but also its principal constituent. "The well-ordered family is a true image of the commonwealth, and domestic comparable with sovereign authority. . . . All will be well with the commonwealth where families are properly regulated".[3] Sir Thomas Smith stressed the patriarchal origins of government.[4] Ralegh thought the first governors were fathers of families, and compared the King to "the master of the household".[5] The introduction to the *Commons Journals* of James I stated that the family was the origin of the state.[6] The patriarchal family is prominent in Bacon's *New Atlantis*. Hobbes used the parallel of household and state in order to emphasize that "the subjection of them who institute a commonwealth among themselves is no less absolute than the subjection of servants".[7] Milton regarded

1. W. and M. Haller, "The Puritan Art of Love", *Huntington Library Quarterly*, V, p. 247. Cf. Cawdrey, *A godly forme of household governement*, Sig. A 7; R. Sibbes, *The Returning Backslider*, p. 272; Geree, *The Character of an old English Puritane*, *passim*; S. Clarke, *The Lives of Thirty-Two English Divines* (1677), p 135, and *The Marrow of Ecclesiastical History* (1675), p. 910; *The Ladies Calling*, pp. 82–4, in *The Works of the . . . Author of The Whole Duty of Man* (1704).

2. See P. Laslett's edition of Filmer's *Patriarcha*, esp. pp. 20–33.

3. J. Bodin, *Six Books of the Commonwealth* (ed. M. J. Tooley, n.d.,? 1955). pp. 6–7.

4. Ed. L. Alston, *De Republica Anglorum, A Discourse of the Commonwealth of England*, by Sir Thomas Smith (1906), p. 24.

5. Ralegh, *History of the World* (1820), II, pp. 104–5; V, p. 107; *Works* (1751), II, p. 53.

6. *C.J.*, I, p. 139.

7. T. Hobbes, *Elements of Law*, p. 105. Eachard correctly pointed out that Hobbes showed no originality on this point (J. Eachard, *Mr.*

marriage and the family as the foundation of the common-wealth, though he came to deny inequality based on patriarchal claims.[1] William Bridge drew an analogy between the marriage contract and the social contract.[2]

John Winthrop thought that a commonwealth resulted from "many families subjecting themselves to rulers and laws". He argued against democracy that it would be "a manifest breach of the Fifth Commandment".[3] The 41 males who signed the Covenant on the *Mayflower* were heads of households: the rest were women, children and servants. In 1629 an attempt was made to establish artificial families among the bachelor male servants of Massachusetts: for some such unit was thought necessary for religious government.[4] Even where communism was practised by the early colonists, it was a communism of heads of households: prentices and servants shared only through their masters.[5] At Providence, most democratic of the Rhode Island towns, before any magistracy was established, "the masters of families have ordinarily met once a fortnight and consulted". In 1636 "some young men, single persons", after promising to be "subject to the orders made by the consent of the householders", became "discontented with their estate" and sought "the freedom of the vote" and "equality".[6] In 1642 Massachusetts passed a law making heads of families responsible for the education of their apprentices; and other colonies followed suit.[7]

The comparison between household and State was a commonplace for the spokesmen of the hierarchy too. Arch-bishop Parker likened the government of a family to that of a

Hobbs's State of Nature considered, ed. P. Ure, 1958, p. 16: published 1672).

1. Milton, *Prose Works* (Bohn ed.), III, p. 279; cf. p. 33.

2. W. Bridge, *The Wounded Conscience Cured* (1643), p. 31.

3. Morgan, *The Puritan Family,* p. 115; R. C. Winthrop, *Life and Letters of John Winthrop* (1867), p. 430, quoted by L. B. Namier, *England in the Age of the American Revolution* (2nd ed., 1961), p. 26.

4. Morgan, *op. cit.*, p. 85.

5. J. Smith, *General History of Virginia* (1626), in Arber, *An English Garner,* II, p. 286. We may compare the servants which Locke's "people" have in the state of nature.

6. Roger Williams to John Winthrop, *Massachusetts Historical Soc. Collections,* 4th Series, VI, pp. 186–7.

7. Morgan, *op. cit.*, p. 45; L. B. Wright, *The Colonial Civilization of North America* (1949), p. 112.

ship, a corporate town or a state.[1] If it was "referred to the judgment of the subject, of the tenant and of the servant, to discuss what is tyranny, and to discern whether his prince, his landlord, his master, is a tyrant, by his own fancy and collection supposed, what lord of the council shall ride quietly-minded in the streets, among desperate beasts?"[2] The equation of household and state was part of the hierarchical theory of degree. "To fathers within their private families Nature hath given a supreme power", wrote Hooker.[3] From Luther onwards, until Milton by implication and Locke specifically denied its relevance, the Fifth Commandment was regularly cited as one of the authorities for obedience to kings.[4]

By Convocation in 1606 a patriarchal theory of monarchy was counterposed to the error that "civil power, jurisdiction and authority was first derived from the people and disordered multitude".[5] The claim of kings to allegiance was like this parental right, Lancelot Andrewes thought, an element in the natural order of the world.[6] Robert Sanderson echoed him: "In a family, the master or *paterfamilias*, who is a kind of petty monarch there, hath authority to prescribe to his children and servants. . . . What power the master hath over his servants for the ordering of his family, no doubt the same at least, if not much more, hath the supreme magistrate over his subjects, for the peaceable ordering of the commonwealth: the magistrate being *pater patriae* as the master is *paterfamilas*".[7] In 1660 he reaffirmed the traditional patriarchal thesis against contract theories which assumed the absolute rights of property.[8] The

1. Strype, *Life of Parker*, II. p. 353.
2. Parker, *Correspondence*, p. 61. Cf. a sermon of 1619 which equates the authority of a father over his family, a landlord over his tenants and a king over his subjects (W. Dickinson, *The Kings Right*, quoted by C. H. and K. George, *The Protestant Mind of the English Reformation*, p. 216).
3. Hooker, *Of the Laws of Ecclesiastical Polity* (Everyman ed.), I, p. 191; cf. A. Nowell, *A Catechism* (Parker Soc., 1853), pp. 132–3, 192. First published 1570.
4. Milton, *Paradise Lost*, Book XII; Locke, *First Treatise of Government*, para. 64.
5. *Bishop Overall's Convocation Book* (1690), pp. 2–6, 25–8, 271.
6. R. L. Ottley, *Lancelot Andrewes* (1894), p. 63.
7. R. Sanderson, *XXXV Sermons*, pp. 230–1; cf. A. Williams "Politics and Economics in Renaissance Commentaries on *Genesis*', *Huntington Library Quarterly*, VII, pp. 209–14.
8. Sanderson, Preface to the Reader in J. Ussher's *The Power Communicated by God to the Prince* (3rd ed., 1710), Sig. E. 2–3. First published (posthumously) in 1661.

contrast between the two theories tells us much about the social outlook of their sponsors. Oxford and Cambridge could only be fitted into the traditional scheme of things by arguing that "the frame of this little commonwealth or body standeth not upon the union of families, etc.", but upon the union of colleges. Undergraduates were urged to look upon their tutor as though he were the head of their family.[1] As late as James II's reign, it was an argument against Father Petre's suitability to hold high state office that he "ne'er was master of a family".[2]

The family was a highly authoritarian institution. Children of all ages stood or knelt in the presence of their parents: a grown son removed his hat when speaking to his father. Until the post-revolutionary generation, Aubrey tells us, "the child perfectly loathed the sight of his parents". The authority of masters over servants, and the loyalty expected in return, were naturally even more complete.[3] The worst thing Joseph Beaumont could say about Judas Iscariot was that he was a traitor to his *master*.[4] Hence the patriarchal theory, with its universally accepted overtones, appealed especially to monarchists.

But the social implications were accepted no less by Puritans like Udall ("Every kingdom or household must be governed only by the laws of the king, or orders of the householder"); by Greenham ("Care in superiors, and fear in inferiors, cause a godly government both private and public, in family, church and commonwealth"); by Perkins ("That person, who by the providence of God hath the place of an husband, a father, a master in his house, the same also by the light of nature hath the principality and sovereignty therein", and rules over wife, children, servants).[5] It was accepted without question by

1. M. H. Curtis, *Oxford and Cambridge in Transition*, pp. 35, 114.

2. *Poems on Affairs of State* (5th ed., 1703), II, p. 149.

3. Brailsford, *The Levellers and the English Revolution*, pp. 42–6, and references there cited. See also pp. 434–5 above.

4. J. Beaumont, *Psyche* (1648), in *Complete Poems* (ed. A. B. Grosart, 1880), I, pp. 226–7.

5. Udall, *A Demonstration of Discipline*, p. 65; Greenham, *Workes*, p. 12; Perkins, *Workes*, III, p. 698; cf. Haller, *Liberty and Reformation in the Puritan Revolution*, chapter 3, *passim*. Baxter, nearly a century later than Greenham, wrote: "In kingdoms, armies and even private families the government is administered by the authority of one single person, although the advice of others may be requisite also; but without

Nicholas Bownde.[1] Even in 1644 Rutherford in his *Lex, Rex* attacked only the conservative monarchical application of the theory.[2]

Some of the overtones of the discussion about the family and the household can be heard in *King Lear*.[3] The fundamental conflict in the play is between loyalty, inheritance, the family on the one hand, and Machiavellian unscrupulousness, egotism and devil-take-the-hindmost on the other. Edmund's early remark about getting lands by wit if he could not have them by inheritance is a key to the whole framework of the play: the bastard (younger son) is a symbol of the individualist in a society of degree: so too is that other traditional self-seeker, the steward. The fool has many remarks about adventurers who succeed by Court favour and intrigue and look upon traditional loyalties as countrified. The same motive appears in all the sub-plots. Cordelia's loyalty is as striking as her filial affection: and Kent exemplifies the same virtues. In Goneril's husband loyalty finally triumphs. Edgar accuses Edmund of being a traitor to himself, his father and his king: in feudal conception "loyalty" is both a public and a family virtue, treason can be high or petty. Lear's feudal following of 100 knights was as much an offence to Goneril and Regan as they would have been to Elizabeth: they were accused of the traditional retainers' vices, brawling and tippling. The scene between Regan and her father in which this is discussed dealt with familiar sixteenth-century topics.

The grandeur of Lear's personal sufferings ultimately transcends the social setting, as do Clarissa's in Richardson's novel. But a knowledge of the setting will help us to grasp the unity of the interwoven plots, and the contemporary significance of the

---

any share in the government" (*Reliquiae Baxterianae*, I, p. 243; cf. Part III, p. 117). For a classic statement of the theory swallowed whole by a layman of average intelligence, see Sir William Waller's *Vindication of his Character and Conduct* (1793), pp. 246–71. Cf. also *The Ladies Calling*, Preface, in *The Works of the . . . Author of The Whole Duty of Man*.

1. N. Bownde, *A Treatise full of consolation for all that are afflicted in mind, or body, or otherwise* (1817), pp. 112–13. First published in 1608.

2. S. Rutherford, *Lex, Rex* (1644), pp. 111–15.

3. Cf. C. H. Hobday, "The Social Background of *King Lear*", *Modern Quarterly Miscellany*, No. 1, pp. 37–56; C. B. Watson, *Shakespeare and the Renaissance Conception of Honor* (Princeton, 1960), pp. 371–6.

theme of loyalty. Otherwise Lear's initial anger and touchiness seem overdone. We may compare Hyde's letter to Lord Mordaunt in October 1659: "I have always believed the greatest piety towards God, and the most exact obedience towards princes, to flow from hearts which are possessed with the strongest and most faithful affections to their other relations; the being good children and good husbands being the best ingredients in the composition of good subjects and good Christians".[1] That was pretty old-fashioned stuff on the eve of the Restoration, as Clarendon himself soon came to recognize;[2] but it makes the point. In the great conflict of our period, between the ethos appropriate to a society composed of feudal households, and the ethos appropriate to an individualist society, the puritan emphasis on the duties of small householders played an important transitional part.

During the revolutionary period even radical theories were often still expressed in patriarchal forms. Milton spoke of domestic liberty as one of the three aspects of liberty essential to the happiness of social life. It would be a contribution to domestic liberty if he could restore to the master of the family that power to put away his wife which the canonists had taken from him.[3] "No effect of tyranny can sit more heavily on the commonwealth than this household unhappiness on the family". "Farewell all hope of true reformation in the state while such an evil as this lies undiscerned or unregarded in the house".[4] Sometimes a new twist is given to the old idea. Fathers are given rule over children, said Robert Norwood in 1653, but the injunction to obey our parents means that we should obey the old English constitution which our fathers established.[5] Yet even in a work of political thought so radical as Gerrard Winstanley's *The Law of Freedom* the family is still the basic unit of society. A father in a family is a commonwealth's officer, though Winstanley is careful to preserve the elective principle which runs through his pamphlet by adding that "the necessity of the young children chose him by a joint

1. Ed. M. Coate, *The Letter Book of John, Viscount Mordaunt, 1659–60* (Camden Soc., 1945), p. 63.

2. See p. 462 below.

3. Milton, *Prose Works* (Bohn ed.), I, pp. 258–9; III, p. 242.

4. *Ibid.*, III, p. 177.

5. R. Norwood, *Pathway unto Englands Perfect Settlement* (1653), pp. 19–22, 56.

consent, and not otherwise".[1] John Eliot's *The Christian Commonwealth*, also a radical work, advocated the grouping of households for electoral purposes, and assumed that the household was the fundamental unit in society, servants having no vote – as indeed they would have had none under the Leveller Agreement of the People.[2] Winstanley speaks of "a bigger family, called a parish".[3] The parish is a federation of households, just as the kingdom is a federation of parishes. This last idea died hard: we find it in the writings of Spence and Godwin at the end of the eighteenth century.

There was thus an inescapable ambiguity in the puritan attitude towards authority. Authority in the state is analogous to authority in the family; but in the family the father's authority is absolute: ergo – authority in the state is that of all heads of households! The double-think recalls the Calvinist attitude to the Church as *both* the whole community *and* the elect only; and the Calvinist theory of revolt, justified when led by the magistrate, not when spontaneously popular. It corresponds to the social position of the unprivileged industrious sort of people, who aspired to a greater share of political influence but had no desire to be swamped by a "mere" democracy.

V

A very early book of guidance on domestic conduct is attributed to Wyclif – *Of Weddid Men and Wifes and of Here Children also* – though it was not printed until the nineteenth century. The Morning Star of the Reformation was no less interested in heads of households than his puritan successors. In fact we can look at the history of the centuries from mid-fourteenth to mid-seventeenth as the period in which heads of households of the industrious sort slowly and ultimately successfully challenged sacerdotalism. Lollardy was a religion of small masters, flourishing especially in industrial areas; Professor Dickens has brilliantly shown how its basic attitudes – scepticism about the miracle of the mass and about priestly pretensions in general, personal piety combined with a practical

---

1. Sabine, *Works of Gerrard Winstanley*, p. 538.
2. J. Eliot, *The Christian Commonwealth* (1659), esp. pp. 3–7. Eliot is best known as the Apostle to the Indians.
3. Winstanley, *loc. cit.*

materialism – contributed to the main stream of popular Protestantism. Tyndale taught that "every man ought to preach in word and deed unto his household, and to them that are under his governance". Laymen should not preach publicly, "but every man ought to endeavour himself to be as well learned as the preacher, and every man may privately inform his neighbours".[1] Sir Francis Bigod and his chaplain, Thomas Garret, both thought that laymen might preach.[2] Professor Tawney once said that "the sufferings of the peasantry in the sixteenth century are due to the printing press", which has made us aware of them. It was perhaps the printing press also which made us aware of the aspirations of godly laymen.

If there were no pastors available, Luther had said, "let each head of a family read the Gospel in his own house, and baptize his children".[3] Family worship would not be needed, Dering agreed, if "every congregation had a sufficient pastor to instruct those that were ignorant".[4] Given the semi-priestly functions of fathers of protestant families, we can see how easily, once the old ecclesiastical régime had broken down after 1640, householders of the industrious sort stepped into the place of ministers. They had been preparing for it through two and a half centuries of history, not only by their increasingly important economic role but also since the Reformation by responding to government demands and – especially from the later years of Elizabeth's reign – by studying the large literature writing up their disciplinary duties.

A special caste of priests no longer mediated between God and man: the residuary legatee was (or in the puritan view should be) the father of the family. He for God only, they for God in him. The man who shirked these responsibilities, still committing his conscience to a priest, Milton compared to a trader who handed all his business concerns over to a factor

1. Tyndale *Expositions and Notes on . . . the Holy Scriptures*, p. 36.
2. A. G. Dickens, *Lollards and Protestants in the Diocese of York, 1509–1558*, pp. 59, 66 and *passim*.
3. Luther's letter of 1523 to the Calixtines, quoted in J. H. Merle D'Aubigné, *History of the Reformation of the Sixteenth Century* (1853), IV, pp. 38–9.
4. E. Dering, *Works* (1614), Sig. A 2v; cf. Baxter, quoted on pp. 430–1 above.

and lived merely on the profit without working himself. Milton even thought it was "an act of papal encroachment . . . to pluck the power and arbitrament of divorce from the master of the family, into whose hands God and the law of all nations had put it".[1]

This elevation of the father of the family thus prepared the way for Independency and separatism. The Family of Love shows this happening. Heads of households were elders and priests: "Every father of a family under the love", said Henry Niclaes about 1560, "hath doubtless the liberty in his family to use services and ceremonies according as he perceiveth out of the testimonies of the holy spirit of love, . . . for to keep his household thereby in discipline and peace".[2] "Every master of a family", wrote Lord Brooke 80 years later, "may and must read, pray, catechize and the like in his own family, if he have none that can do it better than himself". So far that was not too unorthodox; but Brooke drew the logical conclusion: *therefore* such laymen may preach. "If any will come of themselves either to their own families, or send for them, and desire to hear them among some good men, they take this for a call, an outward call, to perform those duties to that congregation"[3] We can see the independent congregation in process of formation here: as an extension of household prayers.[4] All that was needed was to remove the restraining power of the State-ecclesiastical. In 1626 John Etherington, by trade a box-maker, was fined and imprisoned by the High Commission on a charge of expounding the Scripture to others besides his own family. He denied holding coventicles, but admitted that he was "always ready to speak to my neighbour and friend and children, etc., whatsoever I have known and understood of the

1. Milton, *Prose Works* (Bohn ed.), II, pp. 85–6; III, pp. 263–4.

2. H. N., *Introduction to the Holy Understanding of the Glasse of Righteousness*, quoted by G. H. Williams, *The Radical Reformation* (Philadelphia, 1962), p. 481.

3. Lord Brooke, *A Discourse opening the Nature of that Episcopacie, which is exercised in England*, pp. 105–6, in Haller, *Tracts on Liberty*, II, pp. 149–50.

4. Mr. Marchant makes the interesting suggestion that the 6.0 a.m. weekday lectures given at St. Antholin's, and a similar service held at the same hour in puritan Sheffield, were "designed as a communal 'family prayers', perhaps for those too illiterate to read their own prayers and Bible" (*The Puritans and the Church Courts in the Diocese of York*, pp. 173–4).

Word and ways of God".[1] A few years later Jacob Bothomley was excommunicated for repeating a sermon in private meetings before persons excommunicated, and was only absolved as the Long Parliament approached.[2]

In 1583 the Church had prohibited "all preaching, reading, catechism and other such-like exercises in private places and families whereunto others do resort, being not of the same family".[3] We do not know how seriously this was enforced before the Laudian decade, but Whitgift himself followed it up in his Visitation Articles of 1585. At all events it was a significant withdrawal from Tyndale's attitude.[4] Bishop Wren of Norwich, that heretical diocese, had the law of the Church on his side when in 1636 he instructed churchwardens to present those laymen who presumed to discuss religion in their families.[5] But by then the tide was running the other way. Gilbert Ironside, in a treatise dedicated to Laud, expressed alarm about the exercise of private devotions by those who could not read. ("Must they pray in private and secret, otherwise than as the Church hath taught them?") Not all men had attained the Puritans' "imagined perfection of extemporary effusions". There were many who were incapable of repeating a sermon or catechizing their families. Household worship should be extended to the whole family only if "the master . . . be well fitted and qualified thereunto, and presume not beyond his measure". He must "keep himself within the compass of his own charge, not admitting any [worshippers] of other places; for then he becomes offensive to the state, who hath, and that justly, a jealousy over all such assemblies".[6] Here we have expressed with uncommon candour both the pressure from below to extend household worship into something like a conventicle, and the hierarchy's fear of such private discussions because they could not be controlled.

1. J. Etherington, *The Defence of John Etherington against Steven Denison* (1641), pp. 3, 29. The tract had been written 10 or 12 years previously but could not be published before the Long Parliament met.

2. *C.S.P.D.*, *1640–1*, pp. 305–6. Bothomley later became a Ranter, and spoke favourably of the Diggers (N. Cohn, *The Pursuit of the Millennium*, 1957, pp. 335–40). See also p. 346 above.

3. Cardwell, *Documentary Annals*, I, p. 413.

4. See pp. 485–90 below for the significance of the date. For Tyndale see p. 451 above.

5. M. Wren, *Visitation Articles* for 1636, chapter 4, article 31.

6. Ironside, *Seven Questions of the Sabbath*, pp. 267–8.

The outburst of lay preaching in the sixteen-forties is in interesting contrast to the early years of Elizabeth's reign. Then, because of deprivations and the consequent shortage of ministers, tradesmen and other literate laymen had been appointed, by letter from a bishop, as readers in small livings where there was no minister. They were not allowed to preach or to administer the sacraments, but merely to read the prayer book service.[1] One has only to think how impossible it would have been for the bishops to control such readers had they been foolish enough to institute them 75 years later in order to realize what great strides the industrious sort had made in self-confidence during the intervening period.

With Brooke's remarks we may compare Baxter's account of Kidderminster, where "those people that had none in their families who could pray or repeat the sermons went to their next neighbour's house who could do it; so that some houses (of the ablest men) in each street were filled with them that could do nothing or little in their own".[2] The post-Restoration Government naturally was hostile to this attendance of outsiders at anything so seditious as family prayers, as hostile as the Church had been in 1583, or as the General Assembly of the Scottish Kirk had been in 1647.[3] Baxter thought the post-Restoration prohibition of Bible-reading to neighbours was especially hard on "those many thousand families" where no one could read.[4]

Nevertheless, by then even Baxter saw the objections to too much uncontrolled discussion. Without rigorous discipline, he found, he could never have kept *the religious sort* from separations and divisions.[5] We may note too how Brooke, almost as though advisedly, confined the ministerial function to *bourgeois* heads of households: for the aristocracy and

1. Strype, *Annals*, I, part i, pp. 203, 516.
2. *Reliquiae Baxterianae*, I, p. 87. Cf. S. Clarke, *The Lives of Sundry Eminent Persons* (1683), p. 24.
3. *Reliquiae Baxterianae*, I, p. 435 (referring to 16 Car. II cap. 4), III, pp. 111, 117, 159; *Directions of the General Assembly concerning Secret and Private Worship*, p. 8. A Kentish clothworker believed in 1663 that "any man may teach not only his family, but his neighbours that will come to hear him, if he be endued with the spirit" (ed. E. Mellis, *Kentish Sources*, II, *Kent and the Civil War*, 1960, p. 60).
4. Baxter, Preface to the Reader, in T. Young, *The Lords-Day* (1672), Sig. A 4.
5. *Reliquiae Baxterianae*, I, pp. 91–2.

gentry would have their own chaplains, who could pray and catechize better than they. Yet Bulstrode Whitelocke – scarcely more radical in outlook than Brooke – had decided as early as 1630, on the occasion of his wife's illness, that every man ought to be a priest in his own house. He began reading prayers daily to his wife and servants, a custom he henceforth never neglected.[1] Twenty-three years later he explained to the Queen of Sweden that he thought it "as proper for me, being the master of it [his family], to admonish and speak to my people when there is cause, as to be beholden to another to do it for me, which sometimes brings the chaplain into more credit than his lord". Cromwell and the other great officers did the same, the Ambassador assured the Queen.[2]

Once the power of the hierarchy was destroyed, things went further even than Brooke might have wished: and here the New Model Army was the decisive subversive influence. At the beginning of the war Oliver Cromwell's officers had proposed to make their regiment a "gathered church".[3] In 1645, when Parliament was forbidding lay preaching, a right was claimed for persons in authority to read and expound the Bible to those under their charge: "as suppose a master to his family, a captain to his company, a colonel to his regiment, a general to his army, a king to his people, if he hath the grace to do it".[4] A new social and religious unit had been inserted between household and state.

VI

Before 1640 the preachers had proclaimed the rights and duties of men, but they were manifestly thinking almost exclusively of householders. And even when they spoke of heads of households they were thinking not of every peasant's hut, but of a small master craftsman or yeoman farmer controlling his family, his dependent relations, his servants,

1. R. H. Whitelocke, *Memoirs, Biographical and Historical, of Bulstrode Whitelocke* (1860), p. 67.
2. B. Whitelocke, *A Journal of the Swedish Embassy* (1855), I, pp. 247–8.
3. C. H. Firth, *Oliver Cromwell and the Rule of the Puritans* (World's Classics), p. 146.
4. [Anon.], *The cleere Sense* (1645), pp. 3, 10, quoted by W. Haller, *Liberty and Reformation in the Puritan Revolution* (Columbia University Press, 1955), p. 193.

journeymen and apprentices.[1] There were 100,000 such heads of households in London, William Dell guessed in 1651.[2] Thomas Cartwright had thought that only heads of households should have votes in church affairs, and only those heads of families who were in full church communion. Thus the ignorant and unfit would be deprived of influence.[3]

Edmund Coote's *The English Schoolmaster* (1595) was intended not only for those who taught in schools but also for tradesmen and craftsmen who had the responsibility for teaching their prentices and servants.[4] For Bodin only heads of households were citizens.[5] The anonymous *The Lawes of England*, which Miss Judson thinks was probably written by a Puritan in the sixteen-twenties or -thirties, said that one of the rights of "the people" was "those *Jura Familiae*, consisting in wives, children, servants, goods and lands", over which all fathers of families are "lords and kings in their own houses".[6] Heads of families virtually represented their dependants.[7] "The whole family was baptized when the master was baptized", Sibbes told the lawyers of Gray's Inn.[8] Thomas Goodwin made this point conveniently clear when he stated that Christ is "a Common Person representing others", a sort of representative of all mankind, because he is "the head of all the family of them that are named".[9]

1. Cf. a remark from China in the nineteen-twenties: "As to the authority of the husband, it has always been comparatively weak among the poor peasants, because the poor peasant women, compelled for financial reasons to take more part in manual work than women of the wealthier classes, have obtained more right to speak and more power to make decisions in family affairs" (Mao Tse-Tung, *Selected Works*, I, pp. 46–7).

2. W. Dell, *Several Sermons and Discourses* (1709), p. 61.

3. Whitgift, *Works* (Parker Soc., 1851–3), I, p. 456. Cf. the pamphleteer of 1641 who thought that lecturers should be chosen only by scot and lot householders, not by the poor (p. 119 above).

4. I owe this reference to the kindness of Mrs. Joan Simon.

5. Bodin, *Six Books of the Commonwealth*, p. 18.

6. Judson, *The Crisis of the Constitution*, p. 337.

7. The Levellers at Putney stated this explicitly (Woodhouse, *Puritanism and Liberty*, p. 83); so did John Eliot, in *The Christian Commonwealth* (1659), pp. 5–6.

8. R. Sibbes, *The Returning Backslider* (1639), p. 270.

9. T. Goodwin, *Works*, I, pp. 70–4. The interesting conception of Christ as a common or public person, as a representative of mankind, is to be found in John Preston's *Breastplate of Faith and Love* (1634 ed., p. 4: first published in 1625).

The preachers differentiated sharply between such households of standing, from among whose masters lay elders would naturally be drawn, and the really poor or vagabonds. One advantage of being under the rule of a good governor of a family, Sibbes thought, was that there "servants live in obedience to God's ordinances, and not like wild creatures, ruffians, vagabonds, Cains and the like".[1] Dod and Cleaver also distinguished firmly. "Let an hundred vagabonds and runagates play the filthy persons, the unthrifts and the thieves; this brings no discredit to the father. . . .: but if his son that is brought up with him in the family . . . shall do any such things, himself hath not the blot alone, but he bringeth also an evil report upon the family".[2] Herbert Palmer assumed that beggars would be "atheistical".[3] The attitude was accepted by many who were not Puritans. Thomas Heywood, in his *Apology for Actors*, was anxious to stress that players were not vagabonds; many of them were "of substance, of government, of sober lives and temperate carriage, housekeepers".[4]

Professor Notestein indeed has raised the important question of whether farm labourers and the very poor attended church at all. He suggests that it was the sectaries who first began to reach the ignorant members of the population.[5] In theory church attendance was compulsory for all: in 1601 J.P.s were ordered to enforce it.[6] But Grindal regarded the law as more binding on householders than on others;[7] and this was accepted, at least so far as services on Wednesdays and Fridays were concerned, by the 15th Canon of 1604. Clearly vagabonds did not attend. There is some evidence that the ecclesiastical authorities expected paupers to come to church. Already some churches had installed benches marked "for the poor".[8] In

1. R. Sibbes, *The Returning Backslider*, p. 273.
2. Dod and Cleaver, *Ten Commandements*, p. 88. From this passage and another on p. 60 it appears that a vagrant is deemed to have no family as well as no reputation to lose: "masterless men" are social outcasts.
3. Palmer, *The Necessity and Encouragement of Utmost Venturing for the Churches Help* (1643), p. 37.
4. T. Heywood, *Apology for Actors* (1612), Sig. E. 3, quoted by M. C. Bradbrook, *The Rise of the Common Player*, p. 93. Cf. pp. 161–2 above.
5. W. Notestein, *The English People on the Eve of Colonization* (1954), pp. 85, 162; cf. pp. 286–7 above.
6. Neale, *Elizabeth I and her Parliaments, 1584–1601*, pp. 402–5.
7. Grindal, *Remains*, pp. 138–9.
8. Ed. Swayne, *Salisbury Churchwardens' Accounts*, p. 190.

1576 a man brought before the Cambridge Consistory Court for absence from church pleaded that he was too poor to pay his fine. The plea was accepted, and he was discharged with an admonition to attend church regularly in future.[1] Fifty years later John Walls of Stadhampton, Oxfordshire, pleaded that he had been unable to attend church because, through poverty, "he had not clothes fit to come in company; . . . but now he keepeth the swine, and hopeth he shall earn money and will come".[2] This suggests that the very poorest did not in fact go to church. In many parish churches in London there would not have been room for them if they had gone.[3] Some church-wardens seem to have presented only *householders* for absence.[4] We have to wait for the parliamentary ordinance of 8 April 1644 before the obligation of sending rogues and vagabonds to church on Sundays was laid on J.P.s; and this was only six years before the repeal of the statutes enjoining compulsory church attendance. Under Charles II, Matthew Robinson in his Richmondshire parish noted that "many poor people . . . rarely attended the public worship on the Lord's days", though in some counties they would get no parish relief unless they did.[5] A French visitor in 1727 thought that many of the London populace never went to church: "in the country it is different".[6]

If Professor Notestein's suggestion proves to be correct, it may throw a great deal of light on the role of the sects in christianizing the lower classes, as well as bringing them into politics: bringing them into politics through religion. It would also reinforce the point made earlier, about the ability of men of property to dominate their own congregation.[7] In New

1. W. M. Palmer, "The Vicarage as alehouse and smithy", in *History Teachers' Miscellany*, IV, p. 165; cf. Henry Arthington, *Provision for the poore* (1597), quoted by Jordan, *Philanthropy in England*, p. 99. For Arthington see also A. G. Dickens, "The Writers of Tudor Yorkshire", *T.R.H.S.*, 1963, pp. 63–4, and p. 224 above.
2. Peyton, *Churchwardens' Presentments in the Oxfordshire Peculiars*, p. 68.
3. See p. 469 below.
4. H. B. Walters, *Churchwardens' Accounts of the Parish of Worfield* (n.d., ?1904), pp. 148, 150. Even when the poor did attend, they might not sit out the sermon (cf. R. Parr, *The Life of . . . Usher*, 1686, p. 87).
5. Ed. J. E. B. Mayor, *Autobiography of Matthew Robinson* (1856), p. 6: see p. 428 above.
6. Van Muyden, *A Foreign View of England*, p. 220.
7. See p. 229 above.

England John Davenport wished to prevent subordinate members of a household being admitted to church membership on the strength of the master's membership (as his children were); John Cotton took the opposite view.[1] The whole subject deserves more research, since until we know who went to church we cannot be sure what we are talking about when we discuss the relation of Church to "people". So often in the seventeenth century the word "people" excludes "the poor".[2] "Are the poor really admitted to the altar, to communion?" Jeremy Bentham asked of the Church of England in 1817; and he replied: No, only if they can pay for a pew. The fees still exacted for baptisms, marriages, churchings, burials, effectively excluded the poor.[3]

There is little doubt that when sixteenth- and seventeenth-century Puritans spoke of "the people" in connection with church government, they excluded the very poor. "Where the election [of ministers] is freest and most general", Cartwright declared, "yet only they have to do which are heads of families". "All men understand" that fact; it was "a mere cavil" when spokesmen of the hierarchy attributed advocacy of universal suffrage to the disciplinarians.[4] Stoughton was equally explicit. After a passionate and eloquent defence of the "birthright" of the people, he concluded: "When we say that the people of every parish ought to choose and elect their pastors, we mean not that the election should solely be committed to the multitude, but we intend only that the chief fathers, ancients and governors of the parish in the name of the whole should approve the choice made by the holy ministers".[5] The preachers did not emphasize that they were speaking only of and to men of some substance, since the fact was self-evident to them and their audiences. It remains implicit in their tone. Consider how Dod and Cleaver state the great truth that

1. I. M. Calder, *Letters of John Davenport* (Yale University Press, 1937), pp. 263–6; Morgan, *The Puritan Family*, pp. 79–80.

2. See pp. 462–3 below.

3. J. Bentham, *Church of Englandism and its Catechism Examined* (1817), II, pp. 165, 377.

4. In Whitgift, *Works*, I, p. 456. Cartwright's complaint adds plausibility to Professor Macpherson's argument that it was a similar "cavil" when the Levellers' opponents accused them of advocating manhood suffrage (*Possessive Individualism*, Chapter III).

5. W. Stoughton, *An Assertion for true and Christian Church-Policie* (1604), pp. 205–47.

in Christ there is neither bond nor free: "Even bondmen are commanded, notwithstanding their low estate and the baseness of their condition, yet to bring *some* glory to God, and to win *some* reverence to their glorious profession, by their good behaviour. . . . Even a servant, if he be not audacious and arrogant, not given to picking and falsehood, but trusty, diligent and serviceable, patient, meek and humble . . . shall have reward of this service, as well as if he were in a higher and more honourable calling, that the world made more account of".[1]

Men who believed that even those who lived "under good families or good tutors . . . are as wolves tied up",[2] that "the greater part . . . generally is the worst part"[3] and that servants "naturally have an averseness to and hatred of all that is good" (just as children have) would hardly wish to entrust the government of the Church to them.[4] It was only Anabaptists, Gouge assures us, "who teach that all are alike, and that there is no difference betwixt masters and servants".[5] Most of the guides to godliness, though they stress the duties of masters as well as of servants, emphasize the over-riding importance of passive obedience on the part of the latter, however badly the former behaved: a king might be called to account by his subjects, but not a master by his servants. As we have seen, John Winthrop thought democracy was forbidden by the Fifth Commandment.[6] It is easy to understand how the radical sects got their congregations in the sixteen-forties.

In the course of the revolution the preachers' generalizations were taken at their face value. As Hooker had warned, theories devised to justify the rule of a propertied oligarchy as against a nominated priesthood became the slogans of democrats.[7] Congregations began to assert themselves against the elders. The preachers' shrill outcries make their earlier reser-

1. Dod and Cleaver, *Ten Commandements*, pp. 104–5. Cf. pp. 126 note 1, 148–9, 171–5, 236–7, 270 above.

2. Preston, *Life Eternall* (4th ed., 1634), Sermon X, p. 10. This was of course not a peculiarly puritan view: cf. Archbishop Parker's "desperate beasts" (p. 446 above).

3. W. Crashawe, *A Sermon Preached . . . before the right honourable Lord La warre, Lord Governor and Captaine Generall of Virginea* (1619) Sig. F. 2; cf. Baxter, *The Holy Commonwealth* (1659), pp. 92–4, 226–31.

4. S. Clarke, *The Lives of Sundry Eminent Persons* (1683), p. 24.

5. W. Gouge, *Of Domesticall Duties* (1626), pp. 331–2.

6. See p. 445 above.

7. See p. 222 above.

vations clear. As early as 1641 we find Edwards exclaiming "Is it fitting that well meaning Christians should be suffered to go and make churches, and then proceed to choose whom they will for ministers, as some tailor, felt-maker, button-maker, men ignorant and low in parts? . . . They who lay hands on and make ministers should be greater in place and authority and not less, as the common people be. . . . How will this toleration take away . . . that power, authority, which God hath given the husbands, fathers and masters, over wives, children, servants".[1]

Faith cannot be forced, Bayne admitted in 1643; the employer is master only of the body of his servant: his conscience is his own. And yet masters have a duty to compel the outward man to conform. Failure to do this makes "the streets so full of swarms, everywhere openly breaking the Sabbath." For "many of the best servants are . . . so saucy that they scorn to be in any awe."[2] The Independents, said Fuller, "did pick (I will not say steal) hence a master, thence a mistress of a family, a son out of a third, a servant out of a fourth parish, all which met together in their congregation".[3] So religious toleration at once undermined the authority of heads of households and (in the towns) the parochial community which was a federation of households. As late as 1649, a major presbyterian objection to religious toleration was that heads of families would be prevented from compelling their children

1. T. Edwards, *Reasons Against the Independent Government of Particular Congregations* (1641), pp. 23–4, 26; cf. pp. 43–4. Note again the traditional conception of a ministry imposed from on top, by social superiors. With the general point made here, cf. Professor Schlatter: "In their battle with feudalism, the commercial classes made use of revolutionary ideas which could in turn be used against themselves. More than once, bourgeois theorists had to abandon their theories when their revolution had been achieved. Egalitarian principles which helped to destroy the power of kings, priests and aristocrats, were also dangerous allies for the victorious middle classes". The Quakers, Dr. Schlatter goes on to suggest, retained more than any other sect of the egalitarian and revolutionary spirit which had destroyed feudalism and which socialists were to revive later (R. B. Schlatter, *Social Ideas of Religious Leaders, 1660–88*, 1940, pp. 365–73).

2. Bayne, *Commentary on Ephesians*, p. 366.

3. Fuller, *Church History*, III, p. 465. Cf. the no doubt apocryphal story told by the Venetian Ambassador of the Independent peer whose six sons were members of six different sectarian congregations (*C.S.P. Venetian, 1655–6*, p. 308).

and servants to attend public worship, and so their prestige
and authority would be destroyed.[1] By contrast, those who
agitated for religious toleration were driven to question some
of the assumptions behind the elevation of heads of households. They pointed out that family duties were "nowhere
commanded in Scripture", and so "neglected and even disputed against them".[2] So in yet another way the logic of
radical Protestantism led to an egalitarian individualism. In a
famous nostalgic passage Clarendon complained after the
Restoration that "all relations were confounded by the several
sects in religion, which discountenanced all forms of reverence
and respect as relics and marks of superstition. Children asked
not blessing of their parents; nor did they concern themselves
in the education of their children. . . ."[3]

The attitude of the preachers throws light on what political
writers meant by "the people", and helps further to identify
who our "industrious sort" were. Cartwright, Stoughton and
the preachers generally meant responsible heads of households
when they used the word; and this remained true however
many generalizing flourishes they made. The same is true of
parliamentarian politicians, who talked of the liberties of the
people when they meant those of the propertied. Even radicals
spoke of the people when they meant at most heads of households, the freeborn. George Wither's servant would

> *"act an humble servant's part,*
> *Till God shall call me to be free".*[4]

Baxter thought men should not be deprived of civil freedom
unless their poverty was "so great as to make them servants of
others".[5] Colonel Rich at Putney, and the Harringtonian
Captain Baynes in the 1659 Parliament, contrasted "the poor"

1. [Anon.], *The Essex Watchmans Watchword* (1649), signed by 63
ministers, p. 7; cf. [Anon.], *Anti-Toleration* (1646), pp. 31–2 and D.
Cawdrey, *Family Reformation Promoted*, pp. 28–30.

2. Cawdrey and Palmer, *Sabbatum Redivivum*, p. 171.

3. Edward Hyde, Earl of Clarendon, *The Continuation of the Life*
(1759), II, p. 39. For this paragraph cf. K. Thomas, "Women and the
Civil War Sects", *P. and P.*, No. 13, pp. 52–7.

4. G. Wither, *Hallelujah* (1857), p. 294. First published 1641, with
dedication to Parliament. Cf. *Patriarcha and other political works of Sir
Robert Filmer* (ed. P. Laslett, 1949), p. 25.

5. Baxter, *The Holy Commonwealth*, pp. 218–19. Servants got no land
when they were taken to New England.

with "the people".[1] Even the Levellers, who often spoke of the freeborn people's birthright, would have excluded paupers and wage-labourers from the franchise, because they were not economically independent, had no property in their own labour. Servants and apprentices are "included in their masters", said Maximilian Petty in the Putney Debates.[2] In about 1680 the Earl of Shaftesbury stated in so many words that "every paterfamilias . . . has . . . the votes of all his family, man, woman and child, included in his".[3] So the ambiguity in Locke's use of the word "people" has a long preparatory history behind it. His "people" have servants exactly as had those of the anonymous Puritan quoted by Miss Judson.[4]

VII

The conservatives thought toleration dreadful because it allowed family religion without reference to a national Church. Dering had made the point before the civil war when he deplored national toleration "without all superintendency. . . . As much as to say, let every family be a church and have religion as they please".[5] When John Evelyn in 1656 heard the vicar of St. Nicholas, Deptford, preach "that all family assemblies were so many churches, and might have all essentials of a church though no ceremonies", he thought that much of his discourse "savoured of the conventicle".[6] The Presbyterians, who approved of family religion, found toleration especially shocking. "If a toleration were granted", said Thomas Edwards in 1646, ministers, magistrates and people "should never have peace in their families more, or ever after have command of wives, children, servants".[7] When the 5

1. A. S. P. Woodhouse, *Puritanism and Liberty* (1938), pp. 63–4; ed. J. T. Rutt, *Parliamentary Diary of Thomas Burton* (1828), III, pp. 147–8. Cf. my *Puritanism and Revolution*, p. 307.

2. Woodhouse, *op. cit.*, p. 83; C. B. Macpherson, *The Political Theory of Possessive Individualism*, Chapter III. Professor Macpherson's analysis helps to explain why even the Levellers never advocated votes for women, important though the support of women was for their movement. Cf. p. 450 above.

3. *Some Observations*, *Somers Tracts* (1809–15), VIII, p. 401.

4. See p. 456 above.

5. *A Collection of Speeches made by Sir Edward Dering* (1642), p. 165.

6. Ed. de Beer, *Diary of John Evelyn*, II, p. 167.

7. T. Edwards, *Gangraena*, Part III (1646), p. 156.

Dissenting Brethren in the Assembly of Divines demanded a right for laymen to choose their place of worship, exempt from consistorial discipline, a group of London ministers protested. "The whole course of religion in private families will be interrupted and undermined", they said; "the reciprocal duties between persons of nearest and dearest relation will be extremely violated".[1] "Hundreds of people will come to no church at all", Herbert Palmer had already warned the Assembly, adding that nothing was more destructive to "the right performance of family duties than that one should go to one place and another to another".[2]

"Hundreds of people will come to no church at all". That consideration was bound to worry those who attached supreme importance to the Word preached, and especially those who considered all servants naturally wicked. We may recall Edward's story of the servant who gave notice because, he said, "I would have the liberty of my conscience, not to be catechized in the principles of religion".[3] The terrible Ranter, Abiezer Coppe, no doubt put into words what many were thinking when he cried: "Give over thy stinking family duties, . . . for under them all there lies snapping, snarling, biting, besides covetousness, horrid hypocrisy, envy, malice, evil-surmising".[4] But that point of view received no more expression once the censorship closed down again. The social significance of liberty of conscience, as involving freedom for the lower social groups to organize themselves independently of their betters, has often been noticed. But its specific effect in breaking up the discipline of the family economic unit, and so promoting the freedom of wives, journeymen and apprentices, deserves further investigation along the lines initiated by Mr. Thomas.[5]

The point seemed important to Fuller in 1647: "If we should live to see churches of several governments permitted in Eng-

1. *A Letter of the Ministers of the City of London* (1645), in *Somers Tracts* (1748–51), XV, p. 345.

2. Mitchell and Struthers, *Minutes of the Sessions of the Westminster Assembly*, p. 6.

3. Edwards, *Gangraena*, p. 138. The story is also told, as though at first hand, in the anonymous pamphlet *Anti-Toleration* (1646), p. 30, which seems too reasonable in its tone to be by Edwards.

4. A. Coppe, *A Flying Fiery Roll* (1649), in N. Cohn, *The Pursuit of the Millennium* (1957), pp. 369–70.

5. Thomas, "Women and the Civil War Sects", *passim.*

land, it is more than probable that many offenders, not out of conscience, but to escape censures, would fly from one congregation to another. . . . Many servants nowadays will break every man from his master; many guilty persons, abandoning that discipline under which they were bred and brought up, will shift and shelter themselves under some new model of government. . . . Vice, these late years, hath kept open house in England. Welcome all comers without any examination. . . ."[1] In his day Nicholas Bownde had deplored the popular objection to godly household discipline, that it was "the next way to rid themselves of all good servants, and that then they might soon be master and man themselves".[2] When we recall that Paul Bayne's prayer in his family "was not usually above a quarter of an hour long", and that he "diverted others from tediousness in that duty, having respect to the weakness and infirmities of his servants and children" we can imagine what more prolix heads of households must have inflicted on their families. Gilbert Ironside had warned in 1637 that household worship might become burdensome to servants.[3] In the freer air of New England, Ezekiel Rogers in 1658 found it "hard to get a servant that is glad of catechizing or family duties", harder than it had been in Yorkshire. The servants he brought over with him were a blessing: it was "the young brood" that upset him.[4] Bunyan, with more sympathy for the servant's point of view, records that he had "heard some poor servants say that in some carnal families they have had more liberty to God's things, and more fairness of dealing, than among professors. . . . Such masters make religion stink before the inhabitants of the land".[5]

Though it lasted for so short a time, religious toleration may have aided social mobility; the Clarendon Code and the Act of Settlement combined to restrict it again.[6] The nameless servant,

1. Fuller, *Good Thoughts in Worse Times* (1830), pp. 160–1, 174–5.
2. Bownde, *The True Doctrine of the Sabbath* (1606), p. 463.
3. Bayne, *Commentary upon Ephesians*, p. ix; cf. the passage from Gouge quoted on p. 460 above; Ironside, *Seven Questions of the Sabbath*. p. 269. See p. 162 above.
4. C. Mather, *Magnalia Christi Americana* (Hartford, Conn. 1853), I, p. 413. First published 1702.
5. Bunyan, *Works*, II, p. 560.
6. Patriarchal authority is heavily emphasized in many of Dryden's plays – e.g. *The Conquest of Granada* (1669–70), *Aurungzebe* (1675) and *The Spanish Friar* (1681). The imprisoned Ozmyn's remark to his father

whose protest was transmitted to posterity only in the hostile pages of the hysterical Edwards, was fighting for a more real liberty, and one more dangerous to fight for, than many of the supporters of Parliament in the civil war. Just as the priesthood of all believers began with the assumption that believers were a minority, and was only gradually extended by the heretical doctrine of universal grace, so the equality of man was preceded by the equality of heads of households. In each case the extension appeared to the orthodox wildly subversive and dangerous.

The preachers seem to us to have been very short-sighted not to have understood the logical conclusions which could be drawn from the principles which they enunciated; but that is because we live in a different society, a society in which the old communities have been completely split up into their component individual units, in which the large factory and not the household is the dominant productive unit. The social inevitability of the predominance of masters of families seemed so obvious to the Presbyterians that they never mentioned it until it was challenged. The seventeenth-century egalitarians and democrats were men of daring prophetic vision.[1]

---

in the first-named play would have delighted Clarendon: –

Sir, you are just, and welcome are these bands.
'Tis all the inheritance a son demands. (Part II, Act IV, scene i).

1. It is perhaps significant that the abortive meeting of Convocation in 1689 discussed a book of directions for family morning and evening worship; but it was never published. For the Toleration Act deprived it of its main point (Cardwell, *A History of Conferences*, p. 424).

Chapter Fourteen

Individuals and Communities

The church or company of worshippers, whether true or false, is like unto a body or college of physicians in a city; like unto a corporation, society or company of East India or Turkey merchants, or any other society or company in London; which companies may hold their courts, keep their records, hold disputations, and in matters concerning their society may dissent, divide, break into schisms and factions, sue and implead each other at the law, yea, wholly break up and dissolve into pieces and nothing, and yet the peace of the City not be in the least measure impaired or disturbed; because the essence or being of the City, and so the well-being and peace thereof, is essentially distinct from these particular societies; the City courts, City laws, City punishments distinct from theirs.

> Roger Williams, *The Bloudy Tenent of Persecution*
> (Hanserd Knollys Soc., 1848), pp. 46–7.

I know of no more occasion (at least no more necessity) of any distraction, rent or division, than when the father being free of one company, as suppose of Merchant Taylors, shall still upon occasion of the meeting of this company repair to the hall appertaining to it. . . . The members of all the several companies in London dwell scatteringly and promiscuously up and down the City.

> John Goodwin, θεομαχια (1644), p. 31, in Haller, *Tracts on Liberty in the Puritan Revolution*, III, p. 37.

I

MEDIAEVAL society was a federation of communities: members of town gilds and villages, as well as of monasteries and collegiate churches, had a status, rights as well as duties, because of their membership of such communities. But the economic processes of the sixteenth and seventeenth centuries disrupted these communities. Monasteries and many collegiate churches disappeared. Control of gilds fell increasingly into the hands of rich merchants, against whom the small masters looked in vain to Stuart governments or Levellers for protection. Enclosure tended to break up the village community, no less when it took the form of consolidation or enclosure by consent than when it was depopulating enclosure. The same man who despoiled the monasteries filched common lands, we are told: in either case individual ownership replaced community ownership.[1] With the development of a national market and a centralized state, the old communities ceased to protect the interests of their members as hitherto: the London merchant and the royal official were too strong for them. Poor relief became a *national* tax. Parishes were told by the new centralized state how to look after their less fortunate members. Rogues and vagabonds, masterless men, were also men without a community. Their existence as a national problem is the most obvious example of the breakdown of the local community as a unit of employment or of social security. In Professor Hurstfield's words, the mediaeval welfare parish gave way to the Tudor welfare state. The manifest inadequacy of this "welfare state" to cope with its social problems was corrected first by individual charity and then by voluntary organizations.[2]

The House of Commons represented communities, not individuals: sixteenth-century agitations for a widening of the franchise in boroughs, and seventeenth-century agitations for a wider national franchise, had perforce to raise the new doctrine of the rights of individuals: the communities were represented by oligarchies.[3] Coke and Norden still called the manor "a little commonwealth",[4] although it was ceasing to

1. *E.P.C.*, p. 163. I owe many of the ideas in this chapter to the late Dona Torr's *Tom Mann and his Times* (1956) (esp. pp. 101–5, 111–12, 124–9), and to discussions with her.

2. J. Hurstfield, *The Queen's Wards* (1958), pp. xxviii, 333; Jordan, *Philanthropy in England, passim*; D. W. R. Bahlman, *The Moral Revolution of 1688* (Yale, 1957), Chapters 2 and 3, *passim.* Cf. pp. 261–2, 271–3, 416–17, 428 above.

3. Neale, *The Elizabethan House of Commons* (1949), pp. 246–7.

4. Coke, *The Compleat Copyholder*, section 62; J. Norden, *The Surveyor's Dialogue* (1607), quoted by Tawney, *The Agrarian Problem in the 16th century*, p. 350.

be a real administrative and judicial centre. Communal dovecotes, bulls or boars, village ducking stools, are less frequently met with in our period. In 1614 a lady was ex-communicated as a common scold and for using harsh words to her mother-in-law.[1] Here the parish is, or is deemed to be, a real community still; excommunication is the exact equivalent of being sent to Coventry. But parishes, in towns at least, were rapidly ceasing to be communities in this sense.

It was especially in London and the larger towns that the parish was breaking down. Professor Jordan noted how the charitable donors of London "were in no sense parochial-minded", highly developed though their social consciences were. He calculated that in 1540 there must have been about 1,500 inhabitants to each London parish, and perhaps twice as many a century later.[2] But the numbers were unevenly distributed. In 1638 almost certainly none of the parishes within the City walls had as many as 1,500 communicants. The parishes outside the walls must have been far larger.[3] About 1682 Petty suggested that a parish like St. Martin's might contain as many as 40,000 souls; he estimated London's total population at 669,930.[4]

The change manifested itself in the rise of a spirit of individualism. In 1607 enclosure was defended with the novel argument "the good individual is the good general".[5] A London pamphleteer in 1616 declared that "a citizen, however he may be noted for covetousness and corruption in trading; yet under colour of private enriching of himself, he laboureth for the public good".[6] This anticipation of Mandeville's paradoxical doctrine that private vices were public benefits was a sophisticated freak at that early date, even in the capital: yet such views slowly spread throughout the seventeenth century, and were being consciously opposed by protagonists of the old order surprisingly early. In 1600 Nashe, in *Summer's Last*

1. See p. 344 above.
2. Jordan, *The Charities of London*, pp. 33, 297–8.
3. T. C. Dale, *The Inhabitants of London in 1638* (1931), I, p. xxiv.
4. Petty, *Economic Writings*, II, pp. 459, 472.
5. Quoted by L. G. Salingar, "The Social Setting", in *The Age of Shakespeare* (ed. B. Ford, Penguin ed., 1955), p. 40.
6. T. Gainsford, *The Rich Cabinet Furnished* (1616), Sig. E 3, quoted by Wright, *Middle-Class Culture in Elizabethan England*, p. 32. Cf. Tawney, *Religion and the Rise of Capitalism*, Chapter IV.

Will and Testament, was defending the seasonal pastimes of the countryside against puritan arguments for thrift.[1] Nearly half a century later William Grant of Isleworth, a notorious anti-Puritan, was heard to say that all good fellowship was laid aside in his parish, but he would bring it in again and maintain it; "and would have wine and tobacco for all that would come to his vicarage house on Sundays after prayers". Grant "also maintains the Book of Sports". This was an example of the spirit shown in Corbett's "Rewards and Fairies" and by Herrick. Evidence for its widespread existence is slighter than sentimental Merrie Englanders would like to think, and often it covers up peccadilloes like Grant's refusal to accept a lecturer in his parish, although he had pocketed £10 a year as the price of his agreement – or so it was alleged.[2]

But there was something in it nevertheless. The traditional village festivities kept alive a communal spirit that was alien to the new emphasis on the individual. The antithesis between activities by and on behalf of the community, and zest for individual salvation, was neatly illustrated when Bishop Pierce put down sermons because they hindered church ales.[3] Puritans and others opposed the traditional sports because they saw in them vestiges of paganism and magic: so far, however unintentionally, they contributed to the triumph of rationalism. But it was impossible to root out magic without abolishing the communal rites through which primitive agricultural society had tried to control its destinies. In the long run it was the spread of urban values, rather than Puritanism, that defeated magic: though in so far as they worked together Puritanism prepared for industrialization. There is less magic in twentieth- than in sixteenth-century England because there is more industry. Magic is agrarian. But by the seventeenth century magic was already ceasing to be communal: or rather its communities – witches' covens, if these existed – were already voluntary and indeed underground organizations.

In many spheres the secular administrative functions of the parish – taxation, control of vagabonds – were beginning to preponderate over those more ceremonial functions which

1. *Works of Thomas Nashe* (ed. R. B. McKerrow, 1904–10), III, pp. 241–4, 259–63, 785–7, and *passim*.

2. N. Wallington, *Historical Notices*, I, p. 193. For Grant see p. 109 above, and *E.P.C.*, pp. 297, 301.

3. See p. 37 above.

bound the community together. The removal of secular business transactions from the church made it less of a community
centre.[1] The protestant tendency to regard the sermon as the
essential part of worship, the direct appeal to the heart of the
individual believer as against traditional ceremonial processions and the miracle of the mass – this too contributed unconsciously to atomize the parish. The idea that a lawful
minister must be a preacher encouraged individual parishioners to adopt a critical attitude, and increasingly so as the
educational standards of leading laymen left those of the weaker
clergy behind. In large towns at least, men could not be prevented from going away to other parish churches when they
were dissatisfied with their own minister; or they would turn
for spiritual sustenance to lecturers from outside the parish,
or to lecturers of their own appointment, for whom they subscribed to preach against the parochial incumbent. Or men
and women would simply stay away from church and worship
God in their own way in the household.[2] The emphasis on the
repetition of sermons in the family thus also contributed to the
atomizing process: the real religious experience might not be in
church but in the household discussion afterwards, under the
supervision not of the ecclesiastical authorities but of godly
laymen. Religion, for some members of society, is becoming a
matter of lectures and discussion classes: and these are
voluntary activities, catered for more satisfactorily by voluntary associations which choose their own discussion leader.[3]

II

Theoretical controversies were undermining the solidarity of
at least urban parishes no less effectively than economic
developments. One part of the strength of Puritanism, it is
suggested, derived from its attempt to revive the community
of the parish as a reality. The presbyterian discipline was to be
a *local* discipline, imposed in each community by the minister
and elders of that community: it was not to be the work of a
distant lay chancellor, who was neither the pastor nor the
neighbour of those men and women on whom he sat in judg-

1. See Chapter 12 above.
2. See instances in Babbage, *Puritanism and Richard Bancroft*, p. 376.
3. See Chapters 2–3, and pp. 451–5 above.

ment. Minister and elders might or might not be elected in any real sense by the parish as a whole; but at least they had some sort of responsibility to it, and bore some relation to its social realities: the minister was not a divine right sovereign imposed from outside. The presbyterian structure – a federation of parishes – would have attempted to revive the local community as the basis of the social pyramid. The presbyterian discipline was an ingenious attempt to reunite the parish by recognizing its divisions. It functioned on two levels: as an ideology of individualism, of human dignity, for the elect (or for the heads of households); as an ideology of restraint and subordination, of the dignity of labour, for the lower orders; and as a mechanism of social security. The point of junction between the two was the power to exclude from the sacraments, for which the presbyterian ministers fought so stoutly, and which they never succeeded in winning effectively. Without it, the parish community could not be resuscitated.[1]

The forces of disruption had gone too far. Economic processes were atomizing society, converting it from a hierarchy of communities to the agglomeration of equal competing individuals depicted in *Leviathan*. The Reformation had contributed to the process by Luther's subversive doctrines of the priesthood of all believers and of justification by faith alone. These located truth in the heart of the believer, no longer in the law and tradition of the Church: and since the elect were not easily identifiable on earth, it was hard to prevent this doctrine locating truth in the heart of every man, and so becoming a doctrine of absolute toleration, of individualist anarchy. In 1654 the Roman Catholic William Blundell sought the advice of his confessor on how to treat his tenants. A Protestant would have followed his own conscience – i.e. the standards which society was setting. In this case the confessor gave very much the kind of advice that a Protestant's conscience would have given him – err on the generous side of what the market allows; – but then he was advising in a society in which the Church had lost its coercive power and could not hope to regulate economic behaviour.[2]

The economic tension of the community in process of break-

1. Cf. Chapter 6 and p. 356 above.
2. Ed. T. E. Gibson, *Crosby Records: A Cavalier's Notebook* (1880), pp. 254–8.

ing up is focussed on the household, in transition from a patriarchal unit of communal production to a capitalist firm. Mr. Myers pertinently contrasts seventeenth-century family religion with mediaeval community religion. Neither a peasant hut nor the travelling household of the great noble nor the celibate community of the monastery was favourable to home life: that was developed by the middle class in town and country, whose houses began to replace churches as the centres of social life. Middle-class talent and industry were creating homes of unprecedented comfort and privacy, thanks to glass windows, coal fires, upstairs bedrooms, chairs replacing benches. Middle-class houses became places to which friends could be invited, to sing, to play, to discuss. So, especially in towns, new, voluntary communities arose, independent of the parish. These new select groups were united by community of interests rather than by geographical propinquity or corporate worship.[1] For a short time men could even envisage bringing about fundamental reform in the State via reform in the household.[2]

In ideas the crucial issue is religious toleration, because this would not only subvert the episcopal hierarchy, but would also make discipline impossible, and so threaten the domination of the elect over the ungodly, of masters of families over their servants. Religious toleration, consumers' choice in religion, is the natural concomitant of the emerging economic order of free industrial production and internal free trade. But whereas economic freedom benefited the propertied class automatically, free exchange of ideas benefited only truth, if we are to credit *Areopagitica*; the preachers were never as confident as Milton that free trade in ideas would work as automatically to the advantage of godliness.

Professor Haller has taught us to look sympathetically on the dilemma of the preachers, suddenly faced with a demand for religious toleration.[3] Calvinism, with its acceptance of the

1. A. R. Myers, *England in the Late Middle Ages* (*1307–1536*) (Pelican ed.), pp. 66–7, 224; W. G. Hoskins, "The Rebuilding of Rural England", *P. and P.*, No. 4; cf. J. Bossy, "The Character of Elizabethan Catholicism", *ibid.*, No. 21.
2. See preceding chapter.
3. Haller, *Liberty and Reformation in the Puritan Revolution*, *passim*. The whole of this and the following paragraph draw heavily on Professor Haller's work.

traditional mediaeval catholic assumption that the elect are a
small minority, and its insistence on the Eternal Decrees, was
always having to guard itself against opposite dangers. On the
one hand, the preachers might induce despair into their hearers, the majority of whom must be irrevocably damned. After
reading Bunyan one can understand why suicides from despair
were occasionally reported. On the other hand, if the preachers
were too encouraging, there was always the risk that their
simple hearers might fall into the opposite extreme of antinomianism, in the presumptuous confidence that they were
saved in spite of their sinfulness, since they could not be saved
by their own merits. The preachers trod the narrow path as
best they might. Before 1640 despair seemed the greater danger: the covenant theology, and the suggestion that a hearty
desire for salvation might be the first evidence of grace at work
in a man's soul, were desperate attempts to make Calvinism
palatable for mass consumption. The unspoken assumption
was that lay patronage and tithes would ensure an orthodox
ministry, that the hierarchy (or a system of discipline) would
keep down the antinomian heresy among the laity, and that
censorship would circumscribe the field of debate.

But after church courts and censorship broke down? The
Westminster Assembly, caught in the trammels of its own logic
(and of its own belief that truth could be arrived at after discussion among the elect) sought desperately for formulae. But
whilst its members discussed in one idiom, the world outside
was discussing in others. The Eternal Decrees and a godly
discipline had little appeal for the ungodly masses once they
were able to discuss them freely. And even inside the Assembly
the cool wit of Selden brought the plain propertied layman's
anti-clericalism to bear on the assumptions of the Calvinist
theology and discipline. No longer protected by the need for
unity against the dominant Laudians, with a state Church,
tithes and the patronage system called in question, and even
the patrons afraid of a theocracy, the presbyterian ministers
did their courageous best. But the attempt to define turned too
easily into impotent denunciation of the growing numbers of
those who disagreed. The New Jerusalem was a beleaguered
city before it had been built. The sectarian hosts of Midian,
prowling and prowling around, proved on closer inspection
more attractive to many of the defenders than their own

clerical security police. Martial law might be maintained so
long as the war was on; but once it had ended, with the other
side claiming that it was anxious only for reasonable discussion
(as the preachers in opposition had always claimed to be) –
what was to be done? The conditions of debate had changed so
drastically by extending from the elect to the whole community, from the educated to the uneducated, that the divines
abandoned the rules of their own game. They could see no
alternative to blind repression, and to a hysterical denunciation
of the toleration which seemed to them to have created the
new situation.

John Robinson, pastor to the Pilgrim Fathers before they
left the Netherlands, had expressed the social content of the
opposite point of view. To maintain that church government
suffered by being in the hands of the people, he argued, and to
deprive them of their rights in consequence, is to act in the
spirit of those who enclose the commons of their poorer neighbours on the plea that common things are commonly neglected,
and that the value of the commons is increased by enclosure – as though that was all that mattered.[1] "A hedge in the
field is as necessary in its kind as government in the church or
commonwealth", the Rev. Joseph Lee argued in 1656.[2]

The old geographical communities, with their rough-and-
ready but effective hierarchical subordination, their traditional
ceremonies, their succession of popular seasonal festivals, with
the nominated priest in theory directing the spiritual life of the
community: these were passing. The new communities of
the sects which ultimately emerged were voluntary, electing
and paying their own minister, relieving their own poor, imposing a more rigorous discipline on their own members than
the national Church could now do.[3] Contract communities
had succeeded status communities. In between there had come
the state Church, still aiming at being all-embracing, but
representing a national rather than an international community, and completely dependent on the secular power. Just as it
has been said that the early Tudors turned all England into
their manor, so the post-reformation Church became the

1. J. Robinson, *A Justification of Separation from the Church of
England* (1610), quoted by J. Brown, *The Pilgrim Fathers* (5th ed., 1920),
p. 143.
    2. J. Lee, *A Vindication of Regulated Enclosure* (1656), p. 28.
    3. Cf. pp. 365–9 above.

parish of which they were lay rectors and patrons.

We can see problems of the transition in the "backward-looking" revolts against the early Tudor state. In one sense the Pilgrimage of Grace was a revolt of communities against impersonal nationalization under "new men" like Thomas Cromwell. Yet the very existence of this omnicompetent state forced a new attitude upon the defenders of tradition. Sir Francis Bigod said that the commons judged the new Prior of Guisborough no prior, since he had been put in by Cromwell's commissioners. They intended to expel him and choose a new prior by virtue of the whole community. Similarly Archbishop Holgate was expelled by the Commons, who elected a successor; and the Norfolk rebels of 1549 demanded that priests should be elected by their parishioners. Bigod's actions were revolutionary rather than traditional: the "assent" of all the leading men of the chapter of Guisborough to the Commons' nominee hardly disguised this.[1] Yet the assertion of a new communal voluntarism was a reaction, if an extreme one, to Tudor nationalization, to the central control extended over the traditional communities. In a different way, Milton's phrase a century later "a table of separation" criticized the withdrawal of the Church from the people *at the behest of the central power*.[2]

III

Membership of the old communities had been compulsory – initially by the tying of the serf to the soil, latterly by government restrictions on mobility of labour. Tithes were no less legally enforceable than rent or feudal dues. The sects were strictly parallel in their voluntary organization to trading corporations, as so many defenders of religious toleration pointed out.[3] The church covenant was a contract, voluntarily entered into, linking the members for specific purposes. The minister was employed by the congregation on a wage contract, terminable at will by either side. The difference between separatist and conforming Puritans was that for the former the Church was not a community which perpetuated itself through pro-

1. A. G. Dickens, *Lollards and Protestants in the Diocese of York, 1509–58*, pp. 91, 95.

2. R. E. L. Strider II, *Robert Greville, Lord Brooke* (Harvard, 1958) p. 203.

3. For example the epigraphs to this chapter.

pagation, as ancient Israel had been; but a fellowship of the spirit, a voluntary association. The half-way covenant was New England's attempt to find a compromise between the old and the new conceptions.

The transition from parish to sect is from a geographical unit which brings the members of a community together for cultural, social and ceremonial purposes, to a voluntary unit to which men belong in order to hear the preacher of their choice. (Elected ministers, said an anglican pamphlet of 1670, would never reprove the faults of their congregations.)[1] It is of a piece with the process by which religion ceases to be mainly ritual and ceremony and becomes an affair of the heart and the intellect. In the early seventeenth century men broke the law by straying from their own parish to hear a favourite preacher; or they hired a lecturer to preach their chosen theology. Looking back we can see each of these as a half-way stage on the way towards congregational independency. The sectarian congregations after 1640 were united by the agreement of their members on questions of theology and church government: when such agreement ceased, the congregation split. Just as the transition from tribal to village society had involved a shift from kinship, the blood bond, to neighbourhood, so the transition from parish to sect was a shift from a local community to a voluntary organization. The transition to modern society was more complete in the towns than in the villages, where the Clarendon Code defeated nonconformity. Yet even in the villages there was a change, since the Anglican Church after 1660 was dominated by the alliance of parson and squire, no longer effectively controlled from the centre. Just as the abolition of prerogative courts established the dictatorship of J.P.s over the villages, so the abolition of the High Commission established the dictatorship of the squire over church and parish. Free contract in religion existed only in the urban parishes.

It had been of the nature of the old communities, in theory at least, that their decisions had to be unanimous: only one form of cultivation was possible at one time in the common fields. Enclosure thus ultimately helped to make majority government possible, though in the first instance it witnessed to

1. [T. Pittis], *A Private Conference, between A Rich Alderman and A Country Vicar* (1670), pp. 119–20.

and fortified the power of the rich over the community. Majority government, like religious toleration, assumes that society
is composed of a mass of equal atoms: it is natural to associations of free and equal members who have opted to join the
society and so retain their right of dissent. But the idea that
juries must be unanimous survived. A prejudice in favour of
unanimity persisted long after the unanimity was fictitious: it
survives to this day in those feudal bodies, Oxford and Cambridge colleges. We can trace the reluctance of the House of
Commons to abandon the principle of unanimity, to which it
held so long as its function was advisory and critical. It was
forced to adopt majority rule as a normal practice once it had
taken over effective running of the State. The Grand Remonstrance is a turning point in this respect; swords were drawn
in the House in the division over printing it. The peers' right of
registering protest, denied to M.P.s on this occasion, survived
to demonstrate reluctance to be bound by a majority. The
Quaker "sense of the meeting" carried over into the modern
world something of the desire for unanimity which meant so
much to the mediaeval communities.

The antithesis between preaching and praying, between
pulpit and altar, is between a religion stressing salvation by
individual effort and a religion of communal ceremonies.[1]
Roger Williams thought that salvation is gained by individuals, not by churches.[2] The change is illustrated in the internal
arrangements of churches. The protestant emphasis on preaching transformed them from large places in which processions
were held to small meeting houses which are little more than
lecture rooms. The pulpit grows in importance, the choir ceases
to be screened off. The Laudian period of the railed-off altar
was also a great period of screen building. It was the puritan
Earl of Bedford who in 1638 had St. Paul's, Covent Garden,
built as a single rectangular room with no screen dividing
chancel from nave. This departure from the mediaeval plan
later became the model for Wren when he rebuilt London's
churches after the Great Fire. His aim was a building in which
all the congregation could see and hear the minister.[3] Pews for

    1. See p. 69 above.
    2. Jordan, *The Development of Religious Toleration in England* (1932–
40), III, p. 502; cf. R. Williams, *The Bloudy Tenent of Persecution*, pp.
39–41.
    3. G. W. O. Addleshaw and F. Etchells, *The Architectural Setting of*

individual families cut up the space used for processions before the Reformation. Ecclesiastical officers, from bishops to churchwardens, occupied themselves with seeing that members of the parish were seated in due order of social precedence. The purchase of the right to build or occupy a specially grand pew was beginning, but social status was still at least as important in the allocation of seats as cash paid. In the voluntary sects it was normal for pews to be rented; the remaining seats, equal in status, were available for the first comer.[1]

We can see the same thing in theology. Before the Reformation justification by works (drawing on the Church's treasury of merits) mediated by a priesthood; after the Reformation, protestant individualism and justification by faith undermined the position of the priest. The sects for the most part returned to a theology of justification by works; but now the minister is merely the paid servant of the congregation. He plays no significant role in the scheme of salvation. Truth was more likely to reside in the congregation, John Goodwin thought, to be discovered by free discussion, than in the minister or the hierarchy, to be imposed through church courts.[2] The essential basis of the sect is a voluntary contract between its members, all of whom believe the others to be saved. So what we are describing is not a mere cycle – justification by works: by faith: by works. There is a crucial difference in the position of the priest and the sacraments (those bonds of the status community). We can appreciate this if we compare the Arminianism of Laud, which was theologically an attempt to restore sacraments, ceremonies and the priesthood to something like their mediaeval position of honour, with the Arminianism of Milton and the more radical sectaries. Free will in a society safely dominated by an established Church is one thing; free will in a free contract society is something very different.

In a wider sense we might argue that the tension between individualism and collectivism which has often been noted in Calvinism expresses just this search for a new community

Anglican Worship (1948), esp. pp. 38, 50–4, 174; Petty, *Economic Writings*, II, pp. 382–3.

1. *E.P.C.*, pp. 175–82.

2. See Haller, *Liberty and Reformation in the Puritan Revolution*, pp. 149 253.

within the old:[1] it corresponds to the contradiction between the Church as the whole community, and the Church in a different sense as the community of believers only. Hence the discipline which the godly minority wish to impose on the rest of the inhabitants is the crux of the conflict between Calvinists on the one hand, Erastians and sectaries on the other. The protestant emphasis on motive also tried in a more positive way to bridge the gap between individual and community: charitable works have value in so far as they are directed towards the good of the community, of my neighbours, and are not self-regarding as (in protestant eyes) the formal works advocated by late mediaeval catholic theologians had become.[2] Hence the attempt to reconstruct social institutions on new lines by voluntary charity.[3]

The Calvinist emphasis on predestination and discipline had tried to carry hierarchical social subordination and national thought-control over into the modern world: the breakdown of Calvinism in the middle decades of the seventeenth century witnessed to the failure of this attempt. Calvinist theology survived in some of the sects, but the theology without a national disciplinary system was only a shadow compared with that substance which the presbyterian ministers came so near to grasping.

We can trace similar transitions in discipline. National discipline through nominated episcopal officials, remote and impersonal, was challenged by the presbyterian demand for parochial discipline administered by minister and elders, responsible in some sense to the community, and exercising control through exclusion from the sacraments and poor relief. In the sects, excommunication became a purely spiritual censure, administered by the congregation itself: poor relief became a measure of social security within a voluntary community rather than a means of exercising control.[4] With a little

1. Professor Macpherson points to similar tensions between individualism and collectivism in the thought of the Levellers and of Locke; and in Locke between a traditional condemnation of covetousness and a new approval of unlimited accumulation (*The Political Theory of Possessive Individualism*, pp. 157, 237, 256).

2. I have tried to argue this at greater length in "Protestantism and the Rise of Capitalism", *Essays . . . in honour of R. H. Tawney* (1961), pp. 15–39.

3. Jordan, *Philanthropy in England, passim.*

4. See pp. 285–7, 428 above.

forcing we can mark corresponding transitions in relation to the Sabbath. In mediaeval society, seasonal communal festivals on saints' days: in modern society, the regular weekly rest plus bank holidays. In between, a battle for greater sanctity for the Sabbath (with all that it implied in leisure, edification, self-improvement) and a battle against the ruder, less civilized aspects of the parish festivals. The acceptance of Sabbatarianism by virtually all politically effective sections of the population dates from the revolutionary decades. Similarly again with regard to oaths. Their significance in mediaeval and even Tudor society was as links binding the communities to the centre. An oath was still almost a sacrament. In the modern world the doctrine that honesty is the best policy has been established; men keep their covenants made because it is to their mutual advantage to do so. The Quaker refusal of oaths, and insistence that their word was their bond, fought for a principle that is now so universally accepted that it seems odd that anyone ever had to fight for it. In the transitional period, the main significance of oaths was as a means of enforcing national one-mindedness. As the communities dissolved, and new loyalties supervened, so juries of presentment and church-wardens' presentments ceased to function effectively. Whitgift was not the first to discover that heretics could be detected only by means of the oath *ex officio*. As the national battle was fought out, so oaths of loyalty succeeded one another with bewildering frequency, until the currency was hopelessly debased.

With the economic changes of our period, the standards of conduct which church courts tried to enforce became increasingly alien to those of many parishioners, at least in the towns. The rough-and-ready procedures which had held rural society together in the Middle Ages no longer sufficed. By the end of the seventeenth century the "common fame" of the traditional communities has been replaced by the anonymous "due process of law"; the jury is similarly changing its character. Ultimately jurors ceased to be selected *because* they knew the facts at issue (and so were indictable for perjury) and came to be chosen on the opposite principle, so that previous knowledge of the facts is now sufficient to disqualify a juror. A trial ceased to be a communal indictment and became a case between parties.

IV

The importance of the interregnum, from our present point of view, is that the years without censorship, without a national disciplinary or ecclesiastical-judicial system, the years of religious toleration, allowed the voluntary religious communities to establish themselves too strongly ever to be rooted out.[1] This is the difference between the nonconformist sects and all previous underground heretical organizations. Printing was one important new factor in assisting their organization and propaganda. Contact with other countries in which heresy had established itself – heretical views were always strong among merchants – was a further stimulus. The possibility of emigration – revolution by evasion and return – was already opening new vistas of freedom in the early seventeenth century: this explains Laud's desperate attempts to control the English churches abroad, many of them associated with merchant communities.

Hence the paradox that the Independents, who wished to decentralize the Church, needed a stronger state. Under the Tudors the Church, the "State-Ecclesiastical", had been a means of imposing and enforcing national unity. The "Presbyterians" in the Long Parliament wished to destroy the old ecclesiastical machinery and substitute the control of the "natural rulers", locally as elders, centrally as represented by Parliament. They were interested mainly in destroying the old administrative machine: their positive enthusiasm for a full presbyterian system was never very great. The policy of religious toleration which the "Independents" sponsored could be enforced against the hostility of the gentry only by an army. In 1648 the Independents in Kent looked to London for salvation against the leaders of the county gentry whose slogan was "For God, King Charles and Kent!"[2] The Major-Generals enforced toleration on indignant J.P.s. The restoration of parliamentary government in 1660 gave the gentry liberty to persecute again. Charles II failed to implement his indulgence policy, in the last resort, because he had no army. James II failed because his army was papist, and so he lost the support

1. See pp. 331, 463–6 above.
2. A. M. Everitt, *The County Committee of Kent in the Civil War* (1957), p. 52; cf. p. 18.

of dissenters. The Toleration Act gave religious toleration at the price of the continued exclusion of dissenters from politics, thus restoring the hegemony of the "natural rulers" at least in the villages. It was a modified version of the policy of the Clarendon Code and the Test Act rather than the liberty of which Milton and Roger Williams had dreamed. The sects in effect reconciled themselves to the parish as a unit of local government.

The assumption behind a state Church, with ministers paid for by tithes, is that the community, whether parochial or national, is united by geography. Toleration assumes that the nation, and the town, is divided into communities voluntarily entered upon. During the interregnum men opted out of the national (or parochial) community for the separatist congregation: after 1660 dissenters were expelled from the national and parochial communities, and so, if they held out, their loyalty to the voluntary community increased. Church was set against state, religion against politics, with a sharpness which need not have occurred if the relative tolerance of the interregnum had continued.[1] The Tories hoped that the Toleration Act of 1689 would be merely a temporary measure, and the practice of occasional conformity testifies to the strength of the old loyalties; but nonconformity proved strong enough to survive freedom as it had survived persecution.

Puritanism had been especially an urban phenomenon, or rather one whose strength came from the industrious sort of people in town and country. Those who emigrated to the Netherlands after 1660, Downing reported, were "handicraft-and tradesmen", who "pretend the reason thereof to be liberty of their consciences".[2] In one aspect the Restoration was aimed against the missionary work of Quakers and others who were extending radical sectarian ideas into the countryside, just as Cromwell's determination to suppress the Levellers in 1649

1. G. R. Cragg, *Puritanism in the Period of the Great Persecution* (1957), pp. 32, 156–7. Cf. P. Worsley, *The Trumpet Shall Sound* (1957), p. 249: the function of the Naked Cult of Espiritu Santo "seems to be to break all existing ties, of whatever description, and unite people on the exclusive basis of the cult . . . It welds the devotees together in a new fraternity of people who have deliberately flouted the most sacred rules of the old society".

2. T. H. Lister, *Life and Administration of Edward, first Earl of Clarendon* (1837–8), III, p. 218.

may have been influenced by the fact that they too were turning outwards from their main centres, London and the Army,
to undertake propaganda activities in the country at large.[1]
The Clarendon Code failed to eradicate nonconformity from
the towns, because it was too strong among those who formed
the natural ruling classes there. The code was never enforced in its full rigour. There was no return of the pre-1640
state of affairs in towns, no enforcement of full payment of
tithes. Vicars in towns were dependent on the good will of their
congregations. "You are more especially obliged to submit to
our wills", a pamphleteer makes an alderman tell a vicar in
1670, "because your dependence is wholly upon them".[2] The
corporations in the long run proved stronger than the governments of Charles II and James II which tried to purge them
into submission. But the Clarendon Code (plus perhaps the
1662 Act of Settlement) did save the countryside from nonconformity. The existence of organized dissent made effective
reform of the Church of England impossible; but equally the
existence of urban dissent made the Church necessary if the
squires were to retain control of their villages. There was a real
balance of forces, which the Toleration Act preserved by granting only religious toleration, not political equality. Nonconformity did not seriously penetrate many rural areas until
Wesleyanism – and then the second nonconformity might be
said to be following industry.[3]

The Wesleyan movement thus resumed, a century later, the
move of Puritanism into the countryside, which the sects had
started in the sixteen-fifties, but had not been strong enough
to carry through. In the same way political radicalism from
the seventeen-sixties onwards picks up where the democratic
revolutionaries left off, just as Blake and the romantics pick up
from Milton something that the Augustans lost, just as the
Scottish historical school picks up from Harrington. The industrial and agricultural revolutions of the eighteenth century
are based on techniques (the steam engine) and crops first
developed during the interregnum. The Augustan compromise
had held society in stasis for a century.

1. P. Gregg, *Free-born John* (1961), p. 269; Brailsford, *The Levellers
and the English Revolution*, Chapter 23.
2. [Pittis], *A Private Conference between A Rich Alderman and A
Country Vicar*, p. 20; cf. pp. 114–15.
3. Cf. pp. 139–40, 465 above and 494 below.

Chapter Fifteen

Conclusion

> I pondered all these things, and how men fight and lose the battle,
> and the thing that they fought for comes in spite of their defeat, and
> when it comes turns out not to be what they meant, and other men
> have to fight for what they meant under another name.
>
> William Morris, *A Dream of John Ball*, chapter 4.

I

IN the process of writing this book two conclusions forced
themselves upon me which had not been in my mind when I
collected and arranged my material. The first was an interesting coincidence of date. Greenham's and Bownde's treatises
on the Sabbath were published in the early fifteen-nineties.
Sabbatarianism of a sort had previously been part of the
common protestant heritage, but it is from this date onwards
that it becomes the shibboleth of the Puritans, and the spokesmen of the hierarchy came to attack it. Similarly emphasis on
religious duties of heads of households was part of the protestant tradition, since in the early days of the Reformation
governments and reformers had perforce relied on the protestant loyalties of artisans and yeomen. But again there seemed to
be a change from the end of the sixteenth century, though there
is no date here so precise as the publication of Greenham's and
Bownde's books. Household religion comes to be stressed by
the Puritans as a remedy for the shortcomings of the state
Church; the household, ruled by godly fathers of families,
becomes at least a supplement, and almost an alternative, to
the parish ruled by dumb dogs and hirelings. In its turn the
hierarchy from 1583 onwards reveals greater and greater un-

easiness at household repetition of sermons, family prayers and discussions.[1]

Now the later 'eighties and 'nineties are the period in which the High Commission begins to play a new repressive role as Whitgift and Bancroft went over to the offensive against the Puritans. The latent conflict between the presbyterianizing clergy and Puritanism's more erastian lay supporters was brought out into the open, and the Presbyterians found themselves isolated. The classis movement was annihilated, with hardly a protest from Parliament. But Puritanism was not annihilated. On the contrary, the Puritanism which Professor Haller has so lovingly and graphically described really dates from the late sixteenth century, from William Perkins and his like. Perkins had been a member of the underground classis movement; but from the repression of the early 'nineties he abandoned its programme, and became the high priest of the new Puritanism, a Puritanism not committed to a presbyterian system or organization but emphasizing ever more strongly preaching, household discussion and education, the sanctity of the Sabbath. It is a new course to achieve the same ends.

The hope of implementing the full disciplinary programme through Queen and Parliament, or of winning the co-operation of the local magistrates for a parochial discipline, had to be abandoned. The classis movement was never revived before 1640. Henceforth the preachers stressed an individual pietism, with the household as its essential unit rather than the parish, whose secular functions were coming more and more to the fore. I do not suggest that this was a conscious decision, though it must have been for a man like Perkins. But there was no body which could take such a decision for the puritan movement as a whole. We should compare it rather with the working-class movement's shift from direct political action to trade unionism after the defeat of Chartism in England in 1848. But whether deliberate or not, the new tactic was effective. There was great hope of winning support among the industrious sort of householders, whose numbers and wealth were increasing rapidly,[2] just at a time when the hierarchy was beginning to attack some of those elements in the protestant

1. See pp. 165–7, 224–5, 390–1, 433–4, 453 above.
2. W. G. Hoskins, "The Rebuilding of Rural England, 1570–1640," *P. and P.*, No. 4, pp. 44–59 *passim*.

tradition which had most appealed to them, and to enforce an observance of ceremonies which many sober men regarded as innovatory. "Seeing we cannot compass these things by suit nor dispute", said John Field, "the multitude and people" must.[1] This proved a longer way round than capturing the Court through a Leicester, an Essex; but it was far surer.

Because of its abandonment of Presbyterianism, and because of its emphasis on the household, the new Puritanism led very easily – often to the surprise of Puritans themselves – to congregational independency. It did so in exile in the Netherlands and New England;[2] it did so in old England once state power ceased to enforce the monopoly of bishops or presbyteries. In rural New England the ministers and the oligarchy were able to prevent Independency succumbing to religious toleration; that happened only in the political circumstances of the sixteen-forties in the more industrialized centres of revolutionary England. Religious toleration and the development of capitalism in England undermined the authority of fathers of families and led ultimately from the traditional protestant individualism of heads of households to the atomized individualism of Hobbes and Adam Smith.

If these suggestions are at all correct, then the *fin de siécle* is as important in the religious history of England as historians are coming to think it is in the political.[3] (Not indeed that there is a real distinction here. For the new Puritanism was itself a recognition of the fact that the ministers could not achieve the society they wanted without the co-operation of classes who formed part of the electorate of the House of Commons.) In the years after the Armada had been defeated, in which it became clear that Spanish authority could never be restored in the northern Netherlands, there was no longer the same fear that Catholicism would be imposed on England by foreign military force. This fear had preserved protestant unity: the Puritans had been the most loyal anti-Catholics and enemies of Spain. After 1588 the government no longer needed puritan support, and was able to pay more attention to the social dangers inherent in radical puritan doctrine. The

1. A. F. Scott Pearson, *Thomas Cartwright and Elizabethan Puritanism* (1925), pp. 252–3.

2. See pp. 425–6, 450–5, 482–3. above; and Morison, *Builders of the Bay Colony*, p. 40.

3. Cf. P. Crutwell, *The Shakespearean Moment*, (1954), chapter 1.

Marprelate controversy and the rise of separatism revealed this radicalism in its most uncompromising, most popular and least traditional forms; they helped to split the puritan ranks. The defeat of the Armada set men free to think about sacramentalism and divine right episcopacy, without fear of popery; Brownism and the Marprelate Tracts ensured that conservatives began to see the advantages of historical continuity and of those aspects of traditional catholic doctrine which made for social cohesion.[1]

With the abandonment of Presbyterianism, the issue between Puritans and hierarchy ceased to be primarily organizational. Whitgift had had no real theological controversy with Cartwright, but Bancroft, "the capital enemy of all the reformed churches of Europe",[2] asserted divine right episcopacy in his Paul's Cross sermon against Marprelate in 1589, leaving the theologians to work out the doctrine in detail later. Walsingham or Bacon, neither an enemy to the Puritans, described in 1590 exactly how their cause had lost its appeal for propertied classes. "But now of later years, when there issued from them [some] that affirmed the consent of the magistrate was not to be attended; when . . . they combined themselves by classes and subscriptions; when they descended into that vile and base means of defacing the government of the Church by ridiculous pasquils; when they began to make many subjects in doubt to take oaths, which is one of the fundamental parts of justice in this land, and in all places. . . . ; then it appeared to be no more conscience but mere faction and division".[3] When the lower orders looked like taking control of the classis movement, observed Gifford in 1590, "what worldly-wise man will not take it that discipline herself is but a bedlam?"[4] Mr. Worldly Wiseman was not yet the character that Bunyan was to make of him; or, if he was, Hooker is his prototype.[5]

1. Cf. N. R. Ker, "Oxford College Libraries in the 16th century", *The Bodleian Library Record*, VI, p. 498. See C. Read, *Lord Burghley and Queen Elizabeth* (1960), pp. 470, 509, for the shocking effect on men not unsympathetic to the Puritans of Marprelate's appeal to the vulgar.

2. A. Melville, quoted by N. Sykes, *Old Priest and New Presbyter* (1956), p. 57.

3. Burnet, *History of the Reformation*, III, pp. 535–6; cf. p. 390 above.

4. See p. 286 above. Cf. Field quoted on the preceding page.

5. See p. 222 above.

The writings of Hooker, Bancroft, Bilson and many others in the 'nineties, together with the escapades of premature anti-Calvinists like Baro and Barrett in Cambridge,[1] mark the opening of a breach in theological unanimity both among English Protestants and between them and their brethren in Scotland and on the continent. So new was Bancroft's doctrine of the divine right of bishops that Sir Francis Knollys suggested that it was treasonable.[2] James I with great political wisdom appointed Abbot to succeed Bancroft at Canterbury. Abbot was in the protestant tradition of Cranmer, Parker, Jewel, Grindal and Whitgift, and was conspicuous for his loyalty to the Palatinate in the Thirty Years War. But he was very old-fashioned when in 1604 he said "Such as you call Puritans did never differ from the rest in any point of substance but about circumstances and ceremonies, . . . and about the manner of ecclesiastical regiment".[3] The theological divisions were already more real than that, and Abbot was not the man to restore unity: his was a holding operation. The Puritans regarded the Laudians as innovators, not least in the archbishop's attempt to sever relations with continental protestants. Historically the Puritans were right.

Between 1589 and 1640 sacramentalism revived in England under the shadow of the continental Counter-Reformation. These years can be seen as an interlude between the protestant-based anti-Spanish national unity of the half century between Reformation and Armada and the protestant-based anti-French national unity restored by William III. The defeat of sacramentalism in 1640 seemed to have been final; but although the Laudian coercive system was not restored after 1660, the theology (and its political theory) enjoyed a zombie-like existence under the shadow of Louis XIV for another generation. But the Non-jurors were defeated with Louis XIV: the rapidity of their collapse shows how unreal the high-flying position had become in the world of the Vicar of Bray. When sacramentalism revived in the Church of England, in the Ox-

1. See pp. 224–5 above. For a sympathetic account of Barrett and Baro, see Porter, *Reformation and Reaction in Tudor Cambridge*, Chapters 15 and 17. Barrett subsequently became a papist.

2. Strype, *Life of Whitgift*, I, pp. 559–60.

3. G. Abbot, *The Reasons which Doctor Hill hath brought for the upholding of Papistry . . . unmasked* (1604), pp. 101–2.

ford Movement, it was directly inspired by fear of popular liberalism.[1]

I would argue then that the new tactics of the 'nineties, whether consciously adopted or not, still represented a *via media*, aimed at reducing the authority of bishops over the Church on the one hand, and against sectarian separatism on the other. Yet time and again in our analysis we have seen how the new tactics of their own logic led to congregational independency, if not to separatism. The emphasis on preaching stimulated discussion, abandonment of one's own parish church in the quest of sermons, and so voluntaryism and even lay preaching.[2] Parochial independence raised the question of the relations between congregation and state Church.[3] Household prayers, reinforced by the presence of godly neighbours, foreshadowed the formation of separatist congregations, as the payment of lecturers by voluntary contributions foreshadowed the election of ministers.[4] Sabbatarianism and the doctrine of the dignity of labour led to awkward questions being asked about masters and rentiers.[5] After the experiences of the revolutionary decades this difficulty of finding a logical halfway house between congregational independency and complete religious toleration led conservative Puritans to welcome the restoration of a state Church, in the interests of discipline, social subordination and the repression of heresy.[6]

II

A second conclusion which I had not anticipated was that, despite the defeat of religious Puritanism in 1660, and the isolation of nonconformity even after 1689, nevertheless much of the social content of puritan doctrine was ultimately accepted outside the ranks of the nonconformists and even by the apparently triumphant Church of England. Part of the reason for this is of course that many former Puritans con-

1. J. H. Newman, *Apologia Pro Vita Sua* (Everyman ed.), p. 52; *Tracts for the Times*, esp. Tracts I and II and Advertisement to vol. I (1834).
2. See pp. 65–7, 82, 88–9, 102 above.
3. See pp. 420–1 above.
4. See pp. 86–7, 451–5 above.
5. See pp. 171–4, 192, 203–11 above.
6. See pp. 232–3, 242, 249–50 above.

formed to the national church after 1660, but without altogether shedding the habits of thought in which they had been
brought up.[1]

We have seen how the social importance of labour and industry came to be accepted, from dukes down to the writers of
tracts for the poor.[2] "Writers on economic policy after the
restoration", observes Professor Macpherson, "though not
conspicuously Puritan, fully embraced the Puritan view of the
poor".[3] The lower classes were subdued to labour discipline,
even if ultimately by the market, J.P.s and Societies for the
Reformation of Manners rather than by church courts or
presbyteries.[4] The English Sunday exercised its gloomy sway
for the best part of three centuries after the revolution. Oaths
soon lost their crucial significance as social bonds with the
triumph of the self-interest society and when the parish sank
to become a secular organ of local government. Excommunication became a merely spiritual sanction in nonconformist
chapels, whose licensed competition after 1689 rendered nuga-
tory the state Church's thunders. The industrial revolution, to
which labour discipline contributed so much, sapped the
independence of the puritan household and left a society of
atomic individuals, further removed than ever from the organ-
ic geographical communities of the Middle Ages. Voluntary
communities grew in significance in all spheres of English
life.

The puritan emphasis on preaching came to be accepted by
the established Church. Sanderson's post Restoration suggestion that 52 new homilies should be produced to teach
obedience to the people, and to "abate the inordinate desire
of knowing what we need not", though supported by Tillotson, Patrick and Burnet, came to nothing.[5] The last edition of

1. For a good example, see D. C. Coleman, *Sir John Banks* (1963),
esp. pp. 146–7, 198–9. John Locke is another case in point.

2. See p. 140 above.

3. Macpherson, *The Political Theory of Possessive Individualism*, p.
228.

4. Cf. the proposal put forward by the clergy in 1711–12 for a revival
of discipline within the establishment. This was intended as a move
against the Societies for the Reformation of Manners, which acted
through J.P.s and in co-operation with dissenters. But it failed (G.
Every, *The High Church Party, 1688–1718*, 1956, pp. 147–52).

5. I. Walton, *Lives* (World's Classics), p. 395; H. H. Henson, *Studies
n English Religion in the 17th century* (1903), p. 207. Compare Petty's

the Book of Homilies to be printed "by authority" appeared in 1671. In 1678 Joseph Glanvill published *A Seasonable Defence of Preaching*, in which he pleaded for a middle way between those who stressed prayer as against preaching and those who thought only nonconformists knew how to preach. The Church of England took over lectureships endowed by Puritans.[1] The sermon triumphed, with the Anglicans Sanderson, Tillotson, Patrick and Burnet as some of its most distinguished practitioners. Their prose is the plain prose of the Puritans, far removed from the scholarly complexities of Andrewes and Donne. After the Restoration there was an increasing tendency to do away with screens in churches, and the Laudian practice of reading the Altar Prayers at the altar fell into disuse in ordinary parish churches. In most churches men and women did not come up to the altar to communicate. The artificial revival of this practice after the Oxford Movement – a revival made possible only because nonconformity had sufficiently reduced the size of congregations – should not allow us to forget how very "puritanical" Anglican services must have seemed before that other nineteenth-century invention, the surpliced choir.[2]

Wren's acceptance of the architectural aim of making the church an auditorium for the pulpit[3] is all the more significant since he himself was in the High Church tradition. So was Jeremy Collier, who finally led to victory Puritanism's century-old battle against the immorality of the stage. Again we must stress the social aspects of Collier's attitude: "One would think these poets went upon absolute certainty, and could demonstrate the scheme of infidelity. If they could, they had much better keep the secret. The divulging it tends only to debauch mankind, and shake the securities of civil life". Religion is as necessary to government as social distinctions: "To breed all people alike, and make no distinction between a seat and a cottage, is not over-artful, nor very ceremonious to the country gentlemen". Collier's attitude to sex was throughly

---

emphasis on the social and political advantages of having only officially composed sermons preached (*Economic Writings*, II, pp. 472–3).

1. See pp. 119–20 above.
2. G. W. O. Addleshaw and F. Etchells, *The Architectural Setting of Anglican Worship* (1948), pp. 50, 54, 174–9, 213.
3. See p. 478 above.

"Puritan" (in the nineteenth-century sense of the word); but again his interests are social rather than moral. The stage is "the most effectual means to baffle the force of discipline, to emasculate people's spirits and debauch their manners. . . . What disappointments of parents, what confusion in families, and what beggary in estates have been hence occasioned?" That could serve as a summary of the social significance of discipline. Collier carried what later ages knew as "Puritanism" much further than, for instance, Oliver Cromwell or Milton, when he wrote: "Music is almost as dangerous as gunpowder; and, it may be, requires looking after no less than the press or the mint". For "this kind of music warms the passions and unlocks the fancy, and makes it open to pleasure like a flower to the sun". This total hostility to music – not merely to polyphony and organs in church – was echoed by Locke, who in so many respects secularized and bowdlerized Puritanism – e.g. in his labour theory of value.[1]

"The Puritan Revolution was defeated": how often have historians, including myself, repeated that? In the obvious and superficial sense it is true: surplices, Prayer Books, bishops and church courts were restored; nonconformists were excluded from the state Church, and even after the Toleration Act they remained second-class citizens, shut out from political life, with a separate educational system and a separate culture. And yet in all the spheres we have been considering an aspect of puritan values triumphed. But this secret victory of Puritanism was a peculiar one. The object of this book has been to suggest social reasons for which men could hold many of the traditional puritan beliefs. The aspect of puritan values that triumphed was the social one: the form rather than the content prevailed. "Sitting still on Sundays" is a caricature of the strenuous intellectual effort which the Puritans had called for. To place all religion in the ear could, as Puritanism's enemies had suggested, lead to laziness. The class dictatorship of J.P.s was something very different from the potentially egalitarian puritan discipline. A disciplined labour force was supplied for the dark Satanic mills of the eighteenth century; but

1. J. Collier, *A Short View of the Immorality and Profaneness of the English Stage* (1688), pp. 190, 221, 278, 287. For Collier and Locke see also my *Century of Revolution* (1961), pp. 302–3. Cf. F. Antal, *Hogarth and his place in European Art* (1962), pp. 7–11, 220.

Arthur Young's "Everyone but an idiot knows that the lower class must be kept poor or they will never be industrious",[1] expressed an attitude far removed from that of men who believed in the dignity of labour. The Duke of Albemarle's desire that the nobility should take up "good husbandry" in order to prevent them being overbalanced by "the lower and trading part of the people" contrasts strikingly with the relatively democratic doctrine of the duty of labour held by puritan artisans and yeomen.[2] There were fewer cakes and church ales in the eighteenth century than in the sixteenth, but men were not necessarily the more virtuous. A recurrent theme of this book has been the degeneration of puritan ideals into a concern with outward appearances, into hypocrisy.[3] Only after the industrial revolution, as Moses Wall had predicted to Milton,[4] did some of the doctrines of revolutionary Puritanism reappear, not all now taking religious forms.

III

If this analysis is at all correct, it must throw light back on to the main argument of this book. I do not consider that I have "explained" Puritanism by suggesting that its doctrines fulfil a social purpose. If I did, I would not stress so strongly the contrast between the living faith of the puritan revolutionaries and the dry husk of Puritanism which we find alike in the Church of England and in the nonconformist sects of the eighteenth century. Nevertheless, the fact that such distinctions can be drawn suggests that perhaps the attempt to submit pre-revolutionary Puritanism to sociological analysis is not altogether useless. It is wrong to discuss Puritanism – or for that matter the more ephemeral Laudianism – merely in theological terms. Puritanism was a view of life which was deeply rooted in the English society of its day. Hence the profound differences in practice underlying the doctrinal similarities between English and continental Protestantism. To understand Puritanism we must understand the needs, hopes, fears

1. A. Young, *Eastern Tour* (1771), IV, p. 361, quoted in D. Marshall, *English People in the 18th Century* (1956), p. 180.
2. See p. 140 above.
3. See pp. 27–8, 208–11, 248–50, 261, 278–83, 330–2, 400–5, 438–9, 459–66 above.
4. See p. 139 above.

and aspirations of the godly artisans, merchants, yeomen, gentlemen, ministers, and their wives, who gave their support to its doctrines. Like maxims in philosophy for Keats, Puritanism was valid for them only when they felt it on their pulses. It seemed to point the way to heaven because it helped them to live on earth.

Index